DREAMS IN
GREEK TRAGEDY

DREAMS IN
GREEK TRAGEDY

An Ethno-Psycho-Analytical Study

GEORGE DEVEREUX

UNIVERSITY OF CALIFORNIA PRESS

Berkeley and Los Angeles   1976

UNIVERSITY OF CALIFORNIA PRESS

Berkeley and Los Angeles, California

ISBN: 0-520-02921-6

Library of Congress Catalog Card No. 74-27288

Printed in Great Britain

To
KENNETH J. DOVER
Professor of Greek, University of St Andrews
for his early encouragement and constant help
in friendship

Contents

Preface

At each critical moment of history there exists some discipline whose practitioners, like Thoukydides' Athenians, seem to have been "born into the world to take no rest themselves and give none to others". During the Renaissance, these gadflies of the mind were the classical philologists. Today, they happen to be the psycho-analysts. It is perhaps the remembrance of the turbulent beginnings of classical philology—which made possible the birth of the modern mind—that accounts for the generous openmindedness wherewith some of the greatest Hellenists of our time encouraged me to elucidate Greek problems by means of the psychoanalytical method of enquiry.

On the most concrete level, this book seeks to demonstrate the psychological credibility of the dreams Aischylos, Sophokles and Euripides had devised for certain of their personages. There can, of course, be no question of *actually* psycho-analysing a Greek poet long since dead, nor a dramatic personage born from his imagination. What can be shown, is that the dreams one encounters in Greek tragedy are authentically dreamlike: that the dream Aischylos devised for *his* Klytaimestra could have been dreamed by her, had she been a real person, though it could probably *not* have been dreamed by the Sophoklean Klytaimnestra.

But that demonstration is possible only if one goes through the motions of an "as if" psycho-analysis of the fictitious but plausible Aischylean Klytaimestra and of her dream. The conclusions such an operation yields are, strictly speaking, "constructs", whose logical status is exactly the same as that of the equally inferential "construct" that Aischylos, in causing Agamemnon to speak as he does, *meant us to assume* not only that his vocal apparatus was like that of any man, but also that his early training had caused him to speak Greek rather than Persian, and to express himself in a manner befitting a High King instead of like the slack, bitter and brittle usurper Aigisthos. All this, Aischylos assuredly meant us to take for granted, even though he did not say so explicitly in any passage of his *Oresteia*.

I wish to stress that, in taking such inescapable inferences, constructs or conclusions for granted, one adheres strictly to the basic critical principle that one's sole concern is that which is within the drama itself. Moreover, in so doing, one preserves the most essential quality of the text: its status as a work of art. For, the moment one refuses to take these indispensable inferences for granted, the *Oresteia* ceases to be a work of art and is reduced to the status of a mere storehouse of grammatical and lexical problems and puzzles, many of which can—as Chapter 3 indicates— be solved only by re-introducing into one's discourse precisely those inescapable logical constructs which, quite unwarrantably, one had previously rejected on the grounds that they are not *explicitly* mentioned in the text.

My basic methodological position is therefore that a psycho-analytical scrutiny of dreams narrated in Greek tragedy is much more than a wanton intrusion of the psycho-analyst into a discipline not his own, without authority other than his own *ex cathedra* assertion that, since the data fit his method, his enterprise and *modus operandi* are legitimate.

I note, however, from the outset that, since psycho-analysis is a powerful and precise tool of research, I have endeavoured to handle it with the respect a fine tool deserves. I have tried to interpret Greek data as cautiously, patiently and responsibly as I formerly interpreted the utterances and behaviour of my psycho-analytical patients, for "off the cuff", "wild", psycho-analysis is quite as much out of place in the interpretation of Greek data as in that of clinical material.

I concede, of course, that some professional psycho-analysts—and many more who, judging by the fact that they belong to no recognized psycho-analytical organization, are not qualified psycho-analysts, though they are at times mistakenly believed by the general reader to be representatives of that learned profession[1]—fail to display in their "applied psycho-analytical" writings the caution and self-discipline the real psychoanalyst is expected to display in his clinical work and writings. The bad name such performances give to psycho-analysis in classical circles can be counteracted only by showing that psycho-analytically responsible and philologically not grossly amateurish discussions of Greek data have something of value to contribute to the advancement of classical studies. For, though passing rhetorical and ideological fads now and then make fashionable headlines, Gresham's law does not operate in the sciences: in the end good science invariably drives out bad science.

I also concede that the extremely complex logico-epistemological problem of the applicability of psycho-analytical methods and interpretations outside the clinical-therapeutic field has not been carefully thought through even by some authentic psycho-analysts, who regularly write outstanding—and at times inspired—papers on "applied psycho-analysis". But I can plead that I *did* think through nearly every aspect of this problem in the course of the last forty years, helped in this undertaking by my early training in mathematics and in theoretical physics, as well as by my attempt, throughout my working life, to keep in touch with new developments in logic, epistemology and scientific method.

Though in this work the application of psycho-analysis to Greek data is justified only heuristically—by showing that it broadens and deepens one's understanding of texts containing dream-narratives—it is hoped that readers interested in the logical validity of the procedure *per se* will find it to have been demonstrated with the necessary rigour in certain of my earlier publications, whose complex analyses and proofs I cannot begin to outline in the present work.[2]

---

[1] Even so judicious a scholar as B. M. W. Knox (*Oedipus at Thebes*, 1957, p. 197) calls Arthur Wormhoudt's: *The Muse at Length*, 1953, the work of one of Freud's "epigones". For a radically different appraisal of Wormhoudt's status in psycho-analysis, cp. my review of that book in: *Bulletin of the Menninger Clinic*, xviii (1954), p. 121.

[2] *From Anxiety to Method in the Behavioral Sciences*, 1967; *Essais d'Ethnopsychiatrie Générale*

At this point I wish to express the hope that the open-minded reader will not impute to me views which I manifestly do *not* hold. This plea does not seem superfluous. B. M. W. Knox (op. cit., pp. 197 f.), a Hellenist with impeccable credentials, pointed out, firmly but tactfully, that *some* Hellenists have unfairly indicted Freud for holding views about Sophokles' *Oidipous Tyrannos* which Freud had *explicitly and emphatically rejected*. The less temperate Wilamowitz would probably have exclaimed, as he did on another occasion: "Kann man denn nicht lesen?" I make this plea with some insistence, for I know, from my own first contacts with psychoanalysis, that it is "strong medicine" which is not always easy to take: the temptation to set up a straw man, call him Freud and then knock him down, is, at times, almost irresistible.

On the substantive level, the present book advances the thesis that great art is located at the confluence of culturally imposed artistic means and objectives and of a subjectively determined psychological realism. Thus, in Chapter 4, I note that the slowly awakening Erinyes' account of their dream about Klytaimestra's shade—which a moment before was actually performed on stage—is singularly impoverished. They report only that "reproach"—of unspecified origin—smote them in sleep, in dream. In a *drama*, this impoverished account of the dream scene just enacted is aesthetically fully satisfying, though in *epic poetry* Agamemnon's deceitful dream bears being repeated three times, in almost identical words, in the space of some seventy verses.[3] In fact, in the epic, that dream's aesthetic adequacy depends primarily on the recognition of its (deceitfully) oracular quality—and *that* quality of the dream is made evident precisely by its repeated full narration.[4]

But the aesthetic satisfyingness of the Erinyes' impoverished recall of their dream is largely contingent upon the psychologically persuasive evanescence of their dream's actual content. The Erinyes, aroused by their anxiety dream from an induced—i.e., quasi-drugged—deep sleep, struggle hard to wake up: they must fight off both their sleepiness and the lingering imprints of an all too vivid dream. Better still, the one thing they *do* recall —the reproach for their neglect of duty—not only helps them to wake up, but can immediately be used as a self-exonerating device, for they, in turn, at once reproach the god who, by putting them to sleep, made them forget both their duties and their rights.

The requirements of dramatic logic assuredly make some sort of awakening *scene* indispensable after the dream enacted on-stage—but the aesthetic and dramatic *quality* of the scene Aischylos actually devised results directly from its flawless psychological realism. Its beauty is a consequence of its

(1939–1966),[2] 1973; *Ethnopsychanalyse Complémentariste* (1940–1972), 1972; Art and Mythology: A General Theory (in) B. Kaplan (ed.): *Studying Personality Cross-Culturally*, 1961; The Structure of Tragedy and the Structure of the Psyche in Aristotle's *Poetics* (in) Ch. Hanly and M. Lazerowitz (eds.): *Psychoanalysis and Philosophy*, 1970.

[3] Hom. *Il.* 2.11 ff, 28 ff., 65 ff.

[4] An analogy is provided by what happened when an embassy consulted the Delphic oracle: the Pythia raved, the priest "translated" the ravings into cryptic hexameters, and the embassy reported the versified oracle to the King (or City) who had despatched it to Delphi.

finality: once seen, or read, it cannot be imagined otherwise; no alternative is conceivable.

I conclude with two professions of faith:

The Greeks were not buildings, statues, coins, papyri or other relics. They were human beings and, in the Fifth Century B.C., rather more successfully human than we are. Were it otherwise, I would probably be able to write an *Agamemnon* of my own, instead of being reduced to commenting on Aischylos' drama—be it but to remind myself of what greatness "the naked ape" is capable, lest I utterly lose hope in the masochistic orgy of our age, upon which the shadow of tyrannies past, present and still to come falls like a leaden shroud.

The Athenians were Athenians—they did not play at being Athenians. Perikles and Euripides were themselves—not masks put on by actors impersonating "the Athenian", "the statesman" or "the poet". For each culture is at once itself and a complete specimen of Culture, as each man is himself and a complete specimen of Man. And it is precisely the uniqueness of each and every man and culture which enables them to be *complete* specimens of Man, and of Culture. In studying Greece, Aischylos or his *Agamemnon*, we encounter ourselves.

Paris, July 1975 *George Devereux*

Author's Note

Psycho-analytical and Anthropological Concepts are always defined—at times more than once—and, in many cases, illustrative clinical and ethnographical material is cited in footnotes. Further information can be found in Charles Rycroft: *A Critical Dictionary of Psycho-Analysis*, London, Nelson, 1968—a handy and reliable little book (*71*).

Every Greek and Latin word is translated (in parentheses) *every time* it occurs, save only when a whole section is devoted to a particular word. (Thus, in the long passage dealing with the word στίβοι, I translate the word once only: the first time it occurs in that passage.)

The New Translations are as literal as possible, without regard for elegance of style. The three Euripides texts were specially translated by Mr Philip Vellacott.

Spelling: Greek words and names are transliterated strictly and consistently, even when this goes against familiar usage. Thus I write Homeros, not Homer. An added advantage is that Oidipous denotes the mythical personage, while "the Oedipus" denotes that complex.

Klytaimestra, Klytaimnestra. Both spellings are attested, the former being probably the more ancient form of the name. I—not altogether arbitrarily—call the Aischylean (and Euripidean) Queen Klytaimestra, and the Sophoklean one Klytaimnestra, for this distinction saves space.

Place names are given in the modern spelling, for few non-Hellenists own classical atlases. Homeros (if he existed) was never called Homer in his lifetime. Athenai still exists but is now called Athens, at least in English.

Abridgements: When referring to ancient sources, I use the standard—and, regrettably, latinized—conventional abridgements (A. *Ag.* = Aischylos: *Agamemnon*). I deviate from this convention only in respect to Homeros. I write Hom. *Il.* (Homeros: *Ilias*) and not simply *Il.* If Homeros existed, he should not be robbed of his glory. If he did not exist, the non-Hellenist reader is more likely to guess what Hom. *Il.* stands for, than he would had I written simply "*Il.*". At any rate, a complete list of such abridgements is given in the Index of Ancient Authors.

A Modern Author's Name, followed by: "ad loc." refers to his commentary, in his edition, on a certain passage. Thus: "A. *Ag.* 426 and Fraenkel ad loc." refers to Fraenkel's commentary on that verse in his monumental edition of Aischylos' *Agamemnon*.

Some Explanatory Footnotes are of no interest to certain categories of readers, though they are indispensable for others. What is a commonplace for the Hellenist must be explained to the psycho-analyst and to the anthropologist –and vice versa of course. The general reader will do well to read all the footnotes, save only those which simply list ancient sources.

The many references to my own work require a word of explanation.

Clinical Data. Ethical and legal considerations oblige every clinician to "disguise" *some* of his material. By citing data I myself obtained, I could be sure that they represent the actual utterances of patients, for one does not disclose one's patient's identity when one cites only *brief* remarks or incidents.

Ethnological Data are also largely derived from my own field work, simply because every anthropologist knows better the tribes he himself has studied than those he only knows through books.

My Theoretical Work is cited largely because the present book presupposes my theoretical outlook, which I began to elaborate many decades ago.

The Few Repetitions can easily be justified.

(1) The Hellenist, wishing to consult, in the course of his own work on a particular drama, *only* the chapter referring to the dream found in that tragedy, should not be obliged to search the rest of the book for an explanation of a particular psychological process discussed in connection with another dramatic dream. This attempt to make each chapter a self-contained whole parallels my attempt to make the book itself answer all psychological questions that the Hellenist may want to ask, without obliging him to consult technical works.[1]

(2) It has been my experience that readers unfamiliar with *one* of the disciplines used in a pluridisciplinary work, may forget a point made—and made repeatedly—elsewhere.[2]

A *slight* amount of repetitiveness is, therefore, admitted but also affirmed to be purposive: sparing the reader some inconvenience is, I think, a justifiable procedure.

BIBLIOGRAPHICAL ADDENDUM

My Repeatedly Cited Book: Ethnopsychanalyse Complémentariste, Paris, Flammarion 1972, will soon be available in English: *Ethnopsychoanalysis*, Berkeley and Los Angeles, University of California Press, 1976 (?).

My Papers: Art and Mythology; The Structure of Tragedy and the Structure of the Psyche in Aristotle's *Poetics*; Observation and Belief in Aischylos' Accounts of Dreams; Manifestations de l'Inconscient dans Sophokles: *Trachiniai* 923 sqq.; The Psychosomatic Miracle of Iolaos; Stesichoros' Palinodes; The Exploitation of Ambiguity in Pindaros *O*. 3.27 and two previously unpublished papers are now available in book form: Devereux, G.: *Tragédie et Poésie Grecques, Etudes Ethnopsychoanalytiques*, Paris, Flammarion 1975.

---

[1] This implies that the numerous references to modern psychological works are intended only as guide-lines for possible further research. I have done my best to make recourse to psychological works unnecessary for the Hellenist reader.

[2] An exceptionally generous critic of one of my earlier books mildly chided me for some repetitiveness. But, though that book cites perhaps half a dozen times Bertrand Russell's solution of the so-called "Epimenides paradox" (70², pp. 101 ff., 523 ff.), at one point, where it is *not* cited for the *seventh* time, he did *not* think of it himself and therefore accused me of having perpetrated a (non-existent) logical error.

Acknowledgements

My debt is great to a number of scholars who gave help unstintingly, regardless of whether they agreed with my approach and views wholly, in part, or not at all.

Professors E. R. Dodds, K. J. Dover and Hugh Lloyd-Jones read the whole manuscript. The comments they offered are identified either by their names, preceded by their *titles*, or else by their initials (E.R.D., K.J.D., H.L.-J.). Dr C. A. Behr, Professor Walter Burkert, the late Professor Eduard Fraenkel and Professor Sir Denys Page generously answered questions on specific points. Since I have—perhaps imprudently—not always followed the advice given to me, obviously I alone am responsible for this book's shortcomings.

Mr Philip Vellacott kindly prepared literal translations of the three Euripidean dreams.

I owe a genuine debt also to the student-members of the work groups into which my 1968–1969 seminar on the ethno-psycho-analysis of dreams in Greek tragedy was divided:

Aischylos: *Persai*: Mmes A. Castanié, M.A., J. Thibaut, M.A., MM. J.-P. Largillet, Ch. Sanchez. I was also stimulated by an unpublished paper which my friend Miss R. Padel, M.A., wrote for her Oxford tutor.

Aischylos: *Choephoroi*: Melles C. Chernet, A. Payen (now Mme Chapelier), M.A., MM. J.-L. Breton, M.A., J.-B. Chapelier, M.A., R. Notz, M.A.

Sophokles: *Elektra*: Mme M. Boccara, Ph.D.; Melles E. Dervaux, A. Jeinov, MM. A. Prenant, A. Sotto, M.A.

Euripides: *Rhesos*: Mme C. Monpin, MM. J. Comeau, R. Danto, A. Mallet, G. Monpin, P.-M. Rousseau.

Euripides: *Hekabe*: Mmes D. Čakuleva-Diamantis, A. Guerrand-Hermès, H. Vanel, Melles M. Fournier, M. Grandjus, M. J.-L. Mercier.

Euripides: *Iphigeneia amongst the Taurians*: Mmes Olga Perianez, Ph.D., M. Bretin-Naquet, M.A., Melle Ch. Abravanel, MM. G. Perrolier, P.-L. Verheyt, M.A.

For reasons stated in Chapter 1, my personal debt is greatest to the group which studied Aischylos' *Persai*, not because that group worked better than the others, but because my own initial analysis of Atossa's dream was unsatisfactory.

Mrs Jane Wenning Devereux, B.A., edited and typed most of this book, greatly helped me with my research and provided a number of valuable comments, identified by her initials (J.W.D.) in the text.

A visiting Fellowship of All Souls College, Oxford (January to June 1972) gave me, amongst many other things, badly needed leisure to think over and to improve countless passages of this work.

Messrs Basil Blackwell & Mott have put me in their debt by deciding to publish a book on which the opinions of the referees were sharply divided.

The Aischylos translations by H. W. Smyth (from the Loeb Classical Library, *Aeschylus*), are reproduced here by permission of Harvard University Press (Copyright © by the President and Fellows of Harvard University).

The Jebb translation of Sophokles' *Elektra* is reproduced by permission of Cambridge University Press.

The L. J. Beare translation from Aristoteles' *De Divinatione per Somnum*, from *The Oxford Translation of Aristotle* (Volume 3, 1931) edited by W. D. Ross, is reproduced by permission of the Clarendon Press.

The M. Hubbard translation from Aristoteles' *Poetics*, from *Ancient Literary Criticism: The Principal Texts in New Translations* (Oxford, 1972), edited by D. A. Russell and M. Winterbottom, is reproduced by permission of the Clarendon Press.

The frontispiece is reproduced by permission of the Museum of Fine Arts, Boston, U.S.A.

General Introduction

The Technical Objectives

Though addressed not only to the Freud-less Hellenist and the Greek-less psychologist, but also to the lover of great literature, this work reflects my belief that clarity of presentation can make even technical discussions accessible and perhaps interesting to the thoughtful reader, no matter what his professional background may be. It is intended for those who believe in the intelligibility of great poetry and deem the effort to understand it worth while.

"Love that passeth understanding" has no place in the appreciation of art and precludes *a priori* the coming into being of a true science of aesthetics and of a psychology of artistic creation.

The enquiry undertaken here is meant to have a paradigmatic import.

On a purely technical level it seeks to prove the applicability to dream narratives found in surviving Greek tragedies[1] of Cicero's dictum: "even dreams contrived by poets partake of the essence of dreams".[2] This conclusion does not differ greatly from Abraham's finding (*2*) that there are fundamental affinities between myths and dreams.

Before I discuss far greater problems—important alike for the lover of poetry, for the culture historian and for the literary critic—I must specify the *means* which enable one to determine whether a dream devised by a poet is, or is not, authentically dreamlike.

Limitations. I discuss only actually narrated or represented (chap. 4) dreams, occurring in the surviving dramas. I do not study:

(1) *Dreams which are not narrated*, but simply mentioned, in order to indicate that reality confirms their (unspecified) prophetic content (A. *Sept.* 710 ff. E. *Tr.* 921 ff.). Of course, even the clinician occasionally hears a "forgotten" dream mentioned in this manner and is, at times, able to help his patient remember it (*22*, pp. 206 ff.). I believe that Eteokles' dream(s) could be reconstructed and I have, in fact, done so for my own enlightenment, though, in a sense, that was unnecessary, because the rest of the tragedy is but an expanded and decoded narration of Eteokles' non-reported dream(s).[3]

(2) *Brief, metaphorical allusions to dreams.* I did, however, include the

---

[1] For a justification of the exclusion of certain types of data pertaining to dreams, see below.

[2] Haec, etiam si ficta sunt a poeta, non absunt tamen a consuetudine somniorum. Cic. *de divin.* 1.42.

[3] These dreams may have been narrated in Aischylos' (lost) *Oidipous* (H.L.-J.).

snake-spider nightmare metaphor in A. *Suppl.* 884 (chap. 9), because it sheds light on snake and spider *type* dreams in ancient Greece.

(3) *Dreams alluded to in fragments* were excluded because:

    (a) Their context did not survive and therefore cannot provide a substitute for the "analysand's" free associations.

    (b) In my discussion of Menelaos' dream (chap. 3), I show that, had vv. 412 f. survived only as a fragment, the psychiatric and psycho-analytical conclusions one would have drawn from them would have been partially misleading. Only when read in context does their real meaning become fully discernible.

The Psychological Plausibility of a Literary Dream quite as much as the realism of Rembrandt's painting of a beef carcass can be ascertained in terms of specifiable criteria.

All that matters is that the *criteria* in terms of which one affirms that the Aischylean Menelaos' dream is realistic, whereas the Homeric Agamemnon's dream (Hom. *Il.* 2 init.) is not, must have a *counterpart* in at least one *scientific* system of psychology. It simply won't do to assert that the photograph of a running horse is unrealistic because it does not resemble the time-hallowed representation of the "flying gallop"—a gait no *real* horse can assume (*55*, pp. 497 ff.).[4]

The criteria in terms of which I seek to test the psychological plausibility of dreams in Greek tragedy—and the implausibility of the Homeric Agamemnon's dream—are those of psycho-analysis. I know no other technique of ascertaining a literary dream's plausibility or implausibility than that of "psycho-analysing" it. It is hardly necessary to add that this logically valid "as if" procedure no more turns the poet's Menelaos into a real person lying on my analytical couch, than the finding that the texture of Rembrandt's beef carcass correctly represents the texture of high quality steak renders that painting edible.

Last, but not least, the demonstration that Menelaos' dream is properly oniric does not *necessarily* imply that Aischylos carefully set out to contrive a psychologically plausible dream. My goal is not the elucidation of the poet's true intentions, which, unlike certain critics, I do not profess to know. I assume only that he tried to write the best drama (and dream) he could devise. For the rest, I set myself the straightforward task of studying what he had, in fact, done and of ascertaining whether what he did do is "true to life" in terms of the specifiable criteria and techniques of dream-analysis.

The Automatic Production of Psychological—and Psychologically Interpretable— Material, by poet and cobbler alike, is inevitable. The mind is simply *unable* to produce any other kind of material. It can produce the psychologically interpretable *idea* of a nail—it cannot produce an actual nail, which, *qua* object, is psychologically *not* interpretable.

The metallurgically unsophisticated Aischylos described the properties of bad bronze so well that an electrochemist could explain why bad bronze reacts to polishing *exactly* as described by Aischylos in A. *Ag.* 390 f. (see

---

[4] Yet it is precisely in terms of "flying gallop" "psychological" criteria that certain critics assert the lack of plausible and consistent characterizations in Greek tragedy! Cp. also Aristarchos' athetization of Hom. *Od.* 23.218–224 (*13*).

Fraenkel, ad loc.). Since all men dream, we need *not* suppose that Aischylos, Sophokles, Euripides had to read Freud in order to *devise* plausible dreams. But *I* had to read Freud in order to *demonstrate* their plausibility. In short, throughout this book I have put into practice P. Maas' (*60*) maxim: "As regards subject matter the classical scholar must often turn for help to other branches of knowledge (technical, etc.)." The legitimacy of this procedure is beyond doubt. The only question is whether I have applied it competently.

Deliberate "Psychologizing" is of course not to be imputed to most early authors, for recourse to psychology as an artistic device is always a relatively "late" development (*10*). Aischylos described and expressed (psychological) conflicts credibly. The madness of Aias (S. *Aj.*), though *not* analysed psychologically *by the poet*, does furnish *clues* to the clinician. But that is all. Perhaps the first poet not only to describe psychological happenings but also to explain them psychologically—though *not* in terms of a systematic theory (*31*)—appears to have been Euripides. This, in a sense, explains my choice of dramatic dreams as a means of demonstrating the psychological realism of great poets—for just as, according to Cicero, the dreams they devise are *dreamlike*, so are the actual dreams of any human being, be he Descartes, Newton or an Eskimo, none of whom ever heard of modern dream theory. I think I can state this matter metaphorically clearly enough so as not to have to labour it: the pineal gland functioned appropriately long before it was identified—and continued to function as before, even when Descartes believed it to be the seat of the soul.

The Use of the Psycho-Analytical Method needs no defence, at least for the open-minded reader; it has been tested in the crucible of about eighty years of clinical practice, involving tens of thousands of patients. I have, moreover, found many outstanding Hellenists singularly receptive to this approach to Greek problems. I therefore content myself with making two points, which even psycho-analysts do not stress sufficiently.

(1) Being a therapeutic method, psycho-analysis is interested in transforming the "bad" into the "good". It is more interested in sublimation than in neurosis. Sophokles' private—because human—Oedipus complex does not much interest the psycho-analyst; he mainly tries to understand why and how Sophokles—*but not Strepsiades*—managed to turn his private problem into a cultural achievement, by sublimating it. The botanist does not degrade the rose through his attempt to understand how it can absorb manure through its roots and yet produce attar of roses from its flowers. Moreover, by learning to understand how Sophokles managed to turn his private problems into *Oidipous the King*, one also learns the art of helping Strepsiades to use his conflicts in a less self-destructive, more creative manner. If this be "muck-raking", we cannot have enough of it, if men are to be helped to become better and happier (*18*).

(2) No psychological system has, to my knowledge, been found more applicable to—nor is more frequently applied to—the study of literature and of art than psycho-analysis. This too is, I think, a valid argument in favour of a psycho-analytical study of dreams in Greek tragedy.

The Irrational and the Unpleasant in the analysis of the *roots* of a dream—or of a drama—sometimes disturb the non-psycho-analytical reader, though the botanist does not expect the roots of a rose bush to resemble its flowers. In dream it is the repressed that manifests itself—and it stands to reason that no one represses wishes and sentiments noble alike in his own eyes and in those of his group. Io's metamorphosis into a cow shows well enough that the wish her dream expresses is deemed unworthy of a human being (Chap. 2).

As to the non-rational character of dream processes, it hardly calls for comment. Hungry horses do dream of oats, but the oats they "eat" in dream are unreal and they wake up hungry.

The scientific psycho-analyst's task is not to deny that unpleasant material underlies a dream—but to analyse its *transformation* into poetry, in *great* works of art *only*. He may not deny the irrationality of the dream process—he must seek to discover the rules that govern this nocturnal, oniric dementia. The task of the scientist, in all domains, is to discern the rules governing an apparent chaos (*28*, p. xxii).

The query of those who may ask whether these "rules" are there, was answered once and for all by the great physicist-philosopher Ernst Mach: "There are no laws *in* Nature—save only those we *put* into it." I have, in each case, tried to indicate that what I saw in a text *could be* there in Greek, in Aischylean, Sophoklean or Euripidean, in ethnographic and in psycho-analytical terms. The *onus probandi* that I am hallucinating, rests, I think, squarely upon the shoulders of dissenters.

I realize that some of my interpretations are likely to arouse discomfort or anxiety and therefore a defensive rejection. But many myths, as transmitted, also disturbed both the ancients and the moderns.[5]

Man's life is conflict and therefore anxiety. Even bowdlerization cannot obliterate those "nasty" elements of myths which reflect human anguish; it can, at best, thinly disguise them (*16*, *25*). The rejection of an interpretation, just because it is unpleasant, cannot make it untrue. The student of Man must learn to put the anxiety his work elicits to a constructive use (*19*).

Clinical and Ethnographical Parallels are therefore cited without implying that the Greeks in general and the tragic poets in particular were half neurotics and half Hottentots. My approach implies that Greeks, neurotics and Hottentots are equally human; that they could not be Greeks, Hottentots or neurotics, unless they were human to begin with. Unless we understand the Greeks *first* as human beings, we cannot—*pace* Wilamowitz—understand their Greekness at all, nor would their life and culture have any relevance for us (*18*).

I do not consider it necessary to discuss this matter further; a controversy with those who condemn an appeal to such parallel data is hardly useful.

---

[5] Pi. *O.* 9.35: refusal to mention impious tales, which Aischylos tried to moralize; Platon (*Rmp.* passim, etc.) and even Euripides (*HF* 1346) called them the lies of poets. (Cp. also E. *HF* 1317 vs. 1345; *fr.* 292.6 f.) The myths of Ouranos and of Kronos scandalized many: from E. *HF* 1345 to Luc. *philops.* 2; from Preller-Robert (*67*, 1, p. 354) to the self-professed antipuritan Seltman (*73*, p. 12). The detail of a *penile* (non-testicular) castration was implicitly denied by Gruppe (*45*, 1, p. 432; 2, p. 1366). Nilsson (*65*, 1², p. 521) speaks first of a *total* castration, but quickly becomes less specific. Only Wilamowitz (*78*, 1, p. 93 note 1) speaks unflinchingly of a penile castration.

But I cannot refrain from expressing my distress over an authentically great Hellenist's contemptuous remark, that Euripides' Orestes and Elektra are not personages but "abnormal case-studies" (*44*, p. 175). Quite apart from my fundamental disagreement with this opinion as literary criticism, it shocks me to think that any human being—even a deteriorated psychotic vegetating in the closed ward of some hospital—should be thought of as a "case history", rather than as a human being in distress. Three decades of clinical experience have taught me to respect my fellow man and to empathize with the grief and misfortune that led him into so tragic an impasse. Psychotherapy teaches each of its practitioners to say: "There, but for the grace of God, go I." Viewing a psychotic simply as a "case history" makes a humane and efficient psychotherapy impossible. Calling Euripides' Elektra or Orestes "case histories" assuredly precludes all empathy and therefore also valid literary criticism.

The Literary Dream

The Dreamlikeness of a Literary Dream. The means of ascertaining the rightness or wrongness of Cicero's dictum with respect to a particular literary dream constitutes a problem which, I believe, has never been tackled formally, even though countless literary dreams have been studied by psycho-analysts. Although I obviously cannot fill here a major lacuna in the theoretical framework of "applied" psycho-analysis, the criteria or tests I cite do fit the instances studied in this book; many of them doubtless have a wider applicability.

(I) *Dream Metaphors* can be persuasive only if the majority of readers experiences *at once* the shock of recognition. Two examples suffice to demonstrate this point:

(1) Hom. *Il.* 22.199 ff.: Achilleus' momentarily unsuccessful pursuit of Hektor is compared to a dream. Wilamowitz (*77*, p. 100) reacted to it with a shock of recognition; he called the metaphor beautiful but unbearable. This does not oblige one to assume that Wilamowitz once saw himself in dream, clad in Hektor's armour, pursued by Achilleus, or vice versa. Perhaps he only dreamed of running to catch a train and not advancing at all.[6] I note that inhibition dreams of this kind (*22*, p. 253) inspired also a Greek myth and even a Greek philosophical speculation about the nature of the (mathematical) continuum.

(a) Apollod. 2.4.7.: The inescapable Cretan hound pursued the uncatchable Teumessian vixen. Zeus himself could end this paradoxical hunt only by turning both the hound and the vixen into stone.[7]

(b) Zenon's famous paradox of fleetfooted Achilleus' inability to overtake

---

[6] This dream metaphor's *impact* is greatly intensified by the fact that in Hom. *Il.* 21, the scene is anticipated by Skamandros' pursuit of Achilleus in a truly nightmare-like manner —though *that* scene is *not* compared to a nightmare. The postponing of such a *comparison* until 22.199 ff. greatly increases the metaphor's emotional impact (J.W.D.).

[7] Cp. also the Oknos myth (Paus. 10.29.2) and the tale of Penelope's weaving of a shroud (Hom. *Od.* 19.148 ff.).

the turtle that started before he did, is—as regards its form—also in-directly patterned on the experience of an inhibition dream.[8]

(2) A. *Suppl.* 887 f.: The Danaides compare the ruthless Herald both to a spider and to a snake, in a nightmare metaphor. Now, both spider (*1*, *21*) and snake dreams are quite common. I even had occasion to discuss this metaphor with a candidate in didactic psycho-analysis, who had formerly had both spider and snake phobias.

(II) *Type-Dreams* are sometimes mentioned in literature. In S. *OT*. 981 ff. Iokaste tells the anxious Oidipous that many men dream of co-habiting with their mothers. Both Hippias (Hdt. 7.107) and Caesar, (Plu. *Caes.* 32; Suet. *V. Caes*, 7) are *supposed* to have had such dreams and Artemidoros devoted a long passage to dreams of this kind (Artemid. 1.79). But a difficulty arises at once: None of my patients ever reported a flagrant and completed (*heterosexual*) incest dream involving a parent.[9] Similarly, my Mohave informants told me that some persons (and especially mourners) had "type" incest dreams (*23*, p. 172)—but were unable to cite actual parent-child incest dreams. Whether the Greeks and Romans actually had such dreams—or, like modern patients, merely had *dis-guised* (symbolic) incest dreams which, on awakening, they *narrated* as flagrant incest dreams ("secondary elaboration")—I do not profess to know. I merely believe that neither Iokaste's nor Platon's assertions (*Rmp* 9, p. 571d) necessarily prove that the Greeks had such dreams, *in a flagrant and undisguised form*. On the other hand it is probable that ancient audiences, who—like moderns—had only more or less transparent sym-bolic incest dreams, recognized their own (*disguised*) dream experiences in Iokaste's and Platon's sweeping statements and responded to them with something like "recognition".

(III) *Some Type Dreams*, mentioned neither in metaphors nor cited as type dreams, are readily recognizable as authentic: for example Menelaos' sexual frustration dream (A. *Ag.* 420 ff.). This dream credibly combines two separate types of frustration dreams: erotic dreams interrupted just before consummation takes place and mourning dreams in which one tries in vain to clasp the dream-image of the departed. This finding has certain literary consequences. Though Aischylos certainly knew Homeros' (*Il.* 23.65 ff.) account of Achilleus' dream about Patroklos, he *could* have written A. *Ag.* 420 ff. even if he had *not* known Homeros—as Milton *could* have written *Sonnet* xxiii, or *Il Penseroso*, even if he had *not* read Aischylos. All three simply described a common type of dream-experience.

(IV) *The Credibility of Some Dream-Narratives* is enhanced also by the presence of similar events in a myth—for the similarities between the operations of the mythopoeic and of the dreaming mind are manifest.[10]

[8] Major thinkers who have solved difficult problems in dream, in a symbolic form, in-clude: Descartes (*43*, *72*, *79*), Agassiz and Hilprecht (*37*), Kekulé (*19*, p. 318) and Poincaré (*66*).

[9] Worse still, I cannot offhand recall a flagrant incest dream of this type reported in the psycho-analytical literature. I heard from a colleague a *lesbian* patient's dream of incest with her mother, and one of my patients once deliberately had an incestuous masturba-tion fantasy, while another regularly had incestuous (borderline psychotic) fantasies—*but never dreams*.

[10] E.g. snakes in Alkestis' bridal chamber (Apollod. 1.9.15) and in a modern bridal

(V) *Observable Sleeping Behaviour* can also provide clues. Traces of a seminal emission in sleep *usually* justify the inference that an erotic dream had been dreamed (*36*). Men have concluded long ago that sleeping dogs, who whine and whose legs twitch, dream of the hunt (Lucr. 4.991 ff.). This view is indirectly confirmed by the electro-encephalographic finding that predators dream more—and more often—than do herbivorous animals (*53*). This datum has a direct bearing upon the Erinyes' sleeping behaviour (chap. 4). I already noted a further, strikingly persuasive, detail: on awakening, the Erinyes recall only that reproach smote them in dream, but make no reference to the (on-stage) intrusion of Klytaimestra's shade into their dream. Such an impoverishment of the dream's content, on awakening, is quite common.

(VI) *Many "Literary" Dreams* can be shown to be persuasively dreamlike only after they are analysed. I must re-state here my fundamental, if heuristic, principle: if a dream-narrative can be satisfactorily analysed in the usual way—by applying to it the techniques of dream-analysis—then that dream fits Cicero's specification: it is genuinely dreamlike. Most chapters of this book instance this method and indirectly but conclusively confirm it. I confine myself here to entering one *caveat*. No psycho-analyst is perfectly analysed and devoid of all scotomata. I cited, in all humility, an embarrassing example of one of my own scientific oversights elsewhere (*28*, p. 161). A similar blind spot prevented me from seeing at once how authentically dreamlike Atossa's dream (A. *Pers.* 181 ff.) really is; I felt at first that it was only an *un*-dreamlike allegory. Fortunately for me, my scotoma was dissipated in time by a group of my students, who, for some reason, had no unconscious need to scotomize *that particular issue*. Once my scotoma was dissipated, the dreamlike nature of Atossa's dream became evident to me. And this leads me to a further criterion.

(VII) *"Therapeutic" Effect*. In a clinical setting, the correctness of a dream interpretation is usually confirmed by its beneficial effects upon the patient. He gains new insights into his unconscious problems, recognizes the existence—and dissipation—of his scotoma and produces new material which he could not have produced had the dream interpretation *not* abolished the inner obstacles to the recall *and* narration of that material.

Now, neither Aischylos nor his Atossa are on my psycho-analytical couch. Neither of them can "benefit" by the "correct" interpretation of Atossa's dream. But *one* person did profit, exactly as a patient does, from my students' discovery of the key to Atossa's dream: *I am that person*. For their comments not only enabled me to interpret correctly Atossa's dream —they also made me look inward and analyse the *obstacle* which had prevented *me* from seeing at once what was so evident *to them*. Ironically, the point I failed to discern in this particular instance happens to be *directly* related to a theoretical point I appear to have been the *first* to make in psycho-analysis (*12*). Like most psycho-analytical discoveries, it does not concern a pleasant matter. I was able to make this discovery and was

---

dream. A virginal fiancée dreamed that the bedroom she shared with her mother was invaded by snakes. She was very frightened, but her mother calmly picked up the snakes and threw them out of the window, saying: "Don't be afraid! I have been bitten many times by snakes and have suffered no ill effects."

able to apply it in a number of instances. But, in this particular instance, my scotoma returned momentarily—as a different one returned in the instance I reported elsewhere (*28*, p. 161). The psycho-analysed person's fight against the insidious attempts of repression to regain lost ground never ceases: the battle lines move back and forth as long as one lives. This, perhaps, is why many religions hold that lasting wisdom and insight come only at death.

I hope that this frank description of two momentary victories of my repressions over my insight—their temporary regaining of a lost hillock—will encourage the non-psycho-analytical reader who, at some point, finds it difficult to follow my reasoning, to look inward and ask himself what prevents *him* from seeing what is so evident *to me*. I hope he will do so without embarrassment, for I have just shown that even a professional, who had spent years on the analytical couch and had listened to patients for many more years, has occasional relapses. They are unavoidable—but can be overcome if one is but willing to listen; as I was willing to listen to my students, only one of whom, so far as I know, had been analysed.[11]

I must now answer the foreseeable criticism that I have failed to enumerate the objective characteristics of real dreams and, *a fortiori*, of authentically dreamlike literary narratives. Even if it were possible to enumerate them—apart from obvious traits, such as the presence of a dream wish, of a wish-inhibiting dream censor, of symbolization, of overdetermination, etc. (*20*)—I could not do it within the framework of *this* book. Even Freud had not enumerated all characteristic dream mechanisms in his monumental *The Interpretation of Dreams* (*39*); many of his followers have discerned additional ones. Also, my manner of analysing the dreams under consideration implicitly highlights many characteristic dream processes. This being said, I can make up for the unavoidable incompleteness of my list of criteria only by calling attention to the existence of an *external* criterion, which, I hope, will be of special interest to the Hellenist.

The Corruption of a Text by the copyist is—with the exception of deliberate tamperings—governed by the general rules which underlie all parapraxes (*40*, chaps. 6, 7). The copyist usually copies accurately what he understands *and* is able to tolerate, but will make mistakes when copying

---

[11] Though none of the dreams studied in this work requires one *other* type of proof of its dreamlike nature, I mention it at least in a footnote, for the student of Greek dreams may find it useful in determining the dreamlike character of *other* literary dreams. In certain instances an extremely transparent and almost allegorical dream reveals its affinities with real dreams only by the presence of some paradoxical detail. Penelope's dream of the eagle who kills her geese (Hom. *Od*. 19.509 ff.) would seem implausible as a dream, were it not for the paradoxical tears she sheds in dream. Dodds (*33*, p. 123, note 21) tried to explain these tears as manifestations of an "inversion of affect" in dream. However, an inversion of affect in dream *must* have a *discernible motivation*, and such a motivation *cannot* be detected in Penelope's case. I have therefore urged that the no longer young—and, *pace* Homeros, not always faithful—Penelope (Serv. *V. Georg*. 1.16; sch. Lyc. 766; sch. Theocr. 1.3) reacted in dream with *genuine* sorrow to the impending death of her young suitors (and, perhaps, lovers) (*13*). This view suggests that here—as in many other passages (*64*, p. 120 ff.)—the exceedingly proper Homeros had expurgated something unpleasant: in this case an early tale of Penelope's indiscriminate amours—without managing to efface *all* tell-tale *traces* of that tradition.

a badly written, difficult and/or *anxiety-arousing* text. This accounts for what is at least a preliminary finding: "illogical" *and* anxiety-arousing texts, such as dreams, the ravings of insane dramatic personages, etc., tend to be miscopied and to turn into so-called "loci desperati" (E. *Suppl.* 990 ff.)—as is shown by the *length* of the *apparatus criticus* of passages of this type. But the rule is not absolute: a genuinely dreamlike narrative, like that of Atossa (chap. 1), may be so well disguised and seem (affectively) so harmless an "allegory", that the copyist *will* copy it correctly—for its innocuous "surface" permits its anxiety-arousing *latent* content to slip past his "censor"—as it slipped past mine, until my students taught me better.[12] If the existence of such deceptive exceptions is always borne in mind, it is safe to say, in the first approximation, that the *corruption* of the text of a dream narrative *tends* to suggest that the narrative is authentically dreamlike. Also, but again *only* in the first approximation, the emendation of a corrupt and anxiety-arousing dream-narrative is likely to be more difficult than the correction of errors that slipped into a psychologically innocuous text, for the editor of a psychologically perplexing or anxiety-arousing text will occasionally reject precisely the *psychologically most suitable* emendation, because it puzzles or disturbs him as much as it did the copyist(s) or earliest editor(s), as in A. *Ag.* 412 f. (chap. 3).

These criteria for the determination of the dreamlikeness of a dream narrative suffice for present purposes.

Psychologically Implausible Dreams deserve at least a cursory mention. Being both an anthropologist and a psycho-analyst, I have listened to the dreams of jungle-dwelling primitives and of doctors of philosophy or medicine; to those of normals and of borderline or even psychotic patients. What I heard convinces me that, at least in historical times, all human beings' dreams are "dreamlike" in terms of identical criteria—though they assuredly differ a great deal as to the manner in which they are remembered, subjected to secondary elaboration and told to assorted listeners for a variety of reasons (*22*, pp. 139 ff.; *34*, p. 39). In fact, there are, especially in literature, certain "conventions" as to how to *make* a dream (*conventionally*) "dreamlike" (*33*, chap. 4), which do not differ, in their essence, from certain conventions concerning the manner of making a narrative "artistic" (*15*).

For reasons repeatedly alluded to in this book, Homeric dreams containing long discourses are un-dreamlike precisely because they fit the literary-esoteric convention that important dreams should include long speeches.[13]

As to the dream narratives of Ailios Aristeides, the Rhetor (*3*), I must, for brevity's sake, speak apodictically: it is evident that, on awakening, they were subjected to a rather heavy-handed "secondary elaboration", in accordance with the flagrantly neurotic waking needs and wishes of the "dreamer".

---

[12] In fact, in the now wholly superseded first draft of the Atossa chapter, I referred precisely to the excellent state of the transmitted text to support my (erroneous) contention that Atossa's dream-narrative was only an allegory, devoid of any truly anxiety-arousing content. Cp. chap. 1.

[13] Hom. *Il.* 2.6 ff.; 24.682 ff.; Hom. *Od.* 4.787 ff.; 6.13 ff.; etc.

I must speak at somewhat greater length about Artemidoros' _Dream Book_ for—at a time when psycho-analysis was still ridiculed—Freud, casting about for respectable (or at least time-hallowed) precursors, gave somewhat undeserved praise to Artemidoros, in the first (historical) chapter of his _The Interpretation of Dreams_ (_39_). I will content myself with making two points:

(1) Artemidoros (1.79) gives an elaborate classification of _overt_ dreams of (completed) incest between mother and son. Yet, as noted before, such dreams are practically never dreamed, even by the acutely psychotic (supra).

(2) Throughout his book Artemidoros mentions dreams in which the dreamer's _own_ body is deformed in some impossible way. Both my own clinical experience and that of the colleagues I consulted, indicate that so radical a disruption of one's _own_ "body image" in dream is found only amongst psychotics—and rarely even amongst them.

Since Artemidoros (Book 5) credibly asserts that many of the dreams he discusses were actually told to him, in his professional capacity and since his clients were hardly ambulatory psychotics, I suspect that their dreams had lost nothing in the telling. In order to get their money's worth from Artemidoros the dream interpreter, they had unwittingly elaborated the dreams they had _actually_ had, until they _became_ significant in terms of ancient dream-interpretation, and began to reflect primitive theories of organ autonomy (_28_, chap. 13). But, in the process, they became utterly incredible as dreams of _non_-psychotic clients.

Given, then, the striking psychological implausibility of many Homeric dreams devised according to literary conventions and also the near-certainty that the dreams of the rhetor Ailios Aristeides and also those of certain amongst Artemidoros' clients had been subjected to a radical secondary elaboration, one cannot but be struck by the genuinely dreamlike character of dreams narrated in Greek tragedy—dreams whose affinities with real dreams will be highlighted by nearly every page of this work.

Literary Dreams—present already in some myths (Pi. _O._ 13.63 ff.)—_need_ not be psychologically implausible. Both real and invented dreams have found their way into literary works. But even the complete incorporation of a _real_ dream into a drama automatically subjects that dream to a kind of "secondary elaboration". It loses some of its meanings and gains new ones, by being placed into a different setting. I will indicate in due time (chap. 8) that all three surviving Euripidean dreams appear to be poetic elaborations of one of Euripides' own (perhaps more or less recurrent) dreams. But the attribution of two of them to _women_ (to Hekabe and to Iphigeneia) necessarily changed part of the meaning the real model of these dreams had for the _man_ Euripides. (This may explain why the Charioteer's dream seems to me the most dreamlike of the three.) Further sources of secondary elaboration are cultural and literary conventions regarding the manner in which dreams are to be narrated. Conventions regarding the "proper" manner of narrating a dream, even for _non_-literary purposes, exist already in primitive and ancient society (_59, 74, 34_). Dreams and their telling can also be influenced by their being dreamed by a patient "for" his therapist (_22_, passim), or "for" someone else (_74_).

A dream devised by a great poet may be beautiful and rich in unconscious overtones[14]—and yet be more poetry than dream.

The Sophoklean Klytaimnestra's dream is assuredly great poetry. It affects the plot—though less than in A. *Choe.*—and, after one digs through layers of cultural meanings, one does discover its unconscious content (chap. 7). It can be usefully contrasted with the Aischylean Klytaimestra's dream. At first blush the latter's oddly maternal—and even masochistically slanted—dream seems at variance with her virago-like character—enough so to delight those who deny that there is sound psychology in Greek drama (*76, 46, 80,* etc.). But even the lucid commonsense psychologist will readily realize that it is particularly fitting that a manifestly virile and aggressive Klytaimestra should express her *inhibited* feminine-maternal traits *in a dream* (chap. 6).

Whether used in a metaphorical sense only (supra) or actually designated as a dream, a dramatic dream modelled—like that of Menelaos (chap. 3)—on a real dream, impinges like the blow of a sledge-hammer on the audience's unconscious, compelling each man's inner self to participate in the dream-experience which is re-told on stage. It obliges the spectator to cross the *"rim"* and, in crossing it, to abolish it—becoming at once the pursuer and the quarry.[15]

As to Euripidean dreams, their "dreamlikeness" appears to decrease in accordance with their chronological order.[16] The latent content's keynote —the motif of the "primal scene"[17]—is struck by the dramatically almost gratuitous dream of the Charioteer (E. *Rh.*). This key motif then undergoes an increasingly literary elaboration in the other two Euripidean dreams, though this impairs only slightly the oniric character of the latter. In E. *IT* the dream is dramatically almost indispensable. Perhaps the increasing literary elaboration of the key motif—of the nuclear "model"—was compensated for by Euripides' increasing insight into its latent content. That content seems nearest to the surface in his *IT*—where the dream is assigned to a *girl*. It is this that may have enabled the male poet to distance himself sufficiently from what I believe to have been one of his own dreams. I concede that this explanation is, at best, plausible; the real facts cannot be known. Experience simply shows that the more freely a poet exploits his unconscious, the more he learns to tolerate it. In that sense *only*, creative work can *also* be thought of as a kind of self-administered psychotherapy.[18]

Literary Dreams and Dream-Books. Ancient writers on dreams and on their

[14] The role of the unconscious (= inspiration = the Muses) in poetry was probably always sensed by poets. Though noting that he had *not* understood the implications of the dreams he had invented, the novelist W. Jensen (*49*) accepted (*50*) their analysis by Freud (*41*). Cp. also Kris (*54*): a brilliant book, marred, in my estimate, only by the unnecessary concept: "regression in the service of the Ego". I offered elsewhere a theory of artistic creativity *not* involving this concept (*15*).

[15] On the "closed universe" unity of the two in E. *IT.*, cp. chap. 8, note 97.

[16] Ritchie (*68*, p. 345 ff.) proposes the sequence: *Rh., Hec., IT.*

[17] Primal scene: the child's real or imaginary experience of parental coitus. It is plainly mentioned in A. *Dict.* 810 ff.

[18] Cp. Goethe's famous remark: "I had a choice between writing *Werther* and committing suicide." The analysis of defence mechanisms weakens them; that of sublimations strengthens them (*51*)—and creative work is sublimation at its best (*15*).

interpretation fall, in the first approximation, into two categories. Both Artemidoros—though he claims to discuss also some dreams told to him by his clients[19]—and Macrobius appear to use aprioristic systems of interpretation. Pseudo-Hippokrates (*insomn.*) probably, Aristoteles almost certainly (Arist. *insomn.*; *de div. somn.*), use a system which is partly inductive (based upon observation) and partly hypothetico-deductive. I cannot discuss here the various classifications of dreams used by the ancients, for modern scholars still disagree on the exact system of classification they used (*33*, chap. 4; *75*, cp. *3*, pp. 171 ff.); fortunately it is not necessary for me to do so.

What matters is that, since literary dreams are, on *one* level, cultural artefacts, meant to be "significant", one would expect them to fit dream-book systems better than inductive, scientific ones, since, *qua* cultural artefacts, they are, in part, meant to be *consciously* understandable for theatre-goers more or less familiar with traditional systems of dream interpretation. Dream-books are manifestly interested in prophetic or clairvoyant symbols, whose meanings they seek to ascertain. Poets are interested mainly in inner meanings and then (wittingly or unwittingly) cast about for—often traditional—symbols, capable of expressing these "meanings". Hence, dreams devised by a few great poets (e.g., Homeros) and by many minor ones do, in fact, fit primarily "literary" and therefore also dream-book "models". Of course, this does not necessarily imply that even such pre-patterned dreams lack an interpretable latent content, though it becomes discernible only after the layers of cultural meanings and purposes which cover it are, so to speak, "scraped off" and, after being separated from the dream's core, are used as "associations". This is well exemplified by the Sophoklean Klytaimnestra's dream (chap. 7), and by my analysis thereof.

Given this cultural background of the literary dream, it is extremely striking how genuinely dreamlike both Aischylean and Euripidean dreams are. They are *not simply* dream-book type omens masquerading as dreams. In fact, Euripidean dreams appear to be variations on a real dream's theme, though the dramatic personages to whom they are attributed try their best to *make* them sound like oracles and *treat* them as prophetic or clairvoyant.

Still, with one striking exception (A. *Ag.* 420 ff., cp. chap. 3), Aischylean dreams, though plausible as dreams, do differ somewhat from Euripidean dreams. I will attempt to highlight these differences by contrasting the different accounts these poets give of the history of the Delphic oracle (A. *Eum. init.*; E. *IT* 1235 ff.), whose antiquity both of them take for granted.[20]

Thus, Aischylos favoured tales of reconciliation: the peaceful transfer of the oracle's ownership is part of a non-conflictual evolutionary process. There is no hint of such a continuity in Euripides' account of how Apollon wrested the oracle from the chthonian deities: the new "management" turns a haphazardly run self-service workshop into a briskly businesslike

---

[19] Artemid. book 5 also 1.45, 1.78, 1.79.
[20] Brelich (*8*, p. 300) plausibly suggests that Greek ideas about dreams may have a pre-Hellenic origin.

oracle factory, while the dispossessed Earth defiantly sends men dreams that compete with the shrine's high-priced oracles, which profess to interpret the Pythia's inspired ravings. In Euripides, the dream (= oracle) is not immediately processed by experts (E. *Hec.* 87 ff.) : it corresponds to the Pythia's as yet "untranslated" ravings. A faint trace of this is discernible even in Aischylos: Io first tells her recurrent dream and then reports that her father Inachos asked oracular shrines what it meant (chap. 2). According to Euripides (*IT* 1259 ff.), the dreams which compete with the official oracle rise from the depths of the Earth—that probably symbolize the timeless depths of the unconscious. This, "Euripides the Irrationalist" (*32*) may well have understood.[21] The E. *IT* choral passage about the history of the Delphic oracle is, in a sense, an "explanation" of Euripides' *Bakchai*, which instances, *in part*, the "theory of dreams" enunciated in E. *IT*. This, in turn, casts doubt upon the often expressed view that E. *IT*—which I hold to be one of Euripides' most meaningful dramas—is simply an escapist adventure story.

Though I will have occasion to refer repeatedly to the following matter, I must mention here at least in passing one radical difference between many Homeric, etc., dreams and all but one (A. *PV*, chap. 2) of the dreams in the surviving tragedies: it is the absence of articulate speech in the latter, on the one hand, and the occurrence, in at least one drama (E. *IT* 52), of what is certainly an inarticulate human voice. This is quite dreamlike.[22]

Summing up, Artemidoros would have had a field day interpreting most Homeric dreams and also many dreams devised by lesser ancient authors. But he would probably have failed to sense most of the implications of Aischylean and Euripidean dreams: those he would have detected would have been oracular, rather than properly psychological. Culture-historically this means that the manner of *contriving* literary dreams had changed between the age of Homeros and that of the great tragic poets— though the change was by no means complete.[23] The causes of this change are, for the time being, not discernible—at least to me. Since the change is perhaps most manifest in drama, one might think in this connection of the far from negligible similarity between "seeing a dream" and seeing a play (chap. 3, note 287). But that is as it may be. What does matter is that the appearance of psychologically plausible dreams in tragedy seems to have given a more realistic turn to at least one Greek theory of dream interpretation: that of Aristoteles.

[21] Unborn Mohave shamans "dream" the creation myth already in the maternal womb (*23*, pp. 754 f., 770 ff., 775 ff., cp. *30*, chap. 9). Central Australians call mythical times: "dream time" (*69*); this is confirmed even by the most conservative anthropologists (*35*).

[22] Since E. *IT* 291 ff. is somewhat corrupt and also contains a lacuna, I can do no more than note that, *if* certain conjectures as to the meaning of the corrupt text and as to the content of the lacuna are correct, Orestes mistakes inarticulate animal sounds for the voices of the Erinyes. As to the Sophoklean Aias (S. *Aj.*), he apparently did not notice in his madness that the animals he mistook for his enemies produced (like Aischylos' sleeping Erinyes) *inarticulate* sounds. This is psychiatrically interesting. A patient of mine often mumbled to the point of being unintelligible, so as to obliterate "modestly" what she deemed to be "improper" (chap. 8, notes 127, 178).

[23] Dreams of the "old" type are found in Hdt. 5.56; Pl. *Crito* 44a etc.; cp. Deubner (*9*, p. 13) (E.R.D.).

Dreams in Tragedy

Realistic Dreams in Tragedy and their Interpretability. Just as the scholastics'
faith in Aristoteles' greatness as a biologist could be proven right only by
modern biologists, so only the professional psychologist can prove or disprove the—sometimes approving (ps.-Long. *de sublim.*; 15.3 ff.) and
sometimes condemnatory (Pl. *Rmp.* 3.8 p. 396a ff., etc.)—observation of
ancient critics that the tragic poets were perceptive students of the abnormal,[24] i.e., of a condition in which the unconscious plays as great a role
as it does in dreams, which (according to Freud's well-known remark)
are "the royal road to the unconscious." Yet, even though the test case of
the tragic poets' psychological realism is, in terms of this view, their handling of dreams, a systematically psychological and even psycho-analytical
study of Greek tragedy-dreams is, so far as I know, still wanting (*63, 61,
57*). It is this gap my book seeks to fill.

It goes without saying that, both according to Greek thought and modern
research, the dream is, in a sense, a metaphor. And it is at this juncture
that one can, by citing certain Aristotelian texts, not only understand the
basic resemblance between metaphor and dream, but, what is more, get a
glimpse of how the "meaning" of the metaphor (and of the dream) is "encoded" by the poet (or by the dreamer) and how the encoded "message"—
in the sense in which this word is used in communication theory rather than
in occultism—is then decoded.

Metaphor. "For it is the nature of a riddle that one states facts by linking
impossibilities together (of course, one cannot do this by putting the actual
words for things together, but one can if one uses metaphor)" (Arist.
Poet. 1458a24 ff.). "But by far the most important is to be good at metaphor. For this is the only one that cannot be learnt from anyone else,[25] and
it is a sign of natural genius, as to be good at metaphor is to perceive
resemblances" (Arist. *Poet.* 1459a5 ff.; M. Hubbard's translation, *47*,
pp. 121 f.).

Dream Interpretation. "The most skilful interpreter of dreams is he who
has the faculty of observing resemblances. Any one may interpret dreams
which are vivid and plain. But speaking of 'resemblances,' I mean that
dream presentations are analogous to the forms reflected in water, as
indeed we have already stated. In the latter case, if the motion in the
water be great, the reflection has no resemblance to its original, nor do the
forms resemble the real objects. Skilful, indeed, would he be in interpreting such reflections who could rapidly discern, and at a glance comprehend, the scattered [dislocated G.D.] and distorted fragments of such
forms, so as to perceive that one of them represents a man, or a horse, or
anything whatever. Accordingly, in the other case also, in a similar way,
some such things as this [blurred image] is all that a dream amounts to,
for the internal movement effaces the clearness of the dream" (Arist.
de div. somn. 464b5 ff.; J. L. Beare's translation).

[24] Several psychologically sophisticated Hellenists have shown this to be true: Dodds
(*31, 33*, etc.); Bezdechi (*4*); Blaiklock (*5*, chap. 7); cp. *14, 24, 26, 29.*

[25] This fits what I note elsewhere in this work; it is impossible to contrive a plausible
dream by recourse to cognitive processes *only*. Aristoteles' view, that the art of contriving
good metaphors is unteachable, has the same implications.

The *modus operandi* of the poet and of the dreamer on the one hand, and that of the literary critic and of the dream-interpreter on the other hand, are, thus, clearly complementary. The poet *constructs* a metaphor-riddle-dream; the dream-interpreter *disassembles* the dream-riddle-metaphor and then *re-assembles* it "correctly". He *can* do this, for he is able to recognize the hidden similarity between the model and its distorted copy. The poet creates a stylized copy of reality which, despite its enigmatic character, preserves, in a recognizable form—though on several levels (overdetermination)—the *essence* of what it represents ("original").[26] The poet turns reality into a dreamlike metaphor; the dream-interpreter re-converts a metaphor-like dream into reality. Both must be able to discern the "invariants": the latent similarities both hidden and revealed by manifest dissimilarities.[27] Neither psycho-analytical interpretation nor structural analysis go much beyond this Aristotelian insight . . . for example in the case of my demonstration (chap. 8) that all three Euripidean dreams express the same intra-psychic reality, by means of three different metaphors—and therefore produce almost the same effect.

Unfortunately, it is precisely in this respect that the psycho-analytical decoding of a dream (metaphor) sometimes meets with criticism, though already Aristoteles noted that all men are *not equally* skilled either in contriving or in decoding metaphors (dreams). I must therefore seek to strengthen my point by an analogy. Ophthalmologists test colour blindness by showing the patient a piece of paper covered with variously coloured dots (Ischihara test). People with normal colour vision immediately discern that certain dots form a number—a 5. But people with defective colour vision will discern a very different number—a 2. Now, though I have normal colour vision, I can, for some reason, easily *make* myself see the way a colour-blind person does: I first discern the "5" and then, very rapidly, *also* the "2" . . . but never the two simultaneously (complementarity of perception patterns) (*30*).

It stands to reason that a person having normal colour vision may not say that the colour-blind person is "hallucinating" the number "2"—nor vice versa, of course. Charges of "wild" interpretation are often equally unjust. The "2"—discernible almost only for the colour blind—*is* there, even if persons having a *normal* colour vision do not see it.[28] More will be said about this matter in connection with the *inner* complexity that makes Aischylos' seemingly monolithic *outward* simplicity possible.

This being said, it does not matter very much whether a poet "intuitively" contrives a plausible dream or whether, as I believe, the three Euripidean dreams are poetic elaborations of one of his own dreams (chap. 8).

[26] Aristoteles' discussion of the relationship between the object and its distorted mirror image(s) in moving water is perhaps the first allusion to "continuous transformations", such as are studied in topology and in some other branches of modern mathematics.

[27] "Invariant" is used here in an almost mathematical sense: as that part of a (mathematical) expression which does not change when the expression as a whole is subjected to a series of transformations. Thus, when one twists a rubber ball, this does not modify the "neighborhood relationship" between adjacent points on its surface.

[28] A well-known theoretical physicist said to me: "I have no trouble following psycho-analytical reasoning, for, as a physicist, I am accustomed to look behind the façade of things." The colour-blind are good at recognizing camouflaged objects.

Though this was probably a recurrent dream, the actual dream-narratives are so well integrated with the plots of the tragedies in which they occur, that he could not have dreamed all three *exactly* as he re-told them.[29] I simply note that certain peculiar arrangements recur also in the works of other great artists: even the epicene sensuality of a number of Leonardo da Vinci's paintings is psycho-analytically interpretable.[30]

The recurrence of a pattern in an artist's work proves its unconscious importance for him and may represent a—partly effective—attempt to master some trauma or conflict by means of repetitive fantasies or dreams (*56*).[31] Such a recurrent artistic exploitation of the same basic pattern reflects, on the one hand, the stability and continued influence of the conflict—but, on the other hand, also the (at least palliative, and, in the best cases, truly sublimatory) stability of the "counter-measures": that of the *well-controlled neurosis* quite as much as that of the *sublimatorily creative character structure*.

The Problem of Survival: Genius

It is a crucial—and, I think, relatively neglected—question why, after a lapse of nearly 2,500 years, Greek tragedy can still move the modern reader—even in a flat prose translation, even in a capricious "Nachdichtung". Parts of the text are corrupt; our understanding of classical Greek is imperfect; scholars debate the exact meaning even of well-preserved texts; we can never quite think—nor fully feel—the way the Greeks did. What, then, continues to move—and even bewitch—us in these ancient texts, most of whose cultural context is irretrievably lost? Much research is needed before we can understand why Kimon could marry his (presumably paternal) half-sister Elpinike (Plu. *V. Cim.* 4, etc.), *apparently* without undue anxiety—though neither the reader nor the author of this book could do so. But we must also recall that Kimon could not have married his *uterine* half-sister, either without anxiety or with social approval. And, I think, insufficient attention has been paid to the fact that, *at the time* of this permitted but unusual marriage—ridiculed in Eupolis *fr.* 208— Kimon was a dissolute, uncultured, alcoholic boob (as shown by his nickname) and that, apparently, *even later on*, Elpinike was never a decorous Athenian lady (Plu. *V. Cim.* 4,14). "Historical psychology" can explain

---

[29] Their original model can hardly have been a friend's dream which he told to Euripides ... for in that case he would *not* have utilized its latent content and structure, but some of its "manifest content". Also, discussing one's dreams with others was thought to be unmannerly: Thphr. *Char.* 3.3, 16.11, 25.1 f.

[30] Freud (*42*). Another of Freud's interpretations of Leonardo's psychology—the "predatory bird = mother" equation—has, in the meantime, been confirmed by archaeological findings. Bradley (*7*), citing Mellaart (*62*), notes that at Çatal Hüyük (Shrine 1) each of a female deity's breasts contained the skull of a griffon vulture, whose protruding beak represented the nipple.

[31] An outstanding Hungarian novelist, János Kodolányi, whose works have, regrettably, never been translated, utilizes in several of his novels—historical as well as modern—the same family constellation: a stern father, a mother who disappeared inexplicably, a kind stepmother, an envied younger male half-sibling, causing the departure from home of the older son. But this recurrent pattern is, in each case, re-worked in a brilliantly different but equally persuasive manner. This constellation *could be* autobiographical.

why Kimon *could* take this step, as cultural considerations explain why he was *permitted* to take it. But only psycho-analysis—which bears in mind his *early* conduct—can explain why this marriage *did* actually take place.

I cannot retrace here the reasoning of my two studies on the problem of the "appeal" of works of art (*15, 27*). I can only say that whereas our access to most of Aischylos' or Euripides' "tools" is defective or partial, we have *total* access to the *crucial* element of their creative work: to its *unconscious content*, provided we are willing to open the deeper layers of our minds to its impact. For most great Greek tragedies—and other works of great beauty as well—deal with the eternal preoccupations, desires and frustrations of the human mind—and especially of its unconscious layers. Each man must deal *somehow* with his Oedipus complex. Few of us deal with it the way the Oidipous of myth did—even fewer the way Sophokles did: by the sublimation of subjective conflicts into a masterpiece.

I have conceded elsewhere (*15*) that our defective grasp of a great artist's tools and the limited "convertibility" of the "currency" wherewith each culture permits its members to bribe their Super-egos, do create barriers to a full appreciation of works of art not of our time and cultural area. But I hold that we do have a near-complete access to the *nucleus* of each great work of art, *whatever* its historical and cultural setting may be: to its "unconscious" content as reflected in the work of art; we *can* even discern the congruence of the *structure* of the work of art with the *structure* of the human psyche (*27*).

This implies that on one, crucial, level the great artist is also a great realist. He is *psychologically* plausible—and never more so than when he brings to the fore the *latent* problems of everyone partaking of the human estate.

In this sense, then, the present work is a study of the psychological realism of the tragic poets—especially in respect to that (unconscious) portion of the psyche which expresses itself in dreams. And, in demonstrating *this* realism, I hope I contribute something also to our understanding of the possibility of the survival of great art across countless years and culturally seemingly insuperable barriers. I need only define the nature of the great poet's realism.

The Realism of Pegasos is, on anatomical and physiological grounds, totally spurious. Yet, in some peculiar manner, Pegasos continues to "persuade" us. In one sense his persuasiveness partakes of that of the incredible plot of the *Oidipous Tyrannos*, or of that of the inedible beef carcass painted by Rembrandt. We accept the incredible—or the inedible—because the artist endows it with "beauty" (*15*). But Pegasos also has other realistic credentials, the most persuasive of which are his (implausible) wings.

Psycho-analysts have concerned themselves a great deal with the meaning of riding for the unconscious: with the oddly ambiguous symbolic reciprocity between the rider and the ridden, whose roles are surprisingly interchangeable both in rituals and in dreams.[32] The erotic significance of dreams of flying was discovered long before Freud (*39*, chap. 1).[33]

---

[32] Cp. chap. 3, note 104; chap. 8, note 76; chap. 9 note 69, also *11, 14, 17, 52*.

[33] Modern neurological studies of sleep show that periods of dreaming are usually preceded by a brief erection (*6*).

I hold that the persuasiveness of winged Pegasos consists precisely in his *combining* the realistic representation of a horse with a symbolic allusion (wings) to the fantasmatic *core* of what riding (= flying) represents for the unconscious mind.

A very similar problem arises in connection with the "credibility" of myths. I formerly thought that we accept the incredible elements of a myth as part of a "package deal": we pretend to believe the unbelievable, in order to be able to enjoy the tale. Today I feel that this conception reflects only the operations of the *conscious* mind, whose importance no person in his right senses will underestimate. In psycho-analytical terms the situation is, however, somewhat different. We accept the "fiction" as a whole, and particularly its objectively *least* credible elements if—and *only* if—they reflect, symbolically, the unconscious, fantasmatic components of the tale's *credible* part. This permits certain systematically repressed thoughts to become *almost* conscious, for myth-makers and great poets feel and utter the "unthinkable"—but do so in accordance with a special code of the proprieties: with the rules of art (*15*).

The (psychological) realism of Pegasos is inseparable from the truthfulness of Apollon Loxias, the prophet. "The Lord whose oracle is that at Delphi neither speaks nor conceals, but indicates" (Heraclit. *fr.* 93 D–K). Behind the "indication" that is Pegasos, there is, at once, the world of magnificent real horses and the world of actual dreams of riding and flying. Such, too, is the psychological realism of the dream narratives of Greek tragic poets.

At the other end of the spectrum stands the Chimaira, no part of which corresponds to a real and *whole* creature: this juxtaposition of disparate fragments seeks to condense *too many* fragmentary and split meanings into an inacceptable pseudo-whole. For the non-archaeologist it represents *only* the total *negation* of reality: the chimaerical. Having no compelling and unified counterpart even in the affect-laden fantasies subtending weird dreams, it lacks the characteristic *inevitability* which even dreamers of seemingly "absurd" dreams experience. Lacking what is technically called a "system-adequate closure of the configuration" (*Gestalt*), the Chimaira— and Chimaira-like literary productions (including Ailios Aristeides' heavily re-worked "dreams")—can only perpetuate the conflict ruminatively, obsessively, but cannot provide a katharsis—let alone a sublimatory resolution—of the anxiety.

And this brings me to a hypothesis which I can state here only in the most succinct manner. What little is known of satyr-plays permits one to affirm that the Greek tetralogy provided a *double* katharsis. The tragic trilogy made the intolerable acceptable by means of *beauty*—the terminal satyr-play made the *same type* of intolerable material bearable through riotous *humour*. In short, in the tetralogy intolerable ("ego-dystonic") unconscious material was provided with *two* passports to consciousness: the aesthetic passport of tragedy and the humorous passport of the satyr-play.[34]

[34] I discussed elsewhere the equivalence of the two alibis: An "obscene" story becomes socially acceptable if it is told "beautifully enough" (S. *OT*) or "wittily enough" (A. *Dict.* 810 ff. H.L.-J.) (*15*). Cp. chaps. 1, note 34; 8, note 190.

The Complexities of Simplicity. A further foreseeable objection was well formulated by Fraenkel: for Verrall "Aeschylus was too simple and solid ... he wanted him more complex" (*38*, 1, p. 57). Fraenkel then adds (p. 59): "Headlam was more attracted by psychological complexity than by simple grandeur." I fully subscribe to Fraenkel's verdict—but with one crucial *caveat*: Headlam's "psychology" is a home-made "flying gallop" pseudo-psychology and the complexities that Verrall devised resemble those a shrewd lawyer creates to obfuscate a straightforward issue. But that, in a way, is beside the point.

The crucial issue is the distinction to be made between the simplicity (or complexity) of the "*object*" and that of its *explanation*.

It is an almost universal rule that the *appearance* of a streamlined *outer* simplicity—such as the "simple grandeur" of Aischylos—is a direct consequence of the "object's" *inner* complexity. The harmonious and indeed grandiose simplicity of a modern jet-plane's *contours* is made possible by the incredible complexity of its *inner* parts. The jagged, complicated contours of a World War I plane reflected the primitiveness and simplicity of its inner parts: its "complexity" was all on the surface—as it is in Lykophron or in certain modern "poets". Compared to the streamlined dolphin—closest to man in its intelligence—the "Portuguese man-of-war", a very simple organism, is sheer "gingerbread". Equations of incredible complexity underlie Einstein's "simple" conclusion: $e = mc^2$. I confidently affirm that infinitely more complicated psychological processes underlie a two-line Simonides epigram than subtend the cryptic pseudo-ravings of Lykophron's *Alexandra*.

Man's mind—and, *a fortiori*, the mind of genius—is, whether one likes it or not, a singularly complicated device. In studying its operations—and never more so than when that mind comes up with an incomparably lean and spare utterance: with an Aischylean dramatic passage, with a Simonides epigram, with Einstein's basic formula—one must constantly bear in mind the great mathematician Lagrange's warning: "Nature simply does not care how great the mathematical difficulties are wherewith it confronts its students."

Precisely because the solid, majestic, monolithic simplicity of Aischylos is glaringly obvious, the assumption is inevitable that almost incredibly complex thought processes rendered that noble simplicity of the "object" possible. Simple grandeur results from the perfect articulation of *real* complexities.

I italicized the word "real", for much depends on it. The great fugal movement of Mozart's Jupiter symphony sounds simple and smooth: its dazzling contrapuntal sophistication is revealed only by a meticulous analysis of the score. Of course, a conductor wishing to be "different" can easily destroy this impression of total simplicity, by instructing those who play the "middle voices" to play too loudly. That, I think is comparable to the means—condemned by Fraenkel and rightly condemned by him—used by Verrall and by Headlam to make the *interpretation* of Aischylos seem complex. Clever complexity-mongers tend to forget that at the end of their road there still is Aischylos himself, in all his majestic "simplicity".

I must pursue this analogy a little further. During a *rehearsal*, a conductor may well instruct those who play the middle voices to play more loudly, to test the correctness of their performance. This will insure that they will play these middle voices well, but *without* undue loudness, at the actual *performance*.

Given the homophonic character of scientific discourse (*58*, pp. 22 ff.)—though, I feel, not of great poetry (*48*)—I am, throughout this book, compelled to behave as does a conductor *during rehearsals*. I must highlight now the treble, now the alto, now the bass, for the nature of *scientific* discourse offers no alternative. But I have—with love and reverence—always borne in mind that at the beginning of my discourse there is the awesomely complex simplicity of Aischylos or of Euripides and that these same venerable texts also mark the end of my road. I have, therefore, been mindful also of another of Lagrange's maxims: "Seek simplicity, but distrust it!" I have tried to look at the *details* with the microscope, the better to understand their subordination to—and importance for—the *whole*. I have sought to analyse the aerodynamic subtleties of the hawk's anatomy and motion, the better to apprehend in the end the fierce simplicity of its soaring ascent and lethal dive. I have not tried to display *my* subtlety, but to understand the subtlety of the *means* Aischylos used to achieve simplicity.

I hold, in conclusion, that the weaver's art, which produces the seamless web of great tragedy, is greater by far than that of the maker of a crazy quilt, for each of his threads runs *unobtrusively* the whole length of the warp or woof. Nothing in a work of genius is gratuitous and transilient. I also know that I have discerned only some of the threads of the great purple cloth that Agamemnon trod when walking into the immortality of fate and fame. I only ask that it be conceded that I have done so scrupulously and with reverence.

Bibliography

(1) Abraham, Karl: The Spider as a Dream Symbol (in) *Selected Papers of Karl Abraham M.D.* New York, Basic Books, 1953.

(2) id.: Dreams and Myths (in) *Clinical Papers and Essays on Psycho-Analysis.* New York, 1955.

(3) Behr, C. A.: *Aelius Aristides and the Sacred Tales.* Amsterdam, 1968.

(4) Bezdechi, Stefan: Das psychopathische Substrat der "*Bacchantinnen*" Euripides', *Archiv für die Geschichte der Medizin* 25:279–306, 1932.

(5) Blaiklock, E. M.: *The Male Characters of Euripides.* Wellington, N.Z., 1952.

(6) Bourguignon, André: Recherches Récentes sur le Rêve, *Les Temps Modernes* no. 238:1603–1628, 1966.

(7) Bradley, N.: The Vulture as a Mother Symbol, *American Imago* 22:47–56, 1965.

(8) Brelich, Angelo: The Place of Dreams in the Religious World Concept of the Greeks (in) von Grunebaum, G. E. and Caillois,

Roger (eds.): *The Dream in Human Societies.* Berkeley and Los Angeles, California, 1966.

(9) Deubner, Ludwig: *De Incubatione.* Leipzig, 1900.

(10) Devereux, George: Mohave Coyote Tales, *Journal of American Folklore* 61:233–255, 1948.

(11) id. (and Mars, Louis): Haitian Voodoo and the Ritualization of the Nightmare, *Psychoanalytic Review* 38:334–342, 1951.

(12) id.: Why Oedipus Killed Laïus: A Note on the Complementary Oedipus Complex, *International Journal of Psycho-Analysis* 34:132–141, 1953.

(13) id.: Penelope's Character, *Psychoanalytic Quarterly* 26:378–386, 1957.

(14) id.: Obsessive Doubt, *Bulletin of the Philadelphia Association for Psychoanalysis* 10:50–55, 1960.

(15) id.: Art and Mythology: A General Theory (in) Kaplan, Bert (ed.): *Studying Personality Cross-Culturally.* Evanston, Illinois, 1961.

(16) id.: The Exploitation of Ambiguity in Pindaros *O.* 3.27, *Rheinisches Museum für Philologie* 109:289–298, 1966.

(17) id.: Fausse Non-Reconnaissance, *Bulletin of the Menninger Clinic* 31:69–78, 1967.

(18) id.: Greek Pseudo-Homosexuality, *Symbolae Osloenses* 42:69–92, 1967.

(19) id.: *From Anxiety to Method in the Behavioral Sciences.* Paris and The Hague, 1967.

(20) id.: Observation and Belief in Aischylos' Accounts of Dreams, *Psychotherapy and Psychosomatics* 15:114–134, 1967.

(21) id.: The Realistic Basis of Fantasy, *Journal of the Hillside Hospital* 17:13–20, 1968.

(22) id.: *Reality and Dream: The Psychotherapy of a Plains Indian.* (Second, augmented edition), New York, 1969.

(23) id.: *Mohave Ethnopsychiatry.* (Second, augmented edition), Washington, D.C. 1969.

(24) id.: The Nature of Sappho's Seizure in *Fr.* 31 LP, *Classical Quarterly* 20:17–31, 1970.

(25) id.: La Naissance d'Aphrodite (in) Pouillon, Jean and Maranda, Pierre (eds.): *Echanges et Communications* (*Mélanges Lévi-Strauss*), 2.1229–1252. Paris and The Hague, 1970.

(26) id.: The Psychotherapy Scene in Euripides' *Bacchae*, *Journal of Hellenic Studies* 90:35–48, 1970.

(27) id.: The Structure of Tragedy and the Structure of the Psyche in Aristotle's *Poetics* (in) Hanly, Charles and Lazerowitz, Morris (eds.): *Psychoanalysis and Philosophy.* New York, 1970.

(28) id.: *Essais d'Ethnopsychiatrie Générale.* Paris, 1970. (Second edition 1973).

(29) id.: The Psychosomatic Miracle of Iolaos, *La Parola del Passato* 138:167–195, 1971.

(30) id.: *Ethnopsychanalyse Complémentariste.* Paris, 1972.

(31) Dodds, E. R.: The αἰδώc of Phaedra, *Classical Review* 39:102–104, 1925.

(32) id.: Euripides the Irrationalist, *Classical Review* 43:97–104, 1929. (= in *The Ancient Idea of Progress.* Oxford 1973).

(33) id.: *The Greeks and the Irrational*. Berkeley, California, 1951.

(34) id.: *Pagan and Christian in an Age of Anxiety*. Cambridge, 1965.

(35) Elkin, A. P.: *The Australian Aborigines*. Sydney, 1964.

(36) Ferenczi, Sándor: Pollution without Dream Orgasm and Dream Orgasm without Pollution (in) *Further Contributions to the Theory and Technique of Psycho-Analysis*. London, 1926.

(37) Fodor, Nándor (ed.): *Encyclopaedia of Psychic Science*. London (1934?) (s.v.: Dreams).

(38) Fraenkel, Eduard: *Aeschylus: Agamemnon*[2], 3 vols. Oxford, 1962.

(39) Freud, Sigmund: The Interpretation of Dreams, *Standard Edition* 4–5. London, 1955.

(40) id.: The Psychopathology of Everyday Life, *Standard Edition* 6. London, 1960.

(41) id.: Delusion and Dream in Jensen's *Gradiva*, *Standard Edition* 9. London, 1959.

(42) id.: Leonardo da Vinci and a Memory of his Childhood, *Standard Edition* 11. London, 1957.

(43) id.: Some Dreams of Descartes: A Letter to Maxime Leroy, *Standard Edition* 21. London, 1961.

(44) Greene, W. C.: *Moira* (Torchbook edition). New York, 1963.

(45) Gruppe, O.: *Griechische Mythologie und Religionsgeschichte*, 2 vols. München, 1906.

(46) Howald, E.: *Die griechische Tragödie*. Stuttgart and Leipzig, 1930.

(47) Hubbard, Margaret (translator) (in) Russell, Donald A. and Winterbottom, M. (eds.): *Ancient Literary Criticism*. Oxford, 1972.

(48) Jakobson, Roman and Lévi-Strauss, Claude: "Les Chats" de Charles Baudelaire, *L'Homme* 2:5–21, 1962.

(49) Jensen, Wilhelm: *Gradiva*, 1903 (English translation appended to the American edition of Freud (*41*) of 1917).

(50) id.: Drei unveröffentlichte Briefe (Zur Geschichte von Freud's Gradiva-Analyse), *Psychoanalytische Bewegung* 1:207–211, 1929.

(51) Jokl, R. H.: Psychic Determinism and Preservation of Sublimation in Classical Psychoanalytic Procedure, *Bulletin of the Menninger Clinic* 14:207–219, 1950.

(52) Jones, Ernest: *On the Nightmare*. London, 1931.

(53) Jouvet, Michel: The States of Sleep, *Scientific American* 216, no. 2: 62–71, February 1967.

(54) Kris, Ernst: *Psychoanalytic Explorations in Art*. New York, 1952.

(55) Kroeber, A. L.: *Anthropology*[2]. New York, 1948.

(56) Kubie, L. S.: Manual of Emergency Treatment for Acute War Neuroses, *War Medicine* 4:582–598, 1943.

(57) Lennig, Robert: *Traum und Sinnestäuschung bei Aischylos, Sophokles, Euripides* (Dissertation Tübingen). Berlin, 1969.

(58) Lévi-Strauss, Claude: *Le Cru et le Cuit*. Paris, 1964.

(59) Lincoln, J. S.: *The Dream in Primitive Cultures* (Reprint, with a new preface by George Devereux). New York, 1970.

(60) Maas, Paul: *Textual Criticism*. Oxford, 1958.

(61) Meissner, B.: *Mythisches und Rationales in der Psychologie der Euripideischen Tragödien* (Dissertation Göttingen). Göttingen, 1951.

(62) Mellaart, J.: Deities and Shrines in Neolithic Anatolia: Çatal Hü yük 1962 *Archaeology* 16:29–38, 1963.

(63) Messer, J. St.: *The Dream in Homer and Greek Tragedy*. New York, 1918.

(64) Murray, Gilbert: *The Rise of the Greek Epic*[4]. Oxford, 1960.

(65) Nilsson, M. P.: *Geschichte der griechischen Religion* I[2]. München, 1955.

(66) Poincaré, Henri: *The Foundations of Science*. Lancaster, Pennsylvania, 1913.

(67) Preller, Ludwig and Robert, Carl: *Griechische Mythologie*[4]. Berlin, 1894–1921.

(68) Ritchie, William: *The Authenticity of the Rhesus of Euripides*. Cambridge, 1964.

(69) Róheim, Géza: *The Eternal Ones of the Dream*. New York, 1945.

(70) Russell, Bertrand: *Principles of Mathematics*. Cambridge (England), 1903.

(71) Rycroft, C.: *A Critical Dictionary of Psycho-Analysis*. London, 1968.

(72) Schönberger, S.: A Dream of Descartes, *International Journal of Psycho-Analysis* 20:43–57, 1939.

(73) Seltman, Charles: *The Twelve Olympians*. New York, 1962.

(74) Toffelmier, Gertrude and Luomala, Katherine: Dreams and Dream Interpretations of the Diegueño Indians of Southern California, *Psychoanalytic Quarterly* 2:195–225, 1936.

(75) Waszink, J.: Die sogenannte Fünfteilung der Träume bei Chalcidius und ihre Quellen, *Mnemosyne* (Series 3) 9:65–85, 1941.

(76) Wilamowitz-Moellendorff, Tycho von: *Die dramatische Technik des Sophokles*. Berlin, 1917.

(77) Wilamowitz-Moellendorff, Ulrich von: *Die Ilias und Homer*. Berlin, 1916.

(78) id.: *Der Glaube der Hellenen*[3], 2 vols. Basel and Stuttgart, 1959.

(79) Wisdom, J. O.: Three Dreams of Descartes, *International Journal of Psycho-Analysis* 28:11–18, 1947.

(80) Zürcher, Walter: *Die Darstellung des Menschen in Drama des Euripides*. Basel, 1947.

Chapter 1

Atossa's Dream

(Aischylos: *Persai*)

ATOCCA (BACIΛEIA)

ἐδοξάτην μοι δύο γυναῖκ' εὐείμονε,   181
ἡ μὲν πέπλοισι Περσικοῖς ἠσκημένη,
ἡ δ' αὖτε Δωρικοῖσιν, εἰς ὄψιν μολεῖν,
μεγέθει τε τῶν νῦν ἐκπρεπεστάτα πολύ,
κάλλει τ' ἀμώμω, καὶ κασιγνήτα γένους   185
ταὐτοῦ· πάτραν δ' ἔναιον ἡ μὲν Ἑλλάδα
κλήρῳ λαχοῦσα γαῖαν, ἡ δὲ βάρβαρον.
τούτω στάσιν τιν', ὡς ἐγὼ 'δόκουν ὁρᾶν,
τεύχειν ἐν ἀλλήλαισι· παῖς δ' ἐμὸς μαθὼν
κατεῖχε κἀπράυνεν, ἅρμασιν δ' ὕπο   190
ζεύγνυσιν αὐτὼ καὶ λέπαδν' ἐπ' αὐχένων
τίθησι. χἠ μὲν τῇδ' ἐπυργοῦτο στολῇ
ἐν ἡνίαισι τ' εἶχεν εὔαρκτον στόμα,
ἡ δ' ἐσφάδαζε, καὶ χεροῖν ἔντη δίφρου
διασπαράσσει καὶ ξυναρπάζει βίᾳ   195
ἄνευ χαλινῶν καὶ ζυγὸν θραύει μέσον.
πίπτει δ' ἐμὸς παῖς, καὶ πατὴρ παρίσταται
Δαρεῖος οἰκτείρων σφε· τὸν δ' ὅπως ὁρᾷ
Ξέρξης, πέπλους ῥήγνυσιν ἀμφὶ σώματι.

(Smyth's text)

Translation:

Atossa (the Queen): I dreamed that two women in fair vesture, one
apparelled in Persian garb, the other in Dorian attire, appeared before
mine eyes; both in stature far more striking than are the women of our
time, in beauty flawless, sisters of the selfsame race. As for the country
wherein they dwelt, to one had been assigned by lot the land of Hellas, to
the other that of the barbarians. The twain, to my fancy, seemed to provoke each other to a mutual feud; and my son, made aware of this, strove
to restrain and to soothe them, and yoked them both to his car and
placed the collar-straps upon their necks. The one bore herself proudly in
these trappings and kept her mouth obedient to the rein. The other
struggled and with her hand rent asunder the harness of the car; then,
free of the curb [?], dragged it violently along with her and snapped the
yoke asunder. My son was hurled to the ground and his father Dareios
stood by his side compassionating him. But Xerxes, when he beheld him,
rent his garments about his limbs.

(Smyth's translation)

(The exact details of the manner in which the woman in the Dorian garb
frees herself *and*, none the less, drags the chariot along are not altogether
clear; cp. Broadhead ad loc. and my comments, infra.)

Introduction

Atossa's dream confronted me with unexpected difficulties. For reasons to be enumerated below, it struck me as a "literary dream"—as a mere allegory. The "final" draft of this chapter was ready when, in quick succession, two unpublished reports on this dream[1] made me realize that I had missed the essence of its meaning, and that the chapter would have to be completely rewritten. The important methodological implications of this fortunate mishap are discussed in the General Introduction.

The facts that misled me were:

(1) The text's excellent state, not only in comparison with that of other Aischylean dreams, but even with that of the Aischylean corpus as a whole. The few and unimportant errors are easily rectifiable; the *apparatus criticus* of this passage is exceptionally short. Differences of opinion about the meaning of certain details do not create problems of interpretation for the psycho-analyst. At first, I deemed this to be *prima facie* evidence that this text's latent content was not disturbing enough to cause its many copyists to perpetrate defensive mistakes.[2] Such mistakes represent what I call (*17*, chap. 23) the "this far and no further" reaction: "I have heard all I can tolerate".

My failure to grasp this dream's essence well exemplifies such defensive blind spots. The dream's unconscious "message" simply did not *reach* me until the reports of my students and of Miss Padel confronted me with it.

(2) I did not recognize that Atossa was "present" in her dream, let alone that she was doubly present.

(3) The dream is manifestly prophetic and clairvoyant. Its message is duplicated on awakening first by the bird omen, then by the Messenger's report and at last also by the defeated Xerxes' return. Proofs of the dream's oracular character are "laid on too thick". Even Dareios' (non-clairvoyant, 739 ff.) ghost treats it as an oracle. I simply failed to see that, as in actual dreams, the real content of this dream simply reflects the past.

(4) The day's residue exerts almost no influence on the imagery. Only the anxious mood of *many* preceding days is echoed by the dream's outcome—as is the case, for example, also in vv. 133 ff.

(5) No one is puzzled in the least by the dream's meaning; all seek only to avert its disastrous "prophecy" (221 ff.).[3] Since that is less *individual* behaviour than a reflection of Greek *cultural* practices, it caused me to assume that what precedes this series of cultural reactions is also primarily

---

[1] The work-group report of four of my students (Mmes Agnès Castanié, M.A., and Josy Thibaut, M.A., MM. J.-P. Largillet and Chr. Sanchez) and a paper Miss Ruth Padel, B.A., had written for her Oxford tutor.

[2] Patients producing "deep" material fumble and commit many lapses. It is difficult to recall even one's own dream, let alone that of someone else. Analysands often forget all or part of their dreams. Those who jot them down in the middle of the night sometimes cannot reconstruct the dream from their sketchy notes—and are at times even unable to decipher them. On writing down one's dreams, cp. Freud *38*, pp. 89 ff. and Abraham *1*, chap. 5. On the difficulties of remembering the dreams of others, cp. *20*, *passim*.

[3] But I note the absence of an evil-dispelling exposure of the fantasm—or of the dreamer's senses—to the light of day: S. *El.* 424 ff. and schol. *ad loc.*; E. *Hec.* 68 f., *IT* 42 ff.; cp. E. *Ba.* 1264 and my discussion of that scene (*23*), also chap. 2, note 104. On ablutions, cp. Groeneboom ad vv. 201–204.

cultural in nature: an allegory rather than an authentic dream. Atossa is specifically concerned with the shadow her dream casts on her waking experiences (603 ff.). The ritual seeks to control not only the events, but the anxiety reaction as well (*36*), for in Aischylos the waking reaction to a dream is the most effective clue to its "meaning" (*18*). But the bird omen appears to decrease Atossa's faith in apotropaic rituals, for the hawk (= Greece) does not spare the eagle (= Persia) even after it seeks asylum at Apollon's altar.[4]

(6) The literary quality of this dream narrative is not of the highest. It lacks Aischylos' compelling vision and the torrential power of his poetic diction. In trying to contrive something outlandish enough to pass as both dreamlike and "exotic" (Persian), Aischylos seems to have harnessed the racers of his imagination to an ornately cumbersome coronation coach . . . or, better still, to a royal hearse. To insure absolute transparence, he devised a quasi-allegory and not an immediately persuasive dream. Instead of letting fantasy *reinterpret* the real world, turning the commonplace into sheer magic, he tried to manufacture the substance of a fantasy world and therefore (predictably) failed to bring into being the *uncannily realistic* atmosphere of a dream.[5]

In short, the difference between dream and allegory is also the difference between great and merely good poetry. A stylized *heraldic* lion representing Scotland is only an allegory; a *realistic* lion chasing an adolescent dreamer through endless corridors is the stuff of dreams and of great poetry. The great poet grasps reality with his bare hands; in making it his own, he endows it with magic. The merely good poet either plods along, passively stepping into the footprints of a non-thrilling reality or else devises a weird but non-persuasive "world" of his own. Such a contrived world of images and events is queer rather than strange and outlandish rather than poetic, for great poetry's springboard must be, always was and will ever be reality, as the dream's springboard is the real waking experience of the previous day[6] rearranged into an uncanny *pattern*, fitting the requirements of the irrational instincts. Poetry and dream have much in common with the "uncanny", which is at once "homely" (*heimisch* = familiar) and "secretive" (*heimlich*) (*39*).

Thus, the uncannily dreamlike scene in Henry James' *The Turn of the Screw* (*42*), in which the children pretend *not* to notice the "supernatural" happenings all about him, derives its compelling power solely from its intensification of reality. Dream, myth and great poetry re-structure reality in a new way. Allegory and the "literary dream" arrange extravagant elements in a conventional manner[7] (cp. chap. 7). The interpretation

---

[4] On the eagle as a suppliant *not* protected by Apollon, because of Xerxes' sacrileges at Delphi (Hdt. 8.35–39), cp. Broadhead *ad* v. 207.

[5] Of course, the extent of his failure must be appraised by Aischylean standards: what is a failure for Aischylos would, I feel, be a triumph for a Bakchylides. (Though it is inspired in part by professional jealousy, one probably cannot go wrong in accepting Pindaros' estimate of Bakchylides' worth, cp. scholl. Pi. *O*. 2.154b, *N*. 3.143, *P*. 97, 131, 166; cp. also ps.-Long. *subl.* 33.) But I admit that certainty is impossible.

[6] The day residue; cp. Hdt. 7.16; Arist. *insomn.* 461a17 ff., etc.

[7] A somewhat pedestrian analogy will clarify the difference between realistic elements rearranged in a new way and unrealistic elements arranged in a traditional way. A

of a dream must account primarily for the affective and other latent forces responsible for the *distortion* of the usual arrangement of fairly ordinary elements, which need not even be represented by means of symbols in order to create a dreamlike, mythical or poetic sequence and imagery. The structure—in Lévi-Strauss' sense (*47, 48, 49, 50, 51*)—is all that matters. In an allegory, or in a literary dream, the individual symbols alone need be decoded—often simply with the help of a trivial dictionary of symbols. Once this is done, the allegory becomes completely transparent.

But Aischylos asleep is, of course, still Aischylos. Though Atossa's *manifest* dream is, on *this* level of analysis, almost an allegory, it contains enough persuasive touches derived from the world of dreams, myths and poetry to reveal its dreamlike origins, if one can but discern them. I had, at first, failed to recognize these touches. But, enlightened by my young friends, I now hold that this is a genuine "dream", disguised as an allegory. The question is simply: what caused Aischylos so to disguise the dream?

The simplest and most plausible assumption is that, when he decided to devise a dream for Atossa, the first fantasies that flitted in and out of his preconscious mind were so anxiety-arousing that they could not be permitted to enter his conscious mind until they acquired a heavily allegorical varnish, whose (cultural-dramatic) meaning was almost clamorously obvious. This exemplifies the "red herring" resistance I described in connection with certain dreams so startlingly "telepathic" as to distract *certain* analysts from the scrutiny of their *latent* content (*25*, pp. 412 ff.).[8]

The transformation of Aischylos' initial preconscious fantasies into the actual dream-imagery is probably understandable in terms of Aristoteles' observation[9] that, on awakening and while presumably still in a twilight state, the images of the actual dreams are replaced by different ones. This type of secondary elaboration is discernible in several of the rhetor Aristeides' own dreams, and also in the "dreams" which some of his clients told to Artemidoros.[10]

These secondary elaborations helped to smuggle the latent content of *Aischylos'* fantasies past the sentinels of *his* waking mind—though, once written down, the allegorical façade *appears to the dream's modern interpreter* as the means which smuggled its latent content past *Atossa's* dream censor. This, too, is part of the poet's skill, which enables him to represent his fantasies as real and to contrive *psychologically credible* personages.

Of course, this "smuggling" called for the disguising of the latent material: for a borrowing of the appearances of an allegory. And it is by

primitive who acquires a shiny new axe-head and, not knowing its purpose, wears it as a pendant around his neck, is "dreamlike". A unicorn wearing a miraculous talisman on his horn is only "allegorical". This distinction can even be represented more or less mathematically. Let a, b, c be real and x, y, z unreal elements. The realistic arrangement is $a+b = c$; the allegorical one: $x+y = z$. But when dream, myth and poetry *transform* a circle into an ellipse, two qualities remain *invariant*: both are Jordan curves and both can have tangents at every point.

[8] For the layman, nymphomania well exemplifies the "red herring" symptom. He naturally assumes that such women are exceptionally sensual, since they seem to shout it from the rooftops. He is therefore surprised to learn that they are at least orgastically frigid.

[9] Arist. *insomn.* 458b20 ff., cp. 462a25.

[10] Good translations of both sets of dreams exist: *45, 5*.

means of such a disguise that the dreamer (or the poet) "socializes" the latent content of his dream (or fantasy). He tells it in a "culturally proper" manner, which turns the actually dreamed dream—the actually fantasied fantasy—into a "culture pattern dream"[11] in dream-oriented primitive society—and into a work of art in more advanced groups.[12]

There is some evidence that Homeros also indulged in such practices. His long and elaborate dreams are, for all practical purposes, lacking in affective impact and are implausible as dreams. By contrast, his short dream metaphor (Hom. *Il.* 22.199 f.) and Penelope's brief erotic dream (Hom. *Od.* 20.87 ff.) are totally believable. Penelope's medium-length dream about eagles and geese (Hom. *Od.* 19.509–581) is even analysable as a dream (*12*).

The "allegorization" of the initial pre-conscious fantasy may perhaps have been further facilitated by the male poet's need to invent an elaborate dream for a woman, by the Greek's wish to invent a suitably "Persian" dream for Atossa, by that of the Marathon fighter to idealize his foe Dareios and by that of the Salamis and Plataia warrior to represent with compassion Xerxes, the vanquished sacker of his city.

I have shown so far that what prevented *me* from detecting the "dream" behind its allegorical façade also helped shed light on the psychological factors which caused *Aischylos* to conceal, even from himself, the latent content of his fantasy. I can therefore turn at last to the scrutiny of the narrative and to its interpretation, stressing in my Commentary precisely those details of the allegorical façade which permitted Aischylos to ward off a conscious awareness of the latent content of his own fantasy—and which caused me to scotomize the latent content of his text.[13]

An allegorical façade, able to divert even a psycho-analyst from the scrutiny of its latent content, well deserves detailed study, for, like Atossa's audience, I "interpreted it all too lightly" (520) at first.

Commentary

Serial Dreams are fairly commonly encountered in clinical practice. They differ from repetitive dreams in that their manifest content changes, even though their conflictual core remains the same (*2, 4, 40, 29*). In successful psychotherapies, serial dreams reveal the patients' development and maturation.[14] In this instance we may assume that Atossa's dream is not simply repetitive (176 ff.) but serial: it is the worst and least ambiguous (179 f.) of a series of dreams. This is indirectly substantiated by the fact that the dream is immediately followed by an even more catastrophic,

[11] *52*, chap. 1; cp. Dodds *31*, chap. 4. "Official dream": cp. Malinowski (*53*, pp. 92–97).

[12] On the "aesthetic alibi", playing the role of a secondary elaboration, cp. *13*.

[13] I have noted elsewhere (*17, passim*) that an obsessive preoccupation with the immediately perceptible (behaviour, etc.) is animated less by a desire to be responsibly scientific than by the need to use the *appearances* of "scientificality" as a defence against insight into *meaning*. This defensive "scientism" is as obvious in the Kinsey reports (*43, 44*) as in the works of many behaviourists.

[14] "I am shown how to do it. I do it. I show others how to do it" (*19*, pp. 163 ff.).

unambiguous and *dreamlike* bird omen (205 ff.), which, in turn, is followed by catastrophic news and by the defeated Xerxes' return.

The Dream Sequence is quite singular. The narrative refers *first* to the two women and to their pre-existing quarrel. Only then is Xerxes mentioned and it is quite striking that even though the yoking is mentioned, Xerxes' subsequent *mounting* the chariot is not even hinted at. We simply see him thrown *from* it. At that point, Dareios is *also* seen in the dream. The wording suggests—at least to me—that, in a dreamlike manner, he is "suddenly" there, for there is no hint that he was present all along. Schematically represented, the narrative is focused successively on:

The tall women and their quarrel,

Their harnessing by Xerxes,

(Somehow Xerxes is suddenly in the chariot),

The rebellion of one of the women,

Xerxes' fall,

Dareios' "appearance" and compassion,

Xerxes' self-humiliation.

The National Identity of the women is clear. One represents "Persia", the other *Mainland* Hellas. It seems unnecessary to discuss the details of their distinctive dresses.[15]

There is, however, one paradoxical detail which appears to have been overlooked: the Dorian-clad woman rebels only *after* being yoked. This simply does not fit historical facts:

(1) Xerxes' Greek subjects fought quite well for him—especially the Ionianized, though originally Dorian, Halikarnassians.[16] At the time of Salamis, the Mainland Greeks hoped in vain that Xerxes' Greek subjects would defect (Hdt. 8.19 ff.). They rebelled—and then only ineffectually, for the distrustful Persians had already disarmed them—at the end of the battle of Mykale, by which time their mutiny made no difference (Hdt. 9.103 ff.).

(2) Aischylos could not have alluded to the pro-Persian Thessalians and Thebans, who never rebelled.

The initial yoking represents perhaps the occupation by Xerxes of *evacuated* Athens (Hdt. 8.61); the rebellion the now homeless Athenians' continued resistance, chiefly at Salamis.

Only one other alternative is possible. In Greek tragic diction, a planned but frustrated act is sometimes spoken of as though it had been executed.[17] In a sense, this corresponds to wish-fulfilment in dream.

It seems simplest to say that Aischylos is somewhat imprecise in this passage, both as regards ethnic regalia and as regards historical events. While this is understandable in a dream, it does attract one's attention to

---

[15] Cp. Broadhead *ad* vv. 155, 176, 183, 185. The Mainland woman wears a Dorian dress mainly because, as a rule, the women of subjugated Ionia did *not* wear it. Athenian women wore either the Ionian or the Dorian dress. Aischylos—the Marathon, Salamis and Plataia fighter (*Vita* p. 2, Dind.)—certainly did not mean to represent the Dorians as the *sole* champions of Hellas.

[16] The neighbouring Ionians influenced the language of the Halikarnassian inscriptions (K.J.D.).

[17] S. *Aj.* 1126; S. *OC* 1008; E. *Ion* 1500. E. *IT.* 359 is less convincing: the tense is imperfect (K.J.D.); also E. *Cycl.* 665, 669.

the symbolic nature of the scene. A psycho-analytical scrutiny of this vagueness will help reveal the real psychological identity of the two women.

The Sisterhood of the two women can be interpreted in various ways, depending on how broadly or narrowly the ethnic identity of the Persian-clad women is defined.

(1) If she represents the Persians *only*, she is sister to the Mainland Greeks because Xerxes himself is a descendant of Danae (v. 79) through her son Perseus, forefather of the Persians (Hdt. 7.61, 150).

(2) She can represent also the Medes, who—through Medos—are descended from Aigeus—King of Athens—and Medeia (Apollod. 1.9.28, etc.).

(3) If she is meant to represent *also* Xerxes' Greek subjects, the "sister-hood" is self-evident.

These considerations suffice for the elucidation of this narrative *as an allegory*. In the study of its latent content, a different kind of sisterhood will be relevant.

The Sex of the "Horses" is unmistakable. They are women (181, etc.) and sisters (185); they wear women's clothes (182 f.). This is somewhat anomalous. On all monuments known to me, chariots are pulled by stallions. Some texts, such as the *Iliad* (23.295, 409, 512, etc.) do speak of one or two mares pulling chariots. In mule chariot races, female mules were used (Simon. 10P = 7Bgk = 19D). Sophokles, in speaking of Orestes' (imaginary) team, refers to it in the feminine ("mares")—but calls the two animals individually "stallions".[18] Perhaps the collective gender of a pair of yoked horses *could* at times be the feminine plural, even if both members of the pair were stallions.

But in this dream Aischylos clearly *chose* to represent two contending nations as women, though, contrary to Roman and modern custom,[19] at that time the Greeks did *not* appear to have habitually represented their country or nation as a woman, even though the names of countries are feminine in Greek, because γῆ (= earth) is feminine (E.R.D.). Hence, the only explanation of Aischylos' decision to represent nationalities as women is that their yoking could signify also their sexual domination (infra). The chariot is clearly triumphal, and triumph has manifest sexual connotations.[20]

The significance of the fact that this is the Queen Mother's dream will be discussed further on.

Tallness (184 f.). These two women surpass in stature "those of our own time".[21] In Greek thought, tallness was a significant component of female

---

[18] S. *El.* 703 f., 734 f., 737 f. vs. 412 f., 744; cp. W. H. Barrett *ad* E. *Hipp.* 231 (*3*, pp. 204 f.).

[19] Dea Roma, Britannia, Germania, Hungaria, La France = Marianne, etc. Even: La Mère patrie! For earlier periods cp. (*41*). Motherland (μητρίς): Pl. *Rmp.* 575d; Plu. (2) 792E; Paus. 10.24.2, etc.

[20] *33*. Cp. Suet. *J. Caes.* 22. On the eve of a battle, Genghis Khan told his troops that if they were victorious they would mount the choicest *coursers*—which, in the steppes, were *geldings* (*15*)—and the *wives* of the vanquished.

[21] Whether a superlative or a comparative is meant (Broadhead ad loc.) is irrelevant for present purposes. Tall dream messengers: Hdt 5.56, 7.12; Pl. *Cri.* 44a; Tac. *Hist.* 4.83, etc. (E.R.D.).

beauty.[22] Heroines and heroes are always tall.[23] Goddesses appearing in human guise are strikingly tall.[24] The tallness of these women is therefore only to be expected—but no matter what "of our own time" (τῶν νῦν) may mean elsewhere,[25] here it is psychologically more than a manner of speaking.[26] These tall women are representatives of the past: of the world of childhood.

Indeed, since small women can also be beautiful, the *recurrent* connection between tallness and beauty in Greek poetic imagery requires comment. For the small boy, his mother is beauty incarnate, however ugly she may be. Only in one respect are all mothers alike: they are taller than their small sons. Later on, a son grows taller than his mother and, by that time, usually realizes that, because she had aged, she is no longer perfectly beautiful, even if she was formerly lovely.[27] This may help him to surmount, in adult life, most of his earlier oedipal desires.[28]

But the oedipal element can linger on in the form of a systematic linking of tallness with beauty. Perspectives surviving from the infantile past— which is the eternal "present" of the unconscious—make the adult man *feel* that the beautiful young women of his generation are less tall than the mother of his early childhood. There is conclusive evidence showing the survival of infantile "perspectives" in adult life.[29]

The tallness of these women does not suffice, *by itself*, to prove the presence of oedipal elements in this dream. But it greatly strengthens the conclusions drawn from other aspects of the dream.

The Pre-Existing Quarrel represents historically either the Ionian revolt, which the Athenians encouraged (Hdt. 5.97 ff.), or else Dareios' earlier invasion of Greece, or both. What it represents psychologically will be discussed later on. I simply note that this quarrel forces Xerxes to try to reconcile the women by yoking them *together*.

Yoking must be discussed before "yoking together" can be analysed.

[22] Cp. the examples cited by Groeneboom ad loc.; X. *Oec.* 10.2.

[23] Only one source asserts that Herakles was small: Pi. *I.* 4.53—"but at that point he is about to fight a giant" (K.J.D.). Hektor's size *seems* to increase when he dons Achilleus' armour, which he had stripped from Patroklos' corpse (Hom. *Il.* 17.210 ff.). (Cp. Q.S. 7.445 ff.).

[24] Hom. *h. Cer.* 275 f., *h. Ven.* 84 f., etc.

[25] Cp. Fraenkel *ad* A. *Ag.* 532.

[26] But not even the notion that human fathers are images of the universal father Zeus (Plu. *fr.* 46 Sandb.) can justify Murray's translation: earthly.

[27] On the nexus between this fact and the myth of the lost Garden of Eden, cp. Róheim (*55*).

[28] Though uncommon, gerontophilia and marked preferences for ugly women do exist as perversions. A multimillionaire, who could have afforded the loveliest mistresses, was attracted mainly to the slatternly chambermaids of low-class hotels.

[29] I saw in early childhood what seemed to me to be a monstrously tall pig. I subsequently wondered why I never again saw an equally tall one . . . until I realized that I had appraised that pig's tallness in terms of my own childish stature. Such infantile perspectives appear also in what one may call Brobdingnag-ian dreams. In one case, the disproportion between the dreamer's stature and that of objects appearing in dream permitted a fairly exact determination of the period of his childhood to which this adult's dream referred (*8*). Another adult patient reacted with anguish—and with the feeling of reliving his unhappy childhood—to an exhibition of gigantic furniture, meant to persuade parents to buy nursery-size furniture for their children. Even infantile experiences of passive motion (being carried) can reappear in disguise in certain dreams (*14*). The past is always with us.

That yoking—especially that of human beings[30]—represents subduing goes without saying. That the harnessing of women represents also a sexual triumph can be indirectly but conclusively proven through the symbolism of riding, rather than of harnessing. Proof that a "yoking *together*" stands for a complicated sexual relationship will be adduced in a moment.

I begin by noting the Greek poetic practice of calling girls "fillies".[31] The term for "saddle horse" (κέλης) probably had a female and sexual meaning already in Alcm. *fr.* 1.50 P—so West (*63*), with whom I concur. In the comic poets it denotes a sexually active or promiscuous woman[32] and even the female genitalia (Eust. 1539.34). The riding = coitus equation is, so to speak, universal. One of its clearest expressions is Genghis Khan's promise to his troops (note 20). Examples of the Greeks' using captive women as concubines need hardly be cited.

These data suggest that a woman yoked symbolizes a woman sexually subdued. Further indirect, but highly suggestive, evidence is that being attached to a man's chariot *pole* represents for the woman a sexual connection with the charioteer (infra).

The Initial Yoking Together presents, as noted, certain historical difficulties. No already "yoked" Greeks rebelled successfully against Xerxes. The initial yoking together must therefore be treated symbolically. Politically, it reflects the age-old idea that conquest and co-ordination is the best way of ending interminable wars. Poetically, it appears to parallel the "yoke-like" (130 ff.) bridging of the Hellespont, which later on suddenly broke its "yoke" (Hdt. 7.34). I will return to this symbolism in a moment.

In terms of dreaming, the yoking represents an at least incipient wish-fulfilment. In A. *Ag.* 420 ff., Menelaos almost manages to *clasp* Helene in his arms; this corresponds to the initial yoking. But Helene eludes him and the dream ends in frustration. In Atossa's dream too, one, already yoked, woman ultimately frustrates Xerxes by not *pulling* his chariot. Instead, she *breaks loose and spills him.*[33]

The close structural parallelism between Menelaos' manifestly erotic dream and the dream about Xerxes' misadventure is amongst our first indications that the latent content of the latter dream is also erotic.

Now, "to yoke together" (cυζεύγνυμι) commonly denotes marriage; Greek spouses are "yoke-fellows". In A. *Pers.* (133 ff.), a lonesome wife, longing erotically for her husband who is off to the wars, is said to be "yoked *alone*" (μονόζυξ), perhaps because her warrior husband had a camp concubine.

Of course, in this instance the yoke-fellows are *not* husband-and-wife. I will prove later on that they are sisters married to the same King. Aischylos brilliantly translated the relatively egalitarian "yoking together" of technically monogamous Greek couples (S. *Tr.* 539 f.) into Persian

[30] Cp. the still proverbial Caudine yokes.

[31] Though no example of this is preserved in the surviving works of Aischylos, it is common in Euripides (*54*, p. 232). A. *Choe.* 794 concerns Orestes.

[32] Or, perhaps, one assuming a special coital position; coitus inversus: Ar. *Lys.* 60, *Vesp.* 501; Pl. Com. *fr.* 174.18. (K.J.D.).

[33] The equation: unseated by a mount = thrown off by a woman, is commonplace even in humour.

terms. The image of co-wives, yoked to the chariot of their Lord, well reflects the Persian husband's dominance over the women of his harem.

But there is more to this. I will show in due time that the image of the two sisters yoked together (as co-wives) hearkens back to a historical fact which plays, with regard to this dream, the role of a day residue.

Yoke = Bridge = Rape; Sea = Mother. In Persian terms, the yoking of a woman to her husband's chariot reflects her forcible sexual subjection. The yoking of the Hellespont represents violence done to it. One is not surprised to find that—be it intentionally or not—the strophe describing the "rape" of the Hellespont (130 ff.) is answered by an antistrophe which describes the marital yoking of Persian ladies (133 ff.).

Now, the conjoining of horses and ships—both subject to Poseidon—is ancient (A. *PV* 467 f., Tzetz. *Lyc.* 156 f.)—and it is precisely by means of ships tied (yoked) together that the Hellespont was "yoked". Also, in a singularly confusing—because overly exuberant—mixed metaphor Aristophanes (*Lys.* 60 ff.) strikingly commingles the mounting of a horse with the boarding of a ship, in what may well be a hint at *coitus inversus*.[34]

That the forcible yoking of the Hellespont was felt to be an incestuous rape is suggested by the sea being called "undefiled" (578).[35] Indeed, next to the Earth, perhaps the most common maternal symbol is the Sea, precisely because, in the child's imagination, the mother is "pure" and "undefiled".[36]

The bridging = yoking of the "immaculate" sea must therefore almost certainly be viewed as the son's symbolic sexual defilement of his mother.[37]

The Proud Bearing of the harnessed Persian woman is compared by Broadhead (*ad* vv. 190–193) to that of a towering Grenadier guardsman. I do not feel that this comparison is particularly apt. Everyone familiar with horses knows that the stance of a horse just standing around is markedly slack, unless the horse is under tension or strongly stimulated. The firm, "proud" ("collected") stance of a ridden or harnessed horse, *feeling the reins*, strongly contrasts with his ordinary "slackness". This is the most concrete model for the harnessed Persian woman's stance: she feels the reins (193).

---

[34] Here even the ordinarily outspoken translation and comments of Coulon and Van Daele are surprisingly reticent and unclear. And let it not be objected that this is just a comedy quip. As noted (General Introduction, note 34) both comedy and satyr plays represent a *humorous* defence against the *same* anxiety-arousing material which tragedy renders tolerable by *other* means. It is logical that the tensions of the tragic trilogy should have been relaxed by the satyr play which was appended to it. On the basic link between anxiety and humour, cp. Freud (*35*).

[35] Groeneboom also cites Hom. *Il.* 1.314; E. *IT* 1193. Mazon cites the *Avesta*.

[36] Cp. fantasies of parthenogenesis and the conviction, commonly encountered in the analysis of only children: "mother cohabited with father only once: to conceive *me*". The infantile need to deny the mother's "unchastity" explains why many children (repeatedly) repress sexual information given to them (*37*). Some react with rage to any "enlightenment" about parental sexual activities given to them by playmates. As Bertrand Russell once remarked to me: "For the Mediterranean man, his mother is a saint—all other women are harlots." I doubt that the earliest sea deity was Okeanos or Poseidon. It must have been a (mother-) goddess.

[37] The mythical nexus between chariot accidents and inhibited sexuality is mentioned infra.

But there is also a second model, which those who take it for granted that "post coitum omne animal triste" simply cannot envisage.[38] That model was brought to my attention by members of a sexually saner culture. According to the Mohave Indians: "one can always tell who has made love the night before: they carry themselves proudly and their eyes sparkle". As indicated in the preceding note, that was also the classical view. The Persian woman's bearing is proud, for her harnessing symbolizes her sexual gratification, and would have been so apprehended by a non-puritanical Greek.[39]

The Horse Symbol's Choice is heavily overdetermined. Why female (human) "horses" pull the chariot will be shown in a moment.

Riding in a chariot clearly symbolizes Xerxes' triumphant accession to power. A stallion played—*in a sexual context*—a decisive role in Dareios' accession to the throne. From amongst those contending for the throne, it was decided to select the one whose horse, at a gathering arranged for that purpose, neighed first (κληδών = omen). Dareios' groom took his master's stallion to the appointed place one day ahead of the meeting and let him cover a mare. The next day, on being ridden to the same spot by Dareios, the stallion naturally whinnied at once, calling to the mare he had covered there the previous day. This made Dareios the Great King of Persia (Hdt. 3.85–86).[40]

Last but not least, a riding accident of Dareios (Hdt. 3.129 f.), which was an indirect cause of his invasion of Greece (Hdt. 3.134), served as a model for the chariot accident.

The horse symbolism is, thus, heavily overdetermined and therefore appropriately dreamlike also in this respect.

The Disparate and Yet Alike Team is an important feature of the dream. The tendency to distinguish between members of a pair appears to be basic—and not only because the prototypal symbolic yoke-mates are husband-and-wife. The distinction may seem arbitrary at times: in the *equus october* ritual only the right-hand horse of the victorious team was sacrificed.[41] The *Iliad* distinguishes between yoke horses and trace horses (7, p. 143 ff.). Achilleus hitched two immortal and one mortal horse to his chariot.[42] Adrastos' chariot was pulled by the immortal horse Areion and by the mortal horse Kairos.[43] These disparate teams provide a model for

[38] I note that this dictum is grossly distorted by being quoted in *this* abridged form. The complete citation specifically *excludes* from this rule *mankind* and cocks.

[39] That a woman can take pride in "sexual" harnessing was well understood by Freud, who is therefore loathed by modern "feminists". The sartorial fads of an age of "female liberation" confirm Freud's views: "slave anklets", dog-collar necklaces, strong chain belts, etc., are the height of current fashions. Also, according to newspaper reports, the numerous "emancipated" female members of Charles Manson's "family" called him "god" and "devil" and took pride in being his "slaves". Like all *gratuitous* revolts, that of the women, too, is a cry for firm but loving discipline. That the "Women's Liberation" movement should have started in matriarchal America will not surprise the clear-sighted.

[40] The version given in Hdt. 3.87 also concerns the sexuality of mares.

[41] Plu. *Quaest. Rom.* 97, p. 287A; Festus s.v. october equus, p. 178.5; cp. *61*, 273 ff.; *59*, pp. 126 ff.; *24*).

[42] Hom. *Il.* 16.152 and my discussion of such disparate teams in Skythia (*15*); cp. also the modern troika.

[43] Antimach. ap. = Paus. 8.25.9. Mare yoked with stallion: Hom. *Il.* 23.295.

Xerxes' disparate team in Atossa's dream and, ultimately, for that of the soul in Pl. *Phdr.* 246.[44]

The Contentious Team, which causes a chariot accident, has no Homeric precedent. A Homeric war horse throws the team into confusion only when mortally wounded. Even then, it does not break away, destroying the chariot: it is cut loose after dying, in order to save the chariot.[45] Chariot poles, etc., break also in the *Iliad*, but never because *one* of the horses is rebellious.[46] The slight similarities between this dream-accident and Homeric accidents are, thus, not due to Aischylos' imitating Homeros, but to both describing *real* accidents.[47] As to the many tales of *both* horses getting out of control,[48] they are not relevant here.

If a pre-Aischylean model of a contentious team survives, I have not found it. But Platon, while condemning poets, freely borrowed their imagery. The Aischylean dream team may have served as a model for the allegory in Pl. *Phdr.* 246—though with a difference: Aischylos (though not Atossa) *approves* of the rebellious woman-mare, while Platon condemns the "bad" horse. We shall also see that, in Aischylos, the rebellious woman represents the Super-ego, while in Platon the disobedient horse represents man's "lower" nature (the Id).

I must now record a finding which I am unable to explain satisfactorily. Disregarding real chariot accidents in war or during races—which must have been common enough—a surprisingly large proportion of mythical horse and/or chariot fatalities is due to someone's interference with the sexual impulse, be it his own (Hippolytos), that of another person (Oinomaos), or even that of the mares themselves (Glaukos). Also, one such accident leads to a piercing of the groin (Sen. *Phaedr.* 1098 f.); another tale of a chariot accident is a bowdlerization of the tale of Ouranos' castration (Orph. *fr.* 58 Abel = Athenag. s. 20, p. 940).[49]

The existence of a statistically significant nexus between such accidents and sexuality is striking and tends to increase the credibility of my view that sexuality is also at the root of this chariot accident dream.

The Details of the Accident are, on the whole, well discussed by Broadhead (*ad* 194–196). The rebellious woman first frees herself of the reins and the harness; then she breaks the yoke, probably in the middle.

But Broadhead errs in assuming that, at that moment, the pole tilts *upward*, causing Xerxes to fall backwards. In saying this, Broadhead ignores both the Homeric precedent in which Eumelos' chariot pole tilts downward, so that he falls forward (Hom. *Il.* 23.393 ff.) and the laws of physics. Indeed Xerxes, who is obviously alone in the chariot, necessarily "drives" the team, standing *well in front* of the axle: this makes the chariot a lever of the second class. Hence, the moment the yoke snaps, Xerxes' weight forces the pole *downward*, causing him to fall *forward, on his face*.

[44] Rousseau's reference to A. *Choe.* 1021 ff. is far-fetched: the team there is neither disparate nor rebellious (*58*).

[45] E.g., Hom. *Il.* 8.85 ff., 16.466 ff.   [46] E.g., Hom. *Il.* 16.370, 23.391 ff.

[47] On Homeric accidents in general, cp. 7, pp. 98 ff.

[48] E.g., the myth retold in Aischylos' lost tragedy *Heliades* and in Euripides' largely lost *Phaethon*.

[49] Incomplete lists of horse accidents are to be found in: Hyg. *fab.* 250; Tümpel (s.v. Myrtilos *57*, coll. 3318, 3320); Cook (*6*, 1.225.4).

That the pole of a plough or of a chariot symbolizes the phallos, is shown by the oracle's advice to the elderly and childless King Erginos: "fit a new tip to your old plough tree" (Paus. 9.37.4). He is to take a young wife.[50]

What really matters is that being unhorsed (or thrown from a chariot) symbolizes to this day—even in slang—a rebellion of the woman against her sexual partner and represents the latter's "unmanning". This, too, suggests that, in a dream, the chariot *pole* would tilt downward, *even if the laws of physics did not oblige it to do so*. That, in dream, a realistic failure of high ambitions should be symbolized by a castration equivalent is only to be expected, for dreams regularly translate adult problems into infantile symbols. That an infantile representation of *political* ambitions is appropriate also on other grounds will be shown below.

Last but not least, Xerxes' chariot accident may echo Dareios' horse accident (Hdt. 3.129 ff.), which is linked with Atossa's *breast* ulcer (Hdt. 3.133 f.), and which in turn leads to *her* persuading Dareios to invade Greece (infra).

Dareios seems to be suddenly "there", in a suitably dreamlike manner. Two points deserve notice:

(1) The father can only stand there and pity his son. This probably parallels Helios' inability to prevent the fatal fall of Phaethon. Neither father can help his unhappy son.

(2) Dareios appears in Atossa's dream. In accordance with Greek dream theory, this should represent a "real" experience also for his ghost. It is therefore striking that, during the necromantic scene, Dareios' ghost is *totally unaware* of Xerxes' mishap, until he is informed of it (693 ff.). When told what happened, he can only lament, criticize and give advice, which consists mostly of general moralizing, and contains only a few politically unimportant recommendations concerning preparations for Xerxes' return.

When all is said and done, in this great and dramatically impressive scene Dareios' ghost is as unhelpful as his dream image is: in both scenes he can, in the last resort, only feel sorry for Xerxes, but can provide no real help.[51]

Xerxes' Tearing of his Robes, though attested fairly early for Greece, is probably more oriental than Greek. It is, above all, a natural reaction of despair. In mourning for something lost, one regularly *further increases* one's losses: mourning is inseparable from self-aggression. This matter is discussed in Chapter 3.

The Bird Omen, which is both a replica and a sequel of the dream, also supports the dream's sexual interpretation. Riding, including riding in a

---

[50] Here the tip of the pole is equated with a wife. Cp. chap. 7 for a discussion of the symbolic equation: girl = phallos (*32, 22*).

[51] It is noteworthy that Aischylos, the Marathon fighter, never once mentions Dareios' aggressive imperialism. He represents him half as a sage, half as an idealized, Augustus-like prince. That, after Salamis, he was seen in that light *by the Persians* is possible: Stendhal's young protagonists were all Bonapartists, forgetting the flaws of Napoleon's regime and its tragic collapse. But Aischylos' idealization of Dareios is more than poetic empathy; it shows *traces* of an identification with the enemy (*60*), a phenomenon repeatedly observed throughout history (e.g., amongst certain of Hitler's victims, at times in grotesquely excessive form).

chariot, can symbolize flying; Greek myths of winged horses and teams are numerous.[52] As was discovered long before Freud (*34*, pp. 37–38, etc.), dreams of flying are usually erection dreams; landing or falling after a dream flight symbolizes detumescence. Since Atossa is a woman, the motif of flying is—appropriately—*not* part of her dream, but of the omen which follows it.

Other similarities are also evident. Xerxes falls to the ground; the eagle lands on Apollon's altar. Apollon does not protect the eagle; Dareios cannot protect his son, who, like a suppliant, lies at his feet. Both disappointing protectors are male, for a strong and possessive mother tends to feel, both while awake and in dream, that she is the only one able to protect her son. The bird omen even duplicates Xerxes' rending of his clothes, for the falcon plucks the eagle's feathers (208 f.).

But there is also an inversion: in the dream, the danger threatening Xerxes is in front of him; in the omen he is threatened and pursued from behind. Perhaps the dream represents his unsuccessful attack on Greece, and the omen his headlong flight after defeat.

One also notes that the first part of the dream represents an interaction of Xerxes with the women whose *backs* are turned to him; in the second part, Xerxes lies, *probably on his face* (since he fell forward, supra), at Dareios' feet. This much is probable. Whether something can be made of it is questionable.[53]

Interpretation

The Appropriateness of a Dream—its suiting the dreamer and the dreamer's current situation[54]—is the first point to be determined.

The fact that Atossa is not visibly included in the "dream-space" and in the "dream-event", not even as an explicitly included observer, is not a real problem; spectator dreams (*17*, pp. 67 ff.) are far from rare. A good many of the less plausible Homeric dreams are spectator—or, rather, "listener"—dreams. But the wording of Penelope's eagle-geese dream (Hom. *Od.* 19.535 ff.) does tend to indicate Penelope's *presence* in the "dream-space", albeit only as a helpless spectator crying in her dream (*12*). In Atossa's dream, Dareios cries on her behalf.

I thought at first that the A. *Pers.* dream was a Homeric kind of allegory masquerading as a dream, because Atossa *saw* a dream but, unlike Penelope, did not *dream* that *she* was *seeing* these events, nor crying over them.

---

[52] Pegasos, the teams of Helios, Triptolemos, Medeia, etc.

[53] *Coitus [per anum]* with female "eunuchs" is first reported from Lydia: Xanth. *fr.* 19, *FHG* 1.39 = *FGH* 765 *fr.* 4 (Jacoby) = Athen. 12.11, p. 515; Hsch. Mil. *fr.* 47, *FHG* 4.171. Homosexual prostitution of the enslaved Phaidon: D.L. 2.105; Aul. Gell. 2.18. Homosexual threatening of the defeated: Suet. *J. Caes.* 22. Homosexual attack on adulterers: Ar. *Nub.* 1083 (and Dover ad loc.), *Pl.* 168; X. *Mem.* 2.1.5; Catull. 15.19; Hor. *Sat.* 1.2.44; Val. Max. 6.1.13; Apul. *Met.* 12. For a general theory of sexual "retaliation", cp. *27*, chap. 7. Homosexual "attack" by a father-figure: the abduction of Ganymedes by Zeus (Hom. *Il.* 5.265, 20.232, etc.) and of Pelops by Poseidon (Pi, *O.* 24 ff.) (cp. *26*, chap. 6). I cite these *possibly* relevant data, but do *not* assert that they are, in fact, relevant.

[54] Ps.-Hp. *insomn.* 88; Arist. *insomn.* 462a15 f.; Emp. *fr.* 108 D-K; Hdt. 7.16; Cic. *de divin.* 2.67; Lucr. *nat. rer.* 4.963, 5.724; and cp. Dodds *31*, p. 118, etc.

I note, as a general principle, that the "dream-space" is always an extension of one's own body.[55] This implies that the dreamer is always, in some way, present in the dream. That the objects and persons one dreams of are facets of one's own psyche need hardly be demonstrated.

I assumed at first that Atossa was present in the dream only in this very general sense. But the reports of my students and Miss Padel's unpublished paper persuaded me that, though Atossa herself did not realize it, she was definitely present (in disguise) in the dream. Before I can prove this, I must consider Aischylos' and his Atossa's biased appreciation of Xerxes' real ambitions (and their representation in dream) and contrast it with a more objective appraisal of Xerxes' policies.

Filial Piety and Oedipal Rivalry play, in this drama, equal roles in Xerxes' real and dreamed behaviour. His advisers tell him that he must show that he is not an *effeminate*, stay-at-home king (753 ff.). It is his *duty* to avenge his father's defeat and to execute his plans. Xerxes' mobilization of far greater forces than those which were defeated at Marathon is, on the one hand, prudent and, on the other, a sensible admission that only exceptional warriors could have defeated Dareios. Xerxes can hope to defeat Dareios' vanquishers only with an infinitely larger army than the one his great father had deemed sufficient for a kind of colonial expedition. Thus, from the Persian point of view, both royal duty and filial piety impel Xerxes to carry out his father's plans and to avenge his defeat.

But though avenging Marathon was an *obligation* for the Persian Great King this does not preclude that the *wish* to surpass the father was also a neurotic *compulsion* for the son (infra).[56]

The view that Xerxes' attack on Greece was motivated by hybris simply does not fit known facts. It reflects not only a purely Greek attitude, but Aischylos' personal theological stance as well. This being said, the instability of Xerxes' character is probably a historical fact, often highlighted by Herodotos,[57] and quite credible in the case of the son of a great, "self-made" father and of as strong a mother as Atossa (infra).

His dream-behaviour can therefore seem *offensively* grandiose *only* if it is viewed as the reflection of an *oedipal* rivalry with Dareios. The opinion that the son's compulsive attempt to rival his father—and, in *this* instance, to out-perform him—is impiously presumptuous may be safely attributed to Aischylos: he is our oldest known authority for the Phaethon myth, in which a son tries, with fatal results, to rival his father Helios as a charioteer.[58]

The main task of the psycho-analyst scrutinizing this dream is to show

[55] Often "including" the maternal body, *as fantasied* (*56*).

[56] Cp. Xerxes' *personal* reluctance (Hdt. 7.5 ff.) to attack Greece; he is compelled to do so by a deceptive dream, comparable to that of Agamemnon (Hom. *Il.* 2.1 ff.).

[57] The countless passages indicating this are listed by Legrand (*46*, pp. 55 f.), s.v. Xerxes, subsection "Sa personnalité".

[58] I note *very tentatively* that, since Aischylos' self-composed epitaph mentions only his valour as a soldier, he *may* have envied the fame of his (older?) brother Kynegeiros, who fell performing a feat of supreme valour at Marathon (Hdt. 6.114)—fighting (*with* Aischylos) against the very Dareios whom the *Persai* glorifies. I base this tentative interpretation on a modern clinical case, similar, except for glory and genius, to the Kynegeiros-Aischylos precedent. In both instances, the surviving soldier-brother became an alcoholic (*26*, chap. 1; for Aischylos' alcoholism, cp. chap. 4, App. ii).

that this rivalry is *represented* as oedipal in the dream of Atossa, who, in a typically human and even more typically maternal way, *projects* the equivalent of her own Iokaste-like urges upon her son. For this is *her* dream: *she* represents Xerxes *in a manner* which suits *her* repressed impulses and wishes, whose nature is sufficiently indicated by her general attitude and particularly by her hint (851) that Xerxes is her favourite son.

Were this Xerxes' own dream, it could be held that it is a dream of oedipal ambitions brought to nought. But the dream is Atossa's. I concede that, once in a great while, one does encounter cases where A dreams what one would expect B to dream: where A *seems* to dream as B's "deputy" (*11*, pp. 369–372; and cp. chap. 4). But in such cases A's and B's desires and impulses are *parallel*. And it can hardly be urged that this dream represents Atossa's oedipal strivings and their collapse.

Atossa could dream of Xerxes' oedipal hybris and its catastrophic consequences *only* if her dream expressed *her* (ambivalent) "counter-oedipal", Iokaste-like impulses.[59] Her ambivalence is revealed by the contrast between the dream's triumphant initial scene and its wretched ending.

If so, Atossa—i.e., her counter-oedipal Jocasta complex and her rejection of it—is represented by the two women, who are sisters. Their conflict is a reflection of Atossa's inner conflict; this is a very common symbolization of conflict in dream.

The proudly harnessed Persian woman represents the compliantly feminine Id-component of Atossa's counter-oedipal complex.[60] And, even if one disregards the Jocasta-complex element, one is still able to assume that Aischylos' Atossa has, unconsciously, not yet abdicated as a female: The Choros talks explicitly enough about Persian (grass) widows yearning in bed for their husbands' embraces (133 ff.).

If so, the rebellious Dorian woman represents Atossa's Super-ego: the *social* mother who struggles against the demands of her Id. She gives preference to her status as Dareios' widow over her sexual-maternal status.

In this struggle the forces of inhibition win: the chariot is tipped over and Xerxes is blamed and punished—for Atossa's wishes. This fits the adult's tendency to blame his own "improper" fantasies on his children (*26*, chaps. 4, 5). I recall again that Platon turned this image around, by borrowing the poet's means. This is common enough behaviour amongst philosophers.[61] What may have facilitated this jugglery is the subtle contradiction between Aischylos' and his Atossa's appraisal of the whole situation. For, in the last resort, the Greek poet's "good" was the "evil" of the Persian Queen. Though realistically the rebelling woman *seems* to

[59] That, contrary to prevailing opinion, it is the parent's Laius or Jocasta complex which *triggers* the child's Oedipus complex, has been demonstrated by me in several publications (*9, 11, 27*, chap. 7, etc.).

[60] I must postpone for the moment the marshalling of historical arguments favouring this interpretation.

[61] Ploutarchos the Platonist (*de prof. virt.* 10, p. 81 D-E) cites part of Sapph. *fr.* 31 LP but turns its meaning upside down (*21*). Nietzsche's "Alles Unvergängliche ist nur ein Gleichnis—und die Dichter lügen zu viel" deliberately turns Goethe's words into their opposite, by means of the prefix: *un.* Not the poet but the philosopher is the unrepentant liar.

represent *politically* the human striving for freedom, viewed as "nature" (φύcιc)—in a dream, she psychologically represents Atossa's Super-ego and "the law" (νόμοc).

At this point I must turn to the historical substratum, playing here the role of the day residue in *Aischylos'* fantasy (= Atossa's dream). I firmly believe that Aischylos, and perhaps most informed Athenians, knew the facts I cite.

So far I have simply noted the one-ness of the yoked-together but incompatible *sisters*, who are respectively Atossa's Id and her Super-ego. But one must also ask why Aischylos (unwittingly) *chose* the image of yoked-together *sisters*. The question requires an answer precisely because Aischylos makes much of their *being* sisters (v. 185).

The one fact which commentators appear to have overlooked is that Atossa—as Aischylos certainly knew—had *actually* twice been a "yoke fellow" of one of her sisters. Specifically, she and her sister Artystone had both been married to Dareios (Hdt. 3.88).

I now hope to show that Atossa and Artystone did not make *good* co-wives. Herodotos (7.2–3) reports that Atossa's oldest son Xerxes had to contend for his nomination as crown prince with Dareios' firstborn, by a wife *other* than Artystone. Though Xerxes was certainly helped by Demaratos' shrewd—and typically Spartan—legal advice (*30*), Herodotos remarks that Xerxes' success was a foregone conclusion, "for Atossa was *all-powerful*". Yet elsewhere, Herodotos (7.69) notes that Artystone was the wife Dareios *loved most*. Now, even if one assumes that Artystone's two sons did not contend for the throne simply because Xerxes was *their* senior, two facts must be noted:

(1) Artystone, the "best beloved", and her two sons, Artames and Gobryas, only rate one mention each in Herodotos.[62] Artystone's sons held only minor posts and, like their mother, lived apparently in a kind of princely twilight.

(2) The "all-powerful" Atossa—though *not* "best beloved"—rates, however, countless mentions. It is therefore impossible not to conclude that Atossa had successfully contended for supremacy with the "best beloved" co-wife and sister. Even those uninformed of the internal workings of a royal Persian harem cannot but feel that victory over a "best beloved" (which, in that period, meant: sexually most satisfying) co-wife could not be achieved without much struggle and scheming, especially if the ultimately victorious wife was almost certainly the older of the two and was, in addition, sexually already somewhat shopworn (infra).

Thus, wittingly or unwittingly, the image of the contentious sisters and yoke-fellows appears to have been *partly* suggested to Aischylos by Atossa's and Artystone's having been *both* sisters and rivalrous co-wives, traces of whose dissensions are still discernible in Herodotos' account.

But even this analysis is not exhaustive, for we have a great deal of additional and very relevant information about Atossa's sexual life.

Atossa's first husband was her brother Kambyses II (Hdt. 3.31), a mad but legitimate king, son of King Kyros the Great. Subsequently, she had to share Kambyses' favours with *another* of her sisters. This unnamed sister,

---

62 Hdt. 3.88; 7.69; 7.72.

who dared to oppose Kambyses by pleading in favour of their disgraced brother Smerdis, was slain by Kambyses for her pains (Hdt. 3.32). These data suggest that, as a wife and lover, Atossa was inferior also to this other sister—as she was inferior to her in family loyalty, though not in caution and cleverness.

After Kambyses' death, Atossa was made to marry the false Smerdis, who pretended to be her dead brother—and it is striking that, *unlike* another of this usurper's wives (Hdt. 3.68 ff.), *she did nothing to unmask him.* One can once again only admire her prudence, though hardly her integrity—for the false Smerdis manifestly married her only to improve his chances of successful usurpation.

After the slaying of the false Smerdis, she became the wife of Dareios, whose only claim to the throne was that he had dethroned the false Smerdis (Hdt. 3.70 ff.), and had also contrived to outwit by a trick one of his co-conspirators, who had also hoped to become king (supra). Dareios then consolidated his rule by marrying simultaneously (the already twice married) Atossa, her virgin sister Artystone, also a daughter of the defunct *real* Smerdis (i.e., Atossa's niece) and, finally, the daughter of Otanes— i.e., of the man who had done most to unmask the false Smerdis and had therefore felt entitled to contend with Dareios for the throne. These four marriages fully secured Dareios' flanks, linking him by marriage with both his legitimate and his usurping predecessors and with his erstwhile rival for the throne as well. Two of his wives were apparently virgins. As to Otanes' daughter, she had had one husband only, while Atossa had already had two: one was her incestuous brother-husband and the other the murderous (and pseudo-incestuous) impersonator of her brother Smerdis. Atossa was, thus, obviously a woman well able to take care of her interests; outliving husbands and getting the upper hand over all her co-wives— including her virgin sister, who bore two sons to Dareios and was the "best beloved" of his wives. This took some skill in the murderous climate of dynastic chaos and harem intrigues.

It is also noteworthy that Xerxes was the first Great King since Kambyses II to accede to the throne without slaying his predecessor or benefiting by the latter's "suicide" or in some irregular manner (Hdt. 3.64). He managed to achieve this by means of a twisted interpretation of "primogeniture" which was made persuasive less by Demaratos' legal chicanery (which furnished only a pretext) than by Atossa's irresistible influence.[63]

But, marrying two men in succession so as to make them kings,[64] brought Atossa at least the rewards of queenship and royal bedfellows. Giving birth to a king and then having to sleep alone, as dowager queen, was less

---

[63] For traces of other successful manipulations of the rules of succession—be it by primogeniture or by ultimogeniture—mentioned in Greek sources, cp. *(30)*.

[64] It has been argued that Dareios had come to the throne legitimately, since the most legitimate claimant, his father Hystaspes, had, "because of his age", not participated in the conspiracy. But Herodotos does not say so. And old age would *not* have prevented Hystaspes from rulling through his son and other generals and satraps. Hystaspes was clearly set aside *by his son*, though he was hardly decrepit: inscriptions attest that Dareios later on employed his own father, Hystaspes, as a general and even that his grandfather was still alive. This proves that Hystaspes was not senile and therefore also that Dareios had usurped the throne to which his father had a better claim.

satisfying. Something in this woman, who had first married her real *brother* and then a usurper who claimed to be her brother, could well have wondered (preconsciously). why she could not be *also* her *son's* Queen—Queen for the fourth time and for the third time by incest. It is well to recall here that when Oidipous was haunted by the dread that he might commit incest, Iokaste calmly told him that men often dream of bedding with their mothers. This mother of an exposed son took Oidipous' worries surprisingly casually (S. *OT* 980 ff.)—though her exit, when discovery became inevitable (vv. 1056 ff.), showed that she knew well enough whom she had married. Even psycho-analysts do not like to mention that a good many mothers—and especially widowed ones—have quite discernible Jocasta complexes, which trigger peculiar forms of acting out—even if such activities are alleged to be only means enabling such mothers to retain their hold over their sons.[65] Atossa is, in fact, *exactly* the kind of mother modern sociological research shows to be incest-prone (*62*, pp. 85–93, 125).

It will perhaps be objected that Aischylos did not *intend* to represent *this* Atossa. But the fact is that this Atossa *did* exist—*a fact which Aischylos could not but have known*. And I cannot but recall once more that the truth, however much one seeks to conceal it, always slips back into the lie, in some guise.[66] It is a token of Aischylos' genius that the historical truth slipped back into his drama precisely in the form of a *dream* experience. This is what distinguishes the poet from the journalist.

More tentatively, I would like to mention now a historical datum which *may* have unconsciously inspired Aischylos to select a castration-type dream fatality. Dareios had severely injured his leg (ankle) jumping off a horse (Hdt. 3.130 f.). He was cured by Demokedes, who shortly thereafter also cured Atossa of an abscess of the breast (Hdt. 3.133 f.).[67] Better still, incited precisely by Demokedes—who had reasons for wishing to see Greece invaded[68]—Atossa urged Dareios to conquer Greece. In so doing, she used arguments very similar to those which the Aischylean Xerxes' "bad" advisers used to incite him to attack Greece. Thus, Atossa appealed to Dareios' manhood (Hdt. 3.134); the Aischylean Xerxes' "bad" advisers appealed to that of Xerxes (753 ff.). This transposition is, to say the least, curious. Like so many other distortions of fact, this too manages to preserve (in the form of a projection) that which it strives so hard to modify.

Bibliography

(1) Abraham, Karl: Should Patients Write Down their Dreams? (in) *Clinical Papers and Essays on Psycho-Analysis.* New York, 1955.
(2) Alexander, Franz: Dreams in Pairs and Series, *International Journal of Psycho-Analysis* 6:446–452, 1925.
(3) Barrett, W. S.: *Euripides, Hippolytos.* Oxford, 1964.

---

[65] Agrippina and Nero (Suet. *Nero 28*). Real equivalents exist.
[66] Cp. chap. 6 for data; also (*10, 16, 28*).
[67] On the breast = female phallos equation, cp. chap. 6.
[68] Being sent ahead, as a spy, would have freed this captive physician.

(4) Baumann, H. H.: Über Reihenfolge und Rhythmus der Traum-motive, *Zentralblatt für Psychotherapie und ihre Grenzgebiete* 9:213–228, 1936.

(5) Behr, C. A.: *Aelius Aristides and the Sacred Tales.* Amsterdam, 1968.

(6) Cook, A. B.: *Zeus*, 3 vols. Cambridge, 1914–1940.

(7) Delebecque, Edouard: *Le Cheval dans l'Iliade.* Paris, 1951.

(8) Devereux, George: The Psychological 'Date' of Dreams, *Psychiatric Quarterly Supplement* 23:127–130, 1949.

(9) id.: Why Oedipus Killed Laïus. A Note on the Complementary Oedipus Complex, *International Journal of Psycho-Analysis* 34:132–141, 1953.

(10) id.: *A Study of Abortion in Primitive Societies.* New York, 1955,[2] 1975.

(11) id.: *Therapeutic Education.* New York, 1956.

(12) id.: Penelope's Character, *Psychoanalytic Quarterly* 26:378–386, 1957.

(13) id.: Art and Mythology: A General Theory (in) Kaplan, Bert (ed.): *Studying Personality Cross-Culturally.* Evanston, Illinois, 1961.

(14) id.: The Perception of Motion in Infancy, *Bulletin of the Menninger Clinic* 29:143–147, 1965.

(15) id.: The Kolaxaian Horse of Alkman's *Partheneion, Classical Quarterly* 15:176–184, 1965.

(16) id.: The Exploitation of Ambiguity in Pindaros *O.* 3.27, *Rheinisches Museum für Philologie* 109:289–298, 1966.

(17) id.: *From Anxiety to Method in the Behavioral Sciences.* Paris and The Hague, 1967.

(18) id.: Observation and Belief in Aischylos' Accounts of Dreams, *Psychotherapy and Psychosomatics* 15:114–134, 1967.

(19) id.: *Reality and Dream: the Psychotherapy of a Plains Indian.* Second, augmented edition, New York, 1969.

(20) id.: *Mohave Ethnopsychiatry.* Second augmented edition, Washington D.C. 1969.

(21) id.: The Nature of Sappho's Seizure in *Fr.* 31 LP, *Classical Quarterly* 20:17–31, 1970.

(22) id.: La Naissance d'Aphrodite (in) Pouillon, Jean and Maranda, Pierre (eds.): *Echanges et Communications (Mélanges Lévi-Strauss)*, 2.1229–1252. Paris and The Hague, 1970.

(23) id.: The Psychotherapy Scene in Euripides' *Bacchae, Journal of Hellenic Studies* 90:35–48, 1970.

(24) id.: The *Equus October* Ritual Reconsidered, *Mnemosyne* 23:297–301, 1970.

(25) id.: *Psychoanalysis and the Occult* (ed. and contrib.). Reprint. New York, 1970.

(26) id.: *Essais d'Ethnopsychiatrie Générale.* Paris, 1970. Second edition 1973.

(27) id.: *Ethnopsychanalyse Complémentariste.* Paris, 1972.

(28) id. (and Devereux, J. W.): Les Manifestations de l'Inconscient dans Sophokles: *Trachiniai* 923 sqq. (in) *Psychanalyse et Sociologie comme Méthodes d'Etude des Phénomènes Historiques et Culturels.* Bruxelles, 1973.

(29) id.: Trois Rêves en Série et une Double Parapraxe, *Ethnopsychologie* (in press).

(30) id.: Quelques Traces de la Succession par Ultimogéniture en Scythie, *Inter-Nord* 12:262–270, 1972.

(31) Dodds, E. R.: *The Greeks and the Irrational.* Berkeley, California, 1951.

(32) Fenichel, Otto: The Symbolic Equation: Girl = Phallus, (in) *The Collected Papers of O. Fenichel* 2, chap. 1. New York, 1954.

(33) id.: Trophy and Triumph (in) *The Collected Papers of O. Fenichel* 2, chap. 10. New York, 1954.

(34) Freud, Sigmund: The Interpretation of Dreams, *Standard Edition* 4–5. London, 1958.

(35) id.: Jokes and their Relation to the Unconscious, *Standard Edition* 8. London, 1960.

(36) id.: Obsessive Acts and Religious Practices, *Standard Edition* 9. London, 1959.

(37) id.: The Sexual Enlightenment of Children, *Standard Edition* 9. London, 1959.

(38) id.: The Handling of Dream Interpretation in Psycho-Analysis, *Standard Edition* 12. London, 1958.

(39) id.: The Uncanny, *Standard Edition* 17. London, 1957.

(40) Gahagan L.: The Form and Function of a Series of Dreams, *Journal of Abnormal and Social Psychology* 29:404–408, 1935.

(41) Hamdorf, F. W.: *Griechische Kultpersonifikationen der vorhellenistischen Zeit,* ch. 5. Mainz, 1964.

(42) James, Henry: *The Turn of the Screw.* London, 1898.

(43) Kinsey, A. C. *et al.*: *Sexual Behavior in the Human Male.* Philadelphia, 1948.

(44) id.: *Sexual Behavior in the Human Female.* Philadelphia, 1953.

(45) Krauss, Friedrich S. and Kaiser, Martin (translators): *Artemidorus von Daldis: Traumbuch.* Basel, 1965.

(46) Legrand, Ph.-E.: *Hérodote: Index Analytique.* Paris, 1954.

(47) Lévi-Strauss, Claude: *Anthropologie Structurale.* Paris, 1954.

(48) id.: *Le Cru et le Cuit.* Paris, 1964.

(49) id.: *Du Miel aux Cendres.* Paris, 1966.

(50) id.: *L'Origine des Manières de Table.* Paris, 1968.

(51) id.: *L'Homme Nu.* Paris, 1971.

(52) Lincoln, J. S.: *The Dream in Primitive Cultures*[2]. New York, 1970.

(53) Malinowski, Bronislaw: *The Sexual Life of Savages in North-Western Melanesia*[3]. London, 1932.

(54) Ritchie, William: *The Authenticity of the Rhesus of Euripides.* Cambridge, 1964.

(55) Róheim, Géza: The Garden of Eden, *Psychoanalytic Review* 27:1–26, 177–199, 1940.

(56) id.: *Psychoanalysis and Anthropology.* New York, 1950.

(57) Roscher, W. H. (ed.): *Ausführliches Lexikon der griechischen und römischen Mythologie.* Leipzig, 1884–1937.

(58) Rousseau, G. S.: Dream and Vision in Aeschylus' *Oresteia, Arion* 2:101–136, 1963.

(59) Scholz, U. W.: *Studien zum altitalischen und altrömischen Marskult und Marsmythos.* Heidelberg, 1970.

(60) Thompson, C. M.: Identification with the Enemy and Loss of the Sense of Self, *Psychoanalytic Quarterly* 9:37–50, 1940.

(61) Wagenwoort, Hendrick: Zur magischen Bedeutung des Schwanzes, *Serta Philologica Aenipontana*. Innsbruck, 1962.

(62) Weinberg, S. K.: *Incest Behavior*. New York, 1955.

(63) West, M. L.: Alcmanica, *Classical Quarterly* 15:188–202, 1965.

Chapter 2

Io's Dream

(Aischylos: *Prometheus Bound*)

Ἰω

αἰεὶ γὰρ ὄψεις ἔννυχοι πωλεύμεναι 645
ἐς παρθενῶνας τοὺς ἐμοὺς παρηγόρουν
λείοισι μύθοις· " ὦ μέγ᾽ εὔδαιμον κόρη,
τί παρθενεύῃ δαρόν, ἐξόν σοι γάμου
τυχεῖν μεγίστου; Ζεὺς γὰρ ἱμέρου βέλει
πρὸς σοῦ τέθαλπται καὶ συναίρεσθαι Κύπριν 650
θέλει· σὺ δ᾽, ὦ παῖ, μὴ ᾽πολακτίσῃς λέχος
τὸ Ζηνός, ἀλλ᾽ ἔξελθε πρὸς Λέρνης βαθὺν
λειμῶνα, ποίμνας βουστάσεις τε πρὸς πατρός
ὡς ἂν τὸ Δῖον ὄμμα λωφήσῃ πόθου."

(Smyth's text)

Translation

Io: For visions of the night, ever haunting my virgin bower, sought to beguile me with seductive words, saying: "O damsel greatly blest of fortune, why tarry in thy maidenhood so long when it is within thy power to win (mating) of the highest? Zeus is inflamed by thee with passion's dart and is eager to (enjoy with you the gifts of Kypris). Do thou, my child, not spurn the bed of Zeus, but go thou forth to Lerne's meadow land of pastures deep and to thy father's (herds) and where his cattle browse, that so the eye of Zeus may find respite from its longing."

(Smyth's translation modified)

(I replaced the misleading word "union", which suggests a marriage or a durable relationship, with "mating", restored the real sense of v. 650, whose overt sexual nuance Smyth bowdlerized and "flocks" with "herds", scilicet: of *cattle only*.)

(At v. 648 I write, with Page etc., παρδενεύῃ.)

Introduction

The *PV* has so many subtly nuanced references to dreams and oracles (*24*) that one is at first almost disappointed to encounter in it only Io's relatively straightforward oedipal wish-fulfilment dream, which is of a type commonly met with in adolescents, in primitives and even in highly educated members of culturally backward nations (*30*, chap. 6). In fact, were vv. 645–654 a fragment, and were little else known of Io, her dream could be analysed in a very few pages, for this dream's complexity is revealed mainly by Io's and Inachos' *waking* reactions to it.[1]

The focus of this chapter is almost exclusively Io's dream and its immediate consequences. Her "metamorphosis" into a cow—which Kouretas (*45*, chap. 5) interprets as a bouanthropic psychosis[2]—concerns me only in so far as it is a consequence of her dream.

Text and Translation

Since the dream is, at least superficially, very transparent and therefore not markedly disturbing, the copyists did not play havoc with the text, whose state is quite satisfactory. Most modern editions differ only in their spelling of a few words.[3] My translation is based on those of Smyth and Mazon.

---

[1] This finding is, incidentally, responsible for my not discussing here the dreams preserved in fragments.

[2] I disagree only with a few details of Kouretas' analysis.

[3] E.g., v. 650: cυναίρεϲθαι (Smyth, Page), ξυναίρεϲθαι (Mazon, Groeneboom). The differences in spelling do not affect the word's meaning.

Objective Aspects of the Dream

The Dream's Repetitiveness proves it to be partly ego-dystonic. That layer of Io's mind which strongly craves a sexual union with "Zeus" is tenaciously shackled by her Super-ego. Psychologically, the dream reflects this inner struggle; dramatically, it is a kind of *Selbstgespräch*—a dream-debate with oneself. This finding suffices to disprove Lennig's view (*48*, pp. 82 f.) that Io is the wholly passive recipient of a divine command and that she anxiously tries to be—or to play the role of—a totally obedient girl. I will show that Io's demand to be guided by her father's[4] wishes is an unconsciously seductive manœuvre.

The Locale where the dream manifests itself is strongly emphasized: it haunts Io's maiden bower (παρθενών) (646). It could be held that this is simply a poetic way of saying: "the dream haunted me, because I am still unmarried". But it is not altogether improbable that the Greeks may have dimly felt that certain types of dreams tend to be dreamed in certain rooms or in certain beds. I must deal with this hypothesis very briefly, so as not to interrupt the main argument with too long a digression.

(1) Most early Greek dreams are dreamed indoors; that of Rhesos' charioteer (chap. 8) is a striking exception.[5] By contrast (supernaturally caused) visions, hallucinations and illusions tend to occur outdoors.[6]

(2) Most early Greek dreams come to those who sleep alone[7] or at least do not sleep with a person of the *opposite* sex.[8]

(3) Healing dreams visit those who sleep in Asklepios' temple (*34*, 2.145 ff.).

(4) Dreams of a special sort are dreamed when one sleeps on the pelt of a sacrificed ram (Paus. 1.34.5, cp. *33*, p. 126, note 43).

---

[4] The influence of resistances (even on scientific work) is well exemplified by the fact that, even though Aischylos speaks only of Io's *father* (*PV* 656, psychologically anticipated by 653), Lennig (*48*, p. 81) "inexplicably" speaks of her "parents". This lapsus is the more noteworthy as the *PV* does not mention Io's mother *at all*—just as A. *Suppl.* fails to mention the mother(s) of Io's descendants: of the Danaides (chap. 9). By mistakenly speaking of Io's "parents", instead of her father *only*, Lennig unwittingly attenuates the unconscious oedipal provocativeness of Io's daughterly confession. Such lapses, "justifying" the scotomization of the obvious, bedevil also the psycho-analyst, myself included (*30*, p. 161).

[5] I could find no early Greek reference to the kind of notoriously vivid "snapshot" dream one has while cat-napping during the day, at times outdoors—perhaps because *significant* dreams were supposed to be dreamed at night (and indoors?). Rhesos' dream (Hom. *Il.* 10.494 ff.) is flash-like in its brevity, but is dreamed inside the tent and at night.

[6] Hes. *Th.* 1 ff., cp. Q.S. 12.306 ff. Also many passages of the *Iliad*.

[7] Agamemnon (Hom. *Il.* 2.1 ff.; for he declares later on, under oath, that he had never slept with Briseis: Hom. *Il.* 19.258 ff.); Rhesos (Hom. *Il.* 10.494 ff.); Nausikaa (Hom. *Od.* 6.13 ff.); Penelope (Hom. *Od.* 4.787 ff., 19.509 ff., 20.87 ff., etc.). In tragedy: Io; Menelaos (chap. 3); Atossa (chap. 1, indirectly highlighted by A. *Pers.* 133 ff., etc.); Iphigeneia (chap. 8); Rhesos' charioteer (chap. 8). Perhaps for dramatic reasons, A. *Sept.* nowhere mentions Eteokles' wife. One cannot imagine Aigisthos sharing Klytaimestra's bed the night she has her fatal dream (chaps. 4, 7). Cp. Heracl. *frr.* 89 and 73; also Lennig (*48*, p. 226, note 8).

[8] The Erinyes sleep together (chap. 4). Hekabe shares a tent with other captive women (chap. 8).

(5) The sceptical Artabanos "vicariously" dreams Xerxes' dream, while sleeping on Xerxes' throne-bed (Hdt. 1.17).[9]

(6) *Before* dreaming a typically virginal (oedipal) dream (chap. 8), Iphigeneia *first* dreams of being asleep in her girl's room, back home in Argos (E. *IT* 44 ff.).[10]

(7) That the long solitary Penelope should (regressively) have almost virginal (oedipal) dreams is only to be expected. What matters *here* is that she has them upstairs (Hom. *Od.* 19.53), in her quasi-maidenly boudoir, for during Odysseus' absence she does not sleep on her marital couch which, being built around the still rooted stump of an olive tree (Hom. *Od.* 19.190 ff.), was manifestly located on the ground floor.[11]

I do not urge foolhardily that oedipal dreams were thought to hang about every maiden's bower, waiting to appear to its occupant as soon as she fell asleep.[12] But there may well have existed a belief that certain types of dreams tend to come to persons sleeping in certain places. This hypothesis has the added advantage that, if one takes the Aischylos text literally, the dream becomes as firmly located in "space" as are certain Homeric dreams, which specify that the dream stands at the head of the sleeper's bed (*33*, chap. 4).

The Visions (ὄψεις) are referred to in the plural, but probably only in order to stress the dream's repetitiveness. Nothing suggests that more than one dream-personage addressed Io in any one of her dreams, nor that different personages sought to persuade her in successive dreams (on the plural, cp. chaps. 3, 8).

In fact, one cannot even be sure that Io "saw" anything in dream, for these "visions" do not "act"—they only speak. Aischylos probably called them "visions" simply because the Greeks ordinarily said: "I saw a dream."[13]

More important still is that the shape, identity, sex, etc., of these visions is not so much as hinted at; even their voice does not identify them. This lack of information further underlines the dream's endogenous character, for clinical data, daily experience and Greek texts alike prove that very familiar persons can appear in dream in disguise,[14] or may be seen in dream too dimly to be recognized.

I note, *in fine*, that even though Dodds (*33*, chap. 4) is unquestionably right in urging that *most* dream-figures tend to be authoritative father-

---

[9] Vicarious dreams do exist (Hdt. 7.17 cp. *17*, p. 369 ff.), but, despite the bad example set by some psycho-analysts, should not be interpreted as being telepathic.

[10] Dreams of being simply asleep appear to be rare; I have heard only one such dream from a patient. Dreams of dreaming ("a dream within a dream") seem to be more common; one such dream was obtained from an elderly Mohave Indian (*26*, p. 168).

[11] One could argue that the solitary Penelope's dreams unwittingly inspired *later* tales of her grass-widow adulteries (enumerated by Roscher s.v. Pan *63* 3, col. 1380; Gruppe *41* 2.1846). But it could also be argued that Homeros bowdlerized early traditions of this type (*55*). Penelope's dream is also oedipal, since it could have been dreamed by Hippodameia.

[12] Peoples' situation determines both the nature of their dreams and the place where they sleep: a maiden has oedipal dreams in her "bower" (J.W.D.).

[13] Cp. also Lennig (*48*, p. 247, note 112).

[14] Eagle = Odysseus (Hom. *Od.* 19.548); Snake = Orestes (A. *Choe.* 543 ff.); Wolves = Odysseus and Diomedes (E. *Rh.* 783, cp. chap. 8), etc.

figures,[15] the coaxing tone of Io's dream personage shows that she (?) lacks the authority to command. The vision is simply a procuress (infra), whose words derive what little "prestige" they possess from the fact that they are "*heard*" *in dream*. What makes them impressive is not the lofty status of the dream-*personage* but the inherent prestige of anything dreamed.

The Sender of the dream is not specified. This further confirms the dream's endogenous nature, even though the vision acts as a procuress for Zeus. There is no hint that Zeus himself sent this dream to Io, the way he despatched a deceptive dream to Agamemnon (Hom. *Il.* 2.1 ff.). I note in particular that in most early Greeks texts—including, *pace* Lennig (*48*, pp. 199, 201, 291 f.), tragedy—the sender of the dream is usually specified.[16] Where—as in this case—it is neither specified nor clearly inferable, the dreamer perceives external reality "clairvoyantly" (A. *Pers.*), or else is stimulated by sounds perceived in sleep (E. *Rh.*).[17] Only erotic dreams are always represented as endogenous: as motivated by desire.[18] Such dreams are neither "sent" visitors nor mere intruders. They simply "surface", being reflections of the dreamer's own desires.[19]

Even the dream's recurrence—its obstinate efforts to overcome Io's inhibitions—indicates that it reflects a wish. Indeed, the occurrence of a tempting command, not to speak of a complete fulfilment of the wish *in dream*,[20] proves conclusively that the actual gratification of the wish is not (yet) possible *in reality*—and/or is not (yet) acceptable to the *waking* mind.

The Opening Phase of the dream speech—of the only Aischylean dream-oration—differs from the traditional Homeric model described by Dodds (*33*, chap. 4). The speech does not begin with: "You are asleep, Io!" This omission may have two causes:

(1) Unlike what happens sometimes in Homeric epics, the dreamer herself narrates her dream.

(2) The specification that this recurrent dream haunts Io's *room* suffices to situate the dream both in space (bedchamber) and in time (night). This means that this *significant* dream-vision addressed Io—as required by Greek convention—at night, in her own bed, and while she slept.

The Message—which is, for all practical purposes, the sole *manifest* content of the dream—appears to be conveyed to Io in a psychologically noteworthy manner.

I stress also elsewhere (chap. 8) that dreams involving *actual auditory*

---

[15] Or virile mother figures (J.W.D.).

[16] Zeus, supra. Eteokles' dream is sent by Oidipous' curses (A. *Sept.* 709 ff.); Klytaimestra's by the wrath of Agamemnon's shade (A. *Choe.*, S. *El.*); the Erinyes dream of being reproached by Klytaimestra's shade, which appears on stage (chap. 4); Hekabe's dream is "sent" by Polydoros' shade (chap. 8), etc.

[17] On the perception of stimuli in sleep and on their transformation into dreams, cp. Arist. *insomn.* 462a19 ff.

[18] Penelope's dream (Hom. *Od.* 20.87 ff.); Menelaos' dream (A. *Ag.* 419 ff.).

[19] In fact, much of the modern concept of Greek exogenous dreams is barely tenable. Greek accounts of dreams usually indicate, at least implicitly, the presence of a *wish* for a particular *kind* of dream. Dodds (*33*, chap. 4) has proven this for the supposedly highly "exogenous" incubation dreams.

[20] Penelope actually cohabits with Odysseus in dream (Hom. *Od.* 20.87 ff.). That is what παρέδραθεν implies for *spouses* haring a bed—though LSJ does not seem to realize it.

sensations are extremely rare, and dreams of *hearing* articulate speech practically non-existent. Though some dreamers assert that they have "heard" words or sentences in dream, a closer scrutiny nearly always reveals that the dreamer simply "knew somehow" what a personage "told" him in dream.[21]

Now, the Greeks themselves knew that a "message" could be conveyed to a dreamer (or to a person in trance) without his *experiencing* auditory sensations or hallucinations. Such a "voiceless" communication was well described in connection with Sokrates' daimon.[22]

This being said, I *none the less* feel that Aischylos meant to suggest that Io's dream included auditory sensations, accompanying the reception of a message. I deem this to be so even though the text says, in essence, only: "the vision said . . . I understood", and not (more fully): "the vision said . . . *I heard* . . . I understood". I think that Aischylos' omission of "I heard" was due to his text already containing *another* indication that Io had auditory sensations in dream.[23]

I hold that the characterization of the voice as λεῖος (smooth, soft, gentle) necessarily *implies* that Io had auditory *sensations* in dream. Mazon's translation: *mots caressants* seems too literal; λεῖος suits a *voice* better than the *words* it utters.[24] Smyth's translation: "seductive" is even more misleading, for a seductive *voice* would seek to arouse Io's sexuality *then and there* and to direct it *at the speaker*. But, in Io's dream, her sexuality is expected to become aroused only *after* she wakes up and to be directed not at the dream-personage but *at Zeus*, whom that personage actually names, and to whom it refers in the third person.

Though I stress once again that λεῖος refers *primarily* to the quality of the dream voice, characterizing it as smooth or soft, this does not mean that λεῖος cannot secondarily refer also to the crafty persuasiveness of the dream-message. If, however, λεῖος is made to refer also to the message itself, it acquires an added nuance: the "smooth, gentle" voice utters "slick, insinuating" words, brimming with a *deceitful* benevolence—for the

[21] One evening, in January 1970, I discussed this matter with a psychologically sophisticated hellenist, who claimed that he *heard* speeches in dream. The very next morning he told me that he had just had such a dream—rightly adding that "proving me wrong" was one cause—or objective—of his dream. But, after we examined his dream more closely, he conceded that it fully confirmed my views. He had dreamed of hearing a speech emanating from a radio in the room adjoining his—but, owing to the thickness of the intervening wall, that "speech" was *not understandable*. In short, he simply heard in dream the *sound* of speech—and nothing but its sound—for he could not hear *what* was said. What he "heard" in dream was only a kind of mumbling: a type of pseudo-speech whose significance I have analysed elsewhere (*21*). Cp. also my comments (chap. 8) on E. *IT* 52.

[22] Plu. *de gen. Socr.* 20, p. 588E, cp. Chalcidius 255, p. 288 Wrobel. Plu. *V.Lyc.* 23.2: Lykourgos heard a voice; since he could not see the speaker, he concluded that the voice was from heaven.

[23] I.e., Aischylos' omission of "I heard" is due primarily to poetic economy—though the poet may *also* have remembered that dreams of both hearing *and* understanding speeches are extremely rare in reality, though common enough in religious and literary texts, in which the dream-speaker is often not even seen. Cp. Dodds (*33*, p. 109 and p. 125, note 37), also Lennig (*48*, p. 247, note 112), citing E. *IT* 1274, 1276, etc.

[24] On the capacity of a caressing tone of voice to elicit, in a dog, behaviour identical with that which he displayed when actually caressed, and on the tendency of some persons to apprehend the tone of the voice as the *real* message, cp. *30*, chap. 4.

course of action it recommends will, quite predictably (infra), be catastrophic for Io.

The last objective aspect of Io's dream is that it does not seem to have elicited any strong affective reaction *while* it was dreamed. This is in sharp contrast with the distress and perplexity she experiences on awakening and with her somewhat unusual behavioural reactions to the dream's command. For the moment I simply note this discrepancy, which will be discussed in detail in connection with Io's "associations" to her dream.

The Manifest Content

Though as a rule I discuss the various elements of a dream in the order in which they appear in the text, I must, in this instance, discuss first some relatively minor details. Indeed, the dream's two most salient elements: the "vision's" crafty argumentation and its insistence that Io should mate with Zeus at Lerne, must be discussed last and consecutively, for they are not only inseparable logically, but also lead directly to the analysis of the dream's latent content.

Io's Protracted Virginity (648) is emphasized strongly enough to prove that her dream was triggered by her sexual frustration. But this does not imply that Aischylos imagined his Io as being much over sixteen or seventeen years of age—and not only because, knowing that upper-class Athenian girls married when they were still "mere children" (X. *Oec.* 3.13), he probably assumed that this was customary also in mythical times. The main consideration is that, even though the Greek gods did not hesitate to abduct extremely immature *boys*,[25] they do not seem to have seduced barely nubile *girls*. (This can be inferred from the behaviour attributed to such girls both before and after their seduction by a god.)

One of the most significant aspects of this passage is that the dream-voice not only makes *Io* responsible for her unduly prolonged celibacy, but also insists that it is within *Io's* power to terminate this undesirable state. The dream-voice is far more explicit on this point than is, for example, "Athene", who simply scolds Nausikaa for making no preparations in view of her "impending" marriage (Hom. *Od.* 6.13 ff.)—which, incidentally, never takes place.[26]

[25] Ganymedes, the Pindaric (*O.* 1.25 ff.) Pelops, etc.

[26] Considering that, in the surviving version of the *Odyssey*, Odysseus does *not* marry Nausikaa, who appears to be in love with him, it is striking that—unlike that of Agamemnon (Hom. *Il.* 2.1 ff.)—hers is not called a "deceitful dream". Instead—predictably—Aristarchos athetized 6.244 f. I cannot discuss here all the later stories which tell of a marriage between Nausikaa and Odysseus' son Telemachos. They are listed by Wörner (*63* s.v. coll. 32 f.), who does not realize that "bowdlerization" is written large on all of them. I hold, for my part, that the author of *our Odyssey* had bowdlerized an ancient tale describing a third "overseas marriage" contracted by Odysseus who, as is the way of sailors, seems to have had a girl in every port. The later tales simply made a half-hearted about-face, salvaging Nausikaa's marriage, but replacing Odysseus with his son Telemachos—who, in the *Telegonia*, married *another* of his father's forsaken overseas wives, Kirke. I deem it self-evident that *only* the hypothesis of a Homeric bowdlerization of an early tale of Odysseus' *prolonged* stay in Phaiakia, *as Nausikaa's husband*, can explain why, e.g., Page (*59*, pp. 33 ff.) could find so many chronological absurdities precisely in those books of the *Odyssey* which describes Odysseus' "brief" stay in Phaiakia.

One thing, at any rate, is certain: unlike Hippodameia's prolonged celibacy,[27] that of Io was not due *primarily* to her father's interference, nor, as the sexual character of her dream indicates, to a Hippolytos-like sex phobia—which some choose to label: chastity.

It might even be added that both the dream and Io's and Inachos' reactions to it provide perfectly plausible clues as to the *causes* of Io's long and self-imposed sexual frustration. As so often happens in real life, Io's celibacy is due to her oedipal fixation on her father, which—also as in real life—is tacitly reinforced by Inachos' own unconscious "counter-oedipal" daughter fixation (infra).[28]

The Desire of Zeus' Eye (for Io) (654) is to be relieved by Io's sexual compliance. The conventional explanation is that, in Greek thought, the eyes are traditionally the seat of love.[29] But it seems to me that the moment this expression is recognized to be a figure of speech, one is *compelled* to ask just *what* straightforward expression this figure of speech *replaces*, *why* a periphrasis is used at all, and *why*, in Greek idiom, *the eye*, rather than some other organ, should be the seat of love.[30]

I begin by noting striking—and systematically overlooked—differences between A. *PV* 654 and *allegedly* parallel passages. The latter either use the plural, to denote *both* eyes, or the singular, to denote the (*unitary*) sight of (*both*) eyes. Since Zeus is not a one-eyed Kyklops, the fact that Aischylos speaks of Zeus' "eye" *in the singular* should, I feel, be taken into account in interpreting this figure of speech. This singular is especially striking in a myth which mentions many-eyed Argos (677 ff., etc.).

Furthermore, this figurative expression occurs in a dream. Now, it stands to reason that what, in a *waking* discourse, *can* (in the first approximation) be treated as a *façon de parler*, *must* be treated as a vigorously *concrete* symbol when it is part of a *dream*.[31]

But the main consideration is that the ordinary "figure of speech" interpretation of this verse fits neither the Io myth nor the classical Greek outlook, which our still Victorian thought habits cause us to scotomize—and this even though every amour of a god (or goddess) involving a mortal partner tells the same tale and teaches the same lesson. This is so true that I will not waste time on proving that words meaning "to love" are hardly ever found in such stories.[32] Instead, I immediately turn to Io's adventure.

[27] And, perhaps, also that of the girl Penelope, whose father did not want her to leave him (Paus. 3.20.10).

[28] According to numerous sources, Oinomaos delayed Hippodameia's marriage because he himself was in love with her or had actually cohabited with her (Apollod. *Ep.* 2.4 ff.; Luc. *Charid.* 19; Hyg. *fab.* 253; Tzetz. *Lyc.* 156) (*20*).

[29] Groeneboom, ad loc., cites only E. *Hipp.* 525. Barrett, commenting E. *Hipp.* 525, cites further examples. Thomson, seeking in vain to refute Fraenkel's interpretation of A. *Ag.* 418, provides a veritable torrent of "parallel" passages in his edition. Cp. also Malten (*52*).

[30] It is, I think, in his *Physiology of Marriage* that Balzac remarked that men love with their eyes and women with their ears. On ear = vagina, cp. Jones (*42*).

[31] The American colloquialism: "I rode her hard", uttered in a real conversation, means primarily: "I made her work hard and toe the line." In dream, this expression would certainly symbolize a violently domineering sexual act. In waking life, an aeroplane is *primarily* a means of transportation; in dream primarily a symbol of erection.

[32] One exception is perhaps Hom. *Il.* 14.317. But in S. (*Inach.*) (Page *58*, p. 24, v. 10) the word "love" is used sarcastically precisely in connection with Zeus' desire for Io.

The dream speech indicates that the desire of Zeus' *eye* can be appeased only by Io's *sexual* compliance, and both Aischylean and other references to Io's affair with Zeus mention, or clearly imply, *one* embrace *only* (infra). That—if a colloquialism be permitted—is about par for the course. I cannot begin to cite the evidence showing that the same is true of nearly every *authentically mythical* account of such affairs—the data would easily fill a volume.[33] As every Greek girl in her right mind—for example, Marpessa (infra)—knew, a Greek god's "love" is simply a sudden, imperious erection. His "love" disappears as soon as the sexual act is completed and detumescence sets in.[34] Such things are reported even of mortals: a single "wet dream" ended for ever an Egyptian's desperate "love" for the hetaira Thonis, whose high fee he could not afford to pay (Plu. *V. Dem.* 27.5 f.).

The point need not be laboured. I have repeatedly shown[35] that, in most societies, romantic love is the exception rather than the rule, and, far from meeting with social approval, leads mostly to grievous trouble. (Cp. Ps.-Sen. *Oct.* 557 ff.)

For those willing to face facts, the last word on the love affairs of gods with mortals was said by Euripides (*Ion* 436 ff., 1557 ff., etc.). It is in the light of classical texts—and not of penny novelettes—that "the desire of Zeus' eye" must be examined.

That "the desire of Zeus' eye" simply means a divine tumescence would be self-evident even if I were unable to cite—as I will in a moment—massive evidence supporting this interpretation. I moreover assert confidently that Aischylos *intended* to suggest this, and that his fifth century B.C. audience so *understood* this figure of speech—though dry-as-dust scholiasts, both old and new, did not.[36]

This being said, I now propose to justify in detail my view that Zeus' yearning eye is his erect penis.

The eye = penis symbolism is, to begin with, perfectly traditional in Greece. In fact, some Greek monuments show phalloi provided with eyes: *54*, p. 103 (Kyathos, Berlin no. 2095), p. 106 (Paris, Petit Palais, no. 307), p. 107 (Krater, Berlin no. 3206), etc.

Psycho-analytically, Freud's equating Oidipous' self-blinding with self-castration[37] is conclusively validated by the fact that whereas in one

---

[33] I cite, at random, Zeus' Leporello-album of his amours: Hom. *Il.* 14.313 ff.

[34] Most goddesses are no different. Eos, "stuck" with the senile Tithonos, confines him to a palatial padded cell and chases other men (Hom. *h. Ven.* 223 ff.). Thetis leaves Peleus' abode long before the death of their son Achilleus (Hom. *Il. passim*). The tale of Demeter's lasting love for the greying Iasion (Ov. *Met.* 9.422 f.) is not myth but vintage Hollywood, as is that of Eos (Aurora) resting her head on the old Tithonos' shoulder (Sen. *Ag.* 822 f.). Though Odysseus' affairs with Kalypso and with Kirke last a while, these ladies are not authentic immortals, and belong to the folk tale (cp. *8*, pp. 18 ff. and *passim*) rather than to myth.

[35] Cp. *12*; *14*; *26*, pp. 86, 92; *30*, chaps. 10 and 11, etc.

[36] As to Aischylos' earthy approach to sexuality, Ar. *Ran.* 1045 ff. is the *knowingly* absurd quip of a comic poet who had certainly read, e.g., A. *Ag.* 1222, *Choe.* 894 f., 917, (*Tox.*) *fr.* 243N², *Dict.* 810 ff., etc. Aischylos wearing a clerical collar is an unhistorical and, indeed, revolting modern conceit.

[37] But this does not exclude the supplementary conclusion that Oidipous also had many good reasons—in addition to those he himself mentions (S. *OT* 1334 ff.)—for destroying his eyes (*32*).

tradition (Hom. *Il.* 9.453 ff.) the "incestuous" Phoinix is cursed with sterility ("castration"), in another version he is blinded [E. (*Phoinix*) *fr.* 816N[2]; Apollod. 3.13.8, etc.]. Bryas is blinded by the girl he had raped (Paus. 2.20.2), etc. (*32*).

On still another level, the Greek equation: child = eye of the house[38] also exemplifies the eye = penis symbolism, for the child = penis equation is clinically commonplace. It is, moreover, encountered chiefly when "seeing" is conceived as an active, outward-directed performance ("looking").[39] This makes "desire of the eye" = "erection of the penis" a certainty.

As regards *this* text in particular, the correctness of my interpretation is confirmed also by the subsequent—and peculiar—recurrence of the eye motif. As already noted, Zeus' *one* (big?) eye anticipates Argos' *myriad* (normal-sized?) eyes (569, 677 ff.). The *simultaneous* surveillance of the (manifestly rutting) Io by these many eyes is, after the slaying of Argos, replaced by the *recurrent* stings of the gadfly (οἶστρος = rut).[40]

The anticipation of Argos' many eyes by Zeus' *one* eye is rooted in the symbolic equation: big = many. This means of symbolization is commonly encountered not only in dream, but also in the analysis of certain very promiscuous—because oedipally fixated—women, for whom the many organs of their lovers provide, in the aggregate (*16*), the equivalent of the enormous paternal penis of the *little* girl's fantasies—a penis which she never ceases both to crave and to dread.[41]

Excursus. A more indirect argument which, taken by itself, would not be convincing, but which, taken in conjunction with the data cited above, does appear to support my interpretations, is that, in the Io myth, Zeus' penis is symbolized also by another one of his own organs. In A. *PV* 849, etc., and in A. *Suppl.* 312, etc., the touch or caress of Zeus' "hand" upon

---

[38] Cp. Dodds *ad* E. *Ba.* 1308, citing A. *Pers.* 169, *Choe.* 934; E. *Andr.* 406, *Ion* 1467 (but also some exceptions to the rule).

[39] Cp. *29*, p. 406 ff. Cp. cartoons representing active looking by means of rays emanating *from* the eyes. When seeing is conceived as a passive-receptive performance, the eye can represent the vulva (*18*). The sexual ambiguity of the eye is not unique. It is duplicated by that of the nose (*64*), whose further ambiguity, on a different level, is underscored by a German riddle: "What has its back (*Rücken*) in front, its root (*Wurzel*) on top, and its wings (*Flügel*) and tip (*Spitze*) below?"

[40] I recall that, at this point, Io is sexually awakened—the kind of girl whose passionateness Aischylos himself described (*fr.* 243N[2]). More on this point below.

[41] The fantasy of the destructively huge paternal penis, which girls evolve during the oedipal stage of development, continues to haunt many of them even after they are no longer "too small" to be able to admit an adult man's organ. In some cases, this persistent fantasy leads, in adult life, to (unconscious) attempts to "confirm" it, by means of *highly selective* attacks of vaginismus. Painful contractions, making intromission almost impossible, may occur when such a woman seeks to cohabit with a man who represents for her a father figure. A colleague provided especially striking information about a prostitute, who —by definition—has strong, unresolved oedipal fixations: she had attacks of vaginismus only when a client was old enough to be her father. However, the man's relative age may play no role whatever in such attacks of vaginismus: a certain young woman patient *began* to have such attacks when her equally young husband (unexpectedly) became a father surrogate for her. So far as I know, *this* connection between vaginismus and the fantasy of the "huge" paternal penis has not yet been reported in the psycho-analytical literature.

the cow Io's "forehead" helps her both to give birth to Epaphos and to resume her human shape.

Now, Kouretas recognized long ago (*45*, p. 257) that in these passages Zeus' "hand" is really his penis.[42] But Kouretas could have greatly strengthened his argument by pointing out that, according to Cook (*10*, 3.448 ff.), the "neura" of Zeus' hand(s), which Typhon = Typhoeus excises, actually stand for his penis. And both Kouretas and Cook could have made their respective interpretations more compelling had they pointed out *other* similarities between the Io and Typhoeus myths:

(1) Zeus' excised "neura" are hidden in the (furry) pelt of a she-bear[43] (= *vagina dentata*).

(2) Zeus' "hand" touches (in an act of symbolic coitus) Io-the-cow's forehead, which the Greeks often described as "curly-haired".[44]

It is my conviction that in these myths both the bear's pelt and the cow's curly forehead represent the female pubic hair: the female "escutcheon" or "shield".[45] Only in this way can I account for the Greeks' tendency to emphasize the relatively inconspicuous "curliness" of the forehead of cattle (E. *Ba.* 1185 ff., etc.), their preoccupation with the forelock of horses (X. *Eq.* 5.6, etc.), and their conviction that a fleshy "clot" on the newborn colt's forehead acted on mares as a strong aphrodisiac.[46]

What lends added plausibility to this interpretation is that Zeus himself gave birth to Athene from his split *skull*.[47]

With this I can close my demonstration that the "desire of Zeus' eye" is his imperious tumescence. I hold that for any Greek of the classical age the symbolism would have been self-evident (*32*).

The Dream-Speech

The Dream-Voice. As already noted, the word "visions" does not suffice to prove that Io's was a visual dream, nor is there anything to indicate that the (unidentified) dream-speaker was sent by Zeus.

I now propose to show that the surviving fragments of S. *Inach.* (*58*,

---

[42] That Io's *accouchement* should be facilitated thereby is far from absurd. As late as 1900, some country doctors accelerated a protracted delivery by causing the husband to cohabit with his parturient wife. For "breathing upon" (A. *Suppl.* 16) = quasi-coitus, cp. A. *Ag.* 1206.

[43] I have the impression that most individualized Greek mythical bears are female—as are Artemis' young acolytes, the "little bears". (But K.J.D. observes that she-bears with cubs are more aggressive than male bears.) This need mean no more than that the Greeks felt something to be "feminine" about *all* bears—as most people feel that *all* cats, regardless of their sex, are somehow "feminine". [A striking proof of mankind's spontaneous tendency to equate cats with the vulva comes from the Maori (*2*).]

[44] Domestic bovines do occasionally have some curly hair between their horns. Perhaps Greek cattle, less removed than modern cattle from the aurochs, had even curlier foreheads. (I recall that, some years ago, a German zoologist managed to "breed back" domestic cattle to a bovine resembling the aurochs.)

[45] The same may be true of Athene's awe-inspiring Aigis. Ferenczi (*37*) reports that a mother regularly frightened and disciplined her obstreperous little son by a display of her pubis (which mobilized his castration anxiety).

[46] Arist. *HA* 572a21; Ael. *NA* 3.17, 14.18.

[47] All sources discussed by Cook (*10* 3.656 ff.). Cp. chap. 5.

pp. 22 ff.) do *not* permit us to identify the dream-speaker as Hermes. I concede that some echoes of the A. *PV* dream scene are discernible in these Sophoklean fragments. But I also maintain that Sophokles' mind operated so differently from that of Aischylos that he utterly transformed whatever he derived from his great predecessor: it suffices to compare the Sophoklean Klytaimnestra's dream with that of her Aischylean equivalent (chaps. 6, 7). Moreover, the fact that the *PV* is a tragedy, while the *Inachos* is a satyr play, would also automatically increase differences between the two accounts of Io's "seduction".

It is evident that just because, in Sophokles' *Inachos*, Hermes—contemptuously called Zeus' lackey (vv. 2, 23)—acts as Zeus' emissary, this does not prove that he appeared "incognito" also in the Aischylean Io's dream, and this for several reasons:

(1) Though Hermes, the patron of heralds, is, in principle, a persuasive speaker, Io is *not fully* persuaded by her dream. This parallels somewhat the Sophoklean Hermes' failure to persuade Inachos. But there are also crucial differences:

(a) The invisible dream-speaker seeks to persuade Io; the visible Sophoklean Hermes seeks to persuade *only* Inachos—the fragment does not even hint at his addressing Io in any way.

(b) In the *PV*, only the dream-personage speaks—Io does not answer. Judging by what survives of the *Inachos*, Hermes carried on an unsuccessful and scurrilous debate with Inachos, in the form of a stichomythia.

(2) The content of Io's recurrent dream is presumably the same every time. By contrast, though Hermes also appears twice at Inachos' palace, he is visible the first time, and (theoretically) invisible the second time.

(3) The superficial resemblance between the unidentified dream-speaker and the (theoretically) invisible Hermes promptly breaks down when one considers that both the dream-personage and the visible Hermes only speak, whereas, when Hermes returns "invisible", he manifestly does not try persuasion, but is up to a practical trick (v. 21): most probably, an abduction.

(4) In A. *PV*, the dream-speaker remains unidentified. In the *Inachos* (vv. 5 ff.), Hermes, though wearing Hades' cap, is recognized.

(5) The Aischylean dream-speaker's "soft voice" recalls the "whispers, very rapid" (*Inach.* 20), which are relatively dreamlike.[48] But this seemingly striking similarity vanishes the moment one recalls that whereas the (understandable) dream-voice does *not* permit the identification of the speaker, the "invisible" Hermes' (inarticulate?) sounds—recalling the "voice" in E. *IT* 52—promptly disclose his identity (v. 11).

(6) The sounds produced by Hermes present a difficult problem, especially if one assumes—as I think one must—that the sounds which betray his identity (v. 11) are the same as those which madden the hearers (v. 16: μανία). As regards the latter, Page (ad loc.) recalls the sound of the pipes heard by Io in A. *PV* 574. But the effects produced by these two series of sounds are diametrically opposed: the former madden the hearers, the latter are soothing to the point of bringing sleep (ὑπνοδότας). But I concede at once that it is hard to see why the brutally harassed

---

[48] On hearing incomprehensible (blurred) speech in dream, cp. supra, note 21.

and driven Io should consider the pipe's soothing sounds as still another of her many afflictions.[49]

For me, the maddening sounds produced by Hermes recall another sound heard by Io: the angry buzz of the stinging gadfly, which keeps her on the run.[50]

Not wishing to venture on even more slippery ground by re-examining the—in my estimate—still far from clear relationships between Argos, the double of Argos, Hermes and the gadfly, I will conclude my remarks on Sophokles' *Inachos* by reaffirming that, despite its few superficial affinities with the A. *PV* dream-scene, it does not permit us to assume that the dream-voice is that of Hermes. The identity of the dream-speaker can only be established by a psychological scrutiny of the "inner evidence" furnished by the Aischylean text itself.

Super-ego and Id. As a rule, both hallucinated and dreamed voices speak either on behalf of the Super-ego—laying down the law, enunciating taboos and addressing reproaches to the subject—or else proclaim the demands of the Id. But even psychiatrists seldom stress adequately that, in both cases, there is a striking complicity between the Super-ego and the Id.

(1) A voice, which *seems* to express the Super-ego's point of view, not only tends to stress the subject's moral degradation, but also formulates its reproaches *in extremely obscene terms.*[51]

(2) When the voice speaks on behalf of the Id, it tends to borrow its arguments from the Super-ego, in a consummately hypocritical manner. Thus, as will be shown further on, even though the vision urges Io to allow herself to be deflowered, all its arguments are derived from the Super-ego's arsenal of "good" reasons. Hence, Io's craving for coitus—and, as will be shown, specifically for *incestuous* coitus—is *represented* by the dream-procuress as an unselfish act of piety towards the supreme god. This dream-speech is, thus, clearly the work of a dazzlingly perceptive practical psychologist.[52] But I must add also that such a clever hiding of instinctual strivings behind a façade of reasons borrowed from the Super-ego is more common in waking life than in dream—though it is occasionally encountered also in dreams, such as that of Io.

This being said, the role of the Super-ego, both in Io's dream and in her subsequent behaviour, must not be minimized. In A. *PV*, both (the immobilized) Prometheus and (the hounded, errant) Io are represented (in principle) as the "innocent" victims of Zeus. Yet, Io takes it for granted

---

[49] A just barely acceptable explanation may be that these soothing sounds make it even more difficult for her to stay awake and to run. But I note that, so far as I know, only one *domestic* animal is *trained* to respond with increased speed to the sound of a *pipe* even, and especially, when weary: the racing dromedary. As a rule, herdsmen play the pipe so as to soothe their herds and flocks. (The snake-charmer's snake is *not* a domestic animal; only a tamed one.)

[50] Even the buzzing of a gnat disturbs Klytaimestra's light sleep (A. *Ag.* 891 f.). A (figurative) sting awakens the Erinyes (A. *Eum.* 155 ff.).

[51] E.g.: hallucinated accusations of perverted practices, of incestuous propensities, etc., tend to be worded very obscenely indeed—thereby gratifying the reproached person's "condemned" inclinations.

[52] Cp. the striking remark of another good practical psychologist, the banker J. P. Morgan: "Whenever a man does something, he always has two reasons for doing it: a good reason and a real reason." This quip is directly applicable to Io's dream.

that *Prometheus* is punished for some offence (564 f.) and, at vv. 578 ff., she at least wonders what offence Zeus found in *her*. I cannot persuade myself that her bewilderment is purely rhetorical or else motivated solely by the pious conviction that the gods never wantonly harm a mortal.[53] It is by raising this question (578 ff.) that Io confesses her still unconscious guilt: her incestuous cravings.[54]

The childish need to exonerate gods and parents at any cost is, of course, not denied. It presupposes only a fairly naive kind of reasoning:

(1) I am weak and need to be protected by someone all-powerful and good (parent = god).

(2) If I am punished or hurt, it must be because of my wickedness—even if I am unaware of having sinned.[55]

(3) It is more tolerable and more reassuring to assume that I have (unwittingly) sinned than it is to assume that my parents (gods) are bad and wantonly cruel.

(4) If I have been punished because I have (be it unwittingly) sinned, then there is something I can *do* about it: I can accept the punishment and mend my ways. If, however, I am hurt even though I am good, then there is nothing I can do to help myself: I must concede a total lack of control over my fate.[56]

In short, though in real life the "normal" sequence is: "I sin . . . I am punished", in the hidden recesses of the mind the sequence is: "I am punished . . . *therefore* I must have sinned."[57]

The Procuress. Though no explicit statement reveals the identity or even the sex of the dream-speaker, I call that soft-spoken personage a procuress, for reasons which are partly realistic, partly psychological and partly literary.

(1) Since this dream is clearly endogenous, in that the course of action which it advocates is motivated by Io's long inhibited sexual cravings, psychologically the dream-voice is Io's own: it speaks for that part of her mind which struggles against the hesitations and inhibitions of the more conventional—and, in this instance, partly more rational—layers of her mind. In short, though the voice professes to plead the cause of Zeus, it actually advocates—with typically feminine deviousness (infra)—the gratification of Io's own erotic needs.

(2) The gentle-voiced speaker unmistakably musters the arguments every woman wanting—but not quite daring—to be seduced wishes to

---

[53] The clever parallels usually drawn between Aischylos and the *Book of Job* may satisfy the theologian and the moral philosopher—they do not satisfy at least one psychoanalyst: the present writer.

[54] Much of what J.-P. Vernant (*67*, chap. 5) says about Oidipous' self-betraying behaviour in the early parts of S. *OT* can be applied, *mutatis mutandis*, also to Io's wondering about her offence.

[55] Cp. the widely attested willingness of primitives accused of murder by witchcraft to confess that they might have done the deed unintentionally and without even being aware of it (*35*, pp. 121 ff.).

[56] Snell's theory of "action" in Aischylean drama (*65*) overlooks this crucial point.

[57] An adolescent patient, constantly told by his mother that he was "bad", felt obliged to *be* bad, so as to preserve his unconscious but compulsive faith in his mother's infallibility. His delinquency was meant to prove his mother right. This is a perfect example of what I call "being a deputy neurotic" (*17*, *30*, chap. 8).

hear.[58] Better still, these arguments match so closely those of the procuress in one of Herondas' most fiercely realistic mimes that I am almost tempted to believe that Herondas not only imitated reality—as did Aischylos—but also parodied the Aischylean Io's dream.[59]

In short, although I can hardly speak as an expert about this matter, I simply cannot imagine a male procurer reasoning the way the dream-voice does.

The Dream-Voice's Method of Persuasion is as timeless as it is efficient. Like some confessors of royal mistresses, the voice advocates misconduct in the interest of a "higher morality"—it favours that "better" which is pro-verbially the enemy of the "good".

Indeed, if one starts from the assumption that the supreme god is entitled to *whatever* he desires, and that his wanting it suffices to make it good,[60] the "moral" tone of the dream-speech is impeccably lofty. It is, moreover, a commonplace that what a god desires is precisely what he delights in forbidding to man. This is, in fact, *prima facie* evidence of the *divine* nature of his wishes.[61]

All theology ultimately founders on the reef of its attempts to represent the gods as *both* good and omnipotent, for omnipotence can be demonstrated *only* by the systematic transgression of *all* rules. Aischylos knew and accepted this fact, which Sophokles chose to ignore. Euripides, wiser than all theologians and political scientists before or since, faced squarely—and

---

[58] Cp. Freud's dictum, that even in cases of rape, one part of the "victim's" psyche abets the rapist.

[59] "Oh child": A. *PV* 651; Herond. 1.21. Needlessly long chastity: A. *PV* 648; Herond. 1.21. Benefits: A. *PV* 648 f.; Herond. 1.26 ff. Deity: A. *PV* 649 ff.; Herond. 1.26 ff. Glorious lover: A. *PV* 648 f.; Herond. 1.50. Kypris: A. *PV* 650; Herond. 1.62. Holy rites (ἱερὸс γάμοс sacred marriage): A. *PV* 648; Herond. 1.82. Eye or sight: A. *PV* 654; Herond. 1.56. Yearning: A. *PV* 649 ff.; Herond. 1.60. Though both Io and Metriche profess to be reluctant, both listen to the procuress more than once: A. *PV* 645 f.; Herond. 1.10. Etc.

[60] Cp. the problem of whether the gods love what *is* holy or whether their loving something *makes* it holy (Pl. *Euthphr.* 10e and *passim*).

[61] Cp. Sen. *Ag.* 271: the tyrant delights in forbidding others to do what he claims as his privilege. This notion is both ancient and universal. Incest is the jealously guarded exclusive privilege both of the gods and of the divine kings of Egypt, Peru, and much of Polynesia, etc. Also, if an individual behaved the way each and every state so often does, he would be jailed, for "la raison d'État" is, by definition, contrary to ethical rules. I even hold that Kronos did not succeed Ouranos because he was his *son*, but because he criminally *castrated* his father. Lord Acton's remark: "Absolute power corrupts absolutely" must be completed by the insight that absolute power can be obtained and constantly revalidated *only* by actions which, in the case of the private citizen, would be common-law crimes. I cite one example: in an American Arctic tale, an old woman's endo-cannibalism *automatically* turns her into a supernatural being (*4*, pp. 259; *60*, pp. 16 f.). This tale is, in my estimate, paradigmatic, for even Greek oracles were known to have recommended the commission of (ritual) crimes to those seeking to achieve the near-impossible (Orestes is to steal the Taurian Artemis' statue: E. *IT* 85 ff.; Thyestes must commit incest with his daughter: Apollod. *Ep.* 10.5, etc.; to win a war, the Thebans must perpetrate a sacrilege: Ephor. *fr.* 30, *FHG* 1.241). Comparable primitive examples exist: before hunting big game, a Ba-Thonga tribesman commits incest, so that his terribleness will match the awesomeness of the beast he hunts (*43*, 2, p. 68). Paedagogical, sociological and political philosophies alike fail to comprehend that man is, by nature, not a *social* creature (like, e.g., termites)—he is only a *gregarious* mammal, trying to force himself into the strait jacket of the social-insect pattern.

in despair—the *absolute* incompatibility of goodness and of total power, which the one who has that power always dreads to lose: e.g., Zeus in A. *PV*. That is the real thesis of the *Bakchai*: only by going mad can man tolerate the total and eternal incompatibility between goodness and near-omnipotence. Far from deviating, in the *Bakchai*, from his life-long search for truth, Euripides draws, in that drama, the one true conclusion no one, before or since, has dared to draw. Though it is fashionable to claim that Euripides was not a real philosopher but only a poet tainted with the teachings of the sophists, I hold that his *Bakchai*'s philosophical import transcends anything Platon ever wrote. The "enigma" of the *Bakchai* is our own—all too comprehensible—refusal to understand it.

But I am straying from my topic.

I have already noted that, given the right of the gods to an immediate gratification of their sacred whims, the speaker's arguments are flaw-lessly "pious". After the opening verse, not a word is said of Io's sexual needs, nor is she promised ecstasy in the god's embrace. She is simply urged to cater piously to the god's sexual needs.

But the dream-voice's cleverest trick is probably its relative honesty. It promises Io no reward other than the gratification of her avowable— and indeed, princess-like—ambition to acquire immortal glory by a (one-shot) union with the most exalted of lovers.[62] The voice's arguments would be *less* credible were *other* rewards also promised.

Indeed, the tragic fate of girls who had mated with a god was notorious. Even Zeus could not protect his mistresses either from Hera's anger or from abuse by their own kindred. In early Greek texts, the riskiness of divine love-affairs was always taken for granted. Permitted to choose between Apollon's passing infatuation and Idas' lasting love, Marpessa chose the mortal suitor.[63] The attempts of some girls to fight off a divine rapist[64] also prove that divine matings did not tempt prudent girls. Daphne even preferred to be turned into a laurel[65] rather than submit to Apollon's embraces (Paus. 10.7.8, etc.). Kassandra had tricked Apollon into giving her something for nothing, but, by rendering his gift useless, he caused her to perish miserably (A. *Ag.* 1202 ff., etc.).

Summing up, a Greek heroine desired by a god faced what is called today a "double bind": "heads he wins, tails I lose". She was usually punished, whether she yielded or resisted.[66] Hence, many Greek heroines did resist, or at least required a good deal of persuasion before yielding to a god.[67]

[62] The word γάμος (marriage) can even be applied to the rape of a girl by a god (E. *Ion*. 941, etc.). In modern Greek γαμῶ applied to humans, is indecent (K.J.D.).

[63] Hom. *Il.* 9.557 ff.; explained in Apollod. 1.7.8.

[64] Kreusa vs. Apollon (E. *Ion* 10 f., etc.); Kainis vs. Poseidon (Nic. ap. Ant. Lib. 17, etc.).

[65] This, however, obliterated her legs and her genitals (J.W.D.).

[66] The budding Kuanyama Ambo sorcerer asks his mother to cohabit with him. If she does, her sin destroys her. If she refuses, her son fatally bewitches her (50). Nothing reveals better the sickness of our own age than the conviction of certain segments of the lunatic fringe that "total awareness" can only be obtained by subjecting oneself to the Zen Buddhist "double bind". (But Marpessa was not punished, J.W.D.)

[67] In this respect, they were more sensible than were many French ladies of Louis XIV's court. They vied with each other for the title of royal mistress, though all could have foreseen that, like their predecessors, they would end in disgrace or even in a convent.

In fact, mythical heroes dreaded the embraces of goddesses almost as much as heroines dreaded those of the gods.[68]

This explains why, despite her cleverness, the procuress meets with enough resistance to force her to reappear in Io's dream night after night. But I hasten to add that the ascription of resistances to Io, far from disproving the view that the real source of her dreams is *her* sexuality, strongly confirms it. Io's sexuality carries the day only after it turns the tables on her Super-ego and adopts its hypocritical pseudo-morality, which—since the dawn of time—has permitted many women to perpetrate one of the most profitable frauds of history, though they have paid for it with irreparable damage to their femininity and human dignity.

Many a woman persuades her man—and herself—that she has no *spontaneous* interest in sex and derives little pleasure, if any, from it.[69] She may even profess to yield only out of a selfless concern for her partner's pressing needs. This explains why Io's own sexual urge betrays itself only in the speech's initial reference to her prolonged virginity (648).[70]

But even this is not the full story. The Id—which in the psychologically adult woman craves love-and-sex—cannot borrow the Super-ego's lofty hypocrisy without becoming contaminated by the Super-ego's notorious— and always *pre*-genital—corruptibility. This explains why the voice, instead of urging Io to enjoy love's delights, advises her to coin her virginity. Io is told that she is imprudently hoarding a highly marketable commodity: her hymen; the moment to dispose of it, in a seller's market, has come. This argument satisfies Io's Super-ego, for in such a course of action the gifts of golden Aphrodite are gratifyingly contaminated with the pregenital ordure of Ploutos, whose name does not resemble that of the infernal Plouton in vain.[71]

Lerne

For many reasons, Lerne (652 ff., 677 ff.) is a most suitable setting for Zeus' union with Io.

(I) *Mythological Considerations* make Lerne an appropriate place in two respects. But I must, alas, deal with these matters most summarily, for the full proof of what I have to say about Lerne in myth could be cited only in

---

But this stopped them no more than revolutionaries are stopped by the knowledge that, throughout history, revolutions—like Kronos—have devoured most of their children.

[68] Odysseus: Hom *Od.* 10.296 ff.; Anchises: Hom. *h. Ven.* 180 ff., anticipated in vv. 102 ff., 145 ff.

[69] Cp. Hera's pretences and her angry blinding of Teiresias, who had dared to reveal that woman's sexual pleasure is nine times greater than that of man (Hes. *Melamp. fr.* 275 M.W.; Apollod. 3.6.7; Tzetz. *Lyc.* 683; Ov. *Met.* 3.320; Hyg *fab.* 75).

[70] This self-deception, formerly encouraged by the clergy, is today actively fostered by its natural heirs: by the theoreticians of the "Women's Liberation" movement—one of whom at least is reported to have publicly admitted that she is bisexual.

[71] Throughout history, the Super-ego has lived comfortably with dowries, bride-prices, alimony payments, and even with prostitution. But it will never learn to tolerate Love, freely given and reciprocated: the pure gifts of Aphrodite, whom the Greeks alone had sense enough to call ἁγνή (= pure and holy) (*63*, Supplementband 1, p. 54a).

a monograph. I can only state here that the views expressed in the next two sub-sections are—be they right or wrong—based upon a careful study of *all* the evidence. This being said, the sceptic can simply skip the paragraphs devoted to mytho-chronology and mytho-topography, particularly since I cite only a fraction of the sources I have consulted.

(1) *Mytho-chronology.* A. *PV* 652 ff. implies that Lerne was well watered at the time of Zeus' mating with Io. This means that this happening *antedates* another important event: when, in Inachos' time, Poseidon unsuccessfully contended with Hera for supremacy in Argos, he spitefully made Argos a "thirsty country" (sch. E. *Or.* 127). I am convinced that this myth has affinities with Io's adventure. At any rate, Poseidon did not make Argos well watered again until, generations later, he cohabited—*also at Lerne*—with one of Io's descendants, the Danaid Amymone,[72] in what I tentatively believe to have been a water-dowsing rite.[73]

(2) *Mytho-topography.* On the basis of considerable preliminary research, I state, as a general principle, that certain localities are linked with certain *types* of mythical happenings. On the basis of my data, I hold that, in several significant respects, Io's adventure is just the *kind* of thing that is likely to happen *at Lerne*. I cite here—with a summary indication of the main sources—one myth and ritual only: the one which Nilsson (*56*, 1[2], 591) calls the most obscene of all Greek rites. The fact that *such* a rite was performed at Lerne—which also contained an entrance to Hades: the bottomless Alkyoneian pool (Paus. 2.37.5 f.)—will, I hope, make more acceptable my final hypothesis that there corresponded to the Io myth a (far less obscene) pastoral fertility rite, whose locale was almost certainly also the pasture land of Lerne.[74] The myth reports that, trying to keep at least symbolically his promise to the dead Prosymnos (or Polymnos), Dionysos fashioned a figwood phallos and inserted it into his own anus.[75]

With this, I must conclude my discussion of the mythological appropriateness of Lerne as a setting for Io's (forced)[76] mating with Zeus. I must now turn to Lerne's concrete characteristics, which also make it a suitable locale for divine amours.

II. *The Outdoors.* Lerne is the *Draussen*, so admirably discussed by Wilamowitz (*72* 1.175 ff.): it incarnates the non-social and therefore non-human world. Remote from the city (πόλιϲ) governed by law and custom (νόμοϲ), it is the world of nature (φύϲιϲ), represented by domestic animals (A. *PV* 652 ff.)—and even of monsters, such as the Hydra. The

---

[72] Aischylos' lost satyr play *Amymone* (*frr.* 13, 14 N²) dealt with this myth.

[73] Cp. also Hera's annual revirgination in an *Argive* spring, the Kanathos (Paus. 2.38.2 f.), which needs to be re-examined.

[74] That the whole Io myth complex does not contain a single reference to agriculture is manifest. That, for the agricultural Greek, the pastoralist was, in a way, *pre*-human, practising "non-Greek" rites, was ably demonstrated by Vidal-Naquet (*69*).

[75] Paus. 2.37.5; Arnob. *adv. nat.* 5.28; Clem. Alex. *protr.* 2.34. For the many other sources, cp. Hoefer, *63* s.v. Polymnos, coll. 2657 ff. The nature of the annual *secret* rites at Lerne (Paus. 2.17.1) can easily be inferred from the somewhat attenuated forms of that rite recorded in Luc. *de dea Syr.* 16 and in the sch. ad loc. Iconography: perhaps Nilsson, *56* 1. pl. 35, figs. 2, 3 (so interpreted by W. Burkert, pers. comm.) (*7*).

[76] Cp. the Danaides-Aigyptiadai rape-marriage, the satyr's attempt to rape Amymone. Prosymnos' = Polymnos' extortion of Dionysos' consent, etc.

agricultural and city-dwelling Greek usually visualized this world in an unrealistic, fear-inspiring way (*68, 70*).[77]

It is only a slight exaggeration to say that, in the Greek view, the dangerous, mysterious, animalistic *Draussen* encouraged and almost incited impulsive, lawless and, at times, unnatural sexual activities.[78] Greek data confirming this are not hard to find.

(1) Phaidra, haunted by her incestuous cravings, fantasied that she could find relief only "outdoors"—i.e., in the open country (E. *Hipp.* 228 ff.), where she was, of course, likely to meet the hunter Hippolytos. This is by no means an exclusively Greek reaction.[79]

(2) A good many (illegitimate) matings between gods and mortals took place outdoors.[80] All this suggests that the "outdoors" deculturalizes man and incites the gods to be their most divinely lawless selves.

(3) Living outdoors, away from the city, was, at best, felt to be a token of backwardness. At worst, it was viewed as a symptom of perverseness approaching insanity.[81]

(4) In Greece, raving, ecstatic group rites were performed mostly outdoors. The mountain-roaming (ὀρειβασία) of the Mainades is paradigmatic in this respect (*6*).

In short, precisely because Lerne is "the outdoors", it is the ideal kind of place both for unlawful couplings and for the occurrence of hallucinated

[77] This conception of the "outdoors" may explain in part that absence of a "feeling for nature" which so distressed some 19th century, city-dwelling English hellenists, for whom nature in the raw was the Lake District.

[78] Cp. the Prosymnos myth, supra.

[79] A Mohammedan Malay girl, unconsciously, but also irresistibly, attracted to a despised Sakai jungle-dweller, felt that only the nocturnal jungle—where she was likely to run into this Sakai—could cool her "inexplicable" feverishness and alleviate her distress (*9*).

[80] Apollon rapes Kreusa in a cave (E. *Ion* 17, etc.); Poseidon mates with Tyro near a river (Hom. *Od.* 11.235 ff., etc.) and with Io's descendant Amymone in the swamps of Lerne, etc. It was outdoors that a catamite stole Sophokles' cloak (Athen. 13.605). Cp. the mountain roaming Mainades, etc.

[81] Timon (Ar. *Av.* 1548, *Lys.* 809, etc.). Euripides, the alleged misanthrope, was said to have worked in a cave (*Eurip. Genos*, p. 4, 5.ll. 23 ff., Schwartz). His detractors probably put it about that this critic of the gods and the Establishment resembled his own cave-dwelling Kyklops. Bellerophon withdrew from mankind when he became mad (Pi. *I.* 6.44, etc.). Burkert (*6*) noted that the mad women of Greek myth roamed the wilds. Ruth Padel (*57*) found that even some non-mythical Greek psychotics shared that tendency. It is perhaps not fortuitous that our word "idiot" is derived from ἰδιώτης = a person in a private station of life, also: "individual" as opposed to πόλις (city) and even as opposed to "skilled man" (LSJ). The standard Wolof (Senegal) notion of the madman is: he who lives apart from the group (*47*). But the tendency to flee the community is not a universal characteristic of the psychotic. The insane Sedang Moi usually does disappear into the jungle and, unless found, perishes there (*11*). But the psychotic Mohave Indian hardly ever runs away (*26*), perhaps because, unlike the Sedang, who is normally afraid of the surrounding jungle, the Mohave does not dread his semi-desert homeland. The only Mohave Indians who deliberately left the tribe for ever were certain braves, weary of life, who sought to be killed performing some supreme feat of valour in enemy territory (*26*, pp. 426 ff.). The merely "alienated", who insist on staying in the community so as to display *in it* their "social negativism" (*30*, chap. 3) to the limit [Greek cynics, mediaeval "fools in Christ" (*3*), modern hippies, etc.], are in reality clamouring either to be expelled or to be helped to control themselves—both of which societies lacking faith in themselves refuse to do.

experiences caused by solitude, which is a form of sensory deprivation.[82]

But Lerne is not only "the outdoors" in general—it is a *Draussen* of a *special kind*, whose nature further clarifies the meaning of Io's dream.

(III) *Lerne is Pasture Land* for Inachos' *cattle* only.[83] I particularly note the lack of any reference to horse herds, though "horse-pasturing" is one of Argos' regular Homeric epithets.[84] The emphasis, in both A. *PV* and A. *Suppl.*, is on cattle only. This is made clear by a whole series of facts:

(1) Io, the priestess of Hera (A. *Suppl.* 301), is metamorphosed into a cow;

(2) Hera herself is a cow goddess (βοῶπιc = cow-eyed, cow-faced);

(3) Zeus cohabits with Io in a bull epiphany (A. *Suppl.* 301);

(4) Inachos is not only a king but also a river god and, as such, is necessarily horned like a bull;

(5) Argos is a cattle herder (A. *PV* 677, etc.);

(6) Gadflies do harass cattle (Apollod. 2.5.10, etc.).

All this renders meaningful the dream's command, that Io is to cohabit with "Zeus" near or amongst *Inachos'* cattle—behaving sexually like a cow. Whether she actually complies with this order—and I note that, in A. *PV*, the passage concerning the dream and its immediate consequences does *not* mention the cohabitation—and what the consequences of her compliance were, does not concern me in this study.

From the point of view of dream analysis, all that concerns me is the implicit demand that Io should behave in a sexually animalistic manner.[85]

Hence, all that requires elucidation here is the meaning and import of this demand *in dream*.

The simplest inference is that, psychologically, there is *something* about the union advocated by the dream that is incompatible with *human*, but compatible with *animal*, sexuality.[86]

Obviously, I cannot enumerate and discuss here every difference between human and infra-primate, mammalian sexuality. I therefore mention only cursorily some details (which I analysed in full before drafting this chapter): details which concern events postdating Io's

---

[82] Hesiodos appears to have hallucinated the Muses while herding sheep (Hes. *Th.* 1 ff.). On two U.S.A. Pueblo Indian sheep herders hallucinating, cp. *30*, chap. 1. For a basic bibliography of sensory deprivation, cp. *46*, p. 65, note 27; on the relevance of this state for the understanding of certain Greek phenomena, cp. Dodds (*33*, p. 117).

[83] With Italie and Smyth, I take ποίμναc βουcτάcειc (653) to mean: herds of bovines (only). Mazon's "parcs *à moutons* et à boeufs" is even ecologically wrong. Sheep, who crop the grass short, ruin it for cattle-grazing (hence the murderous 19th-century clashes between sheepmen and cattlemen in the American West). The deep grass at Lerne (A. *PV* 653) also suggests that it is not a sheep pasture. Once again, it helps one to assume that the poet knows what he is talking about.

[84] E.g., Hom. *Il.* 2.287 and often. In A. *PV*, Argive horses are mentioned not at all, and in A. *Suppl.* only once: v. 183.

[85] It makes almost no difference whether one assumes that the dream incites Io to behave sexually *like* a cow, or to engage in a *ritual* coitus so as to promote the fertility of cattle, for even the latter would require the union to be as cattle-like as possible. The most compelling argument in favour of this view is that Demeter's sacred union with Iasion, intended to insure the fertility of cornfields, sought to imitate sowing: the two cohabited in a thrice-ploughed furrow (Hom. *Od.* 5.125 ff., Hes. *Th.* 969ff').

[86] I mention only in passing the post-Aischylean, Platonic (*Phdr.* 250e) notion that many sexual acts are inherently animalistic, and worthy only of quadrupeds.

dream and her expulsion—or perhaps, flight[87]—from Inachos' palace.

(1) *The Gadfly* represents Io's state of frenzied rut,[88] which, though she cannot control it, deeply distresses her still relatively human, although mad mind, which survives her metamorphosis.[89] Clinical data also confirm the gadfly = rut equation.[90]

I can do no more than stress once again that *great* poets unconsciously figure such things out, though the literary critic—and sometimes even the psycho-analyst—finds it difficult at times to comprehend the logic of the poets' fantasies.

(2) *The Anonymity of Animal Sexuality* is obvious. Amongst most mammals below the primate level, almost any available partner will do. Conceivably, the normal *a tergo* animal coital position contributes to this non-differentiation of partners.[91] In mankind, a somewhat similar anonymity and indiscriminateness can be achieved by recourse to the *a tergo* position, or at least to positions requiring a minimum of bodily contact (*40*, pp. 170 ff.), or by the use of masks—as in (pre-World War II) Rhenish and Bavarian carnivals and, perhaps, in some ancient sexual rites.

(3) *"Incest"*. As research on the sexual behaviour of animals progresses, it becomes increasingly evident that they can develop spontaneously most of the perversions which a more naive age deemed to be exclusively human. But there is *one* sexual "deviation" no animal can either learn to practice or to avoid: incest.[92] For incest, as distinct from inbreeding, is unimaginable without the concept of kinship.[93]

---

[87] I add this specification for, once expelled, Io can, like a rutting, runaway heifer, race around in search of an aroused bull—as in the most peculiar metaphor found in Q.S. 10.438 ff.

[88] On οἰστράω = to rut in a frenzy, cp. LSJ, s.v.

[89] Cp. a related story in Callim. *fr.* 100h Schr. = 2, p. 356 Pf. Cp. also the distress of certain neurotics who feel "driven" despite their better judgment (*17*, p. 112 f.) and Ainu cases of uncontrollable *imu* seizures (*66, 73*), etc.

[90] A very sensual girl in her twenties had had a number of anxiety dreams in which she was attacked by a gadfly, and this both before and after her defloration. *In dream* she was particularly afraid that she might *swallow* the gadfly (clearly an echo of infantile fantasies of oral impregnation, reinforced by the *real* experience of having had a gadfly enter her nostril), or else that the gadfly might attack her eye. (This reminds one of Argos' many eyes which, in one version (A. *PV* 567 ff.), are replaced after his death by *one* gadfly). (On: eye = vagina, cp. *18*.) In her dreams, she reacted to these "attacks" by covering ("masking") her face with her forearms and by strongly bending her body forward, in a way which recalls the "sexual presentation" posture of rutting female monkeys (*74*). (For the covering of the face instead of the pubis, cp. *19*.) Better still, she *spontaneously* added that a gadfly's bite generates a heat which resembles the heat she feels when sexually excited, and that the itching, which elicits a need to scratch, feels like the need for coitus. I note that this modern Io had not read Aischylos, had never heard the word *oestrus* and therefore did not know that, in biology, it denotes both the gadfly and rutting.

[91] The ventro-ventral position is so deeply ingrained in human behaviour that an ancient statue (Museo Nazionale, Naples, cp. *49*, pl. 25) represents the half-goat Pan cohabiting with a she-goat in a quasi-ventro-ventral position, resembling the traditional position of the Trobriand Islanders (*52*, p. 283 ff.), etc.

[92] One could probably teach a male laboratory animal to avoid cohabitation with his mother, by giving him an electric shock *only* when he tries to mount a female the *experimenter* forbids him to mount. But even that trained male would not have learned to avoid "incest"—he would have learned only to avoid an electric shock.

[93] A human being can even commit socio-psychological incest *without* inbreeding—for

In short, according to his wont, Aischylos (whose incredible terseness is regularly underestimated) says all that matters in the fewest possible words (673 f.): "Forthwith my form *and mind* were distorted." Io's *mental* metamorphosis was a *sine qua non* condition for her being able to comply with the dream's command which, as I will show, urged her to commit "incest"—like a cow.

This being said, I feel that we have no reason to complain that, in the *PV*, Aischylos did not refer directly to Io's bovine coitus with Zeus. For I hold that it is precisely this omission which forces us to see how heavily over-determined the whole incident is and therefore compels us to explain it in terms of *several* frames of reference.[94]

The evidence, so far, can be convergently summed up in terms of two different frames of reference.

(1) Psychologically, Io's dream implies that the sexual union she craves is *not* compatible with human, but *is* compatible with bovine, sexuality: she craves incest.

(2) Socio-culturally, the dream-voice orders Io to perform a (ritual?) act similar to bovine sex acts, in the "shape" and manner of a cow (cp. perhaps, Pasiphae and the "bull", Apollod. 3.15.8; also: Mykerinos' daughter, Hdt. 2.129–131).

As regards Io's madness, the first explanation suggests that she must already have been abnormal to crave an incestuous union. The second explanation suggests that, in order to behave as commanded, she had to work herself into a state of frenzied (bouanthropic) madness,[95] or, at least, had to simulate such a madness so as to do the normally tabooed thing without being impeded by excessive guilt feelings and inhibition.[96]

I hold, in short, that if Io had *not* craved a sexual union of a type forbidden to mankind, though freely practised by animals and by Greek gods, i.e., had she not craved incest:

(1) she would *not* have tarried so long in her virginity;

(2) she would *not* have needed *repeated* anxiety dreams to persuade her, and

(3) the dream would *not* have had to specify that the union was to take place near Inachos' cattle herds—i.e., in a bovine setting and manner.

I must now, for reasons of expository convenience, indicate that "Zeus"

---

example, by cohabiting with his stepmother (E. *Hipp.*; Plu. *V. Dem.* 38). Conversely, he can inbreed without committing incest (socio-psychologically) if—as happened in one case, in the 1950s—he unwittingly marries his sister from whom he had been separated in childhood. By contrast, animals do inbreed, but without committing socio-psychological incest. This basic point was, I think, first made by Lowie (*51*), though I have considerably elaborated its corollaries (*31*, chap. 7).

94 On the basis of rigorous epistemological and logical considerations, I have repeatedly shown (*23*, *27*, *31*) that a myth—or indeed, any human activity whatsoever—which is explained in terms of *one* frame of reference *only* is, so to speak, not explained *at all*.

95 Cp. the initial "warming up" reaction of Madjapahit (Java) soldiers ordered to run *amok* against the Malaccan ambassador (*1*).

96 Cp. the simulation of madness by Solon (Plu. *V. Sol.* 8), or the self-exonerating simulation of madness by the Cretans during rites commemorating the rending of the infant Dionysos (Firm. Mat. *de err. prof. rel.* 6). Comparable primitive data exist (*30*, chap. 1, p. 39).

can, in fact, be Inachos, for, by settling this problem at once, I can substantially abridge my discussion of Io's waking reactions to her dream and of Inachos' responses to Io's revelations.

(IV) "*Zeus*" = *Inachos*.

(1) As already noted, Inachos, being a river god, is necessarily horned like a bull—and Zeus mounts the heifer Io in the shape of a bull (A. *Suppl.* 301).

(2) It is today a commonplace, even amongst the most naive critics of Freud, that man's *image* of the deity is patterned upon the child's *image* of the parent (*45*). Both Platon (*Legg.* 931A) and Ploutarchos (*frr.* 46, 86 Sandb.) saw in the parent the image of the deity. This parallels the Greek notion that Agamemnon's kingship was patterned on that of Zeus, though modern scholars realize that the reverse is true. One should also recall that one of Zeus' principal epithets was: father (of gods and of men), and this even though he personally engendered neither Poseidon, Hades, Hera, etc., nor, e.g., Theseus, son of Poseidon.

(3) According to certain traditions (supra), Hippodameia, whose virginity was also unduly prolonged, committed incest with her father Oinomaos, and her myth is manifestly related to a pastoral (horse, mule) fertility rite (*20*).[97]

(4) If one assumes the existence of a rite, the horned Inachos and Io-the-heifer can suitably impersonate Zeus in a bull epiphany and cow-eyed Hera.[98]

(5) If one considers only the dream, the symbolization of Zeus by Inachos in dream would suitably disguise from Io's "dream censor" (Freud) her incestuous craving for her father.

In short, in the present context, and as regards the dream's command viewed psycho-analytically, it does not matter in the least whether Io wished to cohabit with "Zeus" or with Inachos, whether she "did" so in a human or in a bovine form, nor even whether this "happened" in dream, in fantasy, in a hallucination during a ritual, or simply in the course of a non-ritual incestuous act. All that matters is that the triggering force of all these alternatives presupposes, in A. *PV*, an oedipal-incestuous *craving* on Io's part. Once this is made clear, one understands also why Lerne is explicitly defined in dream as the grazing place of *Inachos' cattle*. For incest, which, as already noted, greatly troubles an ordinary person, does not worry animals[99] or, for that matter, gods and their like. Precisely because Io's dream advocates a *divine* mating, that union must, of necessity, be incestuous from the human standpoint—which, in turn, explains Io's madness.

[97] I note that Nausikaa, whose dream somewhat resembles that of Io (supra), belonged to a royal family which practised brother-sister incest. On this latter point, and on the partial bowdlerization of this clear statement in the *Odyssey*, cp. Vidal-Naquet (*69*).

[98] Cp. Semele demanding, on Hera's advice, that Zeus cohabit with her *the way* he cohabits with Hera (Apollod. 3.4.3; Hyg. *fab.* 167, 179).

[99] Diogenes ap. D. Chr. 10.29; cp. also the comments of Knox (*44*, p. 206) and Vernant (*67*, chap. 5). This realistic view antedates tales of the avoidance of incest by horses (Arist. *HA* 9.47 f; Plin. *HN* 8.156; Varro *RR* 2.7.9; Ael. *NA* 4.7) or by camels (Ael. *NA* 3.47). (I could find no tales of cattle avoiding incest.) These late tales were perhaps meant to condemn the animalistic exhibitionism of the Cynics.

Associations to the Dream

Associations, which help one to interpret the dream, are provided both by Io's reactions to her dream and by Inachos' complementary response to Io's telling him her dream. These responses—which are paired, reciprocal "acting out" patterns—are of exceptional usefulness for the understanding of this dream's latent content.

One of our most telling data is the contrast between Io's affective state *during* her dream and her very different affective response to her *remembrance* of the dream.

Io's Affective State While Dreaming is not clearly specified; this is unusual in Greek tragedy.[100]

Still, Io's emotions during her dream are not beyond conjecture. The use of the word λεῖος (smooth, insinuating) practically guarantees that the dream-affect was not altogether unpleasant; the command she received in dream was not *greatly* at variance with her—already preconscious —sexual desires. None the less, the fact that she had to be urged on in dream, suggests some fear of her desires and so does the perplexity she feels on awakening. In dream, she eludes responsibility for her *wishes* by *projecting* them on "Zeus" (supra), as she projects her *consent* to such a union on the dream-voice, which only provides Io with *reasons* for doing what she already *wishes* to do. Even the fact that the conflict is "solved" *in dream* is a means of exonerating the dreamer (*39*).

But even these indications of struggle do not prove that Io's dream was primarily a genuine anxiety dream. Had the dream been *violently* ego-dystonic, it would presumably have disturbed her sleep—and this Io's dream failed to do. At the same time, the dream was not wholly ego-syntonic either, for otherwise she would simply have dreamed of cohabiting with "Zeus".

Io's Waking Responses to her dream are, as already noted, affectively far more intense and uncomfortable than was the affect she felt while dreaming. This finding is crucial for the correct interpretation of her dream.

On awakening, Io's dominant emotion is: perplexity. The command she receives in dream is twofold:

(1) "Cease to be a virgin", i.e., contract a union;

(2) Contract a union with "*Zeus*" (at Lerne).

I hold that Io's perplexity on awakening is due to the fact that she reacted differently to the two components of the dream-command. The dream did not upset her *while* asleep, for in sleep and dream the unconscious, governed by the pleasure-principle, usually has the upper hand. It is only on awakening that Io becomes disturbed, for the waking mind is subject to the reality-principle (*38*), which includes taking into account also the "reality" of law and custom (νόμος). Most people have had the experience of being disturbed, *on awakening*, by a dream whose *manifest*

---

100 Thus, the dreaming Menelaos' initial happiness soon turns into a mournful frustration (chap. 3). In dreaming of a grieving Dareios, Atossa expresses the grief *she* feels while dreaming (chap. 1), etc.

content *seems* harmless enough: their subsequent distress is caused by the seemingly innocuous dream's *latent* content.[101]

Now, in mythical Greek society, which did not depreciate sexuality even in women, a dream-command to contract a (normal) union would not have distressed, but gladdened, a princess—especially one who had been a virgin far too long.[102] In fact, a Greek princess would not have needed such a dream-command. At most, her dream might have suggested to her that she should marry the particular king or noble she desired.[103] She might even have dreamed of making love with a suitable future mate, and would have felt no distress or shame because of her dream. The classic example is the dream Athene sent to Nausikaa (Hom. *Od.* 6.13–51), which, as already noted, has many elements in common with Io's dream. Yet Nausikaa is not in the least disturbed by her dream's command, for a *suitable* husband is implicitly promised to her: she joyfully hastens to carry out the dream's instructions as soon as she awakens.

Even better evidence is furnished by the erotic dream of a mythical married woman. Penelope is not ashamed of having made love in dream with her absent husband Odysseus. She only regrets that the dream was not reality (Hom. *Od.* 20.87 ff.). Even the Sophoklean Klytaimnestra's erotic dream frightens her only because her dream partner was Agamemnon, the husband she herself had slain (chap. 7).

I therefore hold that if the dream had urged this more than nubile princess, belonging to a society which valued female sexuality, to marry a *suitable* partner, the dream would have elicited no discomfort. In fact, had *that* been Io's desire, she might not have dreamed of being simply commanded to forsake her virginity—she might very well have dreamed of actual love-making.

This indicates that what elicits perplexity and discomfort in Io is not the warning that it is time for her to cease to be a virgin, but the command to surrender her virginity to an *outlandish* partner: "Zeus" (cp. chap. 7).

The perplexity becomes immediately understandable *only* if one assumes that "Zeus" symbolizes a *tabooed* partner: Inachos. It also explains why, in the dream, an initial reference to Io's protracted—and frustrating— virginity is followed *at once* by an elaborate description of the sexual frustration of her prospective partner. This shift of focus constitutes a brilliant description of the self-disculpating, Super-ego-bribing defence by projection ("not I but you desire tabooed sex") commonly encountered both in dream and in waking life.

Summing up, a mythical Greek princess did not need a dream to tell her that sexuality is good—she took that for granted. But she would have needed much dream-encouragement in order to surrender to a *tabooed* sexual partner.

This view is fully confirmed by Io's waking behaviour. The normal

101 In 1956, I developed a projective test whose third part reveals the anxiety the *latent* content of the answers given to the first two questions elicits. The test was recently validated statistically by my student, Dr Mathilde Boccara (*5*).

102 I recall again that many upper-class Athenian girls married soon after reaching puberty.

103 There survives to this day the European folk belief that a girl can see her future spouse in dream, or in a mirror (*62*), etc.

Greek response to a disturbing dream was to "sterilize" it, by telling it to the sunlight and, at times, also by performing apotropaic rites.[104]

But Io does nothing of the kind. Instead, she tells her dream to her father Inachos. This represents a complicated neurotic manœuvre— partly evasive, since she "puts it up" to Inachos. Her telling the dream to her father is less a narrative than a "confession", and a double-edged one at that.

Indeed, on one level, it is an unconscious (or perhaps already pre-conscious) attempt at seduction: in compliance with the dream voice's *latent* advice, Io informs Inachos of her "availability". Such devious seductions are common not only in daily life, but also in psychotherapy and even in projective psychological testing (cp. chap. 3, note 108).

But, on another level, Io's "confession" is a demand for punishment. A scrutiny of Inachos' reactions to Io's account is therefore imperative.

Inachos responds to Io's perplexity and to her attempts to leave the decision up to him with a perplexity reaction of his own. Instead of taking a stand, he consults *two separate* oracles.[105] This is perhaps the only case in which a *ritual* oracle is asked to clarify a *dream* oracle. But the repeatedly consulted oracles' responses are at first riddling and incomprehensible (658 ff.).

At this point, something need be said about oracles in general. Fenichel (*36*) noted that the "misunderstanding" of oracles is psychologically determined. This is true, so far as it goes, but involves the erroneous (implicit) assumption that an oracle's utterances are not only "meaningful", but also that they have *one* "real" meaning only. But the fact is that *no* oracle has a real, *inherent* meaning. It has no meaning *other* than that which the oracle's client *ascribes* to it because of his own subjective needs, fears and inclinations (*25*).[106]

In short, when consulting an oracle, the client unwittingly invites the oracle to substitute for a meaningful though perplexing *real* quandary a *verbal* "riddle", *inherently devoid of any sense whatever*, and which *still* leaves the task of solving his problem—now disguised as an oracular riddle—to the client. In fact, the sole benefit a client derives from consulting an oracle is the dubious privilege of blaming the oracle for his own subsequent mistakes (*25*).[107]

I hold that the first replies the oracles gave to Inachos were inherently

---

[104] A. *Pers.* 200 ff.; E. *Hec.* 68; E. *IT* 43 ff. On the psychotherapeutic use of sunlight, cp. E. *Ba.* 1264 ff., discussed elsewhere (*28*). For the primacy of sight—which is the only sense never normally stimulated before birth—as the principal mediator of reality and as the mind's main defence against the dark world of the instincts and fantasms, cp. *13*, *22* and chap. 1, note 3.

[105] The Athenians consulted the Pythia twice, Hdt. 7.141 f.

[106] The bold Themistokles, grasping at the straw of one word: θείη (holy) Salamis, occurring in a catastrophically discouraging oracle, gave battle and defeated Persia (Hdt. 7.143). The timid Nikias saw nothing but calamity in a favourable eclipse which could have concealed from the foe the Athenians' flight; though everything was prepared, he wasted time, and wrecked his chances (Plu. *V. Nic.* 23). Cp. chap. 6 and chap. 8, note 146.

[107] Cp. Kroisos' blaming of the Delphic oracle for his catastrophic resistance to Persia— and the oracle's self-exculpating reply, which placed the blame on Kroisos himself (Hdt. 1.90). The cynicism of the Delphic oracle, which I take for granted, does not concern me here.

no more riddling than the last. They *seemed* more riddling to Inachos only because *his* mind was not yet made up. When he finally decided to resist Io's tacit seductions, the new oracle suddenly became "understandable" *to Inachos*. For, by then, all he wanted was an excuse for expelling Io, *as though* she had *openly* tried to seduce him and had actually managed at least to tempt him.[108]

In short, while Inachos still hesitates between yielding to and resisting temptation,[109] the answers of the oracles *seem* obscure—*to him*. When his mind is made up to resist temptation, the oracle's *last* answer *seems* suddenly comprehensible—*to him*. I hold that it would have seemed comprehensible to him even if it had consisted of the Hebrew alphabet or the table of multiplication. I stress here a well-documented fact: repeated consultations of an oracle could *not* change the tenor of its response (Hdt. 7.141); all that they could change was the *client's* mood.

Returning to Io, in expelling her from his home Inachos literally *forced* her to comply with the *manifest* dictates of the dream-voice, for the most natural refuge for Io, the outcast, was precisely the half-wild pasture land of Lerne.[110]

The preceding paragraphs presuppose that the daughter's oedipal advances are tacitly, *but well*, understood by the father, who is at first tempted by this stimulation of his so-called "counter-oedipal" (Laius) complex.[111] But, as he sends messenger after messenger to *two* oracles and, as time goes by, his Ego gains the upper hand over his Laius complex, he decides to get rid of the temptation once and for all. Otherwise expressed, in expelling Io, he both punishes her for her incestuous "availability" and protects himself against her tempting "seductiveness". Had he not been tempted, his "understanding" of the oracles would have been, predictably, very different.

One last point to be made is that Inachos is, at this time, apparently a widower, for, in A. *PV*, Io's mother is no more mentioned than are the mothers of the Danaides in A. *Suppl.*, or the mother of Hippodameia in the non-genealogical parts of the tales concerning her. As both common sense and daily experience show, such a familial situation is likely to intensify the attachment between the widowed or divorced father and his

---

[108] Inachos repeatedly sent messengers both to Delphi and to Dodona, but we are *not* told outright *which* of the two gave at last a "clear" reply. I think that *that* reply came from Dodona—partly because Dodona was Zeus' own oracle, partly because, at A. *PV* 830 ff., the oaks "speak clearly, not in riddling terms" to Io and, finally, because, at A. *PV* 668, the oracle threatens Inachos to enforce its orders with *Zeus'* typical weapon: the thunderbolt.

[109] Or, culturally speaking, resisting the order to perform an obscene pastoral fertility rite.

[110] It is well to recall here all the heroes exposed in infancy and saved by herdsmen or even nursed by female domestic animals. Such tales reveal well the way the Greeks *imagined* life in the pastoral "wilds".

[111] I say "so-called" for, as I have shown elsewhere, both ontogenetically and logically the Laius-complex precedes and elicits the child's oedipal reactions (*15, 31*, chap. 7). My theory has the advantage of being based not on adult fantasies, but on experimentally verifiable, biological and physiological facts. It is therefore—needless to say—inacceptable to Klein-ians. But I think it would have been acceptable to Ferenczi, who had a dedication to hard facts, which is becoming increasingly unfashionable amongst certain analysts, more interested in "philosophy" than in science.

unwed daughter. And, as any social worker, psychiatrist or even police-man can tell, in such situations incest is a far from rare consequence of this intensified attachment.[112]

Summary. Io's repetitive dream reflects a breakthrough of the instincts in dream. The inhibiting anxiety is experienced only in daytime. The strife between the two is described with great subtlety. In dream, Io's wish—voiced by the dream-figure—explicitly takes cognizance of the existence of inhibiting forces and crowds them off the stage on which the dream un-folds itself. The dream-voice urges her to yield to her impulses and to overcome her scruples; the inhibiting force is, by contrast, not represented directly in the dream. It manifests itself only in the waking state, eliciting anxiety and forcing Io to indulge in self-punitive acting out, which takes the form of a damaging confession.

APPENDIX

I have deliberately left to the last a striking parallel of father-daughter incest, in which the daughter's quasi-transformation into a cow is a conse-quence of the incest. The Pharaoh Mykerinos raped his daughter, who then hanged herself from shame; her father caused her corpse to be buried inside a handsomely manufactured *cow*, which apparently served as her coffin (Hdt. 2.129 ff.). It is precisely the modification of the narrative sequence—the replacing of the pre-incest metamorphosis into a cow by a post-incest "entombment" into a cow-shaped sarcophagus—that high-lights the importance for the understanding of Io's dream of the notion that incest is animalistic, non-human behaviour. The tale of Pasiphae (submitting sexually to a bull, hidden *inside* an artificial cow) serves, in a sense, as a bridge between the tale of Io and that of Mykerinos' daughter.[113]

Bibliography

(1) Anonymus: *Hikayat Hang Tuah* (H. Overbeck transl.). München, 1922.

(2) Baker, S. J.: Language and Dreams, *International Journal of Psycho-Analysis* 31:171–178, 1950.

(3) Besançon, Alain: *Le Tsarevitch Immolé*. Paris, 1967.

(4) Boas, Franz: The Eskimo of Baffin Land and Hudson Bay, *American Museum of Natural History, Bulletin* 15 pt. 1. New York, 1907.

(5) Boccara, Mathilde: *L'Image des Rapports Interpersonnels à Travers un Nouveau Test*. (Ph.D. Thesis, MS.). Paris, 1969.

[112] Cp. *61, 71*. Two of my students, Melle Elisabeth Pimare, a psychiatric social worker, and Mme Annick Le Guen, M.A., a psycho-analyst, had recently studied a group of girls who became incestuously pregnant. Their data confirm the views expressed above.

[113] For the willingness of a male animal to try to mount the statue of a female animal as a test of its lifelikeness, cp. Paus. 5. 27.3; yet *that* statue represented an *ugly* mare.

(6) Burkert, Walter: *Homo Necans*. Berlin, 1972.

(7) id.: Personal Communication, 1970.

(8) Carpenter, Rhys: *Folk Tale, Fiction and Saga in the Homeric Epics*[3]. Berkeley, California, 1958.

(9) Clifford, Sir Hugh: Tûkang Bûrok's Story (in) *The Further Side of Silence*. New York, 1922.

(10) Cook, A. B.: *Zeus*, 3. Cambridge, 1940.

(11) Devereux, George: *Sedang Field Notes* (MS.), 1933–1935.

(12) id.: Social Structure and the Economy of Affective Bonds, *Psychoanalytic Review* 29:303–314, 1942.

(13) id.: A Note on Nyctophobia and Peripheral Vision, *Bulletin of the Menninger Clinic* 13:83–93, 1949.

(14) id.: Heterosexual Behavior of the Mohave Indians (in) Róheim, Géza (ed.) *Psycho-Analysis and the Social Sciences* 2. New York, 1950.

(15) id.: Why Oedipus Killed Laïus: A Note on the Complementary Oedipus Complex, *International Journal of Psycho-Analysis* 34:132–141, 1953.

(16) id.: Anthropological Data Suggesting Unexplored Unconscious Attitudes Toward and In Unwed Mothers, *Archives of Criminal Psychodynamics* 1:564–576, 1955.

(17) id.: *Therapeutic Education*. New York, 1956.

(18) id.: A Note on the Feminine Significance of the Eyes, *Bulletin of the Philadelphia Association for Psychoanalysis* 6:21–24, 1956.

(19) id.: The Displacement of Modesty from Pubis to Face, *Psychoanalytic Review* 52:391–399, 1965.

(20) id.: The Abduction of Hippodameia as 'Aition' of a Greek Animal Husbandry Rite, *Studi e Materiali di Storia delle Religioni* 36:3–25, 1965.

(21) id.: Mumbling, *Journal of the American Psychoanalytic Association* 14:478–484, 1966.

(22) id.: Rapports Cliniques et Phylogénétiques entre les Odeurs et les Emotions dans la Névrose Caractérielle d'un Hottentot Griqua, *Psychopathologie Africaine* 2 (no. 1):65–76, 1966.

(23) id.: *From Anxiety to Method in the Behavioral Sciences*. Paris and The Hague, 1967.

(24) id.: Observation and Belief in Aischylos' Accounts of Dreams, *Psychotherapy and Psychosomatics* 15:114–134, 1967.

(25) id.: Considérations Psychanalytiques sur la Divination, Particulièrement en Grèce (in) Caquot, A. and Leibovici M. (eds.): *La Divination* vol. 2, pp. 449–471. Paris, 1968.

(26) id.: *Mohave Ethnopsychiatry and Suicide*. (Second, augmented edition), Washington, D.C., 1969.

(27) id.: La Naissance d'Aphrodite (in) Pouillon, Jean and Maranda, Pierre (eds.): *Echanges et Communications* (*Mélanges Lévi-Strauss*), 2.1229–1252. Paris and The Hague, 1970.

(28) id.: The Psychotherapy Scene in Euripides' *Bacchae*, *Journal of Hellenic Studies* 90:35–48, 1970.

(29) id.: *Psychoanalysis and the Occult* (ed. and contrib.) Reprint (hard cover and paperback). New York, 1970.

(30) id.: *Essais d'Ethnopsychiatrie Générale*. Paris, 1970. (Second edition, 1973).

(31) id.: *Ethnopsychanalyse Complémentariste*. Paris, 1972.

(32) id.: The Self-Blinding of Oidipous (Dodds *Festschrift*), *Journal of Hellenic Studies* 93:36–49, 1973.

(33) Dodds, E. R.: *The Greeks and the Irrational*. Berkeley, California, 1953.

(34) Edelstein, E. J. and Edelstein, Ludwig: *Asclepius* 2 vols. Baltimore, 1945.

(35) Evans-Pritchard, E. E.: *Witchcraft, Oracles and Magic among the Azande*. Oxford, 1937.

(36) Fenichel, Otto: The Misapprehended Oracle (in) *The Collected Papers of O. Fenichel*, 2. New York, 1954.

(37) Ferenczi, Sándor: Nakedness as a Means of Inspiring Terror (in) *Further Contributions to the Theory and Technique of Psycho-Analysis*. London, 1926.

(38) Freud, Sigmund: Formulations of the two Principles of Mental Functioning, *Standard Edition* 12. London, 1958.

(39) id.: Moral Responsibilities for the Content of Dreams, *Standard Edition* 19. London, 1961.

(40) Gorer, Geoffrey: *Himalayan Village*[2]. New York, 1967.

(41) Gruppe, Otto: *Griechische Mythologie und Religionsgeschichte* 2 vols. München, 1906.

(42) Jones Ernest: The Madonna's Conception through the Ear (in) *Essays in Applied Psycho-Analysis*, 2. London, 1951.

(43) Junod, H.: *The Life of a South African Tribe*. London, 1927.

(44) Knox, B. M. W.: *Oedipus at Thebes*. New Haven, 1957.

(45) Kouretas, Demetrios: Ἀνώμαλοι Χαρακτῆρες εἰς τὸ Ἀρχαῖον Δρᾶμα. Athens, 1951.

(46) La Barre, Weston: *The Ghost Dance*. New York, 1970.

(47) Le Guérinel, E. N.: *Contribution à l'Etude des Mécanismes de Défense et de l'Adaptation chez des Consultants Africains en Voie de Développement Rapide* (M.A. Thesis, MS.). Paris, 1971.

(48) Lennig, R.: *Traum und Sinnestäuschung bei Aischylos, Sophokles, Euripides*. Berlin, 1969.

(49) Licht, H.: *Sexual Life in Ancient Greece*[8]. London, 1956.

(50) Loeb, E. M.: Personal Communications.

(51) Lowie, R. H.: The Family as a Social Unit, *Papers of the Michigan Academy of Science, Arts and Letters* 18:53–69, 1933.

(52) Malinowski, Bronislaw: *The Sexual Life of Savages in North-Western Melanesia*[3]. London, 1932.

(53) Malten, Ludolfus: *Die Sprache des menschlichen Antlitzes im frühen Griechentum*. Berlin, 1961.

(54) Marcadé, Jean: *Eros Kalos*. Geneva, 1965.

(55) Murray, Gilbert: *The Rise of the Greek Epic*[4]. Oxford, 1960.

(56) Nilsson, M. P.: *Geschichte der griechischen Religion* I[2]. München, 1955.

(57) Padel, Ruth: Unpublished MS., 1970.

(58) Page, D. L.: *Literary Papyri, Poetry* (Loeb Classical Library). London, 1950.

(59) Page, D. (L.): *The Homeric Odyssey*. Oxford, 1955.

(60) Rasmussen, Knud: *Across Arctic America*. New York, 1927.

(61) Riemer, Svend: A Research Note on Incest, *American Journal of Sociology* 45:566–575, 1940.

(62) Róheim, Géza: *Spiegelzauber*. Leipzig, 1919.

(63) Roscher, W. H. (ed.): *Ausführliches Lexikon der griechischen und römischen Mythologie*. Leipzig, 1884–1937.

(64) Saul, L. J.: Feminine Significance of the Nose, *Psychoanalytic Quarterly* 17:51–57, 1948.

(65) Snell, Bruno: Aischylos und das Handeln im Drama (*Philologus Supplement* 20.1). Leipzig, 1928.

(66) Uchimura, Y., Akimoto, H., and Ishibashi, T.: On the Imu of the Ainu Race I [in Japanese with an English Summary], *Psychiatria et Neurologia Japonica* 42:1–69, 1–3; 1938.

(67) Vernant, J. P.: Ambiguité et Renversement (in) Vernant, J.-P. and Vidal-Naquet, Pierre: *Mythe et Tragédie en Grèce Ancienne* chap. 5. Paris, 1972.

(68) Vidal-Naquet, Pierre: The Black Hunter and the Origin of Athenian Ephebeia, *Proceedings of the Cambridge Philological Society* no. 194:49–64, 1968.

(69) id.: Valeurs Religieuses et Mythiques de la Terre et du Sacrifice dans l'*Odyssée*, *Annales: Economies, Sociétés, Civilisations* 25:1278–1297, 1970.

(70) id.: Chasse et Sacrifice dans l'*Orestie* d'Eschyle (in) Vernant, J.-P. and Vidal-Naquet, Pierre: *Mythe et Tragédie en Grèce Ancienne* chap. 6. Paris, 1972.

(71) Weinberg, S. K.: *Incest Behavior*. New York, 1955.

(72) Wilamowitz-Moellendorff, Ulrich von: *Der Glaube der Hellenen²*. Basel, 1959.

(73) Winiarz, Wiktor and Wielawski, J.: Imu. A Psychoneurosis Occurring among the Ainus, *Psychoanalytic Review* 23:181–186, 1936.

(74) Zuckerman (Sir) Solly: *The Social Life of Monkeys and Apes*. London, 1932.

Chapter 3

Menelaos' Reactive Depression and Dream

(Aischylos: *Agamemnon* 410–426)

Preamble

Aischylos' account of Menelaos' dream and, indeed, the passage that leads up to it, are a nonpareil performance, even for one of the greatest poets of all time. The perfect, musical blending of the metre with meaning, quite as much as the alternation of sharp images with appropriately blurred ones combine into a dazzlingly complex and sweeping torrential poetic eloquence, in which image caps realistic image with an absolute parsimony of means. Each word opens new vistas of perception, indispensably clarifies and completes what went before and hints at what is to come. An additional halo of meanings, of singular richness, is provided by means of poetic enumerations, whose impact is further increased by their flawless arrangement. There is perfection in the overall logic of the whole passage, in the complete realism of all details, and in the manner in which their enumeration fits the inherent structure of the objective event. It is extraordinary for any poetry to have all these qualities—great poets at their best often achieve less.

But Aischylos achieved more: this choral passage, shimmering with many-faceted, allusive overtones, is almost more than poetry—it is, at times, sheer archaic magic surging from the depths of the human psyche. It is also the psychologically most persuasive Aischylean account of a dream experience, made more compelling still by the manner in which it is narrated: it is practically an epitome of Freud's great study, *Mourning and Melancholia* (*71*). There are few passages in the world's treasury of poetry which confirm so well Freud's repeated assertion that the poets had *intuitively* anticipated much of his work. This is another way of saying that all great poetry is *psychologically realistic*, in that it reflects objective reality through the medium of psychic reality (fantasy, dream and affect). Even when a merely good poet—not a great one—simply seeks to describe external reality, his writings are poetry not because the reality he describes well is beautiful, but because, in describing it, he reveals—at times unintentionally and even against his will—his own reactions to it.

It is not my purpose to suggest that Aischylos meant to epitomize the symptomatology and psychodynamics of a reactive depression, nor to praise him for having done just that in a poetical form. My analysis of this passage seeks to do more than just interpret the psychopathology of Menelaos' grief and the latent content of his dream. I also try, as best I can, to shed some light upon how a great poet's mind operates: upon the almost incomprehensible sureness of his touch, in saying things both varied and moving in a few words marvellously arranged so as to tighten their interdependence while expanding their scope.

In affirming that much patience and some familiarity both with the things the poet seeks to describe and with the functioning of the human mind enables us to identify nearly all strands of his web and to define their reciprocal relationship, I also affirm the intelligibility of artistic creation and creativity and of the mind of a genius;[1] for I believe that the great poet has—*spontaneously* and simultaneously—access to *all* his inner re-

[1] On this point I disagree with Freud (*69*) who, I believe, abandoned his attempt too soon (*30*).

sources, while ordinary men have access to their's only at different times. I think I have identified most of the components of this passage and have defined most of their reciprocal relationships. But whereas it probably took Aischylos only a few minutes to write these verses, I had to devote three years to the exploring of each word and conjunction of words individually, both in a cultural and in a psychological perspective.[2] I discovered new details on each reading and learned something from each commentary of the text. I think I have discovered *nearly* all that some philological and a not inconsiderable clinical competence can detect, when animated by a passion for poetry. But I have assuredly not discovered all this passage contains, because the poet's genius, quite as much as the psyche of the simplest patient is, by definition, inexhaustible (*74*). My analysis of this passage will not teach anyone to write good poetry, but it may increase one's faith in the intelligibility of even the greatest poetry and of the most creative mind.

I am not analysing here Aischylos the man, nor have I anything to say about his personality, in the clinical sense. I am scrutinizing one of his most magnificent performances. I try to highlight its infinite richness and subtlety and only say: this is how a great poet's mind works. The reader can decide for himself how much of what I say is literary criticism and how much a psychological analysis of the operations of the mind of a genius. For me, the two are not simply inseparable, but almost identical.

The great mathematician, K. F. Gauss, once remarked: "I have had my results for a long time now—but I do not know as yet how I shall reach my conclusions." Sophokles said of Aischylos that he did the right thing—but without knowing what he was doing (Athen. 10.428F). These two remarks do not simply explain the nature of genius; they also guarantee its intelligibility.

Methodological Introduction. Since Menelaos' dream is the climactic symptom of his depression, I must, exceptionally, scrutinize with equal care also the passage which depicts his distress. Indeed, already pseudo Longinos (10.1) noted that poets describe groups of meshing symptoms, forming a syndrome, and an analysis of Sapph. *fr.* 31 LP proved him right (*43, contra 110*).

The length of the passage studied—and its intricacies—inevitably make this chapter somewhat long. But what Lagrange said of Nature also applies to great poetry: it does not care with how great difficulties it confronts its students.

I propose to show, in addition, that not just the content, but also the manner of the narration is psychologically persuasive. In a genuine sense, its poetic perfection is also prima facie evidence of its credibility. In discussing problems, I must, time and again, deal with matters unfamiliar to the student of Greek drama as literature. I would plead that if Fraenkel had to devote a big page of fine print to the elucidation of the metallurgical credibility of a passing and metaphorical allusion to bad bronze (ad A. *Ag.* 391), it stands to reason that the far more complex and important intricacies of a distressed mind call for an even more detailed commentary.

---

2 However, the great poet need simply express himself—he need not identify and label every one of his "moves". Since that is what the creative psychological critic must do, his task is, in a way, harder than that of the poet he studies (J.W.D.).

The Text I print is, with two exceptions—one being v. 413 ἀφημένων Dindorf, and the other v. 426—that of Fraenkel,[3] though I place my quotation marks somewhat differently (infra). Also, for the convenience of the non-Hellenist, I arrange vv. 421 f. like Fränkel, for I regularly refer to him. Unlike a few editors, I place no part of the text between daggers, for I do not think this passage contains any *locus desperatus*.

I note, in fine, that, except for v. 426, I offer no new emendation of my own, for, in each instance, at least one of the emendations already proposed gives a psychologically satisfying sense.

The Corruptions in this passage attest its clinical credibility; Aischylos' text appears to have disturbed at least one copyist enough to cause him to perpetrate errors. Now, clinical experience shows that the nature of a lapsus not only helps to restore the correct sense, but also sheds light upon its *latent* content—for a lapsus is always a compromise between what the poet wrote and what the copyist could tolerate. In that sense, the copyist's lapsus is sometimes similar to a bad pun or to a portemanteau word—as my discussion of the corrupt word in vv. 412–413 (ΑΔΙCΤΟC) will show.

In short, though the philologist cannot but deplore the text's defects, their psychological scrutiny promotes the psycho-analytical comprehension of the text as a whole.[4]

At the same time, one must be extremely vigilant when trying to rectify an error, for lapses are, at times, almost grotesquely contagious.[5]

The Interpretation and Emendation of the text of a "psychiatric" description, which can still convince and move the reader, must make controversial words and meanings fit clinical realities, for the nature of depressions has changed as little since Aischylos' time as has that of inferior bronze. I simply stress that just as Fraenkel (ad A. *Ag.* 391) could cite on this matter the opinion of an electrochemist, without implying thereby that Aischylos owned or managed a bronze foundry, so I do not mean to suggest that Aischylos had read Freud. I assume only that he used his eyes and his empathy, for there was no lack of mourners after Marathon and Salamis. Moreover, the symptoms of depression are both visible and striking; also, the depressed often insistently communicate their thoughts and feelings to anyone who will listen (*71*). This last comment is crucial from the viewpoint of the text-critical rule enunciated by P. Maas: "we must go . . . in matters of content, by the author's presumable knowledge or point of view." Maas also adds that, on certain matters, the editor of a text must consult the outside expert (as Fraenkel did). In plain language, when I discuss Aischylos' description of an *observable* depression, the question is not whether Aischylos had read Freud—but whether I have done so.[6]

---

[3] I disregard here Fraenkel's very tentative emendation of the last word of v. 426, which he, himself, relegated to his apparatus criticus.

[4] For a formal theory of the scientific exploitability of errors, cp. (*39*).

[5] Baker's discussion (*3*, p. 406) of Australian mispronunciations of foreign words includes a reference to the mis*pronunciation* of a name—Courvoisier—which Baker mis*spells*: Courvoissier. X argued with a native of Brooklyn about the correct pronunciation of "oyster". In the end X, annoyed by his interlocutor, said: "At any rate I never oyder örsters."

[6] Having failed to do so, Thomson (ad A. *Ag.* 416) calls Fraenkel's persuasive psychological comments "absurd".

Though I will have to mention this matter again, I indicate that Aischylos himself had had the experience of grievous personal loss. His brother Kynegeiros fell with a good deal of glory at Marathon and I am inclined to think that Aischylos—like some other mourners—partly identified himself with his heroic brother.[7] This may perhaps explain a peculiarity of the epitaph Aischylos wrote for himself. It mentions only his (Kynegeiros-like) heroism when facing the Persian host, but does not even allude to his fame as a poet.[8] As to Aischylos' capacity to describe extreme fear and anguish, it need no longer be demonstrated (*18*). In short, I impute no knowledge to Aischylos which he did not manifestly have.

Still, one *caveat* seems in order. A. *Pers.* 249 ff. (and passim) is poetry and not a treatise on naval tactics, though it does yield information about naval tactics to a historian or to an admiral. Though A. *Ag.* 410–426, too, is primarily poetry and not a monograph on depressions, it tells the psychiatrist that depressions have not changed much since Aischylos' time. Hence, since the non-corrupt and non-controversial portions of the text fit clinical realities perfectly, one's first working hypothesis, as regards the rest, must be that it *also* makes psychiatric sense.[9] This technique is no different from that of emending, e.g., a hypothetical defect in the surviving Aischylean account of Salamis, in the light of a knowledge of seamanship.

The final argument militating in favour of the clinical accuracy of this text is that it describes an *extreme* emotional state, which is psychologically "simpler" than are (culture-bound) logical thought processes or systems of classification.[10]

We can feel Menelaos' elemental grief in our bones, for he writes about timeless human beings—as must every tragic poet if his work is to be more "philosophical" than history.[11] But we respond less to Straton's "love" sorrows, for, being those of a homosexual Greek of the decadence, they are both strikingly (and neurotically) idiosyncratic and also narrowly culture-bound. And yet, though humanly more universal, Aischylos' Menelaos is more differentiated than is Straton, whose individual differentiatedness, like that of a great many people living in periods of socio-cultural decay, is artificial, uncreative and even self-destructive (*52*, chap. 6).

[7] Cp. my comments on the ambiguous phantom in v. 415. On the death of Kynegeiros, cp. Hdt. 6.114.

[8] If one assumes that Aischylos drew for clues upon his own experience of grief, one presupposes self-observation. Cp. Page's (*118*, p. 27) comments on Sappho's capacity for self-observation; also (*43*). Cp. also chap. 4, appendix ii.

[9] For a similar defence of a psychiatrically appropriate old emendation of Sapph. *fr.* 31.9 LP, cp. (*43*).

[10] Cp. the admirable and intricately wrought studies of J.-P. Vernant and his collaborators on the culture-linked aspects of Greek conscious thought processes and systems of classification.

[11] Arist. *Poet.* 1451b5.

ΧΟΡΟΣ
" ἰὼ ἰώ, δῶμα δῶμα καὶ πρόμοι,　　　　　　　　　　　410
ἰὼ λέχος καὶ στίβοι φιλάνορες."
πάρεστι σιγὰς ἀτίμους ἀλοιδόρους ἀπίστους ἀφημένων ἰδεῖν.
πόθῳ δ' ὑπερποντίας
φάσμα δόξει δόμων ἀνάσσειν.　　　　　　　　　　　415
εὐμόρφων δὲ κολοσσῶν
ἔχθεται χάρις ἀνδρί,
ὀμμάτων δ' ἐν ἀχηνίαις
ἔρρει πᾶσ' Ἀφροδίτα.
ὀνειρόφαντοι δὲ πενθήμονες　　　　　　　　　　　420
πάρεισι δόξαι φέρουσαι χάριν ματαίαν·　　　　421–422
μάταν γάρ, εὖτ' ἂν ἐσθλά τις δοκῶν ὁρᾶν,
παραλλάξασα διὰ
χερῶν βέβακεν ὄψις, οὐ μεθύστερον　　　　　　　425
πτεροῖς ὀπαδοῖς ὕπνου †κέλευθοισ†.　　　　　　426
[πτέρωτ' ὀπαδοῦσ' ὕπνου κέλευθα.] (coni. G.D. et K.J.D.)　　[426]

(Fraenkel's text, *modified*)

V. 411 End of quotes. Many other editors end the quotes with v. 426
V. 413 ἀφημένων Dindorf is preferred to ἀφειμένων
V. 426 My *tentative* emendation is given in square brackets. See the
　　　commentary on that verse.

Paraphrase

Given the multivalence of countless words and expressions in this text, as
well as its extreme density, no verbatim translation can render its content
adequately for the Greekless reader. This obliges me, exceptionally, to
provide not a translation but a paraphrase.

"Alas, alas for the palace, the palace and its Head. Alas for the nuptial
couch and for the imprints which Helene's body left on it while, through
her embrace, she expressed love for her husband."

One can see the silence of the (socially and subjectively) dishonoured,
the non-vilifying, the incredulous (and suspicious), who sit apart (from
the others).

The yearning for her, who is beyond the seas, will make it seem that a
phantom (mis)governs the palace (and makes Menelaos himself also
seem ghost-like). The fair forms of the statues (of lovely girls) seem hateful
to the husband. In the inanimate (but, perhaps, also hungrily searching)
gaze of his eyes, all of Aphrodite (libido) is gone to wrack and ruin.

Mournful dream apparitions seem to bring joys that are vain, for
vainly, when in fancy one sees what is good, the vision, slipping sideways
out of the (dreamer's) arms' (embrace), is gone—never again to assume
(follow, imitate) the winged gait ("*allure*") of sleep.

The Choros' Sources of Information are as specifiable as Aischylos' opportunities for direct observation. This greatly enhances the psychological credibility of a tale which refers to events ten or twelve years old. This lapse of time need not cast doubt upon the accuracy of the Choros' recall of (striking) *royal* behaviour or of a royal dream,[12] in a culture which valued dreams and in which Menelaos' personal tragedy affected everyone (vv. 427 ff.)

It is, aesthetically, hardly necessary to ask where the Choros got the information it now transmits to us. But I hold that the psychological persuasiveness of the tale is greatly enhanced if one specifies the Choros' sources of information:

Vv. 409f. The palace prophets lament in public.

Vv. 411f. Menelaos' behaviour is not only observable but also fits cultural expectations. The complete congruence between what the Choros expected to see and what was, in fact, seen, helps one assume a correct recall of correct observations.

Vv. 413–419: It is to be noted that, once past the stuporous state, the depressed *insistently* narrate their feelings and thoughts (*71*). The (inferable) insistence of Menelaos' self-revelations would also insure their correct recall.

Vv. 420–426: We do not know whether Menelaos told his dream to his whole household, or only to a few persons close to him. But, in a dream-valuing culture, the correct recall of this dream would be greatly facilitated by its being a *typical* mourning and sexual frustration dream.

It goes without saying that the Choros' tale—and the personage of Menelaos—are Aischylean inventions. I am simply trying to stress that—were the situation real—one could lend credence to the Choros' narrative —which, in turn, enhances the plausibility of Aischylean fictions.

But there is one important conclusion to be drawn from all this. Menelaos' dream is so "appropriate" (and dreamlike), that—even though he certainly knew the *Iliad*—we are no more obliged to suppose that A. *Ag.* 420 ff., imitates Hom. *Il.* 23.65 ff., than we are obliged to assume that Milton's *Sonnet* xxiii is an imitation of Menelaos' dream.[13] A Seneca's inventions are largely bookish, even if he follows no model. A great poet's inspiration is life, and never more so than when an Aischylos recalls the grieving Homeric Achilleus' dream.

[12] Kroeber (*93*, chap. 51) calls Mohave culture a "dream culture". In such a culture a shaman could tell me one of his former patients' dream in almost the same words in 1932 and in 1938. Studies of modern non-literate folk bards (*105*) also show that people who do not routinely rely on writing can perform impressive feats of memory.

[13] At age 16, I had not read either of these dreams—which did not prevent me from trying, in dream, to enclasp and hold back the elusive dream-vision of my recently deceased brother.

General Comment: Structure and Progression (vv. 410–419)

Verses 410–426 form an organic whole. Each part is linked to every other part, and the points of linkage are also natural points of division; they correspond to "articulations" in Angyal's (*2*) holistic psychology. The very interdependence of the parts presupposes their distinctness: one can speak as legitimately of connecting separations as of separating connections.

I know, moreover, few poetic passages which so clearly reveal what Meyerson calls: *Le Cheminement de la Pensée* (*112*)—that great and realistic inner logic which informs all great poetry, but is seldom as discernible as it is in this instance.[14]

This compels me to devote a good deal of place to this narrative's structure, examining it from several points of view. Though all these diverse scrutinies end up by highlighting Aischylos' genius, I do not think I have, at any point, yielded to the temptation to indulge in the purely lyrical literary criticism so rightly condemned by Kitto (*91*, p. v). For, in my estimate, it is the extraordinary poetic quality of this passage which renders it psycho-analytically so exploitable. Not that Aischylos was familiar with Freud's *Mourning and Melancholia* (*71*)! It was Aischylos' *own* experience of personal (Hdt. 6.114) and national grief, undistortingly transmuted into poetry, that makes this passage superior to many an account of reactive depressions found in psychiatric textbooks.

I note, in fine, that this intricately woven passage is of special interest to the metalinguist. The constant re-evocation of what went before and anticipation of what is to come, gives it a polyphonic quality, which scientific discourse does not possess.[15]

Prophecy, Foresight, Anticipation. Verses 408 f.: "while the seers (προφῆται) of the house with many a groan, spake thus" (Fraenkel), have, I feel, misled certain commentators, causing them to assume that some or all the next 17 verses were uttered by the seers and have a prophetic character;[16] This matter is of some importance for the placing of the quotation marks (infra).

But, just as *non semper arcum tendit Apollo*, so Greek prophets did not prophesy incessantly. The real clue is that, both in S. *OT* and E. *Ba.*, Teiresias, the prophet *par excellence*, mainly defines the situation or problem and gives sensible advice which foretells, non-prophetically, the *logically* previsible consequences of a situation of stress. In other sources, the soothsayer reduces what the client apprehends as an omen to a practical matter.[17] Instead of requiring external information for their elucidation,

---

[14] I have stressed elsewhere that the scientist is constantly biased in two contradictory ways: uncritical over-empathy and defensive under-empathy (*39*). I have done my best to avoid—I hope not without success—both these pitfalls in discussing this passage, which has a singular appeal for me (note 13, supra).

[15] Lévi-Strauss (*98*) rightly deplores the inescapably homophonic character of scientific discourse, but did not note that his persuasive and intricate analysis of a Baudelaire poem (*87*) unwittingly highlights the (implicitly) polyphonic quality of great poetic diction.

[16] Fraenkel, ad loc., even cites the employment of dream-interpreters in some modern Greek households.

[17] Mice gnawed a hole into a superstitious man's sack of meal; the soothsayer he consulted told him to have it patched by a cobbler (Thphr. *Char.* 16.6). For Mohave parallels, cp. *42*, p. 175; *111*, p. 150.

vv. 408 f. tell us that household prophets were often simply spokesmen for the court and advisers in situations of stress.

There is even evidence that these prophets are not in a trance: they *lament* Menelaos' misfortunes. Now, though massive anthropological evidence proves that trance states are painful, almost the only emotionally distraught prophetess in a trance state is Kassandra, who will be *personally* affected by the misfortunes she prophesies.[18] I cannot think of any early Greek account of a prophet, prophesying misfortunes *for others* in a trance state, who is "lamenting". Though the Delphic oracle was traitorously pro-Persian, the cool manner in which it prophesied catastrophe for Athens can hardly be ignored (Hdt. 7.140 ff.).

The view that the prophets do not prophesy because they are not in a trance is confirmed by the fact that their words, as quoted, are grammatically flawless. They are clearly not glossalalic at this point.[19]

These considerations must be taken into account in deciding where the quotes should end (infra).

I hold that the prophets, speaking for the palace, simply lament Helene's elopement and, as reasonable men endowed with normal foresight, know that Menelaos will not leave the abduction of a nonpareil wife unavenged and will mobilize both his own and his allies' resources to obtain revenge, regardless of cost (427 ff.).

If one absolutely insists, one could also take the "those who" formulations of vv. 412–419 as *logical* predictions. If one imagines the prophets to be familiar with reactive depressions, one could—though just barely—view these verses as predictions or prognoses: "anyone who has sustained so great a loss will behave thus and so". There are more than enough examples of "if so . . . then" predictions of the course an illness will take in the Hippokratic corpus.

But though a psycho-analyst might *perhaps* venture to guess that a cuckolded husband would have a dream of the *type* described in vv. 420 ff., I must insist that there seems to be no early Greek example of anyone foretelling the dream someone else *will* have.[20] Even the reverse procedure—the attempt to elucidate the meaning of a dream by consulting oracles (A. *PV* 658 ff.)—is attested, I think, only once.

It is, on the whole, logically simpler and poetically more satisfying to imagine that vv. 412 ff. only record what at least the prophets—who, as crisis-specialists, would be the depressed Menelaos' chief confidantes—had occasion to observe and had been told by Menelaos himself, and which they made public.

What appears to have created the impression that vv. 412 ff. were "prophetic", is a brilliantly employed artistic device: anticipation. Prophecy presupposes an inspired foreknowledge of the future. Artistic

[18] In A. *Ag.* 1072 ff., she is desperate. In E. *Tr.* 308 ff., she is manic (elated) . . . a defence against depression described in any textbook of psychiatry (*63*).

[19] Dodds (*55*, p. 92, n. 68) holds that Kleomenes' bribing of the Pythia (Hdt. 6.66) proves her *not* to have been glossolalic. It seems simpler to assume that when the Pythia knew what she was expected to say, she was *not* glossolalic but only artificially riddling—as was Lykophron's Alexandra (= Kassandra). The simulation of trance is common in all societies which value that state.

[20] Hdt. 7.15 is not a true prophecy, but a working hypothesis.

anticipation presupposes only that the *poet* knew, or "sensed", what *he* would write next. Anticipation tightens the structure and coherence of the narrative; it scatters hints whose full meaning does not become evident until the narrative's climax is reached.[21]

The nature of poetic anticipation is best highlighted by anticipation in music. The melody contains a note, falling on a weak beat, which is dissonant with respect to the accompanying chord. The "premature" melodic note is then *repeated* (or sustained) on the strong beat, while the accompaniment strikes a *new* chord, consonant with the originally "premature" note. The tension created by the discordance on the weak beat is resolved into a harmony on the next strong beat.

One finds many such anticipations in this Aischylean text, only one of which can be discussed here. Doubles of various kinds are mentioned: the imprints (411), the phantom (415), and the statues (416) all anticipate the "(dream) vision" (425). Better still, though "dream apparitions" (in the plural, v. 420) clearly indicate that Menelaos' dream is repetitive, in a way this plural also enfolds in its capacious embrace the three anticipatory references to "doubles" just cited.

But I must insist that these clues are Aischylean anticipations of the dream and not the prophetic utterances of the palace soothsayers. Though already Homeros knew that hungry horses dream of oats (Hom. *Od.* 20.88 ff.), the "imprints of Helene" (v. 411) lead up neither to a prophetic prediction nor to a psychiatric prognosis of Menelaos' dream. The anticipation is the *poet's* artistically and psychologically convincing contrivance: the "day residue" (v. 411)[22] is mentioned before the dream is told.

I seek to state here only a principle: I do not analyse all anticipations in this extremely tautly structured text.[23]

All that matters is that these anticipations make the relentless progression of the passage irresistible: the sweep of its logic is also that of an emotional illness approaching its climax—and that of Fate.

Logical and Chronological Sequence. The moment one discards the untenable prophecy hypothesis, the order of the narrative becomes both logically and chronologically perfect.

Vv. 408–411: As spokesmen of the Court, the distressed prophets lament when they discover Helene's elopement during Menelaos' absence. *Vv. 410 f.* define the place and the personages (Menelaos' and Helene's ghostly imprint). But, in crying "woe", the prophets also foresee (*non*-prophetically) the elopement's impact on Menelaos. The Choros assumes responsibility only for the correct reporting of the prophets' words.

Vv. 412 f. describe Menelaos' first visible reactions on his return—most of them are culturally predictable.

Vv. 414–419 trace the gradual transformation of the initial psychomotor (and partly cultural) symptoms into the affective-ideational symptoms of a prolonged reactive depression.

---

[21] Cp. F. L. Lucas' (*107*, p. 83) comment on an entry in young Napoleone Buonaparte's notebooks: "Ste Hélène, petite île." The number of anticipatory clues in S. *O T* is proverbial.

[22] Hdt. 7.16; Arist. *insomn.* 461a14 ff. Cp. chap. 1, note 6.

[23] Cp. my comment on "non-vilifying" (v. 412). I also note that πάρεστι (412) anticipates πάρεισι (421).

Vv. 420–426 present a frustrated restitutive manœuvre in the form of a dream which seeks (in vain) to restore the *status quo ante*.

A word may be added about Menelaos' "transformations" in the course of this narrative.

In vv. 410 f. he is King.

In vv. 412 f. he is still King enough to respond, even in his stunned state, with socially privileged symptoms (dishonour, sitting apart).

In vv. 414 ff., the King turns into a depressed man, increasingly alienated from reality, which includes his royal status.

In vv. 420 ff., he has achieved the acme of a private status—(Heraclit. *fr* 89D-K)—he sleeps and dreams as would any other deserted lover.[24]

The Psychological Sequence must be scrutinized from a different point of view. Let us imagine that vv. 412–426 are narrated by Menelaos himself. Would he narrate the details *in that order* to his psychotherapist?[25] If the answer is yes, this would enhance the psychological plausibility of the narrative's *sequence* and *structure*, as distinct from its content.

Probably most patients begin the psycho-analytical session with a narration of the last night's dream. A few others, and especially those who resist the treatment, devote the first nine-tenths of the session to providing background material for and comments upon the dream which they do not narrate until no time is left for its analysis. They build up to an *unexploitable* climax.[26]

Deplorable as this procedure is in a psychotherapeutic session, it is a superb literary device; once the dream is told, the Choros' attention shifts from the King to Hellas as a whole. What is a negativistic resistance in a psychotherapeutic setting, exasperating to the therapist, is used here sublimatorily to create suspense in a characteristically archaic Greek manner.[27] The poet simply does creatively what the patient does (auto-)destructively. The latter is as stubbornly "constipated" as a three-year-old; the former is a master of suspense. Anyone unable to grasp the decisiveness of this distinction cannot be trusted to tell a chamberpot from the theatre of Dionysos—nor the extent to which the analysis of a poet's sublimatory use of the *selfsame* mechanisms which the neurotic uses destructively, contributes to our understanding of the poet's genius.

In short, precisely because the psychological sequence—here used to create magnificent suspense—is the same as that of the neurotic's delaying tactics, the sequence itself grips the reader and enables him to experience its psychological realism. It is the great poet's way of speaking to our comparatively mediocre minds in a manner which can stir echoes in us.

The Socio-Cultural and the Subjective Elements in psychiatric illness, and the manner in which they interact, having been one of the main themes of my life's work, I must, even at the cost of some overlaps with what I say

---

[24] Even Artemidoros simply claims special significance for royal dreams; he does not say that their dreams do not resemble those of men in a private station (cp. Hdt. 7.17). And the Greeks are not Malays who designate the sleep of kings by a special word.

[25] I have adduced elsewhere (*45*) evidence for the existence of genuine (recall-and-insight oriented) psychotherapy in fifth century B.C. Greece.

[26] Eteokles (A. *Sept.* 709 ff.) also does this—with magnificently poetic results. In a sense, that drama is, itself, the narration and analysis of Eteokles' never-reported dream.

[27] On the postponement of crucial details, cp. Fraenkel *64*, 3, pp. 805 ff.

elsewhere, devote a brief section to this aspect of the narrative. I hope that the Hellenist—who must so often deal with fragments of tragedies and poems—will feel that the few inevitable repetitions are atoned for by the experiment I propose to make.

I begin with the arbitrary assumption that vv. 412 f. have only survived as a fragment, and will momentarily analyse these two verses as though they were indeed a fragment. The "performances" enumerated in these verses constitute essentially "non-behaviour"; the first symptom listed is silence and all but the last begin with an alpha privative, indicating non-behaviour.

Silence, *per se*, has no immediately discernible psychological or inter-personal dimension. We may imagine that the silent Menelaos "scans" the situation and appraises its social significance; perhaps also its personal relevance.

His feeling "dishonoured" is, on this level of analysis, only a socio-cultural appraisal of his status as a cuckold—a finding congruent with reality.

Non-vilifying introduces the first hint of deviance. He does not exhibit socially expectable behaviour, such as Achilleus, offended and deprived of his woman by Agamemnon,[28] displays. Also, this trait implies, for the first time, the orientation of Menelaos towards another human being: at the absent Helene.

Disbelief-and-suspiciousness broadens Menelaos' "visual" field, since it includes his Court. This "broadening" of Menelaos' "interest" is, however, made possible by a momentary diversion of his preoccupations from Helene (whose elopement his restitutive disbelief negates neurotically) to his Court, whom—with typical disregard for mutually exclusive views, so regularly encountered in the operations of the unconscious mind—he suspects of complicity in an elopement which, simultaneously, he simply cannot believe to be real.

The sitting apart represents a socially predictable, patterned conse-quence of his suspiciousness, but also of his sense of being socially disgraced.

There is, thus, in this imaginary "fragment", an oscillation between idiosyncratic ("improvised") mourning reactions to a personal loss and the exhibiting of socio-culturally patterned reactions to the same stimulus. This is how the situation would appear psychologically, were vv. 412 f. an isolated fragment: the non-behaviour there enumerated appears to be largely socially patterned, exemplifying the type of disorder I call "ethnic" (*48*, chap. 1).

But if we terminate this *Gedankenexperiment* and read vv. 412 f. in its surviving context, we immediately realize that Menelaos does not display *primarily* the "etiquette of distress". His negative symptoms, and especially his sitting apart (and his silence), not only acquire the quality of genuine personal symptoms, but Menelaos' self-isolation is also a *conditio sine qua non* of the deflection of his attention from tangible reality to Helene's phantom, which, obviously, exists only in his own mind . . . and, in the last resort, of a total loss of interest in—of a decathecting of—external reality.

Vv. 412 f., which the student of typical Greek reactions to loss could,

---

[28] Hom. *Il.* 1.106 ff. I note that the war of Troy presupposes Menelaos' being deprived of his woman; the *Iliad* presupposes Achilleus' being deprived of his. The structural parallelism is striking.

within his frame of reference, rightly apprehend only as socially pre-
patterned distress behaviour, appears, in the light of what follows, *also*
as a subjective mourning reaction. The entire passage admirably illustrates
the subjective experiencing and symptomatic utilization of what, on the
cultural level, is clearly the "etiquette of distress". This, in turn, is further
highlighted by the Choros' impersonal ("those who") wording of vv. 412 f.
in particular and by the manner in which, as the narrative progresses, the
"those who" first becomes "the husband" and then the highly individualized dreamer—for in dream even Kings live in a private world. Last, but
not least, after v. 413, the symptoms ascribed to Menelaos become at once
less socially pre-patterned and increasingly severe. This, too, fits a finding
I stated elsewhere (*48*, chap. 1): a psychological disorder which borrows
most of its symptoms from culture ("etiquette of distress") is less severe
than one where culturally pre-patterned distress (or "disorder") behaviour no longer suffices to provide relief[29]—forcing the deeply disturbed
person to improvise his *own* symptoms and, in so doing, to manifest his
"social negativism" (*48*, chap. 3).

I conclude this excursus by pointing out that the proof just adduced,
that vv. 412 f. mean one thing if one pretends they are a fragment, but
have important additional meanings when read in context, further
justifies my policy of not discussing in this work dreams preserved only in
fragments.

Symmetry is evident in two respects:

(1) The narrative begins and ends with simulacra: with the eloped
Helene's imprint on the bed and with the memory of her vanishing in
dream.

(2) Vv. 410 f. are clearly a direct *quotation* of the *prophets' words*. (In
vv. 412–419, Menelaos himself is totally inactive. His behaviour is
"negative": three of the symptoms ascribed to him begin with an alpha
privative, which underscores the *absence* of behaviour. This passage is
purely descriptive.) The first *positive* act the text (implicitly) attributes to
Menelaos is the *telling* of his dream, which otherwise no one would have
known about. In that limited sense, vv. 420–426 are a *quasi-quotation*,
since they reproduce—perhaps third-hand—Menelaos' own tale.

Symptoms Listed

Vv. 412–419 enumerate the following clinical symptoms:

(1) Negativistic mutism;

(2) Subjective self-depreciation echoing a social loss of face;

(3) Inhibition of anger by residual love;

(4) Refusal to believe that the "inconceivable" has actually happened,
and suspiciousness;

(5) Physical withdrawal;

(6) A restitutive hallucination of the absent one, which makes the
hallucinator himself ghost-like;

[29] I recall the general principle that every symptom is a compromise between the
uninhibited wish and the intra-psychic forces which inhibit its overt and immediate
manifestation.

(7) Adverse reactions to beauty;

(8) The typical gaze of the stuporously depressed;

(9) The decathecting of outer reality—its non-investing with libido (which facilitates hallucinations);

(10) The culminating, reality-alien symptom: a *frustrating* erotic dream.

In short, Menelaos' state is compounded of mourning, of melancholia and of what some psychiatrists call a schizo-affective state. Torn between love and hatred, he rope-walks on the boundary between the real and the imaginary, responding now to the external world in terms of inner needs and at other times subordinating inner experiences to the demands of outer reality. The "boundary" between the real and the imaginary, and also between "inside" and "outside", materializes and de-materializes in exactly the same way in which this process was described elsewhere in terms of purely epistemological considerations, which cannot be recapitulated here (*39*, chap. 24; *52*, chap. 2).

General Comment: The Dream Narrative (420–426)

It is hardly necessary to recall once again that Menelaos' dream is one of the most persuasive found in Greek literature. I therefore proceed directly to a general scrutiny of its main characteristics.

Menelaos' Sleeping Behaviour is not even alluded to. This is noteworthy, for the observable behaviour of sleepers who dream preoccupied Aischylos a great deal (*40*); in A. *Eum.* the restless, dream-haunted sleep of the Erinyes is even represented on-stage. This striking omission *appears* to imply that Menelaos had private sleeping quarters making a direct observation of his sleeping behaviour by third persons impossible. But this explanation is insufficient, for·in some instances (*40*) the dreamer herself refers to her light and restless sleep, while in other instances the dream-haunted sleeper's shouts echo throughout the palace (chap. 6).

The simplest, and artistically most satisfying, hypothesis is that the poet advisedly left it to his audience to imagine what the dream-haunted Menelaos' sleep was like.[30]

The Dream's Plausibility is revealed by both positive and negative data.

(1) *Positive Elements:*

    (a) Anyone could visualize Menelaos' dream on the basis of his own experience.

    (b) It none the less contains highly individualized elements, befitting only Menelaos.[31]

---

[30] I note that, quite apart from the experimentally determined fact that men have a brief erection before they begin to dream (*10*), erotic dreams are normally accompanied by visible erections and sometimes even by emissions of semen. If this last hypothesis is considered, at least tentatively, the "imprint" (trace) of v. 411 gains an added anticipatory nuance—one that Thomson refers to (ad loc.) in connection with the traces of an adultery: Liv. 1.58: "*vestigia* alieni viri, Collatine, in lecto sunt tuo"—save that, in this instance, the "imprint" (traces) could *conceivably* anticipate Menelaos' own (hypothetical) dream-emission. •

[31] An analogy: *the* "Oedipus complex" (an inductive generalization) *is not*—a patient's subjective manner of experiencing it *is*—analysable. Similarly, one cannot treat "cholera"; one can cure only a patient who has that illness.

(c) Unlike several of his symptoms, Menelaos' dream has almost no cultural content. This makes manifest the process of a progressive "privatization" (*48*, chap. 15).

(d) The dream is almost wholly visual and only marginally—if at all— tactile. [Housman's ἐc θιγὰc (423) is unconvincing.]

(e) Waking reality is not reproduced mechanically; there is *some* symbolic "distortion".

(f) The recall and narration of the dream are realistic (infra).

(g) The text is more corrupt than that of any other Aischylean dream. This suggests that its latent content disturbed the copyist(s).

(h) Even philologically satisfactory emendations and interpretations do not eliminate all ambiguity, for this is a properly "overdetermined" dream.

(i) The major elements and processes of dreaming are discernible.

(2) *Negative Elements:*

(a) The dream lacks "contrived" or "exotic" touches. One especially notes the absence of conventional but unrealistic details resulting from a retroactive falsification ("secondary elaboration"). In some instances, this tries to make the dream-*narrative* fit cultural criteria which lend it "authority".[32] The traditional dream-speech is one such realistically *excluded* element.

(b) The dream is not prophetic, for the real Helene will finally return to Menelaos' arms. Like real dreams, that of Menelaos is rooted in the past and in the present. Its only future-oriented element is the dream-*wish* to restore the *status quo ante*.

Additional realistic aspects of this narrative are discussed in various connections throughout this chapter.

Recall and Narrative Technique also have a flawless clinical persuasiveness.

The details are vivid but not sharply focused; this fits both daily experience and scientific observations. Nearly all details of Atossa's dream narrative are sharply in focus (chap. 1) here, as in ordinary life, *we* are asked to visualize the scene; thus, only at v. 426 do we learn that the vision was winged. The blurrings and lacunae of real dream narratives are here "provocatively" replicated for artistic ends: we are asked to sharpen the focus and fill the gaps in accordance with our personal experiences.

It is easy for the clinician to imagine that Menelaos himself recalled and narrated his dream in just this manner. For when the affect mobilized by the dream is so *congruent* with reality as to revive, on awakening, a preoccupation with *real* problems, the latter practically obliterate the dream: at times the person barely recalls what his dream "was about" or "implied".[33] In such cases the sadness or frustration—which is *all* one may recall about one's dream—may pervade most of the following day.

---

[32] Diegueño Indian boys, who did not have the "correct" kind of power-giving dream, are told to dream "correctly" the next time (*133*). A Mohave Indian singer quarrelled in dream with his dream-instructor (for songs are supposedly learned in dream) over *how* a certain song should be sung (*52*, chap. 9).

[33] Eteokles' allusive remarks about his *non*-narrated evil dreams (A. *Sept.* 709 ff.) may, perhaps, illustrate this process.

I particularly note that though the vanishing of the dream image is reported, we never learn what waking image *replaced* it (Arist. *insomn.* 458b20 ff.)—for, at v. 427, the Choros switches from Menelaos' grief to that of bereaved Hellas. In short, we are not given "associations" to the dream's manifest content. We can observe only the intensification of the dream-frustration on awakening . . . until one man's despair brings disaster to all of Greece.

In short, the quality of the narrative also enhances the dream's credibility.

The Day Residue[34]—repeatedly mentioned already—can be disposed of in a few words. It is clearly the hollow imprint Helene's body left behind. That vacuum—which "nature abhors"—is inadequately filled by the phantom and by the lovely statues. This makes it foreseeable that the dream-vision will also prove unsatisfactory. Only the real Helene's return—and, perhaps, the slaying of Paris as well—would genuinely gratify Menelaos; the uncompleted erotic dream is but an added source of frustration.

The Dream-Wish is as manifest as is the (ambivalent) counter-wish which, in this dream, practically usurps the role of the dream censor and explains the near-complete lack of symbolization. I note in passing that this *substitution* of a counter-wish for the dream censor, though evident in many dreams, and especially in frustration dreams, is hardly ever mentioned in psycho-analytical literature. The dream censor (or Super-ego) is usually treated as a totally autonomous instance, little attention being paid to the problem of its *mobilization* by an (ambivalent) counter-wish, *not* emanating from the Super-ego.

"Frustration Dreams" belong to more than one category. The two types that interest us here are:

(1) Dreams in which the frustration is part of the dream's *manifest* content. Menelaos' dream is, as the analysis of the text shows, of this type, and is akin to inhibition dreams, in which the goal pursued is not attained.[35] But I note at once that few Greek erotic dreams are frustrating in this sense . . . unless one dreams of Helene (infra). The young man who ceased to love the expensive hetaira Thonis, after he had a gratifying erotic dream about her (Plu. *V. Dem.* 27.5 f.), is a good example, particularly since it indicates that the young man's love was not that of the "soul". In fact, this satisfying dream reminds one of Diogenes' observation that it is a pity one cannot satisfy one's hunger by rubbing one's abdomen, the way one can satisfy one's sexual needs by masturbating (D.L. 6.68–70). One cannot but feel that, like some modern sex researchers who may remain unnamed, neither Diogenes, nor the aforementioned young man sensed that, in order to be satisfying, an orgasm must have an important, inter-personal psychological dimension.[36]

[34] Hdt. 7.16; Arist. *insomn.* 461a14 ff., etc.

[35] Cp. the dream metaphor in Hom. *Il.* 22.199 f., and V. *Aen.* 12.908. Other examples in Cook (*14*, 3.401.1), who cites approvingly Boll's allusion to the Oknos myth, which he rightly assumes to be patterned on an inhibition dream. In fact, I feel that Hom. *Il.* 22.199 f. may, in a way, prepare the ground for Achilleus' frustrating dream about Patroklos (Hom. *Il.* 23.99 ff.).

[36] The similarity between the "sex" stories just discussed and the tale of the pauper who

Though I can hardly agree with Platon's many hints that physical love is incompatible with the "love of the soul"—for truly adult people who "*make* love" do actually *create* thereby their love—Platon's remarks, together with the stories just discussed do hint at a certain affective deficiency in Greek love relationships, or at least in many of them.[37] In fact, completely gratifying spontaneous emissions were even ascribed to Zeus, to Poseidon and to Hephaistos (*44*). But I concede at once that, in a few instances, where a great emotional involvement was present, even symbolic cohabitations (E. *Alc.* 354, etc., the Laodameia myth) gave pleasure. Even a mere kiss (Theocr. 2.126 f.) was supposed to provide an almost complete gratification of body and soul.[38] But this seems true only of heterosexual loves. Skythinos (*AP* 12.22) finds no relief in masturbation, for he is enamoured of a *boy*. I disagree with Professor Lloyd-Jones that Theocr. 12 is an authentic exception to the rule.

(2) Other dreams have a gratifying manifest content, which brings about frustration only on awakening. They are well exemplified by Penelope's erotic dream about the absent Odysseus (Hom. *Od.* 20.88 ff.), which, though it almost certainly involved a dream orgasm, left her bitterly disappointed on awakening: the text calls this dream evil (κακά) (cp. Theocr. 2.58: a love potion is "bad"). Sappho's reaction, in Ov. *Her.* 15.125 ff., is clearly modelled upon this Homeric dream. Its equivalent in myth is the vanishing of the *almost* rescued Eurydike—a scene comparable to an awakening from a pleasant dream only to find that reality does not confirm it.[39]

But Aischylos' tale achieves more than any of these two types of frustration dreams can achieve. Menelaos is frustrated already *in* dream: the vision eludes him. That the near-completion of his desires in dream will be a source of frustration on awakening goes without saying—and to this frustration is added the real Helene's elopement. But, if v. 426 means what I think it means (infra), there is also the further intimation that his subsequent dreams will be even more disappointing.

If this view is accepted, one begins to get a glimpse of just how "dense" a great poet's text can really be: one dream, of great simplicity and persuasiveness, implies four separate levels of frustration. This alone suffices to justify the view expressed in the General Introduction, that a great poet's outer solid simplicity presupposes a dazzling complexity of its inner "works".

Worsening Repetitive Dreams are common in Aischylos.[40] I will cite in due time the two textual intimations (vv. 420, 425 f.) suggesting that

---

ate his bread while smelling the pleasant odours of a cookshop—for which the cook asked to be paid—has, I think, been overlooked.

[37] Conspicuous exceptions exist: Hom. *Il.* 6.429 f., 22.447 ff.; they were discussed elsewhere (*43*). Cp. also parts of X. *Oec.*

[38] As is shown by its being followed by sleep. Cp. Legrand, ad loc.

[39] The Eurydike rescue-motif has uncontestable American Indian equivalents (*76, 22*). This tends to confirm that it is patterned upon a disappointing awakening from a pleasant dream.

[40] *PV*: Io's dream becomes increasingly compelling. *Pers*: Atossa tells the last and worst of her dreams. *Sept.*: Eteokles' dreams seem to get worse. The two "once only" dreams are found in *Choe.* and *Eum.* (See the relevant chapters.)

Menelaos' dream is but the first of a gradually worsening series. Here I mention only clinical considerations.

Even perceptive laymen note that dreams triggered by recent traumata tend to recur.[41] Considering the severe trauma Menelaos had experienced and the ten-year war he then had to wage to restore the *status quo ante*, the non-recurrence of his dream—in an increasingly disappointing form— is psychologically inconceivable. The fact that the initial (narrated) dream was, in itself, frustrating, makes the above conclusion a certainty.

The Spatial Arrangement can best be analysed by assuming that, as in many early Greek dream narratives (*55*, chap. 4), the dreaming Menelaos realistically visualizes himself as lying in his bed. If so, Helene's vision is *above* him and would be above him even if she were not winged.

Though this *coitus inversus* is clearly modelled upon nightmare-inspired representations of the rape of young men by the Sphinx or by certain other female monsters—who, apart from some minor details of their anatomy, are often both lifelike and beautiful (as in the frontispiece of this book), this arrangement also represents a "moral" reality accurately. The eloped and triumphantly amorous Helene is as clearly the "superior" as the abandoned and dishonoured Menelaos is the "inferior" partner in this ghostly embrace.[42]

In short, this spatial arrangement shows that Helene has the whip hand; Menelaos is helpless and unable even to prevent her premature escape.[43]

Quotes: Only vv. 410–411 explicitly quote the words of the prophets. Three arguments—in addition to the psychological ones already cited— militate in favour of this view.

(1) The symptoms listed in vv. 412–413 are said to be visible (ἰδεῖν). This probably means that the Choros reports its own observations, rather than those of the prophets.

(2) Long direct quotations, especially of dreams, are, I feel, an epic[44] rather than a tragic stylistic device. Thus, in Hom. *Il.* 2.8 ff., Zeus tells the Dream to convey *very accurately* a certain dream message to Agamemnon. At 2.23 ff., the Dream scrupulously carries out his instructions. At 2.60 ff., Agamemnon himself narrates his dream exactly as he dreamed it.

[41] Even adults, who had graduated from universities, have at times dreams of "Matura" examinations. Professor Lloyd-Jones tells me that he dreamed of having to take Greats again since becoming Regius Professor of Greek at Oxford. The marked repetitiveness of (1914–1918) combat dreams *seemed* so incompatible with the wish-fulfilment theory of dreaming, that Freud was led to develop the theory of a *primary* "death instinct" (*72*), which I deem clinically unnecessary (*47*, p. 399), though the "repetition compulsion" theory, which accompanies it, is impeccably sound. I hold that the repetition of a real trauma in dream simply seeks to dispose of the psychological repercussions of the trauma, by devising a fictitious "happy ending" for the irremediable. That the Greeks knew of the occurrence of "salvaging operations" in dream is attested by incubation dreams mentioned elsewhere and by the dreams of Ailios Aristeides (*5*).

[42] On the superior vs. inferior position in the sexual act, especially in dreams, cp. chap. 9. For representations of lascivious women mounting men, cp. (*109*): pl. 137 (Athens National Museum); pl. 152 (Berlin Museum, F 2414; Chavalov painter), etc.

[43] That the coitus inversus position affirms woman's superiority was explicitly stated some years ago by a feminist speaking on the French State Radio (ORTF). It is the standard coital posture in a matriarchy invented by Robert Graves (*81*).

[44] And Near-Eastern (*116*, passim).

By contrast, in tragedy the dream is either actually enacted on stage (A. *Eum.*, dream of the Erinyes), or else reported by the dreamer in person.[45] Only in three cases is the dream reported by someone else: in A. *Ag.* by the Choros, in A. *Choe.* also by the Choros and in S. *El.* by Chrysothemis, and in some of these cases (A. *Choe.*) those who report a dream seem to have heard it from the dreamer.[46]

A. *Ag.* admittedly does not specify to whom Menelaos told his dream. Fraenkel's suggestion, that he told it to the palace prophets, is attractive but not inevitable, partly because Menelaos' dream is too transparent to stand in need of an interpretation by experts (though this practice was common enough, E. *Hec.* 87 ff.), and partly because his dream is manifestly *not* prophetic, and is nowhere said to predict the future. The scene depicted in the dream will never take place in reality. It reflects exclusively the affective frustration experienced by the still enamoured Menelaos.

The most obvious alternative would be to place vv. 410–411 and vv. 420–426 in quotes. However, two direct quotes in the same Choral song, separated by only eight verses, seems to me to be alien to tragic diction and especially to a lyrical passage in tragedy.

This being said, the placing of the quotation marks does not affect the interpretation of vv. 410–426 in any way. This explains why certainty regarding this matter is impossible.

The Structural Analysis of vv. 410–411 provides important clues to the manner in which their content, and especially the meaning of the last two words, should be interpreted.[47]

The fundamental datum is that vv. 408 f. specify that vv. 410–411 are a *lament*. This means—in principle as well as in terms of observable clinical facts—that the general content and structure of the lament's first verse will be echoed, with greater specificity and with certain variations, by the second verse. It is also safe to assume that the greater the poet, the more numerous and more complex will be both the affinities and the contrasts between the two paired verses.

The Conceptual Echo is clearly discernible. V. 410 mentions first an object which is at once a material container and a social matrix: the palace, and then refers to its animate content: the prince(s). V. 411, too, mentions first a material container which is also a social matrix (the nuptial couch) and then refers to its quasi-animate content: the imprint of Helene's body.[48] One also notes that v. 411 is more specific than v. 410: there is a passage from the general to the particular; from the social to the individual level.

The second item mentioned in v. 410 is Menelaos (infra), who, at the

---

45 In A. *Pers.* by Atossa, in A. *Sept.* (very briefly) by Eteokles, in A. *PV* by Io; in E. *Hec.* by Hekabe, in E. *IT* by Iphigeneia; in E. *Rh.* by the Charioteer.

46 I note in passing that two of the three dreams told at second hand are the dreams of Klytaimnestra and that, in A. *Choe.* Orestes "teases out" the report of the dream in the course of a swift stichomythia.

47 The following paragraphs owe a great deal to the exemplary analysis of Baudelaire's poem: "Les Chats", by R. Jakobson and Cl. Lévi-Strauss (*87*).

48 This interpretation, and the view that this imprint is felt to be quasi-animate, will be justified further on.

particular moment described by the lament, is not physically in the bed which he formerly shared with Helene. But, in terms of the interpretation offered below of the meaning of cτίβοι φιλάνορες, the *kind* of imprint the eloped Helene had left on the bed once required the amorous co-operation of Menelaos: the weight of his body pressing down on Helene's body during an embrace. Hence, even though the bed may actually have preserved only *one* imprint of *one* body—of Helene's body—*that* imprint was produced by the *combined* weight of two bodies, in the course of an often repeated act.[49] This fully justifies the use of a genuine—non-generic —plural, which none the less has some affinities with the (generic) pseudo-plural at the end of v. 410.

Last, but not least, the syntax of the two verses is the same:

(a) V. 410: repeated expletive, repeated singular noun, conjunction ("and"), generic pseudo-plural.

(b) V. 411: expletive, singular noun, conjunction ("and"), genuine plural noun-and-adjective (with a few overtones of the singular).

The Variations and Reciprocities between these two verses are so numerous and so subtle that, despite a certain repetitiousness which this mode of presentation entails, they must be listed separately:

(a) *V. 410*: a singular followed by a generic (pseudo-)plural.

V. 411: a singular followed by a genuine plural.

(b) The repeated expletive and repeated noun (singular) at the be-ginning of v. 410 are balanced by the plural two-word (plural noun-and-adjective) ending of v. 411.

(c) The terminal one-word pseudo-plural of v. 410 balances the one-word singular at the beginning of v. 411.

(d) If one disregards the expletives and the conjunctions, which help v. 411 to duplicate internally v. 410, one notes that

(α) Vv. 410–411 do not have a single consonant in common.

(β) Amongst vowels they have in common only α and ο, and a single diphthong, which is, moreover, simply a case ending:—οι.

(e) The metres of the two verses are different, but well geared to each other.

A more complete and, at the same time, more varied and complex echoing and balancing of v. 410 by v. 411 is hard to imagine. This does not mean, of course, that Aischylos deliberately and laboriously planned these correspondences and contrasts, any more than Baudelaire planned those which Jakobson and Lévi-Strauss (*87*) highlighted in his poem: "Les Chats". Such subtle and manifold correspondences and contrasts are the characteristic features of great poetry—and *only* of great poetry. The literary critic, laboriously tracking the flight of Pegasos through the air, can at times detect them—but can never predict them. It is the hallmark of great art that it makes the unpredictable seem inevitable in retrospect.

410 δῶμα is primarily an important building: a palace, its great hall or even the city.[50] But the lamenting prophets do not foresee the collapse

[49] Exactly the same is true of the imprint(s) which the enlaced bodies of Sappho and Phaon had (repeatedly) left on the grass, cp. Ov. *Her.* 15.147 f., and *infra*.

[50] The meaning "house-top" appears to be relatively late.

of its walls and pillars, except in a figurative sense.[51] Hence, δῶμα must be
taken here *also* in a sociological sense. It denotes *all* those whom "the
sorrows of the hearth within the home" (427 f.)—the *personal* troubles of
the palace's main inhabitants—affect as directly and as inevitably as
though they, too, *lived* in the palace. The king's private sorrows "involve"
them, no matter how much they murmur and complain (448 ff.).[52] This
much can be safely asserted even of Greek society, in which a "*fictitious*
residence" did not determine a man's social identity.[53] A royal δῶμα
certainly included people who, though they did not actually *live* within its
walls, had to *behave* as though they did; they were part of the retinue.[54]
In short, δῶμα is a "gravitational field"; but even this lends no real
support to the co-residence seemingly mentioned in v. 400.

One other consideration militates at least indirectly in favour of the
view that *this* δῶμα should be taken in a primarily sociological sense.
Though the walls of the palace clearly sheltered the nuptial couch (411),
it is, I hold, not certain just where this palace was located.[55]

What matters aesthetically is the link between the (social) δῶμα and the
πρόμοι, and the nexus between the actual building and the nuptial
couch. It is this *concurrent* exploitation of the various matrices or meanings
of a word which gives poetic diction its durable shimmer (*30, 46*).

410 πρόμοι = prince(s) is morphologically a plural, but functionally a
singular: it is a so-called allusive or generic plural of a type encountered
also in vv. 412–413.[56] One good reason for holding that πρόμοι is such a
spurious plural, is that the plurals of vv. 412 f. clearly refer *only* to Menelaos.
This—as Dr C. A. Behr points out to me—suggests that the pseudo-plural
in v. 410 anticipates or leads up to the pseudo-plurals of vv. 412–413,
which even Fraenkel recognizes as such, and which will be discussed
further on.

I begin by demonstrating the awkwardnesses which result from taking

[51] The collapse of a palace can symbolize a dynastic catastrophe in dream (E. *IT*
46 ff.); the reverse symbolization does not seem to be as common.

[52] This view is Greek: a King's private grievances can cause a war (Hom. *Il.*; Hdt. 1.3);
Aristophanes (*Ach.* 526 ff.) even satirizes this process.

[53] A Sedang Moi bachelor's *body* resides in the village clubhouse; his "fireplace *soul*"—
the basis of his human estate and social affiliation—resides in his parents' hearth-stones
(*21*).

[54] The exact "census" of the δῶμα in question cannot and need not be determined.
I doubt that Helene's oath-bound (Hes. *fr.* 204.78 M.W. = *Pap. Berol.* 10560; cp. Paus.
3.24.10) ex-suitors—two of whom (Odysseus, Achilleus) tried to "dodge the draft"—
should be thought of as being part of the δῶμα the prophets had in mind at this point.

[55] Verse 400 ("house of the Atreidai") does not, in my estimate, shed light on this
geographical problem. In fact, I am not even sure that *verse 400* really indicates that
Agamemnon and Menelaos dwelled under the same roof. Though I cannot argue this
point here, it is surely a finding of some importance that, despite Aischylos' prestige, his
(*alleged*) domiciliary innovation found no imitators. On non-imitation cp. (*53*). V. 410
does not indicate a co-residence, for "princes" is a pseudo-plural.

[56] Cp. Fraenkel on the allusive plurals in vv. 412, 1618, 1625; A. *Choe.* 886; S. *OT* 366,
(and Jebb ad loc.); S. *Ant.* 1263; E. *Her.* 1309; E. *Phoin.* 40 (and Pearson ad loc). But
Fraenkel does not recognize that πρόμοι, too, is such a pseudo-plural. (On plurals of this
type, cp. in general Wackernagel *137*, 1.94 ff.) Why, apart from metrical reasons,
Aischylos chose to use here the generic plural was discussed in the structural analysis of vv.
410–411 (supra).

πρόμοι for a genuine plural, denoting both Menelaos and Agamemnon.[57]

(1) It obliges one, first of all, to deny—as do Denniston and Page—any nexus between πρόμοι and the nuptial couch of Menelaos and Helene. I am not prepared to impute so abrupt a discontinuity of the poetic discourse to Aischylos, who was neither a schizophrenic nor a modern "poet"—two terms which, in times of cultural decay, are practically interchangeable. In their case no normal person—sometimes not even the psycho-analyst—can reconstruct the unconscious connection between two successive but logically unconnected ideas. In the case of great poets and even of some quasi-malingerers, the existence of the inner links of a sequence can always be sensed.[58] I deem it almost sacrilegious to believe Aischylos capable of so totally isolating the nuptial couch[59] from what went before and what comes after. It is conceded that, in a *social* sense, this bed is the core of all that the δῶμα stands for. But the δῶμα was already lamented for; taking the bed *only* as the core of the palace leads to a trivial redundancy.

The fact that in *this* drama[60] Menelaos and Agamemnon supposedly share the same palace may suffice to link the Atreidai brothers with the *palace*, but signally fails to link *both* of them with the *bed*. In fact, stressing this sharing of the abode so as to take πρόμοι as a genuine plural even disrupts the obvious link between the δῶμα and the bed viewed as its social core.

(2) If one assumes πρόμοι to denote Menelaos and Agamemnon, *and* postulates a nexus between both of them and the nuptial couch, one is confronted, first of all, with the fact that, of all the Greek heroes, Agamemnon had the *least* to do with Helene's couch. Not having been one of her suitors, he did not even aspire to it. Not even a hint at a sororate—either successive or simultaneous—can be envisaged here, despite Greek precedents for such matings.[61]

Almost the only hint of a (highly indirect) "sexual" nexus between

---

[57] It cannot very well denote the oath-bound suitors (Hes. 204.81 ff. M.W.), though, in a marginal way, they are part of the Atreidai's "house" (cp. supra). I have even considered the outside possibility that this word might refer to the "royal couple". But, when all is said and done, the poets saw Helene emerging from other peoples' trials and tribulations with her make-up intact, every curl in place and ready to become a goddess (esp. E. *Tr.*, passim). Also, one cannot treat such a distinctly masculine plural as a feminine "generic gender", in the sense in which the feminine plural of "deer" designates the species, or the way "mares" sometimes designates a pair of stallions hitched to the same chariot (cp. *4*, pp. 204 f.). No plural such as πρόμοι designates even a hero and his *warlike* bride, such as Theseus and Hippolyte or Herakles and Deianeira (*53*). Not even Lykophron would have called Menelaos and his ostentatiously (and therefore spuriously) feminine Queen: πρόμοι.

[58] A neurotic, "fearful" (= hopeful) of being diagnosed as a (psycho-analytically untreatable) schizophrenic, regularly suppressed certain of his "crazy" ideas. As a result, his discontinuous discourse sounded almost schizophrenic—though not enough so for me *not* to suspect deliberate omissions, for I could dimly sense that there was some (suppressed) link between two successive but seemingly unconnected ideas (*34*).

[59] The primarily *erotic* bed here (as in A. *Pers.* 133, 543, etc.) contrasts with the primarily *marital* bed in E. *Phoin.* 14; cp. infra.

[60] But apparently nowhere else, cp. note 55. Sophokles, too, failed to impose one of his system-alien innovations (*53*).

[61] Herakles and the fifty daughters of Thestios; Theseus, Ariadne and Phaidra; Tereus, Prokne and Philomele, etc.

Agamemnon and Helene is the marginal tradition that Iphigeneia, the illegitimate child of Helene and of Theseus, was raised by Agamemnon and Klytaimestra.[62] I hold this nexus to be at once too un-sexual and too indirect to justify the leap—from the *two* Atreidai to Helene's couch—which this view would impute to Aischylos.

S. *Aj.* 1311[63] (Teukros to Agamemnon): "Your wife—or your brother's should I say?" is, likewise, hardly evidence for Agamemnon's erotic interest in Helene. The bitter Teukros clearly mocks what he considers to be Agamemnon's (in *his* eyes excessive) eagerness to recover Helene—of which more anon. The point of Teukros' sarcasm is, of course, that even though Agamemnon is *not* Helene's husband, he carries on as though he were. As to Aischylos, he did not depict, either here or elsewhere, Agamemnon's behaviour as husband-like—be it absurdly or otherwise.

The sole purpose of the preceding paragraphs was to show that even a specious distortion of non-Aischylean passages cannot conjure up any erotic link between Agamemnon and Helene's couch.

A further crucial consideration is that even though this passage stresses the erotic distress of Menelaos *the man*, neither early epic poetry, nor Greek tragedy, nor Herodotos explicitly claim that the Trojan war was *erotically* motivated: that its *principal* objective was the recovery of Helene, *as a source of erotic delights*. In Hom. *Il.* 2.70 ff., 90 ff., 255, 285, etc., as in A. *Ag.* 534 ff., the recovery of the stolen treasure is almost as important an objective as the recapture of Helene, who, in E. *Tr.* 860 ff., is meant to be judged and punished. In fact, almost the only ones—except Paris (Hom. *Il.* 7.350 ff.)—to hint that the war's *real* mainspring was Helene *as a source of erotic gratifications*, are the Trojan elders who, seeing her pass, say in effect: "It is worth fighting for so much loveliness."[64]

What really motivated the war—even for Menelaos and therefore, *a fortiori*, for Agamemnon and the Greek host—was that in ancient times no one could afford to let an injury to oneself or to an ally go unavenged, lest the foe get the idea that one can harass members of that group at will.[65] All this has very little to do with Menelaos' private longing for his luscious

---

[62] Paus. 2.22.7; Douris *FHG* 2.470.3 = Tzetz. *Lyc.* 103; Ant. Lib. 27 and Papathomopoulos ad loc.; sch. Hom. *Il.* 13.626; *EM* s.v. Ἴφις, etc.

[63] Which Eustath. 754.21 inexplicably links with Hom. *Il.* 9.327 (cp. Jebb ad S. *Aj.* 1310 ff.), rather than with Hom. *Il.* 9.338–341: The Atreidai went to war for lovely-haired Helene's sake. Are they the only ones to love their [respective] wives (plural!)?

[64] Hom. *Il.* 3.156 ff.; A. *Ag.* 448 ff. does not disprove this view: it refers to the murmurings of the malcontents, who seek to cheapen the larger issues involved—as in Ar. *Ach.* 523 ff. Similarly, in Hom. *Il.* 9.338 ff., Achilleus' outburst is speciously worded, so as to link the Atreidai's *casus belli* with his own grievances over the Briseis matter; it does not reflect the general Greek view of the causes of the Trojan war, as presented, e.g., even in Hdt. 1.1ff.

[65] Shortly after I was adopted into a Sedang Moi village, I fired my revolver at night, to scare off a wild feline which was trying to raid my hen-coop. In a moment all the men came tumbling out of their huts, armed to the teeth, to rescue me from what they believed to be an attack by a not-too-distant Sedang village, which had grievances against the French. Since previous to my adoption the Sedang of my village—who also had a grievance against the French—had been markedly hostile to me, I asked them why they *now* came to my rescue. They replied: "You are now one of us, and if foreigners got the idea that they could attack you with impunity, they would soon get the notion that we had no ingroup loyalty—and would then attack any one of us, in the belief that we would not

bedfellow, and even less with a possible personal nexus between Agamemnon and Helene.

A further difficulty is that the plurals of vv. 412–413 clearly apply only to Menelaos, for no matter how deeply Agamemnon felt for his brother, he was not likely to go into a state of stuporous depression over his brother's erotic distress. This, too, makes it even logically improbable that the text would refer in a single word to Agamemnon (paired with Menelaos) and then forget all about him for countless more verses.

It could be objected, of course, that, since vv. 410 f. are uttered by the prophets, they constitute a prophecy *stricto sensu*: that the prophets, *using their special gifts*, foresee the ultimate doom of Agamemnon, and not only the *logically* predictable hardships of a war. This assumption is not tenable. Vv. 408–409 specify (supra) that the prophets *wail*; they do *not* prophesy. They lament what *is*; they do not bewail what their second sight—or even their logic—causes them to *foresee*.[66] Indeed, though v. 410 could—just barely—imply either a prophecy or a logical prediction, v. 411 can refer only to the present—to what is here and now. This suggests that v. 410 also concerns only the present; that even prophets do not *always* prophesy. Here they simply act as spokesmen for Menelaos' entire retinue.[67]

Hence, both the logic of the affects ("primary process thinking") and that of concepts ("secondary process thinking") justify the view that πρόμοι denotes Menelaos only, for only this assumption renders Aischylos' poetic discourse genuinely coherent. And I hold that the *Agamemnon* must be treated—first, last and all the time—as great poetry, in which no word rattles around in a vacuum. If, like Denniston and Page, one denies any link between πρόμοι and λέχος, the nuptial couch becomes a bit of furniture floating, like Mohammed's coffin, between heaven and earth. Finally, since the essence of great poetry is its inner continuity, the fact that (the plurals of vv. 412–413 included), the whole passage (vv. 410–426) refers *only* to Menelaos also makes it mandatory not to drag Agamemnon into it.

In short, πρόμοι—an allusive or generic plural—designates only Menelaos, for, at *this* point, he is the only man who has a legitimate interest in Helene's indiscriminately hospitable bed.

411 λέχος is not a randomly selected item from the palace's furniture inventory. The prophets lament over a contextually relevant bed—not over an odd chair or frying-pan. They lament over the *marital* couch, which, precisely because it is deserted by one of the spouses, evokes intense erotic longings.[68] Even Greek erotic dreams seem to occur chiefly in bed—almost never while asleep outdoors.

retaliate *en masse*." This, needless to say, is exactly Agamemnon's and Iphigeneia's reasoning in E. *IA* (1274 f., 1374 ff.), and very similar to the reasoning in Hdt. 1.3.

[66] Contra, Thomson ad loc., citing Pl. *Tim.* 72 a–b.

[67] This, I repeat, hints at what Aischylos conceived the status of Mykenaian household prophets to be.

[68] Cp. A. *Pers.* 133, 543. Since humour (i.e., comedy) deals in a different and more defensive way with the anxiety arousing material of tragedy, I feel entitled to cite Dover (p. 119, ad Ar. *Nub.* 734): in vulgar Greek humour, a man alone in bed is likely to masturbate. [But, *pace* Dover (p. 183), I doubt that Ar. *Nub.* 676 refers to masturbation.]

For Aischylos the bed nearly always has a sexual or parasexual connotation.[69] The same is true of many Greek and Roman authors:[70] Q.S. 14.151 ff. is especially relevant here.

The text of v. 411 does not specify whether the bed was *primarily* that of Menelaos, in which Helene joined him,[71] or *primarily* that of Helene, to which Menelaos had free access,[72] or whether it belonged to both spouses equally.[73] Since the text says nothing about the matter of "ownership", I do not propose to discuss it. I simply note that data bearing on this point are available in many Greek sources and deserve to be systematized.

Like the δῶμα, the bed over which the prophets lament has two aspects or dimensions. In one sense it resembles the tangible edifice, in that it shelters the nuclear couple, whose co-*habitation* (and co-*itus*) creates and holds together the in-group. In another sense it symbolizes this human dyad, at the precise moment its members engage in the act which creates and reaffirms their interdependence . . . just as δῶμα symbolizes the household in the very act which is the essence of their interdependence: in the act of dwelling together. Thus, just as δῶμα "is" both the edifice and the dwelling-together of the household, so the bed "is" both the marital couch and the amorous union of those who share it.

This bed must therefore be thought of in sexual terms. This, in turn, means that πρόμοι can denote *only* Menelaos and that cτίβοι φιλάνορες must be linked to what happened in *this* bed. The rejection of both these compelling conclusions would cause λέχος to rattle around in vv. 410–411, unconnected with what comes before and after. I even fear that if this separation of the bed from its context continues, the next step will be to get rid of it altogether, as something that slipped in from a furniture catalogue written on the verso of some old papyrus, and to replace it with a "chaster" doormat, on which properly Ahrens-ian footprints may be left without offence to anyone.

411 cτίβοι φιλάνορες: The meaning of these words has been needlessly obscured by controversies. This obliges me to begin, exceptionally, with a scrutiny of the second of these words.

φιλάνορες has one meaning only and is always applied in a very specific way. Were it not for unwarranted doubts about the meaning of cτίβοι,

---

[69] Λέχος: Sexual: A. *PV* 557, 895; *Ag.* 1224 (despite the doubts of Wilamowitz and Fraenkel; cp. Denniston and Page). Parasexual: nest containing offspring: *Ag.* 50 (51); *Sept.* 292 (where the Choros also fears rape). Λέκτρον: *Pers.* 133, 543; *Suppl.* 39 (anti-sexual); *fr.* 242 N². Εὐνή: *Ag.* 27 (indirect: the couch is the nuptial one), 193, 1447, 1626; *Eum.* 217; *Pers.* 543; *Sept.* 364 (rape?); *Suppl.* 141, 151. Non-sexual (from context): *Ag.* 13 (watchman's bed), 559 (soldier's pallet at Troy); *Choe.* 318 (tomb). Uncertain (mutilated verse): *Pap. Oxy.* 2249.14.

[70] Cp. the constant harping on the bed = coitus equation in Ov. *Her.* 16.20, 35, 156, 264, 268, 318; 17.22, 195, etc. In E. *Med.* 140, Page (ad loc.) suggests that bowdlerization replaced λέκτρα with δῶμα.

[71] Something of the sort is implied by Fraenkel's "husband-loving steps" theory.

[72] A defensible point, since Menelaos moved to Sparta, but cp. E. *Ph.* 14, for Laios' "owning" Iokaste's bed.

[73] As a clinician, I am impressed with the psychological import of a spouse's tendency to designate a double bed as "the", "mine", "yours", or "ours", and also, where twin beds are used, of preferences for making love in the husband's or in the wife's bed (cp. Plu. *V. Dion.* 3.3).

no one would feel impelled to impute to φιλάνορες, as used in A. *Ag.* 411, a meaning it cannot have and does not have anywhere. For the sake of expository convenience, I distinguish between this word's manifest meaning and the use to which it is put.

In the most literal—and only genuine—sense, this word means "man (husband) loving". It designates either the *woman* who loves her man,[74] or one of her (usually erotic) *acts*, which is a manifestation of her love. It cannot, by any stretch of the imagination, denote a husband's love for his wife—not even that part of his love which is a response (ἀντέρως) to his wife's loving behaviour. There is no exception to this rule and the transparent etymology of the word makes any such exception impossible. Hence, Smyth's translation: "the imprint of *her* body *so dear*" (i.e., to the husband) is inadmissible.

The word apparently cannot even designate an action of a loving wife which does not *manifestly* reflect that love. Indeed, though a wife cannot love her husband unless she is sufficiently alive to breathe, her breathing cannot, by any stretch of the imagination, be called "husband loving". The Denniston and Page hypothesis, that στίβοι φιλάνορες means "husband-loving tracks" and represents a condensation of the meaning: "places where the one who loved her husband used to walk" is therefore implausible, for no matter how delightful it may have been for Menelaos to watch Helene's promenade, her walking about did not manifest her love for him. Similarly, even though it took the Trojan elders' breath away to see Helene walk past (Hom. *Il.* 3.154 ff.), her passing by was not a manifestation of her love for the elders. Nor, for that matter, did it express her love for Paris. I can find no text in which a woman is called "husband-loving" *while* she is engaged in an activity which does not reflect her love. Hence, neither the promenading of a still faithful Helene, nor the tracks she left while strolling about, nor the place where she used to walk can be called "husband-loving".

Literary considerations also militate against such an assumption. The image of a lady walking around charmingly in—let us say—a Watteau garden, simply does not fit Aischylos' imagery, nor are promenades—*amoureuses* or other—a classical or even a mythical theme. I cannot think of any mythical lady promenading. If she goes out, she does so with a set purpose: she goes somewhere, to do something definite. The promenade hypothesis introduces a rococo nuance into a lean and virile text.

The notion of a condensation so extreme as to be practically a riddle is also questionable. Such verbal intensity *à propos* of a sentimental tableau, inherently incompatible with the classical taste,[75] could perhaps be expected from Lykophron, Moschos or Ovidius—or the poets of the *Anthologia Palatina*; an Aischylos does not fire a cannon at humming-birds.

Fraenkel's view, that Helene's "husband loving" steps once brought her to the nuptial couch, is neither sentimental nor incompatible with the real sense of φιλάνορες. Fraenkel could even have strengthened his hypothesis by linking these steps with the manner in which Helene's

---

[74] It is never applied to a boy's love for his adult lover, i.e., to homosexual affairs.

[75] Only Sappho's steel-edged objectivity could have depicted such a promenade without violating the canons of classical taste.

dream-image approaches the sleeping Menelaos (v. 420 ff.). The Fraenkel hypothesis is simply unnecessarily complicated, because it tries to take into account Ahrens' erroneous assertion (infra) that cτίβοι must refer to some activity or trace of the *feet* (*1*).

As regards usage, φιλάνορες seems to be applied only to a woman's love *for her husband*. This is true of Aischylos and, so far as I am able to ascertain, also of other poets. It never seems to denote a woman's love for her *lover*, and this despite the fact that the Greeks had no word meaning exclusively "husband"; the primary meaning of ἀνήρ is simply "man".[76] It is precisely this specific meaning of the word ἀνήρ—and of φιλάνορες which is derived from it—which makes Klytaimestra's lying references to her "husband-loving" transports (A. *Ag.* 856), so outrageous. Distorted uses of a word notoriously help one determine its authentic meaning.

Last, but not least, I stress—for reasons which will become apparent further on—that, in Aischylos, φιλάνορες has *erotic* connotations. In A. *Pers.* 136, it describes the erotic yearning of Persian ladies for their absent husbands, for whom they long and grieve, while lying alone *in bed* (A. *Pers.* 133).

This strictly circumscribed application of φιλάνορες renders incomprehensible the attempts of Klausen, Wilamowitz and Mazon to make it apply to Helene's love for Paris, be it before or during the actual elopement.[77]

Indeed, from the purely literary point of view, vv. 410–411 deal exclusively with the chaos *left behind* by the eloping Helene.

From the sociological point of view, the Greek conception of marriage must be differentiated from the Judeo-Christian one. Unlike American divorce courts, which hold that a woman was sufficiently married to be entitled to a ruinous alimony even if her marriage was never consummated, the Greeks did not rate an unconsummated union as a marriage.[78]

This latter finding is of crucial importance since, according to Greek tradition, Helene and Paris did *not* cohabit—even adulterously—*before* their elopement. The union (μίξις) did not take place until after they left Menelaos' palace.[79] This being so, one doubts that even Helene

---

[76] Aischylos even uses this word in order to differentiate between man and woman, cp G. Italie, *Index Aeschyleus*, s.v., 1. (*86*).

[77] The reference to the elopement from the husband in v. 404—specifically by means of the word λιποῦσα, which recalls the λιπεσάνορας of Stesich. *fr.* 46 P and the λειψάνδρους of sch. E. *Or.* 249,—also makes unlikely a further reference to the actual flight in v. 411.

[78] In E. *El.* 1284 ff., the Dioskouroi order Elektra to marry Pylades, on the grounds that her marriage with the good peasant was never consummated; they specify that she is a virgin miscalled "wife". The marriage mentioned by Herodotos (2.181), which, because of the husband's *selective* impotence (cp. Freud 70), was, for a while, not consummated, was *not* a Greek union.

[79] Cp. Paus. 3.22.2; sch. Lyc. 87; V. *Aen.* 1.651 and Roscher (*129*) s.v. Helene, col. 1939. Lehrs' (*97*, p. 16) affirmation that, in the *Kypria*, an adulterous union took place already *before* the elopement, is inadequately documented. Ov. *Her.* 17 and 18 may, perhaps, imply a *desire* to commit adultery already in Menelaos' palace, but the adultery is not *said* to have been consummated before the elopement. In fact, the endless allusions to *plans* of elopement may, perhaps, suggest that even Ovidius did not believe that the adultery was consummated before the flight, though his baroque rhetoric makes certainty on this point impossible.

and Paris considered themselves "married" *before* their cohabitation. In fact, they probably did not consider themselves married before reaching Troy, where a Trojan marriage rite may have been performed. I note here that Ovidius labours the distinction between an affair and a marriage almost *ad nauseam*, and does so specifically in connection with Helene and Paris.[80]

The fact that a Greek god's casual coitus with, or rape of a mortal woman are both called γάμος, does not contradict this view, for that word can also denote simply coitus. Though A. S. Owens (in his edition of E. *Ion*) (*117*) tries to justify the designation of Apollon's rape of Kreusa (in v. 10) as a γάμος (= marriage), by citing E. *Hel.* 190, which so designates Pan's irregular matings, he overlooks a crucial fact: Greek gods simply do not *marry* mortal women, nor even nymphs and their like—though they expected their "inferior" mates to remain faithful to them.[81] This caused Marpessa to prefer the mortal Idas, who would marry her, to Apollon, who would not (Hom. *Il.* 9.557; Apollod. 1.7.9). In fact, paradoxical as this may seem, only goddesses actually *married* mortals or ex-mortals; gods did not.[82] The fact that both Aischylos and Euripides should use the word γάμος to denote precisely the seduction and/or rape of a *mortal* girl by a *god* is, as A. *Ag.* 1207 puts it, "according to custom". It perfectly tallies with a point I made long ago (*42*, pp. 356 ff.; *52*, chap. 7): a marriage rite only consecrates what, in the last resort, remains a forbidden act; hence, the rite cannot abolish all neurotic guilt feelings.[83]

But even if—contrary to tradition—one assumes that Helene and Paris cohabited already in Sparta and that, thereafter—again contrary to custom—they considered themselves "married", and therefore viewed Helene's steps, following those of Paris, as "husband-loving", this still does not give *this* meaning *to v. 411*—and it is the meaning of *this* verse that matters here.

The point is that v. 411 is uttered neither by Helene nor by Paris. It is uttered by the Choros—by Agamemnon's most faithful retainers—who only repeat what Menelaos' loyal prophets said. I deem it inconceivable that *these* men would have considered Paris and Helene married, and would have viewed what Helene did *for Paris' sake* as evidence of her *husband-loving* nature . . . and this no matter what Paris and Helene may have thought about it. Let it not be forgotten that the selfsame Choros stubbornly refused to view Klytaimestra's long concubinage with Aigisthos

---

[80] Ov. *Her.* 16.297, 329 f.; 17.195, etc. He also describes both Hypsipyle and Ariadne as seduced but unwed (*Her.* 16.297).

[81] As Apollon, who never wedded even a goddess, expected Koronis to be faithful to him. (Cp. *Testt.* 21-35 in *57*, i. pp. 21-25.) On divine rapes, cp. chap. 8, note 175.

[82] Eos and Tithonos, *h. Hom. in Ven.* 218 ff.; Hebe and Herakles; possibly Demeter and Iasion, though the only "source" to hint at this is late Biedermeier (Ov. *Met.* 9.422); Peleus and Thetis; Odysseus, Kalypso and Kirke, etc. It was this tendency of goddesses to contract *genuine* hypogamous *marriages*, rather than their casual amours with men, which seemed to have angered Zeus (Hes. *Pap. Berol.* 10560 = *fr.* 204.96 ff. M.W.).

[83] In the works just cited, I highlighted particularly the fact that, among the Mohave Indians, *only* forbidden (incestuous) cousin-marriages involve a marriage *ritual* and only they are *supposed* to be indissoluble.

as a true "marriage"[84]—even though, unlike Helene and Paris, Klytai-mestra and Aigisthos could punish them for their obstinacy.[85]

Summing up, *regardless* of what cτίβοι means—and its meaning is quite transparent—φιλάνορες can only refer to some act—or to the trace of some act—performed by Helene, which was a direct manifestation of her love for her lawful, wedded husband, Menelaos.

cτίβοι must be discussed in detail, for it gave rise to needlessly complicated explanations, devised by editors who unquestioningly accepted Ahrens' sweeping assertion that *all* words derived from the same root as cτίβοι denote the activities of the *feet* and the *tracks* they leave. Yet Schütz, Headlam, Thomson, Verrall and Smyth recognized that cτίβοι refers here to the imprint of the body—but did not justify their (often partly wrong) translations. That is the view I propose to defend here.

1. Imprint of body

(1) S. *Ph.* 33: cτιπτή γε φυλλὰς ὡς ἐναυλίζοντί τῳ. (an imprinted pile of plants, as if for someone who makes his lodgings there). Jebb (ad loc.) correctly comments: "cτιπτή means, pressed down by the body of a person who slept on it".[86]

(2) The soft[87] and inelastic Greek bed preserved the imprint of the sleeper's body until it was remade (cp. for a faint echo: Q.S. 10.131 f.).

(3) cτίβοι is what the prophets saw the morning after Helene's elopement and what Menelaos *may* have seen on his return.[88]

I must now account for the adjective φιλάνορες and for the use of the plural.

(1) The relationship between cτίβοι and φιλάνορες is the same as that between the dream image (ὄψις, v. 425) and the (illusory) sexual delight (χάριν, v. 421) it brings.[89] I recall that in Aischylos (*Pers.* 133 ff.) φιλάνορες is *directly* connected with marital beds and sexuality. Verrall

---

[84] Cp. also Aischylos' underlining of Klytaimestra's brazenness, by making her refer to herself as "husband-loving" (A. *Ag.* 856).

[85] Despite the importance of the distinction between virilocal and uxorilocal marriages in ancient Greece (*136*, pp. 97–143), I doubt that we must bear here in mind that Klytaimestra's marriage was virilocal and that of Helene uxorilocal.

[86] LSJ therefore errs in citing this expression to illustrate the sense: "trodden down". A pallet (cτίβας) would *not* have been trodden down with the feet. The wandering minstrel Homeros (*Od.* 11. 193 f.; cp. 24.255), Aischylos the soldier (A. *Ag.* 411), Sophokles the general (S. *Ph.* 33), Euripides the landowner and soldier (*Rh.* 9, *Tr.* 507), would have known the reasons, as I know them for having repeatedly slept on such pallets while doing anthropological fieldwork: broken twigs have sharp points.

[87] Hom. *Od.* 24.255: μαλακῶν.

[88] One could, somewhat gratuitously, speculate that the bed was not remade until Menelaos' return, so as to prove that Helene had not committed adultery *in it* before she eloped (supra), and also that, like many mourners (*80*, pp. 86 f.), Menelaos ordered that nothing belonging to Helene should be tampered with. Such "pieties" seek to negate the reality of the loss—a psychological defence that will be mentioned in connection with ἀπίστους (infra). Though such supplementary hypotheses, while plausible enough, are not indispensable, it seems worth while to recall that a *physical* tampering with a bed can create a suspicion that it was tampered with also adulterously. This may explain Odysseus' resentment in Hom. *Od.* 23.183 ff. (Liv. 1.58).

[89] For the sexual nuance of χάριν, see infra, on v. 421.

therefore rightly—though in a somewhat Victorian language—writes: "yet printed with her embraces". In plainer terms, cτίβοι φιλάνορες designates the imprint *Helene's* body had so often left on the bed, while making love with Menelaos. It goes without saying that during such acts *only* Helene's body would leave an imprint on the bed.[90] This means that the imprints left by Helene during her marital embraces differed only *in depth* from those *she alone* had left on the bed during Menelaos' absence.

The plural presents no real problem and it is not necessary to assume that it is a "generic plural" of the type found in v. 410 and in vv. 412 f. The last imprint Helene left on the bed simply *evokes*, in a condensed form, the many imprints she had left on it in the course of her years of love-making with Menelaos. It is this *capacity* of the *last* imprint she left on the bed to *evoke* the *many earlier* ones which justifies the use of the plural.

Before discussing the evocative powers of the last imprint, which the prophets—and, perhaps, also Menelaos—actually saw, I must show that traces of love-making interested the ancients ever since Homeros (*Il.* 14. 346 ff.).

(1) Ov. *Her.* 15.148 f.: "Agnoui pressas noti mihi caespitis herbas;/de *nostro* curuum pondere gramen erat." Sappho sees that the bent stalks of grass still preserve the imprint of the *combined* weight of Phaon's body and her own, once enlaced *in an act of love*.[91] The sight of this imprint induces Sappho to lie down upon the still bent grass, so as to *recall* more vividly former erotic joys.[92]

(2) Theocr. 2.136 f. evokes a much more elusive trace: the lingering warmth the husband's body left in the marital bed.[93]

The interest of the ancients in such erotic traces is even more strongly highlighted by the existence of rules requiring them to be *erased*.

(1) A Pythagorean, on getting up in the morning, had to remake his bed and erase the imprint his body had left on it.[94] (Protection against witchcraft?)

(2) Ar. *Nub.* 973. A well-brought-up nude lad had to sit in the gymnasion in a manner which concealed his organs. On getting up, he had to smooth out the concave imprint (εἴδωλον) they left on the sand, so as not to stimulate his lovers or admirers.[95]

[90] A realism of this type may be safely ascribed to Aischylos, who was famous for his (necessarily "obscene") satyr plays (*114*, p. x).

[91] The allusion to the *combined* weight of enlaced bodies contrasts with the subsequent reference (178 ff.) to the present weightlessness of her now solitary body ("Haec mea non magnum corpora pondus habent"), so wasted by love sorrow that if she leaped into the sea, the air would be able to buoy it up. [The allusion here is presumably to the practice of tying birds to the bodies of those who ritually leaped into the sea, in the hope that the birds' wing-beats would slow down their fall. On this practice, cp. C. Gallini's study of Katapontismos (*75*).]

[92] These verses may have been ultimately inspired by Aischylos' cτίβοι φιλάνορες.

[93] Shakespeare refers to the "rank sweat" which pervades the love-couch of Hamlet's murderous mother and uncle.

[94] Cp. P.-M. Schuhl (*132*, p. 255); W. Deonna (*17*, p. 171); O. Weinreich (*140*, p. 180). (References furnished by Professor W. Burkert.)

[95] 975 . . . καί προνοεῖcθαι
976 εἴδωλον τοῖcιν ἐραcταῖcιν ἥβεc μὴ καταλείπειν.

Cp. also Dover ad Ar. *Nub.* 973. A proper Greek lover was interested only in the boy's male organ (*38*).

This Aristophanic passage is crucial for the understanding of the Aischylean expression under discussion.

(1) Aischylos uses στίβοι in a somewhat unusual sense; Aristophanes' use of εἴδωλον to designate a *hollow* ("negative") imprint is so unique that LSJ does not even give for εἴδωλον the meaning: "*hollow* imprint".[96]

(2) Both Aischylos and Aristophanes describe *hollow* imprints capable of eliciting both erotic feelings and a sense of frustration.[97]

(3) Helene notoriously had a sexually arousing εἴδωλον: a double, though,[98] as Fraenkel indicates, it is not really relevant here.

(4) A. *Ag.* 410–426 is full of allusions to doubles (στίβοι, φάσμα, ὄψις and, with some restrictions, κολοσσός).[99]

(5) The foreseeable objection, that Aischylos refers to the imprint of a *female body* and Aristophanes to that of the *male organ*, strengthens rather than weakens the postulated nexus between these two passages. Solid clinical evidence (*62, 37*) demonstrates the existence of the symbolic equation: "girl = phallos (of her father or lover)". Massive Greek mythological data prove the presence of this symbolic equation in ancient Greece (*44*).[100]

The εἴδωλον ("double")[101] aspect of στίβοι—the equivalence of the imprint left by an organ and of the organ itself—is significantly highlighted by the fact that ἴχνος means both the footprint and the foot.[102]

2. στίβοι *and the dream*

The fact that this imprint is on the bed and plays, at least affectively, the role of a double, recalls the fact that Admetos intended to place *in* his bed Alkestis' portrait statue (E. *Alc.* 348) in order to derive (partial) erotic gratification both from the embracing of the statue *and* from erotic dreams: this statue was actually meant to elicit erotic dreams about Alkestis.

Now, like Alkestis' statue, but unlike Helene's phantom (φάσμα and ὄψις) Helene's στίβοι are not only visible, but also *real*. They may therefore be presumed to play, with regard to Menelaos' dream, the role of a

[96] I often wonder whether, in poking fun at the bold complexity of Aischylean tragic diction (Ar. *Ran.* 818 ff. and passim), Aristophanes did not laugh also at the excesses of his own comic diction.

[97] On ἀπηνές in Ar. *Nub.* 974, cp. Dover ad loc.

[98] The myth of Helene's εἴδωλον must be restudied from the start, for the valuable essays of Premerstein (*124*), Pisani (*122*), Zielinski (*143*), Vernant (*136*) and Davison (*15*) do not exploit all the surviving (direct and indirect) references to it (*54*) and are not psycho-analytically oriented.

[99] Cp. Vernant (*136*, p. 257), though I disagree with his interpretation of the Aischylean κολοσσοί (infra).

[100] The Aristophanic hollow double of the convex male organ may *perhaps* be remotely inspired by the *worldwide* fantasy (*25, 44, 48*, chap. 16) of the "reversible" male organ, attested for classical antiquity by Ael. *NA* 6.34. (Chap. 9, note 58.)

[101] On the psychological meaning of the "Doppelgänger", cp. O. Rank (*126*).

[102] Cp. E. *Ba.* 1134. Dodds (ad loc.) cites also E. *fr.* 350, Catull. 64.162. Grégoire cites E. *Hec.* 1058–1059. Compare also Ov. *Her.* 15.186, where "pedem" stands for Phaon. It is perhaps this double sense of ἴχνος which induced Aischylos to use here στίβοι in a slightly special sense.

"day residue" (cp. chap. 1, note 6). The fact that it is located *in* the bed in which *real* love-making once took place, reminds one that Artabanos, when sleeping in Xerxes' bed, had the same dream the king had had there (Hdt. 7.17).[103] In short, Menelaos' dream fills Helene's hollow imprint with her dream-image.

3. The choice of the word στίβοι

This remains the only problem to be discussed, for, as Ahrens noted, words derived from the same root *usually*—though, as we saw, *not* always—refer to footprints, to walking, to walking upon, to treading with the feet. Now, rhythmic movements in general and even rotation and oscillation, which cause vertigo, not only tend to elicit—or, in the case of vertigo, to accompany—sexual excitement, but tend to symbolize such excitement in dream, in fantasy, in magic and even in humour.[104]

(1) *Psycholinguistics* has much to contribute to the clarification of the meaning of στίβοι, for treading has a coital significance in many languages. I deliberately choose Latin examples to illustrate this point:

Calco = the coital activity of the cock (Col. 8.5.24). In the dialect of Picardy *cauquer* (from: *calcare*) signifies: to coitize and evokes, by assonance, the word "coq" (= penis and cock). But *calco* also means to tread (so as to crush, e.g., grapes in a vat)[105] or even to crush in a mortar (Apic. 2.3) —which is notoriously a coital symbol in many cultures.[106]

---

[103] Cp. Ov. *Her.* 15.148 ff. (supra).

[104] It is a psychological commonplace that rhythmic movements can symbolize coitus in dream. This probably sheds new light on Greek rituals involving swings and specifically on the problem of "Phaidra on the swing"—discussed by Picard (*121*) without any real awareness of the sexual symbolism involved. It may also explain why, in Greek love-magic, a wry-neck was tied to a wheel and rotated (Theocr. 2.17)—a practice which reminds one of Ixion tied to a turning wheel (Pi. *P.* 2.40 ff.). (Vertigo-like sensations can occur either during orgasm, or when getting up after coitus.) As regards special types of passive rhythmic movements, it is not without interest that the first cavalry group mentioned in Greek mythology are the Amazons. As I noted elsewhere (*24, 29, 36*), there is a curious equivalence of the rider and the ridden in dream, in fantasy and even in beliefs regarding possession, and this regardless of the actual sex of the rider and of the mount. Indeed, even the male rider spreads his thighs like a coitized woman. As to the mount, I cited in the aforementioned papers the obsessive fantasy of a patient about a phallos-like object protruding from the horse's back and penetrating the rider's crotch. One of my students, M. Jean-Luc Mercier, recently showed me a cartoon sequence, in which a horsewoman is mounted on a horse whose *dorsal* "phallos" penetrates her vagina (cp. Ael. *NA* 6.15 and *78*, p. 21). In a pornographic magazine, there is mention of a woman's bicycle, whose seat is provided with a mobile penis activated by the pedals. Further evidence for the nexus between rhythmic movements and sexual excitement is provided by a Far Eastern ὄλισβος (dildo), which stimulates the woman only while she walks or rocks herself. It consists of a light, thin-walled silver ball containing a small and heavy metal sphere. The latter rolls around when the woman moves rhythmically, and imparts vibrations to the thin walls of the sphere which contains it. It is also to be noted that at least one Greek word (πίτυλος) denotes repetitive rhythmic movements (E. *Hipp.* 1464 and Barrett ad loc.). Even rhythmically swelling and diminishing ("pulsating") *sound* can symbolize coitus in dream, cp. chap. 8, note 124. Human fantasy, at its highest and at its lowest, is much the same everywhere.

[105] Cato *RR* 112 fin.; Varr. *RR* 1.54.2, etc.

[106] Cp. chap. 7, note 66.

"Treading" or "walking upon" has, moreover, usually a specifically triumphal connotation, which degrades the "trodden" partner.[107] Even "climbing" and, *a fortiori*, "climbing on" are marked coital symbols.[108]

From "walking on" to "weighing down upon" (or: compress) is but a short step. In Latin *compressio* means: coitus (Hyg. *fab.* 187, etc.). But *compressio* evokes in turn also a crushing weight on the chest, which suffocates the dreamer—as happens typically in the real nightmare (*Alpdruck*) (*88*). This characteristic of the nightmare is made evident also by its Greek name: ἐφιάλτης = the leaper, he who leaps upon.[109]

(2) *Psychology* also provides support for the views I propound. In fantasy, in dream, and even in slang the foot represents the penis,[110] and, both Mimnermos (*fr.* 15 D.) and a proverb of Rumanian peasant women postulate a nexus between lameness and exceptional male coital prowess.[111]

Also, just as the foot represents the penis, so its imprints or tracks can represent the traces of coitus:

(a) *Prov.* 30.19 describes four kinds of invisible tracks: those of the eagle in the air, those of the serpent on the rock, those of the ship in the sea, and those of the man in the woman.

(b) Two girls, who were friends and were in analysis with different

---

[107] Suet. *V. xii Caes.* 1.22: Caesar seems to imply that he will force his defeated foes to fellate him symbolically. In J.-M. de Hérédia: *Trophées* ("Médaille" v. 14): "l'éléphant triomphal foule les primevères" (*16*), appears to imply that the Malatestas (whose quasi-heraldic animal was the elephant) ruthlessly exercised the *ius primae noctis*. In Stat. *Theb.* 3.208, *calco* means simply "to spurn," and has no *obvious* sexual connotations. I will return to the spurning aspects of coitus in connection with Menelaos' dream. For the moment I note only that Fraenkel's euphemism "spurning" for "spitting" (A. *Ag.* 1192) *unwittingly* sidesteps the sexual implications of a "spurning" expectoration—thereby indirectly highlighting that connection (infra).

[108] A woman patient fantasied that she and her therapist climbed a tree together, but that she was always three branches (3 = male organ, Plu. *Quaest. Rom.* 2, p. 263 F) below her doctor. Finally she got dizzy and climbed down prematurely. Her explicit association to her inability to reach the highest branch revealed her inability to experience a vaginal orgasm. (Frigidity = castration.)

[109] Cp. Sch. B. *Il.* 5.385 and *EM* 403.32 for this etymology. Cp. French: *saillir* = a male animal mounting the female. Of course, in myth, it is sometimes the *female* monster who mounts and rapes the male, whose (anxiety-)erection is only too apparent on some monuments. One of the most interesting of these monsters is the Sphinx = "strangler"— i.e., the one who suffocates. It is of considerable psychological importance that most such rapist female monsters were believed to harm children (Rohde *128*, appendix vi)—for the nightmare is patterned upon the infantile fear of being crushed in bed (= raped) by the fantasmatic sexual mother. Greek humour—or Galgenhumor—confirms this: if a prostitute is nicknamed "Sphinx" (LSJ s.v., 2), that name clearly represents her as a "rapist female"—as a type capable of arousing "erotized anxiety" (*95*) in those psychosexually *immature* enough to cohabit with prostitutes. Indeed, both psychosexual immaturity and a penchant for the erotization of anxiety are manifest in such men, who instance what Freud (*70*) called the most prevalent form of degradation in erotic life.

[110] "Third leg." "Trouver chaussure à son pied" = to find a suitable mistress. Characteristically, foot fetishism occurs in men greatly obsessed with the fantasy of the "female phallos" (*39*, p. 240). There is even a peculiar connection between the foot and the castration of the hermaphroditic Agdistis. A noose was put around her male parts and its end was tied to her foot while she was asleep. When, on awakening, she stretched her leg, the noose tore off her male organs (Arnob. *adv. nat.* 5.5).

[111] "God preserve you from being beaten by a blind man [who can't see where his blows fall] and from being coitized (aggressive slang word) by a lame man [who comes down on you in heavy thrusts]."

analysts, dreamed at approximately the same time that their bed linen was covered with (male) footprints. Both had been deflowered relatively recently and were ashamed of having taken several lovers in rapid succession.

But the traces of unlawful coitus can also be represented by stains of (symbolic) semen, *not necessarily* emitted by a man. In A. *Ag.* 1192, the Erinyes "spit" (ἀπέπτουςαν) on the bed adulterously "trampled on" (πατοῦντι) by the husband's brother. Again, we find that "trampling" denotes forbidden, hostile coitus, and it is a psycho-analytical—and psycho-linguistic—commonplace that spittle = semen and that spitting = ejaculation.[112] In this passage it is admittedly Thyestes who commits adultery and the Erinyes who "spit" on the bed he defiled. But I hold that their spitting actually *stands for* Thyestes' adulterous ejaculation. The Erinyes may be said to "spit" on the bed *by means of* Thyestes' seminal discharge, for, in the last resort, Thyestes' act may be a consequence of the curse weighing on the descendants of Pelops,[113] and therefore also a consequence of the Erinyes' influence upon him: they cause the curse, under which that dynasty lies, to snowball further, by inciting the commission of additional accursed deeds, by Thyestes, Atreus, and their descendants.[114]

Summing up:

(1) In v. 411 cτίβοι denotes the imprint of the whole of Helene's body, *during* the marital embrace (φιλάνορες).

(2) The visible cτίβοι are at once a kind of double, in the mythological sense, and a "day residue" which triggers off Menelaos' erotic dream.

(3) Aischylos probably used this word because walking and other rhythmic movements tend to symbolize coital activity in dream, and footprints the traces of such acts.

If the arguments just presented have one real merit, it is that they dispose of the need to impute to Aischylean diction a *riddling* condensation devoid of psychological validity. For Aischylean condensations always strengthen the impact of his utterance—while here the various *alleged* condensations greatly weaken it, and strip it of all psychological relevance.

412–413: Plurals or Singulars? Our manuscripts have singulars throughout, which the metre—and other considerations as well—render inacceptable. Those who refuse to treat these verses as a *locus desperatus* always modify the case endings—usually turning the singular nominatives into plural accusatives. (But the scansion of these verses and of their responsion is still controversial.)

The first question to be asked is *how* Aischylos' plurals turned into singu-

---

[112] It was, if I am not misinformed, usual in certain areas to call adultery: "spitting on the husband's bed".

[113] In one's preoccupation with Thyestes' curse, whom Atreus had caused to cannibalize his children (A. *Ag.* 1219 ff., etc.), one sometimes forgets that Pelops, too, was accursed for having slain Myrtilos (cp. Roscher *129* s.vv.).

[114] My formulation of the sense in which Thyestes' act is, *in a way*, an act of the Erinyes, is strengthened by Lloyd-Jones' (*104*) discussion of the *sense* in which the supernaturals "cause" men to do evil deeds, and in particular by his comments on A. *Niobe* vv. 15 f. (Page): "God first causes a fault to grow in a man, when he is minded utterly to ruin his estate."

lars in the hands of a not-too-perceptive copyist. I submit that this resulted from the copyist's *correctly* taking πρόμοι as referring to Menelaos only (supra). Having reached this correct conclusion and probably realizing that Agamemnon would not have exhibited the symptoms of a stuporous depression, he failed to understand the plurals—and therefore also the sense—of these verses; he therefore turned the plural accusatives into grammatically and metrically monstrous singular nominatives. I hold with Thomson (ad loc.) that the corruption of these verses began not with the word transmitted as ΑΔΙϹΤΟϹ, but with the corruption of the case endings, the copyist assuming that πάρεϲτι ... ἰδεῖν called for the singular nominative (cp. E. *Tr.* 36 f.).

What, precisely, *is* the sense of the Choros' use of plurals? Realizing that Menelaos cuts a pitiful and most unheroic figure, the Choros deems it best and most tactful (*45*) not to describe his behaviour in a pointedly personal manner. It says in effect: "The distressed visibly exhibit the following symptoms."[115] Menelaos is not mentioned by name, nor are specific—and unheroic—symptoms directly attributed to him. Instead, we are given a description of a "textbook case" of stuporous depression, which Menelaos' behaviour instances.

This procedure is more than merely tactful; it is also supportive. Every psychotherapist has had occasion to soften a painful confrontation or interpretation by saying: "This *usually* means . . ."—for the neurotic is often inclined to believe that he is the *only one* so afflicted, or so depraved; a reference to the similar flaws of others diminishes his sense of total isolation.[116]

In short, the violence the copyist did to the case endings and to the metre is as understandable as the Choros' reason for using a plural of tact ("those who"), instead of the more pointed, but also less delicate, singular ("Menelaos' symptoms are . . .").

The plurals are, moreover, both stylistically and aesthetically appropriate. They effect a transition between the "allusive plural" of v. 410 (πρόμοι) and the singulars used from v. 414 onward. Also, while the symptoms listed in vv. 412–413 are unheroic, those described from v. 414 onward are sufficiently poetic and "heroic" to make the use of singulars and direct references to Menelaos as a person—and not just as a specimen member of the "class of all the depressed"—aesthetically acceptable and even desirable.

412 πάρεϲτι [. . . ἰδεῖν] (= one may, it is possible to [see]) is accepted by most editors, though one hears it questioned now and then, because πάρειϲι occurs in v. 421. The first thing to be noted is that, in v. 421, this similar-looking word has an altogether different significance: "are present". The use of similar-looking and -sounding words, having different meanings, is an acceptable stylistic device, which reminds one of

---

[115] In S. *OT* 1.186 ff. the "generations of men" are an attenuated equivalent of this (but also gnomic).

[116] A girl patient tenaciously insisted that only she was depraved enough to masturbate—but I pointed out that the existence of a word for that activity proved that she was not alone in indulging in self-gratification. Only after this reassurance was given could she admit what, in her opinion, *really* set her apart: certain genuinely unusual masturbation *fantasies* (*45*).

the ancient affinity between poetry and punning. Moreover, if, as seems necessary, one treats the dream as the nocturnal equivalent of Menelaos' waking symptoms,[117] it is stylistically elegant to begin both the list of Menelaos' waking symptoms and the account of his nocturnal symptom— of his dream—with very similar-sounding, though conceptually quite different verbs.

In short, I hold πάρεcτι to be sound, precisely on the grounds on which a small minority of Hellenists would challenge it.[118]

412 cιγᾶc = silence. It is the first listed symptom and the only one which lacks the privative prefix ἀ-. It is therefore a "positive symptom" ("acting silent") and not a "negative" one ("deprived of speech"). It is distinct from the negative symptom ἀλοιδόρουc = non-vilifying.

Now, a hurt or offended Greek would normally either lament or curse, or do both. But Menelaos is silent, partly no doubt because he is stunned ("psychomotor retardation"), but partly also because his silence is a both psychologically appropriate and culturally encouraged "distress behaviour". His mutism differs radically from the involuntary aphasia or aphonia of Sappho (*fr.* 2B = 2D = 31LP), whose seizure does not have even one symptom in common with Menelaos' depression (*43*).

Aischylos, who excelled in composing torrential lamentations (*18*), hardly felt unable to write one for Menelaos. If his Menelaos is silent, it is because the poet so intended it: because he had observed the mutism of stuporously depressed mourners—of whom there must have been many after Marathon and Salamis (cp. Hom. *Il.* 7.425 ff.). Let it also not be forgotten that while some distressed Aischylean personages utter long laments, others indulge in long, ominous silences.[119]

Menelaos' stunned, negativistic, psychologically appropriate and culturally suitable silence is, thus, unmistakably Aischylean. Its mention in the *first* place anticipates Menelaos' *last* (*visible*) symptom: his sitting apart (ἀφημένων, infra), which not only presupposes mutism, but is also the opening gambit of a manœuvre whereby Menelaos expects to regain "face" (infra).[120]

412 ἀτίμουc, though it implies both loss of honour and of "face", does not refer primarily to public contempt for a cuckold still too ena- moured of his wife even to curse her (ἀλοιδόρουc). Verses 412 f. do not emphasize *primarily* Menelaos' *social* handicaps, but his *subjective* symptoms. Menelaos' feeling of worthlessness is a salient symptom of his "mourning reaction",[121] for every loss—even in the absence of sincere

---

[117] Cp. my comments on v. 420: πενθήμονεc.

[118] Cf. also A. *Choe.* 253: ἰδεῖν πάρεcτί. Thomson cites E. *Tr.* 36 f.

[119] Ar. *Ran.* 911 ff. mentions the long silences of his mourning Achilleus and Niobe. Other data in Nauck *TGF²*, pp. 50 f.

[120] Most cultures specify under what circumstances people should be stoical or should display grief. The (still evolving and adaptive) Mohave Indian creation myth blames the forebears of the Americans for being the only ones not to cry at the dead god Matavilye's funeral. But a deserted Mohave husband should not display sorrow (*42*, 90 ff.).

[121] Freud erroneously contrasts the self-depreciation of the melancholiac with the "lack" of self-contempt in mourning (*71*). Every mourning practice is a *ritual* self-degradation and therefore a token of subjective self-depreciation. I hope to discuss the psychology of mourning on another occasion, for I cannot even begin to outline it here.

grief—is experienced as a narcissistic injury.[122] Helene's elopement "proves" Paris to be "superior" to the smug Menelaos, who, unlike Agamemnon, did not even think of providing a chaperone for *his* wife during his absence from home. In societies which take it for granted that a man and a woman left alone will *automatically* copulate (*39*, p. 108), the failure to show anticipatory jealousy is not only socially improper (Hom. *Od.* 11.441 ff.) but also an insult to the wife's sense of her own desirability.[123]

In short, what matters here clinically is not that the cuckolded Menelaos is *socially* dishonoured, but that he *feels* dishonoured by his loss. I note in passing that a great many alleged problems of Homeric and Greek "psychology" would disappear if commentators were more aware of the reciprocity—the complementarity relation—between the socio-cultural and the psychological *explanations* of a given attitude or behaviour (*39, 48, 52*).

412 ἀλοιδόρους (= non-vilifying) does not simply repeat, with an added nuance, something already implicit in Menelaos' silence (cιγᾶc). The Choros once again goes beyond a purely descriptive statement; it appraises the significance of what it observes. In emotional Homeric society (*115*), vituperation was acceptable and even expected behaviour, as was haughty or angry silence and aloofness (cp. infra). These two reactions were acceptable "alternatives", in Linton's sense (*102*, pp. 273 ff.); they could even occur in succession: Achilleus first curses Agamemnon and then sulks in his tent. He first chose one and then another culturally acceptable reaction to a particular socio-cultural stimulus.

By contrast, Menelaos' non-vituperativeness is not a culturally acceptable alternative but deviant behaviour: a symptom and/or a defect.[124]

The Choros, manifestly recognizing that Menelaos had reasons for hating Helene, apparently *expected* him to revile her. Menelaos' failure to do so is therefore noted in a manner which defines his "self-restraint" as a symptom, whose causes are made clear almost at once (414 ff.). The embittered Menelaos is still too much in love with Helene and too obsessed with her to be able to curse the adulteress fittingly. His anger prevents him from lamenting his loss, while his love inhibits his impulse to curse her. This is a classical type of ambivalence, already described by Catullus (85): "Odi et amo" (I love and I hate). The anguish of being torn between contradictory emotions is admirably highlighted by Catullus' choice of the word: excrucior, whose etymology recalls crucifixion.[125]

Ambivalence is always markedly present in depressions and in mourning: the death of the mourned person is also viewed as an intentional

---

[122] Despite the rhetorical question: "Are the Atreidai the only ones to love their wives?" (Hom. *Il.* 9.338 ff.), Achilleus does not grieve over the loss of Briseis; he is angered by the blow to his boundless narcissism (Sch. Hom. *Od.* 3.267, etc.). For the Kwakiutl Indian, any loss or grief is a "loss of face" (*6*, chap. 6).

[123] Cp. Paris' claim that Menelaos was practically throwing Helene at him (Ov. *Her.* 16.299).

[124] Cp. the well-known story of a Spanish knight, who was deprived of his knighthood for responding *inadequately* to a stimulus: instead of killing his wife's lover, he "only" castrated him.

[125] Since the crucified man's weight is supported by his spread arms, his breathing is as inhibited as it is in certain anxiety attacks.

desertion.[126] The selfsame ambivalence is present also in schizo-affective states, in which generalized inactivity (psycho-motor retardation) also results from the reciprocal inhibition of contradictory impulses, contending with each other for the use of the skeleto-muscular system.[127]

It is also important to stress that "non-vilifying" should, in *this* case, be taken as resulting from a simple *suppression*, and not from a total *repression* of anger.[128]

The word ἀλοιδόρους provides the key to Menelaos' dream. *Simultaneously* enamoured and angry in a *waking* state, his conflicting sentiments manifest themselves *successively* in his *dream*: the love he still feels conjures up Helene's phantom, but his anger puts the phantom to flight *before* the sexual union can be completed in dream (infra).[129]

412–413 ἀπίστους = disbelieving, distrustful (suspicious) is Wilamowitz's (1885) emendation, adopted also by Fraenkel.[130]

The codexes (FTr) have ἄδιστος = more pleasant,[131] which makes no sense in the present context, though Sch. Tr tries to justify it by twisting the meaning of vv. 412–413 out of shape. Its absurd interpretations are generally ignored; Sch. Tr. simply proves that the corruption is an ancient one.

The only acceptable emendation is, I feel, ἀπίστους. My objections to other emendations will be enumerated further on.

ἄπιστος (in the nominative) was first proposed and then abandoned by Hermann. Margoliouth retained it, but then violently tampered with both verses. His text is a typical period piece:

πάρεστι σῖγ', ἄτιμος, ἀλλ' ἀλοίδορος
ἄπιστος ἐμφανῶν ἰδεῖν.

Denniston and Page object to this emendation on two grounds:

(1) They assert that ἀτίμους ἀλοιδόρους ἀπίστους "are not comfortable yoke fellows". But Fraenkel cites other typically Aischylean triplets

---

[126] E. *Alc.* 386 λείψεις, 391 προλείπεις; Hopi Indians, cp. (*89*). Laments over a death often have reproachful overtones. Grave gifts are given spitefully (*42*, pp. 442 ff.); they seem to say: "You have taken so much from me, you might as well take it all." Self-aggression in mourning behaviour is a direct consequence of inhibited aggressivity towards the "deserter", which is understandable in terms of Freud's *first* theory of self-aggression, well documented by Dollard *et al.* (*56*). The cannibalistic fantasies and acts of mourners (Hdt. 3.38; cp. the mourning Demeter's cannibalization of Pelops) represent attempts to cancel the loss. Cp. infra: ἀχηνίαις.

[127] The competition between aggressive and passive impulses for the services of the body can even traumatize the articulations and produce psychosomatic arthritis. Euripides may have sensed this: his Iolaos is a classical "arthritic personality type" (*50*).

[128] *Suppression*: "Since, despite my anger, I still love her, I will not curse her, though she well deserves it." *Repression*: "I am *not* angry: I love her, as always." I felt it necessary to clarify this, since even the psychologically perceptive Winnington-Ingram (*141*) confuses these terms. He claims that Hippolytos *suppresses* and Phaidra *represses* her sexuality: the exact reverse is true. Phaidra is only too painfully aware of hers and consciously seeks to inhibit it. Hippolytos claims to feel no sexual urge—but his tongue, which speaks of the hardships his way of life entails, betrays him at once (1367 f.).

[129] The situations here, in vv. 420 ff. and in E. *Androm.* involve differences in the relationship between love and hate. Here, love and hate co-exist, but the former controls the latter. In vv. 420 love is followed by hate (infra). In E. *Androm.* 627 ff. hate precedes the renewal of Menelaos' love for Helene.

[130] Groeneboom writes ἀπίστως, following Schwerdt.

[131] The Doric comparative of ἡδύς.

of adjectives and I hold that three resonant, acoustically and morphologically[132] similar words suit well a tolling, typically Greek and typically Aischylean, enumeration of grievous symptoms.

(2) They find this word's meaning inappropriate: "there is no question of Menelaos *not believing* that Helene has left him". *But that is exactly what Menelaos would do.*[133] In fact, Denniston and Page's bewilderment suggests that the copyist miscopied the word because *he, too,* did not deem such a reaction credible and appropriate. Yet in Greek tragedy even a man personally far less involved than Menelaos can react with dazed disbelief to news of some ghastly misfortune and may even (almost) fail to comprehend it. Theseus' stunned exclamation: "What *do* you tell me?" (S. *OC* 896) is psychologically credible; it is not a gratuitous and conventional comment, whose sole purpose is to keep a stichomythia going and to accelerate its pace.

But ἀπίστουc also has a second nuance: it suggests not only disbelief but also *mistrust* (suspiciousness). Such a reaction is also to be expected from Menelaos, whose love inhibits his anger towards Helene (ἀλοιδόρουc). Failing also to see the appropriateness of this *second* reaction and bewildered by the two concurrent and interrelated meanings of ἀπίστουc, the copyist (almost predictably) perpetuated a *lapsus calami.* The fact that, of all proposed emendations, *only* ἀπίστουc *would have bewildered the copyist,* further increases its plausibility.

The appropriateness of both nuances of ἀπίστουc, in the present context, is easy to demonstrate.

(1) *Disbelief*: Menelaos finds reality intolerable. What *did* happen, *should not* have happened, and therefore *could not* have happened: "denn nicht sein kann was nicht sein darf". This attitude is explicitly foreshadowed by v. 408: Helene dared the undarable (ἄτλατα τλᾶcα).[134] Better still, a denial of Helene's elopement, by means of an outlandish "explaining away" of the real facts, goes back at least to Stesichoros.[135]

I stress at once that Stesichoros' tale is relevant here, *not* because it offers an alternative "explanation",[136] but *only* because Stesichoros, too, *denied the reality* of Helene's escapade.

The following comments will clarify the psychological processes which make possible "disbelief" in observable and observed reality:

(a) One's notion of what is "possible" is all too often congruent with one's preconceptions as to what is "proper".[137]

(b) One's notion of what is "possible" can therefore radically distort one's perception (and/or recognition) of what one sees.[138]

---

[132] All three begin with an alpha privative and even Denniston and Page think that the correct word began with an alpha privative.

[133] Freud asked a visitor for news of his defunct disciple K. Abraham—negating his death. Wilamowitz (1885) understood the disbelief.

[134] An Aischylean thought pattern, cp. A. *Choe.* 929 f.

[135] Stesich. *fr.* 15P = 32 B = 11D: οὐκ ἔcτ' ἔτυμοc λόγοc οὗτοc = "this tale is not true" (*54*).

[136] Fraenkel is right in rejecting the φάcμα = εἴδωλον explanation of v. 415 (supra).

[137] Hom. *Il.* 3.423–426 was rejected by Zenodotos, because he deemed it improper for a goddess to bring a chair for a mortal. Cp. Leaf, ad loc.

[138] I analysed several cases of "fausse non-reconnaissance" (one of them occurring in dream) which resulted from a refusal to admit that one had witnessed an "impossible" (= improper) occurrence (*36*).

(c) Common sense, daily experience and clinical practice alike prove that the negation of painful sense-data is a kind of magic, which defensively seeks to arrest or to undo an emotionally intolerable occurrence.[139]

(d) Conversely, a grievous loss can be negated also by means of a fausse reconnaissance.[140]

(e) Certain private mourning "pieties" also negate the reality of the loss.[141]

At first, Menelaos negates the reality of his loss simply by means of a stunned disbelief; later on, he does so by means of a dream, whose *first half* manifestly begins to restore the *status quo ante*.

Such observations show that Fraenkel is perfectly right in holding that Menelaos is in a state of stunned disbelief. By doubting the reality of his tragic experience, Menelaos wards off *part* of its impact upon his psyche. Such "delaying tactics" account also for cases of "delayed mourning",[142] which occur even in primitive societies (*11*). These delaying tactics make the tragic event more tolerable when its reality is permitted at last to impinge fully on the mind, for some of the "work of mourning" [Trauerarbeit, Freud, cp. (*96*)] was performed (by the unconscious) already during the period of *partial* denial. I use the word "partial" advisedly, for a fausse non-reconnaissance is not a *primary* reaction. The observer *first* recognizes the person and/or the event and then, unable to tolerate reality, "cancels" his initial unpleasant perception and/or recognition, sometimes even replacing it with an acceptable, soothing dream or fantasy.[143] In short, since Helene dared the *un*darable (408), she "obviously" did *not* elope. This justifies Menelaos' defensive refusal to believe the evidence of his senses and the reports of his courtiers. That is how the human—and also the mythopoeic and poetic—mind operates. The logical and realistic psychologist must *accept* the illogical and unrealistic *modus operandi* of the emotions—and then render it comprehensible.

(2) *Distrust* (suspiciousness) is the second aspect of Menelaos' reaction; it can be made comprehensible in two ways:

(a) Paris carried away not only Helene, but also Menelaos' treasure and at least two of her handmaidens.[144] It is of considerable interest that no

---

[139] After a fatal accident, the victim's parents screamed "No! No!" as they flung themselves on the corpse. Newspapers often report that even mere bystanders scream "No!" *while* a suicide's body is already hurtling from a high window. Professor Lloyd-Jones reminds me that "No!" was Mrs Kennedy's first utterance when President Kennedy was shot.

[140] After the death of a close friend, I repeatedly experienced the shock of (pseudo-) "recognition", when seeing in the street some tall and corpulent man, walking with my late friend's characteristic gait.

[141] Cp. Queen Victoria's elaborate negation of Prince Albert's death (*80*, p. 86 f.). In E. *Alc.* 348 ff., Admetos plans to negate Alkestis' death by placing her portrait-statue in his bed.

[142] Well analysed by H. Deutsch (*20*).

[143] Bomber pilots, whose crews had been killed in a crash, were kept asleep until they managed to *dream* of a *happier* ending to the crash (*94*). Psychologically, this therapeutically effective "happy ending" dream is akin to Stesichoros' εἴδωλον (double) device, which also makes a "happy ending" possible.

[144] The theft is repeatedly mentioned in unquestionably ancient passages of the *Iliad*. As to the handmaidens, even if Hom. *Il.* 3.144 should be an interpolation, it almost certainly antedates A. *Ag.*

really ancient source tries to explain why this big theft and group exodus was not detected and prevented. It is, thus, perfectly "logical" for Menelaos to suspect part of his household of complicity;[145] it also permits the still enamoured husband to divert part of his anger from Helene to his household.

(b) Paranoid reactions (suspiciousness) are common in depressions caused by a grievous loss and can even have ritualized consequences.[146] Paranoid suspiciousness after a loss is explicitly mentioned in E. *Alc.* 338 ff., 368, ff.: Admetos now distrusts everyone. In a puzzling passage (A. *Ag.* 838), Agamemnon—whom no friend appears to have betrayed— also expresses distrust of those close to him.[147]

Summing up, ἀπίϲτουϲ denotes two *distinct* but simultaneous attitudes: a defensive disbelief *and* a (psychiatrically predictable) paranoid suspiciousness. Failing to grasp this, the copyist miscopied the word. Also, ἀπίϲτουϲ is the only proposed emendation whose corruption into ἄδιϲτοϲ can be reconstructed in terms of the psycho-analytical theory of parapraxes (slips of the pen, etc.) (infra).

I will now deal with some other proposed emendations, noting at once that those which do *not* begin with an alpha privative (un-) are automatically less likely than those who do. As to the palaeographical probability (or improbability) of the various proposed emendations, I do not discuss it, for it is obvious to the Hellenist and of no interest to my other readers.

(I) Some proposed emendations simply duplicate all or part of another symptom or listed state.

(1) Shame, disgrace (αἴϲχιϲτ', Hermann) feebly duplicates the much more appropriate ἀτίμουϲ.

(2) Unaware, unseeing, unmoved, insensitive, inaccessible (αἴϲτουϲ, Dindorf, ἀδήκτουϲ Blass) could, I think, refer only to the household's inability to "get through" to Menelaos—but that is implicit in the very next word (ἀφημένων).

(II) Not praying (to the gods, presumably for Helene's return) (ἀλίϲτωϲ, Denniston and Page) is, as Professor Sir Denys Page admits, "a very long shot"—though the Lloyd-Jones translation (*103*) accepts it: "not beseeching". The combination: "not reviling, not beseeching" is poetically attractive. Unfortunately, the normal meaning of ἄλιϲτοϲ is: not being prayed

---

[145] I am not raising here a question which did not occur to the Greeks. It is clearly the tradition that Menelaos left his wife without a supervisor during his absence which led, on the one hand, to the view that he had practically thrust Helene at Paris (Ov. *Her.* 16.299) and, on the other hand, to the tale that, before leaving for Troy, Agamemnon entrusted Klytaimestra to a bard's care (sch. Hom. *Od.* 3.267; Eustath. *ad Hom. Od.* 1466.55).

[146] Some Australian tribes alleviate mourning-grief by a paranoid projection: they ascribe even the most natural death to sorcery, and slay a randomly chosen member of the tribe suspected of witchcraft (*58*). This permits the mourner to displace his resentment from the "deserter" (the deceased), whom he cannot *effectively* punish—though at times he tries to do just that (*89*)—to the accessible, hypothetical "murderers".

[147] On the wording of that verse, cp. Fraenkel, Groeneboom and Denniston and Page. Agamemnon's remark that *only* Odysseus was *consistently* faithful to him may, however, hint at Aias' rebellious attempt to avenge a gross injustice. This being said, A. *Ag.* 838 may be meant to be "prophetic" or simply gnomic. Cp. E. *HF* 111 ff.

to.[148] Applied to Hades (contrasted with the Olympians) it means: inexorable, not yielding to prayer.[149] But, though in v. 415 Menelaos is (probably) spectre-like, this does not make him similar to Hades. In short, I cannot accept this emendation.

(III) Fasting, starving (oneself), would admittedly add a further realistic and specific symptom to the list. But words having that meaning would *not* have puzzled the copyist, for in Greek texts fasting is a common symptom of depression and of mourning.

(1) ἄϲιτουϲ (Wecklein, Thomson): Hom. *Od.* 4.788 (the anxious Penelope); E. *Med.* 24 f.; E. *Hipp.* 277; E. *Suppl.* 1105, etc. (cp. LSJ s.v.).

(2) ἄδαιτουϲ (Killeen, *90*, p. 253, cited by Italie, *86*, Addendum, s.v. ἡδύϲ; cp. Hdt. 1.162). But Fraenkel shows that, in A. *Ag.* 151, Aischylos applies that word to human flesh—to that of Iphigeneia—which, by definition, is unfit for consumption. Fraenkel's argument is not weakened by the clinical fact that cannibalistic fantasies do occur in mourning.

(3) ἀπάϲτουϲ has, I think, not been suggested by anyone, though it is Homeric and, with one exception, concerns the depressed and the mourning.[150]

A slight but not negligible further objection to all emendations meaning: fasting, is that it is a behavioural symptom, whereas Menelaos' other symptoms are predominantly intra-psychical.

(IV) Pain, grief (ἄλγιϲτ', Enger, Smyth), is inacceptable for several reasons:

(1) Unlike the other symptoms, it is general, rather than specific.

(2) As such, it should either be listed first (implying: his grief elicits the *following* symptoms),[151] or else last (implying: the symptoms *just cited* reveal his grief). But it is the penultimate symptom mentioned—for "sitting apart" is also technically a symptom.

(3) Smyth, who adopts this emendation, offers a misleading translation. "In the anguish of his grief" suggests an *agitated* depression, of a type Aischylos often described (*18*). But Menelaos' depression is *stuporous*—a state Aischylos *also* described well, e.g., through long silences (cp. Ar. *Ran.* 911 ff.).

(V) Like vapour (ἄτμος ὡς, Murray) is more or less patterned on Hom. *Il.* 23.100 and it may be urged that it anticipates A. *Ag.* 415 (spectre, ghost). But had Aischylos actually written "like vapour", he would hardly have been misunderstood and the word's Homeric background may perhaps even have protected it from corruption. Few accept Murray's emendation.

I disregard Mazon's αὔτωϲ; it adds nothing to the content or syntactical clarity of these verses.

Summing up, not one of the emendations considered is psychologically as suitable as ἀπίϲτουϲ; this, to my mind, is a decisive consideration.

---

[148] In Hom. *h. Merc.* 168, codex Fr gives it as an alternative to ἀπάϲτοι: Hermes and Maia, living in solitude and not yet known as deities, are starved of sacrifices, or are not prayed to. Cp. Page's apparatus criticus of his new Aischylos edition: ἀλίϲτωϲ.

[149] Euph. 98; *AP* 7.643; *IG* 14.1909.3.

[150] Exception: Hom. *Od.* 6.250: Odysseus had not eaten for some time. Hom. *Il.* 19.346 (Achilleus mourning); Hom. *Od.* 4.788 (Penelope fearing for her son); Hom. *h. Cer.* 200 (Demeter mourning for Persephone).   [151] Smyth's *translation* actually puts it first.

The Process of the Corruption of ἀπίστους into ἄδιστος is perhaps not beyond conjecture, though the reader is asked to imagine that every statement made regarding *that particular process* contains the word "perhaps" or "probably".

The transformation of the plural accusative(s) into singular nominative(s) is not discussed here, for I already noted my acceptance of Thomson's explanation of this corruption. For the sake of simplicity, I use in this section only the singular nominative form of words; this does *not* imply that I firmly believe that the corruption of the case-endings antedates the corruption of the word in question.

My initial assumption is that we are not faced here with a deliberate attempt to "improve" the text. Had that been the case, the copyist would not have substituted for the—to him puzzling—"disbelieving + suspicious" the truly inappropriate "more pleasant". For, had he intended to "improve" the text, he would surely have written one of the words conjectured by modern editors, denoting fasting, withdrawal, etc.

My second assumption is that had the slip of the pen been due to fatigue or to inattention, the copyist would *probably* have produced a meaningless word (*vox nihili*) corresponding to an ordinary "misprint": a haplography, a dittography, an anagrammatism, etc. This assumption, while plausible enough, is admittedly slightly less plausible than the first, but still good enough for its implications to deserve study.

These two assumptions lead me to the third and crucial one: Like Denniston and Page, the copyist no doubt felt that "there is no question of Menelaos *not believing* that Helene has left him", though I indicated that that is just what he *would* do *at first*.

Good indirect evidence shows that, like everyone, the Greeks expected a sentence already begun to end in a *foreseeable* way. The comic poets often exploited this anticipation by frustrating it: by writing the unexpected word instead of the expected one.[152] Technically, the already begun sentence seems to have: "Prägnanz", in that only one (expected) "cloture element" seems appropriate at *that* point. The comic poet disrupts this Prägnanz by providing an unexpected cloture element which is, at times, actually the antonym, or quasi-antonym of the expected word.

I conclude that if the copyist felt "disbelief" to be inappropriate, according to the psycho-analytical theory of parapraxes,[153] there would have intruded into his mind that word's antonym: *not* doubting = *not* *un*-believing.[154] Such a word would appropriately begin with an alpha privative: ἀδίσταστος.[155] But that would not *utterly* obliterate the already corrupt word the copyist read: ἄπιστος. The result would be a

---

[152] The locus classicus is Ar. *Ran.* 1206 ff.: Aischylus ends all of Euripides' declamations with "he lost his oil flask".

[153] Even opponents of psycho-analysis seldom question Freud's theory (*67*, chaps. 6, 7) that parapraxes are often very subtle and heavily overdetermined (*73*). Some even rectify an earlier parapraxis (*41*): a dittographic error in numbering paragraphs is sometimes unwittingly rectified by *skipping* the next number, as in: 1, 2, 3, 4, (4), 6.

[154] Greek authors often express a positive state of affairs by means of a *double* negative: "*not un*-mindful" for: "mindful".

[155] For that spelling, cp. Thphr. *Metaph.* 31; sch. Hom. *Od.* 1.100; *Pap. Tebt.* (ii b.c.) 124.26. It fits the parapraxis better than the more usual spelling.

"compromise"—a so-called portmanteau word.[156] The coming into being of a true portmanteau word was, in this instance, facilitated by the fact that ἄπιστος and ἀδίστακτος do not scan alike: the latter has one syllable too many. The compromise word, to scan properly, had to be a real word: ἄδιστος—which (almost predictably) does *not* begin with an alpha privative.

Now, it could be objected that ἄδιστος is not a true portmanteau word, because it is *not* a (meaningless) neologism. But the mere fact that it is meaningless *in this context* makes it psychologically and syntactically into a neologism.[157]

My argument is somewhat strengthened also by the finding that ἄδιστος is highly corruptible and that ἄπιστος can replace a different spelling of the same word.

E.*HF*. 675: ἀδίσταν. Ploutarchos writes: καλλίστην. Stobaios writes: ἡδίσταν. Here, of course, we deal with synonyms.

S. *fr.* 570 N²: ἄπειστος is spelled here ἄπιστος (Hsch. i, p. 242); Nauck holds that Hesychios' ἀπαράπιστος is a corruption of ἀπαράπειστος (Bernard).

These findings, though suggestive rather than conclusive, deserve at least passing mention.

My main argument can be represented schematically as follows:

Basic words	*Their antonyms*
πίστος (trust, belief)	ἄπιστος
διστασμός (disbelief)	ἀδίστακτος

The *intermediate* (mental) corruption (which leads us to the actual corruption ἄδιστος) was ἀδίστακτος, which

(1) preserved many letters of the correct word, but
(2) inverted its meaning (antonym).

It was then trimmed down to fit the (already wrong) metre and became the logically absurd ἄδιστος.

I conclude tentatively that palaeography could benefit from a familiarity of its practitioners with Freud's theory of parapraxes.

413 ἀφεμένων must be emended, chiefly for metrical reasons. Two solutions have been proposed.

(1) ἀφειμένων (Hermann, Fraenkel) = the forsaken, the deserted. This emendation is barely acceptable. It adds nothing new to our understanding of Menelaos' state; this would be surprising in so dense and rich a text. What is psychologically a *facilior* reading is acceptable in a Bakchylides text. In an Aischylean text a psychologically *difficilior* reading is to be preferred: one that sheds *new* light on the situation. Above all, if one insists on this reading, one would have to justify the degradation of con-

---

[156] A slip of this kind—resulting in a portmanteau word—was produced by T. B. L. Webster (*138*, p. XV): he turned the name of the painter A(rnold) Böcklin into Boeckhlin, influenced no doubt by the name of the famous hellenist A(ugust) Boeckh. *Time* Magazine deliberately produces portmanteau neologisms: globaloney (global + baloney) was produced by means of an intentional haplography. Sometimes portmanteau words combine opposite notions. Heinrich Heine: famillionär (familiär + Millionär) (with whom one is seldom "familiar", cited by Freud). An ambivalent schizophrenic called a man he "meant" to praise: "prink" (= prince + prick).

[157] Cp. "spoonerisms": crushing blow = blushing crow.

confused, quasi-negativistic silence, characteristic of a depression, into a stunned speechlessness characteristic of a state of psycho-physiological *shock*; characteristic, like Sappho's (*fr.* 31 LP) speechlessness, of a severe anxiety attack, which, as noted, does not have even one symptom in common with Menelaos' depression (*43*).

(2) ἀφημένων = sitting apart (Dindorf, Wecklein, Sidgwick, Smyth) is more satisfying in every respect: it presupposes and in a sense climaxes Menelaos' previously listed symptoms. It also suggests both a further clinical symptom and a culturally moulded response. Both will be discussed after dealing with Fraenkel's objections.

Fraenkel wonders from whom Menelaos may be isolating himself; obviously, from his household. Given the arrangement of Homeric palaces, even as visualized by the tragic poets, a king seeking privacy, especially when annoyed, could only sit apart, in a manner indicating that he was not to be disturbed. In Hom. *Il.* 1.498, Zeus is not offended or humiliated: he is, at most, annoyed by Hera's partisanship and wishes to be left alone.[158]

Fraenkel holds that Hom. *Il.* 15.106 f. and Hdt. 4.66 are incompatible with the sitting apart of Menelaos. In my estimate, the situation is as follows:

Hom. *Il.* 15.106 f.: Zeus, offended by the rebelliousness of the other gods, sits apart in haughty isolation. Though he is offended, he knows—and Athene reminds the other gods of this fact—that, when the chips are down, he is still the Master. In Hom. *h. Cer.* the mourning and resentfully withdrawn goddess is also able to retaliate against those who have offended her. So, of course, is Menelaos: though cuckolded, he is still the King: he can fantasy and execute a revenge restoring the *status quo ante*. Cp. Q.S. 3.130 ff.

Hdt. 4.66: At the annual victory feast a Skythian warrior, who had not recently distinguished himself, must sit apart from the banqueting heroes. His state of mind is not described, nor need it be. Though humiliated *for the time being* and unable to retaliate directly, he no doubt expects—like Zeus—to recoup himself soon. For the moment his best tactics are to manifest a contemptuous aloofness towards those who despise or pity him. His stance says: "I could not care less!"[159]

Needless to say, an *ostentatious* sitting apart is, in addition, also a veiled—and at times only partly conscious—attention-getting device: the more a man withdraws, the more his fellows will plead to be noticed and listened

---

[158] Cp. Hom. *h. Cer.* 354 ff. and passim for Demeter.

[159] There is excellent evidence in support of this interpretation from another nomadic cavalry group: the Crow Indians (*106*, pp. 35–43, esp. 37–38). Each year two military societies, the Lumpwoods and the Foxes, competed for the biggest "score" of war honours. Any member of the society which scored highest in a given year could take the wife of a member of the losing group if he had ever been intimate with her. Once an unscrupulous man claimed the faithful wife of a member of the losing society. Though the wife tearfully denied having been unfaithful, and though both the husband and the tribe knew that she spoke the truth, her husband sternly ordered her to follow the liar to his tent. His stoicism was, predictably, much admired and made the deceiver lose the face he had gained by belonging to that year's highest scoring society. That, precisely, seems to have been the purpose of the loser's stoicism: it represented what psychiatrists call a "passive-aggressive" counter-attack.

to by him.[160] Last, but not least, the brooding aloofness of a god or of a King is ominous: it suggests the possibility of a sudden and violent retaliation—directed, in this case, at those whose carelessness permitted Helene to escape. Menelaos' aloof sulking is as threatening as that of Achilleus (Hom. *Il.* 15.106 f., cp. Thomson ad vv. 412 f.).

This behaviour is clearly a culturally acceptable and culturally patterned "alternative" (*102*, pp. 273 ff.) reaction to a shaming loss: since Menelaos withdraws into silence (ϲιγᾰϲ), he cannot lament loudly;[161] since love is inhibiting his anger, he cannot curse (ἀλοιδόρουϲ). His apartness is, thus, not only culturally patterned and therefore acceptable; it also permits him to regain some of the lost "face", for even in an exuberant warrior society the stoical bearing of grief is often admired (A. *Sept.* passim).

Viewed in this social context, Menelaos' sitting apart is both a prestige-regaining and dishonour-negating manœuvre.

But the sitting apart can also be viewed as a psychiatric symptom: a token of withdrawal and of inward-turning. If his four previously listed reactions are viewed as culturally "normal" responses to an extreme loss, his sitting apart represents mere sulking: a social response. But if they are viewed *also* as symptoms of a depression, the sitting apart, which climaxes the four previous ones, is predictable on clinical grounds and beautifully balances the first of Menelaos' listed symptoms: his silence,[162] to which it hearkens back. The alternative, ἀφειμένων, does nothing of the sort.[163]

The fact that the *same* stance can have *concurrently* a socio-cultural *and* a psychiatric sense is not surprising. It perfectly illustrates a point I made long ago (*48*, chaps. 1, 2): most of the manifestations (symptoms) of psychological stress (illness) are culturally patterned. This reaction is manifested by countless Greek personages, both in social and in psychiatric contexts; in addition to the social responses of Zeus, Demeter, Achilleus and the Skythian warrior, one notes a symptomatic withdrawal in the case of the mad Bellerophontes, of Phoinix (*26*), of the pain-and-guilt maddened Oidipous (S. *OT* fin.), of Timon the proverbial misanthrope, of Alexandros the Great (Plu. *V. Alex.* 71.2 f.), etc.

This trait is, moreover, placed at the end of the sentence—with great art. It sums up the two preceding verses, just before the next passage obliges one to *reappraise* them retroactively (supra). Its stylistic role is comparable to that of a plagal ending in nineteenth-century classical music: it is half an ending and half a preparation for what is to come. For vv. 414–419 show that the aloof Menelaos is turning away not only from his (suspected) household, but also away from reality and towards fantasy.

The incredible complexity of meaning which Aischylos achieves here

---

[160] Withdrawal can even be seductive (*39*, p. 157), or represent an implicit demand (Hom. *Il.* 9.464 ff.) (*60*, p. 460).

[161] The prophets already did this on his behalf (v. 409); *their* laments are culturally acceptable behaviour.

[162] The Hellenist will note that logically ἀφημένων has a closer nexus with ϲιγᾰϲ than with the other three symptoms.

[163] A deserted husband is not necessarily always silent and non-vituperative. He who sits apart, sulking contemptuously, always is.

with five words only may have no parallel outside music.[164] They build up to a climax: one has the impression of having understood—and the very next verse forces one to revise retroactively most of what one thinks one has understood.

In short, ἀφημένων greatly enriches these verses; ἀφειμένων does not. In the case of an Aischylean text this finding should carry great weight, even though certainty is impossible.

Vv. 414–419: General Sense. These six verses list the last—and most extreme—of Menelaos' waking symptoms. Though seemingly two distinct symptoms are mentioned, the second is a direct consequence of the first and its extension from the particular (beautiful statues) to everything the eyes behold: the *outer* world as a *whole*. After vv. 418–419 nothing further can be said about Menelaos' *waking* reactions: the scene is set for his dream-response.

In interpreting vv. 416–419, one must—as I will have occasion to recall—firmly bear in mind that the *whole* passage (vv. 410–426) is focused on Menelaos' person and behaviour. Everything else is brought in only for the purpose of shedding light on Menelaos' reactions and is therefore alluded to only in passing. None of the "stimuli" to which he responds (at times by a non-response) is elaborated in *any* way *for its own sake*. How true this is, can best be shown by noting that each and every one of the items *external* to Menelaos—each of the "stimuli"—referred to in vv. 414–419 has given rise to controversies, even as regards their ascription to a particular person. This is as true of the phantom (v. 415) and of the statues (v. 416) as of the eyes (v. 418). So much *alleged* vagueness, in the space of six verses only and always with regard to something "external" to Menelaos[165] to which he reacts, is simply not credible in the case of a great poet. Not unexpectedly, all vagueness or doubt disappears the moment one realizes that every word is focused on Menelaos' *reactions to* stimuli, and *not* on the *stimuli* themselves. Vv. 412–426 are not only flawless; they are also extremely concise and always to the point: the point being Menelaos' state. If they are viewed, as they must be viewed; as an exquisitely organized list of Menelaos' symptomatic reactions to various *segments* of reality, culminating in his *non*-responsiveness (which is *also* a reaction) to reality *as a whole*, one understands why, at v. 420, the poet turns from Menelaos' waking reactions to external reality to his dream response to "inner" stimuli.

The correct interpretation is therefore the one which contributes most to a *psychiatric* understanding of Menelaos' distress. This is something all solutions, except those adopted by Fraenkel, fail to do, for their focus is never Menelaos' *response*, but the *stimulus* which elicits it.[166]

---

[164] The key motif of the first movement of Beethoven's Fifth Symphony and of the last movement of Mozart's Jupiter Symphony each contain only four notes. Moreover, whereas in Beethoven's case these four notes involve only two tones in a simple rhythmic arrangement: , in Mozart's case the four different notes are even of equal length.

[165] I treat the "eyes" as "external" because they stand for what they *perceive*. Actually, the key word of vv. 418–419 is Ἀφροδίτα (infra).

[166] Those who do *not* accept Fraenkel's interpretations could be compared to psychologists who focused their attention exclusively on the pitch of the bell which made Pavlov's dogs salivate—or on the brand of meat-powder he used in conditioning his dogs—

414–415 πόθωι δ' ὑπερποντίας / φάϲμα δόξει δόμων ἀνάϲϲειν. = Through longing for her who is beyond the sea, a phantom will seem to rule the palace.[167]

πόθωι δ' ὑπερποντίας. Just as vv. 410—411 state the *concrete* causes of Menelaos' *visibly* abnormal behaviour, described in vv. 412–413, so v. 414 specifies the *psychological* cause of an *elusive* state of affairs, described in v. 415. The italicized words are crucial for a correct interpretation of v. 415, for with vv. 414–415 one passes from the *observable* to the *inferential*: from sense data to psychological interpretations.

V. 415 has given rise to divergent interpretations—probably because the commentators focused most of their attention on φάϲμα and, secondarily, on δόξει. Little attention is paid to what the φάϲμα *seems* to be doing, though it is this which helps one to elucidate the vexing φάϲμα problem.

This obliges me to begin my discussion with the last two words.

δόμων ἀνάϲϲειν. The Choros indicates that the palace is *not* governed *normally*—*not* as it was governed before Helene eloped and Menelaos went into a stuporous depression. It does not take much imagination to assume that, at that point, life in the palace was chaotic. Confronted with an unprecedented crisis, the household displayed a "catastrophic reaction"[168]: only the most indispensable tasks were performed—probably inadequately.

Now, it is of some interest that part of the corrupt A. *Choe.* 131: πῶϲ ἀνάξομεν δόμοιϲ = "how shall we be (become) rulers of the palace?"[169] also refers to a badly, and even lawlessly, governed palace—to the slain Agamemnon's palace misruled by usurpers—which Elektra and Orestes desire to take over and to govern properly and lawfully.

While this parallel passage is not, in itself, conclusive, it does strengthen the impression that *one* of the reasons why Menelaos' palace seems to be ruled by a φάϲμα is that it is in a temporary state of chaos.[170]

I hold, in short, that the ruling of the house by a phantom refers also to the *mis*rule which occurs when not an efficient queen, but an insubstantial phantom holds the reins. The Choros *concludes* that a phantom rules, partly *because* there is misrule and general confusion.[171]

Though this much seems practically certain, both on the basis of commonsense expectations and of everyday experience with homes newly deserted by a wife, or thrown into disarray by her illness or death, the above observations take into account only one—somewhat pedestrian—

rather than on his dogs' conditioned salivation, *in response* to a bell. Hence, not Fraenkel's but Thomson's interpretations of vv. 418–419 are "absurd".

[167] Mazon takes unwarrantable liberties with the first word. He translates: "L'amour le veut."

[168] This term, coined by Goldstein (*79*), denotes the confused behaviour which patients with certain types of brain lesions exhibit when confronted with even relatively minor *unexpected* situations. Groups of normals subjected to extreme and unprecedented stress also manifest "catastrophic reactions" (*23*).

[169] But this verse is corrupt.

[170] Fraenkel cites E. *Androm.* 897, in which Hermione is called δόμων ἄναϲϲα. It may be a coincidence, but it is evident that Hermione, too, miserably misruled Neoptolemos' palace.

[171] That a Homeric royal household was effectively run by its queen should be evident to any reader of the *Odyssey*, though the rough work was done by the servants (A. *Choe.* 84).

aspect of the vivid imagery of v. 415. None the less, this practical side of the situation cannot be disregarded entirely in appraising the meaning of these two verses.

δόξει = "it [the phantom] will seem" must be considered next. As so often, Fraenkel makes the really important point, by drawing attention to the parallelism of φάϲμα δόξει and ὀνειρόφαντοι . . . δόξαι, and by stressing that the φάϲμα is to the waking Menelaos what the dream-image is to the sleeping Menelaos.[172]

I will postpone a discussion of the implications of this remark for an understanding of the word φάϲμα and stress here only that Fraenkel implicitly highlights the *non-concrete* character of that which "seems" to be and to act in a certain way.

Considering that v. 414 specifies a *psychological* cause or motive for the situation described in v. 415, I hold that the future δόξει means that a conclusion *will inevitably* be drawn from *observable* modes of behaviour and situations, in accordance with the (inferential) psychological causes mentioned in v. 414.[173]

The main point is that the conclusion drawn by the Choros is *objectively false*, though metaphorically and psychologically convincing. The Choros does not affirm that an *objectively* real phantom governs the palace; it says that the palace is in the state of disarray it would be in *if* a mere phantom governed it. Its statement is, *on one level*, an "as if" statement. But even this does not illuminate the full scope of the imagery which Aischylos' use of the word φάϲμα evokes. It is therefore to the controversial meaning of this word that I now must turn.

φάϲμα is held by most Hellenists to refer to Helene;[174] but others believe that Menelaos is meant.[175] Smyth's translation leaves the point unsettled, as does the Denniston and Page commentary.

Both Fraenkel, who does take a position, and Denniston and Page, who do not, point to grammatical difficulties in making φάϲμα refer to Menelaos. Denniston and Page also mention grammatical difficulties in making φάϲμα refer to Helene.

This forces one either to tax Aischylos with a slipshod ambiguity or to credit him with a masterfully contrived one. I choose the second alternative, partly because of a methodological principle I enunciated elsewhere (*39*): the most productive datum is the one which seems to present the greatest difficulties.

(1) φάϲμα = *Helene* is, as Fraenkel says, both satisfying poetically and in conformity with human experience: the yearned-for wife *seems* to haunt

---

172 But this does not justify taking—as a distinguished Hellenist suggested to me—v. 415 to mean "he will *dream* falsely that Helene is still queen in his home".

173 Mazon's notion, that the future δόξει means that (already in vv. 412–413) the prophets describe *in advance* how Menelaos *will* react when learning, on his return, that Helene had eloped, has found little acceptance. Thus, Professor Sir Denys Page rejects it (personal communication).

174 Triclinius, Stanley, Pauw, Heath, Brumoy, W. von Humboldt, Klausen, Welcker, Bamberger, Sewell, Conington, Paley, D. Milman, L. Campbell, Wilamowitz, Platt, Murray, Mazon, Fraenkel, etc.

175 Schütz, Blomfield, Scholefield, Ahrens, Nägelsbach, Wecklein, Plüss, Headlam, Groeneboom. Thomson seems undecided.

the palace and everything in it reminds Menelaos of her. One might almost say that Menelaos "feels" her presence, the way an occasional amputee feels his "phantom limb": he seems to experience pain where the now amputated limb once was. But it is a crucial fact that the φάϲμα of Helene can "rule the palace" *only* because *Menelaos* is obsessed with her: she influences life in the palace only *through* the longing she inspires in the distressed husband.

For it is clear that Helene's φάϲμα is not "external" and "real". It is a common mistake to assume that in Aischylos all phantoms and the like are as "real" as the Erinyes in his *Eumenides*; *some* of them are as subjective, as psychogenic, as the Erinyes of Euripides' *Orestes*.[176]

This view, supported by my interpretation of the implications of δόξει, permits one to reject decisively the occasionally still expressed theory that the φάϲμα is Helene's well-known Stesichorean εἴδωλον. Fraenkel rightly questions this view, stressing that the Stesichorean εἴδωλον is a "mythical miracle" while this φάϲμα is a "general and purely human experience".

An additional argument is provided by two—apparently overlooked—aspects of the εἴδωλον story. No version, be it early or late, so much as hints that Helene's εἴδωλον lingered on in Menelaos' palace after her flight—for the simple reason that it came into being only *after* her elopement. Furthermore, the first text in which Menelaos is explicitly said to have met—though only at Troy and during part of his homeward voyage —Helene's εἴδωλον, is Euripides' *Helene* (vv. 582 ff.), and there is no indication that Euripides borrowed *this* detail from anyone else.

I note, however, that when the real Helene first identifies herself to Menelaos, he is afraid and thinks she is a phantom (φάϲμα, E. *Hel.* 359).[177]

Be that as it may, it is possible—but not more than possible—that Aischylos used the *word* φάϲμα because he remembered the tale of Helene's εἴδωλον. It is, however, not only logically preposterous, but also thoroughly unpoetic to hold that he meant to suggest that Helene's *real* double continued to rule the palace in an operationally meaningful way.

This being said, I would go one step further than Fraenkel, while still remaining within the bounds of a purely psychological conception of the genesis of this φάϲμα.

Menelaos is pathologically depressed; both his physical (ἀφημένων) and psychological withdrawal, and consequent imperviousness to external stimuli (vv. 416–419, infra), bring into being the psychological equivalent of an experimentally produced "sensory deprivation", notoriously capable of inducing hallucinations even in normal subjects (*7, 83, 99, 100*). In short, I hold that Menelaos is represented as actually *hallucinating* the longed-for absent Helene.

Such "restitutive" hallucinations, which unconsciously seek to negate the loss (ἄπιϲτουϲ, supra), occur at times even in normal but deep grief. The mourner's attention is diverted from the external, sensible world,

---

[176] This is confirmed by the data cited in chap. 4.

[177] Is it an echo of the Aischylean ὀνειρόφαντοι, that the Euripidean Helene at once assures Menelaos that she is no nocturnal apparition (νυκτίφαντοϲ, E. *Hel.* 570)?

which no longer contains the all-important lost beloved, to the inner world which preserves and keeps "available" her image—an image which is then restitutively "re-projected" into the "outer" world, in the form of a hallucination.[178]

This conception of the φάϲμα as *Menelaos* experiences it, can comfortably co-exist with the notion that, as far as the *Choros* is concerned, the φάϲμα is a metaphorically worded conclusion, derived from the ungoverned palace's disarray. Indeed, more than one passage of vv. 410–426 implicitly contrasts the normal Choros' perception and definition of the situation with that of the pathologically depressed Menelaos.[179]

(2) φάϲμα = *Menelaos*, who is but a shadow of his former self. Taken in so *narrow* a sense, the idea does seem "prosaic" (Fraenkel), but it *need not* be so taken.

Fraenkel also holds that the parallels usually cited in support of this view—and especially S. *Phil.* 994 and S. *OC* 109—are "not pertinent".[180] Both Fraenkel and Denniston and Page feel that it is difficult to attribute such a meaning to the *isolated* word φάϲμα; Fraenkel also urges that in the usually cited parallels the wording is more elaborate. I do not feel that these arguments are really decisive, even if φάϲμα is taken in the very pedestrian sense that Menelaos, *exhausted* by grief, is now but a shadow of his former self.

I think that φάϲμα has far broader implications, not only in this passage, but in general—implications which culturally determined scotomata cause us to ignore. What I am about to say is so contrary to our thought habits that I must lead up gradually to my interpretation.

I begin by noting a self-evident fact: in Greek thought the behaviour of the *non*-violent insane is very similar to that of the shades. The behaviour of Tithonos—an admirably described case of senile dementia (Hom. *h. Ven.* 233 ff.)—greatly resembles that of Patroklos' ghost at the *end* of Achilleus' dream (Hom. *Il.* 23.99 ff.) or that of the gibbering shades of the Nekyia (Hom. *Od.* 11, passim). A seer can see as gibbering shades even men who are still alive, but whose irresponsible behaviour has doomed them (Hom. *Od.* 20.345 ff.)—and it is of special interest that, once they are slain, their shades do behave (Hom. *Od.* 24.1 ff.) very much the way the seer *anticipatorily* saw them.

This similarity between the seer's vision of the behaviour of the doomed and the actual behaviour of their shades proceeding to Hades is explicable in terms of a peculiar Greek thought pattern.

(a) It equates the state *of the* doomed with the state *to which* they are doomed;[181]

(b) Even an outcome as yet only predicted by an omen (Hom. *Od.*

---

[178] While editing his posthumous book, I repeatedly "consulted" the late Professor R. Linton in dream.

[179] Cp. especially vv. 416–417.

[180] Other possible parallels of such a type are: Pi *P.* 8.95 f.; A. *Ag.* 79, 839; S. *Aj.* 125 f.; E. *Phoin.* 1543, etc. In Theocr. 2.110 Simaitha compares herself to a mere wax puppet (δαγύϲ).

[181] E. *Alc.* provides several examples. At v. 387, Alkestis says: "You can say that I no longer exist"; at v. 527 she states: "The one doomed to die *is* dead." At v. 434 Admetos says of the still living Alkestis: "She alone *died* in my place."

20.121 f.), or an action planned but never executed, is at times spoken of as having been performed;[182]

(c) A person *wrongly* believed to have died must undergo symbolic rebirth (Plu. *Q.R.* 4, p. 264C ff.; cp. also chap. 8).

One cannot even object that the doomed suitors of the *Odyssey* are mortal, while Menelaos will be translated alive to the Elysian Fields (Hom. *Od.* 4.560 ff.), for Tithonos could be said to be even more immortal than Menelaos.

More important still is that, in some Greek texts, the behaviour and mood *imputed* to certain shades is barely, if at all, distinguishable from the *actual* behaviour and mood of *real* mourners (E. *Alc.* 347, etc.). The best example is Achilleus' state and mood in Hades (Hom. *Od.* 11. 488 ff.). Conversely, the inevitable result—and implicit purpose—of many mourning customs is to make the mourners' life as joyless as that of the shades is believed to be.[183]

The ultimate equivalence of the mourner and of the one he mourns for is underscored by the belief that one can die in someone else's place. This belief is reflected not only by myths[184] but also by the convictions of historical personages.[185] Such beliefs are not limited to Greek culture and are, moreover, encountered also in clinical practice.[186]

Having indicated the similarity of behaviour of mourners and shades and the equivalence of the mourner and the deceased, I must now scrutinize more closely the behaviour of shades, which closely resembles that of the *non*-violent, depressed insane, such as Tithonos. The facts can be stated even more pointedly: already in Homeric poetry the shades behave "abnormally" in terms of human standards; they gibber, they drink raw blood,[187] etc. In short, the conduct of shades is that of human madmen.[188] Now, since the behaviour of mourners is similar to that of the shades—with whom they identify themselves to the point of seeming at times possessed by them[189]—it is both culturally and "psychologically" appropriate to apply to a depressed mourner the term φάσμα, which can also denote a shade. In other words, Menelaos can be viewed as a φάσμα not only because, exhausted and made ineffectual by his grief, he is only "a ghost of his former self" but, above all, because his *pathologically*

---

[182] Cp. chap. 1, note 17.

[183] Cp. Admetos' elaborate mourning projects in E. *Alc.* 328 ff.

[184] Alkestis dies in Admetos' place (E. *Alc.*); Cheiron renounces his immortality in favour of Prometheus (Apollod. 2.5.4,11).

[185] Ailios Aristeides, the neurotic chronic invalid, firmly believed that various persons close to him had died in his stead—a fact repeatedly mentioned by Behr (5, pp. 9, 97; cp. Aristid. 5.25, etc.).

[186] A patient reported that during his adolescence he believed that, for complicated statistical reasons, either he or his best friend had to die prematurely. He was unable to recall whether he had formed this conviction before or after his friend's premature death.

[187] The drinking of raw bull's blood was believed to be lethal (Plu. *V. Them.* 31.5).

[188] I demonstrated on two occasions (49, 51) that the behaviour of all supernatural beings is explicitly or implicitly considered "mad" by ordinary *human* standards, as is considered insane the behaviour of human beings in *direct* contact with supernaturals. (In A. *Eum.* 17, Apollon himself is possessed; in Hdt. 4.179 so is Triton.)

[189] A symmetrical view is attributed by Ploutarchos (Plu. *Amor.* 16, p. 759C) to Cato: "the soul of the lover is ever present in that of the beloved".

intensive mourning makes him as "abnormal" as Greek shades were believed to be.

(3) φάϲμα = *Helene as manifested through Menelaos*. I specify at once that I do not mean: "An apparition (Helene) will seem to rule the house, by reason of his (Menelaos') longing for her (Helene) who is overseas." (Denniston and Page somewhat strenuously urge that Greek idiom will not admit this meaning.)

As already indicated, our key data—our most productive data—are that:

(a) Equally competent Hellenists could argue *in favour of* either the φάϲμα = Helene notion or the φάϲμα = Menelaos interpretation, and

(b) Grammatical objections (of admittedly limited persuasiveness) can be cited *against* either of these two interpretations.

These findings suggest that, since the two existing alternatives seem to be equally probable and (grammatically) equally questionable, Aischylos —who knew Greek better than any modern scholar can possibly know it— had a purpose in choosing this ambiguous wording.

I repeat: it is safer to credit Aischylos with a superbly contrived ambiguity than to tax him with a slipshod one. I hold that in this passage Aischylos simply evokes—or conjures up—a state of affairs which each reader or theatre-goer can apprehend in the manner which is most likely to move *him*. For one, the most moving image is that of a pathologically depressed Menelaos, similar to a shade: mad, shadowy and ineffectual. Another will be most deeply stirred by the belief that a restitutively *hallucinated* Helene rules the palace.[190] There is evidence that Greek poets so worded certain passages as to permit the reader to understand them in accordance with *his* preferences.[191]

For me, the most logical—and most moving—conception is that Helene is hallucinated (as an internal parasite) by Menelaos who, *by* hallucinating her, not only becomes himself like unto a phantom, but also *mediates* his hallucination to his household. In the negative sense, this means that the household is adrift, as though a mere phantom held the reins: little of what should normally be done is accomplished—and even less is done well. But in the positive sense, much of what *is* happening, much of what *is* done, is done in response to—as a consequence of—Menelaos' total absorption with the hallucinated phantom of Helene. Otherwise expressed, the neglect of *usual* tasks is attributable both to the absence of the flesh-and-blood Helene and to Menelaos' stupor. But many *unusual* activities occur in response to Menelaos' hallucination of Helene. Both the neglect of ordinary tasks and the performance of non-routine acts, in response to the new situation: to Menelaos' grief and to his hallucinating Helene, can be metaphorically described as resulting from the governing of the palace by a φάϲμα.[192] What must be avoided at all cost, is the

---

[190] Cp. my arguments against assuming that a "real" phantom of Helene is meant.

[191] Cp. my discussion of Pi. *O.* 3.27 (*35*).

[192] A somewhat pedestrian analogy will clarify my meaning: the household of a newly bereaved husband will neglect routine activities: it will not sweep the rooms nor cook regular meals. *Instead*, it will perform many non-routine activities, such as comforting the bereaved, fending off intruding visitors, etc.

notion that *others also see* the φάσμα. They cannot see it, for *only* Menelaos hallucinates Helene.[193]

The finding that φάσμα has this double meaning proves the exquisite psychological precision of Aischylos' seemingly imprecise wording: it reproduces observable clinical facts, which the poet apparently senses more clearly than does the literary critic.

The fact that Menelaos' obsession with this hallucinated phantom deeply affects life in the palace turns one's attention to the manner in which Menelaos perceives the *real* world—and it is this which Aischylos describes in the next four verses.

Excursus: Since the crucial point is that—even if the phantom is *only* Helene—no one but Menelaos himself "sees" it, it is useful to consider here, at least in passing, an interpretation of Menelaos' "awareness" of Helene's "presence" which does *not* involve an actual hallucination.

Thus, it could be asserted that since Menelaos' depression is a stuporous one, and also *because* he subsequently sees Helene's image (ὄψις) in dream, he does *not* hallucinate her in a waking state: that he does not project her (intrapsychic) image into the outer world, in the form of a visual hallucination.[194] In short, it could be urged—though not very convincingly—that were Menelaos able to *hallucinate* Helene while awake, he might—but only might—not need to *dream* of her as well. In my own experience, the two are not mutually exclusive. None the less, it is possible to propose a psychological explanation of what is described in vv. 415–416, which does not involve actual hallucinations, but does link these verses with the "imprint" of v. 411.

Helene's phantom, in this frame of reference, would simply be an image (imprint), existing only in Menelaos' mind (memory), though both cultural and subjective factors explain why this image is subjectively experienced as "existing".

In Greek belief, the only posthumous existence partaking of the characteristics of a real "life" is the mark the deceased left in the memory of men: his fame. This shared (cultural) belief made it particularly easy for a mourner to feel that a deceased or disappeared person still "lives" in his memory. This permits Menelaos to experience—and Aischylos to designate—this (internal) "living" image of Helene as her "phantom"— though not as her εἴδωλον (double).

Psychologically the matter is only slightly more complicated. When one sustains a loss, one tries to attenuate the blow by implicitly denying it (supra): one defensively "cathects"[195] the image of the lost person and becomes almost obsessively preoccupied with it. In a way one "introjects"—reconstitutes intrapsychically—the one who disappeared, turning the lost one into an "internal object". This not only diminishes one's sense of a loss and keeps the lost one (partially) "available", but also

---

[193] This view excludes *a priori* Verrall's interpretation that *Menelaos* will think that Helene's phantom rules the palace.

[194] Basically, a hallucination consists in the transposition of an internal experience into the outer world. This definition suffices for present purposes. The complicated problem of what is "inside" and what is "outside" was elucidated elsewhere (*39*, chaps. 22–24, *52*, chap. 2).

[195] Invests with affect, becomes preoccupied with.

compensates one *in part* for the "humiliation" *any* loss involves. Indeed, since the lost one now "exists"—as an introject—"inside" the mourner's self, from which he can evoke the vanished one at will, the humiliation is, at times, partly replaced by a kind of grandiosity, because the (inner) self now "contains" also what it formerly felt to be the most precious thing in the (outer) world.[196]

But the coming into being of such an introject presupposes, as a matter of course, a *de*cathecting of external stimuli, which continue to tempt the psyche to resume contact with reality. It also requires an almost obsessive clinging to this, by nature evanescent (cp. the dream), image of the lost one, which must compete with stimuli emanating from the real world for the occupation of psychic "space". In this sense, too, Menelaos' alienation from external reality is a kind of restitutive manœuvre, since his cherished "internal" Helene inevitably loses some of her intense psychological reality every time he pays attention to the external world.

Last but not least, were Menelaos real, the clinician would expect—and find—that Menelaos had partly identified himself with this introjected image.[197] Now, in so far as this introject is, so to speak, a "phantom", Menelaos who harbours it and who (partly) identifies himself with it, also partakes of the nature of a phantom. It suffices to recall in this context what was said above about the similarity between the behaviour the Greeks *imputed* to the dead and the behaviour they *expected* from the mourners.

In short, whether one holds, as I do, that Menelaos actually hallucinates Helene, or assumes only that he "introjected" her image without (hallucinatorily) re-projecting it into the "external" world, Aischylos' use of the word φάϲμα in this passage is fully justified by psychiatric considerations.

416 εὐμόρφων δὲ κολοϲϲῶν = the shapeliness of statues; this is the most natural and only appropriate translation. The word order stresses the *quality* of the statues *more* than their *nature* and an analysis of v. 417 will justify this emphasis. Hence, the *nature* of the statues is of secondary importance, though some commentators focus their attention only on κολοϲϲῶν and indulge in complicated speculations regarding their nature. As noted, the real objective of vv. 416 f. is to tell something about Menelaos, rather than about the statues. This fits, as noted, the fact that vv. 412–426 are concerned entirely with Menelaos: they list his symptoms, which are made perceptible by the situation in which he finds himself and by the persons and things which surround him, and to which he reacts.

For these reasons I deal only briefly with suggestions regarding the

---

[196] This is to be taken quite literally. When a certain young man's greatly idealized girl-friend behaved in a quite un-ideal manner, he told her: "Go away and do not disturb my happy dreams of you." Compare also the pride of those who knew personally a defunct great man; also the descent of the Holy Ghost on the Apostles.

[197] Cp. infra, my discussion of v. 418. A primitive hunter may eat the heart of a slain lion, so as to become lion-like himself. Cp. also the pious eating of the corpses of deceased relatives, Hdt. 3.99 and amongst contemporary primitives (77). This archaic notion appears to have inspired certain modern experiments, which allegedly show that learning is at least facilitated if the experimental animal is fed the brains of an already taught animal. I hasten to add that the results of these experiments are highly controversial.

nature of these κολοccοί. The correct definition is that given by Fraenkel: they are statues of lovely girls: Attic κοραί, such as adorned Athens, particularly during Aischylos' youth.[198] It is important that even though the sculptors of κοραί may have used models, their statues were *not* held to be portraits. All other interpretations of the nature of these statues are unconvincing.

(1) Portrait statues of Helene.[199] Mythical *palaces* did not contain portrait statues of their *living* inhabitants—and Menelaos going for walks is unimaginable. Admetos planned to have a portrait statue of Alkestis made *after* her death (E. *Alc.* 348 ff.). Laodameia caused a portrait statue of Protesilaos to be made *after* reports of his death reached her (Hyg. *fab.* 104). I know of no evidence indicating that Aischylos' contemporaries or predecessors had such portrait statues in their homes. It could be speciously argued that—like Laodameia in one version[200]—Menelaos had statues of Helene made as soon as she left. But the manufacture of such a statue—and, *a fortiori*, of several statues—would have taken many months and the Choros manifestly describes Menelaos' *initial* stuporous reaction to what happened. Plain common sense suggests that Menelaos' initial extreme reaction could not have lasted long, for he could not have raised and organized an army while in that state. Also, Fraenkel rightly urges that there is a radical difference between his situation and that of Laodameia, even if one accepts the version that she had a portrait statue of Protesilaos made as soon as he left for the Trojan war. Protesilaos was known to be doomed to die,[201] while Helene is always supposed to be alive and well.[202] There is, in short, nothing in this—or in any other—text to justify the hypothesis that the κολοccοί in question were statues of Helene—a finding which has a direct bearing on the problem of the eyes mentioned in v. 418 (infra).

(2) It is far from clear whether Groeneboom's mention of the portrait κολοccοί of the Pharaoh Mykerinos' twenty favourite concubines (Hdt. 2.130) is meant to hint that the Aischylean κολοccοί were portraits of Menelaos' concubines. *If* that is what Groeneboom meant to hint at— which I doubt—two decisive objections arise:

(a) For a mythical Greek king, the husband of the surpassingly beautiful Helene was surprisingly continent.[203]

(b) It is hardly credible that, while Helene was still living with him, he would have cluttered up his palace with statues of his (non-existent) concubines.

(3) I must now discuss the view that these κολοccοί were magical "doubles", presumably of Helene. I cannot undertake here a full discussion of the κολοccόc problem *per se*:[204] I can deal only with essentials.

---

[198] Cp. Fraenkel ad loc.   [199] Schütz, Picard, Denniston and Page, Vernant.
[200] Ov. *Her.* 13, passim.   [201] Tzetz. sch. *Lyc.* 245; Ov. *Her.* 13.90 ff.
[202] E. *Hel.* 289—a difficult and perhaps corrupt verse—refers to a much later event.
[203] The *Odyssey* (4.11 ff.) goes out of its way to explain and to justify his fathering one bastard son. His other bastard appears to have been fathered during his long separation from Helene (Eumel. *fr.* 7 Kinkel = Apollod. 3.11.1). In the *Iliad*, unlike Agamemnon and Achilleus, he has no camp-concubine.
[204] For the data, cp. Fraenkel, Vernant (*136*, pp. 251–264) and the ancient sources and modern authorities they quote.

I begin by briefly recalling some facts:

(a) κολοссός appears to be a pre-Greek word.

(b) It did not acquire the meaning of "colossal" until the κολοссός of Rhodos was built, long after the death of Aischylos.

(c) Herodotos applies this term only to certain *Egyptian* statues[205]— never to Greek ones.

(d) Disregarding Egyptian statues and late Greek "colossal" ones, the term is known to have been applied in early times *only* to the improvised, crude figures used in calling the *dead* at Kyrene,[206] and to crude wax figurines burned at Thera in ritual oathings involving a conditional curse of *death*. Nothing proves that the buried slabs of stone of Mideia (Dendra), or grave-steles, were ever *called* κολοссός (cp. LSJ s.v.).

It is this last set of data which is most relevant in the present context.

Εὐμόρφων means well-shaped (shapely = beautiful) both here and elsewhere.[207] But the true Greek κολοссοί of early times were not beautiful in *any* way—not even in the way some specimens of primitive or folk art can be held to be "beautiful" for *specifiable* psychological reasons (*30*).

Picard (*120*) tried to sidestep this difficulty by translating εὐμόρφων as "exact", thereby implying an "accurate" portrayal. But the real κολοссοί were *not* accurate portrayals; in fact, those of Kyrene *could not* have been portraits, for they represented *unknown* deceased persons.

Vernant (*136*, p. 257) attempts to dispose of the matter by assuming that the Aischylean κολοссοί were not portraits but "doubles". If so, the strongly emphasized word "εὐμόρφων" has no real purpose. This is a hypothesis which, even on purely aesthetic grounds, I am not prepared to accept—and the analysis of v. 417 will show that this word is of capital importance for an understanding of this text.

In my estimate, the problem is not what *real* κολοссοί were, but what *quality* Aischylos meant to attribute to statues of the Attic κοραί type, by *so* designating them, in a clearly *metaphorical* sense. For, as was shown, εὐμόρφων excludes the possibility that he had crude, real κολοссοί in mind, as the absence of any hint at magical practices excludes the possibility that the Aischylean κολοссοί were "magical doubles".[208]

Still another argument, which someone having only a nodding acquaintance with psycho-analysis might perhaps advance, must also be discarded. This argument would run: Menelaos refuses to become unfaithful to Helene even by admiring lovely statues; in so doing, he seeks to show her how she should have treated him. I hope that both what was said so far and what will be said in the next section, will suffice to discard such an assumption.

417 ἔχθεται χάρις ἀνδρί = are hateful to the husband, i.e., to Menelaos . . . and to no one else, for no one else's wife eloped to Troy.

---

[205] Cp. also D.S. 1.67.1 and 1.47.2 and C. H. Oldfather, ad loc.

[206] Admetos intends to call out Alkestis' name while embracing her statue (E. *Alc.* 351).

[207] As Fraenkel points out, also with regard to A. *Ag.* 454.

[208] Also, since only love-magic could be envisaged here, one cannot see how *several* κολοссοί could be used in trying to bring back *one* woman only. In Theocr. 2.110, only one figurine (δαγύς) is used. It is, moreover, unimaginable that κολοссῶν could be a "generic plural" such as those in vv. 410, 412–413. E. *Alc.* 351 does not imply magic or a *ritual* calling of the dead.

Before discussing this reaction, I note that it further militates against the "double of Helene" theory, for in Greek myth the portrait-statue (double) of a deceased person can comfort not only Zeus (Firm. Mat. *de error. prof. rel.* 6, p. 15Z), Admetos (supra), Laodameia (supra), but even grieving dogs (Apollod. 3.4.4).

The saddened, but not pathologically depressed, Choros recognizes the objective beauty of the statues, which would delight any normal person. It is therefore precisely the abnormality—the paradoxical reaction—of Menelaos which it highlights by stressing, through the word order, that it is the *beauty* of the statues which Menelaos cannot bear. One can do no better than quote here a remark Murray (*113*, p. 33) made in another context: honey tastes bitter to a man ill with jaundice.

Of course, one does not have to view Aischylos as a precursor of the Protagorean theory that man is the measure of all things. One need credit him only with the capacity to describe a *common symptom* of severe mourning reactions. And it is certainly a symptom he intended to describe, for I have shown long ago (*48*, chap. 3), that, in order to be able to provide (partial) relief from a pathological inner tension or conflict, a symptom *must* be 'socially negativistic": paradoxical, contrary to custom and provocative, be it only by its "absurdity". The Choros' objective definition of the statues as "beautiful" contrasts with Menelaos' subjective and "absurd" reaction.[209]

Culturally prescribed mourning rites often taboo everything beautiful and enjoyable, replacing at times something inherently beautiful with its deliberately *degraded* equivalent.[210] In E. *Alc.* 430 ff., Admetos forbids all pleasant things for a year. But such taboos, though culturally imposed, also meet psychological needs more than half way. E. *Alc.* 434 ff. appears to imply not only a loss of the capacity for enjoyment, but also, I feel, a negative reaction to beauty, which, in extreme mourning, can be experienced as excruciatingly painful.[211]

Though such reactions, even in Menelaos' case, are in part simply tokens of a "morose delectation", which involves at times a bitter and almost spiteful augmentation of one's distress,[212] the mourner's reaction to beauty is rooted in Beauty's very nature and meaning.

Beauty appears to be intolerable at the *peak* of a great grief (though it can subsequently provide comfort), partly because it mobilizes deep emotions at a moment when one's best defence against grief is self-anaesthesia—a total psychic numbness. For, as Hanns Sachs (*131*) put it:

[209] The same contrast between the objective Choros' expectations and Menelaos' actual subjective response, is also manifest in ἀλοιδόρουc (supra).

[210] E. *Alc.* 425 ff.: Human beings and even horses are to made ugly by shearing. On Good Friday, Greek Orthodox churches replace the musical ringing of bells with a non-musical ("pitchless") rhythmic hammering on planks. Cp. also the "muffled drums" of military funerals.

[211] A distinguished and very musical scientist lost his wife after nearly fifty years of happy married life. For many months he not only found listening to great music unbearable, but could not even hum, as was his habit, great classical melodies while shaving. My own reactions to music after a beloved dog's death were similar.

[212] Cp. a King making a "clean sweep", by spitefully and self-defeatingly killing his last surviving bodyguard during his headlong flight. What matters is not the truth of the story, but the fact that such behaviour was known to, and understood by, the Greeks.

the problem of beauty is not how to understand it, but how to endure it. The unbearableness of beauty in great grief reveals, better than anything else, the power of great art—and of sexuality at its best—to move mankind. For I hold that it is not "piety", but the depth of feeling a strongly experienced embrace can mobilize, which explains why so many cultures taboo love-making during periods of mourning.[213]

In a sense, the points just made simply broaden the scope of Fraenkel's perceptive remark: "Every statue of a beautiful woman is more than the deserted husband can bear, for it reminds him of her whom he has lost." Indeed, one can, on the basis of psychological considerations only, and without anachronistically imputing to Aischylos a true anticipation of Platon's theory of forms,[214] assert that *in so far* as Helene's main—and almost only—quality is that she is the perfect *prototype* of feminine beauty, Menelaos would experience *any* statue of a lovely girl as an attenuated "portrait" of Helene. It would elicit, albeit with a sense of longing[215] for the more perfect original, the kind of reaction Helene herself would elicit.

However, since the real Helene had grievously offended Menelaos, *his* negative reaction to these statues can be viewed *in part* also as an unconscious manifestation of his inhibited anger (ἀλοιδόρους) which, as will shortly be seen, manifests itself also in his dream. The fact that even a widower—not cynically deserted by a beloved but despicable wife—can react negatively to beauty is no counter-argument, for the *irrational* unconscious—and sometimes even culture (*89*)—can view death as a (bitterly resented) "voluntary" desertion. This finding is highly relevant in the present context, for an unconscious resentment towards a real "deserter"—or even towards a person whose death the unconscious *defines* as a desertion—often manifests itself in overt or symbolic aggression towards objects connected with that person.[216] Such a "counter-aggression" permits one to ventilate one's anger, while denying any hostility to the "beloved" (ἀλοιδόρους).

In short, it is on the *subjective* (psychological) and *not* on the *cultural* (magical) level that these statues are *experienced* by Menelaos as genuine—but inadequate—"doubles" of Helene.

This explains why Aischylos *chose* to designate them by the term κολοςςοί

---

[213] This hypothesis is intended to lend further support to Freud's theory that the experience: "this is beautiful" is derived from the experience: "this is sexually arousing" (*68*, p. 156, note 2). A curious happening will confirm this. Some years ago, I was asked, at the last moment, to deliver a lecture on love, before a professional audience. Having had no time to prepare the lecture, I read, with only slight changes, my paper on art (*30*), simply replacing the word "art" with "love".

[214] Which I totally reject.   [215] Cp. infra: ἀχηνίαις.

[216] A deserted or disappointed, but still enamoured, lover frequently loses, mislays or destroys "accidentally on purpose" the gifts or photographs of an unfaithful beloved—often in a manner which greatly inconveniences him: (1) I analysed elsewhere (*41*) the mislaying of a photograph, made possible only by the *simultaneous* mislaying of an urgently needed book. (2) A young man, tormented by his capricious and promiscuous girl-friend, first "mislaid" a cigarette holder she had given him and, after finding it again, "accidentally" bit down on it hard enough to break it—and to chip a tooth as well. The mourner identifies himself with the dead—he inflicts pain on the "deserter" by, e.g., beating his own breast.

—applying a *culture*-oriented term to *subjectively atypically experienced* objects.[217] What is to be noted is that, in clinical experience, the choice of an unusual, though appropriate term, instead of a usual term, is always significant, simply because it has different "overtones".[218] In short, the word κολοccoí does not designate here a *particular* kind of statue. It simply highlights the *unusualness* of Menelaos' reactions to *ordinary* statues. It is a case where the affective climate of a scene determines the choice of a word whose "*halo*-meanings", while not fitting tangible reality, do fit the "mood" which determines one's *reactions* to that reality.[219]

The last point to be made concerns the literary function of Menelaos' negative reaction to these lovely statues: it appears to anticipate *in part* the deceptive joys which lead up to frustration in dream.[220]

This interpretation of v. 417 greatly facilitates the correct understanding of vv. 418–419, which describe the culminating symptoms of Menelaos' waking state.

418 ὀμμάτων δ' ἐν ἀχηνίαιc denotes some deficiency of Menelaos'[221] eyes. Some hold, however, that the eyes are those of:

(1) The statues,[222] or of

(2) The absent Helene—eyes which normally radiate her beauty (A. *Ag.* 742),[223] or of

(3) Both Helene and Menelaos.[224]

I will justify my view that Menelaos' eyes are meant, further on.

There is also disagreement over the *kind* of deficiency the word ἀχη-νίαιc—a word whose use in this passage strikes Groeneboom as "strange" —denotes. Ancient lexicographers gloss it as ἀπορία or πενία (straits, difficulty, need, want). This word often denotes a *partial* or *relative* deficiency only.[225]

(1) Mazon translates: "[les statues] n'ont pas d'yeux"; but statues *do* have eyes.

(2) Denniston and Page suggest that the eyes are the least lifelike part of a statue. But the *painted* eyes of Greek statues were sufficiently lifelike to dispense early Greek sculptors from having to invent the technique of hollowing out the irises.[226]

---

[217] A near-psychotic jazz musician felt that the late jazz saxophonist Charlie Parker was God and actually prayed to him. His *subjective* and deviant behaviour can only be described by using the *cultural* term "worship" in a quite literal sense.

[218] A patient, born in Great Britain but raised in America, one day said "beetle" where American usage would call for "bug". Questioned on this point, he first attributed his choice to his British background. However, his very next associations made it clear, *even to him*, that he had said "beetle" in order to *avoid* saying "bug", which had anxiety-arousing overtones for him ("bugger", a *British* term).

[219] Similarly, a girl complained that her *schizoid* and *depressed* lover handled her body as though it were simply "meat" (*not*: flesh).

[220] I am indebted for this suggestion to my student, M. Alain Sotto.

[221] Butler, Ahrens, Kennedy, Nägelsbach, Wecklein, Wilamowitz, Smyth, Fraenkel.

[222] Klausen, Hermann, Schütz, Mazon, Thomson, Denniston and Page.

[223] Heath, Sidgwick, Headlam, Groeneboom.

[224] Verrall; he postulates an *intentional* vagueness, on the basis of a reasoning which I seem unable to grasp and therefore cannot discuss.

[225] Cp. LSJ: ἀπορία is absolute only when further qualified (ἀπορία τινός). But cp. A. *Choe.* 185: thirsty (δίψιοι) tears (= tears of longing).

[226] A minor oddity of the "eyes of statues" interpretation is its incompatibility with

(3) Others hold that the absent Helene's eyes are meant—an absence which Menelaos experiences as a need. This seems too complicated and I am not even sure that this idea is compatible with the text.

All these alternative interpretations are inspired by the easily documentable[227] Greek view that the eyes stimulate love. For the moment I note one objection only: *despite* or because of the absence or lifelessness of *these* "eyes", Menelaos' ardour is unabated: his dream is erotic.

It is necessary to prepare the ground for my discussion by formulating two general principles:

(1) When, in a descriptive (non-gnomic) passage, a great poet *seemingly* fails to identify explicitly the "thing" he mentions, what he says *about* it usually permits a precise identification of that "thing".[228]

(2) When a great poet is, in fact, ambiguous, the ambiguity always serves a poetic objective (*35, 59*). Since, in this passage, an ambiguity cannot be shown to serve poetic ends, Verrall's ambiguity hypothesis becomes untenable.

What is required at this juncture is a logical analysis of what Aischylos actually says in this passage—because, as a superb realist and psychologist, he could say nothing else.

(1) Throughout vv. 410–419, all statements consist of two verses only. One may therefore even consider replacing the comma at the end of v. 417 with a period—at least mentally.

(2) The *subject* (in the nominative) of the sentence is "Aphrodita". Whatever happens to "her", happens only because of a "deficiency" of (or: in) the eyes. The logic of these verses is the same as that of vv. 414–415; the first verse specifies the on-going (affective) cause of the developments described in the second verse.

(3) Vv. 418–419 describe an *on-going process*. Something is *currently* happening *to* "all of Aphrodita", because something *has* happened—and continues to happen—*in* (δ' ἐν) the eyes. However:

(a) Nothing happened to Helene's eyes—they simply shine now in Troy. The expression δ' ἐν does not fit the view that their passing outside *Menelaos'* visual field is meant.

(b) The statues' eyes *did not* change, for they *cannot* change *objectively*. If they do not radiate love now, they never did, for what is not, cannot cease to be. Two possible objections can easily be disposed of:

(α) Like the statues as a whole, their eyes suddenly ceased to appeal to Menelaos. If so, *only* Menelaos' "eyes" have changed. This implies, moreover, that vv. 418–419 simply duplicate vv. 416–417, which describe the purely *perceptual* degradation of the (objectively still beautiful) statues.

(β) Helene's flight made her statues comparable to an "empty" statue,

ordinary experience, for it tacitly implies that, while Helene was still with Menelaos, the eyes of the statues—rather than Helene's own—aroused his passion. It is only when a beloved wife is *absent* that the husband is stimulated by her "portraits". Yet, in women, dilated pupils = sexual arousal. Hess, E. H.: Attitudes and Pupil Size, *Scientific American* 212:46–54, 1965.

[227] The array of texts cited by Thomson is most impressive—though quite inappropriate in the present context (infra). Cp. also L. Malten (*108*).

[228] Since, in Alcm. *fr.* 1.59, the Kolaxaian horse represents a *lovely* girl, that horse cannot be the *homely* Mongol pony; it can only be the *handsome* Ferghana-type racer (*32*).

in which the deity does not dwell. But there is no evidence that a *live* mythical person could ever "animate" his or her own portrait-statue.[229] Also, a reference to an "empty" statue would be anachronistic. That notion appears to be post-Aischylean and probably Hellenistic (Suid. s.v. Heraiskos).

(4) There is a marked logical *progression* in vv. 410–426: though each detail presupposes the one which precedes it, and prepares the ground for the one which follows it, the poet never back-tracks. However,

(a) If Helene's eyes are meant, vv. 418–419 would hearken back directly to vv. 414–415;

(b) If the statues' eyes are meant, vv. 418–419 would simply "explain" vv. 416–417, which—incidentally—require no explanation. This notion would also disrupt the logical progression in a rather absurd manner: the unattractiveness of the statues *in their entirety* would be "explained" by the relative deficiency of *one part* of the statues: their eyes.[230]

Logic demands that vv. 418–419 should not constrict and particularize, but rather *generalize* and *expand* the statement made in vv. 416–417 about a particular (statues). Vv. 416–417 "explain" vv. 418–419—not vice versa.

(5) The passage as a whole lists *increasingly severe* symptoms. Now, since vv. 416–417 describe Menelaos' *hatred* of the statues, the tension would *decrease* if vv. 418–419 were held to describe merely an *indifference* toward the *eyes* of the statues. This *indifference* could represent an "escalation" of Menelaos' *dislike* of the statues only if it encompasses *all* external reality.[231]

Contextual considerations make it mandatory to conclude that Menelaos' "eyes" have, in some respect, *become* "deficient"—and this quite apart from the fact that only *his* "eyes" can "change".

(1) Vv. 410–426 describe Menelaos' state *only*: his reactions, or his failure to respond—which, psychologically, is also a kind of "response". Other things are mentioned only in order to highlight the abnormality of Menelaos' reaction *to* them.[232]

(2) They make no *psychological* statement about anyone else. Thus, vv. 414–415 mention Helene's *physical* absence only in order to highlight Menelaos' reaction to it. There is not even a passing allusion to Helene's psychological state in Troy.[233] Even the eloped Helene's former love for Menelaos (φιλάνορες) was mentioned only in order to underscore the magnitude of Menelaos' loss.

(3) Vv. 412–419 deal with psychiatric symptoms only—and nothing "psychiatric" can be said about anyone except Menelaos.

(4) Something quite striking *can*, however, be said about the eyes of a

---

[229] No mythical statue ever "behaved" *spontaneously*, in an *operationally* specifiable sense. Even Protesilaos' and Alkestis' statues had to be "quickened" by dreams and by physical contact.

[230] It makes sense to say: "I dislike Kritias—in fact, I loathe all tyrants." It is poor logic to say: "I hate tyrants—Kritias behaved objectionably toward Euthydemos" (X. *Mem.* 1.2.29 f.).

[231] For this meaning of πᾶς' Ἀφροδίτα, cp. my comments on v. 419.

[232] It is the "beauty" of the statues which makes it obvious that Menelaos' dislike of them is pathological.

[233] This is significant, since vv. 406–407 represent her as irresponsibly casual, while Hom. *Il.* 3.171 ff. (and passim) stresses her remorse and shame.

deeply disturbed man. A Greek poet would have had to be both singularly unobservant and ignorant of tradition, had he failed to note an emotionally deranged person's abnormal gaze.[234]

(5) A failure to include so striking a detail into a *list* of symptoms would run counter to the Greek poets' tendency to list *all* of a disturbed person's[235] salient symptoms and to describe them well (Ps.-Long. 15.1)—too well, in fact, for Platon's taste (Pl. *Rmp.* 396a, f.).

(6) The appearance of a severely depressed person's eyes is characterized by a "deficiency". His eyes are dull[236] and usually immobile. They also seem "sightless",[237] for the depressed mourner's attention is focused entirely—and even obsessively—on the "internalized" image of the lost beloved,[238] with whom he identifies himself. In short, the eyes (*qua* organs) are *deficient* in lustre and animation; their gaze is also deficient, for it resembles that of a sight*less* person.[239] In fact, under the impact of a sudden and brutal loss, the depressed may stumble about like a blind man. Though, neurophysiologically, the depressive in a state of shock does "see", he collides with people and things as though he did not.

I note only in passing that the eyes of the depressed sometimes become fleetingly reanimated and seem to search avidly[240] for the beloved (or her φάϲμα)—but, since the beloved is not there for him to see, his gaze soon turns inward once more.

This too leads up, both poetically and logically, to the real meaning of v. 419; The appearance of Menelaos' eyes betrays his lack of interest in what surrounds him. They are *lacking* in sparkle and animation, for their gaze is turned inward: toward the absent Helene's "internalized" image.

This interpretation would be correct even if it were held that vv. 414 f. describe a re-projection of Helene's image into the "outer" world, in the form of a φάϲμα—which, incidentally, would imply a blurring of the boundary between "inside" and "outside"[241]—of a boundary which plays a crucial role in normal psychological functioning (supra).

---

[234] *Iliou Persis fr.* 5: Aias' eyes; E. *HF*: Herakles' eyes, well discussed by Blaiklock (*9*, chap. 7); E. *Alc.* 385: καὶ μὴν ϲκοτεινὸν ὄμμα μου βαρύνεται (my increasingly heavy eyes are getting dark). For the eyes of mad animals, cp. Roscher (*130*, passim). English: "to see red". French: "les yeux foux". Malay: "mata gelap" denotes the appearance of an amok-runner's "black eyes", his supposed visual experiences in that state, and even the state of being "amok" itself.

[235] Sappho *fr.* 31 LP is, *pace* Ps.-Long. 10.1, a non-selective, exhaustive list of symptoms (*118*, p. 27; *43*). Contra: Marcovich (*110*). E. *Hipp.* lists about thirty of Phaidra's symptoms. E. *HF* mentions all the salient symptoms of epilepsy (*9*, chap. 7). E. *Ba.* describes all the major symptoms of possession (*55*, Appendix i) or of hysteria (*8*), etc. On the capacity of Greek poets to sense the coherence—the pattern—of sets of symptoms (= syndromes), cp. Ps.-Long. 10.1 and (*43*). I cannot refute here two critics of my views.

[236] LSJ s.v. ἀχηνία translates v. 418 as: blank gaze.

[237] But this does not justify Vernant's (*136*, 261, note 32) attempt to bring the blind seer Teiresias into the picture.

[238] Cp. my comments on vv. 414–415 and on v. 419.

[239] I stress these deficiencies mainly because Professor Lloyd-Jones rightly objects to the LSJ translation, in which "blank" gaze is, in the *literal* sense, a positive (though bad) "quality" and not a "lack".

[240] "Hunger" (Smyth), "starving" (Fraenkel).

[241] Already Edward Tylor (*134*) suggested that belief in ("external") ghosts is derived from ("internal") dreams about the dead.

What really matters is that even a re-projecting of Helene's internalized image into the "outer" world, in the form of a visual hallucination (φάσμα), may be unable to elicit enough *real* affect in Menelaos to "quicken" his eyes.[242] His preoccupation with this hallucination may even increase Menelaos' depressive "lack of animation" (general psycho-motor retardation).

Appendix

(1) Smyth and Fraenkel translate ἀχηνίαις as "hunger" or "starving". This translation, though semantically unjustifiable, does reflect the principal *psychological* "overtone" of the mourner's *experience* of need (and loss). He *regressively* experiences the loss of love as a (pregenital) oral frustration: as *hunger*.[243] Even cannibalistic fantasies can occur in mourning (*33*), for the "internalization" of the lost person is experienced as a restitutive "oral incorporation". In depressive neurosis (*71*) and even in funeral rites (Hdt. 3.99), the "loss of love" is often compensated by overeating; the affect-hunger is regressively replaced by food-hunger, which often has cannibalistic overtones.[244] Self-starving in mourning[245] can be interpreted as an unconscious defence against "restitutive" cannibalistic-necrophagic cravings.

This summary statement suffices for present purposes, since the nexus between mourning and abnormal feeding patterns (including hunger) is brought to one's attention not by Aischylos' own text but by its (interpretative) translation.[246]

(2) It is possible to explain—at least tentatively and in part—why, apart from metrical considerations, Aischylos preferred the word ἀχηνία to ἀπορία or πενία. His choice appears to have been *partly* determined by a "clang association".[247]

Given the affinities of poetry—and especially of a choral ode—with music, it stands to reason that the poet will choose words not only on the basis of their conceptual content, but also on that of their *acoustic* kinship with other words whose *meaning* has certain *conceptual* affinities with that of the word he actually selects. This procedure has nothing in common with the "clang-associations" of a schizophrenic's discourse, in which the (logically spurious) linking of successive words, in terms of their *acoustic*

---

[242] An affectively frozen, depressed and schizoid patient claimed that his visual fantasies —at once obscene, perverted, sadistic and even "monstrous" in the "Gothick" sense of the word—filled him with "terror". But he described them in a mechanical, *affectless* tone of voice; his facial expression remained wooden and, when pressed for comments, he would reply: "These fantasies and visions mean nothing to me; like everything else, they seem very remote from me" (*34, 37*).

[243] The Greeks were aware of the mechanism of regression: A. *Ag.* 75 compares the old to children. Platon (*Lg.* 672c) even appears to have sensed that all psychological disturbances involve some regression to earlier ways of being.

[244] Thus, Demeter's mourning explains her cannibalization of Pelops (Pi. *O.* 1.40 ff.), etc. A man's wife loved apples; he detested them. But during her one long absence he ate them with pleasure—"on her behalf".

[245] Achilleus: Hom. *Il.* 19.346; Demeter: Hom. *h. Cer.* 200 ff., etc.

[246] I hope to publish eventually the considerable amount of classical, primitive, and clinical data I have assembled on ritual, mythical, fantasied and real feeding disturbances in actual, delayed and neurotic mourning, in a separate study.

[247] This is common in Greek poetry, though I cannot cite here other examples.

affinities *only*, brings into being an almost exclusively acoustic "continuity" of the text. This, in turn, produces an irrational and impoverished, because conceptually discontinuous, discourse.[248] By contrast, even though the poet's choice of one word in preference to another (of similar *meaning*) may be *secondarily* determined by that word's acoustic affinities with another, conceptually *also* appropriate, word, his choice deepens and enriches his discourse by means of *acoustic* evocations of relevant, related *ideas*. It is possible, therefore, that Aischylos chose the word ἀχηνίαις because of its acoustic affinities with ἀχεύω (or ἀχέω) = grieving, mourning.[249]

419 ἔρρει πᾶς' Ἀφροδίτα is psychologically straight out of Freud, since Aphrodite stands here for what she stands for in Empedokles (*frr.* 16–18, 71–75, 86–87, 95, 98, 128, 151 DK), and what Eros or libido stands for in Freud: that which lends the world around us not only the quality of beauty but even the quality of *reality* and *relevance*. It signifies that the resonance of affects gives emotional reality to the sense perceptions. In technical terms, a world animated by *this* Aphrodite is a world "cathected (invested) with libido". A decathected world—like Hades—is colourless, irrelevant and even intellectually just barely apprehended (Luc. *Cat.* 22). As one of my patients put it: "I can see—I know—that this armchair is red, but I do not *feel* its redness. It is all very remote from me."[250] The preceding verses—which reveal Menelaos' loss of interest in a reality so "flattened" that it can no longer feed the hunger of his eyes—prepare us for this bitter summing up.

This reaction is not only psychiatrically predictable; it is also manifestly Greek. Admetos says much the same to the dying Alkestis: "You have taken from me the delight of life."[251]

The word ἔρρει substantiates this interpretation: Fraenkel rightly insists that ἔρρει implies both a degradation and a ruinous—and at times violent—disappearance. It therefore both hearkens back to Helene's abduction—which Menelaos would no doubt like to imagine as involuntary[252]—and anticipates her "flight" in dream (425–426). This degradation of reality, its loss of relevance, is an inevitable result of Menelaos' turning inward.

Aischylos even makes it clear that Aphrodite's disappearance is not an objective event. It is a consequence of Menelaos' reaction. It is *for him only* that Aphrodite has disappeared. The world has no *psycho-affective relevance* other than the one our cathecting it with libido attributes to it. This verse is the proper climax of vv. 415–419 and opens the way for Menelaos'

---

[248] A self-diagnosed schizophrenic even published a kind of schizophrenic theory of language (*142*).

[249] It is quite improbable that he was (even unconsciously) stimulated by ἀχηνίαις's extremely faint acoustic affinities with ἀχέρωις (= the white poplar, of infernal origin) or with Ἀχέρων (= a river of the Nether World).

[250] Such remarks are commonly made by depressive patients.

[251] E. *Alc.* 347: σὺ γάρ μου τέρψιν ἐξείλου βίου.

[252] This conception underlies Stesich. *fr.* 15 P and all myths of her "double" (E. *Hel.*, etc.), as well as passages which emphasize that she was a helpless victim of Aphrodite's will (Hom. *Od.* 23.222 ff., on which see (*28*); E. *Tr.* 948 ff., 1042 f., etc.; Gorg. *Hel. fr.* 11 D.-K.).

dream—for the dream of a man no longer in *affective* contact with reality.

But it is also this verse which foreshadows v. 426, as I read it: the degradation of Aphrodite anticipates the degradation of Helene's dream-apparition.[253]

420 ὀνειρόφαντοι = dream apparitions, clearly hearkens back to cτίβοι (v. 411) and to φάcμα (v. 415) and also to κολοccῶν (v. 416) (Fraenkel). This, too, is an indication of the exceptionally great internal coherence of this whole passage. The repeated hearkening back to what went before and anticipation of what is to come gives this entire passage the taut and manifold internal logic of a strict fugue. It will, moreover, be shown in a moment that the very next word, taken as Fraenkel takes it, further enhances the internal cohesion of vv. 410–426, by linking the dream with Menelaos' depression.

420 πενθήμονεc = mournful.[254] The crucial choice is between:

(1) The view that this word describes Helene's appearance in dream (Denniston and Page).

(2) The view that it represents the dream as a consequence (symptom) of Menelaos' reactive depression (Fraenkel) . . . and as a cause of its intensification. It also foreshadows the frustration and v. 426.

I will now discuss these views, indicating at once that I prefer Fraenkel's interpretation.

(1) Denniston and Page are psychologically correct in urging that Helene appears to Menelaos "as he would have her". Unfortunately, they then proceed to specify that Menelaos visualizes her in dream "not as she is, happily mated with Paris, but . . . sorrowful, returning in tears to her lost husband; and that is gratifying (χάριν), however unreal (ματαίαν)". (But cp. infra, v. 426.)

It is not denied that Menelaos, particularly while awake, might wish a repentant Helene to return to him in tears. But, as indicated above (ἀλοιδόρουc), Menelaos, like nearly all men in his situation, is ambivalent. His waking and relatively rational wish is replaced *in dream* by a less rational, more instinctual wish. The crucial consideration is the *erotic* character of the opening scene of his dream, which begins with an attempted sexual embrace. This suggests that Menelaos does not dream of a *future* scene, for which there is no precedent. He dreams of a particular pseudo-future scene: of a restoration of the *status quo ante*, whose *erotic* character is anticipated by v. 411. I call this scene a pseudo-future one, because the unconscious (which fuels dreams) is "timeless" (Freud): the desired erotic union actually *begins* to happen in dream.

Now, the fact that the dream-image of Helene is capable of triggering an erotic reaction sets certain limits to the manner in which the appearance of that image may be visualized.

What Denniston and Page seem to visualize is, *mutatis mutandis*, the kind of decorous scene depicted in Plu. *V. Dion.* 51.1: Dion receives tenderly the

---

[253] Orph. *fr.* 347 (χειρῶν δ' ὀλλυμένων ἔρρεν πολύεργος 'Αθήνη), cited by Thomson, does not support his view but mine: with the loss of the (artisan's) hands, personified skill (Athene) is gone.

[254] My objections to Housman's gratuitous emendation of this word are relegated to footnote 262.

tearful Arete, whose adultery—unlike that of Helene—was involuntary. Such a scene could lead to an erotic union consolidating the reconciliation. But weighty reasons militate against this manner of visualising the *Aischylean* Helene's dream image.

One must visualize a "sorrowful" Helene, "returning in tears" *in the Aischylean manner*. Now, Aischylean grief-reactions are nearly always extreme (*18*). A repentant and sorrowing Helene, as visualized by Aischylos, would not be a gently and humbly grieving woman. Aischylos would have fantasied a Helene frenzied with despair: dishevelled, clothes in disarray and eyes reddened with tears. He would have visualized her like his Kassandra (A. *Ag.* 1072 ff.) or like that of Euripides (*Tr.* 306 ff.). She would have resembled also Euripides' Phaidra (E. *Hipp.* 170 ff.), and even more his Antigone (E. *Phoin.* 1485 ff.). I submit that a woman resembling a "bakchante of death" (E. *Phoin.* 1489 f.) could not elicit a normal *erotic* reaction even in dream. Even less could a "properly" repentant Euripidean (E. *Tr.* 1025 ff.) Helene—one who meets Hekabe's standards.

I concede, of course, that Mykenaian warriors, as depicted by the poets, did rape distressed female captives.[255] But such a deed is performed by hate-filled men, drunk with blood, and not by grieving husbands like Menelaos—least of all in an erotic dream that brings joy, however vain that joy may be.[256]

In short, χάριν—ματαίαν notwithstanding—automatically excludes an incipient erotic dream scene with a (characteristically Aischylean) despairing Helene, or even with a decorously tearful Ploutarchean Arete. Helene's dream-image is as supremely seductive as ever, at least at the beginning of the dream.[257] The Denniston and Page interpretation of this word therefore cannot be retained either on the basis of literary considerations or on the basis of psychological experience.

(2) Fraenkel holds that this word serves to represent the dream as one of the *consequences* of Menelaos' grief. This is psychologically inescapable, for Menelaos' dream has a psychological plausibility *only* if it is the nocturnal counterpart of his waking depressive symptoms: if it climaxes, in a subtly *contrasting* way, the preceding enumeration of his symptoms. Moreover, it permits—and, indeed, almost obliges—one to visualize Helene's dream-image as totally enchanting and seductive, for, as said above, Menelaos' *first* "dream-wish" (Freud) is to restore the *status quo ante*, with all its delights.

Fraenkel further strengthens his case by stressing that E. *Alc.* 354 was not directly inspired by this Aischylean passage. He insists that both passages simply reflect a basic human experience. In saying this Fraenkel, who professes to be sceptical of psychology, uses precisely the kind of *realistic* psychology commentators of *great* poets should use—and so seldom do.

---

[255] Cp. the rape of Kassandra by the lesser Aias (*Iliou Persis* fr. 1 E.-W.), the Theban women's fear of rape (A. *Sept.* 292, 364), etc.

[256] Examples in which distressed and dishevelled women, stunned by recent misfortunes, were comfortingly taken to bed by a kindly man hardly represent occurrences which are psychologically analogous to Menelaos' straightforward and at least initially joyful erotic dream.

[257] The degradation of Helene's appearance in *subsequent* dreams will be discussed in connection with v. 426.

I concede, of course, that Fraenkel's translation underscores more explicitly than does Aischylos' Greek text the causal nexus between the mourning and the dream and lacks the syntactical ambiguity of the word πενθήμονες. But the fault—if fault it be—is not Fraenkel's; it is a consequence of the nature and limitations of the English idiom;[258] English simply does not permit one to make the causal nexus as allusive—and elusive—as the Greek idiom does.

I must now briefly deal with passages certain commentators cite in connection with this word.

References to E. *Alc.* 348 (or 343–347) are legitimate, even though the eloped Helene is completely unlike the almost dead Alkestis. Admetos relies *both* on the presence of Alkestis' portrait statue in his bed and on erotic dreams to provide at least momentary affective and erotic solace. The recourse to a sculptured double of Alkestis is reasonable in terms of Greek eschatology, for, as I urged long ago (*27*, p. 268.0), the shades of the dead behave like mourners,[259] and are therefore erotically non-stimulating. This explains why, in Hyg. *fab.* 104, Laodameia makes love with Protesilaos' statue, rather than, as in most other traditions, with his returned shade, or else in dream. In both Admetos' and Laodameia's case the portrait statue probably insured that the dead spouse would appear in dream neither as an εἴδωλον, nor as a gibbering, bloodless, sexually unappealing shade, but as that spouse appeared while alive: in a guise capable of eliciting a sexual response, satisfying at least in dream.[260]

By contrast, a number of other passages cited by certain commentators are irrelevant.

In Meleagros (*AP* 5.166),[261] no one appears, nor is expected to appear, to anyone in an erotic dream. The poet simply wonders (hopefully) whether the unfaithful Heliodora has longing and tearful erotic dreams *about him*. This situation differs so radically from the Aischylean one that Denniston and Page wisely refrain from citing it to support their conception of a dreamed *of*—not dreaming!—Helene. Indeed, nothing in the Meleagros text suggests that Heliodora might dream of a repentant Meleagros, comparable to the Denniston and Page Helene—for the good reason that Meleagros has nothing to be repentant about. The citing of this text is simply a token of Verrall's habitual psychological insensitivity, directly connected with what Fraenkel calls his taste for Silver Latin literature (*64* 1, p. 57).

Verrall's two other "parallel" passages are no better or more relevant.

Prop. 4.7.5 refers to a funeral, and does so in a manner which makes any

---

[258] I even tried to "improve" Fraenkel's translation, first in English, and then in French, German and Hungarian. Not one of my efforts was even a shade more exact than Fraenkel's translation; most of them were much inferior to his.

[259] Though Dale (ad E. *Alc.* 343–347) cites E. *Hipp.* 1131 ff., which does *not* describe the future behaviour of the *mourner*, but the future *non*-behaviour of the *dead*, she manifestly had in mind only the "objective", conceptual similarities between the two passages. She did not see that the mourner imitates, by self-denial, the dull existence of the dead, or that the Homeric dead behave like mourners; they mourn the loss of their life.

[260] I note that the commentators I consulted do not quote Ov. *Her.* 13.105 ff., which is relevant at least in connection with E. *Alc.*

[261] Cp. Housman (*85*, p. 269).

appeal to the symbolic equation: departure = death otiose (cp. "Partir, c'est mourir un peu").

In Prop. 4.11.81, a loving, deceased spouse compassionately addresses her mourning husband, speaking of *his* dreams of her. This situation, too, is psychologically totally different from that depicted by Aischylos.

Groeneboom's reference to Milton (Sonnet xxiii) is, if possible, even more irrelevant. Though the dream-image of Milton's wife also eludes his embrace, the scene evoked seems to me tender rather than erotic; in addition, Milton's dead wife was a paragon of virtue. This Sonnet may have psychological affinities with Hom. *Od.* 11.204 ff.; it has few with Menelaos' dreams.

Artificial, psychologically unrelated "parallels" of this kind do not illuminate a text—they obscure it. Hence Fraenkel, showing wisdom quite as much as literary taste and psychological acumen, refrained from citing such pseudo-parallels.[262]

422–423: The Syntax of these verses is said to be perplexing. Denniston and Page speak—perhaps over-emphatically—of "frantic incoherence", and emend the text. Others, including Professor Lloyd-Jones, are prepared to tolerate two anacoluthons, or an incomplete sentence, largely on the grounds that this would be quite dramatic.

I do not presume to settle a point of syntax on which greater experts by far disagree. As a lover of poetry, I have a good deal of sympathy with the argument that the sudden breaking off of a sentence has dramatic impact. But that is beside the point, for I must speak here as a psychologist.

I begin by noting that a dream is an "illogical" experience, while speech is a predominantly logical structure. This explains why patients reporting their dreams often speak haltingly and grope for words. Also, the Choros probably heard the dream narrated by the depressed Menelaos (supra)—and the sentences of the depressed do tend to trail off and not to be completed. Hence, even though the dream is reported in the third person, it is not too far-fetched to suppose that the Choros' syntax was affected by that of the original narrator, Menelaos. I have often enough heard Mohave shamans—and even psycho-analysts—grope for words while

---

262 Housman conjectures πειθήμονες = persuasive, for πενθήμονες. The conjecture is gratuitous, for πενθήμονες, interpreted in Fraenkel's manner, makes excellent sense. Housman's conjecture is, moreover, psychologically redundant, for nearly all dreams are persuasive *while they last*. Exceptions to this rule are dreams which the dreamer recognizes as dreams already while dreaming them, and so-called "dreams within dreams". Headlam's attempts to justify this emendation by citing A. *Ag.* 274: "Is it to persuasive dreams that you pay regard?" is unconvincing; the relatively sceptical Choros' εὐπειθῆ implies a *successful* deception and Klytaimestra herself brushes aside dreams as "hollow fancies" in her reply (v. 275). It is, moreover, very probable that it is Klytaimestra's initial assertion (v. 273), that her proof of the fall of Troy is reliable "unless a god played me false", which gave the Choros the idea that she may have dreamed the kind of Zeus-sent, persuasive but deceptive, dream Agamemnon had in Hom. *Il.* 2.5 ff. Last but not least, the kind of dream the Choros envisages at v. 274 would prove false and deceptive only *after* awakening, when is must stand the acid test of reality, whereas Menelaos experiences frustration already *in* dream, though the sense of frustration is prolonged into the waking state—at which point the deceitfulness of the *whole* dream experience also becomes manifest. In short, the conceptual and factual affinity between v. 274 and v. 420 (as emended by Housman) is too flimsy to justify his unnecessary emendation of a sound text.

reporting their patients' dreams, particularly when, as happens in this instance, the dream-events take an unexpected turn.

Another general point may also be made. I repeatedly cited ancient opinions on the capacity of the tragic poets to reproduce correctly the disordered speech of distressed or insane persons. It is therefore probable that certain parts of such passages, which modern philologists treat as *loci desperati*, may be exactly what Aischylos or Euripides had written. Others may have become corrupted as a result of the attempts of ancient critics and copyists to force an originally relatively incoherently written discourse into the strait jacket of strict grammar and syntax. But I hasten to add that intentionally incoherent passages can easily *become* even more incoherent in the process of being copied.[263]

What matters here is that, *despite* the relative incoherence of the sentence, its *psychological* sense is not only clear, but is not even greatly affected by attempts at emending the text. With this, I can now turn to the details of these verses.

422: χάριν = (sexual) joys or delights. That the context calls for a sexual connotation seems self-evident; that this term often has erotic connotations was shown by Barrett (ad E. *Hipp.* 513 ff., *4*, p. 433). The word ἐcθλά (423), meaning "the good" in general, simply extends the deceptiveness of *erotic* joys experienced in dream to *all* dreamed good and pleasurable experiences. This is only to be expected, for, to the Greek, sexual pleasure was "a good". The psycho-analyst will readily concur with this view.[264]

422 f.: ματαιάν· μάταν γάρ = idle, vain. The crux of the matter is that whereas Penelope feels cheated only *on awakening* after dreaming of making love with the absent Odysseus (Hom. *Od.* 20.87 ff.), Menelaos is frustrated already *in dream*, for the union is *not* consummated even in dream.[265]

At this point, a crucial consideration intervenes: in all classical texts known to me, and in many post-classical ones as well, erotic dreams are fully gratifying *while they last*; the most conclusive example is a young man's dream about Thonis (Plu. *V. Dem.* 27).[266] The exceptions to this rule are the present dream and, strikingly, also the erotic dreams of *other* men about *Helene*.[267] This is not surprising in the case of a woman of whom Stesichoros (*frr.* 15, 16 P.) and others said that only her double cohabited with Paris (and with Deiphobos). In Greek myth and poetry, Helene is the kind of narcissistic, man-destroying woman (vv. 689 ff.) whom her lover possesses the least when he enfolds her most completely.[268] No one ever holds more than her "double" in his arms. Some dim understanding of

[263] Let anyone who doubts this try to copy quickly a specimen of a schizophrenic "word salad", such as can be found in most psychiatric textbooks.

[264] Cp. Freud (*68*, p. 156, note 2 and supra).

[265] Mazon, ad loc., arbitrarily says that the disappointment is due to Menelaos' *premature awakening*. Both πενθήμονες and v. 426 disprove this. The disappointment is part of the dream.

[266] Had Menelaos' dream been gratifying, the Trojan war might well have failed to take place.

[267] Lyc. 820 ff. (Menelaos), 112 ff. (Paris), 171 ff. (Achilleus).

[268] Cp. Catullus' Lesbia, the Abbé Prévost's Manon Lescaut, P. Mérimée's Carmen, etc. In Hom. *Od.* 4.277 ff., Helene plays vocally the "double" of the wives of the men hidden inside the Trojan horse, so as to make them betray themselves.

this fact may have incited Stesichoros to invent *precisely* a "double", rather than some other device which would also have exonerated Helene in the eyes of posterity. And, not surprisingly, this justification—seen psychologically—condemns the shallow Helene *more* than could have done a tale of her consenting, deeply amorous elopement with Paris. The emphasis on this dream's deceptiveness is, thus, legitimate, especially if one considers certain monuments representing male erotic dreams. A glance at the frontispiece of this book shows three facts.

(1) The angle of the erect penis is quite abnormal. Instead of pointing upward, it is forced downward. This would not only be painful, but does not even fit the angle at which the erect penis is (correctly) represented on "obscene" vases.

(2) No insertion has taken place, nor is it likely to occur later on. The tip of the penis barely touches the *introitus* or the clitoris.

(3) The woman's wings are almost spread, and her webbed feet are strongly braced. This, together with her general body posture, with the contraction of her biceps (standing for the *non-representable* contraction of the muscles of her wings) and with the play of her leg muscles, suggests that she is *not* descending upon the sleeper, but is taking to the air, leaving him. Also, the persisting erection suggests that she does so *prematurely*.

Now, one risks misunderstanding this bas-relief if one asserts that it intentionally depicts the phallos for "obscene" reasons—urging perhaps that many genuinely obscene vases *also* show the penis just on the point of being inserted[269]—and this quite apart from the fact that vases of that type do *not* show dreams and that this bas-relief does *not* show an *incipient* insertion that will be completed. This bas-relief must be compared with pictures of female monsters with *clawed* (or otherwise non-human) feet, who *begin* to rape a man in a nightmare scene. In such pictures, too, most of the erect penis is usually visible—and, again, *not* for obscene reasons. This manner of representing rape (in a nightmare) underscores that *real* coitus is *not* performed. What such vases depict (psychologically) are anxiety erections, leading *at most* to a (dream-)ejaculation *ante portas*—as in the case of Hephaistos, frustrated by the sudden disappearance or dematerialization of Athene, whom he was trying to rape.[270]

This does not mean that erotic dreams prematurely interrupted by the dreamer's *awakening* do not exist. Such awakenings are usually due to the "moral" scruples of, e.g., timid and virginal adolescents. By contrast, when the "frustration" is due to a strong though latent hostility toward the (ambivalently desired and hated) dream-partner, the frustration is usually part of the dream: it is not caused by a premature awakening. In such cases, the dreamer usually wakes up only after the dream partner eludes him. This is clearly what happens in this instance. In fact, we learn that Menelaos had *almost* managed to enfold Helene's vision *only* through being told that she suddenly eluded his embrace.[271]

It suffices to conclude with the observation that the unexpected "good"

---

[269] E.g., Sphinx: lekythos, Athens National Museum, 450 B.C. *Pace* Kouretas (*92*), on *that* vase the union is barely approximated.

[270] All texts in Powell (*123*).

[271] The same is true of various accounts of how Athene eluded Hephaistos.

(ἐcθλά) is—or is *first* thought to be—illusory and evanescent (Luc. *Gall.* 5 f., *Tim.* 20, 41, etc.). Mankind, the tragic species, has learned early to be sceptical of hope. Prometheus (A. *PV* 928) takes pride in having *given* hope to mankind; in A. *Ag*, 491 ff., the Choros doubts the good news that Troy had been taken, etc. (Vain terrors: A. *Choe.* 287). Polykrates' consistent good luck was held to foretell a final misfortune (Hdt. 3.43). The point need not be laboured (Luc. *Gall.* 25).

423: δοκῶν ὁρᾶν (ὁρᾷ): Whether or not one emends these words,[272] their basic psychological import remains the same: the dreamer *only thinks* he sees something good (Helene). This excludes from the start the possibility that a "real and external", i.e., Homeric, dream-personage had entered Menelaos' dream. What he *thinks* he sees is an image of his own desires surfacing from his dormant mind.

Excursus: There is nothing to impel Helene herself to intrude into Menelaos' dream from the outside, and no god sends her double to him.[273] If Helene appears, it is because Menelaos wants her to appear—and dreams that she does. This may not fit the earliest Greek dream theory, but it would be well to recall that Aischylos wrote psychologically plausible— and therefore great—poetry. He did not try to provide case material illustrating a Greek treatise on oneiromancy. That is one reason why this dream deviates so much from *routine* Greek literary and "dream-book" types of dreams, and why it is so close to real dreams.

Now, the capacity of men to invite and even to provoke their own dreams (*55*, pp. 110, 294) is attested by tragedy (E. *Alc.* 354 ff.), incuba-tion rites (*19, 57, 84, 139*), clinical experience, and even by such sayings as: "dream brings counsel" or "I'll sleep on it".[274]

But, once one admits that Helene appeared to Menelaos in dream in response to *his* unconscious wishes, one must admit that she eluded his dream-embrace in accordance with *another* of *his* wishes. This makes it impossible to appeal to the Greek theory of the externality and autonomy of dream figures, in order to explain Helene's flight in this extraordinarily plausible dream. Her appearance cannot even be attributed to love magic. No such magic is mentioned and, had it been used, it would probably have brought back the real Helene and not her dream-image. Also, had a magician tried to evoke only Helene's phantom—to furnish an erotic dream to Menelaos—that dream would not have been a frustrating one.[275]

Above all, though Aischylos no doubt knew the theory of the autonomy of dream-visions, he was great enough a poet to sense that the behaviour of

---

[272] δοκῶν ὁρᾶν (Fraenkel, Mazon); δοκῶν ὁρᾷ (Smyth, Groeneboom); δοκοῦνθ' ὁρᾷ (Denniston and Page, Page, Thomson).

[273] Let it not be argued that a god caused this dream, so as to incite Menelaos to start the war of Troy which, in accordance with Zeus' will, is to destroy the race of heroes (*Cypr. fr.* 1, Allen). Neither the *Iliad* nor Helene's conduct at Troy suggest this.

[274] Whether the dream is wish fulfillment (Freud, *66*), problem solving (Rivers, *127*) or reality testing (French, *65*), it is evident that one dreams of something because one con-sciously or unconsciously wishes to dream of it, cp. infra.

[275] In the Eurydike myth the gift is real enough—it is Orpheus' breach of one of the conditions of the gift which cancels it. Cp. a Mohave Indian Orpheus and Eurydike type of myth (*22*).

such apparitions fitted the irrational and unconscious wishes of the dreamer in *every* respect. If he knew that Menelaos' desire invited Helene into his dream,[276] then he must have sensed also that it was Menelaos' anger that put her to flight, *because this insight underlies the theory of the alleged autonomy of dream personages*. The Greeks, like everyone else (*101*), had bad dreams, and dreams which ran counter to the dreamer's *conscious* wishes. I will deal with this problem in the last section of this chapter.

424: παραλλάξασα διὰ χερῶν = (slip) aside, out of his arms. As noted, the twice-mentioned deceptiveness (422 f.) of the joy suggests that the dream embrace was *not* consummated.[277] Now, were Helene a dream-sending, her flight might conceivably reflect her own wish to tantalize Menelaos. But this is clearly an endogenous dream, even by strict Greek standards. This means, in plain language, that Helene's image does not flee but is *put to flight* by Menelaos himself: his desire brings her into the dream as his anger expels her from it, *before* the union is consummated. I have already noted that "unvilifying" (ἀλοιδόρους) (v. 412) reflects the ambivalence of Menelaos: love and hate *co-exist* in a waking state. In dream, these contradictory sentiments appear *successively*: love and longing cause Helene to appear in the dream, but a surge of hatred forces her to vanish before the union is consummated—for, as everyday experience shows, attempts to cohabit with a resented person [278] often fail. In this instance we need not content ourselves with guessing: v. 419 (all libido has gone to wrack and ruin) practically says: Menelaos is made impotent by his anger. This also explains Helene's "flight": it enables Menelaos' (temporary) impotence not to become manifest in dream.

It is, moreover, psychologically only to be expected that a "justifiable" dislike (v. 412), which is denied an outlet in waking life, will find an expression in dream, though *without* an awareness that the dream events have *any* nexus with the inhibited resentment. Therefore Menelaos dreams that Helene eludes him, but is unable to grasp that it is *his* hatred that puts her to flight in dream.

The fact that, in dream, Menelaos does not overtly bid Helene to be gone—that she *seems* to escape of her own volition—is not only properly dreamlike, but fits particularly well into a dream about a woman like Helene, who, being frustrating in reality, is *made* to be frustrating also in dream.[279] Better still, by causing Helene to escape him also in dream, Menelaos manages to acquire yet another grievance.[280] Otherwise ex-

[276] As the hunger of Penelope's loins invited Odysseus into her dream—for the hunger of her soul should not be overestimated (*28*).

[277] For a drunk's futile grabbing at a flute girl, cp. Luc. *Tim.* 55.

[278] In E. *Tr.*, Menelaos' hatred precedes the resurgence of his love (supra).

[279] A psycho-analytical anecdote will highlight this. An old maid dreams that a visibly aroused nude man is approaching her bed. She timidly asks him: "What will you do to me?" The man replies: "I don't know, lady—this is *your* dream!"

[280] The Greek tyrant, Dionysios (Plu. V. *Dion.* 9.5), could, like any primitive, blame, in a waking state, those who harmed him in his dream (*82*, p. 129 f.). But even modern "normals" sometimes take a dislike to those who, in their dreams, have harmed or frustrated them. That some patients blame their analysts for what their analysts "did" to them *in their dreams* is well known.

pressed, the dream reconfirms Menelaos' self-definition as a noble and devoted victim.[281]

The point need not be laboured: the amorous but still resentful Menelaos first *brings* Helene into his dream and then *expels* her from it. And, by dreaming that *she* eludes him, he

(a) repeats the real desertion in dream,

(b) makes Helene responsible *also* for his dream frustration,

(c) accumulates new grievances against her, and

(d) manages to conceal from himself *his* rejection of the faithless Helene.

One thing is clear: in the described dream(s), the vision escapes—it does *not* change shape *during* the dream.[282] That change takes place *here* only between successive dreams.

425: βέβακεν ὄψις = gone is the vision. The wording recalls βέβακεν ῥίμφα (v. 407), which describes the eloping Helene's light, carefree step. Both expressions evoke the image of a casual, thoughtless evanescence. Neither the real Helene nor her dream double are burdened by scruples over the grief their vanishing causes. The day residue of this dream detail is the real Helene's elopement.

But this expression may also have another dimension. It may hint at the totally persuasive (A. *Ag.* 274) feeling of the inevitability of even the most outlandish dream sequences. However strange a turn dream-events take, *in dream* they seem inescapable. The sudden statement: "gone is the vision", creates a feeling of finality, which the next words further reinforce.[283]

425: οὐ μεθύστερον is alleged to have two possible meanings. It goes without saying that the choice one makes will radically affect the meaning of v. 426.

(1) *Forthwith* is wholly present-centred. It excludes neither a bleak, dreamless future, nor the recurrence of similar dreams. Its sole merit is that it conjures up well the feeling of inevitability so common in dream. This alternative needs no further scrutiny, for it obliges one to hold that v. 426 describes an absurdity (see end of next section).

(2) *Never again* does open a vista on the future, however bleak it may be. It expresses a typical mourning reaction, closely paralleling the οὐ . . . δεύτερον (never again) (Hom. *Il.* 23.46) of the mourning Achilleus. But it is important that Achilleus only claims that none of his future sorrows will affect him *as deeply* as his grief over Patroklos' death. The "never again" is only qualitative: it concerns the unique intensity of an ex-

---

[281] Let it not be answered that this is not a Greek stance. The maxim that one should do the greatest good to one's friends and the greatest harm to one's foes would not have been invented, had no Greek been sufficiently masochistic to turn the other cheek: Sokrates proclaimed that it is better to suffer than to do injustice. But this "moral victory" further depreciates Helene and sadistically heaps coals of fire on her head. It permits Menelaos to deny his latent anger: in this respect, one deals here with the well-known "inversion of affects" in dream (*66*, pp. 471 ff.).

[282] As noted above, Arist. *insomn.* 458b20 ff. refers to a change of the dream imagery *on* awakening (retroactive falsification? secondary elaboration?).

[283] In Greek thought, there seems to be little difference between "leaving" and "being left by" a dream or by something comparable to a dream. Luc. *Gall.* 6 says that when the eyes are *left with* the sweetness of a dream it is hard to wake up. But Luc. *Cont.* 17 says that man *leaves* life as if it were a dream.

perience. Achilleus' "never again" forces one to ask here the crucial question: just *what* is it that will "never again" happen?

The notion that a man in Menelaos' position would never again have *any* kind of dream about Helene is absurd even in terms of daily experience. It is also contradicted by the text: in v. 420 ὀνειρόφαντοι is in the plural—though only one Helene appears in the dream. A. *PV* 645 provides the clue to this plural: ὄψεις (visions) is in the plural, though there is only one dream-speaker in each of Io's repetitive dreams. In both instances, the plurals indicate the *repeated* appearance of the personage in recurrent dreams (chap. 2).

But if Menelaos has repeated dreams of Helene, the "never again"—like that of Achilleus—can apply only to some degradation of future dream experiences, most probably through a deterioration of Helene's dream image.[284] In short, deceptive as Menelaos' described dream is, his future ones will be worse, of which more anon.

The sense "never again" also has a purely literary advantage. Unlike "forthwith", it explains why v. 426 is the last to deal with the man Menelaos; with v. 427 Aischylos turns to the sorrows of the household and of all Greeks caught in the turmoil of the Trojan war.

426: General Sense. Most scholars deem this verse to be more or less corrupt. Even Fraenkel, who is almost willing to accept it as transmitted, feels that an emendation of the last word would help matters.[285] Others propose more radical measures.

Though there is, I think, no precedent for such an approach, I propose to tackle v. 426 by *pretending momentarily* that it has dropped out of the text altogether, and by trying to conjecture its probable conceptual content *ex nihilo*.[286]

(I) If οὐ μεθύστερον means "forthwith", v. 426 can concern only the dream vision's *manner* of vanishing or else Menelaos' immediate *reaction* to this disappearance. But since—certain editors and LSJ notwithstanding—it does not have that meaning, this alternative need not be considered.

(II) "Never again" permits various conjectures.

(1) Menelaos will never again dream of Helene. This conjecture has already been discarded on both psychological and textual grounds.

(2) Menelaos will repeatedly have the same dream, feeling *each* time that Helene's vision has eluded him for ever. I doubt that Aischylos would have led up to such a meaning by "never again". Two commonplace psychological observations also militate against this view.

(a) Since each successive recurrent dream uses as a day residue the preceding day's (*variable*) experiences, no two of a series of recurrent dreams can be *totally* alike—*a fact even psycho-analysts seldom stress sufficiently*.

(b) While having a recurrent dream, one is usually aware, already in dream, that one has had that dream before and knows its general out-

---

[284] Admetos, whose situation is different, does not expect his purely palliative dreams of Alkestis to deteriorate (E. *Alc.* 348 ff.).

[285] For three other consecutive plural datives, Professor Fraenkel kindly referred me to A. *Sept.* 747 f.

[286] I have tried to infer the general content of the genuinely missing reply to E. *Ba.* 1300 from its *impact* on Agaue (*45*).

come. This makes a total "never again" reaction *in* dream improbable.[287]

(3) Menelaos' future dreams will be even more disappointing or even worse. Atossa's dream is clearly the last and the most traumatic of an increasingly upsetting series of anxiety dreams (chap. 1). This proves that the gradual degradation of recurrent dreams was known to Aischylos. I therefore feel that, both philologically and psychologically, the most plausible hypothesis is that Menelaos' future dreams of Helene will be even more disappointing *because Helene's image will become degraded.*[288]

These considerations are made very plausible indeed (infra) by a famous precedent for such a dream deterioration: by Achilleus' dream of the dead Patroklos. In Hom. *Il.* 23.65 ff., Achilleus sees in dream a perfect double of Patroklos as he once was: lively and handsome. But the moment he attempts to *touch* him, Patroklos' glorious double turns into a smoke-like, feeble, gibbering shade, such as inhabits Hades in the *Odyssey* (bk. 11). How degraded such shades are, is best shown by their similarity to the non-aggressive insane.[289] The blood-sated ghost of Odysseus' mother is at first also lifelike, but the moment her son seeks to *clasp* her, she too deteriorates into a typical, wretched shade (Hom. *Od.* 11.204).

I cannot stop to clarify the psychological reasons for this degradation of Patroklos' double and of Odysseus' temporarily reanimated mother. I simply note that both become degraded when the men indirectly responsible for their death seek to touch them. I cite these incidents only to show that the degradation of dream-doubles and their like goes back at least as far as Homeros. Clinical examples of the deterioration, in dream, of the image of unfaithful loved women also exist.[290]

A New Emendation of v. 426 is advanced conditionally. It *can* be dispensed with *if* one accepts Franz's translation of that verse—though *not* of οὐ μεθύστερον as "nicht zum *zweiten* Mal"—and if:

(a) one emphasizes "beflügelt" and

(b) bears in mind that the German word "Gang" can mean not only

[287] A patient reported a recurrent childhood dream, patterned upon the Tarzan stories. Lions pursued him and great apes rescued him. But the details were different each time and he recalled being curious *in* each dream *how* he would be rescued *this* time. A Greek, who knew the Elektra myth and had seen A. *Choe.*, would have been similarly eager to discover *how* things would be done in S. *El.* or in E. *El.* I often wonder whether the *idea* of the theatre was inspired by dreams, which are, in a way, private dramatic performances.

[288] The causes and dream-consequences of Menelaos' ambivalence are described in connection with v. 424.

[289] Hom. *Od.* 20.345 ff., Hom. *h. Ven.* 233 ff., etc. (supra).

[290] A man, wantonly deserted by his beautiful and beloved girl-friend, had at first dreams greatly resembling that of Menelaos. But, as time went by and the girl even made an attempt to harm him, her appearance in dream began to deteriorate. His most striking dream during this period was the following: he set out to visit the girl who, in his dream, was imprisoned. After many difficulties and a protracted argument with the female prison-director, he was permitted to see her in a huge, empty, domed, cement rotunda, whose windows (in the dome) were obstructed by heavy steel mesh. The girl herself had greatly changed. Emaciated and rouged, she resembled a middle-aged streetwalker and wore only a poison-green, dirty bikini of sleazy, artificial silk. (This image was inspired by a book illustration, which the dream *also* degraded.) In dream the girl's manner was, moreover, so vulgar, provocative and sulky that the dreamer cut the conversation short and left almost at once. I wonder whether Denniston and Page's notion that πενθήμονες refers to a tearfully repentant Helene does not reflect a relatively correct intuitive appraisal of the meaning of v. 426, erroneously imputed to v. 420.

"the going" but also, very strictly: the gait, the characteristic manner of someone's progression.

Disregarding Franz's translation of the last two words of the preceding verse, he wrote: Das (nie wieder) *beflügelt* nachschwebt dem *Gang* des Schlummers. (My italics.): Which never again *winged* floats-after the *going* (= *gait*) of slumber.

So emphasized, the translation can imply that Helene will never reappear *winged, floating* (like Sleep), but may very well reappear *wingless* and therefore unable to "float" after Sleep *and in the manner* of Sleep.

If *this* interpretation of Franz's translation is accepted, no emendation is necessitated by psychiatric considerations reinforced by ordinary experience. But, since Fraenkel rejects it, only the emendation I advance in the following pages fits the experiences of those who were deserted and therefore also the psychiatric considerations derived from a study of such human experiences. This should be borne in mind, in appraising the validity of my conjecture.

As to the authorship of the emendation: I evolved the *notion* that v. 426 should mean "winged follow (adopt) the 'gait' of sleep", but the *drafting* of the actual emendation is due to Professor K. J. Dover. He comments: "no one would worry if the movement of a bird were so described." For the short last syllable he quotes A. *Ag.* vv. 208 and 239.

426: The Retroactive Model: This much-discussed verse has, so far as I know, never been scrutinized in the light of E. *Rh.* 211 ff.

> . . . . τετράπουν μιμήσομαι
> λύκου κέλευθον πολεμίοις δυσεύρετον,
> τάφροις πελάζων κ.τ.λ.

Dolon, proposing to spy on the Greeks, clad in a wolfskin, says: "four-footed I will imitate the wolf's gait, to the enemies undiscernible, the trenches approaching", etc.

I begin with the external similarities between A. *Ag.* 426 and the first four words of the Euripidean text.

(1) Both opening words refer to a manner of progression (winged, four-legged), which approximates a *non*-human way of locomotion: that of a "bird"[291] or a wolf.

(2) The second word has in both cases the function of a verb in the future tense, which relates this unusual "gait" to what comes after.

(3) The third word is, in both instances, in the genitive and stands for a "species" in general: *the* wolf, *the* sleep ("Sleep").

(4) The fourth words actually have the same root: κέλευθ-. In E. *Rh.* 212, it clearly denotes the wolf's species-characteristic *gait*.

(5) I hold v. 426 to refer to a degradation of Helene's dream image, and note that E. *Rh.* 211 f. manifestly refers to the "degradation" of Dolon into a wolf.

(6) In both cases there is deception: incipient dream-joys and plans of spying both fail.

Some indirect similarities may also be listed:

[291] On winged Sleep, cp. Sauer ap. *129*, s.v. Hypnos; on Hypnos as a bird, cp. Hom. *Il.* 14.290.

(1) The disappearance of Helene's dream-double and perhaps even the *non*-reappearance of her *initially lovely* dream-self are partly replicated by the *non*-recognizability, the *non*-discernibility of the disguised Dolon.

(2) The meaning of ὀπαδοῖc (ὀπαδοῦc') = to follow (= to get close), is also present in E. *Rh.* 213: Dolon will approach the Greek trenches.

So many similarities are not likely to be accidental. Moreover, the *radical* Euripidean transformation of the Aischylean image and of its context (dream into spying) is just what one expects to happen when a great poet's verse resonates—perhaps unwittingly—in the back of the mind of one of his peers.[292]

Let us now examine the individual words of v. 426 in the light of the Euripidean "model"—the "copy" serving to clarify the meaning of the corrupt original.

426: πτεροῖc is almost the only word that could refer directly to some future change in Helene's dream shape. It is usually held to be a dative of manner: winged = by means of wings. But J. Franz translates: *beflügelt* = winged, treating it as the equivalent of what, in English, would be a past participle, used as an adjective. (Winged dream: Luc. *Gall.* 6; cp. E. *Phoin.* 1545.)

If so, the future dreams *could be* about an *unwinged* (wingless) Helene. This would satisfy the demand that the verse should hint at a deterioration. It is obviously not possible to survey here all beings or things imagined as winged by the Greeks. I concede that some monsters were winged, as were the doubles of the dead—but add at once that *not all* the bloodless, gibbering shades in Hades seem winged in the Nekyia (Hom. *Od.* 11). I am therefore inclined to imagine Patroklos' *initial* dream-double as winged, but *becoming* wingless as it deteriorates into a smoke-like shade and slips away. But whether I am right or wrong in making this assumption does not greatly affect the present discussion.

Cases in which wings betoken beauty are fairly common. Like Pegasos, the Alkmanian dream-horse, whose beauty surpasses that of all others, is winged (Alcm. *Parth. fr.* 1.49 P). The Erinyes' *lack* of wings seems part of their monstrousness—precisely in Aischylos (*Eum.* 250). The Peleiades, whose weight increases the burden their father Atlas must bear, are wingless (A. *fr.* 312N²), though in ordinary tradition they are winged doves. Last, but not least, "winged" is a common Homeric laudatory epithet for words.[293]

All things considered, the emphasis in this verse seems to be on: (never again) *winged*.[294] This does not exclude the textually and psychologically valid inference that Menelaos will have future dreams of a *wingless* (deteriorated, perhaps shade-like) Helene.[295]

---

[292] On the error of assuming that a great poet like Euripides would *directly* echo concrete events instead of radically transmuting them, cp. (*31*).

[293] It is a curious coincidence that the moment his mother's shade eludes his embrace, Odysseus addresses her in (formulaic) winged (πτερόεντα) words (Hom. *Od.* 11.204). Could some dim memory of this passage have contributed, *through free association*, to the shaping of this Aischylean text? Such things can regularly be observed even in the didactic psycho-analysis of gifted and normal candidates.

[294] The Greek language tends to emphasize the first word.

[295] Brelich (*13*) underscores the affinity between the dead and "the nation of dreams".

One may sum up by saying that one purpose of repetitive dreams is to master a trauma. Unlike what the sleep therapy of pilots of crashed bombing planes sought to achieve (*94*), the best way for Menelaos to master *his* trauma is to degrade Helene in dream, until she becomes undesirable. And that would easily happen if her initially winged, lovely dream-double became, like Patroklos' double, degraded into a (*wingless*) gibbering shade. This would fit Menelaos' latent anger (involving death wishes) quite as much as the word πενθήμονες applied to the dream apparitions (420).

Last but not least, the supernatural, "ethereal" winged beauty of Helene in the *initial* dream (-series?), itself reveals destructive wishes. Not only do some schizophrenics, haunted by hidden aggressivity, give "ethereal" responses to the Thematic Apperception Test (TAT), but a moment's reflection shows that idealization is, in the last resort, a manifestation of hostility: it is a rejection of the real beloved, *as she is.*[296]

426: ὀπαδοῖς, transmitted by the manuscripts, is deemed acceptable by Fraenkel. It yields the sense: "following the ways of sleep".[297] But Dobree's widely accepted emendation ὀπαδοῦς' gives the sense: "following on wings the ways of sleep".[298] One of the difficulties here is the fact that ὀπαδοῖς is related to a large number of words having other forms[299]—a point I cannot discuss here.

Fraenkel objects to ὀπαδοῦς' on the grounds that this verb should govern the person or thing followed and not its path. But Denniston and Page hold that such an extension needs no defence. The problem disappears if κελεύθοις (κέλευθα) means not "path" but "*gait*"—which is a "thing", that can be "followed" *only* by imitating it. The sense "to follow" = "to imitate, to do like", becomes defensible if κελεύθοις (κέλευθα) (emended) means: "gait" or "*manner* of moving". This does not even require a radical extension of the basic meaning of the word transmitted as ὀπαδοῖς.[300] And, on the whole, it is safer to extend slightly the *nuance* of a word than to widen a grammatical *rule*, especially here, where πτεροῖς (if correct) is a dative of manner.

Vernant (*136*, p. 257) stresses that one can always discern Persephone lurking behind Helene; the nexus between the two is also highlighted by the fact that both had been abducted. Helene may even have further connections with the dead: since D. Chrys. *or.* 11.40 says that Helene did not *sail*, Bowra (*12*) concludes that Hermes carried her off *through the airs*. But, unlike other Olympians, the winged Hermes psychagogos (*125*) carried (guided) *only* the dead. If Hermes did carry Helene off, she must be imagined as a ghostly double. I have also considered a (new) alternative: Helene went to Egypt by using the tunnel Proteus had dug from Egypt to Thrace under the sea floor (Lyc. 120). This, too, would make her like unto ghosts, who notoriously dwell underground.

[296] This is strikingly confirmed by the commonplace finding that some men "idealize" and maternalize their "beloved" wives to the point of being impotent *with them*—but not with "degraded" harlots (*70*). This, of course, serves the purpose of frustrating the "idealized" wife.

[297] LSJ s.v. ἀπήεις II.

[298] LSJ ibid. Professor Lloyd-Jones agrees that ὀπαδοῦς' is probably right.

[299] E.g., with ἕπομαι. I note a curious coincidence: In X. *An.* 7.3.43, this verb is linked with hoofprints: τῷ στίβῳ τῶν ἵππων ἕπεσθε = follow the *tracks* of horses.

[300] Cp. LSJ s.v. ἕπω II.4, which cites Pi. *O.* 2.22: (this saying) befits; Pi. *O.* 13.47: suitable; Pl. *Lg.* 632c: agreeing with; Pl. *R.* 406d: the like to these; Pl. *Lg.* 835c: follow the voice of reason.

In short, there is much to commend ὀπαδοῦσ', especially if the whole verse is held to refer to some *manner* of being or of behaving (in accordance with a model) that will not happen again.[301]

But a word may be said about translations which make the dream (-vision) a "companion of sleep". So far, I have found only one literary text affirming the existence of such a companionship. In Luc. *bis accus.* 1, Dream stays awake with Sleep and is Sleep's interpreter. But the notion that "wings" (whose?) are Sleep's "companions" seems difficult to entertain—particularly since Sleep is represented as winged far more often than is Dream.

It is also worth noting that, in literary texts, the wings of Dream and its flying are mentioned far more often in connection with the Dream's sudden *vanishing*[302] than in connection with its *approach*. This does not *prove* that Aischylos did *not* visualize Dream *approaching* on wings, as does Sleep— but it is another little thing to give one pause.

It also seems very hard to reconcile the notion that dream might *follow* Sleep *going away*—yet the (to me unacceptable) conception of "forthwith" (supra) would require one so to visualize things. So far as I am able to determine, up to Aischylos' time sleep and dream either departed simultaneously, or else the dream ended *before* sleep departed. As repeatedly noted, even Aristoteles did not speak of a continuation of the dream after one wakes up: he spoke only of the *transformation* of the dream images into *other* images. In short, I do not see how one can accept "forthwith" (depart) *and* imagine sleep departing (ceasing) *before* the dream departs. I hardly need to add that I make this point not in order to clarify further what v. 426 says, but to muster another argument against the "forthwith" (departs) conception.

426: ὕπνου = of sleep. This word could be capitalized, to denote Sleep personified or the God of sleep. But it is not indispensable to do so, for the context shows that some *general* characteristic of sleep is meant. Now, in descriptions quite as much as in plastic representations, the god Sleep is most often delicately-winged: his flight is a gentle floating (Hes. *Th.* 763, etc.).[303] In short, Sleep has a *characteristic* "gait" both in its approach and in its departure. Also, even though Dream (-personages) and Sleep are not the same, one cannot imagine dream-personages tramping heavy-footed in the wake of dream's light, floating approach or departure.

This, admittedly, does not *compel* us to visualize *all* dream-personages as winged, though winged dream-beings are far from rare.[304]

But I hold that Helene's image in *this* dream *is* winged, for I have noted above that certain monuments show dreamers seduced or raped by *winged* female creatures. But there is an even weightier argument in support of my view, provided by the learned, versifying librarian Lykophron,

[301] As Denniston and Page point out, the "never again" of v. 425 automatically implies the future, so that there is no need for a future participle.

[302] Luc. *Gall.* 6. Compare the slow-footed approach and swift departure of Riches (Luc. *Tim.* 20, 25, 29), which are compared to Dreams. (Luc. *Tim.* 20, 41.)

[303] Cp. also Sauer, ap. *129*, s.v. Hypnos.

[304] Alcm. *Parthen. fr.* 1.49 P: winged dream horse (Bowra; I concur, for "under the *little* stones" makes little sense: it would not even suffice to make Dream a chthonian); Patroklos' double (supra), etc.

who almost certainly had the correct text before him, and—better still—*all* of whose images are *deliberately derivative*, since they are parts of a series of poetic puzzles, meant to challenge sophisticates.

Lykophron split up the imagery of A. *Ag.* 420–426 into three, partly overlapping, images:

(1) Paris' dreamlike, empty-armed embrace of Helene's traditional double (112 ff.). Significantly, v. 112 contains the equivalent of both the Aischylean οὐ μεθύϲτερον and the Homeric οὐ . . . δεύτερον: never again (δευτέραν . . . οὐκ).

(2) Achilleus' distracting and frustrated dream of Helene (171 ff.).

(3) Menelaos' yearning for the *winged* phantom (φάϲμα πτηνὸν) of his elusive Helene (820 ff.).

Precisely because Lykophron is derivative, I conclude that the text he had before him must have suggested that Helene's (*first* dream-) image was winged, and moved in a manner resembling the gait ("*allure*") of sleep.

This brings me to the last word.

426: κελεύθοιϲ (codd.), Fraenkel holds, is the original seat of corruption: he feels that some copyist had read the word ἀκόλουθος, perhaps in a gloss; Thomson (ad loc.) points out that, in codex *Tr.*, ἀκολούθοιϲ is actually written above ὀπαδοῖϲ—and ἀκολουθέω and related words do imply: conforming to. Hence, Fraenkel may well be right in holding that the corruption began with κελεύθοιϲ—but not the way he visualizes it.

Before discussing this matter, I note that I cannot find any trace anywhere of Sleep having a road, a path or even a wake of its own. There are no data that would permit one to ascribe a path to Sleep—or, for that matter, to Dream. The people of dreams do have a country of their own and true dreams do emerge from the Gates of Horn and false ones from the Gates of Ivory. But these data do not authorize one to claim that Dream—let alone Sleep—has a road or path of its own, not even in the elusive tense in which one can speak of the "road" of migrating wild geese.

What Sleep does have is something else, that the word κέλευθος does, in fact, also denote: a mode of walking, a gait, or, more generally in metaphor: a way or course (of doing). It has *that* sense in E. *Rh.* 211 f., *precisely* where an imitation of the wolf's *gait* is described.[305] The last word should therefore be κέλευθα—for the last syllable need not be long,[306] though opinion on this point is far from unanimous.[307]

At any rate, I find the image evoked by the sense "path" or "wake" (Mazon) aesthetically less appealing that the sense "gait", "manner of moving". Above all, the latter gives a sense which is in better conformity with the dream experiences of *real* abandoned husbands or lovers and also with the psycho-analytical theory of frustration dreams caused by desertion.

I therefore hold that κέλευθα refers to Dream's winged "gait", which

---

[305] τετράπουν μιμήϲομαι/λύκου κέλευθον = four-footedly I will imitate the wolf's gait (supra).

[306] Cp. A. *Ag.* 208, 428 (K.J.D.).

[307] I note a curious detail: Fraenkel tentatively thought of emending κελεύθοιϲ into πελῶϲα (exempli gratia). Now, in the relevant E. *Rh.* passage (v. 213) one finds τάφροιϲ πελάϲων = approaching the trenches. Did the sonorities of this Euripidean passage reverberate faintly *and unwittingly* in Fraenkel's mind, or is it a mere coincidence?

Helene's wingless, degraded image will never again be able to assume in Menelaos' future dreams of her.

But I recall, once more, that this tentative emendation is *not indispensable* if, in Franz's translation, one accentuates *beflügelt* and nach*schwebt* and takes *Gang* to refer to sleep's (winged) "gait" (manner of progression) ;[308] in short, if one holds that these words indicate precisely *what* will "never again" happen in Menelaos' dreams of the flighty Helene. For my part, I insist only on *this meaning* of v. 426 and leave it to better grammarians to decide whether the un-emended verse can—as Franz appears to think—have *that* meaning. As for the non-Hellenist reader, he should bear in mind that great Hellenists often disagree about the grammatical acceptability of a difficult passage.

426: Summary. If this verse is to match the perfect clinical appropriateness of the sixteen preceding lines, it must mean: (never again) will Helene, appearing in future dreams, have the lovely, winged "allure" (gait) of sleep. This *sense* is also that of a palaeographically possible emendation: πτέρωτ' ὀπαδοῦσ' ὕπνου κέλευθα, which I like but neither strongly advocate nor really question.[309]

At any rate, the proposed sense has a proper Aischylean "density" and the difficulties one has with ("mental") punctuation in connection with "never again" tend to suggest that Aischylos condensed, as was his wont, a great deal into a very few words.

Conclusions

The source of Greek—and other—theories and beliefs affirming the externality and autonomy of dream personages is the—perhaps unwitting —attempt to explain why, for example in "bad" dreams, the behaviour of dream personages fits neither the dreamer's rational expectations nor his conscious wishes, and also why some dreams are "deceitful".[310] Needless to say, a dream can be considered "deceitful" only if one generally *expects* dreams to be veridical.[311] Some groups which, unlike the Greeks, who see-sawed between a completely ordered and a relatively capricious conception of the universe, believed in a perfectly ordered universe, resolved the problem of such perplexing dreams in two ways:

(1) They postulated that all dreams mean something, but that one is often unable to discern their meaning (*42*), or

(2) They held that *all* dreams mean the opposite of what they *seem* to

---

[308] Fraenkel cites the translation, but does not interpret it.

[309] The main reason for my hesitation is that ὀπαδοῦσ' governs here an "internal accusative", which can cover a multitude of sins, especially when proposed as an emendation. One of my eminent advisers holds the emendation to be grammatically impossible; another holds it to be correct.

[310] Deceitful dreams: Hom. *Il.* 2.1 ff.; Hom. *Od.* 19.560 ff. Prometheus claims to have been the first to distinguish true dreams from false ones. [A. *PV* 484 ff., cp. (*40*).]

[311] This problem is linked with the observation that one tends to negate sense experiences which do not fit one's criteria of what is "possible". This sometimes leads to fausse nonreconnaissance (*36*).

mean.³¹² In certain respects this theory of the meaning of dreams has marked affinities with a radically pessimistic conception of life and fate.³¹³

At any rate, the Greeks were unable to take the decisive step of concluding, like Freud, that dream figures behave in accordance with the dreamer's *unconscious*—i.e., repressed and denied—wishes which, by definition, are flagrantly *incompatible* with his conscious desires. Indeed, were it otherwise, such wishes would not be repressed and would therefore not need to find an outlet and a gratification in dream. For man does not dream what *no* part of his self does not desire, be it but unconsciously, and much against his conscious will.³¹⁴

Greek myths present Menelaos as a conflict-torn, indecisive man. The dream Aischylos attributed to him suits such a man perfectly. It begins with a near-complete fulfillment of his conscious wish to hold Helene in his arms, but ends with the fulfillment of his unconscious, angry wish to cast Helene out of his life.

In saying this, I do not suppose for a moment that Aischylos figured out all this consciously, in pursuit of an artistic objective. Here, as elsewhere, Sophokles' appraisal of Aischylos strikes the right note: Aischylos did the right thing, often without knowing why and how he did it. (Athen. 10.428F.) That is the hallmark of every great poet.

Bibliography

(1) Ahrens, H. L.: Studien zum Agamemnon des Aeschylus. *Philologus, Supplementband* 1:213 ff., 477 ff., 535 ff., 1860.

(2) Angyal, András: *Foundations for a Science of Personality.* New York, 1941.

(3) Baker, S. J.: *The Australian Language*². Melbourne, 1966.

(4) Barrett, W. S.: *Euripides, Hippolytus.* Oxford, 1964.

(5) Behr, C. A.: *Aelius Aristides and the Sacred Tales.* Amsterdam, 1968.

(6) Benedict, Ruth: *Patterns of Culture.* Cambridge, Massachusetts, 1934.

(7) Bexton, W. H., Heron, W. and Scott, T. H.: Effects of Decreased Variation in the Sensory Environment, *Canadian Journal of Psychology* 8:70–76, 1954.

(8) Bezdechi, Stefan: Das psychopathische Substrat der "*Bacchantinnen*" Euripides', *Archiv für die Geschichte der Medizin* 25:279–306, 1932.

---

³¹² Artemidoros gives examples of misinterpreted dreams (e.g., 5.72) as well as of dreams that must be interpreted "in reverse" (1.4, 2.53, etc.). But one has the impression that he considers both types as somewhat exceptional.

³¹³ Sedang Moi: The unborn child is asked by the Supernaturals what it wishes to be: man or woman, rich or poor, etc. He becomes the opposite of what he desires to become (21). Zaghawa: In a folk tale a man wishing to obtain what he really needs, must ask for something inappropriate and useless; he must also believe the opposite of what the Supernaturals tell him (135). I have read the news media in a similar spirit for decades and have seldom gone wrong.

³¹⁴ Though this is the crux of Freud's theory of dreams (66), even Freud had difficulties with certain dreams of this type. This led him to evolve the logically questionable and clinically useless theory of a "primary" death instinct (72).

(9) Blaiklock, E. M.: *The Male Characters of Euripides*. Wellington, N.Z., 1952.

(10) Bourguignon, André: Recherches Récentes sur le Rêve, *Les Temps Modernes* no. 238:1603–1628, 1966.

(11) Bowers, U. G.: *The Hidden Land*. New York, 1953.

(12) Bowra, C. M.: The Two Palinodes of Stesichorus, *Classical Review* 13:245–252, 1963.

(13) Brelich, Angelo: The Place of Dreams in the Religious World Concept of the Greeks (in) von Grunebaum, G. E. and Caillois, Roger: *The Dream in Human Societies*. Berkeley and Los Angeles, 1966.

(14) Cook, A. B.: *Zeus*, 3. Cambridge, 1940.

(15) Davison, J. A.: De *Helena* Stesichori, *Quaderni Urbinati* no. 2:80–90, 1966.

(16) de Hérédia, J.-M.: *Les Trophées*. Paris, 1895.

(17) Deonna, Waldemar: Quelques Croyances Superstitieuses de la Grèce Ancienne, *Revue des Etudes Grecques* 2:169–180, 1929.

(18) de Romilly, Jacqueline: *La Crainte et l'Angoisse dans le Théâtre d'Eschyle*. Paris, 1958.

(19) Deubner, Ludwig: *De Incubatione*. Leipzig, 1900.

(20) Deutsch, Helene: Über versäumte Trauerarbeit, *Almanach der Psychoanalyse*, pp. 194–207, 1938.

(21) Devereux, George: *Sedang Field Notes* (MS.), 1933–1935.

(22) id.: Mohave Coyote Tales, *Journal of American Folklore* 61:233–255, 1948.

(23) id.: Catastrophic Reactions in Normals, *American Imago* 7:343–349, 1950.

(24) id. (and Mars, Louis): Haitian Voodoo and the Ritualization of the Nightmare, *Psychoanalytic Review* 38:334–342, 1951.

(25) id.: Primitive Genital Mutilations in a Neurotic's Dream, *Journal of the American Psychoanalytic Association* 2:483–492, 1954.

(26) id.: A Counteroedipal Episode in Homer's Iliad, *Bulletin of the Philadelphia Association for Psychoanalysis* 4:90–97, 1955.

(27) id.: *Therapeutic Education*. New York, 1956.

(28) id.: Penelope's Character, *Psychoanalytic Quarterly* 26:378–386, 1957.

(29) id.: Obsessive Doubt, *Bulletin of the Philadelphia Association for Psychoanalysis* 10:50–55, 1960.

(30) id.: Art and Mythology: A General Theory (in) Kaplan, Bert (ed.): *Studying Personality Cross-Culturally*. Evanston, Illinois, 1961.

(31) id.: The Enetian Horses of Hippolytos, *Antiquité Classique* 33:375–383, 1964.

(32) id.: The Kolaxaian Horse of Alkman's *Partheneion*, *Classical Quarterly* 15:176–184, 1965.

(33) id.: The Abduction of Hippodameia as "Aition" of a Greek Animal Husbandry Rite, *Studi e Materiali di Storia delle Religioni* 36:3–25, 1965.

(34) id.: Loss of Identity, Impairment of Relationships, Reading Disability, *Psychoanalytic Quarterly* 35:18–39, 1966.

(35) id.: The Exploitation of Ambiguity in Pindaros *O*. 3.27, *Rheinisches Museum für Philologie* 109:289–298, 1966.

(36) id.: Fausse Non-Reconnaissance, *Bulletin of the Menninger Clinic* 31:69–78, 1967.

(37) id.: La Renonciation à l'Identité: Défense contre l'Anéantissement, *Revue Française de Psychanalyse* 31:101–142, 1967.

(38) id.: Greek Pseudo-Homosexuality, *Symbolae Osloenses* 42:69–92, 1967.

(39) id.: *From Anxiety to Method in the Behavioral Sciences.* Paris and The Hague, 1967.

(40) id.: Observation and Belief in Aischylos' Accounts of Dreams, *Psychotherapy and Psychosomatics* 15:114–134, 1967.

(41) id.: Orthopraxis, *Psychiatric Quarterly* 42:726–737, 1968.

(42) id.: *Mohave Ethnopsychiatry and Suicide.* (Second, substantially augmented edition.) Washington, 1969.

(43) id.: The Nature of Sappho's Seizure in *Fr.* 31 LP, *Classical Quarterly* 20:17–31, 1970.

(44) id.: La Naissance d'Aphrodite (in) Pouillon, Jean and Maranda, Pierre (eds.): *Echanges et Communications (Mélanges Lévi-Strauss),* 2.1229–1252. Paris and The Hague, 1970.

(45) id.: The Psychotherapy Scene in Euripides' *Bacchae, Journal of Hellenic Studies* 90:35–48, 1970.

(46) id.: The Structure of Tragedy and the Structure of the Psyche in Aristotle's *Poetics* (in) Hanly, Charles and Lazerowitz, Morris (eds.): *Psychoanalysis and Philosophy.* New York, 1970.

(47) id.: *Psychoanalysis and the Occult* (ed. and contrib.) Reprint (hard cover and paperback). New York, 1970.

(48) id.: *Essais d'Ethnopsychiatrie Générale.* Paris, 1970. (Second edition, 1973.)

(49) id.: *Wahnsinnige Götter* (Lecture, University of Basel), 1970.

(50) id.: The Psychosomatic Miracle of Iolaos, *La Parola del Passato* no. 138:167–195, 1971.

(51) id.: Drogues, Dieux, Idéologies, *Medica* no. 103:13–20, 1972.

(52) id.: *Ethnopsychanalyse Complémentariste.* Paris, 1972.

(53) id.: (and Devereux, J. W.): Les Manifestations de l'Inconscient dans Sophokles: *Trachiniai* 923 sqq. (in) *Psychanalyse et Sociologie comme Méthodes d'Etude des Phénomènes Historiques et Culturels.* Bruxelles, 1973.

(54) id.: Stesichoros' Palinodes: Two Further Testimonia and Some Comments, *Rheinisches Museum für Philologie* 116: 206–209, 1973.

(55) Dodds, E. R.: *The Greeks and the Irrational.* Berkeley, California, 1951.

(56) Dollard, John *et al.*: *Frustration and Aggression.* New Haven, 1939.

(57) Edelstein, E. J. and Edelstein, Ludwig: *Asclepius* 2 vols. Baltimore, 1945.

(58) Elkin, A. P.: *The Australian Aborigines.* Sydney, 1964.

(59) Empson, William: *Seven Types of Ambiguity*[3]. New York, 1964.

(60) Evans-Pritchard, E. E.: *Witchcraft, Oracles and Magic Among the Azande.* Oxford, 1937.

(61) Fenichel, Otto: A Critique of the Death Instinct (in) *The Collected Papers of O. Fenichel* 1. New York, 1953.

(62) id.: The Symbolic Equation: Girl = Phallus, *The Collected Papers of O. Fenichel* 2. New York, 1954.

(63) Flashar, Hellmut: *Melancholie und Melancholiker in den medizinischen Theorien der Antike*. Berlin, 1966.

(64) Fraenkel, Eduard: *Aeschylus, Agamemnon*[2]. Oxford, 1962.

(65) French, Th. M.: Reality Testing in Dreams, *Psychoanalytic Quarterly* 6:62–77, 1937.

(66) Freud, Sigmund: The Interpretation of Dreams, *Standard Edition* 4–5. London, 1958.

(67) id.: The Psychopathology of Everyday Life, *Standard Edition* 6. London, 1960.

(68) id.: Three Essays on the Theory of Sexuality, *Standard Edition* 7. London, 1953.

(69) id.: Leonardo da Vinci and a Memory of his Childhood, *Standard Edition* 11. London, 1957.

(70) id.: On the Universal Tendency to Debasement in the Sphere of Love, *Standard Edition* 11. London, 1957.

(71) id.: Mourning and Melancholia, *Standard Edition* 14. London, 1957.

(72) id.: Beyond the Pleasure Principle, *Standard Edition* 18. London, 1955.

(73) id.: The Subtleties of a Faulty Action, *Standard Edition* 22. London, 1964.

(74) id.: Analysis Terminable and Interminable, *Standard Edition*, 23. London, 1964.

(75) Gallini, Clara: Katapontismos, *Studi e Materiali di Storia delle Religioni* 34:61–90, 1963.

(76) Gayton, A. H.: The Orpheus Myth in North America, *Journal of American Folklore* 48:263–293, 1935.

(77) Glasse, Robert: Cannibalisme et *Kuru* chez les Fore de Nouvelle Guinée, *L'Homme* vol. 8, no. 3, 22–36, 1968.

(78) Glueck, Nelson: *Deities and Dolphins*. New York, 1965.

(79) Goldstein, Kurt: *The Organism*. New York, 1939.

(80) Gorer, Geoffrey: *Death, Grief and Mourning*. New York, 1965.

(81) Graves, Robert: *The Golden Fleece*. London, 1951.

(82) Grubb, W. B.: *An Unknown People in an Unknown Land*. London, 1911.

(83) Heron, W., Bexton, W. H. and Hebb, D. O.: Cognitive Effects of Decreased Variation in the Sensory Environment, *American Psychologist* 8:366, 1953.

(84) Herzog, R.: Die Wunderheilungen von Epidauros. *Philologus*, *Supplementband* 22, no. 3. Leipzig, 1931.

(85) Housman, A. E.: The *Agamemnon* of Aeschylus, *Journal of Philology* 16:244–291, 1888 (p. 269).

(86) Italie, Gabriel: *Index Aeschyleus*[2]. Leiden, 1964.

(87) Jakobson, Roman and Lévi-Strauss, Claude: "Les Chats" de Charles Baudelaire, *L'Homme* 2, no. 1:5–21, 1962.

(88) Jones, Ernest: *On the Nightmare*. London, 1931.

(89) Kennard, E. A.: Hopi Reactions to Death, *American Anthropologist* 39:491–496, 1937.

(90) Killeen, J. F.: Aeschylus, *Agamemnon* 412 f., *Classical Philology* 55:253–254, 1960.

(91) Kitto, H. D. F.: *Greek Tragedy*. Garden City, New York, 1954.

(92) Kouretas, Demetrios: L'Homosexualité du Père d'Œdipe et Ses Conséquences, *Annales Médicales* (Athènes) nos. 5–6, 1963.

(93) Kroeber, A. L.: Handbook of the Indians of California (*Bureau of American Ethnology*, Bulletin 78). Washington D.C., 1925.

(94) Kubie, L. S.: Manual of Emergency Treatment for Acute War Neuroses, *War Medicine* 4:582–598, 1943.

(95) Laforgue, René: On the Erotization of Anxiety, *International Journal of Psycho-Analysis* 11:312–321, 1930.

(96) Lagache, Daniel: Le Travail du Deuil: Ethnologie et Psychanalyse, *Revue Française de Psychanalyse* 10:693–708, 1938.

(97) Lehrs, K.: *Populäre Aufsätze*. Leipzig, 1896.

(98) Lévi-Strauss, Claude: *Mythologiques I: Le Cru et le Cuit*. Paris, 1964.

(99) Lilly, J. C.: Effects of Physical Restraint and of Reduction of Ordinary Levels of Physical Stimuli on Intact, Healthy Persons, *Group for the Advancement of Psychiatry, Symposium* 2:13–20, 1956.

(100) id.: Mental Effects of Reduction of Physical Stimulation on Intact, Healthy Persons, *American Psychiatric Association Research Report* 5:1–28, 1956.

(101) Lincoln, J. S.: *The Dream in Primitive Culture*[2] (with a new preface by George Devereux). New York, 1970.

(102) Linton, Ralph: *The Study of Man*. New York, 1936.

(103) Lloyd-Jones, Hugh (translator): *Aeschylus, Agamemnon*. Englewood Cliffs, New Jersey, 1970.

(104) id.: *The Justice of Zeus*. Berkeley, California, 1971.

(105) Lord, A. B.: Homer and other Epic Poetry (in) Wace, A. J. B. and Stubbings, F. H.: *A Companion to Homer*. London, 1962.

(106) Lowie, R. H.: A Crow Woman's Tale (in) Parsons, E. C. (ed.) *American Indian Life*. New York, 1925.

(107) Lucas, F. L.: *Tragedy*[2]. New York, 1962.

(108) Malten, Ludolfus: *Die Sprache des menschlichen Antlitzes im frühen Griechentum*. Berlin, 1961.

(109) Marcadé, Jean: *Eros Kalos*. Genève, 1965.

(110) Marcovich, M.: Sappho *Fr.* 31: Anxiety Attack or Love Declaration? *Classical Quarterly* 22:19–32, 1972.

(111) McNichols, C. L.: *Crazy Weather*. New York, N.Y., 1944.

(112) Meyerson, Emile: *Du Cheminement de la Pensée*. Paris, 1931.

(113) Murray, Gilbert: *Euripides and His Age*[2]. London, 1955.

(114) id.: *Aeschylus, The Creator of Tragedy*. Oxford, 1962.

(115) Nilsson, M. P.: Götter und Psychologie bei Homer, *Archiv für Religionswissenschaft* 22:363–390, 1923–1924.

(116) Oppenheim, A. L.: The Interpretation of Dreams in the Ancient Near East, *Transactions of the American Philolosophical Society* n.s. 46 (pt. 3): 177–373, 1956.

(117) Owen, A. S. (ed.): *Euripides, Ion*. Oxford, 1939.

(118) Page [Sir] Denys: *Sappho and Alcaeus*[2]. Oxford, 1959.

(119) id. (ed.): *Euripides, Medea*[2]. Oxford, 1964.

(120) Picard, Charles: Le Cénotaphe de Midéa et les Colosses de Ménélas, *Revue de Philologie* 59: 341–354, 1933.

(121) id.: *Les Religions préhelléniques.* Paris, 1948.

(122) Pisani, Vittore: Elena e l'εἴδωλον, *Rivista di Filologia e di Istruzione Classica* 6:476–499, 1928.

(123) Powell, Benjamin: Erichthonius and the Three Daughters of Cecrops, *Cornell Studies in Classical Philology* 17. New York, 1906.

(124) Premerstein, A. von: Über den Mythos in Euripides' Helene, *Philologus* 55:634–653, 1896.

(125) Raingeard, P.: *Hermès Psychagogue.* Paris, 1935.

(126) Rank, Otto: Der Doppelgänger (in) *Psychoanalytische Beiträge zur Mythenforschung.* Leipzig and Wien, 1919.

(127) Rivers, W. H. R.: *Conflict and Dream*[2]. London, 1926.

(128) Rohde, Erwin: *Psyche.* London, 1925.

(129) Roscher, W. H. (ed.): *Ausführliches Lexikon der griechischen und römischen Mythologie* 6 vols. Leipzig, 1884–1937.

(130) id.: Das von der "Kynanthropie" Handelnde Fragment des Marcellus von Side. *Abhandlungen der philologisch-historischen Classe der Königlich Sächsischen Gesellschaft der Wissenschaften* vol. 17, no. 3. Leipzig, 1896.

(131) Sachs, Hanns: *The Creative Unconscious.* Cambridge, Massachusetts, 1942.

(132) Schuhl, P.-M.: *Essai sur la Formation de la Pensée Grecque.* Paris, 1934.

(133) Toffelmier, Gertrude and Luomala, Katherine: Dreams and Dream Interpretations of the Diegueño Indians of Southern California, *Psychoanalytic Quarterly* 2:195–225, 1936.

(134) Tylor, E. B.: *Primitive Culture* 2 vols. London, 1871.

(135) Verheyt, Paul: *Pour une Approche Synthétique—Psychanalytique et Fonctionnelle—des Contes* (M.A. Thesis, MS.) Paris, 1971.

(136) Vernant, J.-P.: *Mythe et Pensée chez Les Grecs*[2]. Paris, 1966.

(137) Wackernagel, Jacob: *Vorlesungen über Syntax.* Basel, 1920 and 1924.

(138) Webster, T. B. L.: *Greek Art and Literature, 700–530 B.C.* Otago, N.Z., 1959.

(139) Weinreich, Otto: *Antike Heilungswunder* (Religionsgeschichtliche Versuche und Vorabeiten 8, no. 1), 1909.

(140) id. Ein Spurzauber, *Archiv für Religionswissenschaft* 28: 183–184, 1930.

(141) Winnington-Ingram, R. P.: Hippolytus: A Study in Causation (in) *Euripide*, Entretiens Hardt vol. 6. Genève, 1960.

(142) Wolfson, Louis: *Le Schizo et les Langues.* Paris, 1970.

(143) Zielinski, Th.: De Helenae Simulacro, *Eos* 30:54–81, 1927.

Chapter 4

The Dream of the Erinyes

(Aischylos: *Eumenides*)

Text

ΚΛΥΤΑΙΜΗΣΤΡΑΣ ΕΙΔΩΛΟΝ (Vr. 94–116)
(Klytaimestra's ghost appears on-stage and reproaches the sleeping Erinyes.)
ὁρᾶτε πληγὰς τάσδε καρδίας ὅθεν. (Hermann)   103
[She continues to reproach them.]
ὄναρ γὰρ ὑμᾶς νῦν Κλυταιμήστρα καλῶ.   116
ΧΟΡΟΣ
(μυγμός.)
ΚΛΥΤΑΙΜΗΣΤΡΑΣ ΕΙΔΩΛΟΝ
μύζοιτ' ἄν, ἀνὴρ δ' οἴχεται φεύγων πρόσω·
φίλοι γάρ εἰσιν οὐκ ἐμοῖς προσεικότες.
ΧΟΡΟΣ
(μιγμός.)   120
ΚΛΥΤΑΙΜΗΣΤΡΑΣ ΕΙΔΩΛΟΝ
ἄγαν ὑπνώσσεις κοὐ κατοικτίζεις πάθος·
φονεὺς δ' Ὀρέστης τῆσδε μητρὸς οἴχεται.
ΧΟΡΟΣ
(ὠγμός.)
ΚΛΥΤΑΙΜΗΣΤΡΑΣ ΕΙΔΩΛΟΝ
ᾤζεις, ὑπνώσσεις· οὐκ ἀναστήσῃ τάχος;
τί σοι πέπρωται πρᾶγμα πλὴν τεύχειν κακά;   125
ΧΟΡΟΣ
(ὠγμός.)
ΚΛΥΤΑΙΜΗΣΤΡΑΣ ΕΙΔΩΛΟΝ
ὕπνος πόνος τε κύριοι συνωμόται
δεινῆς δρακαίνης ἐξεκήραναν μένος.
ΧΟΡΟΣ
(μυγμὸς διπλοῦς ὀξύς.)
λαβὲ λαβὲ λαβὲ λαβέ, φράζου.   130
ΚΛΥΤΑΙΜΗΣΤΡΑΣ ΕΙΔΩΛΟΝ
ὄναρ διώκεις θῆρα, κλαγγαίνεις δ' ἅπερ
κύων μέριμναν οὔποτ' ἐκλείπων πόνου.
τί δρᾷς; ἀνίστω, μή σε νικάτω πόνος,
μηδ' ἀγνοήσῃς πῆμα μαλθαχθεῖσ' ὕπνῳ.
ἄλγησον ἧπαρ ἐνδίκοις ὀνείδεσιν.   135
(Vv. 136–139: further reproach and incitement to the pursuit. Klytaimestra's ghost vanishes.)
ΧΟΡΟΣ
(Vv. 140–154: the Erinyes wake up and encourage each other to wake up. They feel hurt because Orestes escaped them while they slept. They blame Apollon, who protects Orestes.)
ἐμοὶ δ' ὄνειδος ἐξ ὀνειράτων μολὸν   155
ἔτυψεν δίκαν διφρηλάτου
μεσολαβεῖ κέντρῳ
ὑπὸ φρένας, ὑπὸ λοβόν.—
πάρεστι μαστίκτορος δαΐου δαμίου   160
βαρὺ τὸ περίβαρυ κρύος ἔχειν.   (Smyth's text)

Klytaimestra's Ghost: Mark ye these gashes in my heart, whence they come. (Verse 103) (Vv. 104–115: she further reproaches the Erinyes.)

Klytaimestra's Ghost: 'Tis in a dream I, Klytaimestra, now invoke you. (V. 116.)

Choros: (begins to move uneasily, uttering whining sounds).

Klytaimestra's Ghost: Whine if ye will! But the man is gone, fled far away. For he hath friends not like to mine!

Choros: (continues to whine).

Klytaimestra's Ghost: Too heavy art though with sleep and hast no pity for my misery. Orestes, the murderer of his mother here, is gone!

Choros (begins to moan).

Klytaimestra's Ghost: Thou moanest, slumberest. Wilt thou not arise at once? What task hath been allotted to thee save to work ill?

Choros (continues to moan).

Klytaimestra's Ghost: Slumber and travail, fit conspirators, have destroyed the might of the dreaded dragoness (she-serpent).

Choros: (with whining redoubled and intensified): Seize him! seize him! seize him! seize him! Mark him!

Klytaimestra's Ghost: 'Tis but in a dream thou art hunting thy game and art whimpering like a hound that never leaves off its keenness for the chase. What *work* hast thou afoot? Arise! Let not fatigue overmaster thee, nor let slumber so soften thee as to forget my wrong. Sting thy heart (liver) with merited reproaches; (Vv. 136–139: Klytaimestra's ghost further reproaches and incites to the hunt the sleeping Erinyes.)

Choros (Vv. 140–154). (The Erinyes wake up and encourage each other to wake up. They feel hurt because Orestes escaped while they slept. They blame Apollon, who protects Orestes): Reproach, coming to me in a dream, smote me like a charioteer with goad grasped tight, under my heart, under my vitals (lobe of the liver). 'Tis mine to feel the cruel, the exceedingly cruel smart of the doomster's direful scourge.

(Smyth's translation)

(Words between parentheses are more accurate alternatives to Smyth's somewhat overly lofty expressions.)

Introduction

The magnificent boldness of the Erinyes' dream as theatre tends to divert one's attention from its eschatological complexity and psychological plausibility. Yet, it is the combination of these two factors which turns what could have been mere melodrama into a scene of matchless dramatic tension.

The stroke of genius which put both the dreamers and their joint dream-vision on stage, made the appearance of Klytaimestra's double (εἴδωλον) both a dream and a haunting. By contrast, the dramatically also effective appearance of Dareios' ghost (A. *Pers.* 681 ff.) does not produce deep emotional reverberations, for a mere spectacle, however brilliant and moving, cannot match the penetrating and compelling psychological realism of the Erinyes' dream.

I cannot demonstrate the psychological authenticity of this dream unless I deal first with the purely objective aspects of the scene and then reconsider its eschatological implications, i.e., the far-reaching and striking reciprocities between the Erinyes, Klytaimestra and even Orestes himself. For an eschatologically satisfactory understanding of this scene presupposes its psychological scrutiny, and its psychological comprehension an eschatological analysis.

I. *Objective Features*

The Erinyes' Sleep, induced by Apollon, gives Orestes time to prepare his final exoneration. The theme of one god putting another to sleep, so as to gain time for his protégés, is ancient.[1]

The Erinyes themselves compare their having been put to sleep to the manner in which Apollon intoxicated the Moirai, so as to wrest from them special privileges for Admetos (723 ff., 727 ff.). This, too, is an ancient motif: Dionysos plies the angry Hephaistos with drink, so as to persuade him to return to Olympos.[2]

The Erinyes, asleep on thrones inside Apollon's sanctuary (46 ff.) snort, and rheum oozes from their eyes (53 ff.).[3] When they become visible to the spectators, they whine and moan in sleep.[4] Klytaimestra's comparing them to hounds dreaming of a hunt (131 ff.) strongly suggests that their limbs twitch (infra). It is this comparison which will permit an analysis of their (visible) dream.

FORMAL ASPECTS OF THE DREAM

(1) The visible dream closely parallels Homeric precedents: A dream

---

[1] Hera persuades Hypnos to put Zeus to sleep (Hom. *Il.* 14.231 ff.).

[2] Paus. 1.20.3, etc. Cp. the François Vase.

[3] In A. *Choe.* 1058, their eyes secrete blood. I note, as an aside, that, judging by Aristophanic comedy, inflammations of the eyelids must have been common in Athens. An ophthalmologist told Professor Dover that in severe, chronic conjunctivitis the eyelids can bleed.   [4] μυγμός, ὦγμός, vv. 120–129.

figure appears to the sleeper, stands near him and says: "You are sleeping."[5] The main difference is that, in A. *Eum.* 94, this statement is reproachful and ironic: εὕδοιτ' ἄν.

(2) The fact that *all* the Erinyes have the *same* dream is, by contrast, unique,[6] though psychologically plausible: The Erinyes lack individuality —and not only in this drama. Their "I" is more than a choral convention. In myth, they usually come into being and function as a group. In practice, when viewed collectively, they have no more separate and distinct individualities than have the multiple heads of Kerberos or the three bodies of Geryones, though a single Erinys can exist (Hom. *Il.* 9.571, etc.).

II. *The Nature of the Erinyes*

The Appearance of Aischylos' Erinyes is described at some length. According to tradition, their frightful appearance caused pregnant women in the audience to miscarry (*Vita* p. 4, Dind.). But their *actual* appearance—the costume they wore on-stage—is far less relevant for the understanding of their role and dream than the fact that, in accordance with Greek traditions, Aischylos held them to be both hounds and serpents.

(1) The Erinyes were often called "hounds"—but on the basis of their behaviour rather than because of their actual shape.[7] They track the criminal by the scent of blood which clings to him,[8] and this ghastly odour fills them with joy (253). One may conclude from their whines while dreaming of a hunt that, like hounds, they whine eagerly when they follow a blood spoor.[9] They suck the blood from the (bleeding?) limbs of their living victim[10] and drain him of the last drop.

The criminal is visualized as a hunted beast: Orestes is a fawn or a hare,[11] whose coursing is anticipated by a reference to Pentheus' fate, which was that of a hunted hare (26 f.). This, too, shows that the Erinyes were hounds only functionally, for the human Mainades, who track and rend Pentheus, are also "hounds" (E. *Ba.* 731, 977)—but in this sense only.

At the same time, the Erinyes are functionally not only hounds but also hunters and, specifically, "masters of hounds".[12]

[5] On this detail, cp. Dodds, *17*, chap. 4.

[6] Verrall's claim (*38*, pp. 168 ff.), that, in E. *HF* 815 ff., the Choros has a collective dream, is not generally accepted.

[7] A. *Choe.* 924 f., 1054; *Eum.* 131 ff., 246 f.; S. *El.* 1388; E. *El.* 1342, Ar. *Ran.* 472, etc. (Elektra as a bitch: A. *Choe.* 447.)

[8] A. *Eum.* 230; E. *El.* 1342; Ar. *Ran.* 472.

[9] Confirmed by A. *Eum.* 424, where they screech while hunting. Dreaming dogs: Lucr. 4.991–998.

[10] A. *Eum.* 183, 264; *Ag.* 1189.

[11] A. *Eum.* 111, 147 f., 246, 326; E. *El.* 836.

[12] A. *Eum.* 231, cp. Nonn. *Dion.* 32.100; in art, they are represented as huntresses, cp. Rapp. s.v. *34* col. 1335. In E. *Ba.* the master of the Mainadic hounds is Agaue, representing Dionysos (731, 872), or else Lyssa (977). But there is also a curious reciprocity between these hound-like Mainades and their prey. In E. *Ba.* 731, they themselves are tracked; at 872 they "are" a doe hunted by Pentheus' "hounds". This detail is relevant for my subsequent discussion of the nexus between the Erinyes and Orestes.

What matters most for the understanding of this dream is the comparing of the sleeping Erinyes to hounds who dream of hunting. The ancient and widespread belief that sleeping hounds who whine and twitch dream of hunting, has now received powerful experimental support: brain-wave patterns which indicate dreaming (and which are not unlike waking patterns) occur far more often in sleeping predators (dogs, cats, humans) than in herbivorous creatures (*2, 24*).

Though Aischylos certainly did not originate this interpretation of the behaviour of sleeping dogs, he did use it with consummate dramatic skill and psychological persuasiveness.

(2) The serpentine nature of the Erinyes is, of course, also mentioned (126 f.), for the notion that they are serpents (A. *Choe.* 1050), or own and handle snakes, or sprout snakes is traditional and is reflected also in art.[13] But it is of interest that A. *Eum.* mentions their venom often and their serpentine nature only once (126 f.). These repeated allusions to their venom may be meant to remind one of the serpentine Orestes' poisonous bite in Klytaimestra's dream (chap. 6).

Even more interesting is that Apollon threatens the Erinyes with his own "winged serpents" (= poisonous arrows) (181). It is, thus, a case of serpent threatening serpent and therefore parallels Klytaimestra's dream. For she, who is repeatedly called a serpent in A. *Choe.* (994, 1047) and a (two-headed) amphisbaina in A. *Ag.* 1233, dreams of being bitten in the breast by a serpentine Orestes (A. *Choe.* 527 ff., 928), though in reality her neck or throat will be cut (see Appendix i).

The serpentine character of the Erinyes, of Klytaimestra (who avenges Iphigeneia's death) and of Orestes (who avenges Agamemnon) cannot but underscore that the Erinyes are not only spirits, but also quasi-human beings who kill the kin-slayer. A curious passage (A. *Choe.* 119) perhaps suggests this: Agamemnon's avenger might be either a Daimon or a man.

III. *Erinyes = Klytaimestra*

It is often said that, in calling the Erinyes daughters of the Night, Aischylos (322, 416, 745, 792) implicitly repudiated the earlier tradition (Hes. *Th.* 185) that they were born from the castrated Ouranos' blood, which fell on the earth. But, in my estimate, this is an altogether secondary point. Aischylos may have simply tried to *resolve*, by these means, a more fundamental difficulty: the problem of the existence of the Erinyes *in time*.

The Hesiodic tradition involves a paradox. Since they were born *out of* a quasi-parricide—out of Ouranos' blood—one would expect the Erinyes to harass *Kronos*. Yet, even though, in some traditions,[14] Kronos is subsequently castrated by his own son, Zeus, so that one can speak of an "appropriate retribution", one *expected* element is strikingly missing:

---

13 Rapp., s.v. *34* coll. 1314 ff.
14 Tim. *fr.* 54, *FHG* 1.203; Lyc. 761, 869; sch. Lyc. 869 and Tzetz. ad loc.; Porph. *antr.* 16; Io. Lyd. *de mens.* 4.44, p. 78.13 Bekk., etc.

I know of no text which claims that the *Erinyes* harassed the parricidal Kronos.

This suggests that Kronos' crime simply brought into being a *class* or *type* of avenging deities which, *in practice*, do not trouble the original parricide Kronos, but only *mortals* who commit an equivalent—i.e., *divine*—type of crime. I cannot discuss here at length something self-evident but often overlooked: the commission of "divine" crimes is a fundamental characteristic of gods, of divine kings, and even of mortals who temporarily acquire the supernatural powers that enable them to perform actions forbidden to men. Some such persons actually *become* superhuman (or acquire *temporarily* the power to achieve the near-impossible) precisely *by means of* a (ritual) crime (chap. 2). The greatest Greeks of the classical period apparently failed to grasp this characteristically archaic notion and tried to cope with the "misdeeds" of deities by bowdlerizing them, thereby preparing the ground for the decay of religion.[15]

But the major difficulty lies elsewhere. Regardless of whether the Erinyes were born of Ouranos' blood, or were daughters of the Night, Aischylos and others *also* hint that, like *Gelegenheitsgötter*, they come into being *each time* a person unpardonably insults a member of his family or sheds his blood. I note in particular that in such instances the name: Erinys is at times *in the singular*,[16] and this despite the fact that Hesiodos, Aischylos and many others speak of the Erinyes in the plural: there are usually *three* Erinyes, lacking individuality and working as a team.

This finding justifies the view[17] that the Eriny(e)s was (were) originally simply the vengeful ghost(s), or was (were) at least *born from* the shed blood of a relative whose death could not be avenged because the killer was precisely the one who should have avenged his death.[18] Only later on were these vengeful ghosts re-defined as infernal spirits, having a kind of "continuous" existence in time, but totally inactive until re-animated and mobilized by a kin-murder and *attributed* to the victim. This, rather than the two alternative genealogies of the "original" Erinyes, is the *real* problem.

It would seem that the Greeks held simultaneously *two divergent beliefs* concerning the manner in which the Eriny(e)s "originate(s)". Such double beliefs are quite common.[19]

---

[15] I hope to discuss this copious material elsewhere. Here I note only that the Aischylean Erinyes themselves speak scathingly of Zeus' dealings with the vanquished Kronos (A. *Eum.* 641 ff.), pointing out that this precedent does not justify Orestes' deed.

[16] A. *Sept.* 791 (Oidipous' Erinys); A. *Choe.* 651, etc. Plurals in Hom. *Il.* 21.412, *Od.* 2.135, 11.280; Hes. *Th.* 472.

[17] Propounded by Rohde (*33*, pp. 178 ff., 451 f.); cp. Nilsson (*31* 1.100). Contra (*17*, p. 21, note 37).

[18] I have taught for three decades that criminal law came into being *not* in order to suppress the practice of the vendetta, but in order to permit society to cope with kin-murder, in which the vendetta is impossible. Even nineteenth-century Albania lacked a mechanism for dealing with kin-murder and there is a record of the first attempt of the Cheyenne Indians to deal socially with abortion (= kin-murder) (*23*, p. 436; retold more briefly in *26*, p. 119).

[19] Cp. the two Mohave Indian theories concerning the origin of twins (*4*) and Linton's (*25*, p. 362) discussion of the mutually incompatible beliefs held by modern man about ghosts. These findings imply that the discrepancy between the eschatology of the Homeric

But, as in the case of the two sets of Mohave beliefs concerning twins, it is possible to discern a nexus between the two Greek theories of the origin of the Erinyes.[20]

The basic consideration is that, whether or not they "exist continuously" in time, the Erinyes *become "operational" only* if kindred blood is shed, and *cease to be "operational"* the moment the slayer is punished.[21]

I think it would be anachronistic to consider that the "continuously existing" Erinys are comparable to Platonic "ideal forms", *on which* the "operational" Erinyes, who come into being after a kin-murder, are modelled, and *from which* they are "derived." The real relationship between the inoperative and the "operational" Erinyes can be derived from much more concrete eschatological data.

The Homeric *Nekyia* makes it clear that the shadowy and senseless ghosts of mortals simply "hibernate" in Hades; only when given blood to drink (Hom. *Od.* 11.36 ff.) do they become reanimated and "operational".[22]

Exactly the same thing appears to be true of the Erinyes. In a vague and shadowy way, they "exist in time" even when there is no kin-murder to be avenged.[23] But, just as ghosts in Hades are re-animated by blood, so the Erinyes are re-animated by the thrilling smell of blood (supra) and are supremely active precisely *while* drinking blood. But, once the kin-slayer is sucked dry, the Erinyes—like Homeric ghosts—seem to relapse into a shadowy pseudo-existence.

There are direct references to this alternation of the Erinyes between an active and a passive state. Disregarding for the moment their sleep and awakening (A. *Eum.* 46 ff.), vv. 313 ff. make it clear that they become active only when angered by a kin-murder. When a man does not arouse their wrath they pay no attention to him and remain dormant.[24] There is even a hint that the blood of the victim itself can become dormant or be de-activated by purifications (280 ff.).[25]

Nekyia (Hom. *Od.* 11) and that of the rest of the Homeric epics does not *suffice* as proof of the extraneous, intrusive character of the *Nekyia*. That proof must be adduced by *different* means.

[20] I disregard here the problem of whether my interpretation is simply a "rediscovery" of an actual, unifying Greek belief, in the sense in which Lévi-Strauss holds that the thought patterns *he* detects in myths are *actually* present (in a latent form) in the minds of primitives, or whether I have simply "constructed" a unified conception of the origin of the Erinyes, which the Greeks *could have* evolved, had they cared to do so. It suffices to note that the psychoanalyst's "constructions" (*20*) are, as a rule, sooner or later confirmed by the recovery of repressed memories and/or by the emergence of previously unconscious fantasies.

[21] A. *Eum.* 603: Klytaimestra's slaying atones for the slaying of Agamemnon. This means that Agamemnon's Eriny(e)s cease(s) to "exist" in an operational sense. One also notes that Orestes repeatedly takes it for granted that the slaying of his mother will automatically lead to his own death (A. *Choe.* 438, etc.).

[22] The re-animation of beings normally residing in Hades is a commonplace. Persephone spends part of the year away from Hades. The Dioskouroi alternate between Hades and Olympos (Hom. *Od.* 11. 301 ff.). Only Herakles' shade dwells in Hades; the "real" Herakles feasts with the gods (Hom. *Od.* 11. 601 ff.).

[23] Though "non semper arcum tendit Apollo", *that* god exists even while not engaged in any particular pursuit. The case of the Erinyes is totally different.

[24] This has a bearing also on their role in connection with sterility and fertility (infra).

[25] But the Erinyes' non-active state is far more pervasive than is that of the sleeping

In short, while *not* aroused by the shed blood of kindred, the Erinyes resemble the sword suspended above Damokles' head.[26] When a kin-murder takes place, the hair on which the sword is suspended breaks and the sword—like the active Erinyes—becomes "operational". But, as soon at it pierces its victim, the sword ceases to be operational (until the next occasion); so do also the sated Erinyes.

A physical analogy might also help. When there is no kin-murder to be avenged, the Erinyes "exist" only in the sense in which the "potential" energy of a flower pot placed on a window sill "exists". When there is a kin-murder to be avenged they become "operational"—as, when the flowerpot is jolted and hurtles downwards, its (intangible) potential energy becomes transformed into (tangible) kinetic energy.

The best indication of this is that there is no myth *of* the Erinyes—they appear (as avengers) only in myths centred on great sinners.

But there is more. When the Erinyes of a slain relative vengefully suck the blood of the slayer, the blood they drink is *identical* with the victim's blood. In fact, the key issue of A. *Eum.* is precisely whether the son is his mother's kinsman by blood (606 and passim).[27] By draining him of his blood and thereby turning him into a bloodless shade,[28] they seem to *replace* the blood which the victim had lost with *identical* blood drained from the kin-slayer; this represents a kind of retaliatory blood re-transfusion.

This fact, together with the Erinys' coming into (active) being *because of* a kin-murder and *out of* the victim's blood, proves that, as Rohde indicated, the Erinys (especially in the singular) *is* originally the victim, or, rather a *product of* the victim. This, in turn, explains why the word αὐτόφονος (= self-slayer) designates primarily *not* the suicide, but the kin-slayer.[29]

My final argument is that the Erinyes do not achieve an *active,* continuous existence *even after* turning into Eumenides. I will show, further on, that they continue to be mere potential deterrents (696 ff.) who simply *refrain* from spoiling fertility if man behaves himself, but do nothing to promote that fertility *actively,* so as to reward the just and pious man. This is a culturally primitive notion.

This somewhat long preliminary statement about the existence of the Erinyes *in time* is indispensable for a full understanding of the reciprocity between Klytaimestra's double (εἴδωλον) and the sleeping Erinyes.

It is implicit in Rohde's theory, which my arguments simply sharpen and strengthen, that the Erinyes are, in a sense, Klytaimestra's ghost and, in another sense, a product of her shed blood.[30]

This leads to the *seemingly* perplexing insight that the *dreamed* Klytaimestra is *a product of her own products*: of the Erinyes. Her vengeful "ghost(s)" dream(s) of her vengeful double.

Zeus (Hom. *Il.* 14.231 ff.), for Zeus effectively exists even while asleep, while the inactive Erinyes barely exist.

26 Cic. *Tusc.* 5.21.61; Hor. *Od.* 3.1.7.

27 I note (infra) that their sucking of blood resembles μασχαλισμός; cp. A. *Eum.*230, 253, 261, 264 f., 354 ff., 607, 647 ff.

28 A. *Eum.* 267, 299 ff., 302, 647 ff.

29 Compare Orestes' regret that Klytaimestra and Aigisthos had not been slain by their own kin, instead of their having slain Agamemnon (A. *Choe.* 367). Cp. also A. *Choe.* 438: "Let me kill her and then die."   30 A. *Choe.* 400 actually hints at this.

I begin by noting that the early Greek dreamer usually dreams of things and persons which exist *before* he dreams of them. Thus, Athene must fashion a personage *before* that personage can intrude into the sleep of—be "dreamed" by—Penelope (Hom. *Od.* 4.795 ff.). Klytaimestra's ghost also exists before its intrusion into the dream of her own ghost(s).

There is a curious reciprocity here: if Klytaimestra's double had not intruded (Super-ego-like) into the Erinyes' dream, the Erinyes would have remained inactive, since Apollon had put them to sleep.

But, if the Erinyes had not dreamed of Klytaimestra's ghost, *her* ghost would have remained non-operational. It is the Erinyes' dream of Klytaimestra which enables *her* to exist "actively."

This is clearly a "boxes within boxes" situation: the image in one mirror replicates the image in another mirror and vice versa. Each turns the "potential" energy of the other into "kinetic" energy.

Logically, this situation is quite close to the Cartesian "cogito ergo sum", for the one whose existence his thinking proves is precisely the one who does the thinking which proves his existence. It is not certain that this vicious circle can be satisfactorily resolved even by an appeal to Bertrand Russell's "theory of types" (*35*, pp. 523 ff.), but even if it could be so resolved, what matters is that Aischylos himself lived before Russell's theory came into being. This "boxes within boxes" statement is therefore one which passes for "wisdom" in theology and in metaphysics. It is a kind of idle "wisdom", that fascinates the child quite as much as the adult, because it produces a mental vertigo.[31]

All that matters in this context is that the *image* of the producer being (re-)produced by his product is found also elsewhere in Aischylos. But I stress to his credit that he presents it only as a striking poetic image and not as ventriloquist wisdom. In A. *Ag.* 839 we find the moving expression: εἴδωλον cκιᾶc (= the ghostly double of a shade), which, so far as I am able to determine, is unique in classical literature,[32] and creates a feeling of *emotional* depth—not of philosophical profundity—by a "mirror reflecting a mirror" construction. As so often, it is the poet's correct (emotional-aesthetic) use of affectively rooted symbolism which shows up most cruelly the threadbareness of the philosopher's abusive attempts to turn (real) *affective* elements into (metaphysical) profundities.

Still considering the scene on a purely poetic-dramatic level, I recall

---

[31] As a child, I was entranced by the picture of a girl holding a picture of a girl who held a picture, etc. In the lycée I became fascinated with the notion that our heavenly bodies may only be the atoms of larger bodies, etc., and our atoms the heavenly bodies of a smaller universe, etc. In a novel by James Branch Cabell the gods themselves have gods of their own, etc.—an idea already implicit in Luc. *J. Conf.* (Zeus and the Moirai). Even Platon's doctrine of forms can lead to a "boxes within boxes" vertigo: to the notion that the forms (on which the sensible world is allegedly patterned) presuppose an absolute "perfect" Form (perhaps the sphere). But, if so, there should be an even more esoteric "Form" of perfection, etc. I can foresee the verbal refutations which Platonicians could advance, but do not propose to waste time on refuting *Scheinprobleme*. I hold that any end-less vista of "wisdom" of the "boxes within boxes" type, which cannot be adequately solved by an application of Russell's theory, is *a priori* nonsensical.

[32] Fraenkel (ad loc.) shows that its similarities with S. *fr.* 598N² are purely verbal. Other, even more spurious, "parallels" are cited by Thomson ad A. *Ag.* 839. On the inherent grammatical difficulties of that verse, cp. Denniston and Page, ad loc.

what I noted at the very start: what the spectator's corporeal eyes *saw* as a ghostly haunting, they *knew* to be, *for* the Erinyes, a perception of the inner eye. This, incidentally, decisively militates against the bracketing of A. *Eum.* 104 f.,[33] for it makes the very necessary point that some things are visible only in dream.[34]

In short, since the Erinyes are Klytaimestra's ghost(s)—born from her blood and wrath—her ghost is dreamed by her ghost(s). So far, I have simply pointed out that certain "existence in time" and "independent existence" problems must be solved before one can fully grasp the sheer poetic compellingness of this scene. And the understanding and, indeed, reliving of this scene as poetic drama is an indispensable prerequisite for its psychological interpretation as a dream.

IV. *The Erinyes = Orestes*

While the affinity between Klytaimestra and the Erinyes whom she "produces" is usually taken for granted, the fundamental resemblance between Orestes and the Erinyes tends to be more or less overlooked, perhaps because of the constantly repeated assertion that the Aischylean Erinyes are "objectively" real, while the Euripidean Orestes' Erinyes are simply hallucinations (E. *Or.* 396). This view is questionable, and not only because, in A. *Eum.* 417, the Erinyes are defined simply as (perhaps incarnated) "Curses" (ἀραί), which impinge upon Orestes, or else as punitive delusions (ἄτη) (A. *Choe.* 467). More important is that, in A. *Choe.* 1051 ff., the Choros insists that they are fancies and a close reading of the text shows that even Orestes claims only that *he* sees them and that they are real *to him* (A. *Choe.* 1048 ff., 1053 f.). The specification: οὐκ εἰςὶ δόξαι τῶνδε πημάτων ἐμοί does leave open the possibility of his being *partly* aware of the subjectivity of his "perceptions"—as hallucinating patients are sometimes *partly* aware of the subjectivity of what they seem to see, though they *react* to their hallucinations as though they were real. I cannot assert dogmatically that this loophole reflects an objective insight on the part of Aischylos, for the ambiguity of this passage may well be only that of poetry. But even if the latter were true, it would only prove once again what Freud never wearied of saying: Many of the psychoanalyst's insights were unwittingly anticipated by the poets.[35]

The view that, in one sense, the Erinyes are hallucinations can, in part, be adhered to even in interpreting their actual appearance on-stage, for the *dreamed* double of Klytaimestra *also* appears on-stage. Xenophanes' view (*fr.* 15 D-K), that the Supernaturals are the projections of man's

---

[33] As does Schütz, followed by Thomson.

[34] Perhaps because they vanish when "perceived" by corporeal eyes, as Patroklos' double vanishes when Achilleus seeks to embrace him (Hom. *Il.* 22.99 ff.; cp. *Od.* 11.204 ff.). Cp. also ps.-Hp. *insomn.* 86 f., and Arist. *de div. somn.* 463a17 ff., on the possibility of perceiving an incipient illness *only* in dream—a detail I discuss elsewhere in this book. Mazon inappropriately cites A. *Ag.* 179.

[35] Despite his general outlook and rhetoric, which I deem inacceptable, there is much truth in A. Green's (*22*) assertion that there is a deep and special connection between the world view of tragedy and the psycho-analytical outlook.

mind, lurks, I believe, even behind Aischylos' conscious thought and "will to believe".

Equally important is that, even after their "transformation", the Eumenides never fully accept the view that the mother is not kin to her children —that they do not have the same blood. That theory is propounded only by Apollon (657 ff.). The Eumenides do not *explicitly* accept it; they are simply bribed to behave as if they did. In practice, this means only that they retain the right to punish the matricide under a *new* dispensation: not as a kin-slayer, but as a slayer of a member of the social "in-group"— as guardians of peace within the *city* (infra). And the sociologist will conclude that, even when acting in *that* capacity, they will *continue* to punish the mother-slayer *more severely* that the slayer of a mere fellow-citizen—as Zeus punishes more severely the slayer of a hearth friend than of a random stranger. *In practice*, there can even exist considerable discrepancies between the "closeness" demanded by the formal pattern of descent (kinship) and the closeness resulting from the coming into being of what Befu (*1*) calls "personal kindred". Moreover, it is no accident that, in a manifestly non-matrilineal myth, Ixion's slaying of his father-in-law is called the first *kin*-murder (Pi. *P.* 2.32, etc.). In short, even Apollon's theory of descent fails to negate the *social* closeness of mother and child, which makes mother-slaying so atrocious.

The obvious fact that the Eumenides never *explicitly* accept the view that mother and son are not of the same blood, implies that the Erinyes, which *arise* from the slain mother's blood, are, in a sense, also kin-slayers (filicides), since—for them—the mother's blood from which they spring is *identical* with the matricide's blood which they intend to ingest. In that sense they are the products of both Klytaimestra's and Orestes' (identical) blood.

But there are even more tangible similarities between Orestes and the Erinyes:

(1) If Orestes' hands are bloodstained (280; cp. A. *Choe.* 1055 f.), so are those of the Erinyes (41 f.) and of Aigisthos (A. *Choe.* 72 ff.).

(2) If the Erinyes are serpents (supra), so is Orestes in Klytaimestra's dream; their venom, quite as much as their sucking of blood, closely parallels the avenging—and therefore Erinys-like—Orestes' venomous bite and bloody nursing in the A. *Choe.* dream (chap. 6).

Even more significant are certain functional equivalences:

(1) Like the fugitive Orestes, the Erinyes are *outcasts*. They, too, spread pollution, impair the fertility of everything they touch (infra) and are loathed and despised by both gods and men.[36] One passage is particularly illuminating: like Orestes, they give their (female) "parent"—the country that gave them birth (58 f.)[37]—cause to repent of having reared them. Also, like exiled, fugitive kin-slayers, they too appear to have no home. More will be said of this in connection with their *acquiring* a home after becoming the Eumenides.

(2) As stated above, the Erinyes behave like (kin-)murderers.

[36] E.g., 69 f., 194 f., 347 f., 365 ff., 377 ff., 644 ff., 721 ff., 884, etc.
[37] It is recalled that the Erinyes were born after the castrated Ouranos' blood fell upon the (female) Earth.

(a) As representatives of Klytaimestra, *their* aggression against Orestes amounts to filicide—a filicide which Klytaimestra had attempted but failed to carry out (A. *Choe.* 888 f.): hence, they too are genuine kin-slayers.

(b) A person who commits an infamous murder puts the victim's clotted blood into his mouth and then spits it out (chap. 6). The Erinyes too suck the blood of their victims and can be *made* to spit it out or to regurgitate it (183 ff.); they also drool venom (= blood, cp. chap. 7) (477, 780 ff.).

(c) Such murderers lop off the limbs—and assuredly also the genitals[38] —of their victims (chap. 7), and the Erinyes are explicitly said to preside over various mutilations[39]—especially over the castration of boys.[40] Their symbolic feminization of men is highlighted also by their being the patronesses of impalements (189 f.).[41] I will return to this matter in connection with my discussion of sterility and fertility.

Far more important even than these functional equivalences between Orestes and the Erinyes is an often overlooked fact: A. *Eum.* describes *not one* but *two* purifications and social reintegrations: that of the avenging, matricidal Orestes and that of the avenging, "filicidal" Erinyes (= Kly-taimestra):

The outcast Orestes regains his country and royal status. The wandering, homeless (58 f.) Erinyes find a home in Athens and change from despised, pollution-spreading outcasts into honoured deities.

But there is more. The polluted murderer Orestes is, by definition, doomed to be childless (354 ff.; cp. A. *Choe.* 1006), for such a pollution renders sterile every unpurified (kin-)murderer. Only sch. S. *Ant.* 126 asserts that the Erinyes are not childless. However, as soon as he is exonerated, Orestes takes it for granted that he will now have posterity— or at least that his people, previously polluted and rendered sterile by his deed, will *not* become extinct (762 ff.) This "recovery" can be directly linked with the transformation of the Erinyes, goddesses of sterility, into the Eumenides, (alleged) goddesses of "fertility" (infra).

A parallel evolution can be noted also in connection with Orestes' recovery from madness.

Orestes is clearly mad at the beginning of the *Eumenides* (378 ff.), as he was mad already at the end of the *Choephoroi*. But, at first, the Erinyes are *also* mad;[42] it is *because* they themselves are mad that they are *able* to make their victims mad.[43] However, as soon as they are "reformed", they are

---

[38] For nipple = phallos, cp. chap. 6.   [39] A. Eum. 188: ἀκρωνία, cp. Thomson ad loc.
[40] This detail is not wholly oriental: Periandros sent Greek boys to Lydia, to be made into eunuchs (Hdt. 3.48, cp. *13*).
[41] Cp. Pl. *Rmp.* 361e, *Grg.* 473c. For aggression against the adulterer's anus as a retaliatory "feminization", sometimes accompanied by castration, cp. *12* (Ar. *Nub.* 1083; Ar. *Pl.* 168; X. *Mem.* 2.1.5; Catull. 15.19; Hor. *Sat.* 1.2.44; Val. Max. 6.1.13; Apul. *Met.* 12). Cp. now, D. Fehling, Ethnologische Überlegungen auf dem Gebiet der Altertumskunde, *Zetemata* 61, 1974, pp. 18 ff.
[42] A. *Eum.* 67: μάργους.
[43] A. *Eum.* 306, 328 ff., 341 ff. I have shown elsewhere (*11*) that, as a rule, only those gods who are themselves occasionally mad are inclined to madden mortals.

no longer *expected* to provoke homicidal frenzy *not* caused by drunkenness (858 ff.).[44] This implies that the Eumenides cease to cause violent madness because they themselves (temporarily) cease to be mad. Hence, the exoneration of Orestes and the appeasing of the Erinyes represent also a kind of ritual "psychotherapy" which appeases the rage of *both* the killer and the avenger.[45]

In short, the basic similarity between Orestes and the Erinyes is manifest in various ways, throughout A. *Eum.* This is as true of the similarity between the as yet unexonerated Orestes and the Erinyes, as of that between the exonerated Orestes and the Eumenides.

But, as in the case of all ritual psychotherapy (which does not bring about true insight[46]), one has reason, here too, to expect that its beneficial effects will only be transitory or intermittent. As regards Orestes, this is alluded to already in A. *Eum.* 443 ff.: though *repeatedly* purified, he is *not yet* legally exonerated. Hence—despite moments of relief (vv. 280 ff.), which are psychiatrically plausible—his troubles and madness continue unabated. He is not much better off after his exoneration by the Areopagos. Other myths record his *subsequent* attacks of madness (E. *IT*, etc.). He does not recover *fully* until he *"castrates"* himself—a typical punishment meted out by the Erinyes (188)—at least symbolically, by biting off one of his fingers.[47] Last but not least, Orestes, the dream-snake (chap. 6), finally died of a snake bite (sch. E. *Or.* 1640).

The "incomplete" or "transitory" social rehabilitation of the Erinyes is a more complex problem. It will be scrutinized in the next section, which is less of an excursus than it may seem at first glance.

V. *Erinyes = Eumenides*

Sterility/Fertility: Kinsman/Stranger: Needlessly complicated theological theories seek to explain the role the Erinyes—who generally cause sterility—*allegedly* play in insuring fertility. Even if this role were an active one, it would suffice to stress that, in primitive thought, he who has "control" over something can use it either for beneficial or for nefarious purposes; his "control" is both absolute and ethically neutral.[48] In this frame of reference the Erinyes correspond to the shaman as witch; the Eumenides correspond to him in his capacity as healer.

Speaking strictly of Aischylos' Erinyes = Eumenides, the first part of of the drama stresses exclusively their capacity to render sterile,[49] which is

---

[44] This detail may hearken back to the intoxication of the Moirai (723 ff.).

[45] The rage of Orestes, who still seeks purification, seems to frighten even Apollon (232 ff.). Cp. his rage over his impoverishment (A. *Choe.* 274 f.).

[46] On this point, cp. in general (*15*, chap. 1); for Greek equivalents, cp. (*14*).

[47] Paus. 8.34.2. On real and mythological cases of castration by biting, cp. (*13*). On finger-loss as "castration", cp. Dodds (*17*, p. 130, note 79). Circumcision (mythical) by biting: *21*, p. 245.

[48] The Mohave shaman can cure illness X because he can also kill by inflicting *that* illness—and vice versa, of course (*10*, passim).

[49] 188 ff., 345 ff., 780, 785 ff., 810 ff., 824 ff., 830 ff. There is the same emphasis also in A. *Choe.* 188, 262 f., (perhaps 280), 503, 612 ff. (?), 631, 1005 f.

mentioned both by them and by their interlocutors. This is to be expected, for they overtly dishonour Kypris, goddess of love (215).

Things are different when it comes to their fertility-promoting role. Athene alone speaks of it (895, 907, etc.) as a positive deed the Eumenides will *actively* perform. The Eumenides themselves speak of their role in fertility in a *different way*: at v. 921 ff. they propose to *pray* for fertility; at v. 938 they *hope* that sterility will be *averted*; and at 958 they *pray* that girls will live long enough to *find* a mate.[50] All this does not suggest that the Eumenides have the power to *promote* fertility otherwise than by prayer to superior powers. Even more important is that in the second of these utterances—and, by implication, also in the third—they are talking mostly of *averting* that which could *impair* fertility.

The real point can be made quite briefly: the very primitive Eumenides are bribed *not to* unleash their fertility-*impairing* powers. They are represented as basically evil-doing deities, who can be bought off. The sacrifices and honours paid to them are "protection money". In short, the Eumenides are well-bribed Erinyes; they are given something so that they will not spoil all one has. One encounters such a conception of the gods in many primitive societies.[51]

Even in connection with the punishment of crimes, the "rehabilitation" of the Erinyes is conditional. The moment a man slays his kin, the Eumenides revert to being Erinyes and punish him as brutally as ever (696 ff., 930 ff.).

In short, they correspond to a Damoklean sword, for a fear of retribution is necessary for the good functioning of the city (696 ff.). One might say that the "package deal" offered to them by Athene *includes* the promise that, when conditions warrant it, they will be free to manifest their wrath in their old, Erinyes-like manner (927 ff., 952 ff.).

All told, it is Aischylos and *his* Athene, rather than the (bribed) Eumenides *themselves*, who stress their role in promoting fertility. And, if I may venture a personal opinion, Aischylos shows himself a good psychologist in making the Eumenides' right to function, on appropriate occasions, as Erinyes, part of the "deal". Had this escape clause not been included, the Erinyes would not have accepted the pact. Had they accepted it, their consent would have been psychologically implausible, for the Aethiopian cannot change his skin, nor the leopard his spots.[52]

And this brings me to an Aischylean insight which both Frazer and Freud restated, believing it to be new. There must be a stringent law *precisely* against kin-slaying lest *that* crime become commonplace (496 ff., 513 ff.), for oedipal murder is a constant temptation.

Equally striking and socially even more relevant is the fact that Aischylos twice (545 ff., 270 ff.) links crimes against kin with crimes against

---

[50] Mazon errs in translating: "they will live at the side of their husbands". The Aischylean wording does not exclude *a priori* death in childbed, though too much should not be made of this.

[51] Sedang agricultural rites simply buy off the deities who, without that bribe, would harm the crops. No Sedang deity actively fosters fertility (*3*). Haussa sacrifices also seek only to buy off deities who are primarily spoilers (*30, 37*).

[52] Jerem. 13.23.

strangers.⁵³ This seemingly paradoxical equating of the kinsman with the stranger is not even specifically Greek; it is human.⁵⁴ And let it not be argued that the fact that, in Homeros, "foreigner" (ξένος)—especially in the vocative—means mostly: "friend" is decisive, for the name of a xenophobic Spartan law (ξενηλασία) reveals that that word had also hostile nuances. The relationship between ξένος = friend and ξένος = alien (= foe)⁵⁵ is much the same as that between Eumenides and Erinyes. Both reflect man's basic ambivalence: his Schopenhauerian "normal neurotic" inability to tolerate either excessive distance (strangeness) or complete closeness. The early obliteration of the xenophobic nuance of ξένος by its euphemistic nuance: "friend" reflects—like the invention of a Zeus Xenios—the need to bridle *automatic* (fear-inspired) hostility towards the stranger.⁵⁶ The basic meaning of the word—even when it is used to designate a friend—never loses the meaning: "member of the outgroup"; it designates those who are neither kinsmen nor fellow-citizens.

All this shows that the stranger is the target of hostilities *deflected* (under pressure) from the kinsman, who, being close to us, can wound us more than a stranger can. Aischylos therefore rightly implies that the *same* law protects both, for kin-slaying and the slaying of strangers are psychological equivalents.

This pseudo-dichotomy can easily be linked with the sterility-fertility dichotomy, *as "governed" by the Erinyes-Eumenides*, for in the sexual sphere, too, man must strike a balance between extreme endogamy (incest) and extreme exogamy (miscegenation), both of which were forbidden in Greece.⁵⁷ As with aggression in the kinsman = foe equivalence, so in the course of his psycho-sexual development man regularly deflects his erotic impulses first from his mother to his sister (A. *Choe.* 240 f.) and only then to the "outsider"—wife—and it is hardly necessary to recall here the extent to which A. *Eum.* stresses the "outsider" position of the wife (657 ff.).⁵⁸

Summing up, only in terms of hopeful pieties are the Eumenides to be considered as fertility-protecting "reformed" spoilers. Underneath this euphemistic façade, and despite Athene's stubborn insistence upon the good they *will* do, the Eumenides are only well-bribed Erinyes, spoilers of the good earth's *natural* fertility, who promote fruitfulness only by *not* ruining it, as long as men honour them and behave well. The moment a man sins, the Eumenides promptly resume the old functions of the Erinyes.

⁵³ In 270 ff., these crimes are also linked with crimes against the gods. Vv. 544 ff. link parents and guest: the former are entitled to piety, the latter to respect.

⁵⁴ For the Mohave equation: kinsman = alien, cp. *10*, pp. 128 ff.

⁵⁵ But the meaning "alien" may be a late classical development (K.J.D. and E.R.D.); yet, see now J. Roux; *Euripide: Les Bacchantes* I, p. 32, 1970.

⁵⁶ The selfsame ambivalence is reflected by the verb δέχομαι, which can mean either a friendly welcome or a hostile ambush (7).

⁵⁷ On the latter taboo, cp. my discussion of Hippodameia (6).

⁵⁸ Rohde (*33*, p. 451.75) even argues that, given the patrilocality of Greek marriage, the wife (= mother) stood in especial need of an Erinys protecting her from her husband and affinal kin. The Melanesians of Dobu solved this problem more equitably. The couple lives alternatingly in the husband's and the wife's villages of origin, both spouses being exposed in turn to the malice and witchcraft of their respective affinal kin (*18*, pp. 2 ff. and passim).

And it is of crucial importance in this context that the reformed Eumenides' *appearance* remains as repulsive as that of the Erinyes (990).

In short, any other conception of the Eumenides is inspired by modern pieties and ancient hopes, rather than by Aischylos' mercilessly logical drama.

VI. *Analysis of the Erinyes' Dream*

The Interpretation of the Erinyes' Dream is child's play. Their nature, function and bloodthirstiness make them hunt Orestes. Put to sleep by Apollon —so expert at interfering with Ancient Deities[59] when they threaten his favourites—the Erinyes *dream* of continuing their hunt (A. *Eum.* 131 ff.), and behave like dreaming hounds. This detail is psychologically most realistic. A dream in which one performs a task one has failed to complete in a waking state[60] is a "guardian of sleep" (Freud *19*, pp. 678 ff. and passim). The Super-ego—here represented both by the Erinyes' duty and by Klytaimestra—is temporarily "bribed" by the *dreamed* performance of a task *not* performed in a waking state; this dispenses the dreamer from having to wake up and actually do his duty.[61]

The effectiveness of such self-deceptions or mock performances in dream is regularly reinforced by the extreme vividness of the corresponding dreams, which can even lead to the attenuated or schematic execution, in sleep, of the *ampler* movements and vocalizations which would normally occur in the *waking* performance of the dreamed act (*5*) (cp. chap. 8, n. 146). I feel that these sketchy movements in dream may even correspond to what experimental psychologists call "a preparatory set" (*28*). I note here a curious coincidence. The Erinyes hunt while asleep. In A. *Choe.* 897, the infant Orestes is said to have nursed *while* practically asleep—an anomaly discussed in chap. 6.

In concrete terms, the Erinyes, who *"are"* hounds, behave in dream *like* hounds dreaming of a hunt.[62]

---

[59] A. *Eum.* 172, 723, 728; E. *Alc.* 10 ff.

[60] Some subjects who, in a waking state, could not solve the puzzle: OTTFFSSENT, solved it in dream. These letters are the initials of the first ten numbers.

[61] The substitution of a symbolic act for a real performance is also common in daily life. Good wishes and blessings are often offered in lieu of effective help. The *making* of a promise is sometimes treated as equivalent to *keeping* that promise. Once, when I reminded a person of a promise he had repeatedly made but had not kept, he replied in a hurt tone of voice: "But haven't I *promised* it?" This manœuvre is pithily summarized by a Hungarian adage: "Here is nothing—grasp it firmly (lest it escape you)." Its sublimated and logical form is scientific inference or prediction, expected to be confirmed by experience. James Clerk Maxwell made his equations more symmetrical by adding to them a small term which nothing in his actual experience justified. H. Hertz *assumed* that this term had to have an equivalent in reality—and discovered the Hertzian waves (*32*). Cp. Thales' (logical?) prediction of an eclipse (based perhaps on Babylonian records) and Leverrier's exclusively mathematical "discovery" of the planet Neptune. But it is extremely probable that, both historically and subjectively, such scientific activities are refinements and practical sublimations of the archaic tendency to treat words, symbols, prophesies and the like as full equivalents of reality. One notes in this context the frequency of activities which unwittingly *cause* prophecies to come true (*8*, *27*).

[62] Cp. supra for the experimental evidence.

Of course, the Super-ego cannot be permanently bribed by the *dreamed* execution of the assigned task. Sooner or later it intrudes, in some disguise, into the dream: here, the impatient and vengeful Klytaimestra's double *forces* the dreamers to wake up and attend to their task. But, since this Super-ego representative is actually part of the dreamers' own psyche, it is part of the Erinyes' self which goads them to wake up.

This, too, is clearly represented in the Aischylean dramatization of the dream. Klytaimestra's double compares her reproaches to goads (136: κέντρον) and, after awakening, the Erinyes themselves compare the reproach coming to them in dream—for they do *not* mention having dreamed of Klytaimestra!—to a goad smiting them in the vitals (156).

It is easy to see that the pricking of the Erinyes with a goad is self-goading.

The Goad (κέντρον) is the Erinyes' original and most characteristic weapon, which they use already in Hom. *Od.* 15.234. It is mostly in later texts that they use the whip, rather than the goad.[63] This parallels the evolution of horse-driving technology in Greece.[64] It is an archaic feature of A. *Eum.* that goads are mentioned in connection with the Erinyes' dream only, for in vv. 136 and 156, they do not *wield* the goad against their victims; they are told to jab *themselves* with the goad of self-reproach (136) and, on awakening (156), they admit that the goad of reproach had smitten them in the "vitals" (φρήν).

The analogy between these passages, in which the Erinyes' *own* weapon is turned against them and the one in which Apollon threatens the (serpentine) Erinyes with *his own* (poisoned) *serpentine* arrows is quite striking. This parallelism, too, confirms my demonstration that the Erinyes are, in many respects, similar to their chosen victims (supra).

All this indicates that the dream is psychologically highly plausible.

APPENDIX I

The Throat or Neck plays a curiously prominent role in A. *Eum.* Apollon accuses the Erinyes of being involved with throat-cuttings (187). Orestes claims he stabbed Klytaimestra in the throat (592), and this is confirmed by A. *Choe.* 883 f., 1047. This may, perhaps, explain why he subsequently says that the judgment about to be given will decide between his living and his suicide (?) by *hanging* (746). It is just possible that these recurrent references to the throat were unconsciously motivated by the oral sucking content of Klytaimestra's dream in A. *Choe.* 531 ff. and by the many references in A. *Eum.* to blood-*drinking* and blood-*sucking* from the victims' limbs[65] by the Erinyes. These interpretations clearly hearken back to the biting of Klytaimestra's breast in dream and are greatly strengthened by two considerations:

[63] Rapp, s.v. Erinyes *34*, coll. 1314 ff.

[64] A re-examination of Homeric passages in which goads *or* whips are used is likely to be rewarding, for the whip is a later invention than the goad. I note here an interesting and suggestive fact: the *only* draft animal which must be driven with a goad is the reindeer, for its thick fur protects it against the lash.

[65] 264 f., 299 ff. (?), 357 f.

(1) Though Orestes claims to have cut Klytaimestra's throat—which fits the decapitation mentioned in A. *Choe.* (883 f., 1047)—Klytaimestra's ghost shows the Erinyes a wound in the *breast* (heart) (A. *Eum.* 103),[66] which hearkens back to the A. *Choe.* dream.

(2) Orestes apparently expects to hang himself by the neck, though this is a *most* unusual form of suicide *for a man*.[67]

I suspect that the throat-cutting theme should, in the last resort, be viewed as an echo of the tale about the male echidna's decapitation by the female—precisely because it contradicts the reference to the breast bitten in dream and also the chest-wound Klytaimestra's ghost displays.[68]

APPENDIX II

Drunkenness. Aischylos knew of several types of intoxication: that which reveals man's real thoughts (*fr.* 393);[69] that which clouds judgment (A. *Suppl.* 409), and that which elicits homicidal fury (A. *Eum.* 859 ff.).[70]

This indicates that, unlike what one observes in *some* primitive groups, in Greek culture the effects of alcohol were variable.[71]

While I am about it, I might as well say that I do believe Greek traditions concerning Aischylos' alcoholism.[72] Some modern Hellenists piously insist that this is to be taken figuratively,[73] but I feel that this is as gratuitous and squeamish an *Ehrenrettung* as that which denies Sappho's lesbianism (*12*). Had Kratinos been a greater poet—or had more of his work survived—Victorians would no doubt have denied also his notorious alchoholism,[74] though Kratinos himself admitted it in his Πυτίνη (*The Wine Flask*), which carried off the first comedy prize from under Aristophanes' nose.

As a clinician, I do not consider Aischylos' turbulent eloquence incompatible with alcoholism—quite the contrary! The fact that, in his *Myrmidones*, he turned the relationship between Achilleus and Patroklos—which, in Homeros, is a non-sexual comradeship—into a homosexual affair,

---

[66] So Smyth. Some others translate: "look upon these wounds with your heart", rejecting Hermann's emendation: Murray, Thomson, Groeneboom, Mazon, Rose (also E.R.D. and H.L.-J). I may therefore be wrong in accepting the emendation for psychological reasons. Nothing crucial for my argument is here at stake.

[67] This is documented and discussed elsewhere (*16*).

[68] The fact that a dead mother's ghost still carries the wounds which caused her death is mentioned precisely in connection with *another* father-avenging matricide. In the Nether World Eriphyle's wounds are still visible (V. *Aen.* 6.445).

[69] A common Greek theme: Alc. *fr.* Z.9LP (= 104D = 53 Bgk.), *fr.* Z.43LP (= 66D = 57 Bgk.); Thgn. 500; Ion Ch. *fr.* 1D; Pl. *Tim.* 60a, etc.

[70] Drunken brawls are often described, especially by later Greek authors.

[71] Amongst the warlike Mohave, many drunks peaceably fall asleep (*10*, pp. 505 ff.). By contrast, drunken Plains Indians tend to become violent (*9*[2], pp. 13 ff.), etc.

[72] Plu. *fr.* 130 Sandb. (= Stob. 3.18.32); *Q. Conv.* 1.5 p. 622E, 7.10 p. 715 D-E; Chamael. ap. Ath. 1.22a, 10.428f. (Ploutarchos had access to the works of Stesimbrotos and of Ion of Chios, K.J.D.)

[73] Murray *29*, p. 47; Schmid *35* 1.2.184.5, etc. They disregard the question of sources; this is unhistorical.

[74] Ar. *Eq.* 526 ff.; cp. Crat. *frr.* 182, 183, etc.

further strengthens this view, for the nexus between alcoholism and homo-sexuality—and especially latent homosexuality—is notorious. Peak intellectual performances in a state of intoxication are not uncommon,[75] and my opinion on this point is hardly biased, for I have admitted in print my almost irrational loathing of alcohol and alcoholics.

The time has come to stop treating most Greek biographers as malicious gossips and, instead of wasting time on the "rehabilitation" of great poets like Sappho and Aischylos, to study the manner in which a great poet's sexual perversion (*12*) or alcoholism affected his work.[76]

Bibliography

(1) Befu, Harumi: Patrilineal Descent and Personal Kindred in Japan, *American Anthropologist* 65:1328–1341, 1963.

(2) Bourguignon, André: Recherches Récentes sur le Rêve, *Les Temps Modernes* no. 238:1603–1628, 1966.

(3) Devereux, George: *Sedang Field Notes* (MS.), 1933–1935.

(4) id.: Mohave Beliefs Concerning Twins, *American Anthropologist* n.s. 43:573–592, 1941.

(5) id.: Acting Out in Dreams, *American Journal of Psychotherapy* 9:657–660, 1955.

(6) id.: The Abduction of Hippodameia as "Aition" of a Greek Animal Husbandry Rite, *Studi e Materiali di Storia delle Religioni* 36:3–25, 1965.

(7) id.: The Exploitation of Ambiguity in Pindaros *O.* 3.27, *Rheinisches Museum für Philologie* 109:289–298, 1966.

(8) id.: Considérations Psychanalytiques sur la Divination, Particu-lièrement en Grèce (in) Caquot, André and Leibovici, Marcel (eds.): *La Divination*, vol. 2, pp. 449–471. Paris, 1968.

(9) id.: *Reality and Dream: The Psychotherapy of a Plains Indian.* (Second, substantially augmented edition.) New York, 1969.

(10) id.: *Mohave Ethnopsychiatry and Suicide.* (Second, substantially aug-mented edition.) Washington, D.C., 1969.

(11) id. *Wahnsinnige Götter* (Lecture at the University of Basel, MS), 1970.

(12) id.: The Nature of Sappho's Seizure in *Fr.* 31 LP, *Classical Quarterly* 20:17–31, 1970.

(13) id.: La Naissance d'Aphrodite (in) Pouillon, Jean and Maranda, Pierre (eds.): *Echanges et Communications* (*Mélanges Lévi-Strauss*), 2. 1229–1252. Paris and The Hague, 1970.

(14) id. The Psychotherapy Scene in Euripides' *Bacchae, Journal of Hellenic Studies* 90:35–48, 1970.

(15) id.: *Essais d'Ethnopsychiatrie Générale.* (Second edition.) Paris, 1973.

[75] I was present when two brilliant young mathematical physicists shook, long enough to awaken him, an even more brilliant young mathematician, snoring in an alcoholic stupor and got from him a mumbled—and *correct*—answer to a difficult mathematical problem which they could not solve.

[76] This does not mean that I subscribe to the genius = madman absurdity.

(16) id. (and Devereux, J. W.): Les Manifestations de l'Inconscient dans Sophokles: *Trachiniai* 923 sqq. (in) *Psychanalyse et Sociologie comme Methodes d'Etude des Phénomènes Historiques et Culturels*. Bruxelles, 1973.

(17) Dodds, E. R.: *The Greeks and the Irrational*. Berkeley, California, 1953.

(18) Fortune, R. F.: *Sorcerers of Dobu*. London, 1932.

(19) Freud, Sigmund: The Interpretation of Dreams, *Standard Edition* 4–5. London, 1958.

(20) id.: Constructions in Analysis, *Standard Edition* 23. London, 1964.

(21) Griaule, Marcel and Dieterlen, Germaine: *Le Renard Pale*, Paris, 1965.

(22) Green, André: *Un Œil en Trop*. Paris, 1969.

(23) Hoebel, E. A.: Associations and the State in the Plains, *American Anthropologist* 38:433–448, 1936.

(24) Jouvet, Michel: The States of Sleep, *Scientific American* 216, no. 2:62–71, 1967.

(25) Linton, Ralph: *The Study of Man*. New York, 1936.

(26) Llewellyn, K. N. and Hoebel, E. A.: *The Cheyenne Way*. Norman, Oklahoma, 1941.

(27) Merton, R. K.: *Social Theory and Social Structure*. Glencoe, Illinois, 1949.

(28) Mowrer, O. H.: Preparatory Set (Expectancy): Some Methods of Measurement, *Psychological Monographs* vol. 52, no. 2, 1940.

(29) Murray, Gilbert: *Aeschylus*². Oxford, 1962.

(30) Nicolas, Jacqueline: "Les Juments des Dieux", *Etudes Nigériennes* no. 21, IFAN-CNRS (no place, no date).

(31) Nilsson, M. P.: *Geschichte der griechischen Religion* I². München, 1955.

(32) Poincaré, Henri: *The Foundations of Science*. Lancaster. Pennsylvania, 1913.

(33) Rohde, Erwin: *Psyche*. London, 1950.

(34) Roscher, W. H.: *Ausführliches Lexikon der griechischen und römischen Mythologie*. Leipzig, 1884–1937.

(35) Russell, Bertrand: *Principles of Mathematics*². New York, 1938.

(36) Schmid, Wilhelm: *Geschichte der griechischen Literatur*, I.2. München, 1934.

(37) Tremearne, A. J. N.: *The Ban of the Bori*. London, 1914.

(38) Verrall, A. W.: *Four Plays of Euripides*. Cambridge, 1905.

Chapter 5

Klytaimestra's Dream in Stesichoros' *Oresteia*

Preamble

We possess a Stesichorean, an Aischylean and a Sophoklean version of Klytaimestra's dream. The inner affinities between these three variants are highlighted in the course of this chapter and the next two. The problem I discuss here briefly is whether it is clinically possible for a dream narrative inspired by one, or even two, earlier dream-narratives to be still authentically dreamlike. This question can be answered in the affirmative, on several grounds.

(1) One can start with the assumption that Stesichoros *invented* a (dreamlike) dream for his Klytaimestra, which then *elicited* the invention of (related) dreamlike dreams by his two great successors. The process is the same as that which one observes when, after A narrates one of his dreams to B, the latter partly echoes A's triggering dream in a "responding" dream of his own. I once observed this phenomenon while doing ethno-psychiatric field work amongst the Mohave Indians (*15*, pp. 182 ff.). A dream of my interpreter (night of November 16/17, 1938) heavily influenced the dream one of my informants, E.S. (who had heard the interpreter tell her dream) had the very next night.

(2) All three dreams can also be viewed as credible reactions to the same *strong* stimulus—dream reactions which have many internal affinities. This process is exemplified by the dreams dreamed by several patients in response to the deaths of King George V (*23*) and of President Roosevelt (*31, 35*) and also by the dreams of psycho-analysts and psychiatrists who had seen the previous evening a film showing the subincision rites of Australian tribesmen (*13*, chap. 6).

(3) Since Aischylos doubtless knew the Stesichorean Klytaimestra's dream and Sophokles both the Stesichorean and the Aischylean versions, the three narratives may also be compared to "dreams in series" (*1, 2, 24, 14*, pp. 472 ff., *21*). In serial dreams a key problem besetting the patient is worked through—or at least tackled—in different and yet closely interrelated ways.

In short, three completely discrete sets of clinical considerations validate the hypothesis that a dream narrative inspired by an earlier one can, despite its derivative character, still seem authentically dreamlike.[1]

The Stesichorean Precedent

Stesichoros fr. 42 P (= 42 B = 15 D)—the only surviving pre-Aischylean account of Klytaimestra's dream—influenced both Aischylos and Sophokles. Their versions therefore permit one to settle, once and for all, the exact meaning of Stesichoros' crystal-clear text, needlessly obscured by some hair-splitting interpretations.

The Text is correctly printed by Page, whose apparatus criticus contains

---

[1] I note in passing that considerations (2) and (3) fully fit a theorem I enunciated elsewhere (*10*, pp. 76 ff.; *18*, chap. 16, *20*, chap. 3): The same results can be obtained by investigating one man or one culture exhaustively, or a large number of men or of cultures cross-sectionally. This theorem is derivable from the mathematician's "ergodic hypothesis", which plays a crucial role in the calculus of probabilities.

all that is relevant and rightly ignores gratuitous tamperings (*36*, p. 52) with the manuscript tradition:

τᾶι δὲ δράκων ἐδόκησε μολεῖν κάρα βεβροτωμένος ἄκρον,
ἐκ δ' ἄρα τοῦ βασιλεὺς Πλεισθενίδας ἐφάνη.

Ploutarchos, who cites it,[2] considers this dream to be patterned on life and reality; this justifies a realistic psychological analysis of this fragment.

Translation: [Klytaimestra] dreamed there came a serpent with a bloodied crest, and out of it [crest] appeared a Pleisthenid king [Orestes].

Comments: The two verses together describe a dream about the appearance of the Pleisthenid King.[3] Who Pleisthenes may be is immaterial—only the identity of his descendant matters here—and that identity can be determined solely by the *manner* in which he appears.

The key problem is therefore the *manner* in which the Pleisthenid King appears out of—*what*?

Three theories seem to exist.

(1) Delcourt (*4*, p. 22) translates: "et brusquement[4] ce fut[Agamemnon]".

(a) This might imply an oniric "fausse *non*-reconnaissance" (*12* and my comments on A. *Ag.* 412–413) rectified already in dream. Fausse *non*-reconnaissance dreams do exist (*14*, pp. 415 ff.), but it is almost inconceivable that ἐκ δ' ἄρα should simply mean: ἐκ τοῦ = ἐκτότε (= next), or that the complex process of a misperception and of its subsequent rectification should be described so briefly; Hom. *Il.* 13.70 ff. describes something similar at length.

(b) It might imply the appearance of the snake and then that of the Pleisthenid King (with or without the simultaneous disappearance of the snake).

(c) It might imply the metamorphosis of the snake into Agamemnon. But ἐκ δ' is most unlikely to denote a metamorphosis, even if ἐφάνη = ἐξεφάνη. Basically ἐκ δ' means the emergence of "something" out of "something else". Also, I know of no pre-Aischylean precedent for a *dream* metamorphosis. The analogous metamorphosis described in Hes. *Th.* 190–191 (*16*) is *not* a dream-event. I admit that "snake into man" metamorphoses do occcur elsewhere in culturally significant real dreams.[5] I also concede that in some myths an animal shape must be shed and the

---

[2] Plu. *de sera num. vind.* 10, p. 555.

[3] Wilamowitz holds that the first verse describes a monitory dream and the second *prompt* realization of what corresponds (*dem entsprechend*) to it. The only pre-Aischylean dream which comes true *promptly* is that of Rhesos, dreamed just before he was slain (*32*, p. 75). But in Hom. *Il.* 10.496 ff., the slaying is mentioned *before* the dream which announces it. Also, Stesichoros' poem was (one presumes) sufficiently long to make a condensation of almost half of the Orestes myth into two lines improbable.

[4] This translation implies an acceptance of Hartung's theory of the meaning of ἄρα, which is rightly queried by Denniston (*5*, pp. 32 ff.).

[5] In Mohave Indian dreams the hikwīr (similar to the two headed amphisbaina, A. *Ag.* 1233, etc.) can assume the appearance of—or even be—a man and may resemble a shaman who directs funeral rites (*15*, pp. 118 ff.).

"real" human form assumed in preparation for an effective action,[6] but these arguments are inappropriate, for, after all, Klytaimestra's slayer is not Agamemnon but Orestes.

(2) If one holds that ἐκ δ' ἄρα means: ἐκ τούτου τοῦ δράκοντος (out of the *whole* snake), then the Pleisthenid King emerged (in an unspecified manner) out of the snake *as a whole*—conceivably out of its (sheddable) skin. But this awkwardly leaves us with the snake's shed skin, standing for the snake as a whole.[7]

(3) The Pleisthenid King emerges from the snake's bloody (and split) crest. If so, ἐκ δ' stands for ἐκ τούτου τοῦ κάρατος. Dr C. A. Behr suggests to me that this view is syntactically probable because κάρα (head) is the immediate antecedent.[8] It is this interpretation I propose to defend, less for syntactical reasons[9] than because it fits both Greek thought patterns and beliefs and the different contexts of Klytaimestra's dream in the Aischylean and Sophoklean versions thereof, for that is the *only* way in which this problem can be tackled.[10]

It seems best therefore to analyse what the text says and implies; this, together with Stesichoros' interest in cephalic birth (*fr.* 56 P. and *fr.* 62 Bgk.) should suffice to highlight the inadequacies of alternative interpretations.

(1) The snake is a chthonic creature, representing the wrathful dead (A. *Choe.* 37 ff.): Agamemnon.

(2) The snake's head is bloody and, in Sophokles (chap. 7), Agamemnon's head is stained with gore, both because it is split and because the murder weapon was wiped on his hair. No other major personage of the Orestes myth has a bloodstained head up to, or at this time.[11] What matters most is that no alternative interpretation so far proposed takes into account the crucial and strongly emphasized goriness of the skull which, in A. *Choe.* 546, is retained, but transposed to another protuberant organ: to the nipple, and, in S. *El.* 445, is connected outright with Agamemnon's head.

(3) The serpent with the bloody crest must be Agamemnon also because Ailianos (*NA* 1.24) explicitly compares this myth to the (alleged) reproductive pattern of the ἔχιδνα (viper): the female *decapitates* the male during coitus, but her young avenge their slain sire (Cp. appendix).

---

[6] Proteus: Hom. *Od.* 4.417 ff. Thetis: Pi. *N.* 3.60; Apollod. 3.13.5; Paus. 8.18.1.

[7] A normal (oviparous or viviparous) birth may not be envisaged, for this snake is manifestly a male.

[8] But Professor E. R. Dodds warns me that this rule is not absolute. Professor Sir Denys Page wrote me that κάρα is only an accusative of respect.

[9] Professor K. J. Dover tells me that a choice between "the snake as a whole" and the snake's "head" cannot be made on grammatical grounds.

[10] Professor Sir Denys Page wrote me that the missing verses which followed this fragment *may* have explained the *manner* of the Pleisthenid King's appearance. I think this unlikely. Not even in his *Palinoidia* (192/15P.), only in *fr.* 280/103P., did Stesichoros retrace his steps to explain some already mentioned detail. Having reported this King's appearance in Klytaimestra's dream, logically his next task would have been to describe the impact of this dream on Klytaimestra and its sequelae. I do not think *Pap. Oxyrh.* 2617 *fr.* 4 is a helpful syntactical parallel.

[11] It would be fatuous to bring up here Orestes' *subsequent* purification with pig's blood.

(4) The emergence or appearance of the Pleisthenid King out of his sire's split skull parallels the cephalic birth of Athene, out of Zeus' *split* skull.[12] Other quasi-cephalic "births" are also reported:

(a) Ael. *NA* 9.33 (= Hippys *fr.* 8, *FHG* 2.12 = *22*, test. 422): At Epidauros, the priests of Asklepios decapitate a woman; one of them then extracts manually her tapeworm, through her truncated neck. Her head is then replaced on her neck by the god.

(b) *IG* IV², no. 123.23 (= *22, test.* 423). A tale of dreams and visions: Asklepios' priests seek in vain to remove Aristagora's tapeworm (via the neck) by decapitating her. The god himself puts back her head, cuts open her abdomen, removes the worm and sews her up again.

(c) *IG* IV², no. 123.25 (= *22, test.* 422): A—perhaps visionary—man (Asklepios ?) removes, by abdominal surgery, the masses of tapeworms wherewith Sostrata was ἐκύηϲε = pregnant.

(d) *IG* IV², no. 122.21 (= *22, test.* 423): A mother's dream: Asklepios cuts off her dropsical daughter's head, and hangs up her body upside down, draining off the fluid. [Blood is drained from the ablated penis of the *equus october* by suspending it. (*17*)]

A few details deserve notice:

(α) All four persons from whose body something is extracted are female, though in the Stesichorean Klytaimestra's dream the snake is male.

(β) Before the extraction the woman is, so to speak, "pregnant"; explicitly in Case (c), implicitly in the other three cases.

(γ) (Snake-like) tapeworm = foetus: explicitly in Case (c). This is understandable: physiologically the foetus *is* a kind of parasite or tumour. The draining of body fluids in Case (d) recalls the draining of the amniotic fluid; its sexual significance is further reinforced by the *equus october* analogy.

(δ) Decapitation = caesarean. This is evident in all four cases.

(ε) Caesarean birth recalls Greek beliefs concerning the manner in which young vipers are born.

(ʒ) Somewhat as in Stesichoros, in Case (d) the dreamer is not the patient, but her mother.

(5) Orestes' emergence from the snake's skull is retained in a symbolic, but structurally identical, form by Sophokles: a huge branch (Orestes) sprouts *from one end* of Agamemnon's sceptre and I will show that Agamemnon's sceptre = phallos = snake (chap. 7).

(6) The generative powers of a snake's cephalic end are made manifest by the myth of the Hydra, whose decapitated necks sprout new heads until they are cauterized with fire. This motif, too, is present in Sophokles, but in a *"split"* form, which *links* sprouting and cauterization in a manner familiar both to psycho-analysts and to structuralists. *One* end of the sceptre sprouts when the *other* end is thrust into the fireplace—i.e., is seared. The Sophoklean splitting and re-uniting of this motif may have been inspired, on the one hand, by the Aischylean (*Choe.* 607 ff.) reference to the burning, in a hearth, of a (sceptre-like) log representing Meleagros'

---

[12] All sources fully analysed by Cook (*3*, 3.656 ff.). Could this parallelism shed at least a trace of light on the still puzzling cult-name: Zeus Agamemnon? (Lyc. 335, 1123 sq., 1369 sq.).

"external soul," and, on the other hand, by beliefs in phalloi found in lit fire-places, which can impregnate girls (chap. 7).

(7) Not only is the equation: snake = phallos commonplace, but a snake's split and bloodstained skull greatly resembles the glans: the meatus is cleft-shaped and the glans is reddish and moist.[13]

(8) The view that Orestes emerges from the phallic snake's skull is made even more plausible by certain additional considerations:

(a) Venom = semen.[14]

(b) Venom = blood.[15]

Aischylos (*Choe.* 545 f.) retains the venom+blood+milk (= semen)[16] theme: this motif will be discussed further on.

(c) The sexual element in the venom = semen = blood motif, made evident by the alleged aphrodisiac quality of such a mixture,[17] anticipates the latent erotic element in the Aischylean Klytaimestra's dream (chap. 6).

(d) The Stesichorean imagery implies that Orestes emerges from the snake's head as fully formed as Athene emerges from Zeus' skull. Now, A. *Eum.* 658 ff. affirms that only the father procreates the child. This might imply that, figuratively speaking, the father ejaculates a kind of homunculus (Hp. *Genit.* 1.1.7 p. 470 Littré).[18]

(e) Even the goriness of the snake hints (in reverse) at its generative powers, for the prophylactic mutilation of Agamemnon's corpse (chap. 7) certainly included the ablation of his penis, presumably because of the fear that his ghost (or chthonian snake equivalent) could procreate an avenger.[19]

(9) The notion that the father's skull-phallos ejaculates a homunculus can be readily linked with Hippokrates' belief (*Genit.* 1.1.7 p. 470 Littré). that the semen ultimately comes from the head (brain) (*30*, pp. 108 ff.).

(10) It is not altogether unlikely that even the word "king" is not a purely grandiloquent designation. Orestes could not be called "king" until *after* Agamemnon's death: his "kingship" was, so to speak, "born"

---

[13] Cp. the "bloody bridegroom" of a corrupt biblical passage regarding Moses' (?) circumcision. (*Exod.* 4.24 ff.)

[14] Waste product = semen: a view mentioned but rejected in Arist. *G.A.* 18, p. 724b26 ff. Minos ejaculates venomous insects (Apollod. 3.15.1 and Frazer ad loc.; Ant. Lib. 41 and Papathomopoulos ad loc.). The equation: small creatures = foetus or baby is commonplace. Nessos' ejaculate is poisonous, being contaminated by the Hydra's venom: Apollod. 2.7.6; D.S. 36.4–5. Quilling (in Roscher *34* s.v. Nessos, col. 280) detects a similar hint in S. *Tr.* 580: προσβαλοῦς' ὅσα ζῶν κεῖνος εἶπε, but his opinion does not seem generally accepted.

[15] The Hydra's poisonous blood infects that of the wounded Nessos (Apollod. 2.5.2; Paus. 2.37.4; D.S. 4.11.38; Hyg. *fab.* 30). Suicide by drinking bull's blood: Plu. *V. Them.* 31.

[16] For milk = venom = semen, see chap. 6.

[17] Cp. the Nessos references, supra note 14.

[18] A theory mentioned but rejected in Arist. *G.A.* 1.17, p. 721b12 ff., 1.18, p. 724b36 f. It is also held by the *matrilineal* Hopi Indians (*6*), cp. chap. 7. note 55.

[19] The dead hero Astrabakos fathered Demaratos (Hdt. 6.69), etc. For a direct, if (predictably) sarcastic, reference to this belief, cp. E. *Suppl.* 545. (But I question, with Wilamowitz, the soundness of Dümmler's, Weicker's, Samter's and Nilsson's (*29* I².100) far-reaching inferences from this passage and from Hom. *Il.* 22.72 ff. and Tyrt. 10.25 (Bergk).) Tales of snake paternities abound not only in Greece (Alexandros the Great), but also in many primitive societies.

from Agamemnon's split skull. Needless to say, this view is advanced *most tentatively*, even though such (quasi-punning) allusions are to be expected from an ancient Greek poet.

(11) A further *tentative* observation is that the avowed purpose of many ancient craniotomies may have been the releasing of "something" lodged in the patient's skull.[20] This may *possibly* have (indirectly) led to a tacit belief that an avenging Alastor could emerge from a split skull, by means of a kind of "cephalic caesarean". Viewed in this light, the *man* Orestes was born normally from Klytaimestra, while Orestes the Avenger, the Heir (and King) "emerged" from Agamemnon's split skull.[21]

Summing up, the Stesichorean dream shows Agamemnon, in the form of a threatening chthonian snake, with bloodied crest, approaching Klytaimestra; then out of the gory (and split?) *skull* there appears Orestes, King because avenger and avenger because King (S. *O T.* 132 ff.). The phallic symbolism of the snake and the nexus between the emission of blood = venom = semen and the male cephalic birth of Orestes add an erotic element to the anxiety elicited by the appearance of the snake. The same erotized anxiety will be encountered also in the Aischylean and Sophoklean versions of this dream, for the latent content of a dream or myth is as resistant to change—as invariant (*8, 10, 11*)—as is its structure (*28*). The more general relationship between the Stesichorean theme and its Aischylean and Sophoklean variants will become evident in the course of the analysis of the latter dreams.

In conclusion I note that since, in fantasy, killing is regularly equated with castration, and the killing of a man by his woman with the *vagina dentata* fantasy, the representation, in the Stesichorean text, of Agamemnon as a serpent with a split skull is psychologically and eschatologically appropriate. He is a (chthonian) serpent because he is dead—and, like some other infamously murdered spectres, the wound that killed him is still visible on his spectral body.[22] That the "castrating", murderous Klytaimestra should have guilt-dreams is not surprising. An ancient Icelandic saga records that a man who had had his slave Gilli castrated, had three prophetic dreams that warned him that his slave would kill him—as he actually did. (*26*). The concept of "castration anxiety" has a psychological counterpart and complement: "the anxiety of the castrator"—which psycho-analysts have, so far, chosen to ignore.

---

[20] The Sedang trephined a person who had tried to commit suicide by drinking tobacco, so as to release the poison (*7, 19*).

[21] Cp. the "caesarean" deliveries of Zeus' two potential successors: of Athene the heiress (ἐπίκληρος) (Ar. *Av.* 1653), from the split skull, and of Dionysos, first excised from Semele's womb and then from Zeus' "thigh" (which is probably a euphemism). One notes that both the cranial sutures (Hdt. 9.83, etc.) and (to this day) those of the nether part of the penis and scrotum are called ῥαφή. Much could be said about the role of the latter type of suture in embryology, in congenital genital deformities (*27*), in ritual mutilations (*33*), in perverted ritual practices (*33*), in dreams (*9*), etc., which would shed light upon the nature of Zeus' "paternal womb" (Nonn. 9.11). Unfortunately, an adequate discussion of this matter would take one too far afield. I also feel that A. *Ag.* 1569 ff. implies that another Alastor is still to come: Orestes.

[22] This belief is quite tenacious: Eriphyle's spectre still bears the wound that killed her (V. *Aen.* 6.445). Cp. chap. 4.

Appendix

THE ECHIDNA'S REPRODUCTION

Greek beliefs concerning the reproduction of the viper—which, unlike, e.g., the cobra, is viviparous—are, as already Ailianos (*NA* 1.24) realized, relevant for the understanding of poetic treatments of the Orestes and Alkmaion myths.[23]

Three aspects of that reproductive pattern are relevant:

(1) The male wraps himself around the female (Ael. *NA* 1.24).

(2) The female bites off the male's head during coitus (Hdt. 3.109).

(3) The young kill their mother by emerging not from her vagina, but through her abdominal wall.

I will now discuss these three elements:

(1) In A. *Choe.* 1049 f., the Erinyes are described as interlaced by snakes. The wrapping of the male snake around the female snake thus stands in a symmetrical relationship to the tale that Klytaimestra immobilized Agamemnon by means of a net.[24] Such symmetries are important, both structurally and psycho-analytically.

(2) The decapitation of the male during coitus—which necessarily draws blood—is mentioned by many sources.[25] Only Nikandros indicates that some males manage to escape alive, though wounded. The similarity with the Stesichoros text is manifest.

(3) Two versions of the birth of young vipers exist:

(a) They gnaw their way through the female's abdominal wall, thereby avenging their sire.[26] This recalls the tale that unborn lion-cubs, though apparently emerging from the lioness' vagina, destroy her womb with their claws (Hdt. 3.108). This latter tale is discredited by Arist. *GA* 4.5 p. 773a.

(b) The thin flanks of the female viper simply burst open from the pressure[27]—as do, supposedly, also the flanks of the female pipe-fish (Ael. *NA* 9.60, 15.16).

One source of the absurd tales about the birth of young vipers may be the female's viviparousness, which, as Hdt. 3.109 and Nic. *Ther.* 135 f.[28]

---

[23] Serpents are closely linked with the Alkmaion–Amphiaraos myth. The death of Opheltes links snake and child. Eriphyle was bribed with Harmonia's necklace, shaped like an amphisbaina (Nonn. *Dion.* 5.144 ff.); as to Harmonia, she became a serpent (E. *Ba.* 1330 ff.). Given his life underground, one is surprised *not* to find Amphiaraos regularly represented as a serpent. There is even a decapitation and a split skull in *his* myth: he brings Tydeus the skull of Melanippos, whose brain Tydeus swallows (Apollod. 3.6.8). As to maternal blood, it is mentioned in E. (*Alcm.*) *fr.* 71 N². Though scanty enough, these data justify Ailianos' linking of Alkmaion with viperine reproduction patterns —and my linking the latter with the Stesichorean serpent's split skull. The pattern seems change-resistant.

[24] A. *Ag.* 868, 1115; cp. A. *Choe.* 506, 999, etc.

[25] Hdt. 3.109; ps.-Arist. *Mir.* 846b18; Nic. *Ther.* 128 ff. and scholia ad loc.; Ael. *NA* 1.24.

[26] Hdt. 3.109; Ael. *NA* 1.24 (discredited in Ael. *NA* 15.16).

[27] Ael. *NA* 15.16 citing Theophrastos, whose master, Aristoteles, correctly described the viper's reproduction (Arist. *HA* 558a25, etc.).

[28] And sch. ad loc. (Bussemaker). On these matters the scholl. 129 ff., provide little help. Cp. also *25*, p. 173, on Nic. *Ther.* 128 ff.

note, differs from the oviparousness of many other snakes. This may explain why, in A. *Choe.* 543 ff., Orestes stresses so much his own and the dream-snake's birth from Klytaimestra's womb.

What is most striking about this part of the tale is the conception of the viper's vagina as a "one-way street": it admits the penis but is unable to emit the young.

As regards the tale's two themes, each of the two ascribes to *vipers* behaviour which occurs in *insects*:

(1) At the end of the coitus the praying mantis devours her mate, beginning with his head. Similar androphagous coital behaviour occurs also in other insects (*37*, chap. 7).

(2) Some insects' young actually emerge through the *walls* of the female's abdomen: one of them is the midge Miastor, whose young are born already pregnant (paedogenesis) (*37*, chap. 7).

I note here, once and for all, that human *fantasies* about sexual behaviour can usually be matched by equivalent *genuine* behaviour occurring in other species, such as insects.

Bibliography

(1) Alexander, Franz: Dreams in Pairs and Series, *International Journal of Psycho-Analysis* 6:446–452, 1925.

(2) Baumann, H. H.: Über Reihenfolge und Rhythmus der Traummotive, *Zentralblatt für Psychotherapie und ihre Grenzgebiete* 9:213–228, 1936.

(3) Cook, A. B.: *Zeus*, 3. Cambridge, 1940.

(4) Delcourt, Marie: *Oreste et Alcméon*. Paris, 1959.

(5) Denniston, J. D.: *The Greek Particles*2. Oxford, 1959.

(6) Devereux, George: *Hopi Field Notes* (MS.), 1932.

(7) id.: *Sedang Field Notes* (MS.), 1933–1935.

(8) id.: Why Oedipus Killed Laïus: A Note on the Complementary Oedipus Complex, *International Journal of Psycho-Analysis* 34:132–141, 1953.

(9) id.: Primitive Genital Mutilations in a Neurotic's Dream, *Journal of the American Psychoanalytic Association* 2:483–492, 1954.

(10) id.: *A Study of Abortion in Primitive Societies*. New York, 1955,2 1975.

(11) id.: The Exploitation of Ambiguity in Pindaros. *O.* 3.27, *Rheinisches Museum für Philologie* 109:289–298, 1966.

(12) id.: Fausse Non-Reconnaissance, *Bulletin of the Menninger Clinic* 31:69–78, 1967.

(13) id.: *From Anxiety to Method in the Behavioral Sciences*. Paris and The Hague, 1967.

(14) id.: *Reality and Dream: The Psychotherapy of a Plains Indian*. (Second, augmented edition.) New York, 1969.

(15) id.: *Mohave Ethnopsychiatry*. (Second augmented edition.) Washington, D.C., 1969.

(16) id.: La Naissance d'Aphrodite (in) Pouillon, Jean and Maranda,

Pierre (eds.). *Echanges et Communications* (*Mélanges Lévi-Strauss*), 2.1229–1252. Paris and The Hague, 1970.

(17) id.: The *Equus October* Ritual Reconsidered, *Mnemosyne* 23:297–301; 1970.

(18) id.: *Essais d'Ethnopsychiatrie Générale*. Paris, 1970. Second edition, 1973.

(19) id.: *Sedang Suicide* (MS.). Lecture given before the Institute of Social Anthropology, Oxford University, 1972.

(20) id.: *Ethnopsychanalyse Complémentariste*. Paris, 1972.

(21) id.: Trois Rêves en Série et une Double Parapraxe, *Ethnopsychologie* (in press).

(22) Edelstein, E. J. and Ludwig: *Asclepius* I. Baltimore, 1945.

(23) Fairbairn, W. R. D.: The Effects of the King's Death upon Patients in Analysis, *International Journal of Psycho-Analysis* 17:278–284, 1936.

(24) Gahagan, L.: The Form and Function of a Series of Dreams, *Journal of Abnormal and Social Psychology* 29:404–408, 1935.

(25) Gow, A. S. F. and Scholfield, A. F. *Nicander*. Cambridge, 1953.

(26) Kelchner, G. D.: *Dreams in Old Norse Literature and their Affinities in Folklore*. London, 1935.

(27) Kreisler, Léon: Les Intersexuels avec Ambiguité Génitale, *La Psychiatrie de l'Enfant* 13:65–127, 1970.

(28) Lévi-Strauss, Claude: *Anthropologie Structurale*. Paris, 1958.

(29) Nilsson, M. P.: *Geschichte der griechischen Religion* I². München, 1955.

(30) Onians, R. B.: *The Origins of European Thought*. Cambridge, 1951.

(31) Orlansky, H.: Reactions to the Death of President Roosevelt, *Journal of Social Psychology* 26:235–266, 1947.

(32) Ritchie, William: *The Authenticity of the Rhesus of Euripides*. Cambridge, 1964.

(33) Róheim Géza: Psycho-Analysis of Primitive Cultural Types, *International Journal of Psycho-Analysis*, 13:1–244, 1932.

(34) Roscher, W. H. (ed.): *Ausführliches Lexikon der griechischen und römischen Mythologie*. Leipzig, 1884–1937.

(35) Sterba, R. F.: Report on Some Emotional Reactions to President Roosevelt's Death, *Psychoanalytic Review* 33:393–398, 1946.

(36) Vürtheim, J.: *Stesichoros' Fragmente und Biographie*. Leiden, 1919.

(37) Wigglesworth, V. B.: *The Life of Insects*. Cleveland and New York, 1964.

Chapter 6

Klytaimestra's Dream in Aischylos' *Choephoroi*

ΧΟΡΟΣ
τεκεῖν δράκοντ' ἔδοξεν, ὡς αὐτὴ λέγει   527
ΟΡΕΣΤΗΣ
καὶ ποῖ τελευτᾷ καὶ καρανοῦται λόγος;
ΧΟΡΟΣ
ἐν σπαργάνοισι παιδὸς ὁρμίσαι δίκην.
ΟΡΕΣΤΗΣ
τίνος βορᾶς χρῄζοντα, νεογενὲς δάκος;   530
ΧΟΡΟΣ
αὐτὴ προσέσχε μαζὸν ἐν τὠνείρατι.
ΟΡΕΣΤΗΣ
καὶ πῶς ἄτρωτον οὖθαρ ἦν ὑπὸ στύγους;
ΧΟΡΟΣ
ὥστ' ἐν γάλακτι θρόμβον αἵματος σπάσαι.
ΟΡΕΣΤΗΣ
οὔτοι μάταιον· ἀνδρὸς ὄψανον πέλει
ΧΟΡΟΣ
ἡ δ' ἐξ ὕπνου κέκλαγγεν ἐπτοημένη.   535

(Smyth's text)

Translation

Choros: She dreamed she gave birth to a serpent—such is her own account.
Orestes: And where ends the tale and what its consummation?
Choros: That she laid it to rest, as it were a child, in swaddling bands.
Orestes: What food did it crave, the new-born noxious thing? (stinging or biting beast, cp. A. *Suppl.* 897).
Choros: She herself in her dream offered it her breast.
Orestes: Surely her nipple was not unwounded by the loathsome beast? (the loathsome one).
Choros: No; with the milk it drew in clotted blood.
Orestes: Sooth, 'tis not meaningless—the vision means a man.
Choros: Then from out of her sleep she raised a shriek and woke up appalled.

(Smyth's translation)

(The words in parentheses were added by me; they are alternatives to Smyth's expressions.)

Introduction

Few Aischylean passages reveal the inexhaustible richness of his poetry better than his Klytaimestra's dream. Each nuance belongs to several networks of meaning, for his art transmutes an extremely broad gamut of facts—cultural and other—into dream-poetry. Each detail is linked—at times by almost invisible threads—to many other details.

This is an important fact, for the *great* poet enchants and fascinates not so much by what he *provides* but by what he *demands*: each verse challenges the reader to multiply its echoes by detecting its countless overtones, and its many links both with other passages and with the poet's world as a whole. For, Platon notwithstanding, not the least of the true poet's resources is his capacity to reveal the ultimate truth—which is psychological reality—even, and perhaps especially, through what objectively is an untruth: he highlights the very essence of reality through the metamorphosis of its concrete manifestations. I note again that, more than the finest real racer, the imaginary winged Pegasos conjures up the essence of speed, and especially the *unconscious* meaning of horse back riding. For Pegasos' "absurd" flight is rooted in the symbolic equation: dream-flight = erection or sexual excitement.

It seems to me that Platon's ultimate "reality" is as eerily one-dimensional as the "pure" note, devoid of overtones, produced by the "ondes Martenot". But poetry is like the rich, "impure" note of the violin, whose overtones are audible, and, in a sense, are even amplified by the human ear.[1]

This is why Klytaimestra's lie that she had nursed Orestes (vv. 896 ff.) reveals the psychological truth even more poignantly than does the Nurse's credible affirmation that (only) she had nursed him. It is Klytaimestra's lie which makes her failure to nurse Orestes seem as monstrous as it really is: cp. A. *Ag.* 856, for a similar brazen lie.

It will predictably be objected that, at vv. 544 ff., Orestes himself claims to have been nursed by his mother . . . because that is what he must have been *told*. Far from being the kind of contradiction that delights certain critics, this is the touch of the consummate psychologist. The harsh, possessive mother of a patient had for many years concealed from him the fact that (because of an illness) she had nursed him only for a few weeks and had then entrusted him to one or more wet-nurses. Significantly, when this man, then in psycho-analysis, asked his mother for information about his wet-nurse(s), his mother *claimed* to remember nothing about her (or them)—reasserting once more than she alone was his "real" mother and nurse. This case speaks for itself and disposes of the "contradiction" between the Nurse's statement, Klytaimestra's claims and Orestes' naive belief in his mother's lies.

This, then, is the "lying" art of the poet, which reveals the *undistorted* psychological truth by means of a *misrepresentation* of objective reality. The psycho-analyst can grasp the aliveness of this art only if he is will to defer

[1] Thus, when an orchestra plays only C-E-C, the ear will none the less "hear" the (missing) G, which is present only as an overtone. The ear will therefore hear the whole chord: C-E-(G)-C.

to the poet, who, by means of the extraordinarily multivalent "density'' (*29*) of the poetic utterance, brings into being the wonder of reality, for he alone has the key to it.

In Literary Criticism, one must note, first of all, that, in tragedy, Klytaimestra's dream is told not by her, but by a third party: by the Choros in A. *Choe.*; by Chrysothemis in S. *El.* Also—and this is true especially of A. *Choe.* but to a lesser extent of S. *El.* as well—information about the content of the dream is *elicited* by questioning the informant(s). By contrast, nearly all other dreams in surviving Greek tragedies are reported by the dreamer in person and, moreover, never in the course of a stichomythia. The Erinyes dream (A. *Eum.*) is both represented on the stage and then (partly) narrated.

Though from the literary point of view Klytaimestra's dream is prophetic, from the psychological point of view its "prophetic" character is almost irrelevant. Moreover, Klytaimestra considers it ominous or prophetic only *after* she wakes up, terror-stricken (929). This not only fits Greek belief, but also underscores that the *defining* of this dream as prophetic is not part of the "dream-work" proper, but of the dream's secondary elaboration, on awakening, in response to its affective core. In tragedy, the defining of any dream as prophetic is always an imputation.[2]

The ascription of a prophetic character to this particular dream is facilitated by the fact that it manifestly does *not* reproduce a past *event*, for not Klytaimestra but the old Nurse had suckled Orestes.[3] This leads to the not altogether correct assumption that the dream concerns the future *only*. Actually, it is not the manifest content of the dream but its far more important affective core which is rooted in the past: it reflects guilt feelings and self-punitive impulses related to Klytaimestra's inadequacy as a mother (infra). Moreover, in her dream, Klytaimestra belatedly performs a task she had failed to perform at the proper time. Such dreams are fairly common and are exemplified by the Erinyes' dream (chap. 4). Also, in a psychologically plausible manner, this belated dream-performance of a neglected duty includes a built-in punishment—as does the Erinyes' dream: the snake *bite* anticipates the *goad* of self-reproach in the Erinyes' dream (chap. 4). Thus, there are basic psycho-analytical and structural affinities between Klytaimestra's dream and the dream of her own Erinyes.

These considerations show that, as soon as it goes beyond the obvious, literary criticism leads directly to psycho-analytical insights, simply because great poetry deals persuasively with human personality.

Repetitiveness: Given the complexity of the dream and its countless links with other passages and with various customs, a certain amount of repetition will help the reader to follow my argument, without having to leaf back in order to locate the information needed at a given point. Though aesthetically unsatisfactory, repetition is helpful in following complex reasoning about complex facts.

Dream and Context: The analysis of Klytaimestra's dream would be a

---

[2] Cp. *33*, passim; *66*. "Terror is the dream's interpreter" (A. *Choe.* 929).

[3] Moreover, as is the case in many primitive groups, she nursed him *on demand* and not "on schedule" (749 ff.). This practice is, inexplicably, not mentioned in (*52*).

fairly simple task if it were *all* that survived of A. *Choe.* (cp. chap. 3). But, as is, it must be interpreted in its context. Now, parts of that context *seem* to contradict certain details of the dream—but only in order to reveal, through *objective* untruths and incompatibilities, the dream's underlying *psychological* truth—a poetic technique which I discussed a moment ago.

If, for example, we did not possess the Nurse's credible statement (749 ff.) that *she alone* had nursed Orestes—i.e., if vv. 749–760 were missing—the dream's manifest content could be held to reproduce (with one nightmarish distortion only) memories of Klytaimestra's nursing of Orestes. If so, her subsequent plea to be spared—reinforced by the baring of her breasts which, she claims, once suckled Orestes (vv. 896 ff.; cp. E. *Phoin.* 1568)—would have to be taken as a legitimate reminder of the "debt" a son owes to the breasts that fed him. But the Nurse's account renders both these plausible and "objective" interpretations untenable. The truth of the dream is more psychological—and hence more elusive— than objective.

The dream must therefore be analysed "in situ", with special reference to vv. 27 ff., 32 ff., 535 ff., 749 ff., and 896 ff.

(1) *Vv. 32 ff.*, which describe the outward, observable manifestations of Klytaimestra's dream, provide only one striking datum. This passage mentions a cry of terror *during* the dream—but the actual dream-narrative does not even hint at an outcry. In fact, though the giving birth to a serpent, its savage nursing at the breast, its swaddling and being put to rest are horrible enough, the dream narrative itself does not even hint at any terror Klytaimestra may have experienced *while* she performed these tasks *in dream* (cp. chap. 2). Yet, her matter-of-fact activities in dream would be routine and anxiety-free only if her baby were human. This casualness increases, if anything, the oniric character of her dream—for real dreams, like great art, make the near-impossible seem not only natural and credible, but even inevitable.[4]

How, then, can one reconcile the reported cry of terror with Klytaimestra's tranquil and matter-of-fact dream behaviour?

The simplest assumption would be that Klytaimestra cried out in terror when her horrible dream *awakened* her at night. The text does not forbid such an interpretation, and may perhaps even encourage it.

An alternative would be to suppose that the matter-of-fact behaviour of Klytaimestra's *dream image* is supplemented by the terrified—and terrifying —outcry of the *sleeping* Klytaimestra. This would imply that the calm dreamed behaviour emanates from one level of psychic functioning and the frightened shriek from another level.

Three arguments may be mustered in favour of this interpretation:

(a) Sappho's (*fr.* 31 LP) mind is lucid—all her abnormal reactions to a painful situation are corporeal (physiological). I have shown elsewhere (*39*) that her objectivity is unimpaired precisely because she *somatizes* what, in most cases, would be *psychic* pain.

---

[4] Similarly, an unexpected turn of a Mozart melody or a bold modulation in Schubert are startling when heard for the first time. But, once heard, they seem totally inevitable; one cannot even imagine afterwards that they could have been composed differently. Cp. also (*60*) and chap. 1.

(b) Concurrent verbal and postural behaviour may be contradictory, each reflecting one aspect of an ambivalence.[5]

(c) Klytaimestra's tranquil performance in dream, which contrasts with her terrified outcry in sleep, can *perhaps* be correlated also with the Greek view that dreams are "intruders"; that dream personages (the dreamer's own dream-image included) perform a kind of play before the sleeper's inner eye. But this is certainly the least strong of the three points that can be made in this connection.

The most revealing aspect of Klytaimestra's dream-behaviour is the *actual* activity to which it leads on awakening. Frightened by her ominous dream, she sends libation-bearers to Agamemnon's tomb, so as to appease his angry (278) shade. It is therefore to this rite that I now turn.

(2) *In vv. 27 ff.*, the mourning libation-bearers' behaviour practically duplicates Klytaimestra's dream activity. They, too, *bare* their breasts (cp. E. *Phoin.* 1491; Theocr. 15.134) and then *traumatize* them with blows. Even the libation they offer recalls the mixture of *liquids* Orestes draws in dream from Klytaimestra's breasts (infra).

(3) *Vv. 749 ff.*—patterned in every respect on Hom. *Il.* 9.485 ff.[6]—establish that *only* the Nurse suckled Orestes. Klytaimestra's dream is, thus, not a distorted replica of earlier events, and her demand to be spared (896 ff.), because she had "nursed" Orestes, is a factual deceit—but one which reveals important psychological truths.

Moreover, several details of the Nurse's account echo attitudes present in the dream and in the lie.

(a) Baby = (witless) beast (βοτόν) = snake baby (cp. Hom. *Od.* 19.530).

(b) Nursing is troublesome and saps the woman's "soul" = snake bite (cp. chap. 7 and E. *Phoin.* 1433).

(c) A reward is expected—as in vv. 896 ff.—for the nursing.

Vv. 896 ff. which contain a pack of lies and especially Klytaimestra's claim to have nursed Orestes must be scrutinized further on.

These are some of the facts which I must *repeatedly* recall in the course of my analysis of this dream.

The Observable Aspects of Klytaimestra's dream have already been partly discussed elsewhere (*33*).

Klytaimestra dreams in her bower (μυχός) (35).[7] A terrifying voice, inextricably commingled with the wrathful breath of sleep, echoes through the women's part of the palace. This much is clear. The rest is not—although, except for v. 32, most editors print the same text.[8] But the

---

[5] Cp. the heroic Aratos' fear-diarrhoeas before set battles (Plu. *V. Arat.* 29.5 and passim); Henri IV of France shook like a leaf before riding into combat. As to clinical data, one of my patients spoke lovingly of his brother—but his posture on the couch was that of a pugilist. Cp. Sen. *Phaedr.* 1121, and (*24*).

[6] Even the spotted tunic is "transformed" into soiled diapers. Bowdlerized in Q.S. 3.475 ff. (infra).

[7] Rousseau (*95*, p. 123) tries to represent this bower as a kind of oracular adyton. This borders on the absurd. The dreaming of a significant dream in a particular chamber does not turn it into an oracular shrine.

[8] I disregard, as irrelevant in this discussion, variations in the arrangement of the verse patterns.

translations of Smyth, Mazon and Thomson differ from each other in significant respects. In seeking to decode this cryptic passage, I feel that one must look beyond lexical and syntactical problems: these verses *must* make sense in terms of Aischylean (and Greek) beliefs about dreams and, I submit, also in terms of psychology.

I do not profess to have all the answers. I simply seek to define the difficulties and to comment on them.

The basic problem is whether the shout and the breathing do or do not emanate from the *same source*. But it is best to postpone the discussion of this question until after the other problems have been considered.

The terrifying shout emanates from an unspecified "power", which *interprets* dreams *during* the dream, *to* the household as a whole. Those who hear the shout understand the *meaning* of the dream at once, though they do not know (as yet) *what* Klytaimestra is actually dreaming just then. If, as one must suppose, "interpreting the dream" is to be taken literally, this means that those who hear the shout are given the "interpretation" of an (ongoing) dream (= riddle),[9] *without* knowing (as yet) what the dream is. They simply learn the solution of an *as yet unknown* problem. Another example of this type of procedure is psycho-analytic technique, which consists in discovering the "questions" which the patient's utterances (unwittingly) answer.

This may be contrasted with what happened at the Delphic oracle. The client first heard the Pythia "rave" glossolalically,[10] then the priest told him what the Pythia' utterances "meant".

Yet, one cannot but suppose that here the shout is both inarticulate and "intelligible", in a general way.[11] It conveys *affect*—and, in Aischylos, the basis of dream interpretations is the dream's affective impact, cp. A. *Choe.* 929 and (*33*). It is therefore obvious that the scream—*qua manifestation* of the dream's affective content—rates as its "interpretation": Klytaimestra has a bad dream which, as everyone assumes at once, can only refer to her punishment for Agamemnon's murder. All this the women *infer* from the shout. I stress the word "infer", for I have shown elsewhere (*35*) that the text of the oracles handed to clients simply substituted for a real and meaningful *quandary* a verbal *puzzle* inherently devoid of sense, between whose various possible "meanings" the recipient still had to choose. In this instance, what the women affectively *infer* from the shout happens to be correct.

What reinforces the impression that the shout occurs *during* the dream, but is not part of the dream's *manifest* content, is that Klytaimestra behaves in dream in a very matter-of-fact and efficient way: she gives birth to a snake, nurses it, is bitten by it, swaddles it and then lets it rest. *Not a word* hints at the *experience* of pain or of anguish *in dream*, though one would expect

---

[9] Arist. *Poet.* 1458a24 ff.   [10] Cp. chap. 3, note 19.

[11] A Sedang Moi shaman once shouted in dream: "Ghost! ghost!" and was so obviously in the clutches of a nightmare, that he had to be awakened by those who saw him thrash about. All assumed—correctly—that he had dreamed of being attacked by ghosts, though they did not know exactly *what* he had dreamed until he told them *after* being awakened (*14*). Similarly, if I hear a scream, I can guess that someone is in pain, even though I do not know whether that person has a kidney-stone attack or is being assaulted by a robber, etc.

that to be part of the dream. Then, her task calmly completed, she screams (535).

Now, there are dreams whose affective impact seems incompatible with their manifest content. One may have what *seems* to be a pleasant dream and yet feel very depressed on awakening. (Hom. *Od.* 20.87 ff.) Conversely, a Malay who dreams of being bitten by a snake is cheerful on awakening: his dream foretells luck in amorous intrigues (*11*).[12]

Better still, affect can become totally isolated from symptom and performance.[13] Sappho's mind, as described in *fr.* 31 LP, is totally lucid, for all her anxiety is transposed to the somatic level (*39*).

These data show that it is psychologically possible for Klytaimestra to scream only at the end of a *dream* which "should" arouse anguish, even though her *behaviour* in dream is quite matter of fact. One might even say that her dream behaviour *can* be calm and efficient precisely *because* the horror which the dream "should" inspire is manifested on a *different* level of functioning, in the form of a terminal scream (535).

I therefore accept the view that the scream is, in fact, that of the dreaming Klytaimestra. But I cannot unconditionally agree with Rousseau's flat assertion (*95*, p. 103) that the actual dream event during which she screams is the one when she is *bitten*. While I concede that this is possible, she could have screamed just as appropriately during the pangs of giving birth to the snake. However, v. 535 stongly suggests a scream on awakening, as does the reference to the sleeper's heavy breathing.[14]

On the whole, the text does not permit one to determine *accurately* the dream event which caused the dreamer to scream. Moreover, this vagueness of the narrative, as regards the timing of the scream, only increases its psychological persuasiveness, for the handling of time in dream is notoriously capricious, precisely because the dream is timeless (chap. 8).

There remains the problem that the text *seems* to differentiate between the shouting "power" and the heavily breathing sleeper. This is confirmed by the fact that the shout is frightening, even though one would expect Klytaimestra's scream to express only pain or anguish.

This difficulty is not insuperable. Greek dream theory viewed dream-figures—and the dream itself—as intrusions from the outer world. More important still is Klytaimestra's claim that she is *not only* a mortal woman and wife, but *also* the Atreidai's Alastor (spirit of vengeance: A. *Ag.* 1501)—though the Choros holds that an Alastor simply abets Klytaimestra (1508). This explains, I feel, why the sleeping woman, undergoing a painful experience in dream, does not scream with pain and fright on her *own* behalf, but shouts terrifyingly and breathes wrathfully *in her capacity*

---

[12] I deliberately do not cite here Penelope's *pseudo*-paradoxical tears during her theoretically "encouraging" dream (Hom. *Od.* 19.535 ff.). That dream has, for Penelope as she *really* is, a "discouraging" meaning (*24*).

[13] For certain neurotic housewives, extremely efficient house-cleaning is a means of mastering anxiety (*47*).

[14] One might even imagine the scream to be that of the neonate, physically emitted by the sleeping mother. In one instance an adolescent, while dreaming of being attacked by a lion, growled in *sleep*, just as the lion growled in his *dream*. But such "vicarious vocalizations" in sleep are so rare that they deserve only a footnote. (There may be a human tendency to imitate an aggressive animal's sound, K.J.D.)

as an Alastor[15]—who, at this point, is also the one who will insure that she will be punished. In this sense, her threatening, audible, Alastor-like shout and her matter-of-fact dream reaction to great pain and danger show that the Alastor who shouts *through her* vocal chords is, in the last resort, Klytaimestra's own punitive Super-ego. This is the more credible as, in dream, she herself gives birth to and nurtures her own Alastor: Orestes. Apparently this Alastor uses Klytaimestra's vocal chords as Apollon uses those of the Pythia—for the terrifying shout and the threatening anxiety dream are both products of her Super-ego.

As to the dreaming, the text specifies that it happened at midnight (34: ἀωρόνυκτος), but the awakening probably made it comparable to a traditionally reliable dawn dream.

The Dream's Content

The Stesichorean Model's snake is preserved, though in A. *Choe.* it represents not Agamemnon but Orestes. The model's narrative structure is, however, discarded. The reverse happens in S. *El.*: the snake is replaced by a sceptre, but the Stesichorean narrative's structure remains unchanged[16] (chap. 7).

Before examining the dream's manifest content, detail by detail, a general problem must be considered.

Serpents pervade all of the *Oresteia* and especially the *Choephoroi*. Sooner or later, nearly every important personage is called some kind of snake.[17] Agamemnon is only a partial exception, for the serpent in Aischylos' Stesichorean *model* is Agamemnon (chap. 5). Since, in Aischylos, the dream-snake is Agamemnon's son and avenger Orestes, it is obvious that, in A. *Choe.*, too, the shadow of a serpentine Agamemnon lurks behind the serpentine Orestes.[18] Moreover, whereas in the Stesichorean model the serpent Agamemnon gives (cephalic) birth to a human Orestes, in A. *Choe.* the figurative viper Klytaimestra gives birth[19] to a serpentine Orestes.[20] This development reflects well the pitilessly irresistible progression of even the logically most absurd anxiety dream.

Speaking specifically of Klytaimestra's human image in her own dream,[21] the fact that she gives birth to a snake makes her sufficiently

---

[15] Professor Lloyd-Jones thinks, however, that an Alastor sent the dream.

[16] The tip (head) both of the serpent and of the sceptre "produces" Orestes.

[17] Klytaimestra: *Ag.* 1233, *Choe.* 249, 994f (twice), 1047; Klytaimestra's Erinyes: *Choe.* 1050, *Eum.* 128; Aigisthos: *Choe.* 1047; Orestes: 527, 544, 549, 928; cp. also Apollon's arrows: *Eum.* 181.

[18] Cp. chap. 8 for the equivalence of the avenger and the avenged. Rousseau (*95*, p. 122) complains that interpretations of Klytaimestra's dream confuse the literal (Orestes) and the symbolic (Agamemnon) serpent. He does not see that the two are the same.

[19] Perhaps like a viper (chap. 5), or like a lioness (A. *Ag.* 1258), whose womb her young were thought to destroy (Hdt. 3.108).

[20] Since the slain Agamemnon is, in Stesichoros, a chthonian dream-snake, Klytaimestra, his slayer, is bitten on the breast by her snake-child. See also Mohave beliefs about the snake-like babies of snake-slayers (*38*, p. 253 f.).

[21] Since she puts Orestes to the breast, she cannot be snake-*shaped* in her own dream, though I note that dreams about female snakes are reported from pre-Greek antiquity (*85*, p. 253).

serpentine for the purposes of the dream, even if one ignores both her diabolically serpentine character and the fact that (in Stesichoros) her murdered husband, the father of Orestes, is a snake. The wife and mother of snakes can hardly be anything but a snake (in human shape). The dream requires nothing more than that.

As to the fact that: Serpent = Agamemnon (Stesich.) and Serpent = Orestes (A. *Choe*.), it creates no problem, especially in Klytaimestra's dream. Women fantasy with almost monotonous regularity that they acquire a phallos—that of the husband—by being given a child; i.e., child = phallos (of the husband).[22] There is even striking Greek evidence for this view. Poseidon boasts that the gods always make their women pregnant (Hom. *Od.* 11.249 f.), but, *instead* of impregnating the raped Kainis, he gives her a penis (*25*), turning her into a (penis-proud) man who worships only *his own* spear.[23]

Serpent-Birth is explicitly mentioned (527, 928). Some of my students have argued that this event did not frighten Klytaimestra, for, instead of discarding the young snake, she *promptly* nursed it—which, incidentally, is not realistic, for the newborn hardly ever nurses *at once*.[24] But I think these observations are too literal and disregard, as to fright, the overall impression created by the dream (supra), and, as regards the compression of time,[25] both the timelessness of all dreams and Cicero's accurate observation that nothing is too weird or too absurd to happen in dream.[26]

I feel that the reference to birth has two purposes:

(1) To underscore Klytaimestra's viperine character.

(2) To permit Orestes to assert his identity with the snake, by stressing that both he and the serpent-baby came from the same place (543).

Before I go further, I must scrutinize the details of this birth.

That a live birth—such as that of vipers—is meant, goes without saying. Unlike most serpents, Klytaimestra does *not* lay an egg. This point is worth noting, for her mother, Leda, *did* lay an egg.[27]

I also note that, despite Greek myths about "caesarean births" (Dionysos, Asklepios) (chap. 5), and despite the belief that the viper's young burst through the abdominal wall[28] while the young of the lioness destroy her womb,[29] Orestes must be imagined as being born in the

---

[22] On this equation I cite, once and for all, H. Deutsch's great book: *The Psychology of Women* (*13*).

[23] Apollod. *Ep.* 1.22 and Frazer ad loc. Oddly enough, another Greek spear-worshipper is named Parthenopaios (A. *Sept.* 529).

[24] After giving birth, the mother produces at first not milk, but beestings (colostrum). Real milk is produced somewhat later. In some primitive societies the child is put to the breast only after milk production has begun (*2*, pp. 80 f.).

[25] In dreams, A. *Ag.* 893 f. and chap. 8; in tragedy as a whole, cp. *41*.

[26] Cic. *de. div.* 2.71.146.

[27] Helene: Apollod. 3.10.7; Hyg. *astron.* 2.8, etc. In other versions she was kept in a box (Apollod. 3.10.5). Late tales of the egg-birth of her brothers, the Dioskouroi (sch. Hom. *Od.* 11.298; sch. Lyc. 88; sch. Callim. *in Dian.* 232) were probably inspired by the Moliones myth (Ibyc. *fr.* 285/4P = 16B = 2D).

[28] According to a Tikopian myth, caesarean birth existed *before* birth *per vaginam* (*4*, quoting Raymond Firth). Such notions are rooted in infantile theories of reproduction (navel-birth), also encountered in adult neurotics. (I, myself, treated such a case.)

[29] Klytaimestra = lioness, A. *Ag.* 1258.

normal way. At the same time, one notes that the neutral term: "place" (χῶρος) which Orestes uses, specifies the *place from which* (womb), rather than the *path by which* (vagina), Orestes "left" the maternal body.[30] But the fantasy that birth is an *involuntary* expulsion is not wholly absent. It is simply transposed to a later phase of Orestes' life: as a child he is sent to Strophios (A. *Choe.* 679); later on, he must exile himself after his matricide (A. *Choe.* fin.). This, again, is the process of the "motif-split": the expulsion-fantasy is *detached* from the (active) birth, but *reappears* twice in connection with Orestes' later fate.

In short, there is no direct allusion to a viperine, "abdomen-bursting" birth, though a husband-slaying, viperine wife would deserve that fate. But she gives birth in a manner which does not harm her *at first*.

Still, viperine or leonine models for matricidal births are not altogether forgotten. Like the "expulsion", the matricide, too, is simply *detached* from the birth, and occurs after a certain lapse of time: in dream the matricide occurs during the nursing; in the plot it is postponed until Orestes is an adult.[31] Even so, in at least one text (*AP* 9.126) Klytaimestra mentions two alternatives: a stab in the breast [as in the dream and (with Hermann) in A. *Eum.* 103], or else a stab in the belly (which recalls the viperine birth; also Tac. *Ann.* 14.8).

In short, neither the failure to specify the *manner* of the baby's emergence nor the *non*-synchronicity of the birth and the matricide suffice to obliterate the underlying viperine birth motif. This justifies the ancient view (Ael. *NA* 1.24) that Orestes behaved exactly like a young, father-avenging, mother-destroying viper.

Nursing = Libation. I have already pointed out that the ritual gestures of the libation-bearers, as well as their libations, closely parallel the dream.

I now propose to scrutinize these similarities more closely.

(1) Since both Orestes (in dream) and the dead (chthonian) Agamemnon are "snakes", they are "equivalent" in every significant respect. Thus:

    (a) Orestes = Agamemnon's (human) Erinys = Agamemnon (chap. 4).

    (b) The Avenger = The Avenged. When no avenger is available, the slain man is given a spear, so as to enable his ghost to be his own avenger.[32]

    (2) Agamemnon is given a *liquid* libation (χοή), made of *milk*, honey and wine: Hom. *Od.* 10.518, 11.26. But in ancient times bloody sacrifices were also offered to the dead.[33] We are entitled to ask why no bloody sacrifice is offered in *this* case, by a queen who could well afford it.

---

[30] Interpreters of this dream, who do not read the text carefully enough, might be tempted to view this birth as an allusion to Orestes' (first and/or second) exile from his home, because the neurotic conceives of birth as an expulsion. But the text (ἐκλιπών: quitted) forbids this interpretation. In A. *Choe.*—as in other tales of viperine birth—"being born" is represented as an *active* performance on the part of the baby—*not* of the mother (*44*, chap. 6).

[31] The compression of this interval in the dream is a characteristically dreamlike operation, cp. supra, note 25.

[32] Ps.-D. 47.69; Eur. *Tr.* 1147 f.; Poll. 8.65; Ister ap. *EM* 354.33 ff.; *AB* 237.30 f.; cp. *90*, p. 585.

[33] Cp. *81*, I², p. 180; Hom. *Il.* 23.175 ff.; also Hom. *Od.* 11 passim.

I submit—not dogmatically and yet with some confidence—that bloody sacrifices *revivified* the dead, as in Hom. *Od.* 11.32, etc.[34]—*and that is the last thing Klytaimestra would wish her sacrifice to bring about.* By contrast, like nursing,[35] liquid libations presumably *appeased* (put to rest?) the angry dead—which is what Klytaimestra aims at in dream with regard to the hungry serpent-baby and, in the waking rite, with respect to the angry Agamemnon—but both times too late.[36]

Yet the similarity is even more far-reaching. In reality Klytaimestra caused the Nurse to suckle Orestes in her place. She delegates the libation rite to Elektra[37] and to her house slaves, who actually *comment* on Klytaimestra's *not* performing this rite in person (45 ff., 89 ff., etc.).

But blood—*clotted* blood, on the ground—is none the less mentioned also by the bearers of the bloodless libations (66 ff., etc.) and, in dream, Orestes sucks *clotted* blood from the nipple (533) (infra).

Also, the libation, containing milk, will sooner or later clot,[38] and, as we have already seen, in dream milk is mixed with *clotted* gore. (More on this point below.)

It is this *incomplete* duplication of the dream by the libation that reveals the real nexus between the two. In certain primitive societies, which hold that all dreams must come true, one can avert a major calamity by an anticipatory mock enactment of the dreamed-of catastrophe (*68*, p. 54, etc.), which represents the dream's inevitable but "miniaturized" realization (Aristid. passim).

In short, both the libation and the dream-nursing are meant to be apotropaic, and both fail to achieve their purpose: the libation does not soothe Agamemnon's wrathful shade, nor does the dream nursing render the avenging serpent-baby harmless. For the libation is not offered lovingly and in person, just as the infant Orestes was not lovingly nursed at his mother's breast. The vicariousness and lovelessness of both performances render them ineffectual, though Klytaimestra's deputies perform their respective tasks with loving tenderness. But *that* love comes from them and not from the murderess on whose behalf they act. The psychological spuriousness both of the libation and of the dream nursing renders them ineffective.

A further—and extremely important—similarity between the libation and the dream nursing: the transformation of a "good" libation into "bad" offscourings (vv. 98 ff.), will be discussed further on.

The Fear of a Bite is, in the case of a woman as virile and unmaternal as Klytaimestra, almost certainly a manifestation of the "female castration anxiety", which often equates the (erectile) nipple with the penis, the rest of the breast with the scrotum and milk with semen (*36*).

A literary consideration also suggests this interpretation: the Stesi-

[34] Cp. Odysseus' promise to sacrifice a *fertile* ram and *not* a *barren* heifer (Hom. *Od.* 10.521 ff.) to Teiresias—i.e., to the only ghost whose wits are unimpaired even in Hades (Hom. *Od.* 10.492 ff.).

[35] Hom. *Il.* 22.79 ff.; A. *Choe.* 529.

[36] She is bitten *while* nursing.

[37] Who, in S. *El.*, talks of "nurturing" or "nursing" Orestes (chap. 7) in a manner which recalls the tirade of the Nurse in A. *Choe.* 749 ff.

[38] I am indebted for this point to my friend and student, M. Roger Notz, M.A.

chorean serpent's bleeding crest is preserved or replicated in this dream by the bleeding nipple. The Aischylean modification of the Stesichorean motif presupposes the symbolic equivalence: snake = penis = nipple (cp. the Çatal Hüyük vulture-beak nipples).

It could even be argued that the bitten nipple motif replicates in reverse the bitten penis theme of the *vagina dentata* motif (Folklore Motif F 547.1); an interpretation supported by clinical findings.[39]

It goes without saying that some babies do painfully bite the nipple. But the point is that whereas some women react to this with anguish,[40] other mothers take pride in their *male* babies' violent nursing. What matters here is not that some babies do bite, but that this would make a woman like Klytaimestra *anxious*. After all, in Greek belief, the Mainades nursed young panthers and the like, ostentatiously (counter-phobically) *denying* their fear of being bitten.[41]

I venture to suggest that, underlying the fear of the baby's bite, is the fantasy that nursing represents a kind of cannibalization of the mother,[42] which, in some primitive cultures, is expressed almost explicitly.[43]

Although there seem to have been no Greek tales of children cannibalizing their parents, Herodotos was apparently fascinated by the practice, found among certain "Indians", of a funeral cannibalization of deceased relatives; he mentions this custom twice (Hdt. 3.38, cp. 3.99). Also, I have shown elsewhere (*43*, chap. 5) that the *imputation* of cannibalistic impulses to babies is a projection on the baby of the parents' teknophagic impulses —and it need hardly be recalled that many Greek myths mention the parental cannibalization of children: Kronos, Tantalos, Thyestes, Tereus, (Lykaon?), etc.

The Bite of the Nursing Serpent appears to have more than one root.

(1) Even in modern Macedonia, if a cow's milk contains traces of blood, this is thought to be due to a serpent or a daemon having nursed at her udder.[44] In India, the sacred temple cobras are given bowls of milk. Mohave beliefs about snake-headed babies are cited further on.

(2) For the woman, being bitten by a snake can also symbolize coitus, and especially defloration. Alkestis' bridal chamber was full of snakes (Apollod. 3.9.15). Clinical data paralleling this scene exist.[45] In some folk beliefs snakes may even seek to crawl into a woman's vagina.[46]

---

[39] An analytical patient greatly dreaded injury to his *penis*—and this not only during actual coitus: he carefully wrapped his penis in a blanket before masturbating, fantasying all the while that he was "torturing, oh so gently!"—a girl's *nipple*. (These were the patient's own words.)

[40] Cp. infra: Hera nursing Herakles, and Mohave beliefs about snake-headed babies (*38*, pp. 257 ff.).

[41] Australian women nurse dingo dog puppies (*7*, p. 22). Ainu women nurse bear cubs (*58*), etc.

[42] Cp. the reference, in the next section, to the symmetry between this dream and the feast of Thyestes (note 57).

[43] E.g., the Papuans of Geelvink Bay, infra, note 51.

[44] Information provided by my student, Mme D. Čakuleva-Diamantis, a native of Macedonia (*8*).

[45] Cp. General Introduction, note 10. Phallic giants: chap. 2, note 41.

[46] Even though M. E. Opler (*84*) has tried to prove—absurdly, as La Barre has shown (*64*, p. 327)—that in Japan the snake is *not* a phallic symbol, he mentions the belief that a

That nipple-biting during nursing is related to sexual excitation will be shown in a moment. This indicates that a nursing dream is also a sexual excitation dream.

The Biting of the Nipple is viewed as a major problem in many cultures, and leads to a variety of beliefs, only two of which can be considered here.

In many Euro-Asiatic steppe and tundra cultures, babies born with teeth are believed to become shamans (and witches) later on, and are said to bite the nipple while nursing.[47] I think it is not hazardous to suggest that Orestes resembled an evil shaman in several ways: he committed matricide, he had repeated attacks of madness, he underwent several magical cures, he ended up by (shamanistically) mutilating his finger[48] and even displayed what *may* be lykanthropic traits for, in E. *IT* (296 ff.), he rages in the midst of the cattle like a rabid wolf.

Now, in pleading for her life, Klytaimestra goes out of her way to *deny*, be it only implicitly, that Orestes was born with teeth: she "recalls" that he clasped her nipple with his *gums* (οὖλον) (898). But this idyllic detail is an invention, for not Klytaimestra but the Nurse gave the breast to Orestes (749 ff.) and Klytaimestra's failure to nurse Orestes may well have been traditional, for it reappears, rather surprisingly, in S. *El.* 1143 ff., where the *virgin* Elektra claims to have been the *only* one to "nurse" (figuratively) the infant Orestes (chap. 7). In A. *Choe.* Klytaimestra's spurious claim[49] is part of her attempt to lend force and persuasiveness to the baring of her breasts (infra). Her reference to Orestes' nursing with his gums is therefore automatically suspect. Its main objective is apparently to *deny* that he had teeth that *could* bite, and therefore to deny also the ominous realism of her dream.[50]

This explains her mentioning the "gums"—of which more anon.

Needless to say, the problem here is not whether the "real" Orestes was born with teeth. What matters is that he bites the nipple in Klytaimestra's *dream*. This means that Aischylos represents Klytaimestra as the *type* of (masculine) woman who dreads nursing, fears the baby's ("castrative") bite and views the infant as a destructive, predatory parasite. Such women are not only commonly encountered in paediatric practice, but the con-

snake may crawl into the vagina of a girl who sleeps in the fields. This latter fantasy is so common that even a novel dealing with the Mau Mau revolt (*96*) mentions its exploitation in the interrogation of a captured Mau Mau woman. Among the Jivaro Indians, not a snake but a water daemon enters the vagina of a bathing woman, in the form of a fish or water insect (*63*, p. 221). Alexandros the Great was allegedly fathered by a serpent (Plu. *V. Alex.* 3.1). But in such tales there is *never* an allusion to the intromission of the serpent's *penis*. This forces one to assume that the serpent is thought to crawl into the vagina *head first*, as it does in an obscene novel (*1*) and that its venom plays the role of semen. Professor Verdenius brought to my attentions Onians' (*83*, pp. 108 ff.) finding that, in some Greek beliefs, the semen ultimately originates in the head (as, incidentally, does snake venom!). (Cp. Plu. *fr.* 80, Sandbach and Hes. *Op.* 587≈Alc. Z 23.8 f. LP, also chap. 5 for Greek references to venomous semen.) The fact that in such tales the snake's *entire* body functions as a phallos is almost certainly related to the clinically well-known body = phallos equation (*51*, *69*).

[47] Róheim (*93*) lists many such data; the belief is also found in some American Indian tribes: a nursing Navaho baby was *observed* to hurt its mother (*2*, p. 81).

[48] Cp. Aristid. *Or.* 48.27. This is symbolic self-castration.

[49] Other spurious claims: A. *Ag.* 887 ff., E. *Med.* 256; Ar. *Ran.*, 1469 f. (K.J.D.).

[50] For a further untruth, cp. "Lie Sequence", infra.

ception of the baby as a parent-destroyer is actually a standard belief in various cultures.[51] It was present in Greek culture and is mentioned in A. *Choe.* 749 ff. The Nurse calls the infant Orestes "as witless as a *beast*" (753). In nursing him she had made great sacrifices, spending her "soul" and performing irksome, somewhat disgusting and realistically described tasks.[52]

The biting of the nipple by a snake can be readily linked with a contemporary Macedonian belief (noted supra). Aischylos' dream-imagery probably drew for inspiration on a similar popular superstition.

Even more relevant is the Mohave Indian belief that if a pregnant woman (or even her unborn child's father) *kills* a snake, the baby will be born "snake-headed".[53] Since its poisonous fangs would bite the mother's nipple, it is only fed mush.[54] The mother's killing of a snake and then giving birth to a snake-headed baby likely to bite her recalls Greek tales of the viper's reproduction (chap. 5) and the fact that Klytaimestra herself is called a viper (vv. 249, 994), who, in dream, nurses a snake-baby. In both cases the birth of a snake-baby results from a killing. [The dead Agamemnon is a chthonian snake (chap. 5)].

More significant than any and all these data is the tale of Herakles' nursing at Hera's breasts.

According to D.S. 4.9.6., the infant Herakles was exposed by Alkmene out of fear of Hera, who was, however, persuaded to nurse him herself. But the infant Herakles nursed (and bit?) so fiercely[55] that Hera, unable

[51] "Our children destroy us": Papuans of Geelvink Bay (*94*, p. 91; cp. *22*, p. 307). Nursing is short, for it ruins the mother's breasts and sexual attractiveness: Marquesans (*71*, p. 165), etc. On parent-cannibalizing impulses *imputed* to children, cp. *43*, chap. 5. Greek myths, too, reflect belief in the parent-destroying propensities of *children* (Kronos, Oidipous, etc.). Klytaimestra's dreaming of her fatal nursing *of the baby* Orestes and her being slain *by* the *adult* Orestes show that tales of parricidal adults are derived from fantasies about potentially parent-destroying babies (Oidipous). Gorer and Rickman (*54*) describe the Great Russians' belief that *all* babies are angry and dangerous creatures. That such conceptions of the nature of children are simply projections *of* the parents' hostility to children *upon* their children has been copiously documented elsewhere (*43*, chaps. 4, 5). The "parent-*avenging*" propensities imputed even to unborn vipers (chap. 5) and to *small* children (E. *Suppl.* 1143 ff.; cp. Athene's speech, vv. 1213 ff.) also presuppose their potential dangerousness *to adults*—but in the guise of a socially acceptable reaction-formation against parricidal impulses. Murray's linking of Orestes and Hamlet dimly hints at it (*80*, chap. 8); E. Jones' (*61*) linking of Oidipous and Hamlet enunciates it. One may even speculate that the infant Herakles' slaying of *two* serpents (Pi. *N* 1.33, etc.) should be linked with his having had *two* fathers (Zeus and Amphitryon), one of whom (Zeus) was often represented as a serpent. (But there may have been two serpents because Herakles and Iphikles were twins—but with different fathers, K.J.D.).

[52] Cp. references to defaecation and the washing of dirty diapers (757 ff.). In at least one tribe (*72*) the mother's need to cope with the baby's defaecation apparently puts the child in her debt. In Hom. *Il.* 9.485 ff., the sexually inadequate "man" Phoinix also laments the hardships he endured while raising the infant Achilleus. (Bowdlerized in Q.S. 3.475 ff.) His complaints are, however, less extreme, since, having the body of a man, he *could* not suckle him: he only gave him bread soaked in wine. Achilleus' soiling of his clothes while being *fed* apparently anticipates the Aischylean Nurse's more earthy mention of faeces-soiled diapers.   [53] Probably heredo-syphilitic (*38*, p. 253).

[54] As are all Marquesan babies, as soon as possible—lest the nursing should *spoil* the mother's breasts (supra).

[55] Cp. Genghis Khan's younger brother, infra. His mother—baring her breasts—commanded the angry Genghis Khan to spare him for this reason (*56*).

to bear the pain, threw him away (D.S. 4.39.2.). Under the circumstances, one is not surprised to learn that Herakles subsequently wounded Hera *in the breast* with a poisoned arrow (Hom. *Il.* 5.391 ff.)—i.e., with what Apollon calls a "flying serpent" (A. *Eum.* 181).[56] In these versions, the biting Herakles' rejection by a bad "mother" (Hera) and his subsequent wounding of her breast with a poisoned arrow parallels *point by point* Klytaimestra's failure to nurse Orestes and his biting her nipple in dream, in the shape of a serpent-baby. The two narratives are identical, both structurally and as to latent content.[57]

One begins to see now why, in a society which views babies as devouring beasts and nursing as a hardship which causes pain and drains the woman who nurses (or even a glorified male "wet nurse" like Phoinix), royal babies were regularly entrusted to nurses—and also why Klytaimestra dreams of nursing a serpent-baby.

Mothers in other cultures react differently. Though the Mongols, too, held that biting nurselings born with teeth eventually became sorcerers (shamans), Hoelun's command, that her son, Genghis Khan, spare his rebellious brother *because* that brother had nursed *more vehemently* than he did, betrays maternal pride in such sons. Their violent nursing probably suggested that they would become illustrious warriors (*56*).

I note, as an afterthought, that even though the Mohave also feared the bite of female snake-headed babies, I happen to know of no example of girl babies being said to suck *violently*—nor of a recourse to the "tyranny of the breast" to tame rebellious daughters.

The basic consideration in my linking this dream with various customs from many groups is the *fundamental rule* that what is *custom* in culture A can and does appear as a *subjective fantasy*, etc., in a member of culture B. This rule was justified logically in a work which also instances the possibility of *predicting* from an individual's *private fantasies* the occurrence of a corresponding *formal belief* or practice in *another* culture (*22*, pp. 76 ff.; *44*, chap. 3).[58] These considerations do not exclude, of course, the possibility that Klytaimestra's snake-nursing dream is rooted in part also in some lost Greek popular superstition.[59]

Summing up, Klytaimestra's dream is less prophetic than guilt-laden. Klytaimestra having been a bad mother, it is foreseeable that her son

[56] Endless tales, with many variants, were told about Hera's adoptive nursing and even about her pretended giving birth to Herakles. Preller-Robert (*86*, 2.2, p. 427, note 2 and passim) cite: Paus. 9.25.2. Erastosthenes (ap. Ach. Tat. *intr. Arat.* 24 (in) E. Maass: *Comm. in Arat. reliq.*, p. 55); ps.-Erastosth. *Catast.* 44; sch. Arat. 469; sch. Germ. Caes. BP, p. 104 Br.; Lyc. 1328 ff. and sch. ad loc.; Hyg. *astron.* 2.43; Hsch. s.v. δευτερόποτμος; for vases ibid. 1, p. 171, note 3; 2.2, p. 427, note 1.

[57] I note as a coincidence that the biting = eating of Klytaimestra by her serpent-baby is, in some respects, symmetrical to Thyestes' "unwittingly" eating of his own children. The occurrence of such symmetrical incidents within the *same* group of myths surprises neither the psycho-analyst nor the structuralist.

[58] On the almost incredible variety of cultural and individual ways in which the "inverted penis" idea manifests itself, cp. *20*, *43*, chap. 16. The same is true of the "beings without anus" fantasy (*82*, *21*, *67*, p. 394).

[59] Cp. supra. Harmonia's amphisbaina-shaped necklace is so constructed that the two heads of the "snake" are exactly level with her nipples (Nonn. *Dion.* 5.144 ff.), and I recall that Harmonia herself is eventually metamorphosed into a serpent (E. *Ba.* 1330 ff.).

would retaliate. *Had* she nursed him, she would have given him "poisoned" (un-lovingly given) milk; he repays the quasi-"poisonous" (cp. A. *Eum.* 813) (*non*-maternal) milk given by Klytaimestra's delegate, the Nurse (infra), with a poisonous bite. On a different—and, at this moment, more important—level of (overdetermined) symbolization, Orestes' attack also has an incestuous meaning (infra), symbolized by an oral-biting attack. Seen in this light, the symbolism is plausible. Since the Oedipus complex is infantile, it lends itself especially well to *symbolization* in terms of (infantile) oral-biting aggressivity,[60] rather than in terms of a more mature genital activity.

Maternal Blood is often mentioned in connection with Orestes. This is to be expected for various reasons:

(1) He has to avenge the blood of Agamemnon, by shedding that of Klytaimestra.

(2) The Erinyes never cease urging that Orestes' blood is that of his mother (A. *Eum.* 606 f., etc.), and it is fairly clear that he obtained this blood already *in utero*. In this perspective, the unborn child is automatically a "blood-sucker"—as are the Erinyes (chap. 4). The *real* foetus is fed by the mother's blood stream.

(3) Orestes was purified of the matricide with the blood of a *suckling* pig (A. *Eum.* 448). I note only in passing that purification from filth with filth, though it scandalized Herakleitos (*fr.* 5, D-K), is a fairly widespread custom. What does deserve mention is that, in A. *Choe.* 98, the selfishly sent funeral libations are treated as though they were off-scourings (καθάρματα). But the real problem is why, in Greece, such purifications called for the blood of a *suckling* pig. I do not believe that this was simple due to the relative cheapness of piglets. The use of a pig is understandably because of that animal's chthonian connections. But the need to kill specifically a young—a *suckling*—pig has, to my knowledge, never been fully explained. This rite may hint at an earlier form of purification with the blood of one's *own* child, in which "purification" is combined with punishment[61]—but this is, at best, a guess. I must content myself with pointing out that the use of a suckling pig in purifications presents a problem which I do not feel able to solve at present.

Clotted Blood flowing from a freshly inflicted wound is, as Aischylos the soldier could not but know, an impossibility.[62]

Why then did Aischylos specify *clotted* blood? Two related clues readily come to mind:

(1) The treacherous murderer spits out his victim's clotted blood (A. *fr.* 354; cp. *EM*, p. 118.31).

(2) The Erinyes, whose saliva is venomous (A. *Eum.* 736, 801), or whose heart (*breasts*) secretes venom (813), can be forced to spit out the—*by then clotted*—blood which they have sucked from their victims' mutilated

---

[60] An analysand reported having seen the bathtub full of water and blood when his sister was born. He was told that the stork that had brought the baby had severely bitten the finger of the mother or the midwife . . . he could not recall which (chap. 9).

[61] Cp. the feast of Thyestes; also Harpagos (Hdt. 1.119).

[62] It is one of the body's homeostatic mechanisms (*9*)—lacking in haemophiliacs—that, as blood continues to flow, its clotting capacity increases. This permits the sealing-off of the wound by a blood-clot.

limbs (A. *Choe.* 183). Perhaps Aischylos thought that venomous saliva or snake venom was a coagulant.[63]

But even these suggestive clues do not fully explain why, in the dream, blood clots *at once*, and neither does the reference by the libation-bearers (who bring a *bloodless* sacrifice) to Agamemnon's permanently clotted blood in which the ground is steeped.

The most plausible source of this paradoxical clotting of blood may be the fact that τρέφω (= to nurse) means basically: to congeal, to solidify. In Hes. *Th.* 182, it is even applied to the "congealing" (genesis) of Aphrodite.[64]

Aischylos' repeated references to the eating of *clotted* blood leave little doubt that this practice both horrified and fascinated him.[65] Stimulated perhaps by the meaning: τρέφω = congeal, solidify, he caused the weird dream-baby to drink milk (which will "solidify" *him*) and to suck clotted blood, as do the equally serpentine Erinyes.

In short, the poet disregarded here what the battle-hardened soldier knew; contrary to daily experience, he made *clotted* blood flow from a *fresh* wound—perhaps so as to underscore the snake-baby's affinities with the serpentine Erinyes (chap. 4). This objectively absurd, but symbolically logical, detail therefore increases the authentically oniric character of the dream.

I even venture to suggest that this mention of clotted blood may have been inspired by a paediatric fact, so visible that even primitives like the Navaho Indians have observed it: the neonate sometimes regurgitates (clotted) blood, which he swallowed during birth (*2*, p. 81).

The Mixture of milk and *clotted* blood has an ethnological parallel. The standard food of the warlike Nilo-Hamitic Masai, who originally came from the North, consists of a mixture of milk and blood drawn from the cattle's jugular (= throat!).[66] This mixture is then *clotted* or *curdled* by adding to it cow-urine and ashes.[67] I note that this food contains the three principal fluids that a cow can provide: blood, milk and urine.

The similarity between the mixture which Orestes draws from the breast and the libation offered to Agamemnon has already been discussed.

Orestes' Venom is not explicitly mentioned (but then, neither is the poisonousness of Klytaimestra's milk, infra). Still, vv. 530, 532 do not let us forget that the nursing infant is a snake: the awareness that even a feeble baby-snake's bite is venomous suffuses the entire dream-scene. Orestes is, moreover, called a serpent also outside the dream narrative and is manifestly a human equivalent of his father's serpentine and venomous Erinyes. The avenger of the weak[68]—because dead—Agamemnon, Orestes,

---

[63] Actually, most snake venoms are not coagulants but anti-coagulants.

[64] For a discussion of that passage, cp. *40*.

[65] As it made anxious an anthropologist observing the eating of clotted blood in East Africa (*32*, p. 48).

[66] The Steppe cavalry nomad, who runs short of food or water, also draws blood from his mount's jugular.

[67] Cp. Merker (*79*), or any standard ethnography of the Masai. The A. *Choe.*-Masai parallelism neatly illustrates Róheim's view (*91*) that customs are simply transpositions, to the cultural level, of infantile impulses, fantasies and activities.

[68] Despite A. *Choe.* 323, I take ἀμαυρᾶς (A. *Choe.* 157) to mean "feeble", inefficient (as

is himself weak in dream—a helpless baby-snake—but his bite is nonetheless fatal. At the same time, since Orestes is sent by Apollon to avenge Agamemnon, the baby-snake can be appropriately compared to one of Apollon's poisonous "flying serpents" (arrows; A. *Eum.* 181), wherewith he threatens Klytaimestra's Erinyes, who seek to avenge the slain mother.

In short, the poisonousness of the baby-snake's bite is self-evident. If I say even this much about the matter, it is not because I wish to labour the obvious. I only seek to highlight once again the dazzlingly complex and yet superbly spare texture of each of Aischylos' lines. The moribund Aristophanic myth of hollow Aischylean grandiloquence (Ar. *Ran.* 836 ff.) deserves to be laid to rest at last. Rare are the poets who say half as much as Aischylos, in twice as many words—at least to those willing to listen, willing to let the dramatist's words reverberate in the deeper layers of the hidden mind (*32*, chap. 23). For one must meet the poet's demand for attention not only with the conscious mind, but also with one's unconscious, which mystics call: the Soul. One must give him the rarest of attentions—that which discerns the obvious.

Klytaimestra's Venom = Poisonous Milk. In A. *Ag.* 1260, Kassandra compares Klytaimestra to a "poisoner". In terms of her actual deeds this accusation is undeserved. But if one looks deeper into the matter, the charge may be more than a gratuitous accusation or—as in the Southern United States—a figurative characterization ("she is poison").

As already noted, Klytaimestra is repeatedly compared to various serpents (supra). The Erinyes which she—or her murder—produces are also venomous,[69] and in one instance they are said to produce venom from their *"hearts"*. For the moment I recall only that, even though the real Klytaimestra had her *throat* cut, the ghostly Klytaimestra displays a *breast*-wound (A. *Eum.* 103, Hermann). This recalls the dream far more than the details of her actual slaying.

The notion that Klytaimestra's *milk* might have been thought poisonous therefore deserves close scrutiny.

Before I so much as mention regularly observed clinical facts, I note that—be it intentionally or not—Aischylos himself specifically speaks of the metamorphosis of something "good" into something "revolting". A funeral libation—which contains *milk*—is normally given lovingly and is therefore "good"; it also earns the giver the gratitude and good will of the deceased. But in A. *Choe.* the libation is given not from love but from fear and guilt. Elektra, quite as much as the Choros, discusses at length the cynical and absurd aspects of this "gift". In vv. 97 ff. especially, the libation is called—and treated as—"off-scourings": as the morally and physically contaminated remnants of ritually washed-off soilure (μίασμα). The libation (χοή) becomes (because of the spirit in which it is *sent*—not even given[70]) identical with καθάρματα (= defilements) left over after a ritual cleansing. It earns the sender not gratitude but hatred.

No child analyst could state more clearly the essence of my argument

---

regards the friendly Choros). The equation: child = old = feeble is a commonplace in Greek tragedy—as is the feebleness of dream personages (*33*).

[69] A. *Eum.* 782, 801, 813, cp. chap. 4.

[70] As Orestes was only vicariously breast-fed: by the Nurse, not by his mother (supra).

than does Aischylos: milk given vicariously *and/or without love* is totally evil; it carries contamination, as do the off-scourings of ritual cleansing. In a word, milk *so* given is "poison", even where the hiring of wet nurses is routine, if this causes the *mother* to lose interest in her baby.

This being said, I now turn to a scrutiny of Klytaimestra's performance —or non-performance—as a mother and, in so doing, will cite clinical findings showing that such a mother feeds her infant "poisonous" milk.

Klytaimestra was called a "raging, infernal mother" (A. *Ag.* 1235) *long before* she turned against Agamemnon's children, and A. *Choe.* 749 ff. proves that she did not even nurse Orestes. Yet, for the infant, the giving of the breast represents a gift of love: milk = love. Refused, or reluctantly given, milk is "hate". Hence, one may well ask whether Klytaimestra was ever maternal—even before the sacrificing of Iphigeneia turned her into a wild beast—particularly since, in pre-Euripidean texts, one cannot but feel that that sacrifice is a convenient alibi, rather than the *real* cause of Klytaimestra's savagery. Nor can one forget that, in Euripides' *Telephos*, *she* advised the maimed hero to threaten to kill the infant Orestes, so as to force Achilleus to heal his wound.[71] This is not the behaviour of a good mother, though Euripides was almost the only poet who could—even in his *Elektra*—persuasively attribute ordinary human traits to this she-monster.

In short, it is inconceivable to view Aischylos' Klytaimestra simply as a bad *mother*; in the *Oresteia* she is *all* bad.

Now, from the infant's point of view, the bad mother *par excellence* is one who does not give milk (= love)—or at least does not give it lovingly. This is a commonplace in child psycho-analysis. But, in certain instances, such bad mothering elicits in the neglected child the fantasy of "poisoned milk". The belief of having been fed poisoned milk in infancy is commonly expressed by schizophrenics and also by borderline patients, who had very bad mothers,[72] or whose mothers were unable or unwilling to nurse them, or who were handed over to a wet-nurse (749 ff.), or with whom the mother's milk disagreed,[73] or who were bottle-fed, or were fed mush rather than milk.[74] Of course, the only intermittently insane Orestes is, especially in Aischylos, not a true schizophrenic. He simply has *bouffées délirantes*—a psychiatric disorder common amongst primitive and archaic peoples.[75] He is a "borderline" case.

We can even explain why the son of the unloving, non-nursing, hostile Klytaimestra became not a chronic schizophrenic, but only an inter-mittent psychotic, who finally "recovers" permanently. In view of a case I myself analysed (*28, 30*), and of certain other clinical data, I venture to

---

[71] This radically differs from the advice the Queen of Epeiros gave to Themistokles (Thu. 1.136; Plu. *V. Them.* 24.2). The Telephos myth clearly implies a conditional threat to the baby; the Themistokles story refers only to a Molossian supplication rite.

[72] As did one of my patients, who had this milk = poison fantasy (*28, 30*).

[73] I confidently expect a psychiatric study of such mothers to reveal an unconscious hostility to the child.

[74] The mush-feeding of Marquesan babies is reflected in many myths of man-destroying female daemons (*71*, pp. 204, 214, 226).

[75] On the *bouffée délirante* either as a hysterical psychosis masquerading as a schizo-phrenia in complex cultures, **or** as a schizophrenia masquerading as a hysterical psychosis in archaic or primitive cultures, cp. *43*, chaps. 9, 10).

suggest that he was saved from an irreversible, permanent psychosis by his Nurse, who had lovingly breast-fed him on demand.[76]

But this would not prevent Orestes, neglected by his mother, from fantasying that his mother *had* fed him "poisoned milk", or at least that she "would" have fed him poisoned milk had she nursed him at all. That Klytaimestra *herself* dreams of being bitten *in the breast* by her poison-fanged baby would, in the case of a *real* patient, mean that the dreaming mother herself views her own milk as (symbolically) poisonous. Thus, the infant's venom simply repays the bad mother for the venomous milk she "fed" him—by not nursing him *at all*.

I concede, of course, that the poisonousness of Klytaimestra's milk is not *explicitly* mentioned, but recall that neither is the snake-baby's venom. I feel that the commentators, quite as much as the scholiast(s), make too little of the fact that Orestes draws milk and *clotted* blood from the nipple. I have already discussed the biochemically impossible *clotting* of freshly drawn blood. Here, I simply note that this one verse (533) *suffices* to suggest that it was a *loathsome* mixture (= poison) Orestes had sucked from the breast, and that Aischylos' compliance with the rule of the verse-for-verse stichomythia *enabled* him to say just *enough*, without becoming obvious and revolting.[77] The hypothesis that this mixture is poisonous is indirectly confirmed by A. *Eum.* 184, where the Erinyes *regurgitate* "clotted" blood (sucked from bleeding limbs), mixed with their *venomous* saliva. In A. *Choe.* 533, milk *replaces* the venom of A. *Eum.* 184.

The fantasy of poisonous milk has, moreover, a biochemical model, and this quite apart from the well-known fact that the milk of some ("bad"?) mothers actually disagrees with their babies. Lactose, a major source of calories in milk, can be digested by nearly all babies, for the *immature* organism easily secretes the lactase necessary to digest it. But there appear to be genetic ("racial") differences in the capacity of *adult* organisms to secrete *enough* lactase to digest lactose (75). The Greek "race" *may* have been unable to do so, for *adult* ancient Greeks consumed milk mainly in the form of cheese, in which lactose is already transformed into a substance more digestible for adults. In fact, in Hom. *Od.* 9.297, Polyphemos' drinking of *unmixed* milk is ostentatiously the climax of his *revolting* (cannibalistic) repast.[78]

Somewhat oversimplifying matters: for races whose adult members do *not* secrete much lactase, milk (containing lactose) is a kind of poison—as is *some* mothers' milk for *their* babies.

The folklore equivalent of the mother who yields "poisonous" milk appears to be the sexual "poison damsel",[79] whose close connection with

---

[76] Some psychologically uninformed paediatrists, anxious to please reluctant mothers, still advocate a (psychologically harmful) nursing "on schedule". Most primitives have better sense in this respect, and the Nurse's speech is an important document for the student of Greek child-rearing practices and, therefore, of Greek personality (*31*).

[77] The pace of a stichomythia *can* be slowed if the poet desires it; cp. E. *Ba.* 1269-70 and Dodds ad loc. As pointed out elsewhere (*26*), rules which shackle the poetaster lend wings to the true poet's inspiration.

[78] I note Aischylos' harping upon the fact that the Erinyes repeatedly drink *unmixed* blood (A. *Choe.* 577 f., etc.).

[79] Folklore Motif F582; cp. some "Alexander legends".

serpents is traditional. The poisonous mother's *male* equivalent is Minos, whose ejaculate is venomous.[80] Cp. also Nessos.

Underlying all this is the near-universal conception that *all* bodily secretions have marked (healing or poisonous) magical properties. Milk is no exception to this rule. Though a bad mother's milk is "poison", human milk was also used as a healing medicine in ancient Greece.[81]

The Breast vs. Serpent Motif must be analysed in terms of the fact that both Klytaimestra and Orestes are called serpents—and that Orestes' poisonous bite repays the giving of "poisonous" milk—or the *non*-giving of mother's milk.

A crucial consideration is that a masculine woman like Klytaimestra (A. *Ag.* 11) tends to view the breast as a kind of phallos and its milk as semen (supra). The phallic breast is, in a sense, *pitted against* the phallic snake-baby. The dream therefore reflects a kind of duel of phalloi ... an idea documentable for ancient Greece.[82]

Of course, like all symbolic dream activities, this, too, is ambiguous. A masculine woman pitted her breasts against the phallos, boasting that she could squirt her milk further than a penis could squirt semen (*6*). But other virile women view the breast as obnoxiously hyper-feminine: the Amazons allegedly amputated both their breasts, in order to diminish their femininity.[83] In other traditions the Amazon amputated only her right breast, so that it would not be in the way of the released bow-string.

I propose these interpretations with considerable misgivings: they are possibilities, but no more than that. I mention them mainly to show that I have not overlooked the *possible* "duel of phalloi" element, but refuse to assert that something of the sort was present in Aischylos' mind, be it but in the form of an unconscious fantasy.

The Swaddling Bands are interesting, precisely because their mention seems dramatically so gratuitous.[84] The best guess is that, since son = father,[85] the swaddling bands symbolize the often-mentioned net which immobilized the doomed Agamemnon. But this is, at best, a plausible guess, which sheds less light on the dream itself that upon what caused Aischylos to mention this detail.[86]

---

[80] Apollod. 3.15.1 f., Ant. Lib. *Met.* 41.4 f. Semen = milk is a common symbolic equation. But I note a curious contrast: exposed to air, milk (and blood) *coagulate*, while semen *liquefies*.

[81] Nic. *Alex.* 356, cp. Arist. ap. Plin. *HN* 28.74; also Diosc. 2.70.6; Gal. 6.775, 12.265; Plin. *NH* 28.72.

[82] Cp. the opposing phalloi on a bas-relief from Delos (*76*, p. 55). The avowed purpose of this tablet is to remind one of homoerotic "love". But the (unconscious) aggressive element in homosexuality (*15, 31*) is revealed by the fact that these phalloi face each other in the manner of swords or spears. In Mohave Indian belief, an ithyphallic giant guards the narrow bridge which the souls of the deceased must cross and strikes at them with his phallos. Some phallos-proud young Mohave men boast, however, that they would strike back at him with their own (*38*, p. 229).

[83] As, until recently, the Skopzi also did (*87*).

[84] It is interesting only as information about neonate nursing, followed by swaddling and sleep. But Aischylos hardly inserted this detail for the benefit of latter-day ethnographers.

[85] See chap. 5, especially the comments on the Pleisthenid king.

[86] In addition to countless references in A. *Ag.* to the netting of Agamemnon, I cite, almost at random: A. *Choe.* 492, 506, 529, 557, 982, 998, 1010 ff.; A. *Eum.* 459 ff., 635.

But it deserves mention that swaddling also occurs in a Mesopotamian dream in which Ishtar wraps the king into a baby sling (*85*, p. 207a).

Orestes' Interpretation of the Dream (540 ff.) seems, from the literary point of view, heavy-handed and unnecessary: Athenian audiences were not slow-witted. And, as noted repeatedly, I deny that Aischylos' torrential eloquence was ever over-abundant. What *seems* redundant to the literary critic may contain what, for the psycho-analyst, is an essential datum.

I submit that the dream-interpretation passage has a *purpose*: oracles, as Fenichel (*50*) has shown, are *inherently* ambiguous. I, for my part, hold (*35*) that their ambiguity is a *conditio sine qua non* of their *being* oracles. Hence, they come "true" only *after being interpreted in a particular manner*, which *makes* them come true. This also applies when the interpretation turns out to be "objectively" correct—as when Themistokles *made* the victory at Salamis possible by clutching at the *one* encouraging oracular word: "holy" Salamis (Hdt. 7.143). But it holds true also when the oracle is "misinterpreted". Not the Delphic oracle's utterance, but its "*misunderstanding*" by Oidipous (or by Kroisos), *caused* the predicted misfortune. It is because he seeks to avoid killing his foster-father Polybos and marrying his foster-mother Merope, that Oidipous is led to kill Laios and marry Iokaste. By *thinking* that the great empire which a battle with Kyros will destroy is Persia, Kroisos destroys his own country (Hdt. 1.53 ff., 1.90). (Cp. chap. 2, note 106; chap. 8, note 146.)

Not the prophecy (or dream) but its interpretation makes it "self-fulfilling". In ancient Greece, an *uninterpreted* dream apparently had no consequences.

In short, I hold that Orestes interprets the dream, out loud, in *a* particular way, so as to *make it* come true in *that* particular way. Differently interpreted, the dream's outcome would have been different. Left uninterpreted, it may have had no "consequences" at all. This makes the dream-interpretation passage dramatically indispensable.

I deal here only with the *function* of Orestes' interpretation of the dream. The actual interpretation of the dream must be postponed until vv. 986 ff. are also examined detail by detail.

THE BREAST-BARING SCENE

A careful scrutiny of vv. 896–898 is long overdue, even though the standard text is sound, its meaning clear and the scholion a little less fatuous than usual. What makes this passage interesting is that it contains one brazen lie, one hydrodynamic absurdity and an all but impossible synchronicity of cause and effect. I hope to show that each of these poetic "errors" brilliantly highlights psychological truths.

I begin with a general remark. Literary critics (*95*) have noticed that Klytaimestra's claim is contradicted by the Nurse's credible affirmation that she alone had nursed Orestes—but have not come to grips with the problem. Yet, as already noted, the fact that Klytaimestra had *not* nursed Orestes appears to be traditional, for in S. *El.* 1143 ff. the *virgin* Elektra claims to have been the only one to "nurture" him (chap. 7).

Most critics do not discuss this contradiction. They feel, perhaps, that Klytaimestra is just grasping at cultural straws—or they let it go as an Aischylean lapsus.

Now, as a general principle, when so great a poet *seems* careless, one should enquire whether his "lapsus" has a poetic purpose: whether it is a *means* of highlighting an otherwise elusive and yet important *psychological* truth.[87] It is especially appropriate to envisage this possibility in a drama which contains also another "lie", whose purpose, too, is to highlight an unspoken deeper truth (supra).

The position taken—and justified—here is that the lies and absurdities contained in these three verses shed a great deal of light upon the personality of the Aischylean Klytaimestra and are indispensable for a complete understanding of her dream.

I begin by discussing the concrete details of this passage.

The breast-baring scene replicates in a waking state the baring of the nursing breast in the dream. This is credible behaviour after a dream,[88] and echoes the breast-baring of the libation-bearers (vv. 27 ff.).

The lie—though it cynically and deceitfully claims a right to the respect a child owes the breast that nourished him (Hom. *Il.* 20.80 ff.)—is inspired *also* by the dream (v. 928). Since she had nursed the snake-baby in dream, Klytaimestra may have felt that her claim to have nursed Orestes was valid. The unconscious mind, quite as much as certain primitive and archaic peoples, feels that a dream-performance is real, and that a "right" acquired in dream gives rise to a valid claim in waking life.[89]

But one can also envisage a "legal fiction"[90] which reinforces the previous ones. If, as is likely, the Nurse was Klytaimestra's own slave, Klytaimestra *could probably* have claimed "credit" for the nursing of Orestes. This fantasy of "vicarious physiological functioning" is as striking as it is easy to document, since it is often implemented by actual cultural practices.[91]

But even if Klytaimestra consciously felt that the nursing of Orestes by

---

[87] I have urged elsewhere that the objectively unbelievable gossip that Sappho had been a prostitute and had committed suicide for the love of Phaon indirectly confirms the credible tradition that she was a genuine lesbian (*39*).

[88] Arist. *de div. somn.* 463a25 ff. A man *dreamed* that he broke his leg. The next morning, carelessly descending his home's perfectly safe front steps, he "accidentally on purpose" broke his leg. (Informant: a colleague, cp. *78*.)

[89] A Lengua Indian dreamed that Grubb had stolen his pumpkin and asked for compensation, though he admitted that Grubb *could* not have stolen it, having been away at that time (*57*, pp. 129–130). An Iroquois can claim on awakening the object or favour he had obtained in dream (*98*). Even a modern man may demand that his repeated (but *unkept*) promise be accepted in lieu of its fulfillment (chap. 4, note 61).

[90] Legal fictions are common even in primitive law (*14*).

[91] Cp. the rule evaded by Onan (*Gen.* 38.9). The barren Rachel caused her handmaiden Bilhah to conceive and to bear "her" children (*Gen.* 30). Plinius (*HN* 29.1.19) wrote that slave owners walk with the feet of their (litter-bearing) slaves, etc. A patient, delirious with fever, fantasied that one of his subordinates should *and could* defaecate in his stead. Brigadier M. R. Roberts pointed out to his over-eager brigade major, John Masters—who came running whenever the brigadier left his tent—that even brigadiers had to do their own defaecating (*77*, chap. 11). A systematic exploration of fantasies (and legal fictions) of vicarious physiological functioning—which are patterned upon the foetal state—is long overdue.

her slave *was* vicarious nursing, for which *she* could claim "cultural credit",[92] this did not abolish her subjective guilt feelings. In dream, she herself wittingly puts the snake-baby to her breast, exposing herself to a fatal bite.

This being said, I now pass to the discussion of the actual lie and of the cultural practice which it seeks to exploit.

The Tyranny of the Breast is described in vv. 896 ff.: Klytaimestra bares her bosom to Orestes, half commanding him to stop (ἐπίϲχεϲ) and half demanding shame-respect (αἴδεϲαι)[93]—all on the basis of a lie, or at least of a fiction.

The gesture itself is traditional,[94] but by no means specifically Greek.[95] It exploits the very widespread belief that, by being nursed, the child contracts a lifelong debt. This has a direct bearing on the meaning of this display.

The view that it simply represents supplication disregards the element of *command*—or at least of irresistible persuasion—which is involved in this "dunning" for a lifelong "debt" to the maternal breast. Crucial gestural differences are also disregarded.

(1) *The suppliant* takes hold of his *protector's* chin and knees and beseeches him by these parts of *his* body. He may—ritually or threateningly—also hold his chosen protector's child as a hostage or threaten to defile his altars.[96]

(2) *The dunning mother* displays and lifts *up* her *own* breast and appeals *to it*—to a part of *her own* body. Now, there is ample evidence that the holding or displaying of various parts of *one's own body* is not so much a supplicating as an aggressive, commanding—or even defiant and offensive —gesture.[97]

In short:

(1) The breast-display is maternal role-playing: a commanding *self*-manipulation, representing a dunning for an old debt.

(2) Supplication is infantile role-playing: it involves the manipulation of the *protector's* body; holding on to it *creates*, so to speak, a "debt" of the kind a parent owes to the child.

[92] Even John Locke equated his servant's work with his own (K.J.D.).

[93] On this word and its erotic nuances, cp. infra.

[94] Hom. *Il.* 22.79 f.; E. *El.* 1206 f., *Or.* 527, 841, *Phoin.* 1568 f.; *AP* 9.126. Professor Dover attracted my attention to a vase (*ca.* 500 B.C.) (*74*, pl. 50): a mother (or sister) seeing her son (or brother) off to war, imitates Hekabe rather ineffectively, for she is wearing a vest under her outer garment.

[95] Cp. the Hoelun story (note 55). I note in passing that, like Klytaimestra and Iokaste (E. *Phoin.*), she whom Oriental historians call "Mother Hoelun" was a "strong", widowed mother, who is mentioned mostly *after* the premature death of her husband Yesukai. Like "Madame Mère" (Laetizia Buonaparte), she is much more the strong mother than the pliant wife. This family constellation is that of many conquerors (*27*).

[96] *Telephos myth*: sch. Ar. *Ach.* 332; Hyg. *fab.* 101. *Themistokles*: Thu. 1.136; Plu. *V. Them.* 24. Caricatured in Ar. *Ach.* 326 ff., *Thesm.* 689 ff. In *Gen.* 32.26, Jacob holds the angel until he obtains the blessing he craves. In A. *Suppl.* (787 ff.), the supplication is reinforced by the threat of a temple-defiling suicide; cp. Hdt. 7.141.

[97] *Penis*: Ancient Egypt (D.S. 1.67.6); modern Egypt (K.J.D.); Vietnam (personal observation); Sedang (ditto). *Vulva*: Sparta (Plu. *Lacaen. Ap.* 3, p. 241 B); Persian Empire (Plu. *mul. virt.* 6, p. 246 A. etc.). Cp. Artemid. 4.43. *Anus*: Mohave (*18*). *Breast*: Mohave (*16*). *Thumb* ("fig"): Mediterranean area. *Two spread fingers* ("horns"): Mediterranean area, etc.

This means that Klytaimestra issues a command *and* duns for a debt, in the guise of a supplication.

The details of how Greek mothers bared their breasts are discussed by Leaf,[98] but the gesture itself, in A. *Choe.*, deserves further comment. In Hom. *Il.* 22.79 ff., Hekabe's gesture is described: she *lifts* her aged (and flaccid) breasts with her hands . . . as does many a nursing woman whose breasts are heavy with milk.

Quite apart from the fact that, since Klytaimestra must still be imagined as sexually attractive and therefore firm-breasted (infra)—so that she need not "lift" her breasts—the text gives no details and stage directions have not come down to us. We can be sure only that, since Klytaimestra was played by a male actor, the displaying of the breasts was reduced to a sketchy approximation of the Homeric Hekabe's gesture.[99]

Far more important than the actor's actual performance on-stage is the nexus between the dream and the murder scene. In dream Klytaimestra actually *offers* her breast to the serpent-baby (531). The dream gesture and the stage gesture represent a kind of motif-splitting: the Homeric breast-lifting is inverted in dream; the baby is *lifted to* the breast. The breast-*display* is emphasized only in the murder scene. But this is at best a minor point, requiring no elaborate analysis.

I note in conclusion again, that I know of no example of a maternal command given to a disobedient *daughter* which is reinforced by the display of the breasts that nursed her.

Professor Dover plausibly suggests to me that, since daughters are not fighters, occasions for adjuring them strongly were different and fewer. I accept this as a valid explanation based on reality—but feel I should add a second, more "psychological", explanation: I know of no Greek mention of baby girls who nursed violently and painfully—but admit that girl babies are seldom mentioned. This may perhaps mean that girls owe a *lesser* debt than boys to their mothers.[100]

But there is present here also a deeper and more oedipal element, which deserves to be considered as carefully as the "oral debt" theme.

Sexual components: αἴδεσαι = show shame-reverence. Ἀιδώς—etymologically connected with αἰδοῖα = genitals—has many shadings: shame, reverence, modesty, bashfulness.

Now, in most languages, words denoting affects have many nuances which do not fully overlap with those of their supposed equivalents in *other* languages. The word αἰδώς assuredly has no real equivalent in English.[101]

---

[98] In his edition of the *Iliad* 2, p. 596, App. G-5 f.

[99] Had the actor displayed artificial, flaccid breasts, the comic poets would probably have had a field day with it—either when the play was first produced, or when it was revived—mocking the scene as they mocked the Euripidean Telephos' realistic rags, which were the first of a series (Ar. *Ach.* 414–431).

[100] Both the Nurse and Phoinix complain about the trouble of raising boys (Hom. *Il.* 9.492 ff. cp. E. *Phoin.* 1433). (I recall that the mortality of boy babies is higher than that of baby girls.)

[101] To make matters worse, language A may routinely associate certain affects with certain reactions in a manner which seems wholly inappropriate to persons speaking a different tongue. Thus, I was startled by the information that the (aggressive) Sedang call

I confidently state that αἰδώς *always* has a nuance of sexuality.[102]

The point of the display of the breast is that the *adult* son is shown that which he should *cease to see* as soon as female breasts begin to arouse him sexually. This is why this gesture elicits a sexually tinged shame.[103]

The second meaning of αἰδώς (reverence) has a somewhat different source. The display of the maternal breast is also expected to elicit a *psycho-sexual regression*[104] to the outlook of infancy—to the time when the maternal breast represented nourishing love: the *summum bonum* which elicits reverent awe.

Reaction to the Display: Though his duty as champion of the Trojans prevents Hektor from obeying Hekabe's tender but commanding gesture (Hom. *Il.* 22.80 f.), he is obviously moved by it. He would, one feels, have complied, had it been possible for him to do so, for Hekabe is consistently described as a good mother. We cannot but believe her claim that she had lovingly nursed the infant Hektor, stilling his hunger (= grief).[105] Of course, Hektor displays reverence, and even awe, far more than sexual shame. But even a reaction of awe does not *automatically* exclude a partly sexual reaction.[106]

Before I contrast Hektor's reaction with that of Orestes, I note that the Greek poets also mention the non-maternal, *erotic* display of the female breast as a means of seductive supplication: When the recaptured Helene bared her breast to the wrathful Menelaos, the sword fell from his hand and he kissed his irresistible wife.[107]

Disregarding the sexual element, the baring of the maternal breast represents, as was shown, a "dunning" recall of an old debt. In fact, the display reproduces the opening phase of actual nursing, in the hope of mobilizing memory traces of oral gratification and dependence *only*. Because old Hekabe's breasts are too flaccid to arouse erotic responses,

the erect penis an "angry" penis (suggesting the occurrence of anger-erections) and that a nude Sedang man feels "shame" (*lim*) when seen by another man, but "anger" (*hō*) when seen by a woman. The (drunken) Hungarian's tendency to "rejoice with tears" is a proudly self-ascribed ethnic trait for Hungarians, though it must seem silly or degrading to non-Hungarians (*44*, chap. 6).

[102] Even the Homeric "αἰδώς ᾿Αργεῖοι" (Hom. *Il.* 5.787, 8.228) has a sexual nuance. The Argives are to be shamed into displaying their manhood—which, in Greek thought, includes that *virility* which the effiminate and cowardly Dionysos so conspicuously lacks (*45*).

[103] Oidipous justified his self-blinding by recalling that he *saw* what he should *no longer* have seen (S. *OT* 1271 ff.).

[104] A Mohave woman may insultingly display her breast to a man, and even offer to nurse him; this implies that she regards him as an impotent boy child (*16*). She imputes to him a regression from manhood to infancy.

[105] The Greek expression is hard to translate exactly: "forget worries" (Mazon), "lull pains" (A. T. Murray), "consolation" (Lang, Leaf, Myers). As regards the wording, there is mention of the κόλπος of Hekabe's robe. This word can denote "hollows" in general—including even the vagina and the womb. That sense is attested already in E. *Hel.* 1145 (lyrical passage) and (for a sinus of the womb) in Hp. *Nat. Puer.* 31.

[106] Cp. the worship of the *yoni* in India. On the "phallos-awe" of certain women, cp. *55*; on its presence in Sapph. *fr.* 31 LP, cp. *39*. A grotesque mistake can sometimes highlight an important psychological connection. One of Professor Dover's less able students translated Helene's reverent words to Priamos: "αἰδοῖος τε μοί ἐσσι" (Hom. *Il.* 3.172) as: "You are a foolish man"—influenced by the English idiom: "You're a prick!"

[107] Ar. *Lys.* 155 ff.; E. *Andr.* 628, etc.

and resemble her milk-heavy breasts of yore, she is able to mobilize early and gentle memory traces in Hektor,[108] who must remind himself of his duties as *the* champion of Troy in order to disobey this tender maternal command. He resists it, but in a reverent and loving spirit: the man triumphs over the child and the son. Being psychologically normal, he refuses to "regress".

The neurotic Orestes is in a very different situation. To begin with, Klytaimestra's breasts may *not* be imagined as pendulous, for she had not nursed Orestes—nor, one may suppose, her daughters Elektra and Iphigeneia. Such a multiparous, but non-nursing, beautiful woman's breasts can be firm and attractive even past the age of fifty. This hypothesis is confirmed by at least two references to a *still on-going* sexual relationship between Klytaimestra and Aigisthos.[109] Orestes therefore sees firm and youthful breasts—not the pendulous breasts of an aged or nursing woman—and such breasts can hardly evoke *for him* tender and pious memories of the nursing breast—even of those of his old Nurse. They appear to remind Orestes chiefly of their capacity to thrill Aigisthos the adulterer —and this angers him (904 ff., 917).

Klytaimestra does not improve her chances of survival by ineptly saying: "I was the one who nourished you and with you I would *grow* old" (908). Her remark only underscores that she is *not yet* old and unattractive. Hence, Orestes reacts to her wish to live with him with oedipal horror—as if in response to a maternal attempt at "seduction" (919), which it *probably* is (cp. chap. 2: Io and Inachos).

Last, but not least, one must recall that, since Klytaimestra's tale of nursing Orestes is a lie, Orestes had *never before* had a glimpse of his mother's breasts. For this reason, too, they cannot evoke memories of comforting *milk*. If they subjectively affect Orestes at all, they do so only sexually, as the sight of any pair of firm breasts would affect a young man. What makes him hesitate after the display is not *personal* emotion but a *cultural* reflex.

An anxiety-arousing sexual reaction on the part of Orestes can be inferred also on the basis of other considerations. Having been sent abroad early, Orestes had no time to develop a *sense* of kinship with Klytaimestra. In fact, the *lack* of this sense of kinship between mother and son—which is the legal and psychological theme of A. *Eum.*—no doubt facilitated Orestes' slaying of a woman whom, though she is biologically his mother, he apprehends functionally only as a seductive woman: as his father's sensual, adulterous wife. In this respect the sending abroad of the child Orestes is a psychologically necessary detail of the plot, for it increases the credibility of the matricide.

---

[108] That memory traces of the nursing breast are present even in adulthood is proven by the "Isakower phenomenon" (*59*) and by B. D. Lewin's (*70*) demonstration that the "dream screen"—the background in front of which the dream events occur—is actually the image of the breast, as seen by the nurseling.

[109] Vv. 904 ff., 917; but vv. 132 ff. probably refer to the time of Elektra's first youth. Professor Dover concurs: "I agree that we should think of Klytaimestra as still having strong sex-appeal. The idea that she and Aigisthos are *still* attractive to each other is important." Cf. A. *Ag.* 1654, *Choe.* 594, 893, 905, S. *El.* 589.

This selfsame lack of *daily* familiarity would also facilitate a non-filial, sexual reaction to Klytaimestra's displayed breasts.[110]

I hold, in short, that Orestes reacted to the display of Klytaimestra's breasts not filially but sexually—which only further exasperated his frustrated oedipal jealousies, thereby facilitating matricide.[111]

These findings bring one to a conclusion well known to child psychologists: some mothers—and especially inadequate ones—behave very seductively towards their infant sons. This is confirmed both by clinical data and by primitive and peasant customs.[112]

Now, though maternal seductiveness is a psycho-analytical commonplace, it is always discussed somewhat gingerly, perhaps because, at the beginning of his career, Freud allowed some of his patients to persuade him that they had been *physically* seduced in childhood. After he realized that these tales simply misrepresented the *psychological* seductiveness of parents, he and other psycho-analysts soft-pedalled—though they never denied outright—seductive parental behaviour. Still, so far as I know, I am the only classical psycho-analyst (*19, 23, 44*, chap. 7) to have drawn the inevitable conclusion that the child's Oedipus-complex is triggered by the *pre*-existing Jocasta (or Laius) complex of the parents, which manifests itself in seductive behaviour, particularly on the part of the mother who, as modern experimental evidence proves, is genitally aroused by nursing.[113]

It therefore makes good psychological sense that, in the most famous of all incest myths, Oidipous was exposed at birth—i.e., presumably *before* Iokaste ever nursed him. And, therefore, it also makes excellent psychological sense that, in S. *OT* (707 ff., 980 ff.), this (bad, non-nursing) mother tenaciously ridicules the dreams and hints concerning incest, which greatly alarm her son-husband. The conclusion is inescapable that the possibility that she may have married her son disturbs her *not at all*—

[110] Amongst the Azande, whose kings marry their daughters, the daughters are sent away at an early age, so that no "father-daughter" sentiments may develop and obstruct later on the coming into being of a sexual response (*48*). The following custom, which I quote from memory, has similar implications: in a certain European peasant society, brother-sister marriages were formerly sometimes arranged, so as to avoid the dividing up of the family's land. One of the future spouses was therefore not raised at home, but was sent far away, so as *not* to develop sibling-feelings towards his (or her) future spouse. On familiarity as an obstacle to sexual arousal, cp. Westermarck's somewhat extreme arguments (*99*, chaps. 14–15) and their critique by Loeb and Toffelmier (*73*).

[111] Cp. Hamlet's jealousy of his uncle's sexual intimacy with his mother (*61*). One of my Plains Indian patients left home during his adolescence, when he found his widowed mother in bed with her lover, for he had unconsciously desired to become his father's oedipal successor (*37*, pp. 290 f. and passim)—a hope commonly observed in fatherless boys and, *mutatis mutandis*, also in motherless girls.

[112] Navaho mothers and Hungarian peasant wet-nurses soothe *crying* (boy) babies by stroking their genitals: sexual stimulation replaces or reinforces the soothing and affectionate giving of the breast. A baby boy, taken from the breast before his hunger is stilled, promptly has an (anxiety) erection.

[113] A nursing woman sometimes insists on giving the breast to her husband or lover. Amongst the Navaho, if the woman has "too much" milk, custom demands that the husband draw off the excess (*2*, p. 90). The strict Mohave taboo on a man's kissing his (even non-nursing) wife's breasts constitutes a cultural defence against what appears to be a strong temptation to "imitate" incest by such an act (*17*).

though it panicks Oidipous. A better way of instancing the Jocasta-complex would be hard to devise.[114]

In short, while the display of the breasts is primarily a dunning, it is secondarily also a counter-oedipally actuated seduction, comparable *in part*, to Helene's seductive-supplicating display of her irresistible breasts to the murderously angry Menelaos. One would expect as much from a woman like Klytaimestra, who happens to be also Helene's sister.

The Gums play no role in suction. The baby's lips enclose the nipple hermetically. This permits the creation of a vacuum in the oral cavity, which draws the milk from the breast. It is a matter of hydrodynamics only, discernible by commonsense reflection.

The function of the gums is different. They simply clamp the nipple, keeping it in position and preventing its (accidental or voluntary) premature withdrawal. The more elusive, the more frustrating the nipple is, the harder the baby's gums—and, later on, teeth—will clamp it.

None the less, Klytaimestra's claim that Orestes *nursed* with his *gums*, does have a psychological sense. Had she nursed Orestes, she would have done so *callously* (supra). Hence, her infant son would have *had* to clamp her nipple very hard, to prevent its *premature* withdrawal.[115]

But Klytaimestra was an even more frustrating mother: she did not nurse Orestes *at all*. This is why her *lie* ascribes so great a role to Orestes' gums and why, in dream, the snake bites her nipple. For *only frustrated* babies "bite" the breast, trying to prevent its escape and—as the adult imagines it—"punishing" it for its elusiveness.[116]

Klytaimestra's *lie* about the gums simply means: "had I nursed Orestes, he *would have had* to clamp down hard on my reluctant nipple". Her *dream* says: "I *deserve* being bitten in the breast for *not* having nursed my son."

In short, both the factual lie and the fantastic dream reveal an important *psychological* truth. Furthermore, there is also—in accordance with the law of overdetermination—another nexus between the biting (teeth) of the dream and the sucking gums of the lie: Klytaimestra's absurd reference to gums seeks to *deny* the possibility of a fatal bite conjured up by the dream.

No woman who had *lovingly* nursed her baby would have had Klytai-mestra's dream—and none would have ascribed an absurd role to the gums during nursing. Above all, no mother who had lovingly nursed her son would have been slain by him—probably not even if she had *subse-*

[114] Freud's oft-repeated remark, that his discoveries were anticipated by the poets, is confirmed by the fact that a fine novelist, Mary Renault (*89*, p. 93) highlighted this Sophoklean trait far better than certain psycho-analysts, who keep on writing about S. *OT*—but dissect mostly the nuances of *inaccurate verse translations*.

[115] In Bali, many mothers deliberately tease their nursing babies by repeatedly withdrawing the breast *before* the baby is satiated (*3*) and, as already noted, boy babies react to such frustrations with an anxiety erection.

[116] The frustrated baby is capable of anger and of angry biting. But its nervous system is not sufficiently developed (myelinized) for this biting to be able to represent *for it* a "retaliation", for a baby has no sense of cause and effect, nor can it think or fantasy in any meaningful sense. It is the frustrating mother herself who *views* this angry biting as a "retaliation". But it is worth adding that many adults—including even *some* child analysts —systematically project their own fantasies on infants (*23, 34, 43*, chaps. 4, 5, cp. *10*). In this respect, the Aischylean Nurse is more realistic than are Klein-ian "analysts".

quently killed the boy's father. Hence, no matter what tradition and the text insistently harp on, the *real* (not just: the plausible) cause of Orestes' matricide was Klytaimestra's inadequacy as a mother and, secondarily, her "infidelity" to her emotionally immature son, who hated Aigisthos with an oedipally jealous hatred and felt that his mother had "cuckolded" *him* quite as much as she had cuckolded his father. I cannot do better than cite v. 917: "*Shame* forbids me that I should mention this infamous salary." The full impact of this verse can be felt only by those who sense that this "shame" and silence are not inspired simply by cultural regulations but also (and perhaps even primarily) by Orestes' need to conceal—especially from himself—the oedipal jealousy which motivates so much of his rage.[117]

Nursing Followed by Sleep is the normal sequence. In Hom. *Il.* 22.79 ff., Hekabe recalls that Hektor nursed, was appeased and then slept. *In the actual dream-sequence*, Orestes is swaddled and "sleeps", *after* nursing and biting (526 ff.). But, as already noted, Aischylos *mentions* rest *before* its cause (nursing), but specifies, of course, that it is the *end* of the dream-happening.

By contrast, *in the lie* (896 ff.), the infant is said to nurse *while* very drowsy—a manifest impossibility, as anyone taking the trouble to watch or to ask a young mother will discover. For it is this *lapsus* which makes Klytaimestra's lie a psychologically credible self-betrayal—and her need for punishment is pitilessly revealed by her dream. Indeed, in real life, so obvious a *lapsus*—the affirmation of so manifest an impossibility—in the midst of a lie on whose credibility one stakes one's life, would reveal that the liar had a compulsion to confess (D.S. 2.14.4) and a need to be punished (*88*)—and that is easily inferable from Klytaimestra's dream.

I also note the word order in the *lie*: though sleeping and nursing are represented as simultaneous, sleeping is again *mentioned* first, whereas in the dream-*narrative* the *final* satiated sleep is simply mentioned *before* its cause (nursing), the sleep being realistically represented as the *end* of the tale (dream).

This striking narrative sequence, like the word order in the lie, may, perhaps, be correlated with two facts.

The Nurse's narrative does *not* mention the satiated baby's sleep, but does mention that *her own* sleep was interrupted by the hungry *baby's* cries. As to Klytaimestra, she *herself* is, in fact, asleep *while* nursing her serpent-baby in dream. In her lie, however, it is the *baby* (Orestes) who is drowsy *while* (allegedly) sucking his *non-sleeping* mother's nipple. Since a dream-nursing is, objectively, not real and since very drowsy babies do not nurse, the symmetry between the two fictions—the dream and the lie—is manifest also in this respect.

Such symmetries and echoes cannot be *intentionally* contrived even by

---

[117] Though Malinowski believed he had "proven" the inapplicability of the Oedipus theory to a matrilineal society, which allegedly—but only allegedly (*92*)—denies the existence of paternity, even children in orphanages and adopted children develop full-blown Oedipus complexes in the usual way. Orestes' oedipal jealousy of Aigisthos is as authentic as Hamlet's hatred of his murderous and adulterous uncle (*61*), who behaved exactly as Aigisthos had behaved. On Orestes' affinities with Hamlet, cp. G. Murray (*80*, chap. 8).

the most experienced psycho-analyst, but seem to "come naturally" to a great poet. The literary critic, quite as much as the psycho-analyst—plodding along far behind the poet—can at times, with great effort and patience, follow on the ground the shadow of Pegasos flying effortlessly through the airs.

These findings have some bearing even on a problem of textual criticism. The *order of words* in the lie (sleep before nursing) and the interruption of the Nurse's sleep by the hungry baby's cries explain *in part* why I feel that, in the dream-narrative, vv. 528 f. (mentioning "being put to rest" = to sleep) are in the right place and should *not* be transposed after vv. 529–33, which tell of the nursing which led up to sleep.

Though this point has already been made in the General Introduction (and passim), I wish to stress here once more that, at this juncture, I am not "psycho-analysing" Aischylos. I am simply retracing the relationships between three interrelated passages of his drama and clarifying the nexus between the various images and narrative sequences. It is the manner in which the poet's mind operates that lends to his personages that psychological plausibility which this book seeks to highlight: the great dramatist's personages are real enough to be as analysable *as if* they had existence and being. In analysing the shallower and more obviously contrived personages of a *lesser* poet, one invariably ends up by analysing the author *only*—for he does not create psychologically credible, and therefore analysable, personages.

Interpretation

The Psycho-Analytical Interpretation of the dream should, by now, be self-evident: Klytaimestra, harassed by guilt feelings over not having nursed her son and also over Agamemnon's murder, fuses the two self-reproaches into one, and, in so doing, also fuses Agamemnon with his natural avenger, Orestes. This explains why Aischylos turned the Stesichorean snake, representing Agamemnon, into one representing Orestes.

Before I go further, I must clear up one point of considerable importance. Though the masculine (A. *Ag.* 11) Klytaimestra behaves in a highly non-maternal and sadistic way towards Orestes, in dream she is almost masochistically maternal, since, though bitten in the breast, she swaddles Orestes and lets him sleep. This contrasts sharply with Hera's throwing away the violently-nursing infant Herakles (supra).

This implies that, in her dream-behaviour—which deviates utterly from her real conduct—Klytaimestra does, after all, fulfil her female-maternal potential for nursing a son at her breast. This discrepancy between her actual and her dream conduct only increases the plausibiliy of her dream, for, especially in the case of masculine, non-maternal women, one often observes behaviour which is a *disguised* manifestation of the need to play the mother. Klytaimestra's choice of a weak, effeminate (305) lover, whom she has to protect and who owes everything to her, is typical of certain viragoes, who find an outlet for their inhibited maternal impulses in marrying a weakling.[118]

[118] Her calling the *dead* Aigisthos "valiant" (893) manifestly negates the real facts,

The inference that Klytaimestra does in dream what she failed to do in reality is strongly supported by the fact that in A. *Choe.* she "makes up" in dream for her failure to nurse Orestes, while in her S. *El.* dream she symbolically resumes her interrupted sexual relations with Agamemnon. These differences are only to be expected, for whereas, in A. *Choe.*, she is chiefly a bad mother, in S. *El.* she is mainly a murderous wife. In both dreams she "atones" for her sins of omission (and also of commission)—in each case with fatal results.

One also notes that in A. *Choe.*, though the dream threat emanates from Orestes, Klytaimestra—on awakening—seeks to appease *only* Agamemnon's shade. This is partly justified, since she no doubt feels that only as long as Agamemnon's wrath lasts would he—or his Erinys— incite Orestes to avenge him. However, despite her dream, she is self-destructively blind to the fact that Orestes has also strictly personal and realistic grievances against her—his exile and loss of fortune—as well as two infantile grievances: his mother had not nursed him and had also frustrated his oedipal ambitions, by making not him but Aigisthos Agamemnon's successor in her bed. Klytaimestra's oversight of these resentments is typically self-punitive and explains her subsequent tactical errors: the display of her breasts which, never having nursed Orestes, elicit no tender gratitude, and the implicit seductiveness of her wish to spend her—not yet attained—old age at Orestes' side, which only stimulates oedipal anxiety and anger in him.

The dream therefore clearly reflects the Super-ego inspired need to confess and to atone, commonly encountered in psychiatric practice (*88*) and already mentioned in D.S. 2.14.4. It satisfies self-punitive needs: Klytaimestra herself puts the serpent-baby to her breast and exposes herself to his bite.

There remains to be discussed a matter connected with a major controversy amongst classical psycho-analysts. Freud's first theory asserted that all dreams represent wish-fulfillment. When confronted, during World War I, with repetitive and unpleasant war dreams, in order to preserve his wish-fulfillment theory of dreaming, Freud invented the *primary* death instinct, which such dreams supposedly gratify (*53*). Since this "instinct" has no clinical applicability (*42*, p. 399), and since there is no imaginable way of determining its existence,[119] I refuse to view Klytaimestra's dream as gratifying a (non-existent) *primary* death instinct.

I hold that her dream contains erotic instinctual gratifications, for—as already noted—nursing involves a sexual arousal. Her "gratification" is,

which are constantly stressed in A. *Ag.* and in A. *Choe.* This maternal, older wife—sonlike younger lover, pattern is clearly present in early myths about various mother-goddesses and their juvenile son-husbands. Though partly obliterated, traces of the same pattern are discernible also in the relationship between Iokaste and Oidipous, especially in S. *OT*.

[119] Cp. *97*, s.vv. Instinct Theory, Death Instinct, etc. Attempts to link this "instinct"— as some have done (*5*, *12*, *62*)—with the second law of thermodynamics are absurd, for a system is not *propelled* towards entropy by a "force" (instinct); it only "drifts" towards a statistically more probable state. Also, since inorganic matter cannot "collect" memories, when that matter becomes part of a living system it cannot in any sense desire to *return* to a state *of which it has no memory*. Hence, many classical analysts—myself included— totally reject the death instinct theory (*49*, etc.).

however, tainted by anxiety and by the need for atonement; it therefore occurs in the form of an "erotized anxiety" (discernible also in the repetitive war dreams, which Freud simply did not analyse carefully enough). Otherwise expressed, Klytaimestra's dream provides an erotic gratification *with built-in punishment*. This phenomenon can be observed in many cases of neurotic and perverted (masochistic) behaviour, particularly in the case of women whose sexual conduct is incompatible with their early "moral" education.[120]

The finding that the nursing dream implies both erotic gratification and pain parallels the Nurse's expression of passionate love for a child whose nursing subjected her to so many hardships.[121] I might as well add at once that, in my opinion, some women's insistence that nursing is (primarily or even exclusively) a "hardship", parallels their fraudulent claims, especially in puritanical societies, that marital relations are also an unpleasant drudgery.[122]

In short, considering the Aischylean Klytaimestra's life history and character, her dream is psychologically doubly credible. It gratifies the erotic drives of an extremely sensual woman—but does so by means of a built-in self-punishment. This, in turn, gratifies the bad mother's and adulterous and husband-killing wife's relentless Super-ego, by meting out to her a punishment which her rational Ego dreads, but which her guilt-laden unconscious mind craves. This means that Klytaimestra's dream is one of the most superbly convincing feats performed by Aischylos, the intuitive "psychologist" (*Menschenkenner*).

Bibliography

(1) Arsan, Emmanuelle: *L'Anti-Vierge*. Paris, 1968.

(2) Bailey, F. L.: Some Sex Beliefs and Practices in a Navaho Community, *Papers of the Peabody Museum of American Archaeology and Ethnology, Harvard University* vol. 40, no. 2. Cambridge, Massachusetts, 1950.

(3) Bateson, Gregory and Mead, Margaret: *Balinese Character* (Special Publications of the New York Academy of Sciences vol. 2). New York, 1942.

(4) Belmont, Nicole: *Les Signes de la Naissance*. Paris, 1971.

(5) Bernfeld, S. and Feitelberg, S.: The Principle of Entropy and the Death Instinct, *International Journal of Psycho-Analysis* 12:61–81, 1931.

(6) Briehl, Walter and Kulka, E. W.: Lactation in a Virgin, *Psychoanalytic Quarterly* 4:484–512, 1935.

(7) Buschan, Georg (ed.): *Illustrierte Völkerkunde* 2. Stuttgart, 1923.

(8) Čakuleva-Diamantis, Dobrila: Personal Communication.

---

[120] The first chapters of one of Laforgue's books (*65*) cite striking examples of quests for punishment, disguised as unbridled quests for sexual pleasure.

[121] The Sedang hold that a mother *begins* to love her baby only after she starts to nurse him (*14, 22*, p. 318). Amongst primitives, infanticide seldom occurs after the onset of nursing; exceptions to this rule are quite rare (*22*).

[122] This double fraud provides the basis for the American "alimony racket".

(9) Cannon, W. B.: *The Wisdom of the Body*. New York, 1939.

(10) Chombart de Lauwe, M.-J.: *Un Monde Autre: l'Enfance*. Paris, 1971.

(11) Clifford, (Sir) Hugh: "At a Malayan Court" (in) *The Further Side of Silence*. New York, 1922.

(12) Cochrane, A. D.: Elie Metschnikoff and his Theory of an "Instinct de la Mort", *International Journal of Psycho-Analysis* 15:265–270, 1934.

(13) Deutsch, Helene: *The Psychology of Women* 2 vols. New York, 1944–1945.

(14) Devereux, George: *Sedang Field Notes* (MS.), 1933–1935.

(15) id.: Institutionalized Homosexuality of the Mohave Indians, *Human Biology* 9:498–527, 1937.

(16) id.: Mohave Orality: An Analysis of Nursing and Weaning Customs, *Psychoanalytic Quarterly* 16:519–546, 1947.

(17) id.: Heterosexual Behavior of the Mohave Indians (in) Róheim, Géza (ed.): *Psychoanalysis and the Social Sciences* 2. New York, 1950.

(18) id.: Mohave Indian Verbal and Motor Profanity (in) Róheim, Géza (ed.): *Psychoanalysis and the Social Sciences* 3. New York, 1951.

(19) id.: Why Oedipus Killed Laïus: A Note on the Complementary Oedipus Complex, *International Journal of Psycho-Analysis* 34:132–141, 1953.

(20) id.: Primitive Genital Mutilations in a Neurotic's Dream, *Journal of the American Psychoanalytic Association* 2:483–492, 1954.

(21) id.: The Denial of the Anus in Neurosis and Culture, *Bulletin of the Philadelphia Association for Psychoanalysis* 4:24–27, 1954.

(22) id.: *A Study of Abortion in Primitive Societies*. New York, 1955,[2] 1975.

(23) id.: *Therapeutic Education*. New York, 1956.

(24) id.: Penelope's Character, *Psychoanalytic Quarterly* 26:378–386, 1957.

(25) id.: The Awarding of a Penis as Compensation for Rape, *International Journal of Psycho-Analysis* 38:398–401, 1957.

(26) id.: Art and Mythology: A General Theory (in) Kaplan, Bert (ed.): *Studying Personality Cross-Culturally*. Evanston, Illinois, 1961.

(27) id.: La Psychanalyse et l'Histoire: Une Application à l'Histoire de Sparte, *Annales: Economies, Sociétés, Civilisations* 20:18–44, 1965.

(28) id.: Loss of Identity, Impairment of Relationships, Reading Disability, *Psychoanalytic Quarterly* 35:18–39, 1966.

(29) id.: The Exploitation of Ambiguity in Pindaros *O*. 3.27, *Rheinisches Museum für Philologie* 109:289–298, 1966.

(30) id.: La Renonciation à l'Identité: Défense contre l'Anéantissement, *Revue Française de Psychanalyse* 31:101–142, 1967.

(31) id.: Greek Pseudo-Homosexuality, *Symbolae Osloenses* 42:69–92, 1967.

(32) id.: *From Anxiety to Method in the Behavioral Sciences*. Paris and The Hague, 1967.

(33) id.: Observation and Belief in Aischylos' Accounts of Dreams, *Psychotherapy and Psychosomatics* 15:114–134, 1967.

(34) id.: L'Image de l'Enfant dans deux Tribus, Mohave et Sedang, et son Importance pour la Psychiatrie Infantile, *Revue de Neuropsychiatrie Infantile* 16:375–390, 1968.

(35) id.: Considérations Psychanalytiques sur la Divination, Particulièrement en Grèce (in) Caquot, A. and Leibovici, M. (eds.): *La
Divination*. Paris, 1968.

(36) id.: The Realistic Basis of Fantasy, *Journal of the Hillside Hospital*
17:13–20, 1968.

(37) id.: *Reality and Dream: The Psychotherapy of a Plains Indian*. (Second,
augmented edition), New York, 1969.

(38) id.: *Mohave Ethnopsychiatry and Suicide*. (Second, augmented ed.),
Washington D.C., 1969.

(39) id.: The Nature of Sappho's Seizure in *Fr.* 31 LP, *Classical Quarterly*
20:17–31, 1970.

(40) id.: La Naissance d'Aphrodite (in) Pouillon, Jean and Maranda,
Pierre (eds.): *Echanges et Communications (Mélanges Lévi-Strauss)*,
2. 1229–1252. Paris and The Hague, 1970.

(41) id.: The Structure of Tragedy and the Structure of the Psyche in
Aristotle's *Poetics* (in) Hanly, Charles and Lazerowitz, Morris (eds.):
Psychoanalysis and Philosophy. New York, 1970.

(42) id.: *Psychoanalysis and the Occult* (ed. and contrib.) (Reprint) New
York, 1970.

(43) id.: *Essais d'Ethnopsychiatrie Générale*. Paris, 1970. (Second edition
1973.)

(44) id.: *Ethnopsychanalyse Complémentariste*. Paris, 1972.

(45) id.: Le Fragment 62 Nauck² d'Eschyle. Ce qu'y Signifie ΧΛΟΥΝΗΣ,
Revue des Etudes Grecques 86: 277–284, 1973.

(46) Dodds, E. R.: *The Greeks and the Irrational*. Berkeley, California,
1951.

(47) Ellenberger, Henri: Die Putzwut, *Der Psychologe* 2:1–13, 1950.

(48) Evans-Pritchard, E. E.: Heredity and Gestation, as the Zande See
It, *Sociologus* 8:400–413, 1932.

(49) Fenichel, Otto: A Critique of the Death Instinct, *The Collected
Papers of O. Fenichel* 1. New York, 1953.

(50) id.: The Misapprehended Oracle (in) *The Collected Papers of O.
Fenichel* 2. New York, 1954.

(51) Ferenczi, Sándor: Gulliver Fantasies (in) *Final Contributions to the
Problems and Methods of Psycho-Analysis*. New York, 1955.

(52) Ford, C. S. and Beach, F. A.: *Patterns of Sexual Behavior*. New York,
1951.

(53) Freud, Sigmund: Beyond the Pleasure Principle, *Standard Edition*
18. London, 1957.

(54) Gorer, Geoffrey and Rickman, John: *The People of Great Russia*.
London, 1949.

(55) Greenacre, Phyllis: Penis Awe and its Relation to Penis Envy (in)
Loewenstein, R.M.: (ed.) *Drives, Affects, Behavior*. New York,
1953.

(56) Grousset, René: *L'Empire des Steppes*. Paris, 1941.

(57) Grubb, W. B.: *An Unknown People in an Unknown Land*. London,
1911.

(58) Hallowell, A. I.: Bear Ceremonialism in the Northern Hemisphere,
American Anthropologist 28:1–175, 1926.

(59) Isakower, Otto: A Contribution to the Patho-Psychology of Phenomena Associated with Falling Asleep, *International Journal of Psycho-Analysis* 22:466–477, 1936.

(60) James, Henry: *The Turn of the Screw* (many editions).

(61) Jones, Ernest: *Hamlet and Oedipus*. London, 1949.

(62) Kapp, R. O.: Comments on Bernfeld and Feitelberg's, "The Principle of Entropy and the Death Instinct", *International Journal of Psycho-Analysis* 12:82–86, 1931.

(63) Karsten, R.: The Head-Hunters of Western Amazonas: The Life and Culture of the Jivaro Indians of Eastern Ecuador and Peru, *Societas Scientiarum Fennica: Commentationes Humanarum Litterarum* 7 no. 1. Helsingfors, 1935.

(64) La Barre, Weston: *The Ghost Dance*. New York, 1970.

(65) Laforgue, René: *Psychopathologie de l'Echec*. Paris, 1944.

(66) Lennig, Robert: *Traum und Sinnestäuschung bei Aischylos, Sophokles, Euripides*. Berlin, 1969.

(67) Lévi-Strauss, Claude: *L'Origine des Manières de Table*. Paris, 1968.

(68) Lévy-Bruhl, Lucien: *Les Fonctions Mentales dans les Sociétés Inférieures*. Paris, 1910.

(69) Lewin, B. D.: The Body as Phallus, *Psychoanalytic Quarterly* 2:24–47, 1933.

(70) id.: Sleep, the Mouth and the Dream-Screen, *Psychoanalytic Quarterly* 15:419–434, 1946.

(71) Linton, Ralph: The Marquesans (in) Kardiner, Abram **and** Linton, Ralph: *The Individual and his Society*. New York, 1939.

(72) id.: Personal Communication.

(73) Loeb, E. M. and Toffelmier, Gertrude: Kin Marriage and Exogamy, *Journal of General Psychology*, 20:181–228, 1939.

(74) Lullies, R. and Hirmer, M.: *Griechische Vasen der reifarchaischen Zeit*. München, 1953.

(75) MacCracken, R. D.: Lactose Deficiency, *Current Anthropology* 12, nos. 4–5: 479–517, 1971.

(76) Marcadé, Jean: *Eros Kalos*. Genève, 1965.

(77) Masters, John: *The Road Past Mandalay*. London, 1961.

(78) Menninger, K. A.: *Man against Himself*. New York, 1938.

(79) Merker, F.: *Die Masai*. Berlin, 1904.

(80) Murray, Gilbert: *The Classical Tradition in Literature*. New York, 1957.

(81) Nilsson, M. P.: *Geschichte der griechischen Religion* I². München, 1955.

(82) Norbeck, Edward: Trans-Pacific Similarities in Folk-Lore: A Research Lead, *Kroeber Anthropological Society Papers* no. 12:62–69, 1955.

(83) Onians, R. B.: *The Origins of European Thought*. Cambridge, 1951.

(84) Opler, M. E.: Japanese Folk Belief Concerning the Snake, *Southwestern Journal of Anthropology* 1:249–259, 1945.

(85) Oppenheim, A. L.: The Interpretation of Dreams in the Ancient Near East, *Transactions, American Philosophical Society* n.s. 46, pt. 3. Philadelphia, 1956.

(86) Preller, Ludwig and Robert, Carl: *Griechische Mythologie*[4]. Berlin, 1894–1921.

(87) Rapaport, Ionel: *Introduction à la Psychopathologie Collective: La Secte Mystique des Skoptzy.* Paris, n.d.

(88) Reik, Theodor: *Geständniszwang und Strafbedürfnis.* Leipzig, 1925.

(89) Renault, Mary: *The Bull from the Sea.* New York, 1962.

(90) Rohde, Erwin: *Psyche.* London, 1950.

(91) Róheim, Géza: *The Origin and Function of Culture.* New York, 1943.

(92) id.: The Nescience of the Aranda, *British Journal of Medical Psychology* 17:343–360, 1937.

(93) id.: Hungarian Shamanism, (in) Róheim, G. (ed.): *Psychoanalysis and the Social Sciences* 3, 1951.

(94) Rosenberg, S. B. H.: *Reistochten naar de Geelvinkbaai op Nieuw Guinea 1869–1870.* C's Gravenhage, 1875.

(95) Rousseau, G. S.: Dream and Vision in Aeschylus' *Oresteia, Arion* 2:101–136, 1963.

(96) Ruark, Robert: *Something of Value.* New York, 1955.

(97) Rycroft, Charles: *A Critical Dictionary of Psychoanalysis.* London, 1968.

(98) Wallace, A. F. C.: Dreams and Wishes of the Soul, *American Anthropologist* 60:234–248, 1958.

(99) Westermarck, Eduard: *The History of Human Marriage.* London, 1901.

Chapter 7

Klytaimnestra's Dream in Sophokles' *Elektra*

ΧΡΥΣΟΘΕΜΙC

λόγος τις αὐτήν ἐςτιν εἰςιδεῖν πατρὸς   417
τοῦ coῦ τε κἀμοῦ δευτέραν ὁμιλίαν
ἐλθόντος εἰς φῶς· εἶτα τόνδ' ἐφέςτιον
πῆξαι λαβόντα cκῆπτρον οὑφόρει ποτὲ   420
αὐτός, τανῦν δ' Αἴγιcθος· ἔκ τε τοῦδ' ἄνω
βλαςτεῖν βρύοντα θαλλόν, ᾧ κατάςκιον
πᾶcαν γενέcθαι τὴν Μυκηναίων χθόνα.

(Jebb's text)

Translation

   Chrysothemis: "It is said that she [Klytaimnestra] beheld our father
returned to light, near her [in bed] once more. Then he took the sceptre —
once his, but now borne by Aigisthos—and planted it into the hearth, and
from it [the sceptre] a leafy branch sprung upward, which overshadowed
all of Mykenai's land." [Subsequently Klytaimnestra "sterilizes" her
dream, by exposing it to Helios, the Sun. She (catastrophically) persists,
however, in calling it an ambiguous dream (διccῶν ὀνείρων). She also
hopes that if its omen is good, it will affect her; if bad, that it will affect
her enemies (645; cp. Daniel 4.19).]

Comments: The following views will be justified further on:

(1) "*Near her* [*in bed*]": cp. Bächli (*3*, p. 54): "sich wieder zu ihr legte". Nothing more explicit should be imagined to occur at this point.

(2) "*The hearth*" is, *pace* Jebb (ad loc.), indoors—it is the hearth alluded to also in v. 270.

(3) "*Into*" the hearth; so Mazon (in his ed.) and Vernant (*96*, p. 108). Bowra's translation "on" (*6*, pp. 223 ff.) means the same thing. Jebb's "at" is, in view of what Agamemnon's gesture symbolizes, a euphemism, which he repeats more or less also at v. 270.

(4) "*Leafy branch*": Mazon's "laurier" seems inexplicable.

The Problem. The Sophoklean Klytaimnestra's seemingly transparent (allegorical) dream is far more difficult to analyse than the Aischylean Klytaimestra's dream. The Sophoklean dream's "transparency" is the equivalent of a "red herring resistance" (*34*, 412 ff.) in clinical psychoanalysis. It persuades those who ignore the great mathematician Lagrange's warning: "seek simplicity, but distrust it", that they understand *at once* all that such a pseudo-transparent dream contains.

Actually, the latent psychological content of the Aischylean Klytaimestra's dream lies immediately below the "surface" of its manifest content. In the case of the Sophoklean dream, a thick layer of literary and cultural traditions and meanings separates the two and must be pierced before the dream's latent psychological core can be reached. In short, the latent content of the Aischylean dream is encoded only once; that of the Sophoklean dream is encoded twice, and the two codes are not of the same kind. The technique of analysis to be used here, albeit somewhat similar to that used in the analysis of Atossa's dream (chap. 1), must therefore be a particularly sophisticated one. In fact, the psychoanalyst's task begins where that of the philologist ends.

Stesichoros, Aischylos and Sophokles. Like his two predecessors, Sophokles, too, causes his Klytaimnestra to have *an* ominous dream, but attributes a very different *kind* of dream to her. Yet, this externally innovating dream has a latent content very similar to that of the serpent dreams which Sophokles did *not* choose to imitate. Before this can be proven, a great deal of literary and philological spade-work must be done.

The first point to be made is that, the Sophoklean dream's "perspective" is closer to that of the Stesichorean dream than to that of the Aischylean dream, whose "perspective" is *sui generis*. The Stesichorean and the Sophoklean dreams emphasize the dynastic element: the former mentions the Pleisthenid *king*, emerging from a serpent; the latter the *sceptre* of the Atreidai. They appear to highlight the replacement of one ruler by another: in this perspective the punishment of Klytaimestra is only a means to an end. It may be objected, of course, that Ploutarchos cites the Stesichoros fragment in order to illustrate the delays of divine vengeance[1] and therefore emphasizes mainly Klytaimestra's punishment. But this finding is not conclusive, for Ploutarchos is not above citing a poetical fragment out of context, in order to illustrate a point which is the direct opposite of the point the poet sought to make (*31*). Aischylos stresses

[1] Plu. *ser. num. vind.* 10, p. 555A.

mainly the punishment of Klytaimestra, the bad mother; the reestablish-
ment of the lawful dynasty is, at least in the dream, simply a consequence of
the vengeance successfully exacted for a private offence.

This interpretation is reinforced by the fact that whereas the physiologi-
cal-instinctual element is stressed in the Aischylean dream to the point of
constituting its manifest content (nursing and biting), it is barely hinted
at in the Sophoklean dream (near-coitus with a ghost) and probably also
in the tantalizingly short Stesichoros fragment, whose latent sexual-
procreative content was discussed elsewhere (chap. 5).

Since, in determining the latent content of the Sophoklean dream, I will
have occasion to refer to the Stesichorean and Aischylean models which
Sophokles did *not* replicate, I must prove at once that certain of their
motifs, which Sophokles deliberately *excluded* from his Klytaimnestra's
dream, unintentionally *reappeared* in *other* passages of his drama (*37*).
A careful documentation of this statement is indispensable, not only in
order to avoid the reproach of having taken into account that which is
"outside the drama" (τὰ ἐκτὸς τοῦ δράματος), but also in order to
justify in advance my many references, in connection with Astyages'
second dream (Hdt. 1.108), which Sophokles did imitate, to Astyages' *first*
dream (Hdt. 1.107) which he did not *manifestly* imitate.

I begin by stating a general principle: when an author *deviates* from
a traditional model, the discarded motifs tend to reappear—at times in a
somewhat perplexing manner—in a passage of his work which is largely
unrelated to the passage in which a pre-existing model is wholly or partly
discarded or else radically modified. I have called this unintended and
out-of-context reappearance of discarded motifs: "slippage" (*37*). From
the philological point of view, this resembles the process whereby a gloss
slips into the text, while from the psychoanalytical point of view it
resembles what Freud called "the return of the repressed" (*52*). The
uncontrollable return of the repressed is so well known, that it constitutes the
point of a certain category of jokes which may be summarized as follows:
"You will get your wish if you manage *not* to think of a rhinoceros for
twenty-four hours." This prohibition *causes* the person so instructed to
think of a rhinoceros. I have fully explained the psychodynamics
responsible for such "slippages" elsewhere (*37*).[2]

Before I prove that Sophokles was *unwittingly* influenced by both the
Stesichorean and the Aischylean models which he discarded *intentionally*,
I will discuss first a slippage in E. *El.*, which discards not only the Stesichorean, Aischylean and Sophoklean dream models, but—inexplicably—
even the motif of Klytaimnestra's ominous dream (E. *Or*. 618). I propose
to show that even this radical extirpation of the whole dream-problem did
not prevent a slippage, because of Euripides' awareness of the *sources* of
the Sophoklean dream.

I noted that the Sophoklean dream is modelled *externally*, on Astyages'
second dream, but, anticipating later conclusions, specified that its *latent*
content is related also to Astyages' *first* dream, which Sophokles did *not*
choose to imitate explicitly. Now, Astyages *reacts* to his *first* dream, which

---

[2] In connection with S. *Tr.* 923; a briefer discussion will be found in my analysis of a
"slippage" in Theocr. 2.110 (*31*).

makes him fear that his daughter Mandane's son might dethrone him, by marrying her off to a *Persian*, who, though of high birth, is only a second-class citizen in the empire dominated by the *Medes*. (Hdt. 1.107). This apotropaic or prophylactic device, which is mentioned neither by Aischylos nor by Sophokles, is innovatingly borrowed by Euripides: the usurpers, instead of forcing Elektra to remain single, marry her off to a free peasant. (E. *El.* 34 ff.). In short, while discarding both the dream and the dreaming, Euripides borrowed and brilliantly developed what, in Herodotos, is the *interpretation* of a dream (related to the dreams others ascribe to Klytaimnestra) or, if one prefers: Astyages' *reactions* to his dream and to its interpretation. This "slippage" becomes even more striking if one bears in mind that, in certain cultures, in which much attention is paid to dreams, the dream itself, its telling, its interpretation and the dreamer's reactions to the interpretation must, from the cultural point of view, be treated as a *single* and *indivisible* sequence (*29*, pt. 1, chap. 7).[3] It is even possible that it was this slippage which enabled Euripides to discard so completely both the dream-episode and its content.

I must now turn to the manifest slippages in Sophokles.

Stesichorean Slippages: In the Stesichorean text, there is mention of the snake's "bloody crest". Since the sources of this Stesichorean detail have already been explained (chap. 5), I limit myself here only to this explicitly described image. Aischylos displaced the bleeding from the head to the nipple. Sophokles eliminated it entirely from the *dream*, but mentions *immediately after* the dream (445), that the bloodstained murder weapon was wiped off on Agamemnon's *head*, causing his already cloven "crest" to be doubly bloody. For the literary critic, this detail, mentioned immediately after the dream, is part of its context; for the psycho-analyst, it is a "free association" to it. Be it context or free association, the literary critic, quite as much as the psycho-analyst, must take it into account in seeking to determine the meaning of the dream.

But there is more. The tale of the bloodying of Agamemnon's head is followed *at once* by a description of μαϲχαλιϲμόϲ—of the apotropaic ablation of his corpse's extremities. Since I will show that this practice, too, is relevant for the understanding of the dream, I must consider it here in some detail. This rite manifestly interested Sophokles: he seems to be the only classical author to mention the *amputation* detail twice.[4] Now, it is *inconceivable* that one of the amputated "limbs" should not have been the phallos (*32*) . . . especially in the case of Agamemnon, whose murderers sought to destroy his *lineage*, root and branch (cp. E. *Suppl.* 544 f.). Possibly, the earlier remark (98 ff.): "Aigisthos cleaved Agamemnon's *head* with an axe like a woodman fells an oak" (δρῦϲ), not only anticipates the bloodying of his head, but also indicates that the comparing of Agamemnon to a felled oak—rather than to a slain lion or bull—is doubly significant:

(1) It anticipates the dream-appearance of the sprouting sceptre, for sceptres were made of *wood*, adorned with gold.

[3] Cp. also Dodds' second thoughts on this matter (*40*, p. 39).
[4] Cp. S. (*Troilos*), *fr.* 566 N² = 623 P. For other sources and for the practice as a whole, cp. Rohde (*82*, pp. 582 ff.), Nilsson (*75*, 1², pp. 92–99).

(2) In myth, Dryas' (the *Oak*-man's) limbs are lopped off by his mad father, who thinks he is pruning a vine. (Apollod. 3.5.1).

The assumption that this rite has a bearing on the dream seems supported by a curious fact: the amputation, though mentioned also in A. *Choe*. 439, is *not* echoed by the Aischylean Klytaimestra's dream, in which Orestes sucks blood (and milk) from the nipple. Now, in a fragment from another drama (*fr.* 354 N²) Aischylos mentions *another* aspect of this apotropaic rite: the murderer takes into his *mouth* a clot of the victim's *blood* and spits it out. Thus, just as *this* (oral) aspect of the rite has affinities with Klytaimestra's manifest dream in Aischylos, so the Sophoklean reference to *another* aspect of the same rite may be presumed to have a bearing upon his Klytaimnestra's dream.

Having already mentioned that Sophokles imitated the dynastic perspective of the Stesichoros dream and also its (inferable) latent sexual content, I now turn to:

Aischylean Slippages. The most striking element of the Aischylean dream is the nursing of the serpent at the breast. It focuses one's attention on Klytaimestra's breasts and on the nursing of Orestes *so strongly*, that the Nurse's (genuine) claim to have nursed Orestes from the moment of his birth (A. *Choe.* 749 ff.)—a sacrifice whose fruitlessness she now laments (cp. E. *Phoin.* 1433)—and Klytaimestra's (lying) claim to have nursed Orestes (A. *Choe.* 896 ff., 908) *forcibly* remind one of the dream. The Aischylean dream makes these contradictory claims an integral part of the *essential* warp and woof of the *Choephoroi*.

The Sophoklean *dream* contains, of course, no allusion whatever to nursing. *None the less*, Sophokles took over from Aischylos the contradictory *claims* concerning the nursing of Orestes. That his Klytaimnestra should claim to have nursed Orestes (776) at the breast (μαςτῶν) is perhaps natural enough. What is less so, is that, in S. *El.*, Klytaimnestra's claim is contested *by Elektra*, who, like the Aischylean Nurse, claims to be the *only one* in the house (κατ' οἶκον) to have "nursed" Orestes, and, like the Nurse, laments the wasted devotion (1143 ff.).

Now, had the *Choephoroi* never been written, Elektra's words would *at once* be taken to mean *only* "tender nurturing", which is the secondary meaning of the basic word τρέφω, whose primary meaning is: to nurse at the breast.[5] But anyone familiar with A. *Choe.*, from which the motif of competing claims is borrowed must—be he an Athenian theatre-goer or a modern student of Greek—*stop and remind himself* that, unlike the Aischylean Nurse, the *virgin* Elektra can refer only to tender nurturing; that the Sophoklean Klytaimnestra's claim to have nursed Orestes at her breasts (μαςτῶν) is meant to be believed (776). I do *not* believe Sophokles to have tried to persuade us that Elektra gave Orestes the breast, nor do I feel that he expressed himself obscurely.[6] One's *momentary* bewilderment is due to one's awareness that the Aischylean Nurse, whom Elektra replaces here, *did* nurse Orestes at the breast. It is this *awkward* and incomplete transposition of the competing nursing claims in A. *Choe.* and the *unrelatedness*

---

[5] In A. *Choe.* both the Nurse (750) and Klytaimestra (898, 908) use forms of this word to denote lactation; in S. *El.* (1143, 1147) Elektra uses it to denote mere nurturing.

[6] As he did express himself obscurely in connection with the slippage at S. *Tr.* 923 (37).

of these passages to anything else in S. *El.*, which show that the discarded Aischylean motif of nursing in dream "slipped" indirectly into the Sophoklean text. The only alternative would be to assume that Sophokles knew—and meant to refer to—certain highly unusual biological facts; a hypothesis which I am *not* prepared to accept.[7]

These slippages of elements derived from the Stesichorean and the Aischylean dreams suffice to show that they kept on haunting Sophokles' mind even *after* he decided to discard them. They may therefore be legitimately cited in the course of an attempt to elucidate the latent meaning of the Sophoklean Klytaimnestra's dream. They also absolve me, in advance, from having to justify the use I will make of Astyages' *first* dream (Hdt. 1.107), even though Sophokles borrowed details only from his *second* dream (1.108). Astyages' two dreams encode (symbolize) the same (latent) meaning in two—externally divergent—ways. This statement fits both what we know from various mythologies about recurrent or paired dreams and what psycho-analysts have been able to learn from the analysis of such paired or serial dreams (*1, 4, 38, 57*) which are, in the last resort, variations on a theme. This links them with recurrent dreams— common especially in childhood and adolescence—in which the same meaning is repeatedly encoded in the *same* way. In short, the carefully selected group of non-Sophoklean dreams which I exploit in this chapter are all variations on the same theme: plus ça change, plus c'est la même chose.

Borrowing is, both psychologically and culturally, a complicated process. Not only are traits available for borrowing often *not* borrowed but, when borrowed, they may be discarded after a while, because they do not fit easily into their new context (*65*, p. 46, cp. *66*, pp. 329 ff.). Even useful arts may be lost (*81*)—as the art of writing was lost during Greece's Dark Ages. The impulse to borrow is, moreover, always partly counteracted by inertia and by outright resistances. Items are borrowed *mainly* for more or less unconscious reasons, and these "reasons" continue to *adhere* to the borrowed items even after they are incorporated into a new setting (*36*, chap. 8).

Taken as a *deviation* from the Stesichorean-Aischylean model, the Sophoklean dream is an *innovation*. But, when taken in *conjunction* with an Aischylean metaphor (A. *Ag.* 966 ff.), with two Herodotean dreams (1.107, 108) only *one* of which was manifestly imitated, and also with

---

[7] The production of *milk* by a *virgo intacta* is extremely rare: I know of one reliably reported case only (*7*). A girl's (or a virgin female animal's) mammae can, however, occasionally produce colostrum (beestings). The Mohave Indians claim to be able to induce a flow of "milk" even in a post-menopausal grandmother, who must nurse her orphaned grandchild (*19*). Nic. *Alex.* 64 f. prescribes young girl's milk as an antidote for a poison; this is noteworthy, as Nikandros does not prescribe non-existent remedies. At vv. 357 ff., he says that a man harmed by the βούπρηστις (a poisonous beetle) should nurse at the breast—like a newborn calf butting the udder to *start* the milk-flow. I am unable to say whether this comparison is mere rhetoric or (again) suggests forcing milk from a non-lactating girl. I prefer to avoid hazardous conjectures. The non-lactating Hera's nursing of Herakles is hardly a precedent, for to a goddess everything is possible. (Sources and monuments cited in Preller-Robert *79*, 1.171, 2.2.427.) Equally irrelevant here is the fact that the virginal—but "child-nurturing"—Artemis was represented as polymastic at Ephesos (cp. *51* for psycho-analytical comments).

certain Near Eastern models upon which the Herodotean dreams are patterned, the Sophoklean dream seems *derivative*.

The Aischylean metaphor has *more* elements in common with the Sophoklean dream than has the Herodotean vine dream. But it is the existence (and interpretation) of the latter which probably incited Sophokles to incorporate into his Klytaimnestra's dream *additional* details borrowed from the Aischylean metaphor, but lacking in the Herodotean dream which resembles that metaphor in some respects. Succinctly stated, most of the Sophoklean dream's *elements* were borrowed from an Aischylos passage, but their incorporation into an (innovating) dream was made possible by the existence of the *structurally* somewhat similar Herodotean vine *dream*, whose *content* also has affinities with the Aischylean metaphor.

So far I have shown only *how* the Herodotean dream *permitted* the borrowing of additional *elements* from Aischylos. I must now explain why Sophokles borrowed these elements *for* a dream dealing with the myth of the Atreidai, rather than for one dealing with another myth. It suffices to cite two reasons:

(1) The interpretation of the Herodotean dream is *very similar* to that of the Aischylean and Soophoklean dreams, though totally *unlike* the intended "meaning" of the Aischylean Klytaimestra's lying metaphor.

(2) The Kyros myth has one crucial and *unusual element* in common with Atreus myth. Since Harpagos failed to expose Kyros as instructed, Astyages deceived him into eating the flesh of his own children (Hdt. 1.119), as Thyestes was deceived by Atreus into feasting on the flesh of his children.[8] The only *structural* difference between the two traditions is that Astyages' warning dreams precede, while that of Klytaimnestra follows the cannibalistic feast. Moreover, in the Aischylean Klytaimestra's dream it is the baby who cannibalistically attacks its parent. This "inversion" is not at all surprising, since parental and infantile devouring impulses are symmetrical and mutually reinforcing (*35*, chap. 5).

These two findings suffice to explain why Sophokles borrowed elements from Aischylos and from Herodotos, in order to devise a new kind of dream *for* Klytaimnestra, rather than for another personage, belonging to a different myth cycle.

The process of borrowing having been clarified, one can proceed to a detailed scrutiny of Sophokles' *actual* models.

The Manifest Models of the Sophoklean dream are A. *Ag.* 966 ff. and Hdt. 1.108. In accordance with the programme outlined at the beginning of this chapter, I analyse first the cultural (philological, literary, historical) aspects of these models; the few symbols I mention are of a type which the literary critic is accustomed to take in his stride, and does not consider particularly psychological.

A. *Ag.* 966 ff.—a lying, flattering speech Klytaimestra addresses to Agamemnon—provides most of the *elements* of the Sophoklean dream: I cite (basically) Fraenkel's translation, inserting in square brackets words which help to clarify the meaning of the text.

---

[8] A. *Ag.* 1217 ff., 1594 ff., etc. Even Fraenkel who, in his edition of A. *Ag.* (ad 1594 ff.), stresses differences between the *means* Astyages and Atreus used to deceive the victimized fathers, admits the similarity between the two cannibalistic feasts.

"For as, when the root remains, the foliage returns to the house, stretching over it a shade against the [scorching] dog-star, so, by thy [Agamemnon's] coming home to the hearth of thy house, thou dost signify that warmth has come home in winter, and when from the sour [unripe] grape Zeus is making wine [ripening the grapes with heat], then at once there is coolness in the house, when the consummate master is moving about the house."

Most of the *elements* of the Sophoklean dream are present in this speech: the return of Agamemnon, the hearth, the sprouting of the plant, the great shadow it casts. The sceptre is not mentioned, but what it represents —protective sovereignty—is the theme of the entire passage. The only missing element is the coital theme, mentioned neither explicitly, nor in a transparent allusion.[9]

But the Aischylean passage also differs from the Sophoklean dream in several respects. Though it shares many elements with the latter, these elements are juxtaposed in a different way: the *structure* of the two accounts is *not* the same. For example, the luxuriant foliage's great shadow is mentioned *before* there is any reference to the hearth. A further difference is that whereas both the Aischylean speech and the Sophoklean dream concern imaginary events—the one being a lying flattery, expressed in the form of a metaphor and the other simply a dream—the Aischylean speech is *meant* to deceive, whereas the Sophoklean dream is a *reliable* warning, which the Sophoklean Klytaimnestra simply refuses to believe, and stubbornly holds to be ambiguous.[10] In short, the borrowing of Aischylean *elements* is obvious;[11] the *non*-borrowing of their *structure* is equally manifest.

One must therefore find another source, from which Sophokles borrowed the structure, the designation of the narrative as a dream, and, specifically, *a* dream, which not only contains similar elements, but whose interpretations and consequences are the same as those of the Sophoklean Klytaimnestra's dream. Only if another model, providing precisely the elements *missing* in the Aischylean speech, can be discovered, does one understand why Sophokles was *able* to borrow some of the elements of the Aischylean speech (metaphor). In this borrowing, the second model functions as an intermediary between Aischylos and Sophokles: it serves as a link between the two texts.

Astyages' *second* dream (Hdt. 1.108) is the Sophoklean dream's main model, content-wise, structurally, in its interpretation and, above all, in

[9] I would hesitate to argue that "overshadowing", "warmth in winter", "ripening grapes" and "moving about" hint at a "deep" sexual meaning. Whether they do or do not, could only be determined if one could put Aischylos on the analytic couch. Since that cannot be done, speculations bordering on "wild psychoanalysis" are not permissible (*50, 90*).

[10] S. *El.* 645; cp. *6*, p. 225. One cannot link this detail with the tradition that Kassandra's prophecies fall on deaf ears. Kassandra is unable to persuade; the Sophoklean Klytaimnestra refuses to be persuaded.

[11] Bowra cites (*6*, p. 252) an example of an almost literal borrowing: A. *Ag.* 1343, 1345, cp. S. *El.* 1415 f.

[12] It is hardly necessary to explain why Sophokles did not borrow the *manifest* elements of the first dream. Urination can *not* be fitted into Sophoklean drama, though it is a recurrent theme in Aristophanic comedy (*94*, s. vv. cites about a dozen instances). Comedy regularly breaks taboos.

being, unlike A. *Ag.* 966 ff., a dream. But it can be shown that even though Sophokles did not borrow any of the *manifest elements* of the *first* Astyages dream (Hdt. 1.107), these elements are, none the less, present in the *latent* content of the Sophoklean dream.[12] I will therefore show that *both* of Astyages' dreams are Near Eastern "culture pattern dreams"[13] or resemble certain miracles, which can, both psychologically and structurally, be treated as dream equivalents.

I present here, for the moment, only the raw data, though in some instances I add a word or two in square brackets, indicating the element of the Sophoklean dream with which some detail will eventually be linked.

Astyages' First Dream: The urine of his nubile, but as yet unwed, daughter Mandane floods Astyages' capital and all of Asia (Hdt. 1.107). It foretells Astyages' dethroning by Mandane's son Kyros (Cyrus, Kurush).[14]

Near Eastern Equivalents: A Mesopotamian dream book lists a large number of urination dreams (*76*, pp. 264–266). Moreover, the *only* Mesopotamian dream which foretells the logically unforeseeable accession of a person—of the dreamer's son—to the throne is a urination dream (*76*, p. 265a). There is one major difference only between Astyages' (or Mandane's) dream and the Mesopotamian urination dreams. If I understand Oppenheim's translations and comments correctly, in Mesopotamia only men dreamed of urinating. There were, however, also dreams about the urine (not: the urinating) of females: some men dreamed of drinking their wives' urine[15] (*76*, p. 266a). This finding seems to make Ktesias' attribution of the urination dream to Mandane herself culturally inappropriate, at least within the framework of Near Eastern patterns.

The urination dream has several links with Astyages' second dream. It foretells the same dire event; the same message is encoded in two different ways. In both dreams that which Mandane produces (urine, vine) emerges from her genitals,[16] and both spread inordinately. I note in this connection that in many Mesopotamian urination dreams the urine *spreads out* (divides into several streams?) as soon as it emerges from the meatus.[17] As to the urination dream's link with the Sophoklean dream, I state, *for the moment* apodictically, that it appears in Klytaimnestra's dream in disguise only; it is represented by the hearth: by fire.

Astyages' Second Dream: A vine[18] sprouts from Mandane's vagina and

[13] First called "official dreams" by Malinowski (*70*, p. 92 ff.). Renamed "culture pattern dreams" by Lincoln (*64*, p. 41) and introduced under that name into Greek studies by Dodds (*39*, chap. 4). Their occurrence is understandable both in cultural (*36*, chap. 9) and in psychological (*29*, pt. 1, chap. 7) terms. In some societies the young are instructed to have "correct" dreams (*95*).

[14] Ctes. ap. Nic. Dam. *FHG* 3.399.65 attributes this dream to Mandane herself.

[15] For similar Mohave Indian dreams, cp. *30*, p. 138. Some Micronesian women urinate during the orgasm (*23*).

[16] I specify that in both instances the vagina is meant. In 1.108 αἰδοίων should not be translated as "womb" (Rawlinson). I have yet to encounter a primitive woman who does *not* believe that she urinates from the vagina; even modern female college graduates often do not know that the urinary meatus is located outside and above the vaginal introitus.

[17] Since this actually happens to some men when they urinate after coitus, the Mesopotamian urination dreams may conceivably be "post-coital dreams". But that is as it may be.

[18] The domestic, grape-bearing vine is meant, cp. LSJ s.v. ἄμπηλος. Compare *Gen.* 40.9 ff.; A. *Ag.* 970.

overshadows all of Asia. (Hdt. 1.108). Since this dream is dreamed after Mandane's marriage, she may be presumed to be pregnant at that time.

Near Eastern Equivalents

(1) Xerxes' dream (Hdt. 7.19): the olive garland he wears on his head first sprouts luxuriantly and then vanishes. [The olive recalls item 5, infra; the garland may correspond to the sceptre.[19]]

(2) Nebuchadnezzar's dream (Dan. 4.10 ff.): a huge tree is cut down but not uprooted [A. *Ag.* 966]. It is, for the time being, bound with strips of iron and brass [*golden* sceptre], but the prophet predicts that it will sprout again, later on.

(3) Pharaoh's imprisoned butler's dream (*Gen.* 40.9 ff.): a vine sprouts and divides itself into three branches, which produce grapes. The butler presses them and serves their (fermented?) juice to Pharaoh. [Branching: Mesopotamian urination dreams; drinking the juice: drinking urine(?).]

(4) The miracle of Aaron's rod (*Num.* 17.8): The rod, representing Aaron's headship of the Levi tribe, sprouts during a contest with the rods of other tribal leaders; this makes him supreme in all Israel.

(5) The miracle of Athene's olive tree (Hdt. 8.55): though burned [hearth], it sprouts again, thereby foretelling the (Phoenix-like) rebirth of Athens from its ashes and its ultimate triumph over Persia (*13*). This miracle's links with the Near East are self-evident; I know of no pre-Persian-Wars precedent in Greece, for the Euboian vine (infra) is no real precedent.

Since, in S. *El.*, the sprouting *sceptre* is substituted for the Stesichorean and Aischylean *snake*, another Near Eastern miracle also deserves mention:

(6) Aaron's rod turns into a serpent (*Exod.* 7.10); this is a challenge to Pharaoh's supremacy.[20]

As regards Greek equivalents, the male meaning of trees in Greek dreams was discussed by Bowra (*6*, p. 225). Nothing need be added, save that Klytaimnestra's doubts about the meaning of the dream may, in part, be due to the fact that such dreams tend to be good omens for the *dreamer*, rather than (as in S. *El.* 480 ff.) for someone else.

It is important to stress that such dreams seem to be closely linked with the successful overthrow of established authority. This probably explains why X. *Cyrop.*—in which Astyages' relations with Kyros are affectionate—does *not* mention these dreams.

I note in conclusion that sudden sprouting seem to have interested Sophokles. He mentioned, in his lost *Thyestes* (*fr.* 235 N²), an Euboian vine which sprouted and ripened grapes daily (cp. E. *Ph.* 229 ff.). Since, in this case, *only* the bunches of grape sprout suddenly, that incident is a very incomplete parallel to the S. *El.* dream, but has some affinities with A. *Ag* 966 ff. and with the dream of Pharaoh's butler. I repeat that I cite it here not as an equivalent, but as evidence of Sophokles' preoccupation with this theme.

[19] σκῆπτρον = λυχνίς στεφανωματική (the campion rose, of which garlands are made, cp. Ps.-Dsc. 3.100).

[20] The "contest of shamans" element (cp. Apollod. *Ep.* 5.2 ff. and countless similar contests in many culture areas: *84*, etc.) is represented by the transformation of the rods of Pharaoh's soothsayers into serpents. But Aaron's serpent *devours* the rest. This has affinities with the dream of one of my patients (*35*, chap. 6).

The Hearth

Vernant (*96*, passim) conclusively proves that, even though the Athenian woman had to leave her native hearth and join that of her husband, the hearth is the female centre of the "social space" occupied by the household.

What matters most here is, however, the subjective "dream-meaning" of the hearth. In interpreting the S. *El.* dream as a coital dream, Vernant (*96*, p. 108) necessarily takes it for granted that the hearth represents the female genitals. It is this symbolism which I now propose to document in some detail.

I begin by noting that since what is left of the Stesichorean dream does *not* describe the behaviour and the location of the serpent, and since the Aischylean dream mentions, in addition to the serpent, only the breasts, the hearth may—despite A. *Choe* 49—well be the *one* wholly new element in the *manifest* content of the Sophoklean Klytaimnestra's dream; the sceptre is clearly a substitute for the Stesichorean-Aischylean serpent. It may even be argued that, by using a more allusive symbolism than Aischylos, Sophokles could afford to introduce "coitus" into the *latent* content of the dream: the Aischylean nursing and biting, described explicitly,[21] is replaced in Sophokles by a symbolic coitus. This finding fits my thesis (*24*) that the amount of *tabooed* instinctual material represented in an authentic work of art is proportional to the amount of symbolization.

Before discussing in detail the hearth symbolism, some attention must be paid to the more concrete and pragmatic aspects of this dream hearth.

The Hearth is Indoors. It is, presumably, the one near which Agamemnon was slain (S. *El.* 203, 266 ff.).[22] But it is self-evident that the hearth which Vernant considers to be the female centre of the house was the one located indoors . . . where Agamemnon was slain during the banquet (203). The following considerations also support the view that the hearth was located indoors:

(1) In Homeric passive ("listener") dreams, the dreamer "does not suppose himself to be anywhere else than in bed" (*39*, p. 105). The same is certainly true of several tragic dreams: A. *Ag.* 420 ff., E. *Rh.* 782 ff., and probably also of Io's (A. *PV* 645 ff.) and Atossa's (A. *Pers.* 176 ff.) dreams. Iphigeneia's dream (E. *IT* 44 ff.) manifestly begins with her lying in bed. Though in this dream Klytaimnestra is an onlooker, rather than a (Homeric) listener, she remains passive throughout the dream. This creates a strong presumption that she "supposes" herself in bed—indoors.

(2) Nothing in the text suggests that Agamemnon had to walk any distance, let alone go outdoors, to reach the other sacred hearth.

(3) It is an outside possibility that the reference to the "shadow cast" by the branch might also suggest an indoors hearth, for Vernant (*96*,

---

[21] I recall, however, previously cited experiments (chap. 6, note 113) which prove that nursing elicits sexual excitement.

[22] Contra: Jebb, ad vv. 417 ff., who locates the dream hearth outside, in the αὐλή (court).

p. 124) clearly links both woman and the hearth with the shade:[23] the hearth is equated with the woman (infra).

(4) Much more persuasive is the fact that ghosts tend to reappear *where* they were slain; since the Sophoklean Agamemnon was slain during the banquet, he was necessarily slain indoors, for no Homeric *outdoors* banquet is suggested by any detail or hint.

One can foresee the objection that a Greek queen's *marital* couch was not located in the great hall, near the sacred indoors hearth. But, according to Lorimer (*69*, p. 426), it was located just there, between the back wall and the hearth. An even more obvious retort is that no *plausible* dream reproduces reality *photographically*: it stylizes it. In order to be able to introduce the hearth symbol, Sophokles had to *displace* Klytaimnestra's bed. But there is more: one can actually trace the *deformation* of reality in the Sophoklean dream back to a *realistic* Aischylean detail. The Aischylean Agamemnon was not slain during a banquet, but while being bathed (A. *Ag.* 1107 ff.).

If one could suppose that Sophokles knew the ground plan of the Palace of Pylos (*97*, fig. 35) or of some similar palace, one could urge that at Pylos the bathroom, with a *built-in* bathtub, was located next door to the chamber containing the hearth. But it is more probable that Sophokles had in mind somewhat simpler arrangements: one notes that the slain Aischylean Agamemnon does not fall (as would be more natural at Pylos) into the *bathtub*, but into a (*portable*) hot water *cauldron* (A. *Ag.* 1128 ff.). Be that as it may, the Aischylean bathing scene, which took place—quite realistically—*indoors*, contributed to Sophokles' placing the dream's bed and fire-place indoors, by means of recourse to the mechanism of "condensation" commonly met with both in real and in literary Greek dreams (*39*, p. 106).[24]

Hearth = Vulva is an almost self-evident symbolic equation, which it is easy to document for Greece. I begin by citing Artemidoros' explicit statements:

(1) Hearth = oven = woman in her procreative capacity (1.43).

(2) The hearth represents the life and the wife of the dreamer (1.74).

(3) A woman warms a man the way fire does (2.9).

(4) A frying pan represents a lecherous woman (2.42).[25]

Artemidoros' equations are not late inventions; they are foreshadowed in much earlier works:

(1) Melissa's ghost tells Periandros' emissary to remind her husband that he had "baked his loaf in a cold oven"—that he had committed

---

[23] He lists in this connection some of the following texts: X. *Econ.* 4.2, *Ages.* 1.24, *Hell.* 3.4.19; Pl. *Phdr.* 239c; Plu. *V. Ages.* 9.5, *Ap. Lac.* 13, p. 209C. But in A. *Ag.* 966 ff. and Hdt. 1.108 the shadowing object is *not* in the house (cp. chap. 8, note 53).

[24] A literary consideration deserves at least brief mention. Though the word φῶς assuredly denotes that light which differentiates the Earth from gloomy Hades, it may *perhaps* anticipate *also* the mentioning of the (lit) hearth. Such anticipations are common in great poetry. Like modulations in music, they insure the cohesiveness of poetic discourse, by providing an associative-allusive link between successive images. If this literary argument is accepted, it also helps one imagine a hearth located indoors.

[25] Cp. ibid.: mortar = wife, pestle = husband, cp. note 66.

necrophilia with her corpse (Hdt. 5.92 η, cf. *59*). This tradition has affective affinities with Klytaimnestra's necrophiliac dream.[26]

(2) The hearth, in S. *El.* 266 ff., is the recipient of (semen-like) libations, poured into it by Aigisthos, appersonating (*89*) Agamemnon. This passage is *immediately* followed by a mention of his cohabitation with Klytaimnestra . . . into whose vulva he pours another kind of "libation".

(3) The Roman *equus october* rite[27] is also relevant here, since the sacrificed stallion's "cauda", suspended above the sacred hearth, dripped blood into it. I have, on the basis of *compelling* anatomical and physiological considerations, shown that this "cauda" was not the tail but the penis of the animal (*33*).

I have shown so far that the hearth is a symbol of the vulva and vagina: it is a recipient for the phallos (here represented by the sceptre) and for semen, or semen equivalents.

But, without ceasing to symbolize the vagina as it *really is*, the hearth can at times also symbolize the female organs as they are sometimes *fantasied to be*. The fantasy in question is reported not only by neurotics, but also by *normal* women and children; it is also encountered more than once in myth. It is the symbolic equation: father's phallos = mother's phallos (acquired from father during coitus) = foetus and/or child.[28] I have documented this fantasy for Greece so copiously elsewhere (*32*), that I will mention here only one—very telling—Greek example, already cited in chap. 6:

Though Poseidon boasts that a god *always* impregnates his mistresses (Hom. *Od.* 11.249 f.), he himself does *not* impregnate Kainis. *Instead* of a baby, he gives her a penis: he transforms her into a man (*22*).

Taking hereafter this equation for granted, I will now cite examples which show that the hearth, though often representing the female organs, as they *are*, can also represent them as they are sometimes *fantasied* to be.

(1) At least two hearths *contain* a phallos capable of impregnating an unwed girl and the child so conceived becomes a dethroner or at least a successor of a king.[29]

---

[26] On Greek necrophilia, cp. (*59*) and (*27*). It might, of course, be argued that I, myself, had expressed the opinion (*27*) that *if* there be coitus in Hades, it could only be coitus *per anum*. Now, in Greek, there is actually a connection between "oven" (ἱπνός), the privy (Ar. *fr.* 353; Hsch. = κοπρών) and the dunghill (ἱπνίον) (Callim. *fr.* 216 Pf.). I would *not* think of arguing that Periandros cohabited with his wife's corpse anally. I simply note that both necrophilia and coitus per anum are unfruitful, as is an anal cohabitation with Aphrodite's *statue* (Luc. *Amor.* 14 ff.), and that coitus per anum with women seems to have been common enough in Greece (*27*, *41*, cp. also Hdt. 1.61). Moreover, since both necrophilia and coitus per anum are perversions, both result from a contamination of sexuality by aggression (*44*, pp. 324 ff.).

[27] Plu. *Quaest. Rom.* 97, p. 287A; Festus s.v. october equus, p. 178.5 ff. Modern references, cp. chap. 1, note 41.

[28] The "woman with a phallos" fantasy must not be confused with the "woman = phallos" fantasy, which is both clinically (*45*) and philologically (*32*) documentable.

[29] *Romulus*: Plu. *V. Rom.* 2.3 f.; Plin. *HN* 36.27.204. *Servius Tullius*: Plu. *Fort. Rom.* 10.323B ff. (Cp. D.H. *Ant. Rom.* 4.1 f.; Ov. *Fast.* 6.627 ff.; Liv. 1.39; Plin. *HN* 36.27.204). Numitor's son, killed by Amulius, is called *Aigisthos*. (*85*, s.v. Romulus, cites D.H. *Ant. Rom.* 1.76 ff.; Str. 5.3.2; Serv. V. *Aen.* 1.273; Appian. ap. Phot. *Bibl.* No. 57 p. 16b35 Bekker; Tzetz. *Lyc.* 1232). This murder apparently justifies Romulus' accession to the

(2) Even a hearth which does *not* contain a phallos can emit a spark (= semen) capable of impregnating an unwed girl. The child, so conceived, is named Caeculus and is deemed to be Vulcanus' son.[30] In this case, too, the dethronement motif is almost totally eliminated: Caeculus simply shares with Romulus the trait of having been a bandit before founding a city (Praeneste).[31]

There are, moreover, hearths which contain a baby-equivalent, and female organs which behave as though they were hearths.

(1) Althaia's hearth contains a firebrand which is apparently the "external soul"—or even the "double"—of Meleagros, who has just been born.[32]

(2) Hekabe dreams of giving birth to a firebrand; to the nefarious Paris.[33] The links of this tradition with the structurally symmetrical miracle which announces the birth of the tyrant Peisistratos (Hdt. 1.59) will be discussed further on.

I can mention only in passing the somewhat tangential belief that one can be born, or reborn from the fire or from a cauldron, or can be "reborn" immortal by having fire burn away one's mortal parts.[34]

What is, by contrast, relevant is that fires capable of causing pregnancy, or else symbolically "pregnant", tend to be associated with sexually active, and even hyper-active women. Klytaimestra is notoriously polyandrous (Stesichor. *fr.* 46 P = 26 B = 17 D); Romulus' foster mother is named "Lupa" (bitch-wolf) (Plu. *V. Rom.* 4.3); Hekabe behaves like a rabid bitch (E. *Hec.* 1173; Q.S. 14.347 ff.) and—probably after being stoned—actually turns into a female dog (E. *Hec.* 1265).[35] And let it not be objected that Kyros' foster-mother is called "Bitch", even though Kyros is *not* born from fire, for I will show subsequently that fire is part of the *latent* content of Astyages' *first* dream.

Summing up, the hearth may be said to symbolize the vulva, while the sceptre stuck into it represents the phallos. This leads up to a scrutiny of the relationship between the hearth and the sprouting of the (phallic) sceptre which it now contains.

The Hearth as a "Terrain" motif is seldom given sufficient attention; it is Vernant's (*96*, p. 114) interest in the *social* significance of the hearth which

throne and permits the relative attenuation of the usurpation motif. That motif is also muted in the Servius Tullius myth: he succeeds his father-in-law.

[30] Cp. the numerous ancient sources, cited by Powell (*78*), which mention Hephaistos' premature ejaculation. The spontaneous (non-coital) ejaculations of the gods are also capable of procreating children (*32*).

[31] Caeculus is not only fathered by fire but, after his exposure, is found near a fire; his name may be connected with blinking (perhaps while looking at a bright fire). V. *Aen.* 7.679 ff., 10.544; cp. Varro ap. sch. Veron. ad V. *Aen.* 7.681 and Serv. V. *Aen.* 7.678.; Solin. 2.9.

[32] A. *Choe.* 607 f.; Apollod. 1.8.2 and Frazer ad loc., cp. also (*13*).

[33] Pi. *Pae.* 8; cp. E. *Tr.* 919 etc. To make matters even clearer, in Hyg. *fab.* 91 snakes emerge from the burning torch—a detail derived perhaps from the lost E. *Alex.* (so Frazer ad Apollod. 1.8.2) (cp. *91*).

[34] Rebirth from fire: the Phoenix (Ov. *Met.* 15.392 ff.; Stat. *Silv.* 2.4.36); from a cauldron: Pelops (Pi. *O.* 1.37 ff.; Apollod. *Ep.* 2.3); an old ram (Apollod. 1.9.27). Burning to acquire immortality: Herakles (S. *Tr.* fin.); Demophoon (Hom. *h. Cer.* 235 ff.), Achilleus (A.R. 4.869 ff., Apollod. 3.13.6 and Frazer ad loc.).

[35] On stoning, as the *cause* of the metamorphosis: (*86*).

leads him to stress that the sceptre sprouts only after being thrust into the hearth.

Yet, there is something particularly arresting about this detail. Not one of the *non*-Herodotean models or precedents so much as mentions the "soil" (or soil equivalent) from which the plant sprouts. Even A. *Ag.* 966 ff. simply mentions that the plant is *not* uprooted and there is a hint of the same kind in Dan. 4.9 ff.

By contrast, Hdt. 1.108 specifies that the vine grows *from* Mandane's genitals. For both the structuralist and the psycho-analyst this specification may be held to refer *retroactively* also to the (implicit) "terrain" from which urine is produced (Hdt. 1.107). Its mention in the second dream can, so to speak, be treated as a "once and for all" clause.[36]

Even more striking, particularly from the literary viewpoint, is that the "terrain" *is* mentioned in the *discarded* Aischylean precedent. In A. *Choe.* 543 Orestes goes out of his way to substantiate his interpretation of Klytaimnestra's dream, by stressing that both he and the serpent came out of the same place: out of Klytaimnestra's vulva. In short, whereas the "terrain" is part of the *interpretation* in A. *Choe.*, it is part of the *dream* itself in S. *El.* This falls just short of being a genuine (displaced) slippage, since, as stressed before, in a dream-oriented culture the dream, its telling, its interpretation, etc., form an indivisible whole. By contrast, the serpent's Orestean swaddling bands (A. *Choe.* 544) may *not* be treated as "terrain". They *faintly* recall the iron and brass strips which bind the dream tree in Dan. 4.15. and the gold covering of the Atreidai's sceptre.[37]

The conception of the maternal sex organs as a "terrain" from which something can sprout, fits well Greek ways of thinking. Oidipous, in committing incest, is said to have ploughed (and seeded) the furrow from which he himself was born.[38] (A. *Sept.* 752 ff., cp. E. *Ph.* 17 ff.)

Hearth (Fire) and Urination. Throughout this chapter I stressed a clinically commonplace finding: it is not easy to disregard or to "forget" things at will. What is ostentatiously ejected by the front door, usually re-insinuates itself in disguise through the back door. If Sophokles knew Astyages' vine dream, he also knew his urine dream.[39] Traces of the urination dream should therefore be discernible in the *latent* content of the Sophoklean dream.

---

[36] I have already substantiated this view by citing, in note 16, popular ideas about female urination.

[37] This comparison does not undermine what is said, further on, about such metal bands, since it was shown above that child = phallos. A discussion of the social and psychological meaning of swaddling would, unfortunately, require a great deal of space. Careful studies of this practice show that in some cultures, where swaddling is routine, the infant is viewed as dangerous both to others and to himself: the swaddling serves to restrain him. (*72*, p. 107 ff., with citations of additional literature.) Cp. also the gold leaf covered corpses of royal Mykenaian babies.

[38] The group of my students who, in 1968–69, worked on the S. *El.* dream, drew many interesting parallels between it and the Oidipous myth (and Oedipus complex). Since their findings were more suggestive than conclusive, I do not outline them here, lest this merely suggestive material should prejudice the reader against the genuinely conclusive data presented in this chapter.

[39] Herodotos' "public lectures" preceded the publication of his book, which was in circulation by 429 B.C. Also, Sophokles supposedly knew Herodotos.

Even though Sophokles did not borrow any of the manifest elements of the dream about Mandane's urination, that dream can be linked with the one totally new manifest element in the Sophoklean dream: with the hearth. Though the introduction of the hearth motif is culturally extremely plausible (supra), the fact remains that Sophokles *selected* this symbol from amongst a number of other, culturally *equally* plausible, alternatives, such as the sheath of a sword, etc. His *preference* for the hearth calls for an explanation. Sophokles' "good" (and *conscious*) reason was the *cultural suitability* of the hearth; his "real" (and *unconscious*) reason for selecting it from amongst equally appropriate alternatives was the existence of a *psychological nexus* between fire (hearth) and urination.

Before proving this latent nexus, I propose to recall first the manifest similarities between the S. *El.* 417 ff. and the Hdt. 1.107 dreams.

(1) Both "mean" the same thing; the same warning message is encoded in two different ways. It is encoded in a third way in Hdt. 1.108.

(2) In all three dreams an extremely copious—and, indeed, overwhelming—"thing" emerges from the female sex organs or their equivalent, the hearth.

(3) In all three, the thing produced spreads out *at once*. Since I have already shown that these dreams are Near Eastern culture pattern dreams, it is legitimate to stress again that in numerous Mesopotamian urination dreams the urine "spreads out" (divides into branches?) apparently the moment it emerges from the meatus (*76*, pp. 264–266).

(4) In all three, an almost supernatural *feat* is performed—and urinary feats, particularly in dream, reflect excessive ambition.[40]

(5) Urinary feats are attributed almost exclusively to men, largely because women cannot perform urinary tricks.[41]

(6) In this dream, the feat is not a *qualitative* but a *quantitative* one. This may conceivably—but only conceivably—explain why Ktesias attributes this dream not to Astyages, but to Mandane.[42] Indeed, popular misconceptions notwithstanding, the urinary stream of women is more copious and stronger, since their urethra is shorter and wider than that of men.[43]

(7) The "qualitative" ("trick") feat motif is, however, symbolically anticipated in Astyages' first dream: the vine sprouts *skyward*.[44]

I now turn to the manifest nexus between urination and fire (hearth), on which the evidence is not simply conclusive but overwhelming.

(1) There exists a statistically significant correlation between bed-

---

[40] Cp. Freud: *47*, 201, 204 f., 208 f., 468 ff., *48*, 64 ff., *49*, 175 ff.; *53*, 91 f., *54*, 90; *55*, 102, 187 ff. Cp. especially one of Freud's own urination dreams (*47*, 468 ff.), in which he matches Herakles' cleaning out of Augeias' stables.

[41] Somali folklore stresses this female "handicap" (*83*, p. 202). Child study—even amongst primitives (*10*, p. 285)—shows that little girls try to duplicate male urinary feats. Conversely, some primitive boys perform feats showing their masculine "superiority", by exhibitionistically "urinating backward, like women and mares" (*16*).

[42] Ctes. ap. Nic. Dam. *fr.* 65, *FHG* 3.399.

[43] Information provided by Professor Pierre Aboulker, M.D.

[44] A Mesopotamian *man's* dream of urinating skyward foretells his son's brilliant career and the shortness of his own life (*76*, p. 265b). I note, as a curious coincidence, that anatomists call the urinary system a "tree".

wetting and firesetting (*74*). I, myself, had occasion to study such a case (*18*).

(2) The psychological basis of this nexus was at least briefly outlined by Freud (*56*, cp. *43*), in a paper only a few of whose interpretations are frankly speculative.

(3) In a number of cultures the nexus between fire and urine is explicit.[45]

(4) Myths, literary works and jokes readily link fire with urine.[46]

(5) As regards rites, it suffices to refer briefly to the *equus october* ritual (supra) and to recall, in addition to the equation: blood = semen, also the almost commonplace equation: semen = urine (*76*, p. 265a).[47]

(6) The fire = urine nexus is also confirmed by the finding that the *same* "message" can be encoded *either* by means of a *fire* symbolism, *or* by means of a *urine* symbolism. What makes such symmetrical encodings possible is the well-known technique of "symbolization by opposites" in mythology and folktales, quite as much as in literature, humour and dreams. Both structuralism and psycho-analysis recognize the affinity between structurally or affectively symmetrical narratives. I already mentioned that the nefarious birth of Paris is foreshadowed by Hekabe's dream of giving birth to a firebrand. A symmetrical (water) miracle foretold the nefarious birth of the tyrant Peisistratos: The *water* in the sacrificial cauldrons bubbled over, though *no fire* was lit under them (Hdt. 1.59). I doubt that the overflow of water from the cauldrons—which universally symbolize the female organs—is meant to represent the breaking of the birth waters (amniotic fluid). The "bubbling" clearly suggests that the water represents urine, which does bubble.[48]

It may therefore be asserted with considerable assurance that there is a strong *fantasmatic* nexus between fire and urine. Though Sophokles com-

---

[45] The Mongol is forbidden to urinate into fire (*56*). Yuma Indian woman can render themselves barren by urinating into fire (*46*, p. 159). Sedang Moi men bare their sex organs to prevent jungle fires, when they burn down parts of the jungle to clear new fields (*15*). The staple food of the Masai is a mixture of milk and blood (cp. A. *Choe.* 546) curdled with *ashes* and cow's *urine* (*73*). Even more striking is the alleged tradition that urine (though not water) could put out Greek fire; this idea would never have arisen were the *impulse* to urinate into fire non-existent.

[46] Most strikingly in the case of Gulliver in Lilliput (*92*). Zeus causes both lightning (fire) and rain—and Strepsiades professes to believe that Zeus causes rain by urinating into a sieve (Ar. *Nub.* 373 f.). The relevance of this joke for our purposes is increased by the fact that Zeus the bolt-hurler (καταιβάτηc) is turned into Zeus the excrement thrower (cκαταιβάτου) in Ar. *Pax.* 42 ... and even primitives know that one cannot easily defaecate without *also* urinating (*83*, p. 208). Though the sceptic may say that I risk spoiling a strong case by citing a less plausible (i.e., more symbolic) detail, I will mention also that Prometheus' smuggling of fire inside a hollow fennel-stalk, represents *perhaps* undischarged urine (Hes. *Op.* 50 ff.). By contrast, it would be irresponsible to suggest a nexus between the malodorous vaginal discharge of the Lemnian women and the Lemnian fire rite, now that Burkert's analysis of that fire rite is published (*9*).

[47] At the root of this equation is a so-called "infantile sex theory". I, myself, recall being told by a playmate (age 12?) that men impregnated women by urinating into the vagina. A psychoanalytic colleague informs me that a *mildly* neurotic woman *claimed* that her lover repeatedly urinated into her vagina, causing her extreme pleasure. (This is an impossibility.)

[48] A patient of mine carefully scrutinized his morning urine. If it was foamy, this "proved" that he had masturbated "in sleep".

pletely discarded the urine theme of Astyages' first dream, he reintroduced its *latent* content (fire) into his Klytaimnestra's dream, by inventing a completely new element—the hearth—for which there is no equivalent in his Stesichorean and Aischylean models.

Grapes and Urination

I must now deal with two loose ends.

It is extremely striking that in several sprouting dreams the plant is the domestic grape vine (ἄμπελος). It is mentioned in Hdt. 1.108, in the dream of Pharaoh's butler and in the Aischylean Klytaimestra's metaphor, though not in the Sophoklean dream.[49] The grape yields, of course, *yellowish* wine. In dream, Pharaoh's butler actually gives Pharaoh the (fermented) juice of the grapes to drink and the Aischylean Klytaimestra's reference to *"wine"* seems to imply drinking.[50] Mandane's urine *floods* Asia—and floods usually cause deaths by drowning. Last, but not least, Mesopotamian men dreamed of drinking their wives' urine (*76*, p. 266a).[51] I note these facts, but hesitate to make anything of them: the data are not copious and explicit enough for their interpretation to carry conviction, even if one added that olives—which are mentioned in two analogous accounts (dream of Xerxes, miracle of Athene's olive)—also yield a *yellowish* fluid.

Some speculations may be advanced also in connection with the wine-urine-milk nexus, as long as it is clearly stated that what I offer *here* are *speculations*, and *not* interpretations.

Milk, which is so important a motif in the Aischylean's Klytaimestra's dream, is totally lacking in the manifest content of the Sophoklean dream. However, the principle that nothing is ever *totally* forgotten or discarded makes it desirable to look at least for traces of the milk theme in the Sophoklean dream.

As indicated previously, Mandane's copious urination is a "phallic" feat, "proving" (in fantasy) that she is any man's equal. A relatively minor collateral detail may also be recalled here: the vine in the butler's dream has *three* branches and produces grapes and wine. Now, Ploutarchos did not have to read Freud to discover that the number "3" is a male symbol.[52]

This being said, I recall here again that there is on record (7) at least

---

[49] Cp., however, the Sophoklean and Euripidean references to the miraculous vine of Euboia, supra.

[50] Cp. the Aischylean Agamemnon's falling into a cauldron: he is apparently both wounded *and drowned*; few commentators take this latter detail into account (A. *Ag.* 1128 ff.).

[51] The drinking of female urine—and particularly of that of prostitutes—is a well-known perversion. Pathan women urinate into the mouths of captives. In some areas of Siberia, where only the rich can afford the intoxicating mushrooms, the poor intoxicate themselves by drinking the urine of the rich. A more magical theory of such urine drinking is proposed by La Barre (*60*, p. 178). Even horses lick up their own urine, if they are deprived of salt. For Mohave urine drinking dreams, cp. *30*, p. 138.

[52] Plu. *Quaest. Rom.* 2, p. 264A (probably 1 penis + 2 testes). I note that this passage deals with nuptial torches (fire).

one case in which a woman took great ("phallic") pride in her ability to make her *milk* spurt further than a man's phallic products can spurt: it proved her superior to men.[53] She clearly equated milk with semen and (male) urine. This is not surprising, since in belief, custom and fantasy (dream) alike, all bodily secretions are usually interchangeable.[54] The equation: milk = urine = fire may—but *only* may—thus provide a *faint* connection between the (omitted) milk motif and the (new) hearth motif.

The Sceptre

Though I have tried, throughout this chapter, to discuss first the objective and cultural aspects of the various dream items and to interpret their symbolism only afterwards, this section would become needlessly labyrinthine if I did not discuss the sceptre symbolism first, particularly since this symbol is so transparent that its interpretation is not likely to meet with much opposition.

Sceptre = Staff = Human Helper: S. *OC* 848, 1109.

Sceptre = Serpent is made evident by the fact that Aaron's rod can either turn into a serpent (*Exod.* 7.10) or else bud (*Num.* 17.8) and does so in both cases in a power-contest. Snakes are entwined around Hermes' rod and the equivalence of various types of rods and sceptres is, despite minor differences, fairly obvious (*96*, p. 108, note 2). This makes it fairly certain that, in the Sophoklean Klytaimnestra's dream, a sceptre is substituted for the Stesichorean-Aischylean serpent. I also note, somewhat tentatively, that whereas the Aischylean serpent is swaddled (A. *Choe.* 529, 545 f.), the sceptre of the Atreidai is notoriously covered with gold—of which more anon.

Sceptre = Phallos is implicit in Vernant's view (*96*, p. 108) that the dream represents coitus—and Vernant is *not* in sympathy with psychoanalysis. Cp. also the myths of phalloi in the hearth (supra), and Luc. *VH* 1.22.

The Sprouting of the Sceptre, after being thrust into the hearth, appears to reflect the view that the father is the child's sole progenitor (A. *Eum.* 658 ff.): the father seems to deposit a kind of homunculus into the woman, who then nurtures it.[55] But the sprouting of the sceptre may also hint at continued sexual potency, which in some groups—such as the Shilluk (*87*)—is a prerequisite for the holding of royal power. Though Greek hero myths are less explicit on this point than are Shilluk practices of Greek divine myths,[56] enfeebled old kings often yield the royal power to a suc-

---

[53] The symbolic equations: nipples = penis, breast = testes, are commonly met with in clinical practice (*28*).

[54] One can bewitch a person by getting hold of *any* of his bodily secretions, or of his hair or nail clippings. Being soiled in dream by *any* of one's wife's bodily secretions is believed by the Mohave to cause illness (*30*, p. 138).

[55] This theory of procreation has been somewhat too confidently linked with patriliny: the matrilineal Hopi Indians have identical theories (*14*), while the patrilineal Mohave hold that both parents contribute the seed (*21*).

[56] On the castration and dethronement of gods, cp. (*32*).

cessor:[57] the "overshadowing" motif in A. *Ag.* 966 and in Hdt. 1.108, quite as much as in S. *El.* 417 ff., may well point in the same direction.

Now, I have already indicated that the sprouting of this sceptre is comparable to the sprouting of Nebuchadnezzar's chopped-down tree and of Athene's chopped-down and burned olive—and that all are comparable to the ritual mutilation of a corpse (or body), which Apollod. 3.5.1 explicitly links with the pruning of trees or vines. In addition, I have already noted that it is inconceivable that μαϲχαλιϲμόϲ should not include also the ablation of the corpse's sex organs, since that is an extremely common way of mutilating corpses,[58] and, as said before, the usurpers tried to uproot Agamemnon's entire lineage (even fathered by his ghost?).

I therefore hold that the sceptre represents not simply the phallos of Agamemnon, but, specifically, his *ablated* member. This specification will render more comprehensible what will be said subsequently about the "circulating" sceptre.

We possess a good deal of information about the sceptre in question, which will materially contribute to the clarification of its meaning in the dream.

The Origin of this sceptre already foreshadows its transmissibility: Hephaistos made it and gave it to Zeus, who handed it to Hermes, for transmission to Atreus (Hom. *Il.* 2.101). It may be said that this sceptre "circulated" (Th. 1.9) even before it reached Atreus, and was then transmitted to Atreus' heir (cp. the Trojan royal sceptre: Q.S. 2.136 ff.).

The core of the sceptre is an unspecified kind of wood,[59] stripped of its branches and bark and therefore so permanently dead that Achilleus represents the possibility of its sprouting again as the very prototype of the absurdly impossible.[60] The fact that, in S. *El.* 98 f., Agamemnon is compared to an *oak* sheds no light upon the nature of the wood of which the sceptre is made—but may strengthen the view that a *wooden* object can represent *in dream* one of *his* organs.

The sceptre is "golden"—i.e., either wrapped in thin sheet-gold or else studded with gold nails or rivets.[61] If, as I think, a wrapping in gold foil is meant—for the driving of too many nails into wood might split it—some interesting inferences may be made. The Atreidai's sceptre, which sprouts

[57] Peleus-Achilleus-Neoptolemos (E. *Androm.*); Kadmos-Pentheus (E. *Ba.*); Pheres-Admetos (E. *Alc*); Laertes-Odysseus (Hom. *Od.*), cp. *85*, s.vv.

[58] Copious documentation in (*32*), to which may now be added the impossibility of taking foreskin trophies from the circumcised Aquiyawasa (*77*, p. 21, note 1a), and references to penis trophies in ancient Egypt (D.S. 1.48.2, 1.55.8 f., etc.). Admiral Coligny's corpse was so mutilated during the St Bartholomew's night massacre of the Calvinists—who, incidentally, reciprocated during the uprising in the Languedoc (*63*, pp. 505, etc.). Even a woman's pubis may be "scalped": the Princesse de Lamballe's during the French revolution; Cheyenne Indian women's by the troopers of a Colorado National Guard Cavalry Regiment (*58*, p. 178: a veiled allusion to this fact).

[59] The branch which sprouts from it is, likewise, unspecified; as noted, Mazon's "laurier" is gratuitous.

[60] Hom. *Il.* 1.234. Though Achilleus speaks specifically of the speaker's sceptre and not of the Atreidai, this makes no real difference (*96*, p. 108 ff.), especially as regards the material of which sceptres were made.

[61] Jebb ad vv. 417; cp. Hom. *Il.* 1.15, 246; 2.268; *Od.* 11.91, 369. If golden nails were used, Mykenaian sword handles adorned with gold or silver nails suggest how this was done (*69*, p. 262; *97*, p. 517). Cp. the name (or epithet) Chrysaor.

in dream, is wrapped in gold;[62] Nebuchadnezzar's dream tree, after being cut down, is bound with iron and brass, but will flourish later on. (Dan. 4.15, 23.) Just what purpose these bands of metal served the Biblical text does not tell. Whether they were meant to inhibit the stump's sprouting during that King's madness, or to prevent its splitting and rotting until the time came for it to sprout again—after Nebuchadnezzar became a great and glorious King (Dan. 4.34 ff.)—is anyone's guess. I insist here simply on the *technique* of ringing wood with metal.

I begin with a reference to an ancient Ephesian *stone* pounder or pestle, ringed with tin inlays,[63] which I assume to be decorative imitations of the functional metal bands which prevent *wooden* pounders and pestles from splitting.[64]

The metal sheathing of the Atreidai's sceptre may well be an imitation of bronze-ringed staves, wherewith one occasionally pounded the ground or smote an opponent. Traces of a rough use of sceptres exist in the Homeric epics.[65] Therefore not only wooden pounders, but also early wooden rods ("sceptres") destined for rough use *may* have been bound with metal bands.

Now, the Ephesian pounder in question has a striking particularity: it is *even more* ostentatiously phallic in shape than any pestle *must* be. The glans and the sulcus coronarius are accurately imitated.[66]

Thus, since the sceptre in Klytaimnestra's dream stands at once for the phallos and for the child produced by the phallos, it is of some interest to note that both male organs and babies are, at times, "ringed"—sometimes with metal—both actually and symbolically.[67]

---

[62] As were the corpses of royal babies in Mykenai (supra., note 37).

[63] First published by Cook, *12*, 3.898, fig. 731, pl. 67.

[64] As technology develops, functional elements often turn into mere decorative elements. Though there is no pottery in clay-less Polynesia, the decorations of Polynesian pottery-equivalents show that Polynesians made *coiled* pottery before their migration to their present home.

[65] Hom. *Il.* 1.245; 2.199; 265; *Od.* 2.80. The hypothetical bronze ringed staves I have in mind may have resembled the metal-ringed bamboo *lathi* of policemen in India.

[66] The "pestle = penis" and "mortar = vagina" equations are widespread. Greece: Artemid. 2.42; Mohave (*30*); Betsileo (*65*, p. 45), etc.

[67] *Penis*: The protective tying of a string around the foreskin and the occurrence of penis-sheaths amongst primitives. In parts of Indonesia the skin and glands of the penis may be incrusted with precious stones, etc. Certain South American Indians increase the pleasure of their wives by ringing the sulcus coronarius with a goat's eyelashes. Ancient athletes in training and also certain slaves were infibulated with metal rings (*2*). A neurotic patient sometimes put a padlock around his scrotum (*28*). A neurotic wife, much enamoured of her husband, adorned her husband's penis with ribbons and bows (*68*). A patient had fantasies about a penis tied up with string, like an old-fashioned salami or like a rolled roast and—using rubber bands—once tried to tie up his own penis in such a manner, so as to increase the pleasure of his mistress, after seeing a picture of a Far Eastern hard-rubber ring supposed to promote erection by the compression of the dorsal vein of the penis. Perverts sometimes put metal rings around their flaccid organs, which, after an erection ensues, must be removed with metal saws. Some use wedding rings for such purposes; this sheds light upon the wedding ring symbolism. *Baby*: The most obvious equivalents are swaddling bands, as in A. *Choe.* 529, etc. Even more striking is the tradition that the Egyptian "Kadmos" gilded "Semele's" prematurely born infant, "Dionysos" (= "Osiris") (D.S. 1.23.4 f.). This gold sheath apparently replaces Zeus' "thigh"—which may be a euphemism mentioned by Greek tradition in this context (E. *Ba.* 96, etc.).

I strenuously insist that I do *not* cite these facts so as to suggest that sceptres were gold plated in order to *make* them symbolize a phallos and/or a baby. I seek to indicate only that the gold plating of the sceptre *does not preclude* its being a phallos or baby symbol. Anyone reading more into my remarks than I intended, is irresponsibly indulging in "wild psycho-analysis" which the real psycho-analyst is the first to condemn (*50, 90*).

I will return to the problem of golden organs in Greek traditions somewhat further on.

The Problem of Circular Transmission must now be considered in detail.

Perhaps the most striking example of something that circulates, with the circulation *twice* ending by a return to the one who, at one point of the tale, "emits" or sends it out, is the Hydra's poison. The story is so well known that I do not document each of the steps in the "circulation" of this poison; only unusual versions are substantiated by the citing of an ancient authority.

The Hydra is particularly poisonous; after killing this monster Herakles uses its body-fluids to poison his own arrows. With one of them he slays Nessos who raped—or tried to rape (*37*)—Deianeira. The dying Nessos gives Deianeira his blood and semen, persuading her that, used at the proper time, it would insure Herakles's fidelity to her. When Herakles proves unfaithful, Deianeira sends him a robe smeared with this poison, that kills Herakles. The chain is: Hydra—Herakles—Nessos—Deianeira—Herakles.

Herakles, ready to be burned alive on Mount Oite, gives his bow and arrows to Philoktetes, who consented to light the pyre. Philoktetes is subsequently bitten by *a* hydra (water snake), or, according to Serv. *V. Aen.* 3.402, is wounded by a poisoned arrow (resembling his own). The chain is: *the* Hydra—Herakles—Philoktetes—*a* hydra (poisoned arrow). The pattern discernible in familial curses (*67*) resembles this one.

Subsequently Philoktetes slays Paris with one of his arrows. Then, at Krimisa, Philoktetes builds a temple to Apollon-the-*Wanderer* (Ἀλαιός) (Lyc. 913 ff.).[68] This is one of Apollon's rarer epithets and may therefore be significant, though the fact that the archer Philoktetes should have built a temple precisely to Apollon—an archer god—is natural.

I cite this tale of the circulation of the Hydra's poison since, like the sceptre, it returns to the one "emitting" it—and, in fact, it does so twice (Herakles and Philoktetes). (Cp. Apollon's arrow: Q.S. 3.83 ff.)

The Circulation of the Sceptre, so strongly emphasized by the text, may possibly be cited as an argument militating against the view that the sceptre symbolizes Agamemnon's phallos.[69] Instead of retrenching myself behind Cicero's argument: "Nihil tam praepostere, tam incondite, tam monstruose cogitari potest, quod non possimus somniare" (Cic. *de div.* 2.71.146) (cp. chap. 6, note 26), I propose to show that it is precisely the sceptre's circulation which proves that it represents, in dream, the phallos of Agamemnon.

For gold-leaf covered baby corpses (note 37). For Pythagoras' golden thigh cp. *8*, p. 23.   [68] But that epithet may mean only: absent from home (K.J.D.).

[69] And/or—as Vernant suggests (*96*, p. 109)—his son, which, symbolically (child = phallos), is much the same.

The basic consideration was admirably discussed by Snell (*88*, p. 5, fig. 2), in another context. Some lacunae of the Homeric vocabulary pertaining to the living body and its organs or parts, together with certain early Greek representations of the body on vases, suggest that the Greek's body image resembled a completed "jigsaw puzzle" (contra: Herter). I have shown elsewhere that such a body image—and the notion of a near-total organ autonomy which goes with it—is far from rare and is both culturally (ethnologically) and clinically interpretable (*35*, chap. 13).

I cannot attempt to broach here the immense topic of circulating organs and of vicarious physiological functioning in myth, in belief, in ritual, in informal custom and also in (neurotic) fantasy.[70]

I will therefore define only three of the notions which appear to underlie the sceptre symbolism in this dream, and will illustrate each of them with one Greek example only—asking the reader to take it on faith that many other examples exist.

(1) *Circulating organs*: The three Graiai have only one eye and one tooth between them and use them in rotation. (A. *PV.* 792 ff.)

(2) *The circulating "essence"* (*"mana"*) is exemplified by Cheiron's ceding his immortality to Prometheus. (Apollod. 2.5.4; 5.11.10.)

(3) *Ablated organs continue to function*: At Delphi, women can "awaken" Dionysos' phallos. (Plu. *de Is. et Os.* 35, p. 365A.)[71] I recall in this connection my conviction that, in the course of the μασχαλισμός to which Agamemnon's corpse was subjected, his phallos, too, was ablated.[72]

Of course, *in reality* Agamemnon's phallos was *not* grafted onto the body of Aigisthos and then regrafted onto the "body" of Agamemnon's ghost. Even the manifest dream does not go quite so far: it is the sceptre that twice changes hands. But it seems probable that, underlying this relatively plausible symbolic representation, there is the fantasy of the circulating organ and, *a fortiori*, of the circulating *essence*.

Before I tackle this problem, an important fact must be noted: In vv. 266 ff., which list almost all of Aigisthos' usurpations—including his usurpation of Klytaimnestra's *bed*—the usurpation of the *sceptre* is strikingly omitted.[73] This omission becomes even more striking once one notes that the *dream* mentions *only* the usurpation of the sceptre. Such almost ostentatious omissions are psychologically highly significant.[74] Even purely

---

[70] A study of this notion is on the point of being completed. Cp. chap. 6, note 91.

[71] Cp. also the phalloi in hearths, discussed in connection with the hearth symbolism, supra, note 29.

[72] The corpse's extremities were cut off, so that the crippled ghost could not take revenge. Since dead heroes could father human children (Hdt. 6.69) and since Agamemnon's murderers tried, above all, to destroy his descendants (and avengers), one would have to assume, on these grounds only, that his phallos was ablated, even if the taking of phallic trophies were far less widespread than it actually is (*32*). Cp. Nilsson (*75*, 1², p. 100), also supra.

[73] There is no mention of a sceptre in A. *Ag.* 966 ff. either.

[74] A psychoanalytic colleague could not interpret one of his own dreams, in which there was a fishbowl containing three fishes named Mark, Matthew and Luke. When I said: "What about John?" my colleague replied: "Now I understand my dream—it is about a man named John." (The former Christian symbol: fish = Christ makes this interpretation a certainty, though that symbolism is derived from the initials Ι.Χ.Θ.Υ.C.).

literary considerations require that vv. 266 ff. should be viewed as complementing the dream.

Vernant (*96*, p. 107) considers it anomalous that the (effeminate) Aigisthos should move into (the manly, A. *Ag.* 11) Klytaimnestra's palace, the way an Athenian woman moved into her husband's home. But surely the real point is that, in so doing, Aigisthos behaved like any newly made king of the pre-patrilineal—and even like many new kings of the heroic— period. Menelaos himself moved into Tyndareos' (and Helene's) palace at Sparta, as Oidipous moved into Iokaste's palace at Thebes.[75] Many myths describe the "normal" procedure of killing the king and marrying the widowed Queen; Aigisthos simply inverted this traditional sequence. But even so it is fairly apparent that the moment he began his usurpations and, above all, began to share Klytaimnestra's *bed*, he took over Agamemnon's social niche and functions, for it is only a slight exaggeration to say that Kings were made in the Queen's bed.[76] A Queen, seeking to seduce some youth, offered him not only her favours, but also the throne: she contemplated viricide. But in E. *Hipp.* 1010 Hippolytos spontaneously rejects this potential offer.

In short, a *corporeal* phallos *acquires* the additional quality of being a *royal* phallos, *through* cohabitation with a Queen. It is in this sense that one may find in the dream a trace of the notion of a transmissible, circulating "essence"—the essence in question being royal status. Even sociologically Agamemnon's recuperation of the sceptre in dream is *incomplete*, until he "re-consecrates" it by implanting it into the hearth (= Klytaimnestra). Only then can the sceptre sprout once more.[77]

These findings explain also why Aigisthos' is called a cowardly lion. (A. *Ag.* 1224.) Like Blaydes, Paley, Headlam and Mazon, I hold that "Lion" was the name-title or title-name of the High King of Mykenai.[78] It is perhaps the script Aischylos used which prevented him from writing "Lion" instead of (like the copyists): "lion". It is of great interest that only in A. *Ag.* 1259 (and *nowhere else* in the *Oresteia*). Agamemnon is called a lion . . . whose place in bed is usurped by a mere wolf: Aigisthos. One should perhaps write "Lion" (Λέων) in both instances.[79] Once Lion is capitalized, the expression "cowardly Lion" becomes understandable, for a personally worthless man can still be the Lion King; the insults which Achilleus heaps upon Agamemnon, *the man*, prove this. (Hom. *Il.* 1.122 ff.)[80]

[75] On the socio-historically transitional character of the latter episode, cp. (*25*).

[76] Cp. Atossa's three royal husbands, Hdt. 3.88 etc. (chap. 1).

[77] So physiological a re-consecration is not un-Greek. Hera gave the adult Herakles the breast (supra); some monuments represent Hera as acting out a birth of Herakles. Cp. chap. 6, note 56.

[78] Mylonas notes that the Pelopidai came from Asia, where both real and symbolic lions abounded (E.R.D.). The usual argument is the lion-gate of Mykenai; an additional and perhaps better argument is that *only* Agamemnon wears a lion's pelt (Hom. *Il.* 10.23). "Lion" is a suitable title for a paramount King, cp. "Conquering Lion of Judah". But, I doubt that A. *Ag.* 1258 and A. *Choe.* 938 shed light on *this* problem.

[79] In A. *Choe.* the first and only time Agamemnon's natural heir Orestes (together with Pylades) is called a lion (v. 938) is while he reasserts his claim to the throne by killing his mother. For A. *Ag.* 1224 I cannot accept Fraenkel's explanations.

[80] George III's recurrent psychotic bouts did not abolish his royal status. Similar historical examples exist.

In fact, for the sociologist, the notion that Agamemnon's sceptre-phallos has to be properly re-consecrated by cohabitation with the *Queen* (and not simply with the *woman* Klytaimnestra) *partly* explains why, in the dream, coitus is represented by a thrusting of the sceptre into the hearth, instead of by means of an undisguised coital dream (corresponding to the direct reference to Aigisthos' adulterous coitus in vv. 266 ff.). On the basis of Vernant's analysis of the function of the hearth, it could reasonably be argued that the hearth represents the *Queen's* feminine parts *better* than do the actual organs of the *woman* Klytaimnestra. The symbolic cohabitation of the royal sceptre with the queenly hearth is a better symbolic revalidation of Agamemnon's royalty than would be an explicit coital dream.

I must strongly stress that the arguments I just advanced are sociological and literary, rather than psychological. They deal with more or less conscious and socially moulded symbols. The psychological reasons explaining why the dream represents coitus symbolically, rather than explicitly, will be discussed further below.

Considering the role of royal cohabitation—a ritual act almost approximating a sacred marriage (ἱερός γαμός)—in the dream and its sociological implications, many problems would be left in suspense without a careful scrutiny of the *nature* of Aigisthos' usurpations (listed in vv. 266 ff.), both in strictly sociological terms and in terms of their psychological implications as well. For, as will be seen, so far-reaching and manifold an usurpation, the replication of so many of the absent—and then murdered—King's functions and roles, must have both a socio-cultural basis and psychological consequences.

(I) The socio-functional basis of Aigisthos' usurpations is the fact that, as soon as he began to occupy the segment of "social space" formerly occupied by Agamemnon, he became *socially* the same "person" as Agamemnon. What is involved here is the concept of social representation and of functional substitutability. Indeed:

(1) He who wears a mask *is* the one his mask represents.

(2) If both A and B stand in a relationship *x* to C, then A is functionally substitutable to B (and vice versa), but only

(a) With respect to C (and his equivalents), and

(b) Within the framework of the *x* relationship.

In classificatory kinship systems this functional substitutability (*17*) can even entail a *social non*-implementation of selfhood (*71*), creating the *mistaken* impression (*36*, chap. 6) of a *psychological* lack of the sense of the "self" (*67*).[81]

(II) What, from the sociological point of view, is functional substitutability, is, from the psychological point of view, what Sperling (*89*) called an "appersonation". It seems superfluous to examine one by one the

---

[81] Two Sedang Moi cousins (and best friends) had married the same man. I asked one of them: "Are you jealous when your husband cohabits with your cousin and co-wife?" The young woman—a strong character and an individualist—replied: "Why should I? She is [*for such purposes*] the same person as I." In such societies even subjective feelings may be expressed in terms of a social relationship or role. A planter, who genuinely loved his native mistress, said to her: "I love you; you are a *sweet girl*." She replied affectionately: "I love you—you are *my husband*." Some other forms of social substitutability were discussed elsewhere (*36*, chap. 6). Cp. S. *OT* 258, etc.

psychological consequences of all of Aigisthos' usurpations, though I wish
to stress once more that, in vv. 266 ff., the pouring of libations into the
sacred hearth—which Jebb (ad loc.) rightly deems the same as the one
near which Agamemnon was murdered (203)—precedes a mention of his
"pouring" another kind of "libation" into Klytaimnestra herself. I will
consider only the fact that Aigisthos wears Agamemnon's robes. His doing
so can be fully justified by socio-economic considerations.

(1) In Greek (and Mykenaian) society fine textiles represented much
work and were very valuable. Even Periandros was stingy enough not to
place Melissa's clothes on her funeral pyre (Hdt. 5.92), (75, p. 179).

(2) The robes in question may well have been part of the King's
regalia; they were no more "cast-offs" than the sceptre was a "second-
hand" stick.

But this socio-economically fully understandable wearing of Agamemnon's robes[82] also has psychological dimensions or consequences, which
supplement and complement its cultural dimensions (*32, 36*, chaps. 4, 5).

A wholly convincing—because unexpected—consequence of a superb
experiment was the discovery that clothes are part of the wearer's *body
image*. Subjects were hypnotically induced to develop "agnosia" with
regard to the parts and organs of the *body*. It was then discovered that the
subjects developed *spontaneously* also an agnosia with respect to their
clothes. In simplest terms, they could *name* neither the *arm* nor the *sleeve*;
they could only describe them in a round about way (*93*).[83] Cultural
factors help one understand this merging of the clothes with the body. In
one Greek tradition the Skiapodes' feet also play the role of "clothing".[84]

Two Homeric passages show that the ancients were aware of the
fusion of the clothes with the body in the body image:

(1) Hom. *Il.* 16.41 ff.: Patroklos dons Achilleus armour; he expects to
be mistaken for Achilleus and to behave like his friend.

(2) Hom. *Il.* 17.209 ff.: Achilleus' armour, stripped from Patroklos'
corpse, fits itself (by shrinking?) to Hektor's body. Ares thereupon enters
him (as he occasionally seems to enter Achilleus), so that his (expanding?)
limbs are filled with (Achillean) valour and might. In short, Hektor
becomes—partly even physically—a double of Achilleus, though—*significantly—not* of Patroklos, since the latter also simply appersonated Achilleus.

I hold that these Homeric passages help us understand the psychological

---

[82] A good equivalent is Penelope's demand that her future husband should be able to
bend Odysseus' bow (Hom. *Od.* 21.74 ff.).

[83] A personal experience has similar implications. In 1943, at the end of the day I first
put on the uniform of a U.S. Naval Officer, I dozed off in an armchair. When I began to
wake up, I saw a sleeve with gold braid lying on my lap and woke up completely with a
start: I had not recognized the sleeve (and hand) as my own.

[84] Ctes. *fr.* 89; sch. Ar. *Av.* 1553; Plin. *HN* 7.22.1, etc. Ethnology furnishes even more
striking examples. The men of certain South American Indian tribes routinely bring
about a luxation of the penis, and are therefore able to conceal it inside the skin and the
fatty tissue of the lower abdomen, which plays the role of "clothing" (*11, 98*). According to
the Sedang Moi, the placenta is the cloak (= blanket) of the foetus (*15*). The Mohave
Indian baby's cradle-board not only appears to be treated as part of its body, but even
delimits the "social space" the baby inhabits: the baby is not an inhabitant of the house,
but of the cradle. If a cradled baby dies, only its cradle is burned; only after it ceases to be
cradled is the house burned down at its death (*20*).

dimensions and consequences of Aigisthos' wearing Agamemnon's robes: his complete social usurpation and his psychological appersonation of Agamemnon. He may possibly have worn on occasion even Agamemnon's lion-skin cloak (Hom. *Il.* 10.23). If those who hold that the name-title of the High King of Mykenai was "Lion King" are right—and I think they are—Aigisthos even appropriated Agamemnon's "name".[85]

If, as I think, the sociological concept of "functional substitutability" and the psychological concept of "appersonation" have a bearing on Aigisthos' complete usurpation of Agamemnon's role, functions, (perhaps) name-title, queen, etc., this, too, renders more plausible the view that the circulating sceptre of the *manifest* content of the dream is a reflection of the fantasy of the circulating organ (and "essence"), which I believe to be present in the *latent* content of the dream.

But even if this inference is not accepted, the least that can be said with assurance is that the "circulation" of the sceptre cannot be viewed as evidence disproving the inescapable interpretation of the sceptre as a symbol of the phallos, of the hearth as a female organ and of the thrusting of the sceptre into the hearth as a coital symbol. That much is admitted even by Vernant, who cannot be suspected of being sympathetic to psychoanalysis.

Excursus: Greek tradition knew of golden organs: the "real" (?) golden thigh of Pythagoras (Arist. *fr.* 191 R.) and the (faked) one of Alexandros the false prophet (Luc. *Alex.* 40). Burkert (*8*, p. 23) speaks in this connection of shamanistic dismembering and rebirth rites; Dodds speaks of tattooing (*39*, p. 163). Both theories imply lesions of the body. This view is indirectly supported by the fact that Komaitho *cuts off* Pterelaos' one golden hair (Apollod. 2.4.7., etc.) as Skylla *cuts off* Nisos' purple hair (Apollod. 3.15.8, etc.). The already cited gilding of the prematurely born Osiris (which seems to replace the prematurely lost protection of the womb) tends to suggest that golden, or gold covered, organs or parts of the body are somehow to be linked with bodily lesions: the gold may either be a prosthesis[86] or a protective covering, palliating a real or symbolic defect. I recall once more also the gold-leaf covered corpses of royal babies at Mykenai.

The problem of these golden organs is too complex to be discussed here; it is not even certain that sufficient data have survived to permit them to be satisfactorily interpreted. My sole purpose here is to show that the few existing traditions concerning golden organs do *not* militate *against* the interpretation that the ("golden") sceptre of the Atreidai is, *in dream*, a phallos.

The Evolution of the Dream is inseparable from its affective tone. The trend of the dream can be clarified only if, like Vernant (*96*, p. 108), one admits from the start that it is a transparent female coital dream; such

---

[85] I recall the repeatedly formulated hypothesis that "Minos" was a title also construed as a name—as was perhaps "Pharaoh". I am even in sympathy with the hypothesis, formulated by a fine and scholarly novelist, Miss Mary Renault (*80*), that *every* Eleusinian year-king was simply called Kerkyon, the title serving also as a name. Cp. supra, "Lion", note 78.

[86] In which case "thigh" may well be a euphemism. Cp. Pelops' ivory shoulder, which is a prosthesis.

dreams are repeatedly attested for Greek women,[87] though less often than for men, perhaps because male erotic dreams leave visible traces (*42, test.* 423, no. 14, etc.).

Structural considerations—which I must repeat again, so as to enable the reader to bear them constantly in mind—also support this interpretation. In vv. 266 ff., the libation poured into the hearth *precedes* a reference coitus; in the dream con*cubitus* is alluded to *before* there is a symbolic representation of co*itus* with the hearth.

The dream is manifestly dysphoric and, were it a real dream, the dysphoria would be experienced already in sleep: it is an anxiety dream.

(1) The anxiety dream sent by Agamemnon's wrathful shade[88] is obviously not a simple wish-fulfillment dream. Indeed, in principle all dreams about the dead are ominous.[89] They are more ominous than usual if the dead person is seen to carry something (ps.-Hp. *insomn.* 92)—as Agamemnon carries his sceptre.

(2) Dream coitus with dead persons, who are *not* heroes receiving a cult,[90] is especially harmful, for two specifiable reasons:

(a) Many groups believe that the dead lure the living to the land of the dead, by providing for them instinctual gratifications (coitus, food) in dream (*30*, passim).

(b) In addition to the dream being ghostly and necrophiliac, Klytaimnestra's coital partner in dream is "inappropriate", not only because she herself had murdered him, but also because, in a waking state, she would not find him desirable. I cannot discuss here the vexing problem of such dreams, which *seem* to run counter to the wish-fulfillment theory of dreaming. I must content myself with citing some clinical observations. Dreams of coitus with an inappropriate partner seem to be especially frequent in times of great and realistic psychological stress.[91] This is particularly true of women who unconsciously equate coitus with aggression and are therefore obliged to "erotize anxiety".[92]

The mingling of erotic elements and of anxiety explains why this dream —like that of Menelaos (A. *Ag.* 420 ff.)—can be divided into two acts.

(1) In the first, manifestly *non*-symbolic, part of the dream, Agamemnon simply lies down beside Klytaimnestra (*3*, p. 54). Since this meaning of the opening verses is justified in connection with an analysis of the location of

---

[87] Penelope: Hom. *Od.* 22.88 ff.; Demaratos' mother: Hdt. 6.69; etc. Epigraphic evidence: *42, test.* 423 (= *IG* IV², 1) no. 42 (with a snake), less explicitly in nos. 23, 39, 41, 42; *test.* 426. Several other testimonia concern homosexual dreams of men.

[88] A. *Choe.* 37 ff. and the Argument; S. *El.* 459 ff.; E. *Or.* 618. Dodds, who discusses Greek anxiety dreams well (*39*, p. 127, note 52), cites also A. *Eum.* 94 ff.; Plu. *V. Cim.* 6; Paus. 3.17.8 f.

[89] *6*, p. 225, citing Artemid. 2.67; Achmet, p. 3.26 Drexl.

[90] In Hdt. 6.69 Astrabakos is a hero: he has a heroön and a cult. Is the sending of a libation *after* the coitus dream a first step towards the heroization of Agamemnon, so as to reduce the harmfulness of the coitus dream? The question deserves to be asked, though it would be foolhardy to answer it.

[91] In 1956–57 I obtained an unusual number of such dreams from recent Hungarian refugees. Cp. chap. 2.

[92] Cp. chap. 6, in which it is shown that the Aischylean Klytaimnestra's dream also contained both *latent* erotic gratifications and extremely frightening *manifest* details. For another example of the erotization of anxiety in Greece, cp. (*26*).

the hearth, I consider here only the extent of Agamemnon's activities in these opening verses.

(a) Even though ὁμιλίαν can also designate actual coitus,[93] I hold that, in these verses, it denotes only corporal proximity.

(b) It would be aesthetically unsatisfying if the opening part of the dream included an *explicit* coitus, repeated *symbolically* in the second part of the dream.

It is not denied that this can happen in some dreams—but such a sequence would be highly unusual. A comparison with the sequence in vv. 266 ff. will help clarify matters, even though it does not involve a dream. Coitus is first *symbolically* represented (the poured libation) and is then referred to *explicitly*. This could happen in a dream which is *not particularly anxiety arousing*: the initial symbolic representation of coitus would lead to an increase in the pressure of the instinctual drive upon the "dream censor (*47*, pp. 505 ff.). When the resistances of the latter are overcome, an explicit coital dream can succeed a symbolic one. But Klytaimnestra's dream is an *anxiety-arousing*, guilt-laden and necrophiliac dream.[94] It would be psychologically more plausible if such a dream, beginning with a situation which under normal circumstances would lead to coitus, suddenly turned symbolical, so as to prevent a sudden, panicky awakening.[95] Only by recourse to symbolism, *at the crucial moment*, can the dream continue to perform its function of "guardian of the sleep" (*47*, pp. 233 f., etc.)—though at the cost of depriving the dreamer of a complete gratification. Exactly the same happens, in a somewhat different *way*, in Menelaos' dream, where, despite desire, a complete dream coitus would also be psychologically intolerable (chap. 3).

These considerations require that ὁμιλίαν should *not* be taken to signify coitus—and, so far as I know, it is not taken in that sense by any commentator. Understanding that word to refer simply to a lying down side by side, causes the dream sequence to become psychologically plausible and aesthetically satisfying . . . and it is never superfluous to reinforce accepted interpretations by new considerations.

But this conception of the dream sequence also has a further advantage: it sheds some light upon the paradoxical consequences of the dream: Klytaimnestra's *logically* unjustifiable doubts about the meaning of the dream (645) become *psychologically* understandable the moment one realizes that, while objectively ominous and generally dysphoric, her dream also contained, at least in a symbolic form, instinctually gratifying elements. Her perplexity is a direct consequence of the "erotization of anxiety" in the dream.[96]

[93] S. *OT* 367, 1185; Hdt. 1.182; E. *Hel.* 1400; X. *Smp.* 8.22, *Mem.* 3.11.4, etc.

[94] On ancient Greek necrophilia, cp. (*59*) and (*27*).

[95] Cp. chap. 6 and the references it contains to such awakenings, and especially to that of the Aischylean Klytaimnestra.

[96] The erotization of anxiety is much more commonly met with than one may think. Two sets of data must suffice for present purposes. The first concerns the occurrence of spontaneous ejaculations in adolescents during difficult examinations. The second concerns persons who compulsively seek risks in connection with sexual activities: risks of detection and scandal, risks even of disease or pregnancy. The classical studies are those of Laforgue (*61*, *62*).

Psychological Interpretation: Nearly everything in this section is already foreshadowed by the rest of the chapter. Klytaimnestra dreams symbolically of coitus with her murdered husband's ghost. Were Klytaimnestra a real patient, I would probably try to discover whether her's was a post-coital dream: one in which her real bedmate—the effeminate but murderous Aigisthos—is transformed into a killer of women. After all, Aigisthos was a close kinsman of Agamemnon; under normal circumstances, he would have had to avenge his death. This fact is, so far as I know, rather consistently overlooked.[97]

All that need be added here is that—precisely because she is (defensively) "manly" (A. *Ag.* 11, etc.)—Klytaimnestra is just the kind of woman who would experience coitus as an aggression. She would therefore prefer an effeminate, subordinate husband to a virile and independent one . . . and yet be disappointed by her chosen spouse's lack of virility. The sprouting sceptre in the hearth is a reflection of her phallic ambitions, but is also retrospectively maternal, since she is not about to conceive a child either by Aigisthos, or by the ghost of Agamemnon.

What matters most psychologically, is the close link between coitus and murder in this dream,—a link made more dreadful still by the fact that the "phallos" in question, though certainly ablated in the course of the μασχαλισμός, yet returns: in dream in the form of a circulating sceptre, and in reality in the form of a murderous, exiled son, who also "circulated" —and was believed dead.

But the psychologically most interesting aspect of the dream is its *pseudo*-transparency, which conceals how deeply its true latent content is buried. Genuinely transparent dreams are commonly dreamed by children and hysterics. Genuinely opaque dreams are often encountered in the analysis of obsessive-compulsives. But *pseudo*-transparent dreams, which conceal the dream's real opacity, I have encountered mainly in the analysis of severe character-disorders with manifestly perverted and even criminal leanings, and with almost uncontrollable acting-out tendencies. Since this characterization is fully applicable to Klytaimnestra, the dream is plausible also in this respect.

Yet a caveat must be entered here. Every *part* and aspect of the dream is psychologically plausible. What continues to disturb me about it, is the manner in which these individually plausible aspects, details and structures are *put together*, creating the impression of something *contrived*. Hence, despite everything that can be shown to be psychologically plausible, I continue to feel that, taken in its entirety, this dream is more literature than dream. If a patient told it to me, I would suspect that the actual dream had, on awakening, undergone a considerable amount of (perhaps unwitting) "secondary elaboration".[98]

This finding explains why I have left to the last the scrutiny of this dream as literature.

[97] Kin-murder creates insoluble problems in societies based on the vendetta principle: the murderer is also the avenger. Cp. chap. 4, note 18.

[98] Cp. General Introduction, regarding dreams recorded by Artemidoros and regarding the dreams of Aristeides the Rhetor, which are, at long last, available to the psychoanalyst in Behr's excellently commented translation (5).

Literary Aspects: As a literary device, the Sophoklean dream is less satisfactory and functionally less necessary than is the Aischylean Klytaimestra's dream. Yet, it is a more literary dream than its Aischylean equivalent. Both these findings indicate that the motif of Klytaimnestra's dream had become threadbare through too much use. Sophokles tried to renovate it, by changing its manifest content; Euripides simply eliminated it from his *Elektra,* though he hints at it in E. *Or.* 618.

I hold that the Sophoklean dream is dramatically less satisfactory than the Aischylean one, because it encourages the stay-at-home daughters and the Choros more than it encourages Orestes, who appears only some 600 verses later. In this and other respects, the dream is a far smaller *driving force* in the development of the Sophoklean plot, than in that of the Aischylean narrative. On the whole, except for upsetting Klytaimnestra and encouraging her helpless antagonists, the dramatic role of the dream is negligible.

It is less satisfactory than its Aischylean equivalent also in some other respects. Anyone—be she Klytaimestra, an English charwoman, or a German secretary—would be badly upset by a dream like that of Klytaimestra in A. *Choe.,* whose manifest content is close to basic human anxieties, to fears of mutilation, etc. If the Aischylean Klytaimestra told one her dream, one would seem foolish if one asked her: "*What* about this dream upset you?" One would sound foolish even if one were a simple pygmy hunter, for the anxiety arousing nature of that dream is both self-evident and extreme. By contrast, one would *not* sound foolish if one asked the Sophoklean Klytaimnestra: "*What* upset you about this dream?" Moreover, if one did ask her that question, she would not, like the Aischylean Klytaimestra, reply: "Can't you see for yourself?" She would explain—at length. I have, in effect, done little more in this chapter than ask that question and provide Klytaimnestra's answers, with such commentaries as Artemidoros would perhaps have added to her explanations.

The point I seek to make is that this dream's capacity to frighten the one who dreamed it is *not* due to its *manifest* content—save only for the appearance of a dead person. Its truly frightening content becomes evident only *after* it is *interpreted*—either the way the Greeks interpreted dreams, or the way a psycho-analyst interprets it. What is most frightening about this dream is its *latent* content—and *that* content would be most clearly perceived *in* the dream, for it would be accompanied by a marked dysphoria.

I concede that such dreams do exist and that it is a touch of (unwitting) psychological subtlety which caused Sophokles to devise a dream whose most frightening element is its *latent* content, which would be more clearly perceived during the dream than on awakening. But this subtlety is likely to be lost on the audience, for much cultural, literary and philological spadework had to be done before that latent content could be brought to light.

Another dramatic defect of this dream is that its manifest content does *not* anticipate the climate and deed of terror which it heralds . . . while the terrifying Aischylean dream does anticipate it. That the climactic scene should be simply foreshadowed, rather than fully anticipated, by the dream is defensible from the literary point of view. What is less defensible, is that it should be the *deeply disguised latent* content of the dream which foreshadows it. The understatement is, to my taste, too extreme.

Given the tenousness of the nexus between the dream and the murder, and given also the fact that it is only the hidden, latent content of the dream which foreshadows the murder, two conclusions seem permissible:

(1) The dream, taken by itself, is psychologically plausible enough—though more plausible for the psycho-analyst than for the lay Athenian spectator.

(2) For the rest, I cannot persuade myself that it plays any truly *necessary* role in the Sophoklean tragedy. It is, in some respects, a literary heirloom, which tends to clutter up the scene, simply because one refuses to get rid of it. One moves it from the mantlepiece to the piano and then to a shelf, one tries to renovate it by giving it a new coat of paint (a new manifest content) . . . but it still remains an encumbrance. Stesichoros and Aischylos had already squeezed the last drop of dramatic usefulness out of it. Euripides quietly turned the old battle-horse out to the pasture, and contented himself with an indirect allusion to it, in a drama which dealt with the *aftermath* of the murder only (E. *Or.* 618). It is probably Sophokles' failure to renovate and to rejuvenate this traditional motif which persuaded Euripides that nothing further could be squeezed out of it. It is not without interest that, on the whole, later mythographers and writers ignored the motif of Klytaimnestra's dream.

The main literary conclusion to be drawn from all this, is that a dream can be psychologically plausible and interpretable, without necessarily serving any useful literary end, and the prime literary requirement with respect to any motif is that it should be necessary.

Bibliography

(1) Alexander, Franz: Dreams in Pairs and Series, *International Journal of Psycho-Analysis* 6:446–452, 1925.

(2) Ashley Montagu, M. F.: Ritual Mutilation among Primitive People, *Ciba Symposia* 8:421–436, 1946.

(3) Bächli, Erich: *Die künstlerische Funktion von Orakelsprüchen, Träumen usw. in der griechischen Tragödie.* Winterthur, 1954.

(4) Baumann, H. H.: Über Reihenfolge und Rhythmus der Traummotive, *Zentralblatt für Psychotherapie und ihre Grenzgebiete,* 9:213–228, 1936.

(5) Behr, C. A.: *Aelius Aristides and the Sacred Tales.* Amsterdam, 1968.

(6) Bowra, C. M.: *Sophoclean Tragedy.* Oxford, 1960.

(7) Briehl, Walter and Kulka, E. W.: Lactation in a Virgin, *Psychoanalytic Quarterly* 4:484–512, 1935.

(8) Burkert, Walter: Das Proömium des Parmenides und die Katabasis des Pythagoras, *Phronesis* 14:1–30, 1969.

(9) id.: Jason, Hypsipyle and the New Fire in Lemnos, *Classical Quarterly* 20:1–16, 1970.

(10) Burrows, E. G. and Spiro, M. E.: *An Atoll Culture.* New Haven, 1953.

(11) Caspar, Franz: Some Sex Beliefs and Practices of the Tupari Indians (Western Brazil), *Rivista do Museu Paulista* n.s. 7:203–244, 1953.

(12) Cook, A. B.: *Zeus*, 3. Cambridge, 1940.

(13) Detienne, Marcel: L'Olivier: Un Mythe Politico-Religieux, *Revue de l'Histoire des Religions* 178:5–23, 1970.

(14) Devereux, George: *Hopi Field Notes* (MS.), 1932.

(15) id.: *Sedang Field Notes* (MS.), 1933–35.

(16) id.: L'Envoûtement chez les Indiens Mohave, *Journal de la Société des Américanistes de Paris* n.s. 29:405–412, 1937.

(17) id.: Social Structure and the Economy of Affective Bonds, *Psychoanalytic Review* 29:303–314, 1942.

(18) id.: The Social Structure of a Schizophrenia Ward and Its Therapeutic Fitness, *Journal of Clinical Psychopathology* 6:231–265, 1944.

(19) id.: Mohave Orality: An Analysis of Nursing and Weaning Customs, *Psychoanalytic Quarterly* 16:519–546, 1947.

(20) id.: The Mohave Neonate and Its Cradle, *Primitive Man* 21:1–18, 1948.

(21) id.: Mohave Paternity, *Samīkṣā, Journal of the Indian Psycho-Analytical Society* 3:162–194, 1949.

(22) id.: The Awarding of a Penis as Compensation for Rape. *International Journal of Psycho-Analysis* 38:398–401, 1957.

(23) id.: The Significance of the External Female Genitalia and of Female Orgasm for the Male, *Journal of the American Psychoanalytic Association* 6:278–286, 1958.

(24) id.: Art and Mythology: A General Theory (in) Kaplan, Bert (ed.): *Studying Personality Cross-Culturally*. Evanston, Illinois, 1961.

(25) id.: Sociopolitical Functions of the Oedipus Myth in Early Greece, *Psychoanalytic Quarterly* 32:205–214, 1963.

(26) id.: The Exploitation of Ambiguity in Pindaros *O*. 3.27, *Rheinisches Museum für Philologie* 109:289–298, 1966.

(27) id.: Greek Pseudo-Homosexuality, *Symbolae Osloenses* 42:69–92, 1967.

(28) id.: The Realistic Basis of Fantasy, *Journal of the Hillside Hospital* 17:13–20, 1968.

(29) id.: *Reality and Dream: The Psychotherapy of a Plains Indian.* (Second, augmented edition.) New York, 1969.

(30) id.: *Mohave Ethnopsychiatry and Suicide.* (Second, augmented edition.) Washington, D.C., 1969.

(31) id.: The Nature of Sappho's Seizure in *Fr.* 31 LP, *Classical Quarterly* 20:17–31, 1970.

(32) id.: La Naissance d'Aphrodite (in) Pouillon, Jean and Maranda, Pierre (eds.): *Echanges et Communications (Mélanges Lévi-Strauss)*, Paris and The Hague, 2.1229–1252. 1970.

(33) id.: The *Equus October* Ritual Reconsidered, *Mnemosyne* 23:297–301, 1970.

(34) id.: *Psychoanalysis and the Occult* (Reprint). New York, 1970.

(35) id.: *Essais d'Ethnopsychiatrie Générale*. Paris, 1970. (Second edition 1973.)

(36) id.: *Ethnopsychanalyse Complémentariste*. Paris, 1972.

(37) id. (and Devereux, J. W.) : Les Manifestations de l'Inconscient dans Sophokles: *Trachiniai* 923 sqq. (in) *Psychanalyse et Sociologie comme Methodes d'Etude des Phénomènes Historiques et Culturels.* Bruxelles, 1973

(38) id.: Trois Rêves en Série et une Double Parapraxe, *Ethnopsychologie* (in press).

(39) Dodds, E. R.: *The Greeks and the Irrational.* Berkeley, California, 1951.

(40) id.: *Pagan and Christian in an Age of Anxiety.* Cambridge, 1965.

(41) Dover, K. J.: Eros and Nomos, *University of London Institute of Classical Studies, Bulletin* 11:31–42, 1964.

(42) Edelstein, E. J. and Ludwig: *Asclepius* 2 vols. Baltimore, Maryland. 1945.

(43) Erlenmeyer, E. H.: Notiz zur Freudschen Hypothese über die Zähmung des Feuers, *Imago* 18:5–7, 1932.

(44) Fenichel, Otto: *The Psychoanalytic Theory of Neurosis.* New York, 1945.

(45) id.: The Symbolic Equation: "Girl = Phallus" (in) *The Collected Papers of O. Fenichel* 2. New York, 1954.

(46) Forde, C. D.: Ethnography of the Yuma Indians, *University of California Publications in American Archaeology and Ethnology* 28, no. 4, pp. 83–278, 1931.

(47) Freud, Sigmund: The Interpretation of Dreams, *Standard Edition* 4–5. London, 1958.

(48) id.: Fragment of an Analysis of a Case of Hysteria, *Standard Edition* 7. London, 1953.

(49) id.: Character and Anal Erotism, *Standard Edition* 9. London, 1959.

(50) id.: "Wild" Psycho-Analysis, *Standard Edition* 11. London, 1957.

(51) id.: Great is the Diana of the Ephesians, *Standard Edition* 12. London, 1958.

(52) id.: Repression, *Standard Edition* 14. London, 1957.

(53) id.: From the History of an Infantile Neurosis, *Standard Edition* 17. London, 1955.

(54) id.: Civilization and its Discontents, *Standard Edition* 21. London, 1961.

(55) id.: New Introductory Lectures on Psycho-Analysis, *Standard Edition* 22. London, 1964.

(56) id.: The Acquisition of Control over Fire, *Standard Edition* 22. London, 1964.

(57) Gahagan, L.: The Form and Function of a Series of Dreams, *Journal of Abnormal and Social Psychology*, 29:404–408, 1935.

(58) Grinnell, G. B.: *The Fighting Cheyennes*, Norman, Oklahoma, 1958.

(59) Kouretas, Demetrios: Trois Cas de Nécrophilie dans l'Antiquité, *Comptes Rendus, 56ᵉ Congrès de Psychiatrie et de Neurologie de Langue Française* pp. 705–711. Strasbourg, 1958.

(60) La Barre, Weston: *The Ghost Dance.* New York, 1970.

(61) Laforgue, René: De l'Angoisse à l'Orgasme, *Revue Française de Psychanalyse* 4:245–258, 1930–1931.

(62) id.: *Psychopathologie de l'Echec*². Paris, 1950.

(63) Le Roy Ladurie, Emmanuel: *Les Paysans du Languedoc*. Paris, 1966.

(64) Lincoln, J. S.: *The Dream in Primitive Culture*[2]. New York, 1970.

(65) Linton, Ralph: The Tanala, *Field Musuem of Natural History, Anthropological Series* 22. Chicago, 1933.

(66) id.: The Tanala of Madagascar (in) Kardiner, Abram and Linton, Ralph: *The Individual and his Society*. New York, 1939.

(67) Lloyd-Jones, Hugh: *The Justice of Zeus*. Berkeley, California, 1971.

(68) London, L. S. and Caprio, F. S.: *Sexual Deviation*. Washington, D.C., 1950.

(69) Lorimer, H. L.: *Homer and the Monuments*. London, 1950.

(70) Malinowski, Bronislaw: *Sex and Repression in Savage Society*. London, 1927.

(71) Mauss, Marcel: Une Catégorie de l'Esprit Humain: La Notion de Personne, celle de "Moi" (in) Mauss, Marcel: *Sociologie et Anthropologie*. Paris, 1950.

(72) Mead, Margaret and Métraux, Rhoda (eds.): *The Study of Culture at a Distance*. Chicago, 1953.

(73) Merker, F.: *Die Masai*. Berlin, 1904.

(74) Michaels, J. J.: *Disorders of Character*. Springfield, Illinois, 1955.

(75) Nilsson, M. P.: *Geschichte der griechischen Religion* I[2]. München, 1955.

(76) Oppenheim, A. L.: The Interpretation of Dreams in the Ancient Near-East. *Transactions, American Philosophical Society*, n.s., vol. 46, pt. 3, 1956.

(77) Page, Denys: *History and the Homeric Iliad*. Berkeley, California, 1963.

(78) Powell, Benjamin: Erichthonius and the Three Daughters of Cecrops, *Cornell Studies in Classical Philology* 17. New York, 1906.

(79) Preller, Ludwig and Robert, Carl: *Griechische Mythologie*[4]. 1894–1921.

(80) Renault, Mary: *The King Must Die*. New York, 1958.

(81) Rivers, W. H. R.: *Psychology and Ethnology*. London, 1926.

(82) Rohde, Erwin: *Psyche*. London, 1925.

(83) Róheim, Géza: Psycho-Analysis of Primitive Cultural Types, *International Journal of Psycho-Analysis* 13:1–244, 1932.

(84) id.: Hungarian Shamanism (in) Róheim Géza (ed.): *Psychoanalysis and the Social Sciences* 3. New York, 1951.

(85) Roscher, W. H.: *Ausführliches Lexikon der griechischen und römischen Mythologie*. Leipzig, 1884–1937.

(86) id.: Das von der "Kynanthropie" handelnde Fragment des Marcellus von Side, *Abhandlungen der philologisch-historischen Classe der Königlich Sächsischen Gesellschaft der Wissenschaften* 17, no. 3, 1896.

(87) Seligmann, C. G.: *The Cult of Nyakang and the Divine Kings of the Shilluk*. Khartum, 1911.

(88) Snell, Bruno: *The Discovery of the Mind*. Cambridge, Massachussetts, 1953.

(89) Sperling, O. E.: On Appersonation, *International Journal of Psycho-Analysis* 25:128–132, 1944.

(90) Sterba, R. F.: The Abuse of Interpretation, *Psychiatry* 4:9–12, 1941.

(91) Stinton, T. C. W.: *Euripides and the Judgment of Paris* (Society for the Promotion of Hellenic Studies, Supplementary Paper ii). London, 1965.

(92) Swift, Jonathan: *Gulliver's Travels.* 1726.

(93) Teitelbaum, H. A.: Psychogenic Body Image Disturbances Associated with Psychogenic Aphasia and Agnosia, *Journal of Nervous and Mental Disease* 93:581–612, 1941.

(94) Todd, O. J.: *Index Aristophaneus.* Cambridge, Massachusetts, 1932.

(95) Toffelmier, Gertrude and Luomala, Katherine: Dreams and Dream Interpretations of the Diegueño Indians of Southern California, *Psychoanalytic Quarterly* 2:195–225, 1936.

(96) Vernant, J.-P.: *Mythe et Pensée chez les Grecs.* Paris, 1966.

(97) Wace, A. J. B. and Stubbings, F. H. (eds.): *A Companion to Homer.* London, 1962.

(98) Wagley, Charles and Galvão, Eduardo: The Tapirape (in) Steward, J. H. (ed.): *Handbook of South American Indians* 3 (Bureau of American Ethnology, Bulletin 143). Washington, D.C., 1948.

Chapter 8

Three Euripidean Dreams:
Variations on a Theme

(Euripides: *Rhesos, Hekabe, Iphigeneia amongst the Taurians*)

Introduction

Though the arrangement of this chapter differs appreciably from that of the chapters devoted to the three versions of Klytaimestra's dream, my analysis of the three surviving Euripidean dreams concerns a very similar problem. Klytaimestra's dreams may be compared to dreams dreamed by three different persons in response to the same strong stimulus, which is part of the "residue" of the previous day. The three Euripidean dreams seem to be the equivalent of what, in clinical practice, are called "dreams in series" or "paired dreams": they are repeated dreamed "responses" to some basic and, at times, quite early problem or trauma.

Although I do not neglect the latent content of these dreams, one of my main objectives is to show that countless manifest, latent, structural and psycho-analytical aspects of these three dreams are so deeply inter-related, that the dreams in question must be considered as variations—by the *same* "composer"—on a single theme: on that of the so-called "primal scene", which is the child's real or fantasied, but always anxiety-distorted, experience of his parents' coitus.

If, as I hope, I can demonstrate this, my findings have some bearing on the still controverted view that the drama *Rhesos*, which we possess, is the *Rhesos* of Euripides, and not that of an "unknown author" having the same title as the hypothetically lost Euripidean drama (*134*). Since the whole controversy is most ably discussed by Ritchie (*125*), who, like myself, holds the *Rhesos* to be authentic, I can dispense with a general recapitulation of the problem, limiting myself strictly to a discussion of the fundamental similarities between the dreams of Rhesos' Charioteer (E. *Rh.*), of Hekabe (E. *Hec.*) and of Iphigeneia (E. *IT*)—and, of course, to the psycho-analytical scrutiny both of the dreams themselves and of their basic similarities.

However, since, in this case, what matters most is the presence of a great many similarities, I do not analyse the dreams *individually*. My analysis is focused on the points of similarity, for it is this that interests most the Hellenist. But this does not mean that I short-change the psycho-analyst! Given the fact that nearly every item of each of these dreams has its counterpart in the two others, the analysis of the similarities is also a full analysis of all of their details. Moreover, just as, in clinical practice, one can analyse two or more dreams—especially if they are obviously "serial" or "paired" dreams, dreamed by a patient during the same night—*simultaneously*, so it is legitimate to analyse these dream-variations on a single theme *jointly*. Though this may be an innovation in the psycho-analytical study of literary dreams, it is only very slightly innovating in terms of clinical practice.

I state emphatically that I did *not* set out to prove the authenticity of the *Rhesos*. In fact, I was struck by the similarities between the three dreams *before* I discovered that the authorship of that drama was disputed. Much of the first draft of this chapter was written before Ritchie's excellent book (*125*) fell into my hands. Whatever flaws this chapter may have, that of starting from a preconceived idea is not one of them.[1]

---

[1] Similarly, I did not go to the Mohave Indian reservation to investigate their psychiatric

One last word may be said about the somewhat unusual organization of the material presented in this chapter. As already indicated, the concurrent analysis of "serial" dreams is by no means unusual (*48*, passim). I therefore note only that a separate analysis of each of the three Euripidean dreams would have doubled the length of this chapter. I also realize that I would probably have facilitated the acceptance of my interpretations, had I placed the terminal sections at the beginning of this chapter. But I decided to adopt a different order of presentation, so as to illustrate a relatively new *method* of analysing what the literary critic calls "parallel passages"—such as serial dreams. I am confident that those who read carefully the texts or the translations of the dreams under scrutiny, will have no difficulty following my argument. I concede that this chapter is not exactly "light reading". Those who read it attentively will no doubt decide for themselves whether the effort was worth their while.

---

ideas and practices in order to prove Freud right—for at that time (1938) I was an opponent of psycho-analysis. I was forced to become a Freudian by my Mohave data (*49*, pp. 2 f.).

PHCOY HNIOXOC

καί μοι καθ' ὕπνον δόξα τις παρίσταται·   780
ἵππους γὰρ ἃς ἔθρεψα κἀδιφρηλάτουν
'Ρήσῳ παρεστώς, εἶδον, ὡς ὄναρ δοκῶν,
λύκους ἐπεμβεβῶτας ἑδραίαν ῥάχιν·
θείνοντε δ' οὐρᾷ πωλικῆς ῥινοῦ τρίχα,
ἤλαυνον, αἱ δ' ἔρρεγκον ἐξ ἀρτηριῶν   785
θυμὸν πνέουσαι κἀνεχαίτιζον φόβην.
ἐγὼ δ' ἀμύνων θῆρας ἐξεγείρομαι
πώλοισιν· ἔννυχος γὰρ ἐξώρμα φόβος.   (Nauck's text)

EKABH

ὦ στεροπὰ Διός, ὦ σκοτία νύξ,   68
τί ποτ' αἴρομαι ἔννυχος οὕτω
δείμασι, φάσμασιν; ὦ πότνια Χθών,   70
μελανοπτερύγων μῆτερ ὀνείρων,
ἀποπέμπομαι ἔννυχον ὄψιν,
ἣν περὶ παιδὸς ἐμοῦ τοῦ σωζομένου κατὰ Θρῄκην
ἀμφὶ Πολυξείνης τε φίλης θυγατρὸς δι' ὀνείρων   75
[εἶδον γὰρ] φοβερὰν [ὄψιν ἔμαθον] ἐδάην.
ὦ χθόνιοι θεοί, σώσατε παῖδ' ἐμόν,
ὃς μόνος οἴκων ἄγκυρ' ἔτ' ἐμῶν   80
τὴν χιονώδη Θρῄκην κατέχει
ξείνου πατρίου φυλακαῖσιν.
ἔσται τι νέον·
ἥξει τι μέλος γοερὸν γοεραῖς
οὔποτ' ἐμὰ φρὴν ὧδ' ἀλίαστος   85
φρίσσει ταρβεῖ.
ποῦ ποτε θείαν 'Ελένου ψυχὰν
καὶ Κασάνδρας ἐσίδω, Τρῳάδες,
ὥς μοι κρίνωσιν ὀνείρους;
εἶδον γὰρ βαλιὰν ἔλαφον λύκου αἵμονι χαλᾷ   90
σφαζομέναν, ἀπ' ἐμῶν γονάτων σπασθεῖσαν ἀνοίκτως.
καὶ τόδε δεῖμά μοι· ἦλθ' ὑπὲρ ἄρκας
τύμβους ορυφᾶς
φάντασμ' 'Αχιλέως· ᾔτει δὲ γέρας
τῶν πολυμόχθων τινὰ Τρωιάδων.   95
ἀπ' ἐμᾶς ἀπ' ἐμᾶς οὖν τόδε παιδὸς
μέμψατε, δαίμονες, ἱκετεύω.   (Méridier's text)

ΙΦΙΓΕΝΕΙΑ

ἃ καινὰ δ' ἥκει νὺξ φέρουσα φάσματα,   42
λέξω πρὸς αἰθέρ', εἴ τι δὴ τόδ' ἔστ' ἄκος.
ἔδοξ' ἐν ὕπνῳ τῆσδ' ἀπαλλαχθεῖσα γῆς
οἰκεῖν ἐν "Αργει, παρθενῶσι δ' ἐν μέσοις   45
εὕδειν, χθονὸς δὲ νῶτα σεισθῆναι σάλῳ,
φεύγειν δὲ κἄξω στᾶσα θριγκὸν εἰσιδεῖν
δόμων πίτνοντα, πᾶν δ' ἐρείψιμον στέγος
βεβλημένον πρὸς οὖδας ἐξ ἄκρων σταθμῶν.

Literal Translations

E. *Rh.* 780–788: "And in my sleep a delusion (dream-image) stood by me; for the horses which I tended (fed?) and used to drive standing by Rhesos in the chariot—as it appeared in my dream, I saw that wolves had mounted upon them and were perched (hanging on) their backs; and both of them, beating with their tails the hair of the horses' skins, were urging them on; and they (the horses) were snorting, breathing forth rage from their throats, and tossing their manes high [Reiske]. And I, trying-to-repel the beasts from the horses, woke up; for nocturnal terror was rousing me."

E. *Hec.* 68–97: "O dazzling-light of Zeus, O dark night, why am I in the night thus lifted with fears, with apparitions? O august Earth, mother of dark-winged dreams, I send-away-from-me (= send back?) this vision of-the-night, which, about my son who-is-being-kept-safe in Thrace and about my beloved daughter Polyxene, a fearful sight, in dreams I perceived, I understood. *O gods of the Earth, save my son who, the one anchor still of my house, inhabits snowy Thrace in the keeping of his father's (guest-) friend. There shall be something new, there shall come some tearful tune to tearful women. Never before did my heart shudder and fear so incessantly. Would that I might see here the inspired soul (ψυχή) of Helenos or Kassandra, O women of Troy, that they might judge (interpret) my dreams.*[2] For I saw a dappled fawn being torn by the bloody claw of a wolf, after being dragged pitifully from my knees by force. And this is (also?) the fear I have: there came the ghost of Achilleus above the topmost crest of his tomb and demanded as a gift-of-honour one of the much-suffering Trojan women. Therefore from my (child), from my child turn this away, you gods, I beg."[3]

E. *IT* 42–60: "Now the strange apparitions, which the night has brought to me, I will tell out to the open-sky (αἰθήρ), if indeed it is any help to do this. It seemed in my sleep that I had got away[4] from this land and was living in Argos and that I was sleeping in the midst of the maidens-quarters; and the back (= surface) of the earth (χθονὸς) was shaken with heaving. And I fled and standing outdoors saw the cornice of the building falling, and the whole house in ruin, dashed to the ground (οὖδας; also:

---

[2] Note that "dreams" is twice in the plural (infra).

[3] The middle section, between asterisks, is anapaestic.

[4] The means of escape are not specified. This may *perhaps* imply that not a real escape, but only a regression in time is meant. Cp. infra.

μόνος δ' ἐλείφθη cτῦλος, ὡς ἔδοξέ μοι,   50
δόμων πατρῴων, ἐκ δ' ἐπικράνων κόμας
ξανθὰς καθεῖναι, φθέγμα δ' ἀνθρώπου λαβεῖν,
κἀγὼ τέχνην τήνδ' ἣν ἔχω ξενοκτόνον
τιμῶс' ὕδραινον αὐτὸν ὡς θανούμενον,
κλαίουcα. τοὔναρ δ' ὧδε cυμβάλλω τόδε·   55
τέθνηκ' Ὀρέcτηс, οὗ κατηρξάμην ἐγώ.
cτῦλοι γὰρ οἴκων εἰcὶ παῖδες ἄρcενес·
θνῄcκουcι δ' οὓс ἂν χέρνιβες βάλωс' ἐμαί.
οὐδ' αὖ cυνάψαι τοὔναρ ἐc φίλουc ἔχω·   (Grégoire's text)

pavement, floor) from the top of the roof-trees. And a single column was left, as it seemed to me, of my father's house; and from the capital of it there hung down light-coloured hair;[5] and it assumed the voice of a man. Then I, observing this rite of killing strangers which I have, sprinkled it[6] with water, as if it were about to die—(I) weeping. I interpret the dream thus: the one who had died is Orestes, and he it was for whom I performed the ritual; for the pillars of a house are its male children; and those whom my holy washing touches, die. I have no other friends who fit into my dream."[7]

These translations sacrifice elegance of style to absolute literalness, for here the literal content alone matters.[8]

The Data and their Exposition. The basic data are of three types:

(1) *Dreams* narrated by the dreamer. The texts and translations are given above.

Associations: The passages immediately preceding and succeeding the dream-narratives; also direct allusions to the dreams in the rest of the relevant dramas. Thus, though the appearance of Achilleus' ghost—recalling that of Polydoros in the Prologue—is known to Hekabe only by report, it is an association to the dream, for she says: "And something *else* also frightens me" (E. *Hec.* 92 ff.).

Collateral Material: E. (*Antiope*) *fr.* 203 N[2] duplicates both the content and the spatial arrangement of one element in Iphigeneia's dream: hair (of ivy) tops a column.[9] F. Robert's (*127*) plausible view, that Orestes planned to enter Artemis' temple from above, is also a datum. The collapse of the palace in dream resembles the so-called "Palace Miracle" in E. *Ba.* 586 ff. The obscure manner in which the "descent" of the hair is described somewhat recalls the strange manner (E. *Ba.* 1111 ff. and Dodds ad loc.) in which the tree on[10] which Pentheus is perched, is made to "collapse" (is uprooted), bringing Pentheus within the reach of the murderous Mainades —as the hair ends up within the reach of Iphigeneia's hands. These images seem Euripidean. Other Euripidean images, whose content or structure—but not both—also resemble a dream element, are mentioned either only in passing, or else not at all. As in the other chapters, Greek, ethnological and clinical data are only used to strengthen certain interpretations.

The texts are treated conservatively; they did not have to be strained to

[5] "Hung down"—a vexing expression (M. Hadas: "sprouted forth"; Grégoire: "poussaient"). In this passage the colour ξανθός seems to be light, though in Pl. *Lys.* 217d a dark colour may be meant. In this drama the word is also applied to the colour of blood and of oil (vv. 73, 633).

[6] Presumably the *hair* (M. Hadas: "him"; this cannot be right, for Iphigeneia does not connect as yet the hair and a person. Grégoire: "this column", which E.R.D. thinks may be right).

[7] Interpretation by an exclusion of the unsuitable—perhaps reflecting uncertainty. (The interpretation does prove to be wrong.)

[8] I gratefully acknowledge Mr Philip Vellacott's help with these translations. I, whose native language is not English, would not have dared to brutalize it to such an extent, in order to achieve absolute literalness.

[9] Cp. E. *Ba.* 1170. On the "hair = ivy = curly" nexus. cp. *144*, p. 135, note 1.

[10] On the Greek symbolic equation: tree = column, cp. infra.

yield up their meaning. Unequivocally outlined realistic images are occasionally "completed". Since a realistic wolf *claws* the fawn fatally, *after* that young animal was torn from Hekabe's lap, and since no one else is present in the dream, nor anyone in reality *not* symbolized by the wolf, I see no alternative to the view that the wolf *himself* tore the fawn from Hekabe's lap *with its claws*. The wolf must therefore be visualized, at least to start with, as "arched" over the seated Hekabe's knees: the wolf's front paws on her lap, its hind legs on the ground.

By contrast, in Iphigeneia's dream, I do not "supply" or even imagine the sound the crashing of real masonry would produce, partly because dreams are mainly visual experiences, but mostly because one sound— that produced by the hair—*is* explicitly mentioned in the later part of the dream. In fact, one notes—and can interpret—the absence of sound in the first part of the dream only because there is a sound in its second part.

Finally, I have tried to mention every anomaly and/or *striking* omission in all three dreams and have interpreted some of them.

My description and quasi-structural analysis of the Euripidean dreams' *manifest* content is almost entirely objective, in that I seek to highlight similarities between the three dreams. I identify these patterns by means of a technique comparable to the Aristotelian "decoding" of the changing reflections of an object in moving water; the pattern is revealed by whatever remains invariant in the successive transformations of these reflections. I deliberately refrain from exploiting fully the techniques of structural analysis (*18*), in Lévi-Strauss' sense (*108*, etc.), for that would make this chapter considerably more difficult to read. Besides, since structuralist and psycho-analytical methods are, I believe (*46, 57*), complementary, their interpretations tend to converge. I simply add that my psycho-analytical interpretations are here as conservative as the inherent complexity of psychic processes—and especially of those of a great poet—will permit.[11] Unfounded charges of "wild" over-interpretation will not simplify stubbornly complicated processes. All dream elements mesh and each of them is heavily over-determined even in poetry. This made many cross-references unavoidable. They could be kept at a minimum only by assuming that the reader would thoroughly familiarize himself with every detail of these dreams, before reading their analysis and interpretation.

Some Euripidean Characteristics of the three dreams may now be enumerated. The Euripidean atmosphere and outlook of the dreams, as well as of their pathos is, I think, unquestionable. Also Euripidean is the use of children—or of child-equivalents—to achieve that pathos (note 134). Rhesos' horses are carefully tended and the Charioteer's concern for them is almost maternal. Hekabe's dream-fawn is lap-nurtured. "Orestes'" hair is sprinkled, though in a typically ambiguous, Euripidean manner: the hair of baby brothers is washed protectively; that of sacrificial victims with murderous intent.

The dream personages are quite active—more so, for example, than

---

[11] Freud said that if one could but analyse *fully* one single dream, the patient's analysis would be finished.

in A. *PV*, or in A. *Eum.*—and the imagery's vividness is worthy of a poet said to have studied painting.[12] Yet, the dreams are relatively non-flamboyant: though they have, or are believed to have, a prophetic or clairvoyant dimension—deceptively so in E. *IT*—the imagery is appreciably closer to that of the real dream than to that of the allegory, or of a dream disguised as an allegory (A. *Pers.*, and, to a lesser extent, S. *El.*). Something like a Euripidean dream could, I think, be dreamed also by real Greeks or by modern dreamers. This finding fits both the widely accepted view that Euripidean personages are credible and Dodds' observation that Euripides handled the irrational in a psychologically realistic manner (*63*).

Since I hope to show that all three dreams represent a reaction to the same intra-psychic tension, derived from the same (real or fantasied) "outer" experience, I might as well express here a view which, as my experience of men and the world increases, seems increasingly persuasive to me: reality's *representation* (= science) may well be only the *rational* common denominator of irrational fantasies—a common denominator which strips off Pegasos' wings and the hippocampus' body and tail, leaving only the horse of daily experience and of textbooks of zoology . . . while the winged Pegasos and the real hippocamp continue to haunt our dreams (cp. General Introduction). The great merit of Euripidean dreams is that though they are peopled with the oniric equivalents of Pegasos, they do not stray into the non-world of the Chimaira (as do some of Ailios Aristeides' dreams).

These considerations appear to justify my analysing first the manifest content and structure of Euripidean dreams and only then teasing out also their latent content by psycho-analytical means; I found this procedure useful also in clinical work (*48*). Throughout, I seek to highlight the accuracy of Euripides' observations, the realism of his exploitation of the material and, above all, the dazzling skill he shows in preserving the structure and latent content of his (hypothetical) model—of the Primal Scene—in his three creatively divergent variations on a basic theme.

The Dramatic Function of a dream is to influence the plot.[13] The secondary elaboration which this presupposes does not make the dream psychologically less interpretable than sought incubation dreams.[14] The Charioteer's dream is, strictly speaking, a stylistic device and not a driving force; Lesky (*107*) would probably call it a "reaction". Its "prophecy" (*recte*: clairvoyance) is immediately fulfilled (= verified).[15] The dream barely reaches into the drama. A sluggish spectator in dream, the Charioteer becomes (compensatorily?) hyperactive on awakening.

---

[12] On this tradition, cp. *134*, i, 3, p. 314 and note 3. Cp. *V. Eurip.* 116 ff.

[13] I therefore question Ritchie's (*125*, p. 109) view, that the E. *Hec.* Prologue (which the dream presupposes) could be dispensed with structurally. On the structure of E. *Hec.* cp. infra.

[14] On incubation dreams, cp. *64*, pp. 110–116, 203, note 83 and passim; *67*, 2, pp. 145 ff. Though if an Iroquois dreams that he receives a gift, he must be given it also in reality, his dream, too, is interpretable (*141*) and so are similar "soul wish" dreams from Kamtchatka, etc. Cp. chap. 6, note 89.

[15] This is of Homeric inspiration. Ritchie (*125*, p. 75) notes that the only other Greek dream fulfilled with equal rapidity is that of Rhesos himself, Hom. *Il.* 10: 497.

Guilt-ridden because of his initial inactivity, he irrationally accuses Hektor of murder and horse-theft. Now, according to a number of other sources, Rhesos' invincibility depended on his horses' eating Trojan grass and drinking Trojan water.[16] Only in E. *Rh.* does his invincibility depend on his spending a night on Trojan soil.[17] This slight modification of the tradition was probably necessary, since otherwise even the distraught Charioteer would have realized that it would be self-defeating for Hektor to steal Rhesos' horses.[18] Hektor may simply have cast a longing eye on Rhesos' horses, having just renounced his claim to Achilleus' team in favour of Dolon, whom he hardly expected to fail.[19] What better substitute could there be for that immortal team than Rhesos' horses?[20] Though such a thought might cross even a Hektor's mind, he would certainly never act upon it.

The Charioteer's irrational accusations are mere "projections", motivated by his obsessive preoccupation with his horses, even in dream. The Charioteer did not intuitively read Hektor's thoughts, even though, still befuddled by sleep and by shock, he might have been especially sensitive to subliminal clues. If he is "right", he is accidently so, and Euripides so intended it; he hardly meant to represent the Charioteer as a mind-reader. Besides, the Charioteer's character matters less for the plot than does his dream.

In short, though the quarrel reveals much about the Charioteer, all it tells one about Hektor is that this magnanimous man would deal gently even with a distraught and irrational subordinate.

The dramatic function of the E. *Hec.* dream must be appraised first in relation to that drama's much maligned structure.[21] The presence of a "break" in its middle is a misapprehension of the modern mind, obsessed with the importance of young girls.[22] Athenians may have viewed

---

16 Sch. *Il.* 10.435; Eustath. in *Il.* 817.26; Accius *Nyctegr. fr.* 3, i, p. 230 Ribbeck; V. *Aen.* 1.469; Serv. *V. Aen.* 2.13; Myth. Vat. 1.203. This may be an allusion to an Asiatic manner of demanding fealty. Xerxes asked Greek cities for earth and water; (Hdt. 7.32); according to Hungarian tradition, the conqueror Árpád (IX Cent. A.D.) asked for earth, water and grass (for his horses). Such data may just conceivably hint at a lost tradition that, in exchange for his help, Rhesos asked to be recognized as suzerain, or at least as supreme commander (cp. Gelon's conditions, Hdt. 7.158–162).

17 This, too, may suggest "taking possession". In Central Europe, the room in which a sovereign once slept, was known ever after as the e.g., Maria Theresia room (cp. also England). A Maori king must be carried across land which does not belong to him; were his foot to tread it, the land would become his (cp. also Hippias' loss of a tooth; Hdt. 6.107).

18 Moreover, in E. *Rh.*, the horses presumably grazed on Trojan soil; they were hardly stolen before that, as reported in late sources (V. *Aen.* 1.469 f. and Serv. ad loc., etc.).

19 And rightly so. E. *Rh.* itself highlights the unreliability of primitive and ancient sentinels (808 ff., etc.).

20 According to Patin (*119*, 3, 2, p. 155) the nexus between the two teams was first pointed out by Th. Borel (*10*).

21 Even Ritchie (*125*, p. 109) reluctantly concedes that the E. *Hec.* Prologue is not indispensable. Were that so, one would also have to abandon the dream, which presupposes the Prologue. The dogma of the bad construction of various Euripidean plays should be reconsidered. W. N. Bates (*7*, p. 199) notes that E. *Tr.* gives an impression of unity when performed, though not when read. The appreciation of a Greek drama's unity requires visual imagination.

22 They seldom are cynosures in primitive and non-occidental societies (*103*). Some Hellenists, appalled that no words are wasted on Makaria's consummated self-sacrifice

Polyxene's fate simply as a prelude to the greater tragedy of the last male Priamid.[23] Polyxene's impending immolation only pushed Hekabe to the brink; it took Polydoros' murder to make her topple over it. That this is as it should be . . . by Greek standards[24] . . . would probably have been more obvious in Aischylean or Sophoklean tragedy, since Euripides anticipated at times the modern (and Hellenistic) interest in young girls. At the same time he was also a better culture historian than his peers: myths show that Mykenaian women were freer and socially more important than Athenian ones.[25] Yet even Euripides was sufficiently Periklean— at least in his works—to represent a young girl's death simply as a means to the end that truly matters.[26] Even in Euripides' last play—the *IA*— the key problem is the shore-bound Achaian fleet and not Iphigeneia's doom, and this despite the fact that the poet grew bolder with age.[27] There seems to be no exception to the rule that a young girl's death is incidental,[28] and this quite apart from the fact that it necessarily takes place off-stage, while the main action unfolds on-stage.[29] Hekabe's own reactions also show that Polyxene means less to her than Polydoros. Though briefly grieving and praying in the end over her daughter's *known* plight, she prays first and chiefly for the *hypothetically* endangered Polydoros (59 f.). Also, though she does not beseech Agamemnon to save Polyxene, in order to avenge her son she pleads like a procuress that Agamemnon owes her something for the sexual use of Kassandra's body (824 f.),[30] which is a commodity to be sacrificed for her brother's sake.[31]

(E. *Heracl.*) even assume that a passage has been lost (*133*). Makaria's (and perhaps Euripides') contemporaries felt perhaps that that is what young princesses were there for. But Professor Dover strongly disagrees with this last hypothesis and he may well be right and I wrong.

[23] Helenos, having made his peace with the Greeks, no longer counts. But it is hard to see why Menelaos does not "count" at A. *Ag.* 898.—unless he is still believed to be lost at sea. Fraenkel's notes, ad loc. are implausible, I think.

[24] This is said in the sense in which Wilamowitz (in his ed. of E. *HF*) said that "it is as it should be" that Euripides should have been regularly defeated not only by Sophokles, but also by lesser men. No agreement is implied in either case.

[25] I registered elsewhere (*45*) my disagreement with the customary underestimation of the Athenian wife's role, though I certainly do not concur with its overestimation by C. Seltman (*135*, chap. 7).

[26] E. *Erechth.* seems focused on Athens' fate and on the parents' grief. In S. *Ant.*—an admittedly well-constructed play—Kreon is crushed not by Antigone's, but by Haimon's death, which climaxes and ends the tragedy. The paramount importance of Klytaimestra's death in A. *Choe.*, S. *El.* and E. *El.* does not disprove my point: Aigisthos is only a shabby and shadowy usurper and Klytaimestra matters mainly because Orestes matters even more.

[27] And, as often happens, also more traditional in form (E. *Ba.*); cp. the reappearance of the fugue in Beethoven's late works.

[28] Perhaps because fictitious to Euripides' contemporaries (K.J.D.). But cp. Plu. *V. Them.* 13.3, *V. Arist.* 9.1 f. and the φαρμακός (scapegoat).

[29] On this dichotomy, cp. (*54*).

[30] Cp. Hom. *Il.* 24.477 ff.: for Hektor's sake, Priamus kisses Achilleus' murderous hands. Parts of E. *Hec.* read like a savage parody of the Homeric outlook.

[31] Cp. Plu. *Amat.* 760 B: A Greek sometimes prostituted his wife, but never his *eromenos*. (But cp. Luc. *Cat.* 10.) The men of Sardis apparently contemplated saving their lives by surrendering their spouses to the besieger (Ps.-Plu. *Paral. Min.* 30, 312 E ff.)—a routine practice among the culturally man-centered Australians (*136*) E. *Alc.* is clearly man centered: Pheres is a man, Admetos both man and King—Alkestis is only a woman;

The last word on all this is said by Iphigeneia: it is the sons that matter (E. *IT.* 57). The "break" disappears the moment one overcomes the modern obsession with the *importance* of young girls and re-learns the dynastic outlook.[32] It becomes equally non-existent if one remembers that the topic of a Greek tragedy is an event or problem, and not a personality.[33] The already adequately tight structure of E. *Hec.* is made completely coherent by Hekabe's dream, whose fawn symbol represents both her son and her daughter. Few literary dreams have so high a degree of dramatic functionality.

By comparison, this dream's influence on the plot, while great, is not of paramount importance. It does transform Hekabe's agitated depression and despair into a fierce, scheming, brutal courage; more striking still, her passivity in dream is replaced by a savage activity. Euripides might have achieved the same ends also by some other means, though hardly by a dramatically and poetically more compelling one. What more one could ask from an—admittedly superbly foreshadowed—dramatic dream is hard to see. Moreover, the dream echoes also the appearance of another phantom: that of Achilleus (E. *Hec.* 37 f.).

As to Iphigeneia's dream, in order to avoid repetitiousness, the discussion of its dramatic functions must be postponed until later. I therefore list here only its most salient consequences. The dream practically turns Orestes into a ὑστερόποτμος[34] and makes Iphigeneia bloodthirsty. This, together with her conviction that her brother is dead, decreases Orestes' chances of being recognized and increases the risk that he will be sacrificed. The plot, then, proves the dream's two "occult" interpretations to be wrong, precisely by showing that its psychological implications are right. Each of these consequences is discussed in detail further on.

The Stylistic Function of the dream is identical with that of the poetic metaphor; the dream imagery is a reflection of the dream thought. The possibility that even one and the same dreamer could express the same latent thought through different images was perhaps sensed already by Aristoteles, who noted that, on awakening, a new imagery—presumably *also* related to the dream thought—substitutes itself for the dream imagery.[35]

moreover, having borne sons, she is dynastically no longer indispensable. The dynastic outlook has relevance also for S. *Ant.*, and both Homeros and Aischylos seem to doubt the rightness of going to war over Helene (H.L.-J.).

[32] This was perhaps sensed by A. W. Verrall (*140*, p. 190, note 2). G. M. A. Grube (*85*, pp. 129–130) is explicit: "classical scholars no longer have a dynastic mind".

[33] Arist. *Poet.* 1450a23 ff. This makes it implicitly desirable, though difficult, to draw original characters (1449b36; 1450b19; 1453b22; 1454a33). Euripides met this challenge boldly and brilliantly. In E. *IA.* the traditional myth is not substantially tampered with. But Agamemnon, Menelaos and even Achilleus are shoddy because the Achaians are shoddy for going to war over a worthless Helene; cp. Aristophanes' contemptuous pretence (*Acharn.* 515 ff.) that the Peloponnesian war was fought over the kidnapping of two harlots.

[34] I.e., into a man mistakenly believed to have died abroad, who, when he returns alive, must undergo a kind of rebirth ceremony (Plu. *Q.R.* 5, p. 264 D. ff.). S. *El.* 62 ff. specifies that such a man was then held in high honour. The rebirth ritual involved his entering his old home from above (through the roof). That, precisely, is how Orestes and Pylades intend to burgle Artemis' shrine (E. *IT.* 113 ff.). Cp. F. Robert's excellent discussion (*127*) of this project—though he overlooked its nexus with the hysteropotmos rebirth ritual.

[35] Arist. *insomn.* 458b20, cp, 462a25.

Viewed in another way, in Greek drama the dream narrative is functionally akin to a Messenger's speech.[36] It is, in a sense, "News from Nowhere"—and the reporting of uncanny (dreamlike) occurrences by Messengers is even more characteristic of Euripides than of his two great peers.[37] The Charioteer's account of his dream gives relief to his story and may even suggest that the human wolves were assisted or sent by a Supernatural Being. His sudden transition from sleep to wakefulness explains in part also his wild accusations and perhaps even his (medically premature) wound-delirium at v. 835.[38] In so far as Hekabe mentions the appearance of Polydoros in dream, her narrative is also akin to a Messenger's report. As to Iphigeneia's dream-narrative, it is "News from Nowhere" *par excellence*; technically, it fuses the *functions* of Polydoros' prologue and of Hekabe's dream-narrative into one. Both in E. *Hec.* and in E. *IT.* the dream narrative is so closely integrated with the prologue that it can be distinguished from it only by means of purely external criteria. Psychologically no separation is possible: the content of the prologue is, in both cases, funnelled into the drama by means of a dream—as off-stage happenings are funnelled into E. *Rh.* through the Charioteer's dream.

The Psychological Appropriateness of Dreams increases their plausibility. The dream is a highly individualized product of the psyche; the Charioteer could not have dreamed Iphigeneia's dream.[39] A real dream fits the dreamer at a given point of his existence; in literature, a plausible dream must also fit the plot.[40] All Euripidean dreams satisfy these requirements. I examine here only the general appropriateness of the dream for a given dreamer at a certain point in time; the appropriateness of the symbolization, of regression in time, and so forth, is discussed in the corresponding sections.

The Charioteer is almost obsessively preoccupied with his horses; he sees all life and his own duties in a horse perspective. Though Rhesos is murdered *first*, the Charioteer is awakened only by his dream of danger to his horses. This is not only psychologically subtle, but also echoes the Homeric *Doloneia* (Hom. *Il.* 10) in which—save for a final whistle (10.502) —both the murder and the theft are apparently committed in complete silence.

Also, I can attest from personal experience that even the Charioteer's heavy sleep is plausible: Rhesos' army had been a long time on the march and had, no doubt, faced dangers en route. For the first time in many weeks the Charioteer need not sleep with one eye open. Objectively, his

---

[36] Characteristically, Klytaimestra's dream is told not by herself, but by the Choros (A. *Choe.* 523 ff.) which, in this instance, does not comment but informs—at least to begin with. In S. *El.* her dream is reported by Chrysothemis.

[37] E. *Ba.*, *HF.*, *Hipp.*, *IA.* etc., cp. (*54*).

[38] Ritchie (*125*): added relief, pp. 75, 138; delirium: p. 131.

[39] A hysteric does not dream like an obsessive, nor a woman like a man, nor a child like an adult (*75*, passim). An Eskimo does not dream like an Indian (*64*, chap. 4). Several adolescents boarding in a therapeutic school for deviant youngsters tried to deceive their respective therapists, by exchanging their dreams. The fraud was detected almost at once; the borrowed dreams simply did not "fit" the alleged dreamers (*32*, pp. 271 ff.).

[40] Ps.-Hp. *insomn.* 88; Arist. *insomn.* 462a15 ff.; Hdt. 7.16; Emp. *fr.* 108 D-K; Cic. *de divin.* 2.67; Lucr. *nat. rer.* 4.963, 5.724; Patin (*119*, 2, p. 164 and n. 1); Dodds (*64*, p. 118), etc.

dream is a symbolic understatement: it phrases a military disaster in terms of a horse theft. Even this is perceptive: the survivors of bombings may obsessively—and defensively—grieve most over the loss of a keepsake.

Hekabe's dream is equally appropriate, because its symbolism is both regressive, and present-centred. In dandling her "baby" (= fawn) on her knees, the old *woman* regresses to the happy times before the siege of Troy, while the old *Queen* hopes that her son would avenge the fall of Troy and rebuild its razed walls. Her maternal dream is tragically appropriate. Unlike young Antigone, or Intaphernes' wife, this old widow cannot say: "Ah well, I can always have another child."[41] But, at the same time, the old *Queen's* dream is present-centred: she is the only possible leader and defender of the captive Trojans.

Iphigeneia's dream also fits her. Hekabe is a Queen, for whom the state is more important than its ruler; Iphigeneia is a princess in distress, more family (= dynasty) than state oriented. For her: "l'Etat c'est Papa!" —or at least Orestes, who may yet restore the might of the House of Agamemnon, as distinct from that of still mighty Argos.[42] Her own dream-horizons are almost as narrow as those of the Charioteer, and, as befits a formerly sheltered princess, who is now a privileged captive, her dream is the most self-centred of the three.

Not one of the three dreamers could have dreamed the dreams of the other two; each dream fits *only* the one to whom it is attributed. The general appropriateness of these dreams may therefore be held to have been proven already, though the analysis of their other features will furnish further proof of their appropriateness.

The Manner of Dreaming is unusual in all three dreams, though whether Euripides realized this is uncertain, for most people take it for granted that their own manner of dreaming is the natural one.[43] Even Greek dream books have relatively little to say about atypical ways of dreaming.

The E. *Rh.* dream is not only unusual, but of a type well understood already by Aristoteles.[44] It is elicited by the impact of *sounds* on the sleeper's sensorium; these, the dream-work converts into appropriate *imagery* and then incorporates into the dream, with relatively little distortion. In so doing, the dreamer denies their external origin, by "properly" reacting to them in dream; this dispenses him from waking up at once, in order to respond to these stimuli also in reality (chap. 4, note 61). Such dreaming is a lip service which the dreamer pays to reality, for it helps the dream fulfil its role of guardian of sleep.[45] Reality's contribution to this dream is

41 S. *Ant.* 909–912; Hdt. 3.119. Even Euripides' Andromache will bear another child (E. *Androm.*), to comfort her for the loss of Astyanax (E. *Troad.*). But, in Homeros, Polydoros is not Hekabe's son and is killed in combat.

42 The contrast is even more complete: the Trojan dynasty was autochthonous; the Pelopidai, like many other mythical rulers, were outsiders, immigrants or even usurpers. E. *IT.* 510 implies only misrule (cp. Thu. 1.12.).

43 A clinical psychologist discovered only during his own analysis that his dreaming in colour was relatively unusual.

44 Arist. *insomn.* 462a15 ff.; *de div. somn.* 463a5 ff.; cp. Dodds (*64*, p. 114) for Greek dreams of this type.

45 S. Freud (*75*, passim). This brilliant hypothesis has now received experimental confirmation. Subjects permitted to sleep, but awakened as soon as their electroencephalogram indicates that they are beginning to dream, do not feel rested. If this is done

at least as great as the contribution of the dreamer's psyche; the Charioteer's dream achieves almost the maximum of reality awareness a dream can achieve. Moreover, the external sounds which triggered the dreaming process ultimately awaken the sleeper.

Hekabe's dream has similar characteristics, though more in terms of dream-book theory than of psychology. It, too, is said to have been elicited by an "external" stimulus: by the appearance of Polydoros' phantom (cp. chap. 4). The spectator probably expected him to appear to his mother as he appears to them: in his "real" shape (εἴδωλον). However, Hekabe's "dream work" transforms this "stimulus" (= double) into a fawn. This is less realistic than the Charioteer's transformation of sounds into a very appropriate imagery. Still speaking in terms of dream-book theory, the anxious Hekabe's contribution to the content of the dream is therefore greater than that of the tired but unanxious Charioteer; the reality awareness of her dream is, moreover, less great than that of the E. *Rh.* dream.

Iphigeneia's dream is unusual in several respects. It is a dream in colour: the hair is light coloured (ξανθός).[46] Sound, barely, alluded to in the Charioteer's dream (snorting), plays a great role in it. It is not clear, either psychologically or in terms of dream-book theory, just what *triggered* her dream, but it is clinically conceivable that a real sound, perceived (heard) in dream, *terminated* it. Iphigeneia's own contribution to her dream's manifest content is maximal, while her dream's reality awareness is minimal—a fact underscored by its *double* misinterpretation. Its most striking feature is that Iphigeneia *dreams* of being *asleep* (resting); there is no typical Greek dream-figure to tell her that she is asleep.[47] This makes her dream seem a *forme fruste* of the somewhat more common "dream within a dream". None of my analysands ever reported dreaming simply that he was *asleep*.[48] There are, moreover, faint hints that dreaming that one *sleeps* was known to Homeros,[49] but the evidence is too allusive to warrant its being discussed here. What is certain, is that nothing in E. *IT.* indicates that Iphigeneia has a "dream within a dream". In a sense, Iphigeneia is simply *doubly* asleep: in reality as well as in dream. This implies both a double distortion and a double repudiation of the dream-thought and dream-wish: one notoriously feels less responsible for one's dreams than for one's waking acts and thoughts (*80*). Dreaming that one sleeps or dreams represents, from the viewpoint of the Ego, a double denial of responsibility; from the viewpoint of the Id—of the world of the instincts—it means that the dream wish must crash through two barriers. The text actually hints at a double distortion (sacrificial priestess,

several nights in a row, neurotic symptoms appear. W. Dement (*16*) well summarizes these experiments. Cp. also (*94*).

[46] One notes that the Charioteer does not mention the whiteness of his horses, though that would be compatible even with a routine "black and white" dream. The fawn, too, *could* seem dappled even in a black-and-white dream.

[47] On such dream personages cp. Dodds (*64*, chap. 4).

[48] A borderline patient dreamed that he was in bed; whether he had *also* dreamed that he was *sleeping* could not be ascertained.

[49] The figure appearing in dream says: "you are asleep". Hom. *Il.* 2.23, 23.69, *Od.* 4.804, cp. Dodds (*64*, p. 122, note 13) for other examples.

mourner), perhaps determined by an ambivalence: the dream makes the formerly gentle princess bloodthirsty (348 f.).[50] The conjugateness of the two affective polarities: "compassionate vs. bloodthirsty" and "sacrificing (killing) vs. mourning" may also reflect the two-fold layering of the dream and its ambivalence—and so might its *double* misinterpretation.

What is remarkable in all this, is the progressive increase in the three consecutive dreamers' contributions to the manifest content of their respective dreams. The decrease in the dream's reality awareness which this entails is compensated for by its increased awareness of the unconscious (infra). Moreover, in all three instances, Euripides plausibly manipulates and varies the "depth" of the dream and this is something none of his predecessors even attempted to do.

Symbolization, an essential part of the dream work, distorts, and therefore attenuates, the intra-psychic stress sufficiently to prevent it from disrupting sleep. When a dream actually awakens the sleeper, as in E. *Rh.* and perhaps in E. *IT.*, this represents, in part, a failure of the symbolization process. In the first approximation, the amount of symbolization in a dream is a moderately reliable measure of the disharmony between the Ego and the (ego-dystonic = inacceptable) latent material reflected by the dream.[51] The symbols are, moreover, not contrived haphazardly. They are heavily overdetermined: constructed out of day residues, personal experiences, cultural elements and the like, in accordance with the dreamer's personality. Even the *articulation* of symbol *A* (representing *X*) with symbol *B* (representing *Y*) is part of the symbolization process. While it is impossible to construct comprehensive dictionaries of *symbols*, it has become increasingly evident that certain types of intra-psychic *problems* are likely to seek expression in dream.[52] The relative predictability of the emergence of certain *types of problems* in dream—though in an unpredictable *form*—is an important determinant of the interpretability of dreams.

Amongst the best clues to the identity of dream-thought *X*, represented by symbol *A*, is that which, in commonsense terms, is *atypical* either about *A* itself or about its setting. The silence of the wolves, their un-wolf-like failure to use their fangs, their human use of their limbs, etc., reveal that they are human. Moreover, their failure to bite eliminates from the dream the intolerably anxiety-arousing element of cannibalism (56, chap. 5). The fawn presumably behaves in a fawn-like manner, but its position in space on Hekabe's lap shows it to be a child.

The contribution of the day residue to dream symbolism will be highlighted by the analysis of the wolf symbolism in the E. *Rh.* Cultural considerations also help one identify the X represented by symbol A. In all three dreams the victim is light in colour (infra). This, together with certain psycho-analytical considerations (infra), suggests that the victims are—or are viewed as—female. This inference is further supported by the

---

[50] This may perhaps be understood as a delayed reaction to her having almost been sacrificed at Aulis: she now "hands on the trauma" (infra).

[51] On degrees of distortion in dream, cp. Pl. *Rmp.* 571c–572b.

[52] Periods of dreaming, as determined by means of electroencephalograms, are almost invariably preceded by a brief tumescence, even in the case of very old men (*11*).

finding that on most Greek vases women are lighter in colour than are men—an indication that they lead an indoor life (*139*, pp. 97 ff.), though the tendency to *think* of women as lighter in colour is not exclusively Greek.[53]

All I tried to determine in the preceding pages is the *manner* in which dream-personages are represented by means of diversified but invariably overdetermined symbols.

The self-representation of the dreamer in his dream is inferable mainly from his self-referable dreamed sensory *experiences*. I insist on this specification, for two reasons. First, every dream personage being a product of the dreamer's own psyche, it *also* represents him, or at least part of him. Second, a dream may seem to imply a dreamed sense-experience, though, on closer scrutiny, that experience may *not* be part of the dream: though one may dream of touching or lifting an object, sensations of texture and weight may not be present in the dream. A statement may be part of the dream but not the (dreamed) experience of *hearing* it (chap. 2, note 21 and infra). Iphigeneia says that a "voice" emanated from the hair: in this case one may infer an acoustic dream experience precisely because the voice makes *no* statement (infra). At times, the dreamer may not even dream that he is present and is actually witnessing the dreamed occurrences, though this is often obscured by the Greek formula: "I *saw* a dream."[54] I know of no case in which a Greek *dreamer* simply said that he "knew *somehow*" that certain things were happening in dream.

Significantly, the only *human* personages in these dreams are the dreamers themselves. This suggests that the dreamer's body-Ego (or nuclear Ego) is, in that respect at least, intact. Only the portions of the body-Ego projected outward, onto *other* "personages", are distorted sufficiently to assume a non-human form. It may well be that the integrity of the dreamer's body-Ego is preserved, wholly or in part, precisely *by* this projection, or extrajection, of disharmonious material.

E. *Rh.* The Charioteer's self-representation is realistic; the dream even shows him sleeping on the ground. He is definitely "present", though he turns acoustic stimuli into visual images, and then "amplifies" the marauders into wolves.[55] His regression in time is quite minimal: the dream's wolves may recall those of his native Thrace, which he just left.

E. *Hec.* The dreamer's self-representation is also realistic, though less so than in E. *Rh.* She regresses to the time of her last (?) maternity, and visualizes herself as seated. She specifies (credibly) that she had had visual experiences. On the other hand, though (objectively speaking) large areas of her body seem to be in contact with "outer" objects (seat, fawn, forepart of wolf), no tactile or weight experiences are reported. Also,

---

[53] Nearly all classical Malay texts stress the light colour of beautiful women. Though the (Mongolic) Hungarians were originally yellowish, Hungarian peasants call women: *fehérnép* = white folk, though they too work outdoors. Cp. E. *Ba.* 457 f. and Dodds ad loc., cp. chap. 7, note 23.

[54] A dreamer saw, in a vivid dream, an object *the way* he could see it only if he were lying flat on his stomach in front of it. Yet he specified that he did not feel that he had personally witnessed some of the dream scenes. He just "knew it" somehow (*46*, chap. 6, case 39, Dream H-ii).

[55] On such amplifications, cp. Arist. *de div. somn.* 462b10 ff.

though a real wolf would growl, acoustic experiences are not mentioned.

E. *IT*. Self-distortion is most marked in Iphigeneia's dream: a ripe adult, she regresses to her girlhood. Only some parts of her dream activity are congruent with present realities. Though it is in Taurike that she actually lies on her bed and sleeps, she thinks she does so in Argos. Later on, she stands and officiates as a priestess. Visual experiences are explicitly mentioned; auditory ones—though probable—are only implied.[56] The earthquake dream implies the experience of being shaken or rocked; psycho-analytical considerations make this a near certainty. Objectively, her (washing) hands should have tactile sensations, but this is not explicitly mentioned. External objects are, so to speak, kept at arm's length; in Hekabe's case, all objects are in contact with her body. Yet, on the whole, Iphigeneia's self-representation is adequately realistic, for a dream experience.

Other dream personages are represented symbolically, either as animals behaving in unusual ways,[57] or as inanimate objects in unusual motion, or "behaving" in peculiar ways. Three animal species are represented: wolves, horses and a fawn, and we fortunately possess extensive information about Greek beliefs concerning them.[58] In addition, both Freud and E. Jones had analysed the role of wolves and of horses in fantasies, in dreams and even in folk beliefs concerning dreams.[59]

The Wolf Symbolism. Greek beliefs concerning wolves were numerous and varied. I mention here only a few salient facts. Except for Leto's connection with pregnant (sexual) she-wolves, the few known mythical wolves seem to be male and are associated primarily with Apollon (who, like his sister Artemis, is associated also with the wolf's prey: the deer) and secondarily with the cult of Zeus on Mount Lykaion. As a dreaded, eerie, nocturnal predator, the wolf suitably symbolizes the father of the primal scene (infra).[60] The Greeks' awareness that male wolves mate with female dogs may have a bearing upon the (inferable) arched posture of the wolf in the dream of Hekabe, who later on turns into a female dog.[61] In E. *Rh.* the wolves "ride" the white "horses"; the sexual meaning of this symbol was well known to the Greeks. The real problem is therefore not *what*, but precisely *whom*, the wolves in E. *Rh.* and in E. *Hec.* symbolize. This uncertainty is characteristically dreamlike.

E. *Rh.* The primary source of the wolf symbolism is a day residue. Ritchie (*125*, p. 76) plausibly conjectures that Odysseus had stripped Dolon of his wolf-pelt and had put it on, as a disguise; he holds that Odysseus appears, so disguised, as early as vv. 565 ff. and that the word

---

[56] She says: the hair *assumed* the voice of a man; she does not say: I *heard* its voice. Cp. supra, and chap. 2.

[57] Animal dreams are far more common among children than among adults. Primitives also tend to dream of animals and so, apparently, did the Greeks, even in drama. Ritchie cites (*125*) A. *Ag.* 1258 f. and E. *Hec.*; he could have added Klytaimestra's dream (chap. 6).

[58] (*120*) s. vv. Hirsch, Pferd, Wolf; also O. Keller (*97*) s.vv., Artemid., passim.

[59] Wolf: (*79*). Horses (*76, 79, 93*).

[60] Cp. U.S. slang: "wolf" = sexually predatory male. "Neither beast, nor father" (A. *Dict.* 781; Lloyd-Jones' conjecture).

[61] As did an Ephesian woman for a while: Callim. *fr.* 100h Schn. = 2, p. 356 Pf.

cκυλεύματα (spoils) (592) alludes to this pelt. In the dim light the Charioteer saw *two* prowlers (773) but speaks of only *one* murderer (741). This shows that the wolves derive primarily from the two (seen) prowlers and only secondarily from the one (unseen and inferred) murderer. Also, it is just barely possible that the two wolves represent additionally a splitting into two of the one murderer on the one hand and, on the other hand, a "contamination" of the pelt-less Diomedes by the pelt-wearing Odysseus. This hypothesis is attractive, because the exactly symmetrical opposite happens in E. *Hec.*: Polymestor and Odysseus are "condensed" into one wolf.

Cultural influences in this symbolism are more complicated. Some commentators unjustly ridicule Dolon's disguise, both in the *Iliad* (10.333 f.) and in E. *Rh.* (208 f.). Yet, many primitive hunters successfully disguise themselves as animals.[62] Moreover, given the Greeks' dread of wolves, anyone who saw at night something that looked like a wolf would hardly stay long enough to take a second look.[63] Besides, even an educated modern may feel uncomfortably anxious in the dark, which upsets his visual habits and makes him think he "sees" things.[64] This means that Dolon's plan was sound, both psychologically and in terms of the neurophysiology of night vision: the dimly seen, wolf-skin-clad prowler Odysseus was transformed in dream into a real wolf. This day residue is supplemented in this case by culturally determined associations of the "A usually implies B, etc." type. In the *Doloneia* (Hom. *Il.* 10), the Achaian chiefs wear fur robes at night.[65]

One (preconscious) chain of associations is thus: cold night—fur robe—furry wolf (in dream). A second chain has as its starting point the nexus between spies and bows and, perhaps, between bowmen and pelts.[66] A third one may be rooted in the equation: spy = outlaw (= "wolf").[67]

These latter chains of associations, reinforced by the first chain and by the day residue, would also lead to *a* wolf dream. The convergence of these associations with the day residue accounts for the overdetermination of the dream symbols. Also, Odysseus' wearing of Dolon's wolf-pelt exemplifies the Euripidean dual-unity of aggressor and victim (infra). A further source of the wolf symbolism is regression: in Thrace, the horses' main enemy was the wolf. Last but not least, Odysseus and Diomedes *are*

[62] Cp. European prehistoric cave paintings; bushman rock paintings in South Africa (also Aktaion?). Cp. now my *Tragédie et Poésie Greques*, Paris 1975, chap. 9.

[63] The Cumans (Kipchaks) deliberately bred huge *white* cattle-herding dogs (still surviving in Hungary under the name of "komondor"), so as not to mistake them at night for wolves. The French call a certain moment of nightfall: "entre chien et loup"—when one can no longer tell the two apart. Professor Dover tells me that the present-day sheepdogs of the Epeiros look like wild beasts ("polar bears") and are very fierce.

[64] This has a neurophysiological basis. At night peripheral vision is sharper than macular vision. If one sees something from the corner of one's eye and then turns full face towards it, to take a "better" look, the object may "disappear". Commandos operating at night were therefore trained to use—and to rely upon—their peripheral (lateral) vision (25).

[65] Lion: Agamemnon (10.23–4), Diomedes (10.177–8); panther: Menelaos (10.29).

[66] Odysseus' bow: 10.260 ff. Bowman's pelt: Paris in Hom. *Il.* 3.17 ff. Cp. vases on which bowmen wear a pelt over their left arm; this may possibly explain why the *Iliad* does not mention the archer's gauntlet.

[67] Cp. the well-known Greek equation: "outlaw = wolf".

wolves for Rhesos' horses (as Hektor and Dolon would *wish to be* for those of Achilleus).

E. *Hec.* It is less easy to account for the wolf in Hekabe's dream. Some of its sources may be the automatic pairing of a fawn with its principal natural enemy, the wolf, and Polymestor's residing in Thrace, which, as noted, was wolf country. This symbolization may also anticipate Polymestor's blinding, which makes him walk on all fours, like a wild beast (E. *Hec.* 1058 f.). The wolf = Odysseus problem is even more difficult. Once before Hekabe had seen Odysseus in a (different) disguise (*Hec.* 241 ff., cp. Q.S. 5.278 ff.). Some hold this to be a Euripidean invention, mainly because sch. E. *Hec.* 243 calls this story implausible. Possibly the equation: Polymestor = wolf, led—by a "contamination" of the type just discussed—to the equation: Odysseus = wolf. The condensation of two men into one wolf echoes, in reverse, the splitting, in E. *Rh.*, of one killer into two wolves. Such symmetries are both structurally and psychoanalytically important. Both Polymestor and Odysseus are, moreover, predatory. The former preys on Polydoros' gold; the latter acquires Achilleus' armour by questionable means.[68] A third consideration is of a different kind: Odysseus is twice represented in dream as a wolf; both times in Euripides. A third—non-Euripidean—reference compares prudent Odysseus to prudent wolf-torn horses.[69] This is a further example of "representation by opposites", already known to Artemidoros. One also notes that, in the Charioteer's dream, Odysseus the wolf actually "attacks" horses. Not even Athamas, Lykaon or Danaos is so systematically brought into conjunction with wolves. The "naturalness" of this symbolism does not weaken the arguments just advanced.

The preceding considerations only explain why Hekabe *could* represent Odysseus as a wolf. The real source of this symbolism is probably different: having made Odysseus into a wolf in E. *Rh.*, Euripides simply repeated this symbolization in E. *Hec.* This hypothesis further strengthens the view that the *Rhesos* was written by Euripides: a great poet does not repeat himself *mechanically*: Euripides substituted for the "splitting" in E. *Rh.* a "condensation" in E. *Hec.*

The Horse Symbolism is well motivated in the E. *Rh.* dream. On *one* level the horses are not symbolical at all; they are simply "themselves". On another level they represent Rhesos, whose "badge" they are, by means of the *pars pro toto* device.[70] In so far as the horses represent Rhesos, the dreamed attack on them is a symbolization by understatement, whereas the symbolization of the attackers by wolves is a symbolization by overstatement or amplification. A further argument is Euripides' unusual proneness to call a young person metaphorically: πῶλος = colt, filly.[71]

---

[68] The traditions concerning this matter are contradictory. Their form depends on whether an author favours Odysseus or Aias. Euripides' un-Homeric dislike of Odysseus is notorious, cp. note 148.

[69] Plu. *Smp.* 2.8.1 p. 615 F. For wolf-torn horses in general cp. *38*, esp. p. 179, note 9.

[70] This is made certain by the substitution of Rhesos' having to spend one night on Trojan soil, for the tradition that his horses had to be fed and watered there, cp. supra, note 18.

[71] On this peculiarity cp. Ritchie (*125*, p. 232). Others use this word in the sense of "young person" more seldom.

The determination of the sex of these horses is difficult but important. Though Orestes' chariot *team* is spoken of in the feminine plural ("mares") each of the individual animals constituting it is called a stallion.[72] Yet one cannot claim that for the horse, as for the deer,[73] the Greek generic gender is feminine. This kind of epiceneness is not limited to horses; in Greek ox (or cow) (βοῦc) and bull (ταῦροc) are time and again used interchangeably.[74] I do not profess to know whether these curious fluctuations regarding the sex of animals should, or should not, be correlated with the polyvalent sexuality of the Greeks (*45, 60*).

It is possible that some (Homeric ?) Greeks harnessed mares because the Greek chariot harness did not give the charioteer much control, and most mares are gentler than stallions.[75] Yet on most vases the horses harnessed to a chariot are clearly stallions. To complicate matters further, in classical times the cavalry horse was apparently always the stallion and yet, paradoxically, "charger" (κέληc) also meant a sexually loose woman (LSJ s.v. III) (riding = cohabitation) (chap. 1, note 32). The symbolic confusion between the horse and the cavalier, between the rider and the ridden, is also quite widespread. In Haitian voodoo belief—as in those African beliefs from which voodoo is derived—the possessed ("ridden") human is at times ridden by a spirit-horse, and yet, at the same time, the possessed (ridden) one is the spirit's horse.[76] In the night*mare* the "mare" (= phallic mother) lies suffocatingly upon the "ridden" dreamer (*93*).[77]

To these considerations may be added the Greeks' manifest dread of being bitten by their horses and also their myths of man-eating mares (*59*).[78] The Charioteer's dream vision must, thus, be decoded on more than one level. Objectively, Rhesos' horses respond to the wolves' attack with violence and it is important to recall that a range-bred stallion, or even an occasional mare, is quite able to handle—and even to kill—an attacking wolf (*38*, p. 182, note 5).[79] Yet, in dream, the Charioteer feels that his team must be rescued by him. This is a typical "primal scene" rescue fantasy; it does not reflect an *objective* appraisal of the "danger" threaten-

[72] Cp. W. S. Barrett (*6*, pp. 204–205, ad v. 231). Sch. E. *Rh.* 239: Euripides turns the Homeric Achilleus' stallions into mares.

[73] LSJ s.v. ἔλαφοc.

[74] As in A.R., in respect to the brazen-hooved bovines.

[75] J. K. Anderson (*4*, passim) seems at times to say as much. Even in quite recent times, the Arab's war-horse was the mare (*124*). Very ferocious mares exist; lactating mares can be quite dangerous.

[76] The same article (*27*, cp. *43*) cites a Euro-American clinical case, involving obsessive doubt about whether the ridden or the rider is "masculine". One source of the confusion may be that the rider *straddles* the mount (cp. chap. 3, note 104).

[77] Jones' book is a work of great erudition, which cites many popular beliefs about the nightmare. The situation corresponds to "coitus inversus" (e.g., as in the case of Sphinxes and other female monsters shown in Greek vases), derivable, in part, from the small child's fear that the mother, whose bed he shares, would "sexually" roll upon him and suffocate him (chap. 9).

[78] X. *Eq.* passim, also Anderson (*4*). Cp. the mares of Diomedes and of Glaukos. It was shortly after her mating in the form of a mare (Paus. 8.25.4) that Demeter partly cannibalized Pelops. Cp. (*39*) on mourning cannibalism and zoöphiliac fantasies.

[79] Around 1930, in Arizona, a stallion, repeatedly put into a ring to fight a mountain lion (puma), regularly killed the big cat, which is larger and more dangerous than a wolf. Rhesos' "mares" are in a state of rage (786).

ing Rhesos' horses or the "victimized" mother of the primal scene.[80] That these particular horses are *not* helpless is suggested also by their belonging to Rhesos: the figure of Rhesos, blended with that of Bistonian Diomedes, of the savage, man-eating mares (*59*), notoriously lurks behind the figure of the still problematical "Thracian Rider".[81] The mother's violent erotic response in the "primal scene" is often misinterpreted by the child as panic.[82]

It is noteworthy that whereas the horses "attacked" by the wolves survive, Rhesos, whom they represent, and the Charioteer, who wishes to rescue them, are killed or at least mortally wounded. This fits the primal scene fantasy perfectly (infra).

Psychological considerations cannot help us solve the objective (philological) problem of the sex of Rhesos' horses. They only highlight the characteristically dreamlike confusion between—or merging of—the sexes in primal scene fantasies and dreams; and it is this that matters here.

The Fawn Symbolism is, if possible, even more complicated, both as regards the fawn's identity and (despite the gender) its sex. I begin with a minor aspect of the problem. For modern man, the deer is a symbol of dove-like gentleness. This is zoologically untrue,[83] and, moreover, does not fit Greek belief. Euripides (*frr.* 740, 857 N²) is one of our earliest sources on the horned Keryneian hind, whose dangerousness was explicitly underlined by various authors.[84] Euripides seems to be the first to have offered an explanation of the hind's harmfulness; it ravaged the fields; this puts her in a class with the boars of Erymanthos and of Kalydon (E. *HF.* 377 ff.). It is, moreover, hard to visualize the savage Artemis' animal as being harmless, especially since it was by turning herself into a hind that Artemis caused the Aloadai to kill each other "accidentally" (Apollod. 1.7.4). I do not claim that the fawn in the E. *Hec.* dream should be visualized as (already) dangerous, though Hekabe clearly hoped it would be fierce some day. I only seek to forestall the *automatic* assumption

[80] A regrettably anti-Freudian friend challenged the validity of this stricture, urging that though a cat is normally able to fight off an attacking dog, he would none the less come to the cat's rescue. Though I would, of course, do the same, his example could not but elicit a smile. For, as *regularly* happens when anti-Freudians cite *personal* data in order to contradict a psycho-analytical interpretation, my friend's remark more than confirmed my interpretation . . . by selecting as the attacked animal a cat ("pussy") rather than, say, the kind of courageous billy-goat a wolf attacks in a well-known tale. His choice of a cat therefore indirectly confirms what his example tried to negate: the horses attacked by wolves do, in fact, symbolize the "victim" of the "primal scene", *in dream.*

[81] The Rhesos-Bistonian Diomedes-Thracian Rider nexus is already mentioned in Roscher, *Lex.* (*131*) s.v. Rhesos (for further data cp. *42*, esp. p. 131, note 7.) Euripides knew and used the story of Bistonian Diomedes: *Alc.* 483 f., *HF.* 382 f.

[82] Female erotic violence is easily documentable both for earlier times and for modern primitives. At Hastings, the shoulder of Harold's corpse allegedly bore the tooth-marks of his beloved. Violent erotic clawing in the Trobriands: (*112*), pp. 217–218, 280–281, 398, 400; among the Sedang of South Vietnam: personal observations of young men bearing erotic scars (*19*). Cp. Catull. 66.13 f.

[83] L. von Bertalanffy, a great biologist, contrasted, in a lecture, the stag's murderous attacks on does and fawns with the "chivalrous" behaviour of wolves. Tamed(?) stags have even killed men. Reindeer are only tamed—*not*: domesticated—wild animals (*86*).

[84] V. *Aen.* 6.801–2; bronze hooves; Hyg. *Fab.* 30.

that, for the early (though perhaps not for late) Greeks deer were totally gentle creatures.[85]

How did a fawn stray into Hekabe's dream? Since no day residue accounts for its presence, its appearance, *in dream*, is to be explained primarily not in terms of Hekabe's psychology, but in terms of that of Euripides. I already indicated that the wolf probably strayed into E. *Hec.* from the E. *Rh.* dream; the fawn seems to anticipate Iphigeneia's associations to her dream.[86] Moreover, I deem it self-evident that, in E. *IT.*, the cattle-slaying (296 ff.) Orestes' madness is lykanthropy; there is, thus, a symbolic "wolf" also in E. *IT.*—and *Rh.*, *Hec.* and *IT.* are the only surviving Euripidean dramas which contain dream narratives. This suggests a certain continuity in Euripides' fantasy—of his "idea" of what a dream par excellence is about. Were Hekabe "real", we could account for the appearance of a fawn in her dream only if we assumed that she knew that her tragedy was made possible by the (Iphigeneia =) hind sacrifice at Aulis, so reminiscent of the foreseeable fate of her daughter Polyxene. Whether *Hekabe* "knew" this, is anyone's guess. That *Euripides* knew it is proven by his *IT* and his *IA*.

This, in turn, brings me to the vexed problem of the dream-fawn's identity and sex. In appraising this problem, one must bear in mind that, though it is a primal scene dream, Hekabe's dream is dreamed from the *mother's* and not, like the other two, from the *child's* point of view. The, fawn-child is between her and the aggressor; this is a (neurotic) maternal version of the primal scene, and may account, in part, for the uncertainties regarding the fawn's sex, which is indissolubly linked with the problem of whether the fawn stands for Polydoros, or for Polyxene, or for both.

That the fawn represents Hekabe's child is certain, both from the philological and from the psychological point of view; the symbolization of small children by small animals is extremely common (*123*, etc.). One notes, however, that, later on, the Choros calls Polyxene, in the Euripidean manner (note 71), a "filly" (142). The Greek language gives no help: ἔλαφος in the feminine is the generic word for deer of both sexes. British Hellenists translate the word as "fawn". But Schmid (*134*), Bächli (*5*) and some other Germans translate: "Hindin"; Méridier and also Duclos translate in French "biche". This would be conclusive if one could be sure that the dream is about Polyxene *only*. Unfortunately, Polyxene' ghost *tells us* that *he* appears to his mother (in dream, v. 30 and sch. ad loc.), and it is on behalf of Polyxene that Hekabe supplicates the gods. The fawn must therefore—be it wholly, or in part—symbolize Polyxene.[87]

---

[85] In Anacr. *fr.* 63 P (= 51 B = 39 D) Zenodotos even tried to emend "horned" (κεροέϲϲην) to "lovable" (ἐροέϲϲην) (Sch. Pi. *O* 3.52, 1.120 Dr.).

[86] The hind sacrificed in Aulis is mentioned in E. *IT.* in v. 28; only 14 vv. before the dream-narrative begins (42). For the appearance of a dream element now in a dream and now in an association to a dream, cp. infra. That the "preface" to a dream is also an association to it, need hardly be argued.

[87] One could argue, perhaps, that, since Polydoros' ghost is transformed into a deer in dream, the dream-work may also have changed his sex. One could even cite as a parallel —albeit a feeble one—the fact that the corpse of Kaineus was found to be that of a woman (Hyg. *fab.* 14.5; Serv. V. *Aen.*, 6.488). (Sir J. G. Frazer's note to Apollod. *Epit.* 1.22 refers to a passage in Serv., which alleges that Platon or Aristoteles spoke of a change of sex in

The theory that the fawn may represent *only* Polyxene is, thus, hard to accept: the evidence of Polydoros' speech seems conclusive. Moreover, one dreams more often about vague anxieties and worries than about concrete fears, and Polyxene's impending fate is a source of fear, rather than of some vague anxiety. Only *after* telling her dream does Hekabe specify that something *else* also troubles her. Save for a brief allusion in v. 75, it is then only that she proceed to speak of Polyxene. This hardly permits one to put Polyxene squarely in the centre of Hekabe's dream. In fact, it is psychologically probable that her fears about Polyxene made her anxious also about the supposedly safe Polydoros and caused her to dream about him.

Of course, we may not eliminate out of hand the possibility that a second dream—about Polyxene—dropped out of the text. But Hekabe is apparently *almost conscious* of a condensation: the plurals in v. 89 and also in vv. 74–75 are therefore to be construed as allusions to this insight. The blending or condensation of the two children into one is psychologically greatly facilitated by the fact that both their names begin with *Poly*—and also by the *inner* connection between the two second halves of their names: (guest) gift (δῶρον) and guest-friend (ξένος). The two are, moreover, the last of Hekabe's surviving children that are still hers: she specifically stresses that Helenos (who had made his peace with the Greeks) and Kassandra (Agamemnon's concubine) are no longer accessible to her (87–88). If these interpretations are acceptable, there is no need to suppose that the text of a second dream (about Polyxene ?) fell out after v. 91.[88]

The condensation theory has other advantages as well: it supports the view that Hekabe's dream also condenses Polydoros' enemy Polymestor and Polyxene's persecutor Odysseus, into a single wolf. These two sets of condensations not only greatly increase Hekabe's anxiety but are also dreamlike enough to give the dream imagery the necessary oniric ambiguity. The final advantages of the condensation hypothesis is that (despite the feminine gender) it leaves the "true" sex of the fawn as indeterminate as the sex of Rhesos' horses seems to be (chap. 1, note 18, and supra, note 72).

Before examining the column symbolism, a word may be said about the reference to Polydoros as an "anchor" in Hekabe's associations (80), for reliable data show how tremendously this symbol (= metaphor) is overdetermined and how intricately its various determinants mesh. Hektor's son was generally called Astyanax (King of the City) because his father was Troy's sole guardian (Hom. *Il.* 6.403 ff.). Hekabe's associations call *Polydoros* the "anchor" (ἄγκυρ') of Hekabe's (= Priamos') house. We know, however, that *Hektor* (Ἕκτωρ = the holder = stay, prop) *can also* mean "anchor".[89] The allusion is, thus, psychologically identical with

reincarnation. The authority of that passage is said to be somewhat dubious. See, however, Pl. *Rmp.* 10.16 p. 620 b–c: Atalante, Epeios and Odysseus. More relevant might be the unconscious tendency to evolve the symbolic chain: death = castration = feminization, but I hesitate to appeal to it here.)

[88] See on some aspects of this passage also (*143*, 4, pp. 225 f.).

[89] Sapph. *fr.* 157 Bgk = 180 LP (uncertain); Pl. *Crat.* 193 a; cp. also Hsch. (with respect to Zeus); Lyc. 100 (with respect to the ship on which Helene eloped); Luc. *Lex.* 15. (Polydoros mentions Hektor in vv. 18, 21.)

Iphigeneia's designation of Orestes, the man-child, as a "column" of Agamemnon's house.[90] It is perhaps the presence in her mind of Hektor's name which caused Hekabe to choose the "anchor", rather than the equivalent "column" symbolism. Also, the old Queen might have thought here in terms of the time-hallowed "ship of *state*" imagery, since she apparently hopes that Polydoros will rebuild *Troy*. By contrast Iphigeneia, the largely family-minded Princess, would more plausibly think of a column, supporting her father's *house*.[91]

What is psychologically relevant, is the occurrence of the "stay" or "prop" motif in both Hekabe's and Iphigeneia's associations, albeit in two different forms: anchor vs. column. This element, too, unifies the imagery of the two dreams.

The Column Symbolism is particularly overdetermined. The representation of a human being by a mere object (in dream) occurs only in E. *IT*.[92] and it is only in that drama that the *dreamer* behaves aggressively (sacrificial priestess) towards someone she should actually protect. The symbolization is therefore obscure enough to permit a typically Aristotelian state of ἄγνοια (non-recognition) in dream. Were the disguise less impenetrable, Iphigeneia's aggressive behaviour would be intolerable to her even in her dream. This interpretation is psychologically the more convincing as misidentifications of this kind are common not only in Greek myths and dramas—as when Agaue mistakes Pentheus for an animal (*52*)—but also in abnormal states preceding crimes.[93] The impenetrability of this disguise, on *one* level, is proven by Iphigeneia's "aggressivity" in dream; its transparency on *another* level is revealed by her shedding tears in dream: yet, her affective recognition fails to cancel her intellectual non-recognition (E. *Ba.* 1147). In this instance, the mechanism of "isolation" apparently does not extend into the waking state, since Iphigeneia does realize in the end that the column is Orestes. Isolation reappears, however, in a modified form: she "denies" that *she* killed Orestes (in dream) and believes instead that he is already dead.[94]

[90] Agamemnon as a ship's cable and as a column: A. *Ag.* 897 f.

[91] One can hardly correlate the two distinct symbolizations with maritime vs. non-maritime interests, since, in the *Iliad*, one hears nothing of Trojan ships, while Archil. (*fr.* 333 L.-B) calls the two deceased champions of the maritime state of Naxos, Megatimos and Aristophon, "the tall pillars of Naxos". Cp. also A. *Ag.* 898, Pi. *O.* 2.98. Agamemnon as "only son". A. *Ag.* 898 and Fraenkel, ad loc.

[92] Polydoros is called an "anchor" only in Hekabe's associations.

[93] Demeter alone, of all the deities, failed to recognize that she was eating human flesh: Pelops' shoulder. An Ojibwa Indian, in the throes of the cannibalistic "windigo" psychosis, which made him want to eat his children, first hallucinated them as fat beavers . . . an Ojibwa delicacy (*106*, p. 216); other examples in (*137*). Two psychotic Acoma Indians hallucinated their "persecutors" as witch foxes and tried to shoot them; they hallucinated a State Policeman as a deer before shooting him dead (*56*, chap. 1). Such hallucinations decrease guilt-feelings and make the crime possible. Evidence that the creative artist can "invent" such subtle traits is provided by C. Chaplin's film "Gold Rush": the starving bully hallucinates Chaplin as a fowl *before* trying to cannibalize him.

[94] In E. *Ba.* Agaue's "isolating" manœuvre (Pentheus = animal) is "analysed" and destroyed by Kadmos, esp. vv. 1277 ff. (*52*). The parallelism is quite close also in other respects. Pentheus is, in a way, also sacrificed to a god; he perches on a tree (= column) before being killed; at vv. 1169 f. his hair is called "ivy" (cp. E. *Antiope, fr.* 203 N²). Shortly afterwards (vv. 1184 ff.) it is seen as the hair-mop of a young bull.

In the E. *IT.* dream Orestes must be sufficiently well disguised not to be recognized intellectually; this aim is achieved by his being represented by an inanimate thing: by a column. But, at the same time, his disguise must also be sufficiently defective to permit affective recognition (tears); this is made possible by the object being vocal and behaving as though it were alive. This is no mean feat of ambiguity.

It was noted that the other Euripidean dream victims are neither altogether helpless nor harmless. The horses fight back savagely. Hekabe had hopes that her fawn-child, grown to man's estate, would fight back and rebuild Troy. In E. *IT.* the victim's (counter?) aggressivity is even more marked. The column is part of the structure that almost crushed the dreamer. Moreover, the real Orestes plans a criminal sacrilege and, seized by lykanthropic madness, slaughters the Taurians' cattle. In his initial interview with Iphigeneia, his sullen hostility postpones the recognition.

Iphigeneia herself is not gentle in her dream (sacrificing priestess), nor does she subsequently claim to be still compassionate (348). There are more than mere hints of her identification with Orestes.[95] I will stress below that, in behaving aggressively towards Orestes, Iphigeneia indirectly attacks also her father Agamemnon, who had once attacked (attempted to sacrifice) her. In that frame of reference, the column topped by hair is not only Orestes, but also Agamemnon, and, specifically, Agamemnon's phallus.[96] Last, but not least, the building threatening to collapse and to crush Iphigeneia, quite as much as the heaving earth, clearly represent the parents who, during their embrace (primal scene), crush the child between themselves.

One other noteworthy point is the curious "dual unity" of aggressor and victim in all three dreams . . . a unity which psychiatric studies of brain-washing have taught us to understand better (*89, 99*). The applicability of insights derived from the analysis of brain-washing to Greek data requires no further proof here (*65*, pp. 77 ff., *110*). The tormentor and the tormented form a dual, reciprocal unit, interacting completely and intensely—each provoking the other, each provoked by the other—in a relationship of mutual induction, until a veritable ritual of oppression comes into being.[97] This "modern" understanding of sado-masochism is foreshadowed with almost intolerable revulsion (μιᾰρος)

[95] She calls her hair "light coloured" (173), like that of Orestes. This similarity between Orestes and his sisters is traditional: A. *Choe.* 166 ff., E. *El.* 520, 529, etc. Iphigeneia herself was almost sacrificed, as Orestes is almost sacrificed, etc. Emotionally she is almost as unstable as Orestes. Orestes killed because Apollon told him to kill; Iphigeneia prepares men for the killing in obedience to the wishes of Apollon's sister, Artemis, etc. On the aggressivity of mourners (*78, 98, 39, 49*, pp. 431–459, etc.), cp. chap. 3.

[96] Son = father, brother = father are common dream symbolizations. For the important son = phallos equation, cp. infra, where Greek data bearing on the column = phallos symbolism are also given.

[97] Cp. (*36*). For a brilliant literary characterization of the "closed universe" in which the two move, cp. T. H. White: *The Once and Future King* (*142*): the children torture the donkeys and the donkeys torture the children with their provocative stubbornness. They move somnambulistically in a narrow world: in a small capsule in which the giving and taking of pain is equally anxiety arousing and perversely satisfying. (Cp. Hom. *Il.* 11.558 ff.: children and donkeys.)

arousing-intensity in the three Euripidean dreams—all concerning *only* sons. (As noted before, Helenos no longer counts.)

Perspective—the angle of vision in dream—is discussed here only in relation to the organization of space in dream. Its psychological implications will be considered further on, in connection with the problem of regression and of the latent content.

In Euripidean dreams the gaze of the dreamer is never level (horizontal). In E. *Rh.* the Charioteer not only seems to know, even in dream, that he is lying prone on the ground, but the details he sees suggest that, in dream, he looks diagonally upward, as he would were he awake. The centre of his field of vision is occupied by the backs of his horses and by the lower halves of the wolves' bodies; neither the horses' legs nor the wolves' heads are mentioned. This suggests an angle of vision about 45° *above* the horizontal.[98] Hekabe's angle of vision is also about 45°—but *below* the horizontal: she looks downward, since she sees only the fawn on her lap and the wolf's claws. Iphigeneia's angle of vision is variable. At first she looks upward: at the falling cornice and at the hair topping the column. Later òn, she necessarily lowers her gaze, looking down at the hair she sprinkles. The angle of vision, while she is looking upward, cannot be estimated with any assurance; while looking down at the hair and at her hands, her gaze is probably at least 45° below the horizontal.

This consistent deviation of the gaze from the horizontal is striking. The upward-directed gaze often characterizes dreams in which the dreamer regresses to his childhood and looks up to adults (chap. 1, note 29); the downward-directed gaze is occasionally maternal: the adult looks down to the child. The change in Iphigeneia's angle of vision in dream may perhaps be correlated with the "Phantasy of the Reversal of Generations" (*92*). The young girl of Argos, protected by adults, becomes Orestes' protector. In my clinical experience a *strikingly non*-horizontal gaze tends to occur mainly in anxiety dreams (*46*, pp. 67 ff.).

Space can be experienced in dream only as a Leibnizian "order of bodies" and its symbolic meaning is still not fully understood. Dream-space appears to be an extension or projection of the dreamer's body; in very regressive dreams it may represent also the maternal body (*129, 130*). I will discuss for the moment only the arrangement of objects in the three dreamed spaces. Their relation to the dreamer's body (perspective) and the symbolic implications of their arrangement will be analysed in due time.

Euripidean dream space is consistently made up of four horizontal layers. Interest in the vertical may possibly be a Euripidean[99] characteristic. There are not many obvious Aischylean (A. *Ag.* 1 ff.) and Sophoklean parallels to Antigone on the terrace, Orestes on the roof, Pentheus in a tree and—if F. Robert's hypothesis (*127*) is accepted—to Orestes' plan to enter Artemis' temple from above.[100] Euripides' propensity to use the elevated *theologeion* may also be relevant.

---

[98] The Charioteer sleeps near, though certainly not under, his horses' hooves. A suitable distance would be 5–6 feet. In Euripides' time, a fine Greek horse stood about 14–15 hands (4′ 8″–5′) at the withers (*4*). This gives approximately a 45° angle of vision.

[99] And Aristophanic: *Nub.* (the suspended Sokrates and the clouds), *Av., Pax* and *Ran.*

[100] E. *Phoen.* 88 ff.; *Or.* 1567 ff.; *Ba.* 1063 ff. Cp. also Hom. *Il.* 3.161 ff.

The lowest supporting surface is, with one exception, the naked earth; only in the first part of the E. *IT.* dream is it necessarily the floor of a room. This is striking since, in most early Greek dreams, the Dream visits the dreamer in his sleeping quarters, which have a floor.

This principal surface supports in turn objects arranged in three layers.

The bottom layer is an object whose schematic form is the same in all three dreams (Fig. 1). It has connections with Hekabe's antecedent and subsequent waking experiences. The antecedent one might have been the old tale—or, if one prefers, the Euripidean invention—that, when Odysseus entered Troy as a spy, he had to crawl, asking for mercy, to Hekabe's feet (E. *Hec.* 245). The subsequent event is that the "wolf" Polymestor, blinded by Hekabe and her fellow-captives, crawls on all fours like a beast (E. *Hec.* 1058 ff.).

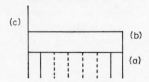

These objects consist of: (a) slender vertical supports, (b) a substantial horizontal element and (c) at one end of the latter, a short, upward projecting element.

(a) The horses' legs. The (seated) Hekabe's calves (and, if she is imagined as sitting on a chair, also the legs of the chair) and the wolf's hind legs (*blending*). The legs of Iphigeneia's bed *and,* later on, the columns of the palace (*duplication*).

(b) The horses' bodies. Hekabe's thighs (lap). The horizontal part of the bed *and* the roof of the palace (ditto).

(c) The horses' necks and tossing heads. The seated Hekabe's torso and head. The head of the bed *and* the metope of the palace (ditto).

One notes the duplication of all three elements in Iphigeneia's dream.

Owing to differences in perspective, the position of this last object with respect to the dreamer is variable. In E. *Rh.,* it towers above him; in E. *Hec.* it is Hekabe's own (maternal)[101] body; in E. *IT.* it is at first underneath the dreamer (bed); later on it surrounds her (palace). The colour of this object is, either definitely or probably, the lightest or the most brilliant of all objects seen in the dream: Rhesos' famous (301 ff.) white horses; probably Hekabe's robe; almost certainly the bedding and perhaps the columns.[102]

The topmost object is always darker than the others and is usually hairy or shaggy: in E. *Rh.* and E. *Hec.* the wolves, in E. *IT.* perhaps the roof and possibly the hair. The latter is suggested by E. (*Antiope*) *fr.* 203N[2], since ivy is dark. The hair is called ξανθός, variously translated as blond,

[101] In dream, the support *par excellence* is the symbolically represented maternal body (37).

[102] Too little is known of Greek house painting to make anything but tentative statements about the colour of the various parts of the palace. The columns were probably either light in colour or else painted in brilliant hues.

reddish, light brown. Whatever its colour, it is probably less brilliant than the colour of house paint. This colour-name occurs four times in E. *IT.*, always with ominous or funereal connotations: the frightening hair (52), blood (73), Iphigeneia's own hair which is to be shorn in mourning (173), oil for Orestes' funeral pyre (633). This does not suggest that, in dream, the hair has a cheerful brilliance;[103] moreover, I already noted the tradition that Orestes' hair resembled that of his sisters.[104] The roof is, of course, not shaggy, but the hair, which *replaces* it on top of the column, is. This is a common form of displacement in dream and is, moreover, duplicated by the displacement of sound in time, in a similarly incongruous (= dreamlike) manner.

All or part of the topmost object is hairy, pendulous and mobile: in E. *Rh.* the whipping wolftails; in E. *Hec.* the (presumably) hanging tail of the rampant wolf; in E. *IT.* the descending hair. This is invariably balanced by some lighter, long hair in one of the three lower layers: the snowy manes; Hekabe's (inferable) white hair; and, perhaps, doubly in E. *IT.*, for Iphigeneia's hair, though also ξανθός, may be imagined as lighter than that of her brother[105] and, if the inference that the already descended hair is that of the *infant* Orestes is correct, it, too, might be imagined as lighter than that of the adult Orestes, which tops the column representing him. This interpretation is advanced with due caution, precisely because too complete a parallelism would be suspect. The meaning of this contrast will be interpreted further below.

Another characteristic of these topmost objects is that all of them are in the "wrong" place.[106] Wolves should not ride horses, nor should one almost climb onto Hekabe's lap; hair on top of a column is out of place.

By contrast, each lower object is in the "right" (natural) place. This finding can be correlated with the *symbolic* representation of the (anxiety arousing) topmost objects and the *naturalistic* representation of the (victimized) lower ones. The upper objects are, predictably, the aggressors; the lower ones are the victims. It may also be noted that none of the three dreams mentions supporting, or being supported, *as an experience*. This may conceivably indicate that these dreams do not represent regression to babyhood, for dreams involving such a regression occasionally include that experience (*37*).

Summing up, in all three dreams space is divided into three layers, supported by a fourth. Their arrangement is much the same in all cases. Even if one grants that the dream space is modelled upon the structure of the body, the mathematical probability of these extensive structural congruences being due to chance is very small.[107]

[103] It is the most ominous object in the dream and dark objects in dream are of ill omen, cp. Ps.-Hp. *Insomn.* 91.

[104] A. *Choe.* 166; E. *El.* 520, 529.

[105] Cp. women's hair on a few vase paintings.

[106] No "out of place" element can be properly appraised unless one bears in mind that *one* customary scientific definition of "dirt" is "something out of place". But I hasten to add that a far broader definition of "dirt" has recently been proposed by a brilliant young Australian anthropologist, in an all but inaccessible periodical (*88*).

[107] In fact, my attention was first attracted to these dreams by their striking structural congruences with respect to space.

The Parts of the Body and Their Use. Though the bodies of the dreamers and of the animals present no particularities, it is desirable to differentiate between named parts, parts implied by the mention of their functions and parts whose use or non-use is, for one reason or another, anomalous enough to attract one's attention to their existence.[108] This is directly related to the problem of the routine use, the anomalous use and the non-use of certain limbs. A pattern is discernible, even if one treats the column representing Orestes as a person.

The dreamers' limbs are named in only one case: *Hekabe* mentions her knees (= lap). Iphigeneia mentions her own hair only in her associations (*174*). The organs implied by a mention of their function are slightly more numerous. The least important of these are the eyes (seeing), since the Greek "saw" dreams. The Charioteer uses no other part of his body. As regards Hekabe, the statement that she holds a fawn on her lap and the mentioning of her knees (= lap) can only mean that she is seated; this in turn implies an allusion to *both* sides of the middle portion of her body. Iphigeneia's crying constitutes a second allusion to her eyes, her running an allusion to her legs, the "watering" of the hair an allusion to her hands. In a sense, her eyes and hands are paired: her eyes metaphorically[109] sprinkle the hair which her hands sprinkle in fact. Her ears are also alluded to, in that she hears a voice; so are those of the Charioteer, who apparently hears in his *sleep* the (*real*) snorting of his horses, which helps elicit his *dream*. It is noteworthy that, if one disregards references to sight (eyes), neither the head nor the hands—man's most reality-oriented and "rational" organs—are mentioned in E. *Rh.* and in E. *Hec.*, though both are indirectly alluded to in the E. *IT.* dream. The mobility of the dreamer's body is nil in E. *Rh.*, at best hypothetical, and even then limited, in E. *Hec.*, but considerable in E. *IT.* This progression is significant, in that it suggests a decrease in the immobilization of the sleeper-dreamer by anxiety.

Few of the aggressors' limbs are mentioned. E. *Rh.* only mentions their tails; E. *Hec.* names the wolf's claws; in so far as the shaky column = Orestes (= Agamemnon in the primal scene) is a potential aggressor, his hair is mentioned. Limbs whose *function* at least is named are: in E. *Rh.* the riding wolves' hind legs and crotches; in E. *Hec.* the wolf's hind legs and his body arched over Hekabe's knees. No organ of the aggressor is *visually* inferable from its function in the E. *IT.* dream. The conspicuous absence of any reference—direct or indirect—to the wolves' heads in both wolf dreams is especially striking, since the Greeks dreaded the wolf's eyes (*132*). The omission in E. *Rh.* has already been interpreted; that in E. *Hec.* is interpretable. Since this wolf is human, any mention of his head (maw) would evoke the spectre of cannibalism. This would raise the level of anxiety to an intolerable pitch (*56*, chap. 5) and would weaken the human implications of the (man-like) use of the forepaws and claws (= hands).[110] In both wolf dreams the functioning of named and inferable

---

[108] Striking omissions in a dream are always clues to its meaning (*46*, p. 306). Cp. chap. 7, note 74.

[109] "Shed tears over"—"arroser de larmes"—"mit Tränen benetzen".

[110] Professor Dover momentarily visualized the E. *Hec.* wolf with hand and dagger (cp. δόλων = stiletto). (A slippage?)

limbs alike is not wolf-like but human: paws seem to climb and claw; hind legs straddle horses or else permit the wolf to stand on them like a man; tails are used as whips. Finally, the aggressors are always silent; manifestly so in E. *Rh.* and E. *Hec.* and probably—with some reservations —in E. *IT.* (infra). Their mobility will be discussed further on.

The victim's organs and limbs are more frequently named or at least implied. E. *Rh.* names the hides and the hair of the horses (though not their proverbial whiteness), their manes, their backs and their nostrils; their heads and necks are implied by the tossing of the manes, their legs by their bucking. They are, moreover, noisy (snorts). In E. *Hec.* only the spotted hide of the fawn is mentioned; this (perhaps) implies a scotomization of the head of this non-vocal victim, since a fawn's least conspicuously *spotted* part is its head. In E. *IT.* only the vocal (potentially sacrificial) victim's hair is mentioned and—except symbolically—no other of its limbs is so much as implied by its functioning.[111] The general behaviour of the victims is appropriately horse-like in E. *Rh.* and probably adequately fawn-like (helpless) in E. *Hec.* In E. *IT.* the column "behaves" as columns do in an earthquake; only the hair's behaviour is anomalous. One notes that the long-haired victims are vocal, while the short-haired fawn is not.

In the first approximation, the consistent inappropriateness of the aggressors' behaviour and the perfect appropriateness of that of the victims suggest, but do not suffice to prove, that the former reflects the child's *distorted* "vision" of the primal scene, in which father, the nocturnal ogre, does "terrible" things to mother. Similarly, at this point, the appropriate behaviour of the victims may only tentatively be correlated with the relatively undistorted self-representation of the dreamers, which suggests that they identify with the victims. This interpretation will be substantiated in later sections.

Three other points must also be noted:

(1) The emphasizing of the forepaws and hands must not be over-interpreted: man is hand, rather than foot, oriented, though perhaps less so in the first weeks of life than later on. This gives a faint clue to the "*psychological* date" of these dreams.

(2) Iphigeneia's running outdoors is appropriate emergency behaviour, even for a modest girl.

(3) In the temporal sequence: *Rh. Hec.* and *IT.*, the increasing mobility of the dreamer contrasts with the decreasing mobility of the victim: bucking horses, huddled fawn, inanimate column.

Though the many parallelisms and contrasts just cited are interesting, the importance of some of them is decreased by the interdependence of the various parts of the body; for example, a wolf cannot very well claw and bite *simultaneously*. These strictures notwithstanding, the similarities and conjugate contrasts in question are probably significant.

Movement being extremely important in all three dreams, a careful distinction must be made between various types of motility.

I. *Active Movements*:

(1) Rhythmic movement is represented in E. *Rh.*[112] by the bucking,

111 Cp., however, below: column = phallos = body as a whole.
112 On E's interest in such movements, cp. Barrett, ad E. *Hipp.* 1464 (πίτυλος).

heaving and mane-tossing of the horses and by the whipping motions of the wolf tails. Their heaving parallels the heaving of the earth (earthquake) in E. *IT*. The whipping is so typically dreamlike in its plausible absurdity, that it first suggested to me that this might be the poetic elaboration of a real dream. Yet, paradoxically, it is *this* detail that has possible literary antecedents. As a riding whip, a tail is as inappropriate as the bow, used by Odysseus in the *Iliad* (10.550).[113] In E. *Hec.*, gross or ample *rhythmic* movement is lacking in the dream, but is implicit in the associations. Hekabe mentions her "black-winged" dream (71, 704). This transposition is psychologically sound: in psycho-analysis, one observes in the course of successive dreams that certain elements pass freely from the manifest content to the associations and back again. In E. *IT.*, *rhythmic* active movement is faintly represented by Iphigeneia's running, but this is rhythmic movement on a symbolic level only.[114] Descriptively, it parallels the rhythmic movements in E. *Rh.* and E. *Hec.*

(2) Repetitive, scrabbling movements occur, in a properly dreamlike (absurd) manner, in all three dreams, and always involve the forelimbs. Since the Greeks had no stirrups, in mounting horses they relied more on their hands than we do. In E. *Rh.* the wolves probably "clawed" their way up to the horses' backs, in a very human manner. In E. *Hec.* the wolf claws at—but does not bite—the fawn. In E. *IT.* Iphigeneia waters (sprinkles) the hair, or the column, or even—as Hadas ambiguously [and wrongly, for she does not equate the pillar with a person until vv. 56 ff. (K.J.D.)] translates—"him". The little that can be made of this is briefly discussed in connection with the primal scene.

Muscular effort *not* involving movement is limited to the lower (hind) limbs and is quite peculiar in two of the three dreams. In E. *Rh.*, the wolves obviously *straddle* the horses; in E. *Hec.*, the wolf *stands* on his hind legs; in E. *IT.*, Iphigeneia, quite appropriately, stands while washing the hair. This limited locomotion pattern is compatible with the interpretation that these are primal scene dreams.

II. *Passive Movements*, especially of the rhythmic type, probably antedate (ontogenetically) even spontaneous foetal movements. Being extremely archaic, this movement pattern often occurs in dream, though usually in a heavily disguised form.[115] In infantile autism, pathological self-rocking is apparently first experienced as *active* movement, though the *experience* rapidly changes into that of being rocked, *passively*. This is, psychologically, a regressive experience—for the mother's rocking comforts the child—which is sometimes actually exploited for religious ends, as in the ecstasy-inducing behaviour of Mainades,[116] and also in grief (E. *Tr.* 116 f.).

---

[113] This is practically the only "inappropriate" use of a weapon in the *Iliad*.

[114] In dream, walking and running are experienced as strongly rhythmic and often represent sexual activity (cf. chap. 3, note 104).

[115] An analysand often dreamed of being alone in a moving automobile, which *seemed* to mean that he drove it. Not until he had a dream in which he experienced movement the way a child carried in his mother's arms would experience it—though being carried was *not* part of the manifest content—did he realize that in his automobile dreams he did *not* drive, but was simply "transported" alone in a moving car, interpretable as a womb (*37*).

[116] *64*, appendix I; cp. *9*, *115*, Iconography: *69*. "Sought" fatigue (leading to ecstasy)

More important still, for present purposes, is the *illusion*, usually experienced in states of mild regression, that the body is spontaneously rocking or oscillating. If this happens during a psycho-analytical session, it usually heralds the return of repressed memories (or fantasies) about the primal scene (*71*, p. 215).[117] This matter is discussed further in the appropriate section; here I postulate only that dreamed *passive* motion of this type is also a manifestation of an oniric primal scene "experience".

This movement is most conspicuous in the *IT.* earthquake which, in terms of Greek belief, can only be caused by Poseidon, the Earth Shaker ('Εννοσίγαιος).[118] It is also quite fitting that the fall of the House of Pelopid Agamemnon should be due to an earthquake caused by Poseidon, who had helped the immigrant Pelops to found a dynasty: the ambivalent notion that the creator is also the destroyer is theologically, mythologically and psychologically a commonplace. To these two determinants a third may now be added. An ancient theory correlates Poseidon the Earth Shaker with Poseidon of the Horses ("Ιππιος), relating earthquakes to the vibrations set up by stampeding horses; moreover, Poseidon and the Earth goddess Demeter once coupled in the form of a stallion and a mare (infra). These observations lead directly to the horses of Rhesos, whose bucking necessarily tosses the wolves about, exactly as the quaking earth tosses about the Palace[119] and, of course, Iphigeneia herself as well. Though the Charioteer, sleeping near by, presumably felt the earth shake under the bucking horses' hooves, he apparently condensed the shaking earth and the maddened horses into one image. Hence, Euripides postponed a direct mention of the earthquake motif until the E. *IT.* dream. Such postponements are fairly common in serial dreams.[120] In E. *Hec.*, passive movement of this type is lacking.[121]

Experiences of passive movement often give rise to subjective misinterpretations; for example, an *involuntary* shaking of one's body may be experienced as being of external origin.[122]

---

may be a form of toxicomania (fatigue = autointoxication: *56*, chap. 11). I believe that the more moderate self-rocking of praying Hassidic Jews induces apparently not ecstasy, but only a so-called "oceanic feeling" (Freud) (*81*); it is therefore *not* interpretable as a toxicomania equivalent. Self-rocking in schizophrenic and preschizophrenic children is an alarming symptom, suggesting a very poor prognosis.

[117] The same is true of oscillation sometimes experienced in the dark (*25*) or after sedation (*28*).

[118] Earthquakes symbolize physiological changes or upheavals. ps-Hp. *insomn.* 90.

[119] Significantly, there is an earthquake, which destroys a palace, also in E. *Ba.* (586 ff.) —i.e., in a drama in which nearly everyone is a more or less sublimated voyeur: Teiresias observes coupling snakes and/or Athene in the nude, and, though blind, is a seer and "observes" (how?) the flight of birds (see, however, S. *Ant.* 988 ff., 1012 ff.). Cp. note 158. Voyeurism is rooted in the primal scene.

[120] For the primal-scene implications of Iphigeneia's (logically justifiable) flight reaction, cp. infra.

[121] Hekabe's rocking of the fawn and her possible warding-off leg movements would be purely logical constructs and our task here is to analyse the *text*. Hekabe rocks herself in E. *Tr.* 116 f.

[122] A French *maquisard* had to flee across the fields at night, but his severe heart ailment repeatedly forced him to lie down and rest. During one such pause, he "heard" hoofbeats and "felt" the vibrations they set up. Only when the hoofbeats did not come any closer did he realize that he had simply heard the beating of his overtaxed heart and had felt *it*

Sounds are uncommon, and *heard* (articulate) speech is altogether exceptional in real dreams which, for reasons still not fully understood, are
primarily experiences (infra). Since articulate speech is very common in
Homeric dreams, while pure sound is seldom mentioned, the total absence
of speeches in Euripidean dreams and the superb handling of sound are
evidence of his realistic treatment of the dream. As repeatedly noted
(chap. 2, etc.), psycho-analytical experience indicates that it is at times
almost impossible to determine whether a speech seemingly "heard" in
dream actually involves a *dreamed* auditory *experience* or is simply something "understood" as having been "told" in dream. (Plu. *de gen. Socr.*
588D, f.; Chalcidius 255, p. 288 Wrobel.) In most cases, it is definitely the
latter. The reverse is true of *inarticulate* sound: whenever it is part of the
manifest dream content, it is always something "heard" in dream. This is
only to be expected: the dream is affective rather than conceptual. In fact,
at times external *sounds* impinging upon the sleeper's sensorium are—as in
E. *Rh.*—immediately *translated* into visual images.[123] At other times, a
dreamed *sound* is simply a transposition into the auditory sphere of more
primitive coenesthetic sensations.[124]

The one overt reference to sound is in the E. *IT.* dream: the column's
hair has a human voice, though what is "said" is not reported.[125] Three
alternatives may be considered; a fourth—that Iphigeneia forgot what the
voice said—must be discarded from the start, since she says nothing to
suggest this. Given the Greeks' fondness for dream speeches (chap. 2), had
the voice spoken, Iphigeneia would have said so.

(1) The "voice" was glossolalic, like the Pythia's.[126]

(2) The voice "mumbled"; this would represent an attempt to super-
impose a blurring noise on an ego-dystonic utterance.[127] Mumbling only
communicates affect, but withholds the conceptual content. (Cp. also
32, pp. 244 ff.)

(3) The voice moaned or groaned inarticulately. This is the most
plausible assumption. Since Iphigeneia "wept" in dream, and, perhaps,
also on awakening, she must have felt that the voice was mournful. Since
she misinterprets the visual and conceptual part of her dream, her appreciation of the affective quality of the voice, too, is probably at least
partly erroneous. It seems likely that this misinterpretation should be

shake his frame (Ἵππιος = Ἐννοσίγαιος). Conversely, a half-asleep analysand misinterpreted a few slight seismic shocks as illusory oscillations and reacted to them with
primal scene hypnagogic reveries.

[123] I am told this also happens when one takes certain drugs.

[124] A female analysand recalled at first only the tremendous crescendos and decrescen-
dos of a huge choir heard in dream. As soon as its analysis showed that these changes in the
volume of sound simply echoed strong, localized erotic pulsations, the patient recalled
that the dreamed auditory experience gradually shaded over into a manifest sexual dream,
which she had at first "forgotten".

[125] Voice of the house: E. *Androm.* 923, *Hipp.* 417 f., 1073 f., *Phoin.* 1344, cp. A. *Ag.* 37 f.
But the ship Argo speaks intelligibly (Apollod. 1.9.19) as do Sedang objects in myths
(*19*).

[126] Pythia non-glossolalic: (*64*, p. 74); contra *62*.

[127] On mumbling and related peculiarities of speech, cp. *56*, chap. 4; *40*; and *32*,
p. 244 ff. Cp. note *178*, also the General Introduction (note 22). Barking obliterates
human speech: Apollod. 3.2.2.

linked with the child's tendency to mistake the mother's *pleasurable* erotic moans for the moans of a person *in pain*—a hypothesis strengthened by the fact that these are the sounds small children most frequently hear at night and therefore most commonly associate with darkness. They are therefore also the sounds which are most commonly "heard" in dream. (For a further discussion of this important detail, cp. infra.)

The seeming mournfulness of this sound is, in a way, replicated by Iphigeneia's weeping in dream. This does not necessarily mean that she "heard" herself weep in dream—that *that* part of her dream was *also* an acoustic one. We may not even assume, *a priori*, that she *actually* shed tears while she slept, though some people do cry in sleep. As regards the former, I have never, either in clinical practice or in my readings, come across a dream in which the dreamer hears *himself*. In fact, even in a waking state one actually hears one's own voice "objectively" only in slightly dissociated states, in which one *hears* oneself talking. Moreover, the text permits perhaps the inference that Iphigeneia cried again on awakening; this seldom happens when one has already cried in sleep.

Equally interesting is the absence of sound *experiences* in the first part of the dream, though a real earthquake, causing the masonry to crash, would make an enormous din. This lends added significance to the subsequent (logically inappropriate) vocalness of the hair. Psycho-analytically, it probably represents a *deferring* of the earthquake's sound: its displacement in time. This postponement would affect the meaning of the deferred sound in a highly dreamlike (plausibly absurd) manner. There may even be another displacement in time: Iphigeneia does not seem to cry out while fleeing from the palace, but subsequently cries over the hair, and it so happens that delayed grief is a common manifestation of the displacement of affect in time (cf. chap. 3). In short, just as the noisy earthquake is silent while the silent hair is vocal, so Iphigeneia does not cry out *when she should,* but cries *inappropriately* later on.[128]

The E. *Rh.* mentions one sound only: the snorting of horses—i.e., a sound the Greeks found impressive.[129] I note in passing that this snorting sound, too, resembles bedroom sounds. More interesting still is the already briefly noted *transformation* of sounds impinging on the sleeping Charioteer's sensorium into visual imagery. His dream is manifestly triggered[130] by the sound of the struggling and snorting horses, whose crashing hooves shook the earth. From this sound and vibration an appropriate, and mainly visual, imagery is constructed; in the *dream itself* the only sound is the snorting. The (*suppressed*) thunder of hooves reappears only in the E. *IT.* dream's earthquake (Poseidon of the Horses = The Earth Shaker). In short, though, like the crashing palace, the hooves of Rhesos' horses, too, make much noise, this is *not* perceived *as sound* in the *dream*; only their loud snorting appears to be "heard" in sleep. The

---

[128] Delayed mourning of a primitive child (Assam) (*12*); cp. chap. 3, note 142.

[129] Three times mentioned by Aischylos: *Sept.* 391 f., 461 f.; *fr.* 181 Sm. (326N²) (L.C.L. ii, p. 487). The Greeks tended to muzzle horses, for fear of being bitten (X. *Eq.* 5.3) and the muzzle amplified the sound. Cp. the sexual neighing of a stallion: Hdt. 3.85–86. (Chap. 1, note 40.)

[130] Iphigeneia's dream *ends* with an apparently intrapsychically originated sound.

Charioteer clearly views his dream as a primarily visual experience, though he does so partly because (despite dream-speeches) in Greek one always "sees" a dream. This notwithstanding, the transmuting of sound into an appropriate imagery is a superb touch.

In both these dreams, the sounds lack a conceptual content and convey only affect. In both, moreover, the aggressors are silent and the victims vocal, though real crashing masonry and live attacking wolves do make loud noises. By contrast, human thieves are silent. A significant contrast may now be noted. The paradoxical *vocalness* of the hair reveals that it represents a man, while it is the paradoxical *silence* of the wolves that proves them to be human. This means that in these cases important revelations are made by diametrically opposite acoustic means. In fact, the Charioteer "constructed" the dream-wolves *out of* the noise made by the struggling horses, for only wolves would alarm Rhesos' Thracian horses.

Hekabe's dream contains no sound: nothing permits us to infer that the fawn whimpers or that Hekabe cries out. There is, none the less, a special kind of sound *in the associations*, implicit in the mentioning of the "black-winged dream" (71, 704). This image, lacking even a Homeric "winged dream" precedent, suggests another type of sound. The beating of wings sets the air in motion, as does an earthquake and falling masonry. In E. *Rh.*, too, there is a sound produced by masses of violently displaced air: the horses only snort, or blow; they do *not* whinny.

A further peculiarity of these dreams is the recurrent nexus between sound and some kind of moisture: hair—crying—sprinkling; snorting—blowing—(inevitably) foaming and sweating [and (possibly) a slight bleeding]. In Hekabe's dream itself there is no sound, nor can moisture—other than blood—be plausibly inferred. This matter would hardly deserve mention were it not for a Euripidean peculiarity: a check of *every* relevant passage in his complete surviving dramas shows that whenever sleep or dream are mentioned,[131] there is, every single time, also mention of *some* kind of fluid—be it water or something else—either just before or just after that word—never more than about 30 lines away. This nexus between sleep (dream) and moisture is at least puzzling.

What is to be retained, is Euripides' psychologically realistic and superbly plausible handling of sound in dream, though in this respect literary dreams, both before and after him, are singularly unrealistic and deficient. Equally important are the extensive manifest and latent, parallel or symmetrical, congruences between the handling of sound in these dreams.[132]

Time: Regression and Wish. The handling of time in dream must reconcile

[131] As listed in J. T. Allen and G. Italie, *A Concordance to Euripides*, 1954 (2). Possible nexus suggested by J.W.D.: bedwetting and/or nocturnal pollution. I suspend judgment on this hypothesis.

[132] I would like to advance here a new explanation of the visual nature of most dreams. In sleep, sight is the *only* sensory sphere which *cannot* be fully stimulated without awakening the dreamer. By contrast, the sleeper continues to have auditory, tactile, kinesthetic and coenesthetic experiences of moderate intensity (75). It is therefore possible that, in order *not* to be awakened by them, the dreamer *transmutes* them in dream into imaginary visual experiences, since *that* sensory sphere is not "occupied" by *real* (external) stimuli in dream. This is precisely what the Charioteer does. Also, since the only stimuli which the

two sets of paradoxes. The Ego is time-conscious; the Id and at least some segments of the Unconscious are timeless. The dream is inherently regressive; the wish it expresses is technically progressive. The resolving of these two pairs of conflicting orientations in dream occasionally leads to a circularity of oniric time.

The manifest content is experienced in the present tense, though it may imply the future in the form of a dread or wish. The Charioteer apparently plans *already in dream* to save his horses; Hekabe's narrative at least hints at a frustrated wish to save the fawn; Iphigeneia flees from the Palace so as to save herself. This is little enough, but it is precisely the cursoriness of these allusions that is dreamlike. The past is hardly ever "remembered" in the manifest content. Though always implicit in it, it is experienced—so to speak—in the present tense. In dream, Iphigeneia does not remember her girlhood; she *is* a young girl. Hekabe does not "reminisce" about her babies; she actually dandles one on her knees. Only the Charioteer's narrative alludes directly to the past ("the horses that I tended")—but that, as Professor Dover points out to me, is natural, for by the time the dream is *told*, the horses *have* been stolen. It is, thus, the narrative (*111*), rather than the dream itself, that contains an (explicative) reference to the past. Psycho-analytically, the past tense is here part of the secondary elaboration which results from the *telling* of the dream to Hektor. The dominance of the present is strikingly highlighted by the fact that, e.g., Iphigeneia is in an unusual place in dream, but does not know (or say) how she got there; the "because . . . therefore" sequence is little stressed in real dreams.[133]

The manifest representation of regression gives a clue to its *depth*.

(1) It is almost negligible—a matter of weeks or months—in the Charioteer's dream, as shown by his (now inappropriate) fear of (Thracian?) wolves. This detail probably implies a thought-habit lag, rather than a genuine regression.

(2) In Hekabe's dream, the regression is represented by the maternal stance. Its depth cannot be calculated with any precision, since the fawn may be either Polydoros or Polyxene—or both. The latter is of marriageable age. As to Polydoros' age, the data (vv. 4 ff.) are ambiguous. They seem to imply that he was sent abroad when the tide began to turn against the Trojans, but they might just as well mean: when Troy began to be besieged (= in danger, κινδύνος). Hekabe's advanced age supports the latter alternative. Polydoros therefore cannot possibly be an infant.[134]

foetus does *not* experience are visual ones, sleep and foetal existence notoriously have much in common. It is especially interesting that man's *most reality-oriented* sense (*25*): sight, should *also* be the sphere of his *maximally unrealistic* dream-experiences.

133 It is, moreover, so unusual in Mohave Indian myths, that its occurrence in one place is specifically pointed out by Kroeber (*101*, p. 65, note 137).

134 Were he alive, we might, considering Euripides' habit of giving speaking roles to children (*7*, pp. 48 ff.; *15*, p. 190; *84*, p. 103), extrapolate from A. M. Dale's attractive suggestion (in her edition of E. *Alc.*) that, since Eumelos is given a speaking role, he must be about 8 years old. [Dale could have added that, on vases, many children are represented as being about 8 years old; but this may only be a bad artistic representation of head/body proportions (K.J.D.).] The difficulty here is that the speaker is Polydoros' phantom I do not think Euripides made careful calculations, though much is grasped intuitively by a great poet. On children in ancient literature see now Kassel (*96*).

(3) Iphigeneia's degree of regression can be determined with precision. She was already of marriageable age at Aulis (E. *IT* 25, *IA* 98 ff., etc.); to this, one must add the duration of the ten-year Trojan war, of Agamemnon's return voyage, the growing up and matricide of Orestes and perhaps an additional year, needed to bring him to the land of the Taurians. Hence, in E. *IT.*, Iphigeneia cannot be a *very* young adult; her captivity was clearly a long one. We also have a second clue. Initially, the hair topping the column is high above her, since, by now, Orestes is necessarily taller than she is. Then it descends low enough for her to "water" it; formerly Orestes, her baby brother (v. 231), was much smaller than she. Regression is also suggested by our not being told *how* the hair descends; such things just "happen" in dream, partly because each element is over-determined.[135] The apparent inarticulateness of the hair's voice may, on the *manifest* level, imply that Iphigeneia regresses to the time of Orestes' early (v. 231 f.) childhood.[136] But the latent meaning of this inarticulate voice implies also a regression to Iphigeneia's own childhood and not only to that of Orestes: a brilliant exploitation of overdetermination.

On the manifest level regression is, thus, reflected by the dreamer's self-representation. On the latent level it is reflected by the dreamer's affective reactions to external objects and events in the dream, though the latter are, of course, *also* created by the dreamer. The latent regression is, as will be shown, much greater than the manifest one. The Charioteer probably and Iphigeneia certainly regress, in person, directly to their own childhood; Hekabe regresses to hers only by the circuitous route of her (latent) identification with the endangered fawn on her lap. This, too, represents an effective exploitation of overdetermination.

Matters become even more involved when one also considers the matrices into which the dreams are embedded.

The dream in context, as a phenomenological unit, has boundaries wider than those of the manifest and the latent content. Taken out of context, the manifest dream has primarily stylistic functions. Seen in context, one of the dream's most striking aspects is the conscious and/or unconscious "acting out" to which it leads (Arist. *insomn.* 463a27 ff.) and of which the demand that it be interpreted is only one manifestation. Only the articulation of time into past, present and future, and the manner in which its circularity is *brought about*, need be discussed here, particularly with respect to the dream's oracular functions.[137]

The circularity of time in the largely present-oriented E. *Rh.* dream is

---

[135] For a different meaning of this hair, cp. infra. The hair may descend because the column *collapses*; though, in so far as it is crowned by Orestes' hair, the column perhaps *shrinks*. Other explanations seem implausible. It cannot be the victim's cut-off hair since at that point, it is sprinkled. It is hardly lowered like a flag. The supposition that it grows long, like *real* hair or ivy, is less implausible. V. 74 makes decapitation possible, but the wording of vv. 51 f. may preclude that hypothesis.

[136] Euripides knew how to make slightly older children speak articulately and yet childishly. Cp. Greenwood (*84*, pp. 103 ff.) on the pathos of the orphaned children's warlike chantey (E. *Suppl.* 1139 ff.), seen as a manifestation of human folly.

[137] The articulation of time in the unconscious is so ill-understood that exploratory work is still possible (*41, 54, 55*).

minimal.[138] What seems to be a premonition in dream is, at most, clair-voyance, or even a simple elaboration of synchronous, external stimuli (Arist. *insomn.* 462a18 ff.). One can, at most, speak of a fusion of the present with a pseudo-future.

In E. *Hec.* the fusion of the psychological tenses is more complicated, chiefly because of the ambiguous definition of the present. Unlike what happens in A. *Eum.*, where the dreaming Erinyes and the intrusive spectre of Klytaimestra are simultaneously present on-stage, the sleeping Hekabe, when she "saw" Polydoros' spectre, present on the stage, was, assuredly sleeping inside the captives' tent and therefore invisible. Also (30 ff.), Polydoros' spectre probably floated above the stage, on the crane. More-over, though Hekabe's dream supposedly results from Polydoros' Kly-taimestra-like appearance (present), he does not inform Hekabe of his present state ("I am dead"). Instead, he speaks of past ("I was murdered") and future ("my mother will bury me") events (45 f.). His appearance motivates Hekabe's change of conduct. The psychological tenses are, thus, confused both in the dream itself and in reality. It is left to Hekabe to protect (if she can) the fawn no longer sheltered, even in distant Thrace, by Hektor's prowess and Troy's might. In dream she foresees that the fawn is (= was = will be) torn from her lap: this is the Polyxene and/or Polydoros problem. Awake, she must seek to forestall, if she can, Polyxene's ritual murder and to take revenge for Polydoros. The complex meshing of the *psychological* tenses is a brilliant means of bringing into being an over-determination which is further enhanced by the uncertainty as to whether the dream is retrocognitive or prophetic. The circularity of time also has an affective basis. Worried by Polyxene's *foreseeable* fate, Hekabe begins to worry *also* about what *might have happened* to the—supposedly safe—Polydoros.[139] The dream also contributes to the shaping of the future, by partly disinhibiting Hekabe's aggressivity.[140] Finally, her anticipations prove to be correct.

The articulation of time in E. *IT.* is particularly complicated, especially on the manifest level. This strengthens the view that hers is the most literary of the three dreams. Though its dramatic function has been dis-cussed many times,[141] some of its most important dramatic aspects have been overlooked. The complexity of the problem necessitates discussing its real and its oracular implications separately.

The most direct consequence of the dream and of the subsequent mourn-

[138] The circularity of time may be an orphic idea (cp. perhaps Ar. *Av.*). On circular time cp. *(8)*.

[139] This is typical crisis behaviour. In 1939, a research team was told by many German-Jewish refugees that their families, living in constant danger in Germany, obsessively worried about *them*, who were safe in America.

[140] Which leads to her being stoned. This, in turn, *causes* her transformation into a bitch. [On stoning *causing* such metamorphoses, cp. Roscher *(132)*.] It is just possible that the wolf's arched posture in dream faintly anticipates this metamorphosis, and the suicide (Cp. Krimisos' and Segesta's mating: Lyk. 961 f.; Tzetz. ad *Lyc.* 953; Serv. *V. Aen.* 1.550; 5.30; Myth. Vat. 1.137, 2.193; and Segesta coins. Also the shame suicide of a woman who had been temporarily turned into a bitch and then became human once more: Callim. *fr.* 100h Schn. = ii, p. 356 Pf.

[141] References in W. Schmid *(134,* i, 3, pp. 522–523). Not discussed in Platnauers's annotated edition of E. *IT.*

ing is that it makes Orestes into a man who, having erroneously been believed dead, must be reintegrated into society (supra).[142] This enables Iphigeneia to "lie the truth" to Thoas convincingly. She *pretends* that the victim *should be* purified; she *knows* that a man erroneously believed to be dead *must be* purified.[143] Active in dream, she is also active in the drama, first prolonging her dreamed sacrificial role into the waking state and then reversing it. Moreover, her sadness in the dream anticipates her subs quent sadness. Her sacrificial role in dream foreshadows her confession that she had become bloodthirsty (343 f.), though psychologically her dream presupposes an antecedent—and perhaps not yet conscious—disinhibition of her aggressivity.[144] Her belief that Orestes is dead increases the probability that he might not be recognized and would therefore be sacrificed, thereby gratifying Iphigeneia's bloodthirstiness, so similar to that of Artemis, to whom she herself had been "sacrificed" at Aulis.

The dream also influences Iphigeneia's behaviour precisely by being treated as an oracle.[145] It is this way of *viewing* a dream which leads to its being made self-fulfilling, by means of the acting out it elicits.[146] Much of Iphigeneia's behaviour is determined by her *double* misinterpretation of her ostentatiously prophetic dream.[147] This is striking, in view of Euripides' obvious preference for dream oracles, as against those of Delphi.[148] Later on, Iphigeneia complains that the dream misled her (569 f.), though it showed her as a sacrificial priestess and not as a mourner. Oracles deceive because men insist on being deceived (72, 20, 47).[149]

In dream, she makes preparations for a ritual murder. On awakening,

---

[142] Euripides did not labour this problem. There are many such men in times of war and the topic is a painful one. [Phrynichos was heavily fined for staging his *Capture of Miletus* (Hdt. 6.21).] (It has often been noted that S. *OT.* soft pedals the Theban plague. Whether he had the Athenian plague in mind, or simply some other plague, is anyone's guess, for the date of S. *OT.* is unknown.)

[143] On this type of lying, cp. infra.

[144] Changes, both for the better and for the worse, often manifest themselves first in dream, next in behaviour, and last in projective tests. (For dreams and behaviour, cp. *48*, passim; for psychological tests, cp. Holt's notes, ibid., p. 493.) Iphigeneia's tears in dream do not disprove her aggressivity, cp. E. *Ba.* 1147, and (*33*).

[145] Oracles influencing events: *14*. E. Bächli (*5*) only skirts the insight that the same applies also to dreams. Cp. also *72*, *47*.

[146] Arist. *de div. somn.* 463a4 ff.; cp. *64*, p. 120. Clinical evidence: *114*. A dream can be *made* to come true, by acting out already *during* the dream: an adolescent analysand tried, in dream, to avoid a collision by jumping off his motor-bicycle; in reality, he threw himself out of the top bunk of his double-decker bed (*31*).

[147] By contrast, the other two Euripidean dreams do come true and are correctly interpreted.

[148] E. *IT.* 1235 ff. Amphiaraos is a noble figure in E. *Hyps.* (132 ff., 152, 204 ff. and passim, Page), and is spoken of with respect in *Phoin.* 1111 f., *Suppl.* 158. This, of course, is traditional, but Euripides did not always respect traditional heroes, such as Odysseus. (Chap. 3, note 147 and supra, note 68.)

[149] Unlike Euripides, the old-fashioned Hesiodos (*Th.* 26 ff.) calmly accepts the occasional untruthfulness of the Muses (or gods). The existence of vicious gods does not shock—though it may anger—real primitives (*21*, pp. 667 f.) Psychologically, this is rooted in the child's (partly justified) notion that all adults are psychopaths, since they so behave towards children (*29*). In a still family-centered society, Autolykos can be a hero and Aigisthos "blameless". A. W. H. Adkins (*1*, esp. p. 81, note 11) understood the sociological, but not the psychological, meaning of this "blamelessness". [But one does not really know what this epithet meant for Homeros (K.J.D.).]

she believes that Orestes is dead. Psycho-analytically, this can only mean that she treats the human sacrifice, prepared in dream, as a *fait accompli*. This is reminiscent of a peculiarity of tragic diction, which at times speaks of an intended murder as though it had actually been executed.[150]

The circularity of time is brought about in E. *IT.* by means which, in some respects, resemble those which make times circular in Hekabe's dream: while dreaming, Iphigeneia's behaviour "prophetically" anticipates what she *will (almost)* do in reality; yet, on awakening, she treats her dream as *retro*cognitive. Misleading as a clue to the past, her dream also fails as prophecy. This is brilliant, persuasive *and* poetic psychology:[151] she sacrifices in dream, but not afterwards. She misinterprets the dream while awake: she cries over Orestes, who is actually alive.

The articulation of time in the three dreams is as follows:

E. *Rh.*: Past: (habit lag?), feeding and driving the horses; Thrace (dangerous wolves). Present: the real (= dreamed) attack. Future: the wish to protect the horses and the quarrel with Hektor.

E. *Hec.*: Past: regression and the retrocognitive interpretation of the dream. Present: the dream is caused by Polydoros' dramatically earlier but onirically synchronous (cp. A. *Eum.*) appearance; the dream crisis and the real crisis are, moreover, similar. Future: bad news about Polydoros will reach Hekabe, bad things will happen to Polyxene.

E. *IT.*: Past: regression and the retrocognitive (mis-)interpretation of the dream. Present: the sacrificial priestess role in dream and the ostentatious denial (by means of regression) that she is amongst the Taurians; transposition, with changed meaning (sacrifice = mourning), of the dream activity into waking activity. Future: she will (almost) sacrifice Orestes; ostentatious denial of that possibility by the conviction that Orestes is already dead.

In all three cases a circularity of time is brought about by varied and subtly nuanced means.

Summary: Real dreams, especially when taken in context, show at least some articulation of time, even on the manifest level. In some pre-Euripidean Greek literary dreams, time tends to be either badly articulated, or else over-articulated in a manner which is *not* authentically dreamlike. Though these Euripidean dreams also articulate time somewhat too well to be accepted as *undistorted* accounts of real dreams, this slight over-articulation is brought about by nuanced, varied and, above all, characteristically dreamlike means. The supernatural meaning imputed to them largely determines their dramatic function. Theirs is the role dreams were expected to play in Greek tragedy and Euripides managed, without diminishing their plausibility, to make his dreams achieve what was expected from them in terms of tragic convention.

Latent Content: The Primal Scene. Three dream-narratives, which are structurally variations on a single theme, necessarily have the same latent content or meaning, to whose probable nature certain external charac-

---

[150] S. *Aj.* 1126 ff.; cp. E. *IT.* 60, 359 f. (?), E. *Ion* 1497 f., etc. Cp. chap. 1, note 17.

[151] Psycho-analytical scrutiny shows that "retrocognitive, clairvoyant, telepathic and prophetic dreams" fuse the past and the unconscious wish. All clinical psycho-analytical papers on this subject up to 1951 (including those of Freud) are collected in *55*.

teristics of these dreams furnish a clue. Since they are anxiety dreams, their content must be painful; the amount of symbolization indicates that it is not in harmony with the Ego's strivings (ego-dystonic). The regression shows that the roots of these dreams are infantile. On a wholly different level, the recurrence of the same theme in three tragedies implies not only the conflict's persistence *in Euripides' unconscious*, but also its partial sublimation, since he expressed it in the form of great poetry. This sublimation was perhaps partly facilitated by the fact that the theatre, like the most common type of primal scene, is a primarily visual experience, which permits a sublimatory gratification of the infantile wish to "see something". Great drama deals with this "something" in such a manner that the anxiety it arouses leads to a katharsis and to subsequent sublimation.[152]

The basic latent theme is the "primal scene": the child's anxiety-distorted experience or fantasy of sexual relations between the parents. It underlies also certain themes of both Greek and non-Greek cosmogonic myths and is represented in an almost undisguised form in Hesiodos' *Theogony* (159 ff.) (*51*). Turned (defensively) into grotesque comedy, several aspects of the primal scene experience are mentioned in words that leave nothing to the imagination in Aischylos' *Diktyoulkoi* (*Net Fishers*) (810 ff., H. L.-J., etc.). Last but not least, nearly every one of the primal scene's twenty constituent elements occurs, often in an undisguised form, in a variety of Greek myths and texts. The material will be presented in a numbered, itemized form; cross-references are indicated by the corresponding numbers in parentheses. Some other Greek sources, which also mention these elements, are given in footnotes: they constitute only a fraction of the relevant Greek material I was able to assemble.

In all three dreams realistic current preoccupations furnish the Aristotelic raw material (day residue) for the symbolic reconstruction of the primal scene in dream. In my opinion, this pouring of new wine into old bottles, so characteristic of dreaming (and of neurosis), appears to insure the continuity of the psychic life and the unbroken evolution of the temporal Ego (*41*), particularly in the course of alternations between sleep and the waking state. In a sense, the need for such a continuity in the experiencing of the "self" *in time* may explain *in part* the circularity of time in so many dreams.[153]

In analysing these three dreams, one must bear in mind that in E. *Rh.* the poet describes the primal scene from the small boy's point of view, in E. *IT.* from that of the little girl, and in E. *Hec.* from the viewpoint of the mother (= father's wife). This latter psychological feat is the more impressive as even psycho-analysts seem little interested in the primal scene *as fantasied* (or acted out neurotically) *by one or both parents*. Yet in at least two Greek traditions, the child is literally invited by one of the parents to participate in the primal scene. In Hes. *Th.* 159 ff., Gaia asks her children to intervene during the act itself (*51*), while in A. *Dict.* 810 ff.

[152] It may or may not be a coincidence that the three primal scene dreams occur in dramas which would *not* have scandalized Aristophanes' "Aischylos," (Ar. *Ran.* 1044 ff.): no *amorous* women appear in them.

[153] I suspect that the fusing of the present with the past—the patterning of present conflicts on infantile models—may be an important determinant of the process of falling asleep. I hope to deal with this problem in a psycho-analytical publication.

(H. L.-J.), the infant Perseus' prospective "father", Silenos, literally invites him to witness the primal scene: "(you) can make a third in bed with your mother and with me, your father, And daddy shall give the little one his fun" (Lloyd-Jones' translation).[154] While nothing quite so extreme occurs in Hekabe's dream, such data prove that there is also a parental (i.e., maternal) way of imagining the primal scene. It is this manner of viewing it which finds expression in Hekabe's relatively normal dream.

Before listing and scrutinizing the twenty constituent elements of the real primal scene, as reflected in these dreams, I note that these ways of experiencing that scene are clinically quite commonplace. That the experience itself was fairly common in the fifth century B.C. Athens is best shown by A. *Dict.*; had the primal scene experience been exceptional, the "joke" would have fallen flat. Moreover, as noted, Aischylos' satyr plays appear to have been admired by the ancients (*116*, p. x). That would hardly have been the case had they dealt with material to which his audience could not respond. Judging by the few surviving samples, the psychological "detonator" in satyr dramas was the presentation of some anxiety-arousing infantile fantasy as grotesque "fun". In short, as already noted, the satyr play deals with the anxiety-arousing material of tragedy in a radically different mood.[155] (Cp. chap. 1, note 34.)

As regards the primal scene elements in the three Euripidean dreams under consideration, it may be useful to make first three points:

(1) In talking about the primal scene, one *automatically* talks *also* of the Oedipus complex—and vice versa, of course.

(2) Though any one—and perhaps more than one—of the twenty primal scene elements listed below can occur also in other types of experiences, fantasies and dreams, their *co*-occurrence, in the form of a *pattern* or *configuration* (syndrome) can characterize *only* a primal scene dream. Already ps.-Long. (*de sublim.* 10.1) understood that syndromes, and not isolated symptoms, matter.[156]

---

[154] Since this aspect of the primal scene is, unaccountably, still neglected by psychoanalysts, a few clinical examples may help clarify matters. An intermittently impotent man "complained" that his children "intruded" into the bedroom at "inopportune" moments. Unconsciously, he *desired* these "intrusions". Indeed, despite repeated psychoanalytical interpretations and, finally, despite direct advice, it took him three months to get around to having a key made for the bedroom door and then he regularly "forgot" to use it. A neurotic woman enjoyed marital relations only if she *concurrently* fantasied that she was pregnant with a boy, that her husband's phallos intruded into the foetus' mouth and that the unborn ingested the semen. The second and third of these fantasies are duplicated, in every detail, by Mohave beliefs about pregnancy (*22*, *24*). Thus, parental exhibitionism complements infantile curiosity. Moreover, in a sense, parental exhibitionism is both a "handing on" of the trauma to the child and a vicarious gratification of the parent's incompletely outgrown curiosity. (I.e., "I am showing my own parents how they should have treated me!") This is a common neurotic manœuvre.

[155] The primal scene: E. *Ba.* vs. A. *Dict.* 810 ff. The cannibalization of someone *relatively* small (= teknophagy): A. *Ag.* 1218 ff. vs. E. *Cycl.* Blinding: S. *OT* vs. E. *Cycl.* Whether the (folk tale) motif of the aggressive, clever baby and his outwitted (stronger) foe occurred not only in satyr plays (S. *Ichn.*), but also in tragedy, is uncertain. That motif may *conceivably* lurk also behind the tragic theme of exposed but saved children, who return later on and harm their persecutors (S. *OT*, etc.).

[156] On the importance of appraising Sappho's seizure (*Sapph. fr.* 31 LP) in terms of the configuration (syndrome) as a whole, and on her independence of Homeric models in the description of her experience, cp. *50*.

(3) It is safe to ascribe to Euripides an interest in the primal scene. The ("off-stage")[157] climax of his greatest tragedy is the rending of Pentheus, who seeks to spy upon the (hypothetical) sexual misconduct (E. *Ba.* 223 ff.) of the Mainades—*including specifically his mother* and aunts (E. *Ba.* 229 f.).[158] Since he made *this* the climax of his *Bakchai*, it is not surprising that he should have devised primal scene dreams for some of his earlier dramatic personages.

This being said, the following primal scene (experience, fantasy, dream) elements occur in the three Euripidean dramas containing dreams:

(1) *Infantile spying* and, at times, parental counter-spying.[159] E. *Rh.*: the spy and counter-spy motif. E. *IT.*: Iphigeneia watches the collapse of the house; Orestes and Pylades spy out the temple which they intend to burgle [cp. (6)]. E. *Hec.*: Polydoros' visible spectre probably appears to (is seen in dream by) Hekabe.[160]

(2) *Horror and fascination.*[161] *Rh., It., Hec.*

(3) *Scotomization.* Anxiety blurs some of the details. At times a haze covers part of the visual field (*82*). At other times the visual field is so restricted as to approximate so-called "tubular" vision. However, in the Euripidean dreams, the *non*-perception of certain details is, strictly speaking, not due to a scotomization, but to the dreamer's (small child's, mother's) angle of vision (cp. the section on "Perspective").[162] E. *Rh.*: the dreamer's vision is almost "tubular": he mentions neither the wolves' heads, nor the horses' legs. E. *Hec.*: the wolf's head *is* apparently *not* seen; in a maternal (wifely) perspective, the wolf's "tail" (penis) *could not* be seen.[163] E. *IT.*: possibly the unexplained descent of the hair. As already noted, the perspective is peculiar though appropriate in all three dreams.

(4) *Non-recognition* (total or partial) of the parent(s): this implies a repudiation of the *intolerable* evidence of one's senses.[164] Usually, it is the mother who is "not recognized", though there are exceptions to this

---

[157] On the connections between "off-stage" and "the irrational" (= unconscious), cp. Arist. *Poet.* 1460a26 f. and *54*.

[158] Two other points may also be made. (1) The two other named male personages of that tragedy have, at some point, *also* indulged in "sexual spying": Kadmos enquired into the amours of Zeus with his sister Europe (Apollod. 3.1.1); Teiresias saw Athene in the nude (Callim. *Lavacr.* 75 ff.), revealed Zeus' amours with Alkmene (Apollod. 2.4.8), saw snakes copulate (Apollod. 3.6.7), and disclosed that women enjoy coitus more than do men (Hes. *fr.* 275 M.W.). (2) Gossipy biographers asserted that Euripides himself caught his wife *in flagrante* with his slave Kephisophon (Anon. *Genos*, etc., p. 6 Schw.; Satyr. *V. Eurip. fr.* 39, pp. xii f.). Not the truth of this incident, but its ascription *to Euripides*, matters. (On information that can be drawn from inauthentic anecdotes, cp. *50*.)

[159] I.e., "Is the child safely asleep?"—but also: "Is the child masturbating?"

[160] Cp. Hom. *Od.* 9.329 ff. (Ares and Aphrodite); Thphr. *Char.* 13.8, 20.7 (mother's childbed); X. *Smp.* 9.2 (erotic dance); A. *Dict.* 810 f. On the ambiguousness of the many-eyed, sex-spy Argos' role, cp. chap. 2.

[161] Caricatured defensively in reverse in A. *Dict.* 810 ff., as "fun".

[162] Athene blinds Teiresias. Semele is (perhaps) blinded by Zeus seen as lightning. For Oidipous' explanation of his self-blinding, cp. S. *OT.* 1369 ff. For Stesichoros, cp. below. Possibly Epizelos: he saw a foe whose immense beard *covered* his shield (Hdt. 6.117); (goat skin aigis?). Other suggestive cases are to be found in Escher (*70*), though the unpsychological Escher did not understand them (*58a*).

[163] Both Greek and Latin equate "tail" and "penis" (*53*).

[164] Cp. my comments (chap. 3) on A. *Ag.* 412–413: ἀπίστους, also (*43*).

rule.[165] But, in Euripidean dreams it is the aggressor (father) who is most heavily disguised. This may well be a Greek peculiarity;[166] the most striking exception is the tale of Stesichoros' blindness.[167] The relatively transparent representation of the "victim" (mother) and the opaque disguise of the "aggressor" (father) in Euripidean dreams, though less easy to explain, are perhaps not beyond conjecture.[168] At any rate, in all three dreams the least recognizable personage is the aggressor. E. *Rh.*: the non-recognition of the wolves makes accusations against Hektor possible. E. *Hec.*: the real (double) identity of the wolf is revealed only by analysis; by contrast, though the sex of the fawn is uncertain, the fact that this animal represents one or two of Hekabe's children is obvious—at least on the affective level—already in the dream. E. *IT.*: the identity of the falling roof is never recognized; the column's identity is not only ambiguous, but the dream concerning it is *twice* misinterpreted.[169]

(5) *Father* = *ogre*.[170] E. *Rh.*: the wolves ride (= coitize) the horses [κέλης = sexually active woman, cp. LSJ s.v. iii, 1 and 2; perhaps at times—but *not here*—coitus inversus (chap. 1, note 32)]. E. *Hec.*: the wolf *must* be arched (in a sexual posture) over Hekabe's knees, since he claws the fawn on (or: off) her lap; later on, Hekabe herself turns into a bitch—and the Greeks knew that bitches mate with wolves. E. *IT.*: The roof threatens to crush (= coitus = *compressio*) Iphigeneia [cp. (16)]; the collapsing column may also be dangerous [cp. (18)]. I note that the horses are not really harmed—only stolen. The fawn is harmed. Iphigeneia remains unscathed . . . though, at Aulis, she was "sacrificed".

(6) *The Paternal phallos*, seen as a dangerous organ,[171] fascinates but

---

[165] An adolescent Plains Indian did not "recognize" his widowed mother's lover and only "inferred" that this person was "another" (*sic*) man from the fact that he tried to hide (*48*, p. 290 f.).

[166] The invisible or disguised lover motif: Zeus and Semele; Zeus and Alkmene; Eros and Psyche; also other tales of divine or heroic paternity. A young woman dreamed that a purple-clad jester capered and grimaced at her. On awakening she recognized, with a start, the jester as her father and concluded that the shadowy woman, also present in her dream, was her mother. I.e.: father disguised, mother shadowy.

[167] The initial recognition that "the most beautiful of women" (= mother) misbehaves (Stesich. *frr.* 10–14P) causes blindness, which is cured as soon as the poet rejects the evidence of his "eyes" and writes two retractions (Palinodes): Stesich. *frr.* 15–16P. (Chap. 3, note 98.) (*59a*).

[168] Euripides' foes would not have consistently jeered at his mother ("the vegetable seller") had their attacks not hurt him. This suggests that he was greatly attached to her—more so than to his father, who was seldom directly attacked: the story that he was a peddler was probably an extrapolation from the gibe that the mother sold vegetables; data in Schmid (*134*, i.3, p. 313, esp. note 4). [But the joke's basis may be its incongruousness: the son of a vegetable seller is writing about kings (K.J.D.).] Possibly the "brutality" of the aggression against the "helpless" mother made recognition tolerable. These are admittedly conjectures, though they are not lacking in plausibility, especially in view of Euripides' sympathy for women, and also for the oppressed.

[169] The dream collapse of *this* palace anticipates that of Pentheus' palace in E. *Ba.* 386 ff.

[170] A. *Dict.* 781: "neither beast nor father" (H.Ll.-J). Myths of male deities cohabiting with mortal women in animal shape (snake, bull, swan, serpent, dog. etc.) are common.

[171] Cp. (perhaps) the Axiokersos myth. Also (perhaps) the spear worship of Kainis-Kaineus (sch. A.R. 1.57) and of the well-named Parthenopaios (A. *Sept.* 529 ff.). For Kainis, cp. *34*. On phallos awe, cp. *83*, cp. chap. 6, note 106.

also frightens the child.[172] E. *Rh.*: wolf "tails" whip the horses. E. *Hec.*: the tail (and, of course, also the penis) would, plausibly, be invisible in a *maternal* primal-scene dream. E. *IT.*: the (apparently collapsing or shrinking) column could be dangerous to the dreamer.[173]

(7) *Father does dreadful things to mother*; he is killing her.[174] E. *Rh.*: the wolves seem to harm the horses. E. *IT.*: the falling roof might first crush Iphigeneia and then smash the flooring (= earth). E. *Hec.*: by attacking the fawn on her lap, the wolf implicitly harms Hekabe as well.

(8) *Mother heaves about*, seemingly trying to fight off the attack. This, together with the father's rhythmic movements, is the principal determinant of the nexus between rocking sensations and the recall of the primal scene.[175] E. *Rh.*: The horses buck and heave. E. *IT.*: the earth quakes. E. *Hec.*: No data.[176]

(9) *Mother cries out*, partly "in pain" and partly "asking to be rescued".[177] At times, this misinterpreted erotic sound is fused—or confused—with the father's erotic moans. E. *Rh.*: the horses' snorting is interpreted as a call for help. E. *Hec.*: there is no sound, and no *call* for help is needed, since the fawn is attacked before Hekabe's eyes. Moreover, parental erotic vocalizations usually play no role in *maternal* primal scene fantasies.[178] E. *IT.*: the mournful(?) inarticulate (male?) voice of the hair which tops the (phallic) column. The dream of the oedipally fixated Iphigeneia appropriately emphasizes the *male's* erotic moans.

Needless to say, items (8) and (9) are gross distortions of reality. They reflect the child's anxious, defensive misinterpretation of what the

---

[172] "Truly this little one loves the penis:" A. *Dict.* 786. (Professor Dover thinks that "penis-lover" may be a common gibe, directed at over-enthusiastic boy-lovers and that Silenos is here applying it jestingly to the baby, who takes hold of Silenos' outsize phallos.) For phallos-born Aphrodite as "she who loves the penis" (or, as Professor Burkert suggests: "der der Phallos eigen ist."), cp. *51*. For the penis—(and not buttocks)—centredness of the "proper" Greek boy-lover, cp. *45*.

[173] That: "column topped with hair" (cp. one topped with ivy, E. *Antiope fr.* 203 N²) = "tree" is well-nigh inescapable. Tree = phallus, cp. ps.-Hp. *insomn.* 90. That the column is the paternal phallus is suggested by the disproportion between its size and that of Iphigeneia. Clinical data show that this disproportion is a source of anxiety for the oedipally fixated little girl, cp. chap. 2, note 41.

[174] Ouranos' cohabitation with Gaia is repeatedly called "evil" in Hes. *Th.* 159 ff. Zeus' lightning kills Semele. Minos' poisonous semen kills his bedmates (Apollod. 3.15.1; Ant. Lib. 41.5).

[175] Rape is exceptionally common in Greek myths (*45*). Ouranos "rapes" the reluctant Gaia (Hes. *Th.* 164 ff.) Poseidon the stallion mates, as Hippios, with the unwilling mare Demeter (Paus. 8.25.5. f.). (Compare Kronos' mating with Philyra.) He also rapes Kainis, but rewards her with a penis (*34*). Apollon rapes Kreusa (E. *Ion*) and tries to rape Kassandra (A. *Ag.* 1206 ff.). Cp. chap. 3.

[176] But cp. E. *Tr.* 116 ff.: Hekabe speaks at length of rocking her body in grief. Coincidence? The self-rocking of certain psychotics is known to be sexual (autoerotic). Rocking, like an intense orgasm, produces vertigo: Phaidra on the swing see chap. 3, n. 104.

[177] Explicitly: Gaia in Hes. *Th.* 159 ff. (*51*).

[178] Exceptions exist, as in the case of the previously mentioned woman: "When I moan, my children must think that my husband is killing me!" In this case, the identification of the mother with the child, who *might* be both puzzled and upset by bedroom sounds, was perfectly obvious. Throughout her life, this woman had anxiously tried to identify partly obliterated, murmurous (= bedroom) sounds (*40*), cp. note 127.

mother's tossing and moaning—that is, her active and pleasurable participation in the act[179]—"means".

(10) *The child clings to—or flees into—sleep.* E. *Rh.*: The Charioteer wakes up too late. E. *IT.*: Iphigeneia is doubly asleep (εὕδειν). E. *Hec.*: apparently no data.[180]

(11) *Denial of the reality of the sense-experience*: "I am only dreaming it" or: "I am only seeing things in the dark". This defence is closely related to the defensive scotoma (3) and non-recognition (4) manœuvres.[181] E. *Rh.*: at first, the Charioteer mistakes reality for a dream. E. *Hec.*: the "real" apparition of Polydoros' spectre is not experienced as a vision, but as a dream. E. *IT.*: Iphigeneia first dreams that she is asleep and then (still asleep) that she wakes up; the transition from the former to the latter is quite vague and does not entail a real awakening. There is only a transition from being "*doubly* asleep" to being *simply* asleep.

(12) *Immobilization* of the child by fright and anxiety.[182] E. *Rh.*: the Charioteer is immobilized by sleep. E. *Hec.*: Neither Hekabe nor the fawn seem to move. E. *IT.*: No relevant data, except, possibly, the *double* sleep.

(13) *Flight-reaction.*[183] E. *Rh.*: only after waking up. E. *Hec.*: No data, nor could one expect them in a maternal dream. E. *IT.*: flight from the shaking palace.

(14) *Identification*, usually with the "attacked" mother, especially before the mother-child so-called "dual-unity" is *entirely* outgrown. In boys, such an identification often leads to passive homosexual tendencies. E. *Rh.*: perhaps the fact that an attack on the horses is also an indirect attack on the Charioteer, who is subsequently gravely wounded, while the horses escape unscathed. E. *Hec.*: the same considerations with respect to the fawn, but seen from the mother's viewpoint. E. *IT.*: the evidence being both complex and allusive, any interpretation can only be tentative. In so far as Iphigeneia is about to sacrifice "Orestes", she identifies herself with her own aggressor: with her father Agamemnon, who had tried to sacrifice her at Aulis.[184] But, in so far as she is a woman who might sacrifice a man—and, moreover, one who stands for Agamemnon and is his natural avenger—she identifies herself with Klytaimestra.[185] Subtending both

---

[179] Cp. the accusation (Ar. *Ran.* 1044) that Euripides' women were too sensual.

[180] Unless one so interprets the twofold layering of Hekabe's experience (apparition = dream), which parallels Iphigeneia's twofold sleeping.

[181] This echoes, in a way, E. *Phrix.,fr.* 838 N²: "is life not really death and death life?" Visual illusions are common in E. *Ba.*, passim. Cp. A. *Ag.* 412 f.: ἀπίϲτουϲ (disbelieving), chap. 3.

[182] Cohabitation with a goddess (= mother figure) usually weakens, unmans or even paralyses the mortal man. Cp. Tithonos, Anchises, perhaps Endymion; cp. Hermes' warning to Odysseus, who is about to become Kirke's lover (Hom. *Od.* 10.293 ff.). Ixion is punished both by immobilization and by being whirled around (primal scene "oscillating" sensations). Paralysis = impotence, caused by oedipal fixations and fantasies.

[183] The flight (= exile) motif is common in Greek myth. De Romilly (*17*) notes the tendency of Greek dramatic personages to exclaim that they wished they were elsewhere.

[184] Identification with the aggressor is clinically commonplace (*74*).

[185] Let it not be objected that, at this point, Iphigeneia does not know, as yet, that Agamemnon had been murdered; what matters is that Euripides knew it—and the poet's unconscious sometimes plays tricks on him (*58*). I am not prepared to urge that Iphigeneia "guessed" that her mother would try to avenge her "slaying" at Aulis.

these *tentative* interpretations is the symbolic equation: coitus = killing ("sado-masochistic infantile theory of coitus"), cp. (7).

(15) *The "millstones"*. Motivated partly by identification with the parents and partly by the desire to separate them, the child inserts itself *in fantasy* between the two and then feels caught and crushed between two millstones. This fantasy may be accompanied by rocking sensations (8) and by erotized anxiety.[186] This fantasy may, perhaps, account in part for the Greek mythological motif of being hammered on a bed or on an anvil.[187] E. *Rh.*: no "millstones". E. *Hec.*: the fawn is caught between Hekabe's lap and the (arched) wolf's claws. E. *IT.*: Iphigeneia risks being crushed between the heaving Earth[188] and the collapsing roof, but escapes, and retreats to a spectator position, to one side of the "parents". (Cp. the Charioteer.) In Euripides' works, the evolution of this important image is circular: E. *Rh.*: the spectator is to one side; E. *Hec.*: the crushed (clawed) fawn is not the dreamer herself; E. *IT.*: the dreamer escapes being crushed by retreating to a peripheral position, but remains close enough to "touch" the "hair".[189]

Since I expect to be challenged on this point by non-clinicians, I can do no better than cite Professor Dover's comments: "Last night at the Film Society I saw a Polish short film which was presented as a comedy and was so taken by most of the audience,[190] but it actually portrayed twenty minutes in the life of a psychotic, hospitalized but inadequately diagnosed and tormented by hallucinations. At one moment his parents are in the room,. dressed as they were when he was a *baby* [my italics]; he takes refuge *under the bed* [Professor Dover's italics]; they dance round the room and end up dancing on the bed, while its underside bounces up and down

---

[186] On erotized anxiety, cp. *104* and *105*. On the fantasy of being run over (crushed), cp. *91*. This fantasy can degenerate into a suicidal perversion: a hospitalized borderline psychotic sometimes crawled under parked automobiles: he had developed a technique of being run over by started cars without sustaining real injuries.

[187] Prokroustes: *13*, 2, pp. 626 ff. Idaian Daktyls: (anvil—Ἄκμων) (*13*, 2, 312 f.). If Dionysos the man-smasher (ἀνθρωπορραίϲτηϲ) was an axe-god (*13*, 2, 522, 662), his epithet may also be relevant. In defence of *her* father, Athene crushes Enkelados under the island of Sicily; she fells Herakles with a stone, in defence of *his* father (E. *HF* 1004 f.). An observation of one of my students deserves mention at least in a footnote: Iphigeneia has, so far, escaped marriage (defloration = piercing by the penis). Orestes, destined to be sacrificed (pierced with a knife), also escapes. Iphigeneia (*in the primal scene*) witnesses Klytaimestra's piercing by Agamemnon's penis, but escapes (*in dream*) from the collapsing palace.

[188] I recall that, by becoming mobile, the (maternal) Earth ceases to be merely a supporting surface and becomes an "actor": the lowest of the dream objects, the lowest of the *active* strata into which the dream-space is divided.

[189] There are perhaps traces of this fantasy-imagery also in E. *Ion* 16 ff.: Ion is (*fide* LSJ) exposed in a *wheeled* cradle. But Professor Dover thinks—and I concur—that he was exposed in a *rocking* cradle, in the very cave where Apollon had raped Ion's mother, Kreusa. Apart from the inherent appropriateness of the place of exposure, one might perhaps interpret the exposure in a *rocking* basket as a "displacement in time" of the "lethal" primal scene. I recall once more that sensations of oscillation often precede the emergence, in psycho-analysis, of primal scene memories (or fantasies) (supra). For other Euripidean displacements in time, see the section on circular time. Whether sensations of oscillation reactivate (hypothetical) prenatal sensations is uncertain.

[190] Cp. my comments on the traumatic latent content of satyr plays, and the katharsis they afforded. (Cp. General Introduction, note 34; chap. 1, note 34.)

on his head as he flattens himself on the floor!" Obviously, as Freud insisted, the unconscious is timeless.

(16) *Variant of the "millstone" fantasy*: Instead of being caught between the parents, the child is attacked *in utero*.[191] E. *Rh.* no data. E. *Hec.*: knees = lap = womb; this is common enough a euphemism. E. *IT.*: house = womb, the womb being often held to be the foetus' house, especially in dream.[192]

(17) *Rescue fantasies* are elicited by the primal scene and especially by the mother's misinterpreted moans (calls for help). (Hes. *Th.* 164 ff.)[193] If such rescue fantasies take root, the wish to save women "from a life of shame" may become a neurotic symptom.[194] The rescuing of the mother by her son ("mother's hero") is a frequent theme in Greek myth.[195] E. *Rh.* The Charioteer wishes to rescue the snorting horses already in dream. E. *Hec.*: this being a maternal dream, it is Hekabe (cp. Rhea and Zeus) who presumably wishes to rescue the fawn-child. No call for help is needed, since the fawn is on Hekabe's lap and before her eyes. E. *IT.*: the mournful (?) voice. In the end, Iphigeneia does rescue Orestes (= Agamemnon = his house) and is simultaneously rescued by him.

(18) *Rescue = counter-attack*. The parents are separated; the father is killed or mutilated.[196] E. *Rh.* The intended counter-attack on the wolves is displaced to Hektor. E. *Hec.*: Her dream "causes" Hekabe to counter-

---

[191] Kronos is definitely "inside" Gaia (Hes. *Th.* 174, 178), whose pregnancy is apparently artificially prolonged. Cp. the postponement of Herakles' birth until after that of Eurystheus (*81*), also Kleo's five-year-long pregnancy and Ithmonike's three-year pregnancy, *IG.* IV², 1. no. 121 (*67*, 1, pp. 221 ff.). Cp. a widespread folktale motif: the (aggressive) "clever baby" dodges, while inside the "mortar", the giant's "pestle" (*22*). Cp. also the widespread taboo on cohabitation with pregnant women. Where this taboo is lacking, atypical modes of cohabitation may be thought to harm the foetus (*49*, pp. 248 ff.).

[192] Cp. my discussion of the meaning of "space" in dream, supra, citing (*129*, *130*). For: womb = house of the foetus, and: cradle = house of the baby, cp. (*23*). In order to be socially reborn, a man wrongly believed to have died had to lower himself *into the house* from above (note 34).

[193] Experimental data show that the expression of certain *extreme* emotional states is easily misinterpreted as an expression of the polarly opposite state (cp. *3* and much subsequent work).

[194] Cp. Freud (*77*), on the wish to "save" prostitutes by marrying them. This is a common plot element in New Comedy, whose forerunner was notoriously Euripides (*118*). Coincidence?

[195] Gaia asks Kronos to rescue her (Hes. *Th.* 164 ff.). Other rescues: E. *Antiope*, E *Hyps.*, etc. Perseus must rescue Danaë from Polydektes; A. *Dict.* is, I suspect, a parody of this theme, Polydektes being perhaps anticipatorily caricatured as Silenos. This motivation is inverted in the Phoinix myth: the son must avenge the sexual frustration of his mother, Hom. *Il.* 9.44 ff.; perhaps: E. *Phoenix*; this is a counter-oedipal fantasy (*30*). Lydian "mother's hero" examples in Herter (*87*).

[196] Kronos (inside Gaia) attacks Ouranos with a, twice specified, curved, jagged (= toothed) weapon. This is a variant of the *vagina dentata* motif: the weapon must represent Kronos' teeth, especially since he later on devours his own children (*51*). Cp. dogs "defiling" (eating) an old man's genitals: Hom. *Il.* 22.75; echoed in Tyrt. *frr.* 6–7 D. (*11*, Edm.) vv. 25 ff. (v. 25, *pace* Edmunds (*68*) should *not* be emended). Grey squirrels castrate red squirrels (*109*); strong male onagers castrate weaker males (*138*). Child grasping his own penis for balance: (*113*, pl. 29.1). Given Dodds' (*65*, p. 43) interpretation of Ailios Aristeides' finger sacrifice dream, Orestes' biting off of his own finger (Paus. 8.34.2) must also be so interpreted. Actual and/or fantasied castration by biting was copiously documented elsewhere (*51*).

attack Polymestor. E. *IT*. After escaping crushing, Iphigeneia prepares the column (= Agamemnon's phallus) for sacrifice. In so far as (additionally) column = Agamemnon's son, Iphigeneia—like other Greek women—hurts a man by killing his child.[197] In E. *IT.*, attack, counter-attack and rescue form a heavily overdetermined whole: Agamemnon "sacrifices" Iphigeneia at Aulis to Artemis, who rescues her and substitutes a hind.[198] In E. *IT.* Orestes attacks the herd; he plans to "attack" (rob, kidnap) Artemis (= Iphigeneia). Iphigeneia (a hypostasis or double of Artemis) counter-attacks: Orestes is to be sacrificed. Yet, ultimately, Orestes kidnaps (= rescues) both Artemis and Iphigeneia. Thus, the attack and counter-attack lead to a reciprocal rescue. Agamemnon attacked Klytaimestra via Iphigeneia; for Iphigeneia's sake Klytaimestra counter-attacked and killed Agamemnon: in dream the column, representing Agamemnon's maleness, collapses.[199]

(19) *Reactive sexual arousal*: this leads to occasional autoerotic activities.[200] E. *Rh.* E. *Hec.*: Apparently no data. E. *IT.*: Probably hinted at, albeit in a heavily disguised form: Iphigeneia washes "hair".[201] (But I recall that the Athenian woman's pubis was shaved (Ar. *Thesm.* 590 etc.))

(20) *Screen memory*. The primal scene experience is almost always deeply repressed and then leads to the formation of a substitute—spurious and distorted—pseudo-memory ("screen-memory"), whose equivalent is so-called "second sight".[202] E. *Rh.*: The Charioteer's unjust accusation of Hektor. E. *Hec.*: The Prologue's apparition (a man-shaped spectre) is

---

[197] S. *Tereus*; E. *Med.* This is the third time Orestes is in jeopardy; the first two times he manifestly incurred mortal danger because he was Agamemnon's infant son: E. *Teleph.* (from Telephos); A. *Choe.*, S. *El.*, E. *El.* (from Aigisthos).

[198] Hence: daughter = hind (E. *IT, IA*); child = fawn (E. *Hec.*).

[199] This is the commonplace "detumescence = castration = death" symbolic equation, cp. the Somali proverb: "the vagina is the place where the penis goes to die". (*128*) For: "tumescent phallus = symbol of life", cp. Nilsson, (*117*, 1² pp. 118 f.) This equation is basic and widespread: some Micronesians try to prolong a dying man's life by attempting to produce a tumescence of his organ. (*100*).

[200] Hermes envies Ares in Aphrodite's arms, Hom. *Od.* 8.339. (Since humour seems resistant to cultural change, I mention that, only ten lines earlier (329), one reads: "the *slow* (Hephaistos) overtook the *fleet* (Ares)." This is precisely the point of a modern anecdote about an autoerotic reaction to the primal scene.) X. *Smp.* 9.7: after seeing an erotic dance, the aroused married men rush home to their wives and the bachelors vow to get married at once. Explicit references to the child's arousal by the primal scene: A. *Dict.* 810 ff. Understandably, autoerotism is not mentioned in myth (except in the Dionysos-Prosymnos story, chap. 2, note 75, reported only by late authors, though the ritual suggests that it is ancient). There exist, however, several myths of spontaneous or premature divine emissions, cited elsewhere (*51*). The Egyptian god Atum even masturbated, (cp. *131*, s.v. Schow, col. 567). Such evidence should neither be strained nor ignored.

[201] Cp. Tyro pouring water erotically in her lap (Luc. *DMar.* 13.1) and Danae impregnated by a rain of gold falling in her lap. S. *An.* 944 ff. Whenever Euripides mentions sleep or dreaming, within less than 30 lines there is also *always* an allusion to water or to some other fluid, supra, note 131.

[202] Athene deprives the peeper Teiresias of his sight but grants him second sight: Callim. *Lavacr.* Moreover, though blind, he can, when helped by a seeing assistant, interpret the flight of birds (S. *Ant.* 998 ff., 1012 ff.)—though he does not always seem to have a seeing assistant. The (obviously imagined) flight of birds is an excellent screen memory for the primal scene, since the dream symbolization of tumescence by flight was known long before Freud (*75*, chap. 1) and has now been experimentally confirmed (*11, 94*).

seen apparently only in dream, and then only in the guise of a fawn.[203] E. *IT.*: The dream is misinterpreted once in dream and (differently) again on awakening. The relationship between the *retroactive* defensive contriving of a screen memory and the *immediate* defence of scotomization (3) and/or of non-recognition (4) is highlighted by Hekabe's and Iphigeneia's attempts to "ward off" their respective dreams. The former utters a prayer and the latter hopefully tells her dream to the daylight—an old Greek apotropaic manœuvre,[204] which evens the path for the formation of screen memories, whose coming into being is, of course, already facilitated by the *anxiety-distorted* perception of the primal scene.[205]

The presentation of the component elements of the real or fantasied primal scene in an itemized form, susceptible of statistical analysis, is only a preliminary step towards an understanding of the broader human implications of this *total* experience, which plays an important role in the formation of mankind's species-characteristic (*102, 57*, chap. 7) Oedipus complex. Not only children, but also some emotionally immature mothers feel that marital relations disrupt their almost symbiotic communion.[206] Traumatic for the child, it is also derivatively traumatic for the parents, though the extent to which the child is traumatized depends on whether the witnessed embrace was loving and proud or shamefaced and cold (*26*). It may well be of great significance for the understanding of Greek character structure, that, in the Kronos myth, they contrived a *triumphant* (though savage) solution for one of the most traumatic conflicts of childhood. May this not explain, at least in part, their intellectual and emotional freedom and spontaneous creativeness? This query leads directly to the problem of the sublimation of this experience, *via* screen memories and their oniric equivalents; they provide the raw fantasy material from which the *manifestations* of this sublimation (e.g., of tragedy) are constructed.

The three Euripidean dreams were probably patterned upon one or more of Euripides' own dreams (= screen memory equivalents). Of course, we lack information about his own initial experience, his waking screen memories and his actual dreams, which underlie the sublimation of his experience into three poetically compelling and psychologically plausible dreams. We can, however, get an indirect glimpse of this process, by scrutinizing the many variants of the myth of Iasion's and

---

[203] This is an extremely striking detail. The consciously *not* perceived elements of a tachistoscopically presented picture impinge none the less on the sensorium and become part of the "day residue" of the following night's dream, though sometimes in a symbolic form only (*121*). (These epoch-making findings have been repeatedly and completely confirmed by subsequent experimental work.) On the perception, in dream, of subliminal sense impressions, cp. ps.-Hp. *insomn.*, passim and Arist. *de div. somn.* passim. The belief, that one is parapsychologically more "sensitive" in dream than in the waking state, is ancient and requires no documentation.

[204] Psychologically, Iphigeneia pits reality and daylight against fantasy and dream. So does Kadmos, while trying to bring Agaue back to her senses, E. *Ba.* 1264 ff. (*52*). Cp. chap. 1, note 3; 2, note 104.

[205] On the protean manifestations of screen memories, even in the state of transference, cp. (*41*).

[206] Cp. the widespread taboo on cohabitation with lactating women; also clinical data. A young mother felt "sawed in half": "the upper part of my body belongs to my baby, the lower to my husband" (*57*, chap. 7).

Demeter's sacred marriage; variants which range in quality all the way from magnificent epic sublimations to the cloying novelette, depending on the way a particular author handles certain elements of that myth.

The exact date of the authors cited is immaterial, since no unilinear evolution of the myth is postulated.[207] The evolution of this myth deserves close scrutiny, since it reflects paradigmatically both the success and the failure of the sublimatory process.

The Basic Myth: Demeter cohabits in person, lovingly and voluntarily, with the mortal Iasion, in a thrice ploughed fallow land (Hom. *Od.* 5.125 ff.; Hes. *Th.* 969 ff.).

(1) *The Evanescence of Demeter*: She is involved in her own person in Hom. *Od.*, Hes. *Th.*; probably also in Strabon[208] and almost certainly in Apollod. 3.12.1. Only her cult statue (ἄγαλμα) is mentioned by Skymnos (685, *GGM.* 1.223) and by Hellanikos (*fr.* 129, *FHG.* 1.63 = sch. A.R. 1.916). In Konon (*narr.* 21) we are left only with her phantom (φάςμα.) She is present in person—though only *after* the act—in Ovidius (*Met.* 9.422 ff.), of which more below.

(2) *Love vs. Rape*: Only in Hom. *Od.*, Hes. *Th.* and in Ovidius (infra) does she voluntarily unite with Iasion in love. In the other sources just mentioned, and also in D.H. (*ant. rom.* 1.61), she herself, or her statue, or her phantom is sacrilegiously assaulted.[209]

(3) *Completed vs. Non-Completed Union*: Several of the sources cited say— or seem to suggest—that the attempted rape was unsuccessful.[210] An imitative, euhemeristic and rationalizing author (D.S. 5.49.3) even denies that a union was attempted; he interprets the myth as meaning that Iasion acquired great merit by discovering agriculture.[211]

(4) *Innocence vs. Sin of Iasion*. Hes. *Th.* praises the union. In *Hom. Od.*, Kalypso obviously does not consider Iasion a sinner, since she insists that he was struck down by a pettily selfish Zeus. By contrast, nearly all later authors call him a sinner. Yet, though he is usually struck down before, during or after the union, no one—not even a late author—claims that he was also *further* punished in Hades. This suggests that he was originally *not* felt to have been guilty of sacrilege. But Diodoros the Sicilian *makes* him "sinless", simply by denying that a union was so much as attempted; he can therefore grant Iasion a well-deserved place in the halls of the gods. In Ovidius, too, he is a commensal of the gods: despite his greying locks, a Biedermeier Demeter loves him still. (Or. *Met.* 9.422 ff.).

The evolution of this myth is paradigmatic of the evolution of the primal scene experience in general, both towards sublimation and towards

---

[207] And neither may one postulate a unilinear progression from the primal scene to its sublimation in the case of the individual; there is always much zig-zagging and back-tracking.

[208] Str. 7.49 (50) Jones, is, unfortunately, only a fragment.

[209] Cp. Ixion's attempt to rape Hera (= Nephele). (Pi. *P.* 2.21–49, etc.)

[210] The topic so embarrassed late authors that in a few instances the wording is inconclusive. Incomplete rape: Nessos and Deianeira (S. *Tr.*, etc.) (*58*); also Hephaistos and Athene (*122*).

[211] As usual, the cloven hoof is visible behind the bowdlerization. As a rule, it is Triptolemos who, taught by Demeter, teaches agriculture to mankind. Now, for a Greek fond of etymologizing, *his* name evokes the "thrice" (furrowed field)—and this is precisely what D.S. tried *not* to evoke. Cp. E. *Phoin.* 18.

the failure of sublimation and its replacement by denials and defences. Predictably, the poetically most powerful versions are the least disguised and expurgated ones: those of Homeros and of Hesiodos, simply because the most creative sublimations are those *stable* enough to come to terms with the unvarnished psychological truth (*35, 90*). This is the atmosphere of epic poetry and often also that of tragedy. A less complete sublimation corresponds, roughly speaking, to the moralizing novel, represented here by all our other sources (except D.S. and Ov.). With the former we enter the world of bloodless, speculative intellectualizations, while Ovidius represents the nadir of this myth's degradation: his cloying genre-picture reflects the failure of sublimation on all fronts.

The degree of sublimation attained by Euripides in these three dreams is not much inferior to that attained by Homeros and by Hesiodos, in their accounts of the Iasion myth, though, on the manifest level, his dramatic dreams *seem* non-sexual.[212] But Euripides did preserve in them the *basic structure* of the primal scene experience, and therefore did not attenuate its immense *affective* charge. He also made up for this slight defect of his sublimatory potential by learning to tolerate uncertainty to an extent seldom matched by other poets.

As Friedrich Schiller said: "The poet is one who remembers his childhood." He is also one strong and human enough to dare remember it *creatively*.

Appendix: The Rhesos Problem

An incidental finding of this chapter is the striking similarity between the E. *Rh.*, E. *Hec.* and E. *IT.* dreams: descriptively, structurally and psycho-analytically. *Mathematically, the possibility that these many similarities could be due to chance appears to be negligible, even though some of the common elements are technically not independent variables.* These dreams are, moreover, so highly individualized that no psychological system (other than the pseudo-psychology of the mystic C. G. Jung) could account for them in terms of *basic* human characteristics, nor do the similarities between them appear to be due to a specifically Greek cultural patterning of dreams, for I was unable to find an ancient Greek dream which resembles these three more than superficially.

The possibility that the Charioteer's dream is a deliberate imitation of the other two Euripidean dreams must also be excluded. Aristoteles himself stressed the unteachableness and individualized character of the metaphor, and therefore (implicitly) also that of the dream—especially of the "literary dream" (General Introduction). The scientific psychologist can only concur—and I might add that I myself have tried and failed to contrive a dream which resembles these three in *fundamental* ways. It is also nearly impossible to entertain the notion that the E. *Rh.* dream was simply lifted either from the hypothetically lost Euripidean *Rhesos* or from some other lost Euripidean dream narrative: the Charioteer's dream fits its existing context far too well to warrant such a hypothesis.

212 Perhaps because of his inferable attachment to his mother (supra).

Since these basic similarities *do* exist, a refusal to explain them would be scientific nihilism. It therefore seems simplest to conclude that they lend solid support to Ritchie's sober and scholarly arguments in favour of the authenticity of the *Rhesos* we possess and also to his view that it is Euripides' earliest surviving work (*125*).[213]

Bibliography

(1) Adkins, A. W. H.: *Merit and Responsibility*. Oxford, 1960.

(2) Allen, J. T. and Italie, Gabriel: *A Concordance to Euripides*. Berkeley, California and Cambridge, 1954.

(3) Allport, G. W. and Vernon, P. E.: *Studies in Expressive Movement*. New York, 1933.

(4) Anderson, J. K.: *Ancient Greek Horsemanship*. Berkeley, California, 1961.

(5) Bächli, Erich: *Die künstlerische Funktion von Orakelsprüchen, Träumen usw. in der griechischen Tragödie*. Winterthur, 1954.

(6) Barrett, W. S.: *Euripides, Hippolytos*. Oxford, 1964.

(7) Bates, W. N.: *Euripides, A Student of Human Nature*. Philadelphia, 1930.

(8) Besançon, Alain: Chronos et Cronos (in) *Histoire et Expérience du Moi*, chap. 4. Paris, 1971.

(9) Bezdechi, Stefan: Das psychopathische Substrat der "Bacchantinnen" Euripides', *Archiv für die Geschichte der Medizin* 25:279–306, 1932.

(10) Borel, Th.: *Examen Critique de la Tragédie de Rhésus*. Genève, 1843.

(11) Bourguignon, André: Recherches Récentes sur le Rêve, *Les Temps Modernes* no. 238:1603–1628, 1966.

(12) Bowers, U. G.: *The Hidden Land*. New York, 1953.

(13) Cook, A. B.: *Zeus*, 2. Cambridge, 1925.

(14) Crahay, Roland: *La Littérature Oraculaire chez Hérodote*. Paris, 1956.

(15) Decharme, Paul: *Euripides and the Spirit of his Dramas*[2]. London, 1909.

(16) Dement, W. C.: The Psychophysiology of Dreaming (in) Grunebaum, G. E. von and Caillois, Roger (eds.): *The Dream in Human Societies*. Berkeley, California, 1966.

(17) de Romilly, Jacqueline: *La Crainte et l'Angoisse dans le Théâtre d'Eschyle*. Paris, 1958.

(18) de Saussure, Ferdinand: *Cours de Linguistique Générale*. Paris, 1916.

(19) Devereux, George: *Sedang Field Notes* (MS.), 1933–1935.

(20) id.: Principles of Hà(rhn)de:a(ng) Divination, *Man* 38:125–127, 1938.

(21) id.: Religious Attitudes of the Sedang (in) Ogburn, W. F. and Nimkoff, M. T.: *Sociology*. Cambridge, Massachusetts, 1940.

(22) id.: Mohave Pregnancy, *Acta Americana* 6:89–116, 1948.

(23) id.: The Mohave Neonate and Its Cradle, *Primitive Man* 21:1–18, 1948.

---

[213] But, in the meantime, the sceptics still persevere (*66, 73, 95*).

(24) id.: Mohave Paternity, *Samīkṣā, Journal of the Indian Psycho-Analytical Society* 3:162–194, 1949.

(25) id.: A Note on Nyctophobia and Peripheral Vision, *Bulletin of the Menninger Clinic* 13:83–93, 1949.

(26) id.: The Primal Scene and Juvenile Heterosexuality in Mohave Society (in) G. B. Wilbur and W. Muensterberger (eds.) *Psychoanalysis and Culture (Róheim Festschrift)*. New York, 1951.

(27) id. (and Mars, Louis): Haitian Voodoo and the Ritualization of the Nightmare, *Psychoanalytic Review* 38:334–342, 1951.

(28) id.: Psychological Factors in the Production of Paraesthesias Following the Self-Administration of Codeine, *Psychiatric Quarterly Supplement* 27:43–54, 1953.

(29) id.: Charismatic Leadership and Crisis (in) Muensterberger, Warner (ed.): *Psychoanalysis and the Social Sciences* vol. 4. New York, International Universities Press, 1955.

(30) id.: A Counteroedipal Episode in Homer's Iliad, *Bulletin of the Philadelphia Association for Psychoanalysis* 4:90–97, 1955.

(31) id.: Acting Out in Dreams, *American Journal of Psychotherapy* 9:657–660, 1955.

(32) id.: *Therapeutic Education*. New York, 1956.

(33) id.: Penelope's Character, *Psychoanalytic Quarterly* 26:378–386, 1957.

(34) id.: The Awarding of a Penis as Compensation for Rape, *International Journal of Psycho-Analysis* 38:398–401, 1957.

(35) id.: Art and Mythology: A General Theory (in) Kaplan, Bert (ed.): *Studying Personality Cross-Culturally*. Evanston, Illinois, 1961.

(36) id.: La Psychanalyse et l'Histoire: Une Application à l'Histoire de Sparte, *Annales: Economies, Sociétés, Civilisations* 20:18–44, 1965.

(37) id.: The Perception of Motion in Infancy, *Bulletin of the Menninger Clinic* 29:143–147, 1965.

(38) id.: The Kolaxaian Horse of Alkman's *Partheneion, Classical Quarterly* 15:176–184, 1965.

(39) id.: The Abduction of Hippodameia as "Aition" of a Greek Animal Husbandry Rite, *Studi e Materiali di Storia delle Religioni* 36:3–25, 1965.

(40) id.: Mumbling, *Journal of the American Psychoanalytic Association* 14:478–484, 1966.

(41) id.: Transference, Screen Memory and the Temporal Ego, *Journal of Nervous and Mental Disease* 143:318–323, 1966.

(42) id.: The Enetian Horse of Alkman's *Partheneion, Hermes* 94:129–134, 1966.

(43) id.: Fausse Non-Reconnaissance, *Bulletin of the Menninger Clinic* 31:69–78, 1967.

(44) id.: La Renonciation à l'Identité: Défense contre l'Anéantissement, *Revue Française de Psychanalyse* 31:101–142, 1967.

(45) id.: Greek Pseudo-Homosexuality, *Symbolae Osloenses* 42:69–92, 1967.

(46) id.: *From Anxiety to Method in the Behavioral Sciences*. Paris and The Hague, 1967.

(47) id.: Considérations Psychanalytique sur la Divination, Particulière-

ment en Grèce (in) Caquot, André and Leibovici, Marcel (eds.): *La Divination*, 2, pp. 449–471. Paris, 1968.

(48) id.: *Reality and Dream: The Psychotherapy of a Plains Indian*. (Second, augmented edition), New York, 1969.

(49) id.: *Mohave Ethnopsychiatry and Suicide*. (Second, augmented edition), Washington, 1969.

(50) id.: The Nature of Sappho's Seizure in *Fr.* 31 LP, *Classical Quarterly* 20:17–31, 1970.

(51) id.: La Naissance d'Aphrodite (in) Pouillon, Jean and Maranda, Pierre (eds.): *Exchanges et Communications (Mélanges Lévi-Strauss)* 2.1229–1252. Paris and The Hague, 1970.

(52) id.: The Psychotherapy Scene in Euripides' *Bacchae*, *Journal of Hellenic Studies* 90:35–48, 1970.

(53) id.: The *Equus October* Ritual Reconsidered, *Mnemosyne* 23:297–301, 1970.

(54) id.: The Structure of Tragedy and the Structure of the Psyche in Aristotle's *Poetics* (in) Hanly, Charles and Lazerowitz, Morris (eds.) *Psychoanalysis and Philosophy*. New York, 1970.

(55) id. (ed. and contrib.): *Psychoanalysis and the Occult* (Reprint). New York, 1970.

(56) id.: *Essais d'Ethnopsychiatrie Générale*. Paris, 1970 (Second edition, 1973).

(57) id.: *Ethnopsychanalyse Complémentariste*. Paris, 1972.

(58) id. (and Devereux, J. W.): Manifestations de l'Inconscient dans Sophokles: *Trachiniai* 923 sqq. (in) *Psychanalyse et Sociologie comme Methodes d'Etude des Phénomènes Historiques et Culturels*. Bruxelles, 1973.

(58a) id. The Self-Blinding of Oidipous. *Journal of Hellenic Studies*, 93: 36–49, 1973.

(59) id.: Une Note sur les Chevaux Anthropophages dans les Mythes Grecs, *Revue des Etudes Grecques* (in press).

(59a) id. Stesichoros' Palinodes: Two Further Testimonies and some Comments, *Rheinisches Museum für Philologie* 116: 206–209, 1973.

(60) id.: Le Fragment 62 Nauck² d'Eschyle. Ce qu'y Signifie ΧΛΟΥΝΗC, *Revue des Etudes Grecques* 86: 277–284, 1973.

(61) id.: Quelques Traces de la Succession par Ultimogéniture en Scythie, *Inter-Nord* 12:262–270, 1972.

(62) id. and Forrest, W. G. G.: La Folie de Cléoménès (in preparation).

(63) Dodds, E. R.: Euripides the Irrationalist, *Classical Review* 43:97–104, 1929. [= (in) *The Ancient Idea of Progress*, Oxford 1973].

(64) id.: *The Greeks and the Irrational*. Berkeley, California, 1951.

(65) id.: *Pagan and Christian in an Age of Anxiety*. Cambridge, 1965.

(66) Ebener, H. (ed.): *Rhesos. Tragödie eines unbekannten Dichters*. Berlin, 1966.

(67) Edelstein, E. J. and Ludwig: *Asclepius* 2 vols. Baltimore, Maryland, 1945.

(68) Edmunds, J. M. (ed.): *Greek Elegy and Iambus* 1. London, 1931.

(69) Edwards, M. W.: Representation of Maenads on Archaic Red-Figure Vases, *Journal of Hellenic Studies* 80:78–87, 1960.

(70) Escher, Albert: *Das Antlitz der Blindheit in der Antike*[2]. Leiden, 1961.

(71) Fenichel Otto: *The Psychoanalytic Theory of Neurosis*. New York, 1945.

(72) id.: The Misapprehended Oracle (in) *The Collected Papers of O. Fenichel* 2. New York, 1954.

(73) Fraenkel, Eduard: Ritchie, The Authenticity of the Rhesus of Euripides, *Gnomon* 37:228–241, 1965.

(74) Freud, Anna: *The Ego and the Mechanisms of Defense*. New York, 1946.

(75) Freud, Sigmund: The Interpretation of Dreams, *Standard Edition* 4–5. London, 1958.

(76) id.: Analysis of a Phobia in a Five-Year-Old Child, *Standard Edition* 10. London, 1955.

(77) id.: A Special Type of Choice of Object Made by Men, *Standard Edition* 11. London 1957.

(78) id.: Mourning and Melancholia, *Standard Edition* 14. London 1957.

(79) id.: From the History of an Infantile Neurosis, *Standard Edition* 17. London 1955.

(80) id.: Some Additional Notes on Dream Interpretation as a Whole, (B) Moral Responsibility for the Content of Dreams, *Standard Edition* 19. London, 1961.

(81) id.: Civilization and its Discontents, *Standard Edition* 21. London, 1961.

(82) Greenacre, Phyllis: Vision, Headache and the Halo, *Psychoanalytic Quarterly* 16:177–194, 1947.

(83) id.: Penis Awe and its Relation to Penis Envy (in) Loewenstein, R. M. (ed.): *Drives, Affects, Behavior*. New York, 1953.

(84) Greenwood, L. H. G.: *Aspects of Euripidean Tragedy*. Cambridge, 1953.

(85) Grube, G. M. A.: *The Drama of Euripides*[2]. London, 1961.

(86) Hančar, Franz: *Das Pferd in prähistorischer und früher historischer Zeit*. München, 1956.

(87) Herter, Hans: Lydische Adelskampfe (in) Wenig, Otto (ed.): *Wege zur Buchwissenschaft* (Bonner Beitrage zur Bibliotheks- und Bücherkunde 14). Bonn, 1966.

(88) Hiatt, L. R.: Mung, *Balcony* (Australia) no. 3:15–21, 1965.

(89) Hinkle, L. E. Jr. and Wolf, H. G.: Communist Interrogation and Indoctrination of 'Enemies of the State', *Archives of Neurology and Psychiatry* 76:115–174, 1956.

(90) Jokl, R. H.: Psychic Determinism and Preservation of Sublimations in Classical Psychoanalytic Procedure, *Bulletin of the Menninger Clinic* 14:207–219, 1950.

(91) Jones, Ernest: The Symbolism of Being Run Over, *International Journal of Psycho-Analysis* 1:203, 1920.

(92) id.: The Phantasy of the Reversal of Generations (in) *Papers on Psycho-Analysis*[3]. London, 1923.

(93) id.: *On the Nightmare*. London, 1931.

(94) Jouvet, Michel: The States of Sleep, *Scientific American* 216, no. 2:62–71, 1967.

(95) Kannicht, Richard: W. Ritchie, The Authenticity of the Rhesus of Euripides, *Gymnasium* 73:295–297, 1966.

(96) Kassel, R.: *Quomodo quibus locis apud veteres scriptores Graecos infantes atque parvuli pueri inducantur describantur commemorantur* (Dissertation). Würzburg, 1954.

(97) Keller, Otto: *Die antike Tierwelt* 2 vols. Leipzig, 1909–1913.

(98) Kennard, Edward: Hopi Reactions to Death, *American Anthropologist* 49:491–496, 1937.

(99) Kouretas, Demetrios: Brainwashing and its Ancient Greek Prototype, *Medical Annals* (Athens), 6:935–955, 1966.

(100) Krämer, A.: Truk (in) Thilenius, Georg (ed.): *Ergebnisse der Südsee-Expedition 1908–1910* (2-B-5). Hamburg, 1932.

(101) Kroeber, A. L.: Seven Mohave Myths, *Anthropological Records* 11 (no. 1), pp. viii+1–70, 1948.

(102) La Barre, Weston: *The Human Animal*. Chicago, 1954.

(103) id.: Social Cynosure and Social Structure, *Journal of Personality* 14:164–183, 1946.

(104) Laforgue, René: On the Erotization of Anxiety, *International Journal of Psycho-Analysis* 11:312–321, 1930.

(105) id.: De l'Angoisse à l'Orgasme, *Revue Française de Psychanalyse* 4:245–258, 1930–1931.

(106) Landes, Ruth: *The Ojibwa Woman*. New York, 1938.

(107) Lesky, Albin: Psychologie bei Euripides (in) *Euripide*, Entretiens Hardt 6. Vol. Genève, 1960.

(108) Lévi-Strauss, Claude: *Anthropologie Structurale*. Paris, 1958.

(109) Lewis, N. D. C.: The Psychobiology of the Castration Reaction, *Psychoanalytic Review* 14:420–446, 15:53–84, 304–323, 1927–1928.

(110) Lifton, R. J.: *Thought Reform and the Psychology of Totalism*. New York, 1961.

(111) Lincoln, J. S.: *The Dream in Primitive Cultures*[2]. New York, 1970.

(112) Malinowski, Bronislaw: *The Sexual Life of Savages*[3]. London, 1932.

(113) Mead, Margaret and Macgregor, Frances C.: *Growth and Culture*. New York, 1951.

(114) Menninger, K. A.: *Man Against Himself*. New York, 1938.

(115) Métraux, Alfred: *Le Vaudou Haitien*. Paris, 1958.

(116) Murray, Gilbert: *Aeschylus*. Oxford, 1940.

(117) Nilsson, M. P.: *Geschichte der Griechischen Religion* I[2]. München, 1955.

(118) Norwood, Gilbert: *Greek Comedy*[2]. New York, 1963.

(119) Patin, H.: *Etudes sur les Tragiques Grecs* 3: *Euripide* 2 vols.[7]. Paris, 1894.

(120) Pauly, A. and Wissowa, G.: *Real-Encyclopädie der classischen Altertumswissenschaften*. Stuttgart, 1893– .

(121) Pötzl, Otto: Experimentell erregte Traumbilder in ihren Beziehungen zum indirekten Sehen, *Zeitschrift für die gesamte Neurologie und Psychiatrie* 37:278–349, 1917.

(122) Powell, Benjamin: Erichthonius and the Three Daughters of Cecrops, *Cornell Studies in Classical Philology* 17. New York, 1906.

(123) Rank, Otto: *The Trauma of Birth*. London, 1929.

(124) Raswan, Carl: *Drinkers of the Wind*. New York, 1950.

(125) Ritchie, William: *The Authenticity of the Rhesus of Euripides*. Cambridge, 1964.

(126) Robert, Fernand: *Homère*. Paris, 1950.

(127) id.: Le Haut du Décor dans "Iphigénie en Tauride", *Latomus* 114:96–114, 1970.

(128) Róheim, Géza: Psycho-Analysis of Primitive Cultural Types, *International Journal of Psycho-Analysis* 13:1–244, 1932.

(129) id.: *Psychoanalysis and Anthropology*. New York, 1950.

(130) id.: *The Gates of the Dream*. New York, 1952.

(131) Roscher, W. H.: *Ausführliches Lexikon der griechischen und römischen Mythologie*. Leipzig, 1884–1937.

(132) id.: Das von der "Kynanthropie" handelnde Fragment des Marcellus von Side, *Abhandlungen de philologisch-historischen Classe der Königlich Sächsischen Gesellschaft der Wissenschaften* 17, no. 3, 1896.

(133) Schmid, Johanna: *Freiwilliger Opfertod bei Euripides* (Religionsgeschichtliche Versuche und Vorarbeiten 4). Berlin, 1921.

(134) Schmid, Wilhelm: *Geschichte der griechischen Literatur* 1.2. München, 1959.

(135) Seltman, Charles: *Women in Antiquity*. New York (Collier Books), 1962.

(136) Spencer, Baldwin and Gillen, J. G.: *The Arunta* 2 vols. London, 1927.

(137) Teicher, M. I.: The Windigo Psychosis (in) *American Ethnological Society, Proceedings of the 1960 Spring Meeting*, Seattle. Washington, 1960.

(138) Time Magazine: *Noah's Park* p. 34, col. 2, 28 August 1972.

(139) Vernant, J.-P.: *Mythe et Pensée chez les Grecs* chap. 5. Paris, 1965.

(140) Verrall, A. W.: *Euripides the Rationalist*. Cambridge, 1913.

(141) Wallace, A. F. C.: Dreams and Wishes of the Soul, *American Anthropologist* 60:234–248, 1958.

(142) White, T. H.: *The Once and Future King*. New York, 1958.

(143) Wilamowitz-Moellendorff, Ulrich von: *Kleine Schriften* 4. Berlin, 1962.

(144) Winnington-Ingram, R. P.: *Euripides and Dionysus*. Cambridge, 1948.

Chapter 9

The Dream Metaphor of the Danaides

(Aischylos: *The Suppliant Women*)

Introduction

The text of A. *Suppl.* 885–901 is defective. Without radical emendations, vv. 896–897 are practically unintelligible.[1] Moreover, it does not describe a dream experience: it simply compares a real happening to a dream. I was therefore tempted not to discuss this problematic passage at all. But I soon realized that my wish to ignore it was motivated less by my conservative attitude towards the textual tradition than by the desire not to jeopardize the credibility of the rest of this book by offering here an analysis which may strike some *non*-psycho-analytical readers as "wild". At that point I recalled Freud's advice to make no concessions, for that will not persuade those who refuse to look beyond the obvious. I therefore decided to tackle this passage psycho-analytically, letting the chips fall where they may, though without deviating from a conservative approach to the textual tradition. Hence, even though the emendations of vv. 896–897, printed by Smyth, are not implausible, my analysis takes into account only the two intelligible words of the MS:[2]

(1) ἔχιδνα (= viper) is both legible and reinforced by the ὄφις (= snake) of v. 895. The mention, in one breath, of two names of snakes in manifestly Aischylean.[3]

(2) δακοсάχ (or δάκοcαχ); the last two letters cannot belong to δάκοc. This makes it certain that a stinging monster (δάκοc) like a spider or a snake[4]—or, perhaps, a noxious stinging (δάκνω)—is referred to. What the rest of vv. 896–897 means—what this serpent is actually *doing*—is purely conjectural. Though I give the plausible conjectures printed by Smyth both in the text and in my translation, I do *not* use them in my analysis. I simply note, once and for all, that both in reality and in Greek thought, spiders and snakes have many points in common:

(1) On several occasions, Nikandros (*Ther.* 8, 715 ff., *frr.* 31, 32) discusses spiders either together with or immediately after snakes. Thus, he notes that the Psylloi are immune to the bite of both (*fr.* 32).

(2) Most spiders immobilize their prey by means of webs. Some snakes do so by means of their coils.[5]

(3) The bite of both is poisonous.

(4) The snake is a commonplace phallic symbol, even though in Greek myth some serpents are female.[6] The spider *inside* its net is a phallic symbol; *outside* its net, only its body (minus the legs) is a phallic symbol (infra).

As to the emendations printed by Smyth, I simply note their objective (but *not* necessarily textual) plausibility:

(a) Snakes do tend to bite primarily the (conveniently located) foot.

---

[1] But Mazon goes too far in putting 77 verses (825–901) between daggers.

[2] There is only one manuscript of A. *Suppl.*: M (Laurentianus Mediceus 32.9, X or XI Cent.). The other five listed by Page in his edition of Aischylos are apographs.

[3] In A. *Choe.* 994 Klytaimestra is called by the names of two kinds of serpents, one of which is the viper.

[4] Cp. Fraenkel, ad A. *Ag.* 824.

[5] Typically in the famous Laokoön group.

[6] Delphyne, the guardian of the Delphic shrine (AR 2.706, etc.); the she-serpent to whom Typhon entrusts Zeus' excised sinews (infra), etc.

(b) A snake wraps itself around the mad Dionysos' legs like shackles (Nic. *fr.* 30 = *fr.* 27 Jacoby).

In short, like Klytaimestra (note 3), the Herald is compared to two beasts which have many traits in common. This being said, the reader is free to accept or reject the conjectures printed by Smyth, or replace them with other conjectures regarding the snake-Herald's behaviour—or, as I do, assume nothing whatever regarding his serpentine activities. This, as far as I am concerned, closes the discussion about the role of the serpent in this dream metaphor.

The time has now come to print the text (as emended by Smyth) together with my translation. Plausible emendations of the text and inferences regarding its all but inescapable meaning are placed between square brackets: [ ]; attractive but uncertain conjectures are placed between angular brackets: ⟨ ⟩.[7]

[7] Both here and throughout this chapter I have greatly benefited by Professor Dover's comments on the first draft of this chapter. His comments are identified by his initials (K.J.D.) or name.

Text, Translation and Comment

ΧΟΡΟΣ·

Οἰοῖ, πάτερ, [βρέτεος ἄρος	885
ἀτᾷ] ⟨μ᾽· ἁλαδ᾽⟩ ἄγει	886
ἀραχνος ὡς βάδην	887
ὄναρ ὄναρ μέλαν	888
[᾽Οτοτοτοτοῖ·]	889
μᾶ Γᾶ μᾶ Γᾶ, [βοᾶν]	890
φοβερὸν ἀπότρεπε	891
ὦ πᾶ, Γᾶς παῖ, Ζεῦ.	892

ΚΗΡΥΞ·

Οὗτοι φοβοῦμαι δαίμονας τοὺς ἐνθάδε.	893
οὐ γάρ μ᾽ ἔθρεψαν, οὐδ᾽ ἐγήρασαν τροφῇ	894

ΧΟΡΟΣ·

Μαιμᾷ πέλας δίπους ὄφις	895
ἔχιδνα δ᾽ ὡς μέ ⟨τίς	896
πόδα⟩ δακο⟨ῦς᾽ ἔχει⟩.	897

(Vv. 889–892 repeated)[8]   Smyth's text.

Danaides: Alas, father, the idol's help [is my perdition]. Like a spider he gradually drags me ⟨seawards⟩. A dream—a black dream! Alas, Mother Earth, Mother Earth, avert the terrifying shout, O Father(?), Earth's son, Zeus! (Sch. M. is plausible; L.S.J.'s βᾶ = βασιλεῦ is not.)

Herald: Mark that I do not dread the gods of this place. They did not foster me [nor will they nourish my old age].

Danaides: Eagerly approaches the two-legged snake. Like a viper ⟨he grabs my foot and bites it⟩. Mother Earth, Mother Earth, avert the terrifying shout, O Father, Earth's son, Zeus!

   [8] Cod. M gives for vv. 896–897:

ἔχιδνα δ᾽ ὡς με < – >	(response to – – UUU –)
τι πότε ν < <u>uu</u>U – >	(response to UUU – U –)
δακοσάχ < <u>uu</u>U – >	(response to UUU – U –)

ἔχιδνα is scanned UUU, these being dochmiacs, i.e. <u>U</u> <u>UU</u> <u>UU</u>–(K.J.D.). Speaking with pessimism, one has: Like a snake (me?) (but μ need not be μ᾽ or με). What ever ... (it) (but ν need not be νίν). Monster? grief? (but the syntax of that word is unknown) (K.J.D.).

I must now consider this dialogue point by point, justifying it and clarifying its manifest meanings and implications. Only after this is done can a psycho-analytical interpretation of the dream-metaphor be attempted.

The idol's help [*is my perdition*]. Though usually translated as: "may cause", the text is almost certainly in the present indicative (ἀτᾷ); classical Greek has no potential subjunctive (K.J.D.). The Danaides presumably feel that they had erred in relying on the safety of the sacred precincts; they should have continued their flight.

⟨*Seaward*⟩. The MS contains the nonexistent word μαλδα. From the purely palaeographic point of view, this "word" can be a corruption either of μάλα δ' (= very much, exceedingly; Bothe, followed by Mazon) or of μ' ·ἅλαδ (= seaward; Schütz, followed by Smyth). Psychologically, only μ' ·ἅλαδ' can be right, for the Herald actually means to drag the Danaides towards the ships waiting to carry them off. Schütz's emendation therefore adds a further *concrete* detail to the Danaides' nightmarish plight. And, as a general rule, the dreamlike atmosphere of certain great tales of supernatural danger is due to the accumulation of highly realistic *details*, arranged in an uncanny manner.[9]

On a different level, being dragged "seaward" echoes the Danaides' wish to drown themselves (796 ff.), which the Herald intends to prevent (873 f.). It hardly requires lengthy proof that there is an intimate relationship between the wish to drown and the threat to commit suicide by hanging (465), not only in this drama and in Greek thought,[10] but physiologically as well (*suffocation*.)[11] Last, but not least, I will show in due time that "seaward", especially when conjoined with "leaping into the sea" and with "hanging", is compatible also with this dream metaphor's *latent* content.

Drags me. Elsewhere (*fr.* 39 N²) Aischylos described the carrying (dragging) away of a fawn by *two wolves*. This reinforces my conviction that he intended the Danaides to visualize themselves as being dragged away by a spider (and/or serpent?). Indeed, the fragment just cited, which concerns *two* wolves, makes the (inferable) "*duplication*" of the dragging by a spider and/or a serpent (?) also a clue to Aischylos' way of *visualizing* such scenes: he apparently felt that *two* draggers were necessary. Since there is only *one* Herald, Aischylos resorts to a duplication of images: *in fantasy* a "spider" and a "snake" attack the Danaides "*successively*". But it is probable that *on stage* the Herald had grabbed only one member of the Choros. However, the *duplication* of the *described* attack(s) must have helped the spectators to *imagine* the Herald as perhaps multiple or many-armed, and therefore capable of seizing *all* of the Danaides.[12]

[9] A critic—perhaps T. S. Eliot—noted how effective Kipling's precise reference to "Portugal laurels" (and not just to "laurels") is at the end of one of his tales of the supernatural. Cp. also Freud's cogent observation that "*Das Unheimliche*" (*42*) is related at once to *heimlich* [= secret(ly)] and to *heimisch* (= home-like, i.e., "homey"). The uncanny is, thus, simply the highly familiar, appearing in disguise or out of context.

[10] Parthen. *Erot.* 31; Apul. *Met.* 12 init. Cp. (*68*).

[11] It is just possible that the reference to a leap into the depths also seeks to evoke allusively ritual leaps into the sea. *Katapontismos* was admirably discussed by Gallini (*43*).

[12] One often sees more than one insect caught in a cobweb. In the Laokoön group, each

Spider. The word used here can denote spiders in general, though usually it denotes the common, web-weaving (house-)spider.[13] Thus, the Aischylean image suggests the *netting* of the Danaides by the Spider-Herald, of which more anon.[14]

But, be he viewed as a hunter or a netter, the Herald is here—as in some other instances (E. *Tr.*, E. *Heracl.*, etc.)—a ruthless kidnapper, with scant respect for sanctuaries.

Black dream. The word ὄναρ can, in theory, refer either to the dream as a whole, or to the Herald's figure seen in dream. The dream can be "black" either because "Egyptians are black in Greek eyes" (K.J.D.), or because black things seen in dream are ominous,[15] or because "black" denotes here the painful and ominous quality of the "dream"(-like) experience. Smyth's translation: "nightmare" is semantically incorrect: in later times the nightmare was called ἐφιάλτης (perhaps: leaper-upon).[16] But I propose to show further on that this "dream" has all the qualities of a nightmare *stricto sensu.*

I do not fear the gods of this place. They did not foster me (i.e., in my childhood [*nor nourish my old age*]. This is the usual translation (Smyth, Mazon). But the text *seems* to say: "nor did they grow old through ⟨my⟩ nourishing of them". "This is a simple *polarity*; a Greek feels he is 'brought up' and 'fed' by his father until he becomes old enough to take over the οἶκος (household), after which he has the responsibility of 'feeding' his father" (K.J.D.).

I concede that this polarity is Greek (Ar. *Av.* 1355 f.) and that aged mortal kings who abdicate do rely, in myth, upon the protection of their sons or grandsons.[17] I even concede that, despite their access to nectar and

serpent entwines more than one person. But I must note that, in this drama, Aischylos *did not* make the Herald *wolf*-like, though his principals, the sons of Aigyptos, are called wolves (351 f.), and even the Danaides themselves are compared to wolves (760). In another myth, Danaos is represented by a wolf vanquishing a bull (Paus. 2.16.1, 19.3 ff., 38.4). (Exile = wolf is commonplace.)

[13] The girl Arachne, an excellent weaver, was turned into a spider after being defeated by the challenged Athene in a weaving contest (V. *Georg.* 4.46, etc.). Several persons known to me, who greatly dislike spiders, regularly visualize spiders (in general) as sitting on the edge of their webs, ready to pounce on their victims—and this even though they *know* that some spiders simply hunt. In short, unless otherwise specified, the word "spider" makes most people think of *web-weaving* spiders. Nikandros, who does not mention the spider's web in his poems, never once calls a spider ἀράχνης; the generic term he uses is: φαλάγγιον (a poisonous spider). But it is significant in this context that he *does* use (Nic. *Ther.* 733) the term ἀραχνήεντα (full of filaments?), thus showing that the word ἀράχνη evoked for him *mainly* the spider's *web*.

[14] But the scene can also be visualized differently: "the image made me think not of a web, but of a hunting spider which chases its prey and drags it off when it has killed it. When I read the Greek text before reading [the first draft of this chapter] I thought of: (a) the fact that crabs walk backwards or sideways, as often observed by the ancients, (b) the close affinity between crabs and spiders, (c) the fact that a man *dragging* a woman is bound to walk backwards or sideways: βάδην seemed to me to emphasize this image" (K.J.D.). But I feel that the Herald dragging away the Danaides by their *hair* or by their *garments* need not walk backwards or sideways. Pulling at these "leashes", he can walk straight ahead. Still, it is interesting to contrast the divergent mental images the same text can conjure up for two different readers.

[15] Cp. ps.-Hp. *insomn.* 91. [16] Sch. B. Hom. *Il.* 5.385.

[17] Laertes and Odysseus (Hom. *Od. passim*). Kadmos and Pentheus (E. *Ba.* 1308 ff.), etc.

ambrosia,[18] the Greek gods relied for their nourishment also on the smoke of sacrifices.[19] But I have shown (*30*) elsewhere that the Greek gods were imagined as "smoke-inhalers", probably lacking an anus, as legendary "odour-feeders" so often do.[20]

But one decisive detail militates against the view that the Herald speaks of *his* feeding the gods: it is the mention of *old age*. Though some Greek supernaturals were believed to be old—e.g., the Graiai (= hags)—their great age made them neither helpless nor dependent.[21] I am therefore *not* prepared to assume that, because of their dependence on sacrifices, the Greek deities were—be it only unconsciously—imagined as senile and *therefore* as standing in need of human "nurturing".

Thus, the text can only mean: the gods of Argos neither nursed the Egyptian Herald in childhood, nor will they sustain him in his old age. If it is held that the text, as it stands, *cannot* mean that, then it must be emended.

What matters most here is, however, the Herald's impiety.

I begin by noting a minor detail: he only mentions the child's and the old person's dependence on divine nurturing. Perhaps, like Aias (S. *Aj.* 767 ff.), he arrogantly felt that a man in the flower of his strength has no need of divine assistance (921).

But it is more probable that the Herald's impiety is simply ethnocentric (922): he feels he owes much to the divine Nile, but nothing to the alien gods of Argos. This is, however, contrary to the outlook of the Greeks, who held that Xerxes was punished for his destruction of *Greek* temples (Hdt. 8.54).[22] A Greek revered even alien deities, though he owed them no personal debt.[23]

I note, *in fine*, that the Herald's arrogant disregard of the Argive gods radically differs from the Danaides' desperate threat to defile the sanctuary

---

[18] That ambrosia was a hallucinogen is a near certainty for La Barre (*50*, p. 468 and *passim*). I believe it to have been imagined as a euphoric (*30*).

[19] Hom. *h. Cer.* 310 ff.; Ar. *Av.* 580, 1230 ff., 1262 ff., 1516 ff., etc.

[20] The gods do not defaecate (Plu. *Reg. imp. ap.*, Antig. 7 p. 182C). As odour-feeders they were perhaps similar to the Mysian καπνοβόται (Posid. *FHG* 3.291.91 = Str. 7.3.3, p. 296). On other odour-feeders, cp. Plu. *V. Artax.* 19; Plin. *HN* 7.25; Aul. Gell. 9.4.10 (the latter two probably derived from Aristeas; *3*, p. 28 ff.), Luc. *VH* 1.23. Cp. καπνος-φράντης *Com. Adesp.* 1025, Alciphr. 3.49 and the Greek anecdote in which kitchen odours serve as a condiment. Ethnological and clinical parallels often include also the denial of the existence of the anus (cp. *60*; *52*, p. 392; *62*; *48*; *14*).

[21] The only senile and helpless "immortal" known to me is Tithonos—a mere mortal rendered immortal, but not granted also eternal youth (Hom. *h. Ven.* 233 ff.). I hold that his decline was due primarily to his having mated with a goddess. In the same hymn, Anchises dreads a similar fate and is later on actually lamed (V. *Aen.* 2.647 ff.) or blinded (Serv. *V. Aen.* 1.617, 2.687)—punishments recalling both Oidipous' hurt ankles and subsequent blindness (*33*). Odysseus had to be told how to avoid such a fate (Hom. *Od.* 10.281 ff.). Psycho-analytically expressed: not old age but incest with a mother-imago (goddess) causes the "paralysis" (= impotence = loss of manhood) of mortal men.

[22] This alone should perhaps have indicated that A. *Suppl.* postdated Xerxes' invasion of Greece. Had it antedated it, this scene would have unpleasantly reminded the Athenians of their *own* sacrilegious burning of Sardis (Hdt. 5.105, 6.30, 7.8.β, 7.11, etc.).

[23] This attitude probably prepared the ground for the later philosophical view that the gods were entitled to reverence, even though they did not intervene in human affairs. This view preserved the first half of *do ut des*, but abolished the second half.

by hanging themselves in it, if the asylum failed to protect them (787 ff.).[24] That threat implies a recognition of the existence and power—if not of the *spontaneous* benevolence—of the Argive gods.[25]

Two-legged viper. As in the spider metaphor, the Herald is once again visualized (or described) in a distorted manner. The points of similarity between spiders and serpents justify his being called by both these names. The "two-legged viper"[26] corresponds to the "two-legged lioness" Klytaimestra (A. *Ag.* 1258), who, in the rest of the *Oresteia*, is mostly called a snake. The alleged obstetrical affinities between the lioness and the she-viper (cp. chap. 5) justify her being called by both these names.

Of course, we cannot be sure that Aischylos expected us to imagine that the Herald was actually "misperceived", rather than simply called appropriate derogatory names. I incline towards the second alternative: the Herald is a spider = snake only morally and in his actions.[27]

Moreover, *qua* "serpent", the Herald is a chthonian being—as is, at times, also the patron of his profession, Hermes (A. *Choe.* 1). It is even conceivable that it is precisely the *chthonian* character of the viperine Herald that causes the Danaides to appeal for protection to Mother Earth[28] and to designate Zeus by the unusual title: "Earth's son". This epithet probably forbids us to assert that the desperate Danaides simply appeal here *both* to a Chthonian and to an Olympian deity.[29] But I concede at once that this argument is appreciably weakened by the fact that the invocation occurs *first* in connection with the (non-chthonian) spider, and is simply repeated after the verses in which the Herald is called a serpent. Whether the first invocation "meant" to *anticipate* the serpent imagery or else unwittingly "*suggested*" it to Aischylos, I am unable to decide on the basis of psycho-analytical considerations. But, be it the

---

[24] Cp. the similar threats of the Athenians, when the Delphic oracle gave them a discouraging response (Hdt. 7.141). On blackmail disguised as supplication, cp. chap. 6.

[25] A Greek hero occasionally fought or threatened a god, but, in so doing, recognized his power and existence. He who fights the gods—the θεομάχος—may be a contemptor of the gods, but he is neither an agnostic nor an atheist, nor does he feel that the gods do not concern him.

[26] Structurally related to the two-headed snake, A. *Ag.* 1233. Two-headed scorpion: Nic. *Ther.* 812.

[27] By contrast, the good serpentine Kekrops and the bad serpentine Typhon are both morally and behaviourally "human".

[28] Who, in E. *IT* 1262 ff., is represented by the slain Delphic she-serpent and who, when dispossessed, sends oracular *dreams* to men, in competition with the usurping Apollon's oracle. And let it not be objected that Euripides' account differs from that of Aischylos (A. *Eum.* 1 ff.)! I have conclusively shown that the same persons can hold two mutually contradictory sets of beliefs (*8*) and also that that which a culture (or a theology) affirms on one level of discourse, it tends to deny on another level (*29*, chap. 16). The Aischylean and the Euripidean tales are therefore not incompatible, but complementary.

[29] This way of addressing Zeus *may* indirectly hint also at his fight with the *serpentine* Typhon. That tale is doubtless of Egyptian origin: a replica of Osiris' fight with Typhon [Plu. *de Is. et Os. passim*, now confirmed by a newly discovered papyrus text: Pap. Jumilhac, cp. (*45*)]. The fact that the tale of Zeus' fight with Typhon is mentioned only in *late* Greek sources (Apollod. 1.6.3; Nonn. *Dion.* 1.137, 2.712) does *not* mean that Aischylos, who was notoriously familiar with Egyptian matters, did not know it and did not have it in the back of his mind while describing the clash between the Danaides (whom he considers to be mainly Greek) and the serpentine Herald of the Aigyptiadai (whom he views as barbarians).

witting anticipation or the unwitting root or inspiration of the snake passage, the first invocation greatly tautens the texture and coherence of vv. 885–901.

Stinging beast (or, perhaps, stinging bite) provides the one non-conjectural clue to the behaviour imputed to the serpentine Herald in the second (snake) part of the dream metaphor. The two previous references to serpents (ὄφις, ἔχιδνα) do *not* authorize us to take it for granted that the dream-snake behaves as snakes usually behave. For, were the text of E. *Hec.* 90–91 defective, one might conjecture that the wolf *bit* the fawn. But in the surviving, *non*-defective text one finds the wolf "clawing"—in a *feline* manner—or, better still, using his forepaws the way a man uses his hands. Similarly, were the text of E. *Rh.* 784 defective, one would never guess that the wolves use their tails as riding crops (chap. 8).

I have noted objective similarities between real spiders and real serpents: web = coil, sting = bite. But this only makes it likely that the dream-snake behaves like the dream-spider—it does *not* guarantee the correctness of the conjecture.

The words "snake" and "viper" make a bite no more than probable. But δάκος makes a poisonous bite as probable as any conjecture can be, because δάκνω means: to sting (poisonously). This detail can therefore be exploited in the interpretative section.

Discussion

Before I can analyse the latent content of this passage, some general comments are in order.

These verses describe a real event in the form of a dream metaphor. This necessarily indicates that spider (and snake) dreams were common (or proverbial) enough in Greek culture for the metaphor to elicit an affective response from the audience. Similarly, the "running inhibition" dream metaphor in Hom. *Il.* 22.199 ff. elicits a strong response to this day: Wilamowitz (*73*, p. 100) called it "unbearable".

But, in Hom. *Il.* 22.199 ff., it is the *poet* who speaks; in A. *Suppl.* 885 ff., the Danaides *themselves* describe their present experience through a dream metaphor.[30]

One must also distinguish between what the *dramatist* sought to achieve by these means and what a recourse to a dream-metaphor would mean to a *real* woman, who described her experiences in such a manner.

Clearly, Aischylos sought only to *heighten* the affective impact of the scene, by mobilizing the spectators' spider phobias[31] and perhaps memories of spider dreams as well.

Matters are different when one imagines the Danaides as real—or at least as psychologically plausible—personages.

---

[30] Other alternatives exist. In A. *Choe.* 527 ff., the Choros narrates Klytaimestra's giving birth to and nursing a serpent in dream. But, *at v. 928*, it is hard to say whether Klytaimestra recalls her actual dream or (much less probably) simply claims that she *metaphorically* bore and suckled a serpent.

[31] "About one-third of the persons I know well have some phobia of spiders" (K.J.D.).

The description of an *on-going* experience as a "dream" reveals, first of all, how shifting and tenuous the boundaries between reality and dream are for primitives (*53*, etc.), the ancient Greeks (*36*, chap. 4) and neurotics (*19*).[32]

But there is more to it. The comparing of a horrible experience to a dream—though it may heighten its ghastliness *for the audience*—indicates that a defence mechanism is at work: the *reality* of the actual *experience* is practically negated, by recourse to a "de-realization"[33]: "I must be dreaming—this cannot be true!" But the *descriptive* intensification of an "uncanny" horror is sometimes made possible precisely by taking one's affective distance from it—i.e., by means of the defence mechanism of isolation.[34]

This being said, the analysis of a dream-metaphor raises a basic methodological issue. In analysing Menelaos' dream (chap. 3),[35] etc., one analyses his personality *as revealed* by his *dream*. Similarly, though all three Euripidean dreams (chap. 8) have as their latent theme the primal scene,[36] each of the three Euripidean dreamers reveals his (or her) *personality*—and distinctive *predicament*—through the *manifest* content of the dream (*26*).

By contrast, this dream-metaphor must be analysed primarily as a "type dream": "What does a spider (or snake) dream *mean* to anyone—especially in Greek culture?" There are three sets of clues to its overt "meaning":

(1) The primary clue is the manner in which Aischylos elaborated this *simple* theme[37] and provided clues to its latent meaning in the rest of the drama.

(2) The secondary clues are Greek beliefs about spiders and snakes.

(3) Tertiary clues are ethnological and clinical parallels.

I must now return for a moment to the matter of "shifting boundaries," which I did not discuss fully before, in order not to interrupt my main argument. This scene contains one of the most brilliant manipulations of "boundaries" I have ever come across either in poetry or in the dreams I have heard as a practising psycho-analyst.

The spider captures and immobilizes its victims by means of its web, i.e., by means of *filaments* it produces out of its body. He can even suspend himself by—hang from—his own filament, which is so definitely a part of the spider that in Greek ἀράχνης denotes the spider, and ἀράχνη its web.[38]

---

[32] For another "boundary shift", see below.

[33] For a different type of denial (by means of a hallucination: A. *Ag.* 414 ff.), cp. chap. 3.

[34] One of my patients could afford to wallow in ghastly and obscene, nearly hallucinatory, *fantasies*, simply by reacting to them impassibly (isolation): "All this is very remote from me" (*20*, *23*), though his actual *dreams* were neither truly horrible nor obscene.

[35] Or that of Penelope, Hom. *Od.* 19.555—which fits her personality as Homeros described it, though *not* the idealized personality literary critics ascribe to her (*16*).

[36] Parental coitus and the child's reactions to it.

[37] Compare what Beethoven did—and others failed to do—with a truly trivial theme in his "Diabelli Variations" (op. 120).

[38] But ἀράχνη can also mean the spider. Latin: *aranea* = spider = cobweb. Cp. German *Spinne* (related to: "spin"). The rope (an object) with which Arachne hanged herself becomes a secretion of her spider-body (Ov. *Met.* 6.144 f.).

Now, in A. *Suppl.* a "web" or rope is *not* part of the spider-*Herald's* equipment. It is a part of his *victims*! The Herald proposes to drag the Danaides along by *their* (filament) *hair* (884, 909) or by *their* (web) *woven* garments (903)—*not* by their arms or necks. That the "woven" robe which immobilized Agamemnon is called a spider's web (A. *Ag.* 1492, 1516) as well as a "net" (A. *Ag.* 868, 1115; A. *Choe.* 999, etc.) strongly suggests that Aischylos visualized the garments by which the Danaides are to be dragged along as spider-web equivalents. In fact, even the spider's ability to hang from (and by) its own filament is duplicated by the Danaides' threat to *hang* themselves (465).[39] Once again we are face to face with the tendency of many mystics to equate the aggressor with the victim; the hunter with his prey.

These considerations make it almost certain that Aischylos expected us to visualize a "trapping" (web-weaving) spider and not a hunting one.

I must comment further on netting = immobilization, for it will be an important element of my analysis of the dream-metaphor's latent content. The *Oresteia's* countless references to Agamemnon's immobilization (by "netting"), which far outnumber mentions of the act of slaying, suggest that the horror of being netted (immobilized) may have been an *Aischylean* character trait. But it was assuredly also a *Greek* trait, for it is a recurrent motif in Greek myth.[40]

In short, the spider metaphor not only gives a logically acceptable sense, but also one compatible—as will be shown further on—with the nature of the anxieties the dream-metaphor expresses.

Interpretation

The attempted kidnapping sought to force the Danaides into unwanted unions: it prepared the ground for their being "legally" *raped* by their

---

[39] For hanging as the standard Greek female suicide, cp. *32*. Rope used to hang oneself with = spider's filament: Ov. *Met.* 6.144 f. Cases of suicide by hanging (choking) oneself with one's own hair are on record (*74*, p. 209).

[40] Perjured gods become paralysed (Hes. *Th.* 775 ff.). Hera is glued to her throne by Hephaistos (Paus. 1.20.3, etc.) and is also tied up by Zeus (Hom. *Il.* 15.18). Aphrodite and Ares are netted by Hephaistos (Hom. *Od.* 8.272 ff.). Prometheus is chained. Ares is chained by the Aloadai, one of whom is named Ephialtes (= leaper-upon, nightmare, sch. B. Hom. *Il.* 5.385 ff.: *EM* 403.32). In Hades, Theseus is attached to his seat by many snakes (Apollod. *Ep.* 1.24), or by chains (Hor. *Carm.* 3.4.79), or by his own flesh growing to the seat (Paus. 10.29.9). (Cp. Arachne's rope = bodily secretion, supra, note 39). These alternatives prove that "fetters" and garments can either be external to, or part of, the prisoner himself (*69*) (chap. 7, note 83). An amphisbaina immobilizes the mad Dionysos' legs, sch. Nic. *Ther.* 377. The Greeks, who used hunting nets extensively, were certainly able to empathize with the plight of an insect caught in a net. For, as I have shown elsewhere (*10*), one's *choice* of a particular means of aggression—and even of a particular curse—always reveals what the aggressor himself dreads *most*. One need not even be a psychologist to reach this obvious conclusion. The pivotal point in Nevil Shute's novel: *Most Secret* (1945) (*67*) is that the Germans invented the *Flammenwerfer* because *they* dreaded fire *more* than other people. I am inclined to connect the Greek's fear of immobilization with the swaddling of Greek infants (A. *Choe.* 529). An analysand, who had been swaddled, broke with a charming girl-friend because he could not endure her tendency to wrap herself tightly around him in bed. Moreover, the same analysand *punished* his cat *exclusively* by hog-tying the animal whenever it misbehaved.

kinsmen. The Danaides reacted to this with threats to hang themselves and with the wish to drown; in short, they reacted to the Herald's threats of *immobilization* with the striking *alternative* of suffocation fantasies (*68*).

We have here *every* element of the nightmare *stricto sensu*: incest, sexual aggression, immobilization and suffocation (*47, passim*).

Oedipality. I must begin my discussion of the dream-metaphor's latent content with a discussion of the incest element, discernible in *all* genuine nightmares (*47*).

Incest (oedipality) is *not* definable by rote, in purely bio-genealogical terms. There can be no incest, in an operational sense, where there is no kinship system: animals can inbreed, but cannot be incestuous (*31*, chap. 7). Coitus between an adoptive father and an adopted daughter is operationally and experientially incestuous, *without* being also inbreeding. Coitus between a brother and a sister, unaware of their biological kinship, is not incestuous, though biologically it is in-breeding (see also chap. 2) (*55*).

Incest, *as an experience*, depends on arbitrary social rules: an Athenian could marry his paternal, but not his uterine half-sister, though in childhood he presumably developed psychologically identical—tenderly fraternal, rather than sexual—feelings towards both. The incest element is latently present also when one marries a (biologically unrelated) father or mother "substitute". It can appear even in the course of a *non*-incestuous marriage, if the nature of the marital relationship gradually manœuvres one or both of the spouses into a psycho-socially parental role. (Cp. chap. 2, note 93.[41])

In short, the incest element intervenes when a pre-existing psycho-social "kinship type" relationship between a man and a woman:

(1) causes them to *avoid* coitus "virtuously";

(2) *incites* them to engage in coitus:

    (a) to lend it a tabooed "spice", or

    (b) because it is, e.g., a royal privilege (Egypt, etc.), or else

    (c) because it is a socially standardized ritual crime, having "desirable" consequences,[42] etc.

In the case of the Egyptian-born royal Danaides, what highlights most their *subjective* obsession with incest is the routine character of Pharaonic brother-sister marriages, which one may assume to have been known to Aischylos. But I note that, throughout this drama, he represents the Danaides *as Greeks* and their cousins, the Aigyptiadai, as *Egyptian barbarians*. It is possible that, by means of this differential characterization, Aischylos sought to assert the superiority of Greek customs to those of the

---

[41] Du Bois (*37*, p. 96) recorded a striking statement made by an Alorese man: At night, half asleep, one sometimes calls one's wife: "Mother". Ferenczi (*39*) noted long ago that a decrease of sexual interest in the spouse may result from a growing tendency to *perceive* the spouse as a parent-surrogate (husband = paternal provider; wife = maternal nurturer).

[42] Cp. the purely "instrumental" (goal-directed) incest of Thyestes with his daughter Pelopeia (chap. 2). On the possibly political-instrumental character of Oidipous' incest, cp. (*18*). On Kuanyama Ambo sorcerers (*54*) and chap. 2, note 61. On incest and kinship in general, cp. *31*, chap. 7.

Egyptians (cp. 760 f.). If so, he did not attain his objective, for, as noted, an Athenian could marry his *paternal* half-sister.

In short, what underscores the oedipal element in this *whole* drama is precisely the Danaides' socially disingenuous *pretence* that a marriage with their (paternal) cousins would be incestuous.[43]

The fact is that neither Aischylos nor any other Greek author who retold this myth seems to have accepted as valid the Danaides' claim that a marriage to their paternal cousins would have been "incestuous" (socially objectionable). Hypermnestra's happy union with her cousin Lynkeus also disproves the validity of the Danaides' clamourings about incest.

What their *untenable* claims and arguments *do* underscore is that the Danaides were *personally* hostile to men and to sexuality—an attitude which the Greeks did not condone—and tried to *disguise* their loathing of sex as a horror of incest. But it is precisely their *choice* of this particular (*15*, pp. 55 f., etc.) futile rationalization which reveals their real motivation: the Danaides (subjectively) experienced *all* sex as "incest". Such an outlook is commonly met with in daughters having a strong oedipal fixation on the father—and the Aischylean Danaides' father fixation has been conclusively demonstrated by Kouretas (*49*) on the basis of altogether *different* data and reasonings.[44]

The importance of the incest element in this drama—and in nightmares —must be borne in mind throughout the following discussion, which is focused on the sexual-aggressive role of the phallic mother (rather than on the father) in the *typical* nightmare experience, which the dream-metaphor replicates.

Spider Symbolism was well understood by Abraham (*1*), whose interpretations were subsequently verified by others, for spider dreams appear to be fairly common.[45] Artemidoros (4.56) compares spiders to contemptible people who, despite their weakness and insignificance, can cause great harm. One also notes that certain Greek authors grossly exaggerated the

---

[43] I stress that the Danaides and the Aigyptiadai are kindred mainly through their common descent from two brothers, even though in most of their speeches the Danaides refer mainly to their common ancestress Io (but less often and also less explicitly to their common ancestor Zeus). But one notices at once that they *harp* on this kinship mainly in order to validate their claim to asylum in Argos. Thus, they barely mention the obvious symmetry of their (virginal) flight with that of (pregnant) Io (351 f.). Also, they never once mention that the *Aigyptiadai's* descent from Io entitles them, too, to the sympathy of the Argives. In fact, even the Herald fails to make this very obvious and telling point. These omissions suggest that Aischylos did *not* seek to persuade the Athenians of the validity of the Danaides' incest argument—for example, by recalling the Athenian taboo on marrying a *uterine* half-brother (or maternal kinsman?), a taboo made largely inapplicable here by the fact that the Danaides and the Aigyptiadai were primarily paternal parallel cousins and remote descendants of Io only in the second place. On the sociological aspects of such marriages, cp.—with some reservations—G. Thomson (*70*, chap. 16).

[44] A further, indirect but revealing, proof of the Aischylean Danaides' father fixation is the lack of any reference to their mothers (infra).

[45] I have the impression that, during the years when I had a psycho-analytical practice, I usually had at least one patient who had spider dreams or spider fantasies, or who had a pathological fear of spiders. In one area—in what was formerly Magna Graecia—the spider phobia is actually institutionalized in the form of tarantism (*5, 44*).

poisonousness of *most* spiders,[46] though the bite of many species is at most unpleasant.

The most striking thing about the mental *image* of the spider is that this creature is so often felt to be *feminine*—albeit in a peculiar way (infra)—in part perhaps because spinning-and-weaving is, in most of the Mediterranean area, a female occupation.[47] Spiders are specifically compared to women (Ael. *NA* 1.21) and even to female geometricians who sit in the centre of their webs (Ael. *NA* 6.57). Certain "four-jawed" spiders[48] were apparently hostile to men, for they attacked the *men* of an Indian nation and almost exterminated them (Ael. *NA* 17.40).

This choice bit of *pseudobiologia phantastica* is of special interest, for I have often noticed that even the most outlandish bits of "unnatural history" tend to have some sort of counterpart in reality. In several spider species, the female—larger than the male—devours her mate after coitus (*72*).[49] Figuratively speaking, such a female spider's *whole* body is a *vagina dentata*.

PW-*RE* (Spinnentiere) doesn't say whether the Greeks knew of the cannibalistic mating habits of spiders. It would almost be better for my argument if they had *not* known of them—for it would suggest that "something" about spiders makes them seem to be *female* monsters (cp. sch. Nic. *Ther.* 11).

The spider seems to be imagined as a *vagina dentata* also in two other ways:

(1) According to Nic. *Ther.* 716 and Ael. *NA* 3.36, a certain spider, called "grape", has its mouth and teeth in the centre of its abdomen (which makes *me* think of the "four-jawed spider", supra): Nikandros adds the striking information that a *man* bitten by *this* spider will have a pathological erection, a foul discharge from the urinary meatus and a paralysis of the legs. These symptoms, which clearly combine erection and paralysis, will be discussed in greater detail later on. The symptoms of bitten *women* are *not* mentioned—this, too, makes one think of the *man-killing* "four-jawed" spiders.

(2) For some normal informants,[50] "the *vagina dentata* is the cobweb tube up which the spider lurks—especially the various species of house spiders which build webs in corners" (K.J.D.).

In short, the "grape" spider has an *abdominal* (inguinal?) maw (resembling the *vagina dentata*); its bite produces symptoms affecting the male genitals.

As regards spiders that weave a tubular web (vagina), the web's "teeth" are represented by the spider lurking in it.

[46] Nic. *Ther.* 8, 715 ff.; in both passages, spiders are mentioned immediately after snakes. Cp. also Ael. *NA* 17.40, etc.

[47] Amongst the Hopi Indians of Arizona (*6*) and the Reungao Moi (*7*), the weavers are men. "Persian" carpets are also woven by men.

[48] "Four-jawed" may *conceivably* imply an allusion to the *vagina dentata*. Cp. infra. Vipers bite the groin, and so do scorpions (Nic. *Ther.* 545 ff., 783).

[49] In one species, the tiny male lives as a parasite inside the female's genital tract; this automatically protects him from being devoured by his mate. But I must, in fairness, cite an at least superficially contradictory bit of *pseudethnographia phantastica*. The nation of the Psylloi was immune to both spider and snake bites (Ael. *NA* 16.27); and ψύλλα is the name of various noxious insects, including a venomous spider (Arist. *HA* 622b31).

[50] Questioned by Professor Dover on my behalf, lest it be said that *my* psycho-analytical outlook influenced their responses.

In my own clinical experience, spider webs, hairy spiders and swarms of spiders represent mainly the female pubic hair surrounding the dangerous (toothed?) vagina (which the pubic hair both conceals and implies).

Since this point—which is of considerable importance in this discussion —may bewilder (and perhaps shock) the non-clinician, several concrete examples, which will substantiate this finding, will now be cited.

Example 1. A depressed, apathetic and asthenic male analysand (with a "devouring"—but also seductively "food-stuffing"—mother) dreamed of an electric wall socket, literally covered with swarms of spiders. He immediately understood—without any interpretation from me—that the socket was his mother's vulva[51] and the spiders her pubic hair (*25*).

Example 2. An inexperienced pubescent boy felt repelled by his barely nubile girl friend's scanty pubic hair. It seemed to him that spiders were crawling over her otherwise bare *mons veneris*.

At times, the spidery female pubic hair is fantasied as *behaving* like the tentacles of certain small marine animals, or like the arms of cephalopods, which sweep their victims into their maw. In other instances, the hairy vulva is fantasied as a *vortex*, which, by *suction*, draws the victim into the vagina.

Example 3. A very severely disturbed borderline patient once practically hallucinated his mother's whole body as a huge, hairy pubis and feared that her vagina would suck him in, "the way a vacuum cleaner sucks in dust" (*20, 23*).[52]

This terrifying conception of the spidery, "traplike" female pubic hair may perhaps even explain why the pubis of Athenian women was depilated.[53]

In short, a woman whose spidery pubic hair entraps the man is a good symbol of the kind of rapacious and sexually seductive woman Americans call a "man-trap".

Still another fantasy centred on the symbolic equation: female pubic hair = swarms of spiders = cobweb, is that the pubic hair conceals the female penis, or actually "is" the female penis.

Example 4. A statistician in analysis reported seeing his mother in the nude only once: at the age of six or seven, when he was not yet (consciously) aware of anatomical differences between the sexes. *Expecting* to see a penis, he *did* "see" a penis—but did *not* see his mother's pubic hair (perhaps because, at that age, he himself had none). His associations to this misperception were striking: "Perhaps my lifelong tendency to see

[51] In the U.S.A., such sockets do not have round holes, but narrow slits; cp. U.S.A. slang: "split" or "slit" = vulva.

[52] The vortex has always fascinated mankind. The Mohave believe that small dusty whirlwinds carry ghosts (*27*, p. 435). The vortex played a major role in the thought of the Pre-Socratics. Cp. the Index, s.vv. δίνη, δίνος, of Diels-Kranz; also Edgar Allan Poe's tale of the Maelstrom (*61*). The Greeks even mythologized sea vortexes (Skylla, Charybdis), and Greek seamen could not but know that one must swim away from a foundering ship, lest one be sucked into the depths by the vortex its sinking creates. (Cp. the Danaides' drowning fantasies.)

[53] This interpretation is reinforced by the anxiety dream a Somali man—belonging to a nation whose women are depilated—had after cohabiting with a (*non*-depilated) European prostitute. In his dream her pubic hair appeared as an inguinal (male) beard— i.e., as something which (necessarily) surrounds a (tooth-filled) mouth (*64*).

what I expect, and not what is really there, accounts for my deficiencies as a proof-corrector."

Since I have related the Herald's threats to drag the Danaides by the *hair* to spider *webs*, I must demonstrate that there can be a *cultural* nexus between *head* hair and spiders, even in tribes where the spider plays a "good" role.

One of the main souls of the Sedang Moi is the "spider soul" (cp. the Greek winged soul: ψυχή), which is said to perch just above the forehead, in the *parting* of the hair.[54] It requires little imagination to realize that the parting of the hair greatly resembles the "parting" of the female pubic hair.[55]

During an important annual ritual, each Sedang catches a live spider and puts it on the parting of his (or her) hair, so as to reinvigorate the "spider soul", which perches on that spot.[56]

The Phallic Female. Throughout the preceding paragraphs I have spoken of the spider as a symbol of the *vagina dentata*, and this even though I underscored also the Danaides' father-fixation-motivated neurotic obsession with incest. I must therefore answer the foreseeable and quite reasonable objection that I have treated the spider (and its net) as a female symbol—seemingly ignoring all the while the fact that the spider-Herald is a *man*.

I begin by noting that the child views the penis as the main symbol and attribute of power. Hence, since the mother is larger than the child, the child fantasies that she simply "must" have a penis. In *Example 4*, one actually witnesses the transformation of the (*not* perceived) maternal pubic hair into a (*mis*-perceived) female phallos. It is, moreover, a traditional characteristic of the *vagina dentata* that it deprives the male of his phallos, so as to *retain* possession of it. The child, the neurotic and even myth easily circumvent the hollowness of the female organ by means of the fantasy that the woman has an anal *hollow* penis (*40*, chap. 42).[57]

---

[54] This portion of the skull, where, in the neonate, the fontanella is located, plays a major role in Sedang "physiological" beliefs. One informant flatly asserted that one breathes *with* the fontanella. Another said only that the fontanella was "somehow" connected with breathing. Now, in the Sedang language, *ihiàm* means both breath and (violent) affectivity; its seat is the solar plexus. To have "much ihiàm" is therefore practically an equivalent of the Greek μεγάθυμος, which corresponds exactly to *magnanimità* (as used, e.g., by Macchiavelli) (*56*).

[55] The Romans parted the hair with a little spear called *hasta* (Ov. *Fast.* 2.560). That word can also denote the penis (Auct. Priap. 41.1). The equation: hair = pubic hair is discernible in I *Corinth.* 11.10 ff., and also in the tradition that the cow Io gave birth to Epaphos after Zeus touched her *forehead* (A. *Suppl.* 576 ff., *PV* 850 ff., etc.), for the Greeks emphasized the curly-haired forehead of bovines both in poetry (E. *Ba.* 185 ff.) and in art (cp. chap. 2, note 44). Cp. the belief that the aphrodisiac "hippomanes" is a fleshy clot in the *forehead* of some colts (Arist. *HA* 572a21, 577a9; Paus. 5.27.3, etc.). [In Theocr. 2.48, it is a mare-maddening hallucinogenic *plant* (Datura stramonium). Contra: Dover, ad. loc.]

[56] How "naturally" spiders evoke a woman's *head* hair is shown by a rather beautiful modern love poem (*2*, p. 5), which I happened to read while writing this chapter. The poet *refuses* to compare this beloved's hair to corn silk or to spiders—and, in so doing, *does* of course compare it to spiders. This comparison is particularly significant in the case of this poet, who mentions his beloved's *pubic* hair far more often than her (head) hair.

[57] Abraham (*1*) even cites, in connection with spider symbolism, the infantile fantasy that, during coitus, the man's small (but external) penis penetrates the large (but internal) female phallos.

Another way of circumventing this difficulty is to assert (symmetrically) that the penis (or the scrotum) can withdraw into the abdomen, becoming inverted and turning into a kind of vagina.[58]

Now, as regards ancient Greece, it is easy to demonstrate in myth the existence of both the "woman provided with a phallos" (*66*) and the "woman = phallos" (*38, 28*) ideas. Moreover, in so far as the vagina is "*dentata*"—i.e., a weapon of aggression—it is "necessarily" a phallic organ, for the phallos appears to be the prototypal weapon (A. *fr.* 44 N²), which can pierce,[59] club (*24*, p. 229) or cut (*34*).

But there is more to it. Citing striking clinical data, Abraham (*1*) shows that, at times, the longlegged spider's *legs* are seen as female pubic hair and the spider's *body* as the "female penis". If, however, the spider lurks *inside* its web, the cobweb is both the female pubic hair and the vagina, while the spider itself (*in* its net) is the "hidden" female penis. The statements—and, in one case, the drawing—of Abraham's patients are clear enough to convince anyone—except, perhaps, the obtusely mechanistic, know-it-all behaviourist.[60]

It seems almost otiose to cite so many data showing the commingling of male and female sex organs in fantasy, when the Hellenist can easily think of countless Greek stories of hermaphroditic beings, of generic plurals in the feminine gender, of a pair of stallions spoken of as "mares" when hitched as a team to a chariot (chap. 1), etc. Nothing is more characteristic of fantasy—and this regardless of whether it masquerades as myth, mysticism, wisdom, neurosis, or "Female Liberation Movement" ideology (complete with "unisex" fashions)—than to juggle and to commingle opposites, and particularly *sexual* differences whose existence and symmetry appear to have anguished mankind since the dawn of time (*24*, chap. 15).

The Phallic Mother in the Nightmare. This commingling of the sexes is nowhere more manifest than in the nightmare, in which the sexual aggressor, mounting and suffocating the dreamer, is—*regardless of the dreamer's sex*—nearly always the phallic mother (*47*). She assumes with regard to the female dreamer the male role, in a manner well described in Luc. *DMeretr.* 5. As to the male dreamer, she immobilizes and rapes him in the *coitus inversus* position, as does, e.g., the Sphinx on a red-figure (*circa* 450 B.C.) lekythos in the National Museum of Athens, etc. I specifically note

---

[58] Greek evidence: castors (Ael. *NA* 6.34); cp. *28*. Urology: luxation of the penis. Deliberate performance: the routine acts of certain South American Indians (*4, 71*); the deed of a German psychotic (*63*); perhaps the practices of some Japanese sumo-wrestlers (retraction of the testicles). Myths, tales, jokes, lies, alibis, beliefs, etc., of this type are reported from many areas: South China, Indonesia, Zoroastrian Central Asia, Greenland Eskimos, Mohave Indians, Renaissance France, etc., and neurotic fantasies from the U.S.A., Central Europe, etc. (*13, 28, 29*, chap. 16). The underlying "primary process" "logic" appears to be that the possibility of inverting the penis (causing it to resemble a vagina) "proves" the existence of a female "internal" penis.

[59] Cp. *hasta* = penis, supra, note 55.

[60] Since I have already compared the Sedang's spider soul to the Greek winged soul (ψυχή), it is worth noting that, according to Abraham, the butterfly's wings are sometimes visualized as (opening and closing) labia and its body proper as the female phallos (*1*). As to the equation: soul = phallos, it is both ethnologically and clinically commonplace.

that, in that picture, the horrified young man visibly has an anxiety erection[61]—and recall the painful erections the "grape" spider's bite is said to cause (supra).

A further element, which also highlights the quasi-interchangeability of the sexes in the nightmare is the curious reciprocity of the rider and the ridden. This point, which is of considerable importance, is taken up briefly further below.[62]

Thus, the *theoretical* femaleness of the sexually aggressive and, indeed, murderous mother who oppresses the dreamer in the nightmare, does *not* imply that she lacks a "penis". The dreamer himself imputes it to her— often simultaneously with the possession of a vagina.[63] Indeed, underlying the nightmare there is always a great deal of obsessive doubt (*17*) based on *fausse non-reconnaissance* (*22*), especially as regards the distinctive anatomy and reciprocal coital roles of the sexes. It is noteworthy that in the myth in question, though not in A. *Suppl.*, there is also a further element pointing to a confusion of the sexes: I refer to the curiously masculine character of the Danaides themselves, who build a temple, construct and row a ship and decapitate their unwanted cousin-husbands (Apollod. 2.1.4 ff.). It is even significant that traditions should diverge on just why Hypermnestra alone did *not* kill her husband, Lynkeus. Some say she spared his life because he had spared her virginity (Apollod. 2.1.5). But Aischylos says she spared him because his embraces had delighted her (A. *PV* 865 f.). That delight necessarily involved the acceptance of the feminine role, for it is precisely the woman's feminity which permits her to "acquire"—in a suitably mature manner—a penis "all her own". By contrast, in the Apollodoros version, only Hypermnestra was allowed to preserve (temporarily) her *immature* virginity, whose loss her murderous sisters experienced as a castration justifying the retaliatory castration (decapitation) of the deflowerers.[64]

Defloration = Snake Bite: Remains to be considered the inescapable conjecture that the serpent representing the Herald—or rather, the Aigyptiadai whose deputy he is—bites the girls with his poisonous fangs.[65]

---

[61] Anxiety erections even permit women to rape a man at gun point—as did, some ten years ago, three women hitchhikers in America. Hungarian informants reported, in 1957, cases of Russian female soldiers forcing men (in 1945–46) to cohabit with them at gun point.

[62] Cp. note 69. Also: (*11*, *22*) and chap. 3, note 104.

[63] The patient referred to in *Example 3*, though he dreaded being sucked by a vortex into his mother's vagina—which would have caused his *entire* body to become *her* penis (*20*, *23*)—none the less had the recurrent obsessive thought: "my mother's penis is bigger than my vagina". The body = phallos symbolic equation, which is frequently encountered in clinical practice, was briefly mentioned in chap. 6. For detailed evidence of the occurrence of this fantasy-equation in ancient Greece, cp. *28* and especially the Phil. Bybl. passages referred to in it (*FHG* 3.568.18; 3.569.24).

[64] On defloration = castration, cp. Freud (*41*) and Yates (*75*). Certain Australian aborigines even believe that the virgin is a phallic-daemonic being, whom only a rape-defloration can feminize and humanize (*65*, p. 236).

[65] In accordance with my principle of interpreting only the intelligible textual tradition, I do not interpret the plausible conjecture: "bites *my foot*". For those who are willing to consider this conjecture as conclusive, I simply mention that foot = penis is a common symbolic equation (*24*, p. 240) and that the female-foot = female-phallos equation is at the root of foot fetishism. If so: bitten foot = defloration = castration (feminization of the "boyish" virgin).

The equation: snake bite = coitus and especially: snake bite = defloration has already been discussed in chap. 6.[66]

The equation: snake venom = semen, and its consequence: injection of venom = injection of semen during coitus, have been discussed in detail (chap. 5) in connection with the Nessos-Deianeira and Minos-Prokris myths.

Since the Herald does, in fact, try to drag the Danaides towards nuptial couches and defloration, the occurrence of a poisonous bite in the dream-metaphor can, in the light of the word δᾶκος, be confidently taken for granted.

This brings me to a crucial point: throughout the preceding pages one repeatedly encountered, via the *vagina dentata* motif, the theme of the equivalence of maternal biting (devouring) and rape. A passage in Pindaros (O. 1.24 f.) permits one to assert that, for Aischylos' illustrious contemporary, these two activities were equivalent. Furthermore, in the passage in question, there is a curious blending of the "mother" with the "father"—the latter being *substituted* for the former, and, moreover, substituted in a context as *homosexual* as is the latent content of the nightmare, in which the phallic mother rapes the dreamer, regardless of the dreamer's sex.

Indeed, Pindaros, deliberately bowdlerizing the tradition that the mother-goddess Demeter had devoured Pelops' shoulder, asserted that the handsome boy had simply been "respectably" abducted by the enamoured Poseidon. Now, in *this* context, Poseidon is clearly a "father-god," for he is not only Pelops' lover and protector, but also Demeter's husband. The (purely external) bowdlerization simply transforms the mother's cannibalistic attack into a homosexual "rape" by the father. Copious clinical data show that many children have fantasies of being devoured by the mother and/or of being homosexually attacked by the father[67]—and react to both of these fantasies with erotized anxiety. Thus, the Pindaric bowdlerization—quite as much as lies in general (*15*, pp. 55 f. = *31*, chap. 3)—leave intact the psychological core and the structure of the original version (*21*).

Summing up, the fantasy of the *vagina dentata*, the "abdominal" (inguinal) maw of the "grape" spider, the myth of the man-raping, "man-eating"[68] and man-strangling (infra) Sphinx, etc. all show the infantile-neurotic equivalence of oedipal coitus and devouring. The entrapper, the biter, the (deputy) deflowerer—in short: the Herald—is therefore quite appropriately at once spider and serpent and is, because of his (fictitious) sexual ambiguity, just the right kind of epicene *nightmare* figure to haunt and terrify the virile, man-hating, incest-obsessed Danaides, who can visualize defloration only as castration and devouring and can experience an orgasm—triggered by anxiety (*51*)—only in the form of suffocation (hanging, drowning), involving biting (*68*).

---

[66] Snakes in Alkestis' bridal chamber (Apollod. 1.9.15) and in the dream of a modern bride. For bleeding stork-bitten finger = bleeding during childbirth, cp. chap. 6, note 60. In some cultures, bleeding during defloration is implicitly equated with bleeding during delivery (*9*).　　　　[67] For traces of the latter fantasy in the Oidipous myth, cp. *12*.
[68] U.S. slang: a promiscuous, man-destroying woman of the Manon and Carmen type.

Indeed, for the Danaides, hanging or drowning are the *alternatives* to rape. I propose to show now that the latent meaning of these alternatives is the same as that of the rape which they wish to avoid.

Having, in the last paragraphs, repeatedly referred to the *erotized* anxiety manifested by the Danaides, I must now turn to an aspect of the nightmare in which the same tendencies are evident.

The nightmare assailant *regularly immobilizes* and *suffocates* the victims of his (her) oedipal aggression, by its weight as well as by its tight embrace. This tendency is well exemplified by beliefs concerning the Sphinx, a creature whose origin is to be sought in the nightmare experience.[69]

Tradition defines the Sphinx as a "Strangler" ("suffocator"): some scholars even hold that this is the correct translation of that creature's name.[70] If so, the Sphinx is a strict equivalent of the Alp (*Alpdruck*). It has already been indicated that the Sphinx invariably rapes men in the *coitus inversus* position—as do the Seirenes,[71] etc. I note only in passing that both the Sphinx and the Lamia are—as one might expect—also cannibals: their raping, strangling and devouring tendencies are, for all practical purposes, inseparable.[72]

But this is less important than the Sphinx's, the nightmare's, the spider's and the snake's immobilizing-suffocating tendencies.[73] I have already noted that the suffocation theme is present in the Danaides' conception of both hanging and drowning as *alternatives* to—i.e., as means of escape from —unwanted coitus.

I now note a crucial fact: a mild inhibition of breathing is a *normal* female experience in ventro-ventral coitus.[74] In fact, for some women, whose pseudo-masculinity simply masks a strong, if latent, masochism, this "suffocation" is an important condition of their sexual gratification.[75]

Other indications of a "suffocating" erotic element in this dream-metaphor are (perhaps) also discernible.

[69] It has been suggested elsewhere (*11*) that the voodoo (*58*) possession rite, in which the possessing spirit (sometimes called: horse) *rides* the possessed—who is *also* called the "horse" (*of* the possessing spirit)—is simply a ritualization of the nightmare.

[70] Cφίγξ is related to cφίγγω, which means: to bind, though cφίγξ can also denote a rapacious person (Anaxil. 22) or even a (predatory) prostitute (Call. Com. 23). [However, the *Boiotian* form of that name, Φίξ, cannot have that meaning (K.J.D.).]

[71] See frontispiece.

[72] It is striking that Demetrios' favourite hetaira (older by far than he) was named Lamia—and quite appropriately so, for she used to bite him as savagely as the lion that bit Lysimachos (Plu. *V. Dem.* 27.3). This fits the well-known, but seldom discussed, fact that amorous—and often quite savage—biting is almost exclusively a female sexual practice.

[73] I recall the belief that the "grape" spider produces an erection but *also paralyses* the legs. Nikandros' wording underscores, I think, the *contrast* between these two symptoms. Now, those snakes, whose venom is a neurotoxin, do paralyse those they bite. Spiders also "net" their victims (which approximates suffocation). Large serpents can crush their victims (e.g., the Laokoön group, supra).

[74] The Trobrianders consider this position uncomfortable for the woman (*57*, p. 284).

[75] A relatively small girl always chose extremely heavy partners; her *main* source of pleasure was that their weight nearly suffocated her. If one of her partners was not heavy enough to make it difficult for her to breathe, she would hold her breath in order to be able to have an orgasm. Cp. the fantasy of being run over (*46*), which occurs also in men (*26*, pp. 217, 463, 596), cp. chap. 8. It is almost certain that infantile oedipal fantasies, involving desire for the "huge" parent, cause suffocation to be experienced as

The leaping into the depths has already been briefly mentioned. Falling and leaping downwards in dreams is often a symbolic representation of detumescence, or of a decrease of excitement after an erotic dream.[76]

The leaping into the *sea* may very probably also symbolize sexual excitement. Psychosexually mature women—which the Danaides are *not*—tend to compare a vaginal—but *never* a clitoral—orgasm to being engulfed by a great, surging wave, or by a vortex.

I hasten to concede that the "falling" (leaping downward) and the "jumping into the sea" themes would, *by themselves*, not suffice to reveal the presence of erotic components in the dream-metaphor. But they may be tentatively treated as such indications because they reinforce other, unquestionably sexual, symbols.[77]

I have left to the last a thorough discussion of what is perhaps the most telling argument in favour of the view that this dream-metaphor is patterned upon the nightmare. I note, to begin with, a curious fact: in no other suriving Greek tragedy are *all* the personages, with the *exception* of the Choros, males. What matters most is, however, the already briefly noted fact that there is not even a passing mention of the Danaides' mothers. Their place is totally usurped by their daughters' defunct bovine ancestress Io, whose frightened, gadfly-*stung* flight *after* her dreaded —and probably oedipal—premarital defloration and *during* her pregnancy (which aroused the mother-imago Hera's anger), is practically duplicated (351 f.) by the terrified flight of the Danaides *from* defloration, *from* a dreaded (incestuous) marriage (represented by a snake bite) and, of course, *from* pregnancy. This drama therefore exemplifies the clinically familiar "splitting" of the real mother into two separate "images": the "good" (but sexually abused) mother is Io; the "bad" (devouring, tormenting, jealous) mother is, in the Io myth, Hera. In this drama the "bad" (nightmarish) mother *image* is incarnated by the symbolically epicene Herald of the dream-metaphor, in which he (acting on behalf of his principals, the Aigyptiadai) is represented as a spider and as a snake and, on the latent level, as the phallic mother of a waking nightmare. I hold that this (delegated) horribleness of the (never-mentioned) phantasmatic mothers strongly supports Kouretas's (*49*) view that the Danaides are the victims of a—both thrilling and anxiety-arousing—father fixation.

Summary. Since the text in question does not contain a real dream, but only a metaphorical allusion to a *familiar type* of dream, in interpreting it one does not "analyse" either Aischylos or the Danaides. One analyses a *type-dream* of great antiquity and world-wide distribution. In so doing, one erotized anxiety. I also cite (from memory) the case of a man who repeatedly hanged himself and ejaculated when on the point of suffocating. He did it once too often—and died of strangling.

[76] This is not an absolute rule. A normal adult once told me that his erotic dreams never ended in falling and contained no other unpleasant experiences. Conversely, his rare dreams of falling never contained *manifest* erotic incidents. Whether they contained *symbolic* erotic elements could not be ascertained, since this information was not obtained in the course of a psycho-analysis, but during a conversation.

[77] Nightmare, suffocation-hanging-drowning and, above all, the fact that hanging and drowning are represented as *alternatives* to coitus. As a former parachutist, I well remember that, as one begins to fall, one tends to catch one's breath and to hold it until the parachute opens and arrests the fall.

also examines its poetic and dramatic appropriateness and persuasiveness, and determines what it signified in Greek culture.

On the strictly factual level, the scrutiny of this metaphor proves once more that Aischylos, the perceptive observer of dreams, was capable of exploiting to the utmost the dramatic potentialities of oniric imagery.

On the most generalized phenomenological level, his Danaides' dream-metaphor is persuasive *qua* dream, precisely because it does *not* pretend to be prophetic: like real dreams, it is rooted in the remote past and in the present.

The dream-metaphor also stands up well under psycho-analytical scrutiny. The Danaides' comparing of the Herald's behaviour to that of a spider and of a snake in a black dream (nightmare) rings true psychologically, for the situation has *all* the characteristics of a genuine nightmare. Its components: suffocation, immobilization and counter-oedipal aggression by a phallic mother, converge into—or, if one prefers, diverge from—an infantile fantasy of (inguinal) devouring. The fact that the Herald is male, while the spider = snake symbolizes the "bad" mother's devouring inguinal maw, is almost to be expected. The evil and powerful mother of the nightmare is the "phallic" (and man-slaying) woman[78] of Greek myth (*66, 28*), and the phantasmatic character of the Danaides' *mothers* is highlighted precisely by the absence of *any* reference to them in A. *Suppl.* and by the ostentatiously phallic character of their daughters.

That these phantasmatic mothers's threatening sexual organ(s) should be visualized as a spider (= snake) is also to be expected, since, for the Greeks, though not for the Romans, the female genitalia were a symbol of Evil (*59*, 1.118 ff.).

Thus, this spider-snake dream-metaphor satisfies every criterion of a genuine nightmare. Its psycho-analytical interpretation is not only congruent with Greek beliefs but also fits perfectly the Danaides' psychological make-up and dramatic predicament *as delineated by Aischylos*. The metaphor is manifestly the poetic echo of a common *type* of anxiety dream and attests the existence of spider and snake nightmares in ancient Greece.

Bibliography

(1) Abraham, Karl: The Spider as a Dream Symbol (in) *Selected Papers of Karl Abraham M.D.*, chap. 19., London, 1927.

(2) Benton, Walter: *This is My Beloved*. New York, 1947.

(3) Bolton, J. D. P.: *Aristeas of Proconnesus*. Oxford, 1962.

(4) Caspar, Franz: Some Sex Beliefs and Practices of the Tupari Indians (Western Brazil), *Revista do Museu Paulista* n.s. 7:203–244, 1953.

(5) De Martino, Ernesto: *La Terra del Rimorso*. Milano, 1961.

(6) Devereux, George: *Hopi Field Notes* (MS.), 1932.

(7) id.: *Sedang Field Notes* (MS.), 1933–1935.

(8) id.: Mohave Beliefs Concerning Twins, *American Anthropologist* n.s. 43:573–592, 1941.

[78] Cp. ἀνδρόβουλος: A. *Ag.* 11; Phryn. *PS* p. 31; ἀνδρόφρων: S. *fr.* 857N² (= 943 P).

(9) id.: The Psychology of Feminine Genital Bleeding: An Analysis of Mohave Indian Puberty and Menstrual Rites, *International Journal of Psycho-Analysis* 31:237–257, 1950.

(10) id.: Mohave Indian Verbal and Motor Profanity (in) Róheim Géza (ed.): *Psycho-analysis and the Social Sciences* 3. New York, 1951.

(11) id. (and Mars, Louis): Haitian Voodoo and the Ritualization of the Nightmare, *Psychoanalytic Review* 38:334–342, 1951.

(12) id.: Why Oedipus Killed Laïus: A Note on the Complementary Oedipus Complex, *International Journal of Psycho-Analysis* 34:132–141, 1953.

(13) id.: Primitive Genital Mutilations in a Neurotic's Dream, *Journal of the American Psychoanalytic Association* 2:483–492, 1954.

(14) id.: The Denial of the Anus in Neurosis and Culture, *Bulletin of the Philadelphia Association for Psychoanalysis* 4:24–27, 1954.

(15) id.: *A Study of Abortion in Primitive Societies*. New York, 1955,[2] 1975.

(16) id.: Penelope's Character, *Psychoanalytic Quarterly* 26:378–386, 1957.

(17) id.: Obsessive Doubt, *Bulletin of the Philadelphia Association for Psychoanalysis* 10:50–55, 1960.

(18) id.: Sociopolitical Functions of the Oedipus Myth in Early Greece, *Psychoanalytic Quarterly* 32:205–214, 1963.

(19) id.: The Perception of Motion in Infancy, *Bulletin of the Menninger Clinic* 29:143–147, 1965.

(20) id.: Loss of Identity, Impairment of Relationships, Reading Disability, *Psychoanalytic Quarterly* 35:18–39, 1966.

(21) id.: The Exploitation of Ambiguity in Pindaros *O*. 3.27, *Rheinisches Museum für Philologie* 109:289–298, 1966.

(22) id.: Fausse Non-Reconnaissance, *Bulletin of the Menninger Clinic* 31:69–78, 1967.

(23) id.: La Renonciation à l'Identité: Défense contre l'Anéantissement, *Revue Française de Psychanalyse* 31:101–142, 1967.

(24) id.: *From Anxiety to Method in the Behavioral Sciences*. Paris and The Hague, 1967.

(25) id.: The Realistic Basis of Fantasy, *Journal of the Hillside Hospitaι* 17:13–20, 1968.

(26) id.: *Reality and Dream: The Psychotherapy of a Plains Indian*. (Second, augmented edition), New York, 1969.

(27) id.: *Mohave Ethnopsychiatry and Suicide*. (Second, augmented edition), Washington, D.C., 1969.

(28) id.: La Naissance d'Aphrodite (in) Pouillon, Jean and Maranda, Pierre (eds.): *Echanges et Communications (Mélanges Lévi-Strauss)*, 2.1229–1252. Paris and The Hague, 1970.

(29) id.: *Essais d'Ethnopsychiatrie Générale*. Paris, 1970. (Second edition, 1973).

(30) id.: Drogues, Dieux, Idéologies, *Medica* no. 103:13–20, 1972.

(31) id.: *Ethnopsychanalyse Complémentariste*. Paris, 1972.

(32) id. (and Devereux, J. W.): Manifestations de l'Inconscient dans Sophokles: *Trachiniai* 923 sqq. (in) *Psychonalyse et Sociologie comme Méthodes d'Etude des Phénomènes Historiques et Culturels*. Bruxelles, 1973.

(33) id.: The Self-Blinding of Oidipous, (Dodds *Festschrift*), *Journal of Hellenic Studies*, 93:36–49, 1973.

(34) id.: Auto-Caractérisations de Quatre Sedang (in): Poirier, J. and Raveau, F., (eds.): *Je et l'Autre*, (Mélanges R. Bastide) (in press).

(35) Diels, H. and Kranz, W.: *Die Fragmente der Vorsokratiker*[10], 3 vols. Berlin, 1960–1961.

(36) Dodds, E. R.: *The Greeks and the Irrational*. Berkeley, California, 1951.

(37) Du Bois, Cora. *The People of Alor*, Minneapolis, Minnesota, 1944.

(38) Fenichel, Otto: The Symbolic Equation: Girl = Phallus (in) *The Collected Papers of O. Fenichel* 2, chap. 1. New York, 1954.

(39) Ferenczi, Sándor: Psycho-Analysis of Sexual Habits (in) *Further Contributions to the Theory and Technique of Psycho-Analysis*, chap. 32, London, 1926.

(40) id.: An 'Anal Hollow-Penis' in Woman (in) *Further Contributions to the Theory and Technique of Psycho-Analysis* chap. 42. London, 1926.

(41) Freud, Sigmund: The Taboo of Virginity, *Standard Edition* 11. London, 1957.

(42) id.: The 'Uncanny', *Standard Edition* 17. London, 1955.

(43) Gallini, Clara: Katapontismos, *Studi e Materiali di Storia delle Religioni* 34:61–90, 1963.

(44) Gloyne, H. F.: Tarantism, *American Imago* 7:29–42, 1950.

(45) Hani, Jean: Plutarque et le Mythe du Démembrement d'Horus. *Revue des Etudes Grecques* 76: 111–120, 1963.

(46) Jones, Ernest: The Symbolism of Being Run Over, *International Journal of Psycho-Analysis* 1:203, 1920.

(47) id.: *On the Nightmare*. London, 1931.

(48) Keiser, Sylvan: Orality Displaced to the Urethra, *Journal of the American Psychoanalytic Association* 2:263–279, 1954.

(49) Kouretas, Demetrios: Ανώμαλοι Χαρακτῆρες εἰς τὸ 'Αρχαῖον Δρᾶμα, Athens, 1951.

(50) La Barre, Weston: *The Ghost Dance*. New York, 1970.

(51) Laforgue, René: De l'Angoisse à l'Orgasme, *Revue Française de Psychanalyse* 4:245–258, 1931–1932.

(52) Lévi-Strauss, Claude: *Mythologiques 3: L'Origine des Manières de Table*. Paris, 1968.

(53) Lévy-Bruhl, Lucien: *La Mentalité Primitive*. Paris, 1922.

(54) Loeb, E. M.: Personal Communication.

(55) Lowie, R. H.: The Family as a Social Unit, *Papers of the Michigan Academy of Science, Arts and Letters* 18:53–69, 1933.

(56) Macchiavelli, Niccolo: *The Prince*. 1513.

(57) Malinowski, Bronislaw: *The Sexual Life of Savages in North-Western Melanesia*[3]. London, 1932.

(58) Métraux, Alfred: *Le Vaudou Haitien*. Paris, 1958.

(59) Nilsson, M. P.: *Geschichte der griechischen Religion* I[2]. München, 1955.

(60) Norbeck, Edward: Trans-Pacific Similarities in Folklore: A Research Lead. *Kroeber Anthropological Society Papers*, no. 12: 62–69, 1955.

(61) Poe, E. A.: A Descent into the Maelstrom (in) *Tales of Mystery and Imagination*. (First published in *Graham's Magazine*, May 1841.)

(62) Raum, O. F.: Female Initiation among the Chaga. *American Anthropologist* 41:554–565, 1939.

(63) Reuss, H.: Ein Fall von anatomischen Narzismus (Autocohabitatio in Urethram). *Deutsche Zeitschrift für die gesamte gerichtliche Medizin* 28:340–346, 1937

(64) Róheim, Géza: Psycho-Analysis of Primitive Cultural Types. *International Journal of Psycho-Analysis* 13:1–224, 1932.

(65) id.: Women and their Life in Central Australia. *Journal of the Royal Anthropological Institute* 63:207–265, 1933.

(66) id.: Aphrodite or the Woman with a Penis. *Psychoanalytic Quarterly* 14:350–390, 1945.

(67) Shute, Nevil: *Most Secret*. London, 1945.

(68) Sterba, R. F.: On Spiders, Hanging and Oral Sadism. *American Imago* 7:21–28, 1950.

(69) Teitelbaum, H. A.: Psychogenic Body Image Disturbances Associated with Psychogenic Aphasia and Agnosia. *Journal of Nervous and Mental Disease* 93:581–612, 1941.

(70) Thomson, George: *Aeschylus and Athens*². London, 1946.

(71) Wagley, Charles and Galvão, Eduardo: The Tapirapé (in) Steward, Julian (ed.): Handbook of South American Indians, 3. *Bureau of American Ethnology*, Bulletin 143. Washington, D.C., 1948.

(72) Wigglesworth, V. B.: *The Life of Insects*. Cleveland, 1964.

(73) Wilamowitz-Moellendorff, Ulrich von: *Die Ilias und Homer*. Berlin, 1916.

(74) Wisse, J.: *Selbstmord und Todesfurcht bei den Naturvölkern*. Zutphen, 1933.

(75) Yates, S. L.: An Investigation of the Psychological Factors in Virginity and Ritual Defloration. *International Journal of Psycho-Analysis* 11:167–184, 1930.

Indexes

I Ancient authors and works

II Modern authors

Aboulker, P. 235
Abraham, K. xvii, xxii, xxxvi, 3, 20, 96, 332, 335, 336, 341
Acton, Lord 40
Adkins, A. W. H. 298, 312
Ahrens, H. L. 82, 84, 86, 89, 106, 117, 140
Akimoto, H. (see Uchimura, Y.)
Alexander, F. 6, 20, 171, 178, 225, 251
Allen, J. T. and Italie G. 294, 312
Allport, G. W. and Vernon, P. E. 307, 312
Anderson, J. K. 279, 285, 312
Angyal, A. 65, 140
Anonymous, see *Hikayat Hang Tuah*
Arsan, E. 194, 214
Ashley-Montagu, M. F. 240, 251

Bächli, E. 221, 247, 251, 281, 298, 312
Bailey, F. L. 190, 194, 198, 209, 214
Baker, S. J. 36, 53, 61, 140
Balzac, H. de 33
Bamberger, F. 106
Barrett, W. S. 8, 20, 33, 79, 89, 127, 140, 279, 289, 312
Bates, W. N. 268, 295, 312
Bateson, G. and Mead, M. 210, 214
Baudelaire, C. 65, 76, 77
Baumann, H. H. 6, 21, 171, 178, 225, 251
Beach, F. A. (see Ford, C. S.)
Beare, J. L. xvi, xxx
Befu, H. 158, 166
Behr, C. A. xv, xxv, xxviii, xxxvi, 5, 21, 75, 78, 109, 140, 173, 249, 251
Bekker, I. 152
Belmont, N. 190, 214
Benedict, R. 94, 140
Benton, W. 335, 341
Bergk, Th. 165, 175
Bernard, E. 101
Bernfeld, S. and Feitelberg, G. 213, 214
Bertalanffy, L. von 280
Besançon, A. 44, 53, 297, 312
Bexton, W. H., Heron, W. and Scott, T. H. (see also Heron, W.) 107, 140, 143
Bezdechi, S. xxx, xxxvi, 120, 140, 290, 312
Blaicklock, E. M. xxx, xxxvi, 120, 141
Blass, F. 98
Blaydes, F. H. M. 243
Blomfield, C. J. 106
Boas, F. 40, 53
Boccara, M. 50, 53

Boll, F. 73
Bolton, J. D. P. 326, 341
Borel, Th. 268, 312
Bothe, H. 324
Bourguignon, A. xxiii, xxxvi, 71, 141, 152, 166, 274, 308, 312
Bowers, U. G. 97, 141, 293, 312
Bowra, Sir (C.) M. 136, 141, 221, 227, 229, 247, 251
Bradley, N. xxxii, xxxvi
Brelich, A. xxviii, xxxvi, 135, 141
Briehl, W. and Kulka, E. W. 202, 214, 225, 237, 251
Broadhead, H. D. 2, 4, 7, 8, 11, 13
Broustra, J. (see Nicolas, J. or Monfouga-Nicolas, J.)
Brumoy, P. 106
Buonaparte, Lt. N. 67
Burkert, W. xv, 43, 44, 53, 54, 87, 236, 241, 246, 251, 304
Burrows, E. G. and Spiro, M. E. 235, 251
Bussemaker, U. C. 177
Buschan, G. 193, 214
Butler, S. 117

Cabell, J. B. 156
Čakuleva-Diamantis, D. 193, 214
Campbell, L. 106
Cannon, W. B. 197, 215
Caprio, F. F. (see London, L. S.)
Carpenter, R. 34, 54
Caspar, F. 245, 252, 336, 341
Chombart de Lauwe, M.-J. 210, 215
Clifford, Sir H. 44, 54, 215, 288
Cochrane, A. D. 213, 215
Conington, J. 106
Cook, A. B. 13, 21, 36, 54, 73, 141, 174, 178, 240, 252, 306, 312
Coulon, V. 10, 11
Crahay, R. 298, 312

Dale, A. M. 125, 295
Davison, J. A. 88, 141
de Balzac, H. 33
Decharme, P. 295, 312
de Heredia, J.-M. 90, 141
Delcourt, M. 172, 178
Delebecque, E. 12, 13, 21
De Martino, E. 332, 341
Dement, W. C. 273, 312

III Ancient persons, gods, beings, etc.

IV Persons, non-Graeco-Roman

V Places, peoples, groups

VI Proper nouns